IN PURSUIT FOR IMPROVEMENTS:

A MEMOIR BASED ON A FOREIGN SERVICES OFFICER'S CAREERS WITH A U.S. AGENCY FOR INTERNATIONAL DEVELOPMENT AND AS AN INTERNATIONAL FINANCIAL CONSULTANT

1962 -- 2000

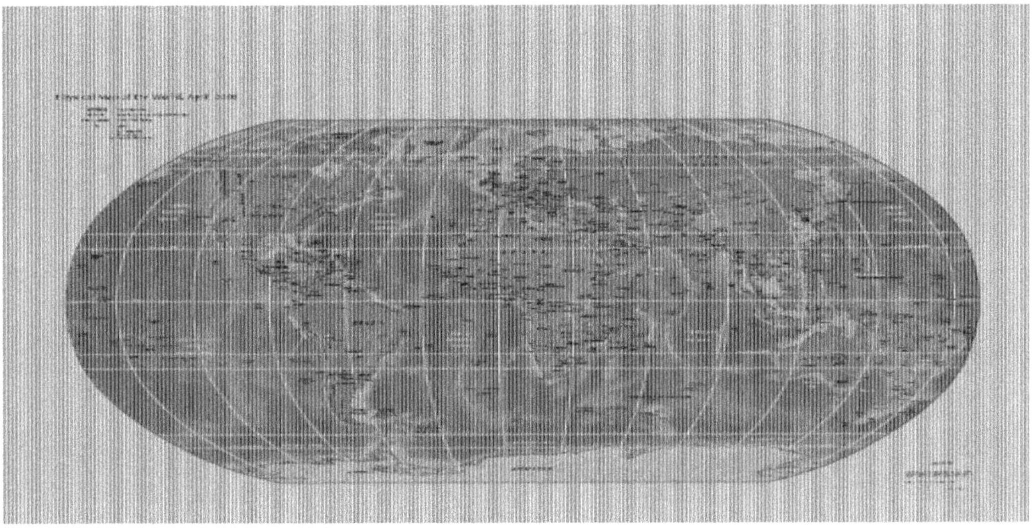

Jose M. Pena

In Pursuit For Improvements

Printed in the United States of America

First Printing 2022

ISBN: 979-8-218-12708-4

TABLE OF CONTENTS

NOTE: The detailed table of contents is attached at the end of the book.

AUTHOR'S PREFACE

PART A. THE PROLOGUE

Background: This book represents the story of my life, my career as a Foreign Service Officer (FSO), as an International Financial Consultant, and parts of the lives of my family. With the exceptions noted later, the great majority of my life, my family's life, and my career can be classified as Excellent. For this reason, I have six objectives in writing this book; these are to:

a) *Record and pass a brief description of USAID programs, my technical knowledge, experiences, and analytical procedures to others who read my book.*

b) *Disseminate this book to colleges and universities so that majors in Business Administration can use programmatic evaluation in their reviews.*

c) *Suggest to current Inspector Generals that they adopt the practice of hiring younger Universities graduates and continue to "upgrade" their analytical experience levels through progressive "on the job training and further studies."*

d) *Request the current USAID Directors, Program, Project Officers, Inspector General, the Council of the Inspectors General on Integrity and Efficiency (CIGIE), and OAS Officials to review and learn from past problems so they can be avoided in the future and at the same time explore ideas, stated in Chapters 19 and 22, for adoption in the future.*

e) *Describe our (my family and myself) lives while on overseas assignments so that future FSO potential candidates can make informed decisions on their careers.*

f) Discuss the negative periods in my career and thereby leave a comprehensive story of the adverse events and provide complete closure of my life.

Here is a Brief Overview of My Life Experiences: First of all, let me clarify that I wrote this Prologue so that it could be "the Executive Summary" for the avid reader.

Here is the beginning of my story. I was born in Laredo, Texas, over 90 years ago. My parents were born in Guerrero, Tamaulipas, Mexico, and were very poor, but they were extremely hardworking and honest. They migrated to the U.S to escape the violence of the Mexican Revolution of 1910. They settled in Laredo (Texas) -- what was then a small town. Being so close to the Mexican border, about 95.5 percent of the people were Hispanic and spoke mostly Spanish. Because of this Spanish-speaking majority, so called "Anglos," were also fluent in Spanish. These facts are presented to account for the way I was brought up and my ethnic feelings. As a result, growing up – in a town with a 50,000 population and where 95.5 Percent were Hispanic -- I did not feel much of the "discrimination" that was felt in other Texas Cities and states. It was this social exposure and environment that made me – and other Hispanics from Laredo – have life-long mixed feelings and attitudes toward any discrimination that we might have felt later. In other words, being Hispanic from Laredo had many attributes and many challenges and, it was much later that I experienced – and I tried my best not to be influenced – by the wrath of some discrimination.

In any event, I attended public schools. I cannot say that I was the best of students. However, I nevertheless graduated from High School. After my high school graduation, I served in the U.S. Air Force for 4 years. I went in as a Private and came out as a Staff Sergeant. Thanks to the U.S. Air Force and GI Bill, I went to a Laredo Junior College and graduated from the University of Texas (UT) in the upper 10 percent of my class. After my UT graduation, I worked for the U.S. Air Force as a civilian auditor for 4 years at General Dynamics Corporation in Ft. Worth, Texas. I did extraordinarily well during this period, and I was promoted three times. Although my career with the U.S. Air Force, as a Civil Servant was assured, I decided to work in an international environment and chose what was then the International Cooperation Administration (ICA). Since the emphasis is on my Foreign Services Officer's (FSO) Career, Chapters 1 and 2 discuss my achievements during these early periods of my life.

With the passage of the Foreign Assistance Act on January 1, 1961, the U.S. Agency for International Development (USAID) was created and took over the ICA functions. ICA ceased to exist, and USAID has now been in operations for over 60 plus years. So, the story of my life-long career really begins from the time I became a FSO, January 4, 1962, and I worked for the USAID for 28 years. Once I retired from USAID, I worked as an International Financial Consultant, under Personal Services type of contracts, for two private international companies and the Organization of American States (OAS), as follows:

- The first contract was with the Construction Control Services Corporation (CCSC), that was implementing the Afghan Construction and Logistical Unit (ACLU) Project. I was stationed in Peshawar, Pakistan, for six months.

- The second contract was for close to two years with Clapp and Mayne Inc. as a Director of a Child Survival Health Project in Guatemala.

- My final work was for a 4-year period with the Office of Inspector General of The Organization of American States (OAS). Let me say that working for OAS, a highly political and diplomatic institution, was quite an experience.

I have been semi-retired ever since. During this time, I have written and published two books, written numerous Essays, lectured, and have been busy all the time. In short, my presentation, in this Prologue, will follow the above sequence.

Career with U.S. Agency for International Development (USAID): What is the history of USAID, and what is the Organization all about? Chapter 3 shows a panoramic profile of USAID, its history- from 1945 to the Present, its

Organizational charts, and a sample of the 134 countries and sectors it currently helps. This is a "must-read chapter" because it represents a fabulous description of what USAID is all about and what it does. Nonetheless, in my many years with USAID, I have always noted that there seems to be a great deal of confusion on the programs. In fact, a great many people think that USAID "gives money away" to other countries. As you read my book, you will learn that this line of thinking is a total misconception, and then, I hope that you will agree with me that USAID has a fabulous policy in place for awarding assistance to countries. The policy prescribes a two-way beneficial effect. For instance, most financial assistance to countries returns back (to the U.S.) – through astute contractual marketing procedures -- to help businesses in the United States. **The only exception I take to this policy is that it should have more dispersive economic effects so that the U.S. aging infrastructure will also receive significant benefits.**

As Foreign Services Officer (FSO), with the USAID, I can proudly say that, based on my qualifications, I was selected – and served -- as the first Mexican American Person to hold the Position of Deputy Regional Inspector General for Audit (DRIG/A) and to act, intermittently, as an "Acting RIG/A" -- in both Egypt and for Latin America for six years.

Briefly, many things happened to me and my family during my 28 years of work with the USAID. These years were the most productive period of our lives. With USAID, alone, my family and I were assigned – and lived – in nine different countries, and I also went on Temporary Duty Assignments (TDY) to 26 other countries. In addition, because of the dangers that existed in some countries, the whims of those in power, and/or health problems of my family, I lived in some countries by myself. For instance, I served in South Vietnam during the war and was there during the Tet Offensive. I was also alone in Pakistan (1 ½ Years), Egypt (8 months), Kenya (2 years), and Guatemala (2 years).

This book describes the lives led by my family in those countries, and there was some rough and light side of my personal self. We lived in nice furnished homes or apartments. My wife lived very nicely but had two car accidents caused by wild host country drivers. My children went to excellent schools. All of us experienced the fear or excitement that exists while military person, dictators, or someone takes over through a "country coup." There were times when we were being exposed to the customs of the country for the first time. As you read my book, you will also see me experiencing the excitement of helping President Jimmy Carter when he officially visited Egypt in 1979; or my crazy auditioning as Bullfighter in Ecuador; or the hair-raising experience when – I was in an extremely dangerous situation, in Vietnam, and, to save my tail, I shook hands with 10 Vietcong; or the dangerous feeling of witnessing a "human rights situation," near the country of Burma (now called Myanmar); or that of being told to immediately leave the area; or the reactions of a "Madam' when I unintentionally visited her "Thatched Brothel" in Bangladesh; or the horror in seeing a person in the last stages of Leprosy; or the "bloated experience" of undergoing an ancient Colonoscopy; and/or the cultural experiences of holding hands, dancing, and hugging and kissing other men on the cheeks. Yes, this is all true. I (we) have done all these things.

Chapter 4 shows my professional Biodata and a synopsis of the types of studies and reviews I made during my working years and FSO career. However, without hesitation, let me say that I was nowhere prepared to be a Chief Auditor in (Peru), my first post with USAID overseas. The university and my work with the U.S. Air Force, as a civilian, had done an excellent job of preparing me for financial type of reviews. However, I was very ill-prepared – and had some initial number of adjustment problems – with the Programmatic Evaluations that USAID required.

Nevertheless, together with the experience at my first post and those learned over time, the training has lasted me for a lifetime and enabled me to reach the pinnacle of my profession and capabilities. They certainly helped in giving me the discipline and the start of my expertise so I could do the most complicated audits that one can imagine. You will see some fabulous examples as you read chapters, especially Chapters 7, 11,13, and nineteen on Colombia, Washington, Pakistan, Egypt, and my final chapter on USAID. **For instance --- while doing a review of a Certain Foundation – one of my findings resulted in changes to an erroneous ruling by the American Institute for Certified Accountants (AICPA) – related to the way the AICPA interpreted "accrued expenditures." These changes produced immeasurable savings for USAID and other U.S. Government Agencies. Yes, my professional maturity consistently improved throughout my career.**

Throughout this book, you will note that the lessons learned in Peru had a lifetime benefit. Therefore, one of my objectives is to see if we can influence the Universities to include or share with students the field of Programmatic Evaluations within their curriculum. My suggestions to the Universities are included in the book. In the interim and as an alternative, I believe that Active Inspector Generals should consider employing young university graduates and "bringing their level of experiences" through progressive "on the job training."

In any event, Chapter 5 to Chapter 22 in this book show some brief details of the many country assignments I had. I also include many examples of the technical reviews and work I made in the different countries – Peru, Ecuador, South Vietnam, Colombia, Panama, Honduras, Washington, Pakistan, Egypt, Deputy RIG/A (in Washington, Kenya, Peshawar (Pakistan), Guatemala and in the Organization of American State (OAS).

Yet not everything was rosy for me. I encountered a few very rough roads during my work with USAID and at the Organization of American States (explained later). For instance, two USAID Auditor Generals and/or the first USAID Inspector General (I will refer to him as IG#1) made some erroneous or really bad decisions that adversely affected me – and many others -- along the way. A brief explanation follows:

a) One newly assigned Auditor General made the ridiculous decision to close the Office in Panama, fire the local staff, and move all the FSO Audit Staff to Miami, Florida. Yes, you are reading right. The plan was a failure from the start. Nevertheless, both the Panama Office and the planned office in Miami were closed. As a result, all the U.S. audit staff moved to Washington D. C. and, we lost all our very valuable local staff and the logistical Panamanian location.

b) My tour in Washington was most productive but was shortened because – after being 15 years on overseas assignment with no additional formal education -- I met with another Auditor General, and I told him that he needed to establish a Policy so FSOs, on "Rotation Assignments," could improve their University Education. He did not like what I was telling him; so, he "exiled" me to Pakistan. This

Auditor General was replaced within a year, and I was transferred to Egypt. The book describes my experience and work in Pakistan, Bangladesh, Afghanistan, Yemen, Egypt -- and the position I served during my tour in Egypt.

The last Inspectors General (I will call him IG#1) I worked with had an exceptional background and was a good manager for about 7 years; however, he occupied his position too long (17 years). One proverb expresses the problem well. "Absolute Power Corrupts. Absolutely!" This I.G. became entrenched and created many problems for USAID FSO's, in general, and this affected me. He brought 8 people from another U.S. Agency (GAO), made them FSOs without them serving in developing countries before, or observing FSO hiring rules, promoted them to higher positions, and tried to implement erroneous policies. Since I was the DRIG/A – and Acting RIG/A for Latin America at the time and based on feelings expressed by my staff, - I expressed all our disagreements with the erroneous policies the I.G. and these people tried to implement. Since the IG had no "Dissent Channels," (at that time) all kinds of retaliation against me followed. For instance, I was demoted from the DRIG/A/LA Position, falsely accused of insubordination, given a bad and vicious PER, persecuted, investigated, and harassed in many ways. L**et me clarify that the problem was the I.G. and not the USAID. He thought that he was not accountable to anyone. So that something like this never happens again, I make a strong recommendation to the CIGIE to set a fixed lower term for present and future Inspector Generals and to review their management of their staff and organizational employees in a periodic manner.** Chapters 16 to 18 must be read because they show details and the conclusion of the retaliations.

In turn, Chapter 19 is a directed summary and referrals to be read by very high officials of USAID, Inspector General, and the Council for Inspectors General on Integrity and Efficiency (CIGIE). It represents my final parting from USAID, and I use my 28-year experience with this fabulous organization to present many salient – good and bad -- memories of the past with a vision towards preventing the repetition of the same type of errors in the future. I also include some new theories, ideas, suggestions, and recommendations in areas that USAID should explore for probable future adaptations.

Since I had the years and saw no future with IG#1, I retired from USAID on December 31, 1989. However, I still love USAID and firmly believe it is an exceptional Organization. I know that whoever reads this book will gain a tremendous insight into the past and current USAID history, the way that USAID works, many of the programs it was implementing, many of the problems I found, and some ideas I am proposing for further consideration.

The Afghan Construction and Logistical Unit (ACLU) Project: As mentioned earlier, my next work was under a Personal Services Contract with the CCSC that was implementing the ACLU Project from Peshawar, Pakistan. The ACLU Project was designed in a manner that it would create incentives for the Russians to leave Afghanistan. I served as the Chief Administrative and Financial Officer and worked on computerized accounting and inventory systems; refined the terms and mechanics of the Solatium Fund (a type of health and life insurance for the Mujahedeen); and visited some of the projects being developed from Peshawar to Kabul.

Let me say that my description of Peshawar, Pakistan, as a tinderbox, and the ACLU Project as being a "Cauldron of Warring Mujahedeen" is very precise and descriptive. As I will later explain, the project was financing the ACLU Project to support the Mujahedeen in their effort to get the Russians out of Afghanistan, consequently, Peshawar was full of Afghan guerillas. The guerillas separated the city into factions. All were armed to the teeth, crazily running in trucks everywhere, protecting important warlords and at times firing into the air (and sometimes at each other or anyone around), and crossing into Afghanistan to do their thing. Many never came back; the Solatium Fund helped the families. Stray and aimed bullets abounded; a number hit my house a few times. Mujahedeen groups came and went to the ACLU Project to pick up financial and other help; so, I might have met some of Mujahedeen's main warlords, but only the name of Gulbuddin Hekmatyar now sticks in my mind. Some of our people could not take the stress and "cracked up" and were quickly evacuated. One of my colleagues left a very "creative Termite Army" behind. And, when one of my colleagues was shot five times – but survived – I was "very politely asked" to leave the country because my life was no longer guaranteed. Two days later, I was gone. Chapter 20 describes the six months of my contract.

<u>The Guatemalan Child Survival Health Project (PAI/TRO):</u> My next contract was with Clapp and Mayne Inc. I served as the Director of a Child Survival Health Project in Guatemala; I hired and led the efforts of 50 professional doctors, nurses, administrative and clerical personnel. Since my children were now grown-up, I served alone.

This Project had seven objectives: (a) reactivate the project (which had failed because the prior contractor had been embezzling funds); (b) reactivate the cold chain, which included an Expanded Program for Immunization (PAI); (c) repair and restore the transportation system of vehicles and motorcycles; (d) introduce a new element, which included The Oral Rehydration Program (TRO); (e) the procurement and provision of computer equipment to Health Areas; (f) improve budget execution of the MOH; and, (g) support decentralization effort by employment and use of "Gestores" (Field Representatives) who were to be assigned to, and coordinate all requirements, in the 24 Health Areas.

When I got to Guatemala, my original team consisted of 4 excellent people and a subcontractor, who would be my Deputy and who had already hired 2 computer specialists. With the help of the original team members, I hired 45 more professionals (doctors, nurses, Accountants, Administrative, Transportation Personnel, and Clerks) that were needed during the implementation of the project. Although the subcontractor (my Deputy), turned out to be narcissistic and ineffectual, there were no surprises in relation to the Guatemalan team. They proved to be exceptional. With their help, we did a fabulous job and achieved most of all desired objectives. Since USAID expressed an exigency for a Public Health Doctor to implement the second phase of the project – and I did not have the desired doctoral qualifications -- my contract was not renewed. See Chapter 21 for full details on our problems, achievements, and a number of awards I got from the Government of Guatemala.

<u>The Organization of American States (OAS):</u> Between 1994 and 1998, I was contracted and worked, for the Office of the OAS Inspector General, as an International Financial Consultant. During this time, I did many evaluations, audits, risk assessments, and studies covering: the Problems of the Land Mines, Employment Mechanisms, Trade Programs, Flow of Funds, Payment Procedures, Payroll, Inventories, the Internet, Procurement System,

Electoral Observations, and several Special Reviews. Most studies required radical changes in the way OAS conducted some of its administrative and operational affairs because:

> Every review I made showed numerous -- and complex – types of problems. As an International Organization, OAS could be exceptional. However, I found it in urgent need to improve its overall administrative operations in a radical manner because OAS (and specifically one office of the General Secretariat), in my opinion, OAS was not performing its personnel requirements, managerial, administrative, financial, Activities, Internal Controls, and/or Operations in the most efficient, effective, economical, or accurate manner. Hopefully, OAS has implemented all our recommendations and has taken the required steps toward improving its operations.

Chapter 22 shows a synopsis of our major findings. OAS is an extremely important International Organization. It is, however, highly political and, working there can be difficult. For example, high officials are/were appointed using a political criterion. Once appointed, some officials act like kings and are not amenable to strong criticism. Working under two "strong" Inspectors General during this four-year period, I called attention to several weaknesses which management was correcting. However, most reports described very explicit problems, and the findings obviously alienated one important Official. For instance, one problem related to the fact that its Statement of Financial Condition contained significant material distortions, omissions, and errors. In addition, OAS also had a problem related to numbers and levels of hired personnel. As a result, a high official was attempting to reorganize his six departments in an ill-conceived, haphazard manner, and without considering the needs of the OAS, as an organization; in effect, he abolished the position of the very important Chief Accountant and filled some accounting positions with non-accounting personnel; he also weakened the very important Treasury Department, and there were other similar erroneous organizational changes. At the end of my work, as it related to that office, we held an "Exit Conference" and I told him that there were too many erroneous problems with his plans. As required by our work, we included those findings and required recommendations in an issued OAS/ OIG reports. Nevertheless, this official refused to implement four (4 of 70) recommendations which related to his faulty reorganization plan.

For expressing my Professional opinions, reprisals against me were vicious. Once the I.G. retired, I became a "Persona-Non-Grata" and was not permitted to work in OAS or even enter its buildings anymore. Here is how it happened. When I no longer worked for the new OAS/IG, I was asked to meet two Technical Office Directors; they liked my work and wanted me to do studies *to help them on some of their projects. No more than 10 to 15 minutes into the meeting, a* guard came, telephone conversations went back and forth, and I was told that "someone high up" had told him to escort me out of the building. As if I was a criminal, the guard escorted me out of the building, and I was never again allowed to work in OAS or even allowed to enter its buildings. Although I never officially found who had instigated the reprisals, the source seems so obvious. Also, my two letters, explaining problems, to the Secretary General were never answered by him. Response to my letters was delegated to the very people who treated their office as a "Fiefdom." The responses to my letters can well be imagined by the reader. Even now, I find this incredible - especially that the reprisals took place in a diplomatic organization like OAS. But it happened; the adverse effects of the reprisals, by a narcissistic person, deprived OAS of the desperately needed help -- which I could have given -- to OAS's Technical Projects' and the Field Offices' operations. I wrote a letter to the then U.S. Ambassador to OAS, and that was the end of my appeals.

> ***In my opinion, the operations and administration of OAS could be top-notch. However, back when I did my reviews, OAS needed to: (a) rescind and correct the ill-conceived reorganization plans; (b) relocate, adequately staff, and empower the Office of Inspector General so that it reports directly to the Permanent Counsel of the General Assembly, (c) relocate, adequately staff, and empower the Department of Financial Service so it can perform the functions of a true Financial Manager or Controller; (d) review functions desired, and relocate, if needed, the Treasury Office; (e) inculcate high-level operational officials that reprisal is not within their purview; (f) improve its way of determining human capital***

requirements for administrative and financial operations in a radical manner; and (g) others stated in Chapter 22.

In My Retirement: Despite the career setbacks and except for the loss of three members of my immediate family (mentioned later) and fearing the COVID -19, I have enjoyed my retirement, and to continue my "Pursuit for Improvements." In this connection, I have done the research, written, and published two books, several articles, and have given lectures. Thus, my life and career have been most satisfactorily fulfilled. In Part B, I want to express my appreciation to the people who helped me in drafting my book.

PART B. MY ACKNOWLEDGEMENTS

I owe special thanks to members of my family, my friends, relatives, and work colleagues whose help, contributions, constructive criticisms, guidance, editing, and different forms of assistance are hereby acknowledged and appreciated. They include:

My friends and work colleagues in the USAID: Carlos R. Cabrera and his wife Carmencita Cabrera (who is unfortunately very sick); Eugene and Thu Lan Treasau; Mervin Boyer and his wife. (Note: may Carlos, Gene and Mervin Rest in Peace.)

The two OAS Inspector Generals and my good friends: Alfonso and Cristal Caycedo (may he RIP); Dr. Guillermo and Nora Belt. Their review on the OAS drafts audit reports were tremendously helpful and invaluable. Dr. Larry Posner, CEO for Clapp, and Mayne; his help during my work in Guatemala was plain fabulous.

A special mention and love also go to my relatives and family. They include David and Mary Jacobs; Arthur and Belinda Jacobs; and Diana Noble, and Russell (her husband), and their extended family. They offered great leads and help. (Note: May David and Arthur Jacobs Rest In Peace.)

A special mention goes to Jason and Laureen Fontenot -- my next-door neighbors and excellent friends -- Jason has a fantastic all-around gift in a multitude of disciplines and has been particularly helpful with his computer expertise. He solved many of my computer problems.

With all my love, this book is dedicated to my remaining extended family, including Jose M. Pena III, my oldest son, and his family Lucy Sanchez Pena, and my granddaughter Estela Pena; to Lauren Marie Bucher Delaney -- my second Granddaughter -- and Andrew Delaney, her husband (and their brand-new baby Natalie Marisol Delaney); to Melissa Gisela Pena, my beautiful youngest daughter; and, to Leticia Martinez, my niece.

In addition to my dedication, my son, Jose M. Pena III, deserves a very special mention; he did a fabulous job reviewing and editing my drafts of this book. His reviews went beyond simple editorial, and his research, suggestions, and recommendations resulted in a tremendous improvement of this book.

A special dedication goes to my parents (Jose M. and Hortencia Pena), Pauline A. Pena, my wife for over 61 years, who passed away July 14, 2019; to Linda Marisol Pena Bucher, my daughter who passed away February 10, 2004; and, to Jerry (Gerardo) Javier Pena, my second son, who died August 24, 2017, because of a hospital nurse giving him an accidental overdose of one medication. We miss all of you: my parents, Pauline, Linda, and Jerry very much. The moral support and help they gave to all my extended living family and me during your lifetime was most needed, welcomed, and appreciated. May they now Rest in Peace. Please see the Epilogue for our concluding thoughts on them.

List of Acronyms follows:

PART C. LIST OF ACRONYMS

ACLU	**Afghanistan Construction Logistical Unit**
AIC	**Analyst or Auditor-in-Charge**
AG	**USAID Office of the Auditor General**
AAG	**Assistant Auditor General**
AAG/LA	**Assistant Auditor General for Latin America**
AAG/W	**Assistant Auditor General for Washington, D.C.**
AICPA	**American Institute of Certified Public Accountants**

A/R	**Audit Reports**
BOR	**Banco de la República de Colombia**
BAVINC	**Banco de la Vivienda de Nicaragua**
CAC	**Cairo American College**
CABEI	**Central American Bank for Economic Integration**
CCSC	**Construction Control Services Corporation**
CIA	**Central Intelligence Agency**
CIACOP	**Inter-American Training in Public Communications.**
CIGIE	**Council for the Inspectors General on Integrity and Efficiency**
CIP	**Commodity Import Program**
CPA(F)	**Certified Public Accounting Firms**
CRDA	**Costa Rican Demographic Association**
CVC	**Corporación Autónoma Regional del Cauca**
CWDD	**Converse Ward Davis Dixon**
CPA	**Certified Public Accountant**
DR/IG/A	**Deputy Regional Inspector General for Auditing**
RIG/A	**Regional Inspector General for Audit**
EER	**Employee Evaluation Report also referred to as PER**
EHB	**Ecuadorian Housing Bank**
ESSB	**Ecuadorian Social Security**
EMCALI	**Empresas Municipales de Cali**
FASB 93	**Statement of Financial Accounting Standards No. 93**
FSO	**Foreign Service Officer**
GOC	**Government of Colombia**
GOE	**Government of Ecuador**

GOE	**Government of Egypt**
GON	**Government of Nicaragua**
GOS	**Government of Sudan**
GVN	**Government of South Vietnam**
ICA	**International Cooperation Agency**
IDB	**Inter-American Development Bank**
IG	**Inspector General**
IPPF	**International Planned Parenthood Federation**
MICIVIH	**International Civilian Mission to Haiti**
ISK	**International School of Kenya**
M/T	**Metric ton**
NGO	**Non-Government-Organizations**
OAS	**Organization of American States**
OAS/OIG	**OAS Office of Inspector General**
OAS/UPD	**OAS Unit for the Promotion of Democracy**
OAS/DFS	**OAS Department of Financial Services**
OAS/CPR	**OAS Contratos Por Resultado**
OAS/PSC	**OAS Personal Services Contracts**
OAS/SICE	**OAS Foreign Trade Information System**
OAS/TA	**OAS Travel Advances**
OAS/TEC	**OAS Travel Expense Claims**
OICI	**Opportunities Industrialization Centers International**
OIG	**Office of the Inspector General**
PAI/TRO	**Guatemalan Child Survival Health Project**
PER	**Personnel Evaluation Reports also referred to as EER.**
PIF	**Colombian Private Investment Fund**

PIO/C	**Project Implementation Order for Commodities**
PIO/P	**Project Implementation Order for Participant Training**
PIO/T	**Project Implementation Order for Technical Support**
PVO	**Private Voluntary Organizations**
RAF	**Report of Audit Finding**
RFMC	**Regional Financial Management Center**
TDY	**Temporary Duty Assignment**
THC	**THC Tetrahydrocannabinol**
USAID	**U.S. Agency for International Development**
USAID/RIG/E	**Regional Inspector General for Egypt**
USAF	**United States Air Force**
UT	**University of Texas at Austin**

Part D. List of Qualifications, Pseudonyms And/or Pen Names

As noted in the Prologue, this book covers my careers that expands a period of nearly 40 years. As such, I include many facts, events, analyses, and interpretations in this book; if there are errors in facts, analysis, and/or judgments, in any of this information -- these are solely mine. Moreover, throughout this book -- whenever I think is proper -- I will use the first names, or even full names, to attribute events and/or personalities that affected me in a *positive manner*.

However, because of the complexity and interrelations of some of the different issues that affected me and other people in a negative manner, I will present the details of my positions in five separate Chapters 15, 16, 17, 18, and 19. In such instance, however, whenever the events and/or personalities affected me in a *negative manner,* I will attribute these to a Pseudonym or "Pen" person who I will name "IG#1" or "Guy X," in place of actual names. I do this because most events took place 30 years ago. To me, the adverse issues and/or events are the ones I deem important. Using pseudonyms or attribution system enables me to "…air our adversarial disputes…" but attribute the event to a nebulous Guy. If I were to use proper names, it could adversely affect his/her current family, which I do not wish.

The following chart shows a list of Pseudonyms that I will use. Some like Guys 1, 2, 3 were in Vietnam or Pakistan and not related to IG#1 problem. Those beginning of Chapter 16 and ending in Chapter 19 were related to my problems with IG#1. For instance, Guys 4, 5, 6, and 7, in the chart, used to work for GAO. They were converted, without following rules or actual USAID experience, by the IG#1, to a very high FSO Grade and appointed as Regional Inspector Generals in different locations. To avoid repetition of these facts, I will only say, "New FSO appointed to X position." Here is the chart:

Guy Number - New or Old FSO, Designated Positions Filled by Employee

IG#1	**The first Inspector General who is no longer with USAID.**
1	**Do not recall name. We were In Vietnam.**
2	**Do Not recall we were in Vietnam.**
3	**An Auditor in Pakistan not related to I.G. Problem.**
4	**New FSO appointed as RIG/ A/Washington, later to IG/Policy, and Procedures Office (PPO).**
5	**New FSO appointed as RIG/A/Senegal, then to Washington.**
6	**New FSO appointed IG/PPO and then as RIG/A/ Philippines.**
7	**New FSO appointed as RIG/A/Nairobi.**
8	**A USAID Employee who was Deputy Director in RFMC and who was rancorous and erroneously questioned the SHCEA and SMA after Controller was transferred.**
9	**Joe Feri, An excellent New FSO professional who worked well with all our staff.**
10	**Old IG FSO who replaced Dean H. as RIG/A/LA.**

11	**Old IG FSO who is not a nice Employee, has psychopathic personality, and replaced me as DRIG/A/LA**
12	**Old Time IG Office of Inspector General Investigations.**
13	**Inspector with OIG/N/ He did crazy things for Advancement.**
14	**The USAID I.G. Executive Officer in Washington.**
15	**She replaced the Previous Executive Officer in Kenya,**

CHAPTER ONE
MY EARLY LIFE

PART A. INTRODUCTORY COMMENTS

This first chapter covers my birth, life with my parents, my life in Laredo, the Laredo economic conditions, joining the U.S. Air Force, Junior College, and my University of Texas Years. It is divided into the following nine (9) Parts:

- Part A. Introductory Comment.
- Part B. Birth, Family Life, and Life Growing Up.
- Part C. Elementary School Years.
- Part D. High School Years.
- Part E. The 1950 Economic Outlook of Laredo.
- Part F. U.S. Air Force Military Service.
- Part G Japan, My First Overseas Assignment.
- Part H. Junior College and University of Texas Education.
- Part I. Concluding Remarks.

PART B. BIRTH, FAMILY LIFE, AND LIFE GROWING UP

Introduction: Born over 90 years ago in Laredo, Texas, I was the sixth child of a very poor Mexican family. Honest, hardworking, loving, and stable, my parents were absolutely beautiful people who lived in the house that they built, in 1927, until they passed on. I discuss my family's origins in my previous book, "Inherit the Dust from the Four Winds of Revilla" Here are the names of my family of origin:

José María Peña (father), Hortencia Garcia Peña (mother), Maria Estela Peña (sister), Maria Angelina Peña (sister),

Gloria Hilda Peña (sister), Jose M. Peña (me), Arnoldo Ramon Peña (brother), and three others who died at birth. Maria Angelina died when she was 3 months old; Gloria Hilda was victim of senseless killing when a young boy shot a stone with a slingshot, at me and missed. He hit my sister in the head; the doctor did not diagnose the problem correctly; she died 4 days later (may they all Rest in Peace).

Both of my parents were born in a Mexican town known as Guerrero Viejo. This town was later submerged and destroyed as result of the construction of the Falcon Dam (my book: "Inherit the Dust from the Four Winds of Revilla" provides a history of this town) My parents migrated to Laredo during the tumult of the Mexican Revolution of 1910; and did not become U.S. Citizens until the 1940's. We were poor and life in Laredo when I was a child was hard. Spanish was the only language we spoke until I began attending public school. All my siblings and parents are now gone. So, as I write this – the story involving parts of my life – I do so proudly remember the rough-road I have traveled and my constant pursuit of improvements on the lives and organizations I have touched in different parts of the world – particularly the ones of my family and my own.

As shown in later chapters, life of a Foreign Services Officer is not easy. In fact, my life (and that of my family) was full of achievements, challenges, trials, and tribulations – but with plenty of on-the-job education. This is what the first few chapters attempt to summarize – my life, in brief -- so that I can move to describe, with more details, certain parts of my years (and those of the family) with the U.S. Agency for International Development (USAID) and as a consultant with several organizations that operate in developing countries.

This book is not meant to be a chronology of everything or every circumstance and/or event that happened to me in life, in the Foreign Service, in foreign countries, and/or any organizations. I certainly do not intend to make an in depth organizational, programmatic, and/or financial, analysis or critique of any organization that I worked for. Rather, the emphasis here is to look back, reminisce, and write on a most productive part of my life and to give some examples of interesting things and experiences that I encountered along the way.

Nevertheless, there are certain situations that have weighed in my mind for a long time; as will be stated in Chapters 16, 17, and 18. These situations relate to questions I made over proposed policies that would affect negatively on USAID; these questions resulted in very serious retaliation against me by people who came to USAID from another agency. I will discuss these briefly by way of closure to those bad times in my career.

As much as possible, I will avoid full names of persons and use the first name of the person only. In the case of negative aspects, I will not use the names of the people involved; in those instances, I will briefly cite the different cases only, attribute them to a synonymous person named "Guy," and avoid personal attributions. My work papers do contain the details of these factual situations.

Family life: My years growing up were rough ones. Like my siblings, I was delivered by a mid-wife and was born at 517 Clark Street (now 517 Clark Blvd), in Laredo, Texas. The house, which is pictured as it currently appears (below) had four fair sized rooms. When I was seven or eight, my father built handsome, nice "Greek style" cement pillars. I sold the house about 15 years after my parents died; even now, the house and pillars are still in place. The house now serves as a beauty shop.

My family was poor. In those days, women did not work, and my father was the only one that earned a very meager salary. For 19 years, my father worked for a company as a Chief Clerk for a private company. President Roosevelt's signing the Social Security Act of 1935, would have enabled my father to retire after serving 20 years with the company, but instead, the company found a weak pretext to fire him so as not to have to pay him a penny in social security for all the years of work. This took place during the Great Depression. So, without work or savings, my father and mother courageously struggled to keep an optimistic outlook on life and to feed us. For a time, during this period of unemployment, my father worked as a common laborer cleaning yards and doing menial types of job – just to get food on the table. But my parents were exceptional hardworking people and had good friends and with their help, we managed to survive until he found another job. He worked for the second company for over 23 years, given increasing levels of clerical responsibilities until his retirement. My father never owned a car; he had a used bike. He got up at 4:30 each morning; my mother would prepare a breakfast, some lunch, and he would pedal 6 miles each way to and from work.

From left to right:
Jose M. Pena Jr, Hortencia G. Pena, Estela Martinez,
Baby Letty Martinez, Arnoldo Pena, Baby Joe III with Pauline A. Pena
In Back Alonzo Martinez (my sister's husband)
My Father, Mother, Sister, Niece, Brother, Baby Joe III, Pauline

On the other hand, my mother was a very noble but courageous and supportive woman. She was an excellent cook. Everyone really liked her. Although her name was Hortencia, everyone called her "Tenchita" -- a sign of love and respect. This sign of respect also extended to my father; he was addressed as Don Jose Maria. Even 30 years after their death, people still talk nicely about my parents, especially about my mother. Both were exceptional people and parents.

In my case, I tended to be skinny and shy. I always have had leadership traits, an independent mind, and an ability to select friends and people. Avoiding gangs and drugs (mostly Marihuana), I formed a baseball team, and functioned as the team's manager while at the same time playing second baseman. In managing the team, I was able to judge an individual's playing capabilities well and gave fair opportunities to all participants. However, I was not an exceptional baseball player myself; later, in high school, I tried out for the baseball team, but did not make the cut. I learned to box and had my share of fights – I won some, lost some.

Popularity in Neighborhood: In our neighborhood, we were the only ones that had a telephone. It was an ancient wall telephone, and it also served as a party line. For that reason, neighbors would come and borrow it every day. They would come to the house and say: "Tenchita, me presta el telefono por favor" (Tenchita, may I please use your phone). We knew everyone in our neighborhood, and everyone knew us. For many years, we did not have running water or showers inside our home. The outhouse was about 50 yards away from the house; the ground hole had been dug by my father and friends. To take a bath, we would go to a little shed in the yard and fill a wash tub. We did not have electricity for many years. Laredo gets extremely hot in the summer and bone cold in the winter; we had many of those. Because of the heat, there were many nights that my father, my brother, and/or I would sleep outside on the front porch. Way back then, it was a peaceful time and people slept outside without fear of attacks or violence from outsiders. Everyone knew each other and the neighborhood was poor; so, what could anybody steal?

Groups of us learned to swim and swam at a beautiful round swimming pool, operated by Mr. Jose Gallegos called Buenos Aires. Mr. Gallegos was a Spaniard from Galicia and a tremendous entrepreneur for his time. He certainly was the wealthiest man of the neighborhood. He had the swimming pool, as well as a movie theatre. He owned a lot of land, some of which he donated to build the Buenos Aires School, which still exists? A few years ago, the City of Laredo finally recognized his societal contributions and renamed the Buenos Aires School the "Gallegos School."

Entertainment: When my parents finally put electricity in our house, they bought an old, used radio and we liked to wake up in the morning listening to Mariachi and Mexican Music. Singers of the time included: La Tariacuri, Lucha Reyes, Jorge Negrete, Agustin Lara, Pedro Infante, Trio Los Panchos, and others. We were also glued to the radio listening to novelas about "Maximilian and Carlota," (the man that Napoleon III of France installed as emperor of Mexico) and about "Chucho El Roto" (where Jesus Arriaga, a Robin Hood-type, robbed the rich to give to the poor, and never got caught.) We would go to the movies and see Gene Autry, Roy Rogers, Mario Moreno (Cantinflas), Jorge Negrete, Pedro Infante, Maria Elena Marquez, Maria Felix, Libertad Lamarque, El Pachuco Tin Tan and others. I liked "El Peñon De las Animas," and some scary series, like, "El Monge Loco" (about a crazy monk who played a huge organ and laughed weird). We tried to imitate Pachuco Tin Tan by wearing pants that were wide overall and narrow at the bottom. Since my mother came from a large family (12 in all), I loved our frequent visits with her sister (Adelfa Jacobs) and my cousins (Dolores, Joe, Arthur, and David). Their father (Jose Jacobs) was a well-known photographer who owned one of the best-known photography shops in Laredo. He owned an old Studebaker and in today's politics, my uncle would have been known as a liberal Democrat; he liked to help the most deprived people, i.e., the underdog. He gave me summer work one time. During these few months, I swept and cleaned the photo shop; he held classes on photographic processes; and he increased my pay incrementally each month, until I went back to school. Although Dolores passed on a few years back, the remaining cousins and I remain in touch. Joe and (Arthur and David, now deceased, may they RIP) were extremely successful professionals –Joe was a multi-Language professor; Arthur was a former Internal Revenue Service Regional Director (and an international consultant), and David was a high union leader. Even close to the time he died, David continued to amaze me with his fabulous genealogical collection and historical knowledge. I consulted him frequently.

Sexual Subjects: Certain subjects – especially related to sex, pregnancies, and others. -- were taboo for "kids;" these subjects were only for "grown-up" conversations. Sex education was non-existent. At four or five years of age, with an ever-present curiosity for life and seeing a young woman in what people then called "estado interesante" (interesting state, i.e., pregnant), I asked what was wrong with her, why she had such a big belly, and how did she get that way? Smack! I got a light slap on the back of my head and told not to ask, "impertinent questions." I was told that adults could only discuss these subjects. When a young unmarried neighbor girl got pregnant – and the morning sickness came – all the neighbors followed the strict cultural line that "she is sick because she ate an avocado and milk that were bad." The baby was born eight months later; the baby's father took off and we never again saw him. There were a few divorced or separated ladies that eventually got lovers (married or otherwise); at given days of the week, we would see the ladies, all dolled up and pretty, walking, trying to be very discrete, to meet their "friends" in their encounters; in several ways and not surprising, neighbors whispered. Abortions were illegal and there were no family planning clinics that engaged in such practices. One young girl, who lived a block away from the house, got pregnant. The man refused to marry her, and she got a clandestine abortion. It was done under very unsanitary conditions and for those reasons a horrible infection and gangrene set in. She suffered tremendously and died. That one was a tragedy which could have been prevented.

(Note: At this writing, many years later, Texas recently passed a law which would close legitimate family planning clinics and place several roadblocks against needed or wanted abortions. Its constitutionality was challenged in the courts. At the Federal Level,, the courts recently reversed a 47 year law that permitted abortions. Thus, we are back in square one and abortions are now considered illegal. In my opinion, this law is wrong and will force women back to clandestine abortion practices. If this happens, some women might die, just like my neighbor; these are preventable and unnecessary deaths if done under sanitary conditions of a certified clinic. Let's hope that this law is revoked, and a sensible law codified.

In any event, kids being kids, we had other ways of finding out that there were differences between boys and girls. A little neighbor girl and I had begun experimenting with our differences many times; we would meet in the Buenos Aires School, across the street from my house, hide under closed-in stairwells, and "experiment." I do not think we went "all the way" because her mother (Aurora) would frequently catch us. Running after me, she would chase and yell at me: "…huerco cabron, si te pesco, te voy a capar… (Damn you, if I catch you, I am going to cut them off). Either I was too fast for her, or she was deliberately slow, but she could never catch me.

There were five in Aurora's family – the mother (a widow), two girls, and two boys and they were a hardworking group. The lady's husband had been a police officer who had answered a call on a robbery and had been killed in action. A pretty lady, she later found a "married friend" and was in a "Casa Chica" relationship. A "Casa Chica" relationship is one where the man is married to his wife; he gets a mistress on the side and after that supports two separate families. Both families know each other; they accept and remain silent of their triangular relationship. Despite our childhood explorations, the family liked me and would often take me to the field where I experienced the real hard way of life – picking cotton, picking tomatoes, picking cucumbers, and planting onions. One time, I spent one month in Corpus Christi, working like this with the family. Without a doubt, this was an extremely hard way to make a living.

PART C. ELEMENTARY SCHOOL YEARS

My School Years: Like others in my neighborhood, I only went to public schools; we were too poor to attend private schools. The name of my first school was Buenos Aires School (it has now been renamed as "Gallego School). It was located right across my house.

My first-grade teacher was an elderly lady, perhaps in her late 70s and on the plump side. She was mean-looking and usually dressed in dark-drab-color dresses that reached all the way to the floor. (Note: Although teaching was a very honorable profession, back in those years, teachers did not have a retirement or health plan; so, the teachers worked until old age, or they passed on). In line with her appearances, she was a strict disciplinarian. Of course, being saints ourselves; we would try to escape to the bathroom to flee the monotony of the classes! *After raising our hands to be excused, the teacher would most times point her finger at us and make us tremble by saying: "Alli se cagan o se mean, Pero no me salen." (You can either pee or pooh in your pants, but you are not going any other place."* .... *And so, it was bound to happen that a little girl who sat in front of me had diarrhea one day, raised her hand; the teacher pointed her finger and said the dreaded words. Being refused, the little girl began to cry uncontrollably, and then –* ***IT*** *began to flow all over the seat and onto the floor. Pandemonium broke; I jumped and ran away. The smell was terrible. Some kids gagged, some threw up, others burst into nervous laughter, and some ran out of the room. The teacher stood stoic. The poor little girl was beyond herself. When it was all over, the poor janitor – the grandfather of a good friend of mine – had to come and clean up the mess.* Did the teacher change her ways? No! Not a bit! She certainly was a tough one.

Getting past that teacher, the rest of my schooling times were much easier to handle. By the fourth grade, the U.S Government had a school feeding program and we were given hot chocolate milk each day. I liked that. I also had a young teacher who had a beautiful face, body, and leg attributes. She usually wore nice dresses; anklets that jingled, and she always crossed her pretty legs just right so that her pretty thighs could be seen; my friends and I learned quickly where to position so we could get better views.

Corporal Punishments in Those Days: In the seventh grade, a friend, who died some years ago, and I were caught playing, joshing, and pushing each other in class. *The teacher got mad with us, gave us a note, and we went to the Principal's Office—* ***bad referral****. Back then, Principals were judges, jury, and executioners – and there was no appeal. That chubby principal read the note, took out his wide belt, told my friend he was first, made him bend over the desk, and that belt whistled through the air about five times. Every time the belt was swung, my friend whimpered and cried softly, the principal's face became redder, the cracking noise became more ominous, my eyes got wider, my facial grimacing got weirder, my body language got more contorted, and I got close to sh.ing in my pants. Then, it was all over for my friend, and it was* *my turn on the desk... I still do not know which was worse – the torment of watching or getting the whipping. When we walked out of the office ("shuffled" is a better word -- giddy with nerves -- the other kids looked at us knowingly, some gave us subdued consolations, and no one dared to get close to us. We were pariahs for a few days. At home, that afternoon, we stayed away very quietly and sheepishly from our parents. I don't remember telling them about it. What was the use? They would only side with the principal.*

PART D. HIGH SCHOOL YEARS

High School Years: Many things took place during my high school years. Some friends and I did some hunting and catching rattlesnakes so we could sell them to the pharmaceutical companies for the venom. Two friends were terrific sportsmen, marksmen and hunters; they killed deer, wild boars, and even a small black bear. One (Ernesto Trevino) – together with his uncles -- even caught a small alligator which he kept in his yard; some neighbors reinforced their fences in fear that the creature would escape from its cage. Sometimes we would spend the nights fishing and hear splashing--we always wondered if the splashes were from the alligators.

I liked girls, went to school (and home) dances, danced decently, and had my preferences of girls, but was not an extremely popular guy. The schools had weekly or monthly dances with the "Big Band Sound Orchestra of Laredo." Girls sat on one side of the room and boys asked them to dance; ballroom dancing was gracious and fun.

> *Dances in different homes were fun and funny. I remember dancing in the home of two brothers (Cristobal and Santos Luna – now deceased). With an old-school of record player and 78 revolution records going round and round, dancing was usually in the dusty yards, among the various trees, and the hanging lightbulbs. Music (polka, paso doble, boleros, and others.) was always rhythmic, and the swirling of the couples – at the fast-moving musical paces -- raised a tremendous amount of dust. In the heat of the summer, everyone would be sweating profusely. Sweat and dust formed a hilarious combination. By the end of the night,*

everyone's normal black hair became a matted dark or blondish- brown; and, most faces were powdered, in different clownish shades, by the dust of nature. It was a hilarious scene to say the least. Yet, everyone had fun and enjoyed themselves. Those were beautiful times, in my life, that I will always cherish.

The 1950 high school yearbook says that I was "…strictly the silent type, but congenial…" I took vocational education classes—essentially because I had no money to go to college. I liked building radios and fooling around with the electronic equipment of the time. I used to fix radios in the outlying towns, like Zapata (Texas), and later go to dances. Sometimes, while fixing radios, I would get terrifying electrical shocks a few times; the electrical sizzling lifted me from a stool, transferred me to the floor, and blasted my hair straight up – but I survived.

Anyway, I also took Reserve Officer Training Corps because it was mandatory; but I did not have the inclination or discipline to do well in the Corps. What is funny is that nearly sixty years after leaving high school, while attending a class reunion, a person who had been a "ROTC Sergeant" in High School said very seriously to me: "Joe, you were no good in ROTC. I had a lot of problems with you." I just looked at him and shook my head. I found it so sad that he had been carrying this load – of childhood events and pranks -- etched in his mind, all this time. I don't even recall the pranks we all played on each other; so, they could not have been either that bad or that memorable. But, after so many years gone by and many positive achievements later, what improvements could I now possibly make? So, here is my resolution: I will make improvements in my ROTC discipline on my next go-around on this earth.

In all fairness, though, I was not the best of students, overall. Looking back, I barely graduated from high school on May 31, 1950. However, the reader will find it most interesting that 55-years after just barely making it through high school, I was awarded a very prestigious award (The Tiger Legend Award) from this – my Alma Matter--Martin High School in Laredo. What a turn-around, huh?

Part E. The 1950 Economic Outlook In Laredo

Economic Situation In Laredo: Back in the 1950s, Laredo was a very small, friendly little town; but it was controlled by one family and it was economically deprived. It offered very few economic opportunities. The "Partido Viejo" (Old Party) controlled everything; if a person dissented on their political policies, those people were ostracized and not given jobs and were treated badly. One of my cousins was subject to that type of treatment and for a great deal of time, he was not allowed to get a job as a teacher – for which he was professionally qualified (president of his high school class, a graduate of a university, multi-Language speaker). People left Laredo either after withdrawing or graduating from school.

Like other people in my situation, I was very confused about what to do in the future once I graduated from high school. College was out; my parents could not afford the costs and I lacked both the maturity and discipline to attend college, much less a university. A number of my friends were in the same shape.

Part F. U.S. Air Force Military Service

U.S. Air Force: Thus, it was that around May 25, 1950, a few of my friends and I, walking in the center of the city, passed the Army and Air Force recruitment offices.[1] The U.S. Air Force (USAF) recruiter, who was an expert at seeing a lost soul when he saw one said, "Come in, I would like to talk to all of you." And so we did. The next thing we knew, we were taking a written test. All passed. I passed with flying colors – though to this day, I don't know how. The next thing we knew, those that had passed were taking a semi-physical exam. Being so skinny, I did not weigh the required minimum to serve in the U.S. Air Force. The intrepid recruiter found a nifty solution to that. He took me aside, had me drink up tons of water -- and **voila! Although I peed all afternoon,** I was in the USAF. Several of us went into the USAF Military Service on June 1, 1950.

The first few weeks were awfully hard for me (and my friends). We went through the usual physical exam and shots immediately – hernia check (finger up your groin and cough), bend over, spread them, and a line of nurses giving you a series of injections. Some new recruits fainted. All of us from Laredo were "Macho" though. We got woozy – but acted as if we had only been stung by a fly. Chow was good and I ate well. I liked the SOS, which consisted of a cream sauce with meat in it over toast (usually described Sh..t on the Shingle) in the morning. Although I had forgotten it, a friend reminded me that I ate meatloaf in the early days, became allergic to it, and was sent to the infirmary.

I remember drill Sergeant Arocha putting his face in front of mine, yelling obscenities and Accusations at me, when I did some insignificant thing wrong. I was sent to clean the latrine with a brush and leave it "sparkling-clean." That happened two times. My mama and papa were not there to console me. Making my usual informed analysis, I knew these were battles I could not win. I was on my own -- like Don Quixote de la Mancha, without his trusted sidekick Sancho Panza's, fighting the wild windmills. Unlike Don Quixote, for me, it was enough. I straightened out and flew right from then on.

We were given aptitude tests. Although I had been good with radios and electronics, the Air Force --- in its infinite wisdom --- concluded otherwise. So, I was designated exceptional for the supply field. My other friend's aptitudes were for administration, airplane mechanics, and other things. I guess the assessment by the Air Force was correct; we all did well in life.

All hell broke loose on June 27, 1950, when the Korean War broke out. Some of my friends were sent there. I was more fortunate. During my four-year stint (until 1954), the Air Force gave me education and discipline. As an auditing and supply clerk, I went to a school in Denver, Colorado, and later posted to Watertown, New York, and afterwards stationed in Iwakuni, Japan. I came to Laredo on furlough before transferring to Iwakuni, Japan.

PART G. JAPAN, MY FIRST OVERSEAS ASSIGNMENT

Iwakuni, Japan: Before leaving for Japan, a Laredo girl had promised to wait for me. She was a beautiful girl, nice, a good dancer, and had a gentle personality. She had gone to high school, been my favorite dancer, and graduated with me. So, we liked each other. But other guys were also interested in her and waiting for me to come back in two years was too long. I got a nice "Dear Joe" letter, explaining that she was on the way to the Church

Alter with another nice man. They are a real nice couple, and they continue to be my friends even today.

Iwakuni, Japan, was an interesting assignment. World War II had ended barely five years before and there were no formal barracks. So, we lived in tents – six or eight people in one tent. I was assigned as the tent chief to a group where three people were from the same town in Tennessee. These guys were tough. No one wanted to live with them – and certainly not as Barracks Chief -- because each night they would get drunk and pick fights with everyone. In a very diplomatic manner, I had a talk with higher up officials (I think he was a Captain), and two of the troublemakers were reassigned to units and tents that were a mile away from each other. That was the end of the problem, and I was tagged by the Air Force as a problem solver.

While in Japan, there were a few labor-saving ideas that I promoted, and which were used. One time, the officers wanted to move bins holding thousands of airplane parts to various locations. The bins turned out too heavy, so I devised a pair of bottom wheels, and the bins were more easily wheeled around. Another idea saved a great deal of re-typing parts requisitions. Since computers were nowhere in sight, parts were ordered on "Parts Requisitions" forms. There were times that we did not have parts; so, the requisitions were “back-ordered,” and filled as parts became available. This system required typing and retyping the full requisition over and over. By cutting and pasting on the requisition, My system reduced the retyping aspect.

Iwakuni was a small little village that was 45 minutes away from Hiroshima. It was an agricultural village, and I would see, each day, the hard-working Japanese people plant their rice and carry the “honey-suckle buckets” (buckets full of feces) to fertilize the rice. I was able to visit Hiroshima a number of times. The destruction was horrific. I saw buildings and people that had been burned in the blast; their physical state is still vividly etched in my mind. I met a Japanese girl, in Hiroshima, who had been repatriated from Peru during the war and spoke excellent Spanish. She and I used to have long conversations. I liked Iwakuni, and Hiroshima.

I got to go on a train ride to a training conference in Tokyo. A beautiful city even five years after the war. I saw Emperor Hirohito's home and got to visit the awesome Central Command Headquarters of General Douglas MacArthur. To my way of thinking, General Macarthur was the brightest general – though not the best politician – that the U.S. has ever had.

Anyway, as all soldiers tend to do, I contributed to the local economy by visiting most local bars, drinking Saki and beer, and sharing revelry with the Geishas. The Japanese girls made fabulous companions – very friendly, clean, and reared to be hygienic oriented. I particularly remember "the before…. and…. after hibachi hot baths," and there were quite a few always with a nice companion. The Japanese had tubs of water, which were heated with wood fires from underneath; the hot water was so relaxing. They also had a public hot water pool where anyone could go, take all clothes without any inhibition, and dip in. Drunk, some of us did that once or twice. What terrific customs! I was in a local bar when we were told that Hank Williams, country music singer, had died. I also heard that Jorge Negrete died from Cirrhosis of the Liver and that Pedro Infante had died in a plane crash around that time. I learned a few Japanese songs. When I remember the lines -- over 60 years later -- I keep wondering if the Japanese, unknowingly, invented Saki as way of improving memory retention…. Also, toward the end of my tour in Iwakuni, we were visited, and I saw, Marilyn Monroe and Joe DiMaggio in a show they put for the Thousands of us – the 1000's of us, soldiers. Boy! Back then Marilyn was something to look at….and when she looked at ME (among the 1000's) I almost melted….

Anyway, I went into the Air Force as a buck private and left as a Staff Sergeant, with possibilities of getting additional promotions.

Part H. Laredo Junior College And University Of Texas Education

College and University: For me, the Air Force was an investment of my time which turned my life around. When I got out, I knew that I wanted to take a chance at college and university. If I failed, I could always return and have a very nice Air Force career. A few of my friends did that. They got discharged from the military, tried college, could not adjust, went back, and enjoyed excellent careers.

So, using the G.I. Bill, I enrolled in Laredo Junior College (now known as Laredo College) in September 1954. Thankfully, I had sent my papa and mama a little savings, which they never spent and saved for me. They had also bought a small piece of land where they thought I could build a small house. I sold it and with the money, I bought a used 1950 Ford, learned to drive, and used that car for 7 years. I was lucky in other ways. During my junior college years, I lived with my parents and paid little rent and food. With the recently acquired maturity and discipline, I made the Honor Roll, the upper 10% of the Class, and Phi Theta Kappa in all four semesters. Although I continued to be shy, there were a few girls that were particularly good friends. One girl was special; we went together for close to two years. However, our priorities of life came into conflict and things did not work out for the two of us.

I transferred to the University of Texas at Austin, Texas, and majored in accounting. Barely existing on what the U.S. Government sent, a group of us rented, and lived in, old and beat-up houses and/or apartments and shared rent and food. We took turns at cooking, washing dishes, and cleaning our home. There was no air conditioning, and the heat was terrible. Flies were all over the place. I remember one guy continuously saying "…moscas desgraciadas…" (damn flies). Not much could be done.

Because of the heat, some of us did our studies at the library. All of us studied hard. I took two accounting courses and other required courses in the first semester. One was Theory of Accounts; that one I will always remember. Although I studied like crazy, I got an "F." That was a shocker; this was my major and I had flunked it. Luckily, I took it again and passed it with a "B." After that scare, the rest of the University was easy. I remember that I got "A's" in Cost Accounting and Statistics; these were tough courses. For the first time since its foundation, the University included a course on Computer systems, and I took it. At that time, computers were "the cutting edge of technology and wave of the future…" The IBM 360 Computer was the state of the art--a monster the size of an 8ft X 11ft wall with punch cards for use in programming the computer and tape drives for storage. I was initially overwhelmed, but I managed to get a "B" and lose some fear to what was then considered new technology. This training later served me well, particularly when I worked for USAF as a civilian and at the time when USAID in the 1970s adopted the Wang computer for word processing.

I graduated with a BBA, in accounting, on May 31, 1958. For a person who 0had barely made it through high school, I say that is "...pretty darn good..." Later, I will explain the type of on-the-job liberal education that I got in place of further higher university degrees.

PART I. CONCLUDING REMARKS

This chapter has described my early life, my high school years, my years in the U.S. Air Force, and my graduation from the University of Texas. Although I come from a very humble beginning, thanks to my tour of duty with the U.S. Air Force, the G.I. Bill of Rights, and the sacrifices and love of my parents, I was the first and only person from my parental family to graduate from a university.

CHAPTER TWO
MY EARLY PROFESSIONAL LIFE

PART A. INTRODUCTORY COMMENTS

Introduction. This chapter is divided into 5 Parts:

- **PART A. THE INTRODUCTORY COMMENTS.**
- Part B. Civilian Employee of USAF in General Dynamics
- Part C. Marriage and Family Life.
- Part D. Efforts to Join the International Cooperation Administration.
- Part E. My Concluding Remarks.

PART B. CIVILIAN EMPLOYEE OF USAF ASSIGNED TO GENERAL DYNAMICS

Background information. After graduating from the University of Texas, I was accepted and worked for the U.S. Air Force as a civilian employee for four years.

USAF Civilian Employee: My good grades and my status as a veteran resulted in my being accepted by the USAF as a civilian employee. The acceptance was given before I graduated from the University of Texas. I started my professional career on June 1, 1958, as a GS – 5 Junior Contract Auditor, assigned to audit the General Dynamics Corporation in Ft Worth, Texas. General Dynamics was, at that time, producing the supersonic B-58 bomber. The computer courses at the University of Texas helped me a great deal. During my four-year tour at General Dynamics, I did several computer studies. I found serious problems with General Dynamics' computerized payroll systems as well as the contractors' scheduling and ordering and production systems. Here are only two examples of my findings:

- In the study of the Payroll System, the contractor was paying enormous -- in fact, excessive -- amounts of overtime costs to employees. This way of doing work was not cost-effective to the USAF. My calculations showed that the contractor could hire more employees with the amount of overtime costs and, also, produce the same number of parts in a more economical manner.

- During my study of the Scheduling and Production Department, the contractor had two types of problems: (1) he was scheduling the production of spare parts too early; .and, (2) producing too many parts. The way the Contractor was scheduling and producing the spare parts created a terrific cost problem because many of spare parts would, later on, become obsolete and thus wasted.

General Dynamics curtailed these practices. I ended my assignment, as a GS-11, on January 1, 1962.

PART C. MARRIAGE AND FAMILY LIFE

Marriage: It was in the early stages of my career that I married my wife over sixty-some years ago. My wife, Apolonia "Pauline," was from a town called McNeal that had been absorbed by the city of Austin. I met her at a dance at the Palmer Center when I was still at the University of Texas. We married in Austin, Texas. After we married, we had two sons, both of whom were born in Ft. Worth, Texas. Subsequently, we had two daughters, one of whom was born in Lima, Peru on September 3, 1963, and a second who was born in Bogota, Colombia, on October 26, 1968. Here is my extended family:

- Pauline Aguilar Peña (wife), son Jose M., Gerardo J., Linda M., and Melissa. As I write this part of the chapter, my son Gerardo, Linda, and Pauline have passed-on (died) to, as they say, "…a better world…". I loved them dearly and will carry all of them in my heart until my death.

- Jose M. is married to Lucy, and Estela is their daughter. Jose graduated from the College of William and Mary with honors, is a former Peace Corps Volunteer posted in Costa Rica and Ecuador and got a master's degree from the University of Kentucky. Both he and Lucy are exceptional professional people who work in Washington

D.C. Joe works for the Federal Government, and Lucy recently retired from the Inter-American Development Bank (IDB).

- As I said earlier, Linda Marisol Peña Bucher was born in Lima, Peru, on September 3, 1963. She married, divorced, and sadly died on February 10, 2004. Linda was a redhead, truly beautiful, creative, intelligent, quick, exceptional, and an inspiration to all of us. As the reader might surmise, we miss her terribly. She left a beautiful, red-haired daughter (Lauren), who lived with her father (Kendall) and the other grandmother in California for a few years. Lauren's father died, and Lauren – at this writing – is 26 years old, lived with me for 8 to 10 years, and is now married to Andrew De Laney. At this writing, they have a baby girl (Natalie Marisol De Laney). She is just fabulous. She is now 7 months old. They are so happy together.
- Jerry graduated with two Associates in Arts Degree, one from the Northern Virginia Community College in Annandale, Virginia, and a second from the Austin Community College in Austin, Texas. Jerry taught himself to speak and write Arabic quite well. He died because of a nurse's terrible mistake in administering a medication known as Temazepam which is used to enable people to sleep. Instead of giving him 7.5 milligrams of medicine, the nurse gave Jerry 75 milligrams.
- Melissa is a deeply religious person. Neither Jerry nor Melissa ever married.

Anyway, during our life in Ft Worth, we first lived in a tiny apartment, then we moved to a house near the former Carswell Air Force Base where General Dynamics was located. I remember sharing our bathroom with raccoons and possums, who somehow, would find ways of entering the house. Since we were just starting, we had no air conditioner; we had a window cooler – the old kind which was covered by straw. To cool off, we had to hose down the straw, which got wet. The fan sucked the water. On the plus side, it did provide cool air. On the negative side, it spewed water into the living area. The pay was decent, but for many years, we still drove my old 1950 Ford.

PART D. EFFORTS TO JOIN THE INTERNATIONAL COOPERATION ADMINISTRATION

Desire to Enter the International Cooperation Administration. As I entered my third year as an Air Force civilian employee at General Dynamics, I began to hear of the work done by the International Cooperation Administration (ICA) in other countries. The more I researched, the more I liked the idea of helping people in Less Developed Countries.

The concept of ICA had started right after World War II with the Marshall Plan. Military and non-military assistance was indistinguishable. There was economic, technical, and military assistance going into the different countries. So, my expectations were to provide technical support in some areas and in some other countries.

After I asked ICA for information, I got a telephone call asking if I was really interested. Of course, I was. ICA was very picky in its selection and vetting procedures. They sent me an application, and I filled it out.

> *The next thing I knew, they sent me a timed test that I took in a U.S. Government Office. They called me again and told me to pick an "ICA Official," by a certain name, at the airport. All they told me was he would talk to my wife and me. So, on the indicated day, I picked him up. While the window fan kept humming and spewing water, he visited with us for about three hours. We offered him a beer; he took a coke. So, we drank cokes the entire time he was there. There was question after question, and we seemed to have talked about everything – home life, national and international economics, politics, and others. With some of the questions, I flew by the seat of my pants; even after more than 66 years – the questions still boggle my mind:*

- Are you humble? How humble are you on a scale of 1 to 10?
- Have you ever been arrogant? On a scale of 1-10, how arrogant?
- Are you diplomatic with people? How diplomatic, on a scale of 1 to 10?

How do you respond to such questions? If I answered low or too high, I would be a fool, a nincompoop, a rascal, or a security risk. For three hours, the dammed window fan kept humming, spewing water on all of us, the questions kept coming, and I kept going for the middle ground.

To this day, I do not know what the guy was – a psychologist, investigator, FBI, CIA, DOD, and others. And to this day, I do not know whether I was being interviewed as a technician or a CIA agent. So, it was such a relief to take him to the airport, and I never expected to hear from ICA again. But hear, I did. The next thing I knew, I was being investigated very thoroughly – and I mean very thoroughly. A couple of months went by, and they sent me papers authorizing my family (Pauline, Joe, Jerry) and me to take a physical exam in a U.S. Public Health Office. We all passed with excellence.

The next call was to ask if I would accept an assignment in British Guiana (now Guyana). I knew the country was in South America (it's by Venezuela), but I did not know anything about it. Taking a risk that they would not even consider me any further, I asked them if I could do some research on it. They sent me the "Post Report," and I did a further study. Guyana was not for my family. So, I wrote a nice letter explaining that I had Spanish capabilities that ICA could better use me elsewhere. The wait and uncertainty were interminable.

PART E. CONCLUDING REMARKS

While I was being processed through the employment procedures, the U.S. Congress passed the Foreign Assistance Act of September 4, 1961 (FAA). This FAA emphasized long-term development assistance to countries and totally reorganized the way development and military assistance was to be provided. Various assistance venues – social, economic, development loan funds, and certain local currency functions of the Export-Import Bank, Public Law 480 (Food for Peace), and others. – were consolidated, and the philosophical concepts of U.S. foreign assistance changed.

Ten months after President John F. Kennedy was sworn in, the name of the International Cooperation Administration was changed to the U.S. Agency for International Development (USAID). Kennedy also created the Peace Corps and, there was renewed political and economic interest in Central and South America under a Kennedy initiative known as the Alliance for Progress. The Alliance for Progress was a ten-year plan that increased the amount of U.S. assistance to Latin America.

After a long delay, I was asked if I would take an assignment in Peru. I said: "perfecto." And so, it was that I went to Washington D.C. for training on January 4, 1962, embarking on a career full of education, adventure, personal hardships, sacrifices, and the greatest opportunity of an excellent lifetime.

Before going overseas, we finally exchanged the old Ford for a huge 1961 Dodge Dart that had Push Buttons in place of an automatic stick shift.

My immediate family lived with me in six of the nine overseas posts – Peru, Ecuador, Colombia, Panama, Egypt, Kenya (and, of course, in Virginia). We also traveled together to many other countries. The numbers of family separations, three required forced assignments, the many temporary assignments, certain personality differences and temperaments, certain tendencies towards selective repressed memories – and my own ways of dealing with personal problems – created some problems in our marriage; but we stayed together until Pauline recently died (on July 14, 2019).

CHAPTER THREE
THE U.S. AGENCY FOR INTERNATIONAL DEVELOPMENT (USAID)

PART A. INTRODUCTORY REMARKS

Some Background: After being in U.S. Air Force and working as a civilian for the Air Force at General Dynamics Corporation, in Ft. Worth, for a few years, I joined USAID on January 4, 1962. I spent my career being posted in several countries. This will be stated in more detail in a series of Chapters in this book. I retired on December 31, 1989, i.e., after a total of about 36 years in government service.

Because this chapter presents a series of complicated information, it is divided into the following twelve (12) Parts:

- Part A. Introductory Comments.
- Part B John Kennedy Greeting USAID Mission's Directors and Deputy Directors.
- Part C My Preliminary Observations.
- Part D A View of the 2021 USAID Organizational Structure.
- Part E. Profiles of Assistance per AID/W Documents.
- Part F. Distinction Between a Project and Non-Project in the Field.
- Part G. Some Types of Projects Conducted at Field Levels.
- Part H. Some Types of Non-Projects Conducted at Field Levels.
- Part I. Some Other Types of USAID Assistance.
- Part J. Assistance Highlights Per "The Front Lines."
- Part K. El Otro Sendero (The Other Path) An Excellent Treatise On How to Help the Under-Served Informal Sector.
- Part L. Concluding Remarks.

PART B. JOHN F. KENNEDY GREETING USAID DIRECTORS AND DEPUTIES

Here is a photograph of John F. Kennedy greeting the many USAID (Mission) Directors and Deputy Directors six months after the USAID was born:

JFK greets USAID directors and deputy directors on the White House lawn, June 8, 1962.
Picture by Robert. Knudson

PART C. MY PRELIMINARY OBSERVATIONS OF USAID

When I joined USAID, I found that, although it receives foreign policy guidance from the U.S. Department of State, USAID is an independent organization, extremely complex, whose programs, equally complex, were designed to address isolated, bilateral, multilateral, and multilevel type of problems, the world over, all of which were authorized by the Foreign

Assistance Act of 1961, since amended. USAID is affected by frequent political directions that the U.S. Congress or the President might take. Thus, it is a most dynamic organization that evolved significantly during my employment and is in a frequent state of adaptation to changing conditions.

When USAID was conceived, its objectives were broad, and they were designed to address the many problems of an ever-changing world, i.e., budgetary assistance, balance of payments, technology, agriculture, health, globalization, population growth, conflicts, weapons, drugs, terrorism, micro-credit-assistance techniques, finance, and others.[1]

Its objectives were revised and narrowed by the Foreign Assistance Act of 1973. In effect, this amendment called for new functional assistance categories aimed to help the "poorest majority" or the "poorest of the poor." It concentrated assistance into many categories such as food and nutrition, health and family planning, education, and human development.[2]

In 1978, President Jimmy Carter created a new organization, known as the International Development Cooperation Agency, which was supposed to coordinate all the assistance being provided by the U.S. This organization existed mostly on paper, did not have much authority, and did not survive. This organization was abolished in 1998.

PART D. A VIEW OF THE 2021 USAID'S ORGANIZATIONAL CHART

Statement of Mission, Vision and Values: Both the statement and the organizational chart that follows were obtained from the following web site: https://www.USAID.gov/who-we-are/organization

[1] Foreign Assistance Act of 1961 and own experience.
[2] An Internet Document called "Overview of the US Foreign Assistance Acts, p2

On behalf of the American people, we promote and demonstrate democratic values abroad, and advance a free, peaceful, and prosperous world. In support of America's foreign policy, the U.S. Agency for International Development leads the U.S. Government's international development and disaster assistance through partnerships and investments that save lives, reduce poverty, strengthen democratic governance, and help people emerge from humanitarian crises and progress beyond assistance.

USAID Washington and Field: The above Vision of Responsibility and the following organization chart represents major components as of the Year 2021. According to the Chart, USAID was reorganized in September 2021. The website is excellent: However, the reorganization shows the limits which I must make to my book. The Chart and the new USAID way that the Agency will carry-out its new responsibilities is beyond the scope of this book. We present this data as a matter of information only.

US AGENCY FOR INTERNATIONAL DEVELOPMENT STRUCTURE

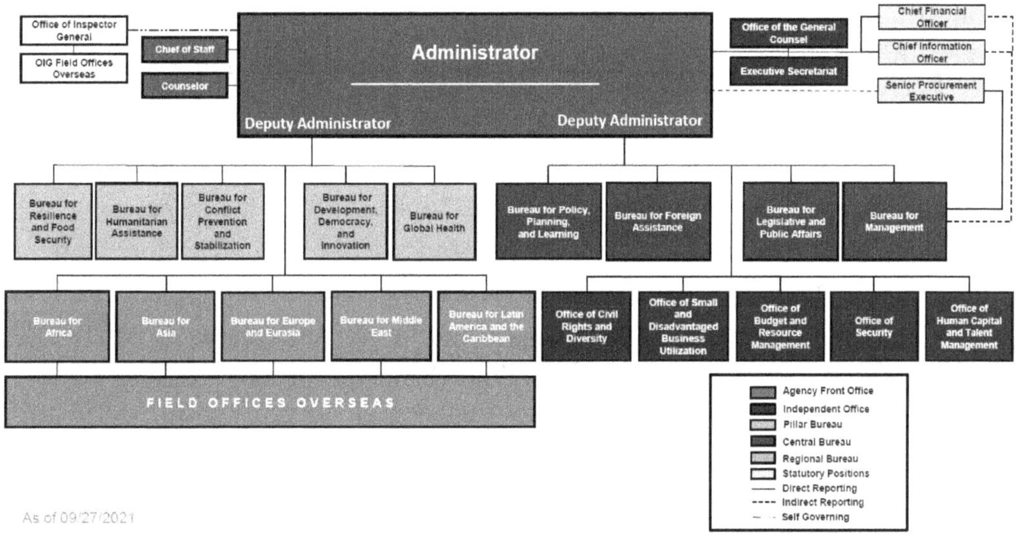

When USAID was conceived, its objectives were broad, and they were designed to address the many problems of an ever-changing world, i.e., budgetary assistance, balance of payments, technology, agriculture, health, globalization, population growth, conflicts, weapons, drugs, terrorism, micro-credit-assistance techniques, finance, and others.[3]

Its objectives were revised and narrowed by the Foreign Assistance Act of 1973. In effect, this amendment called for new functional assistance categories aimed to help the "poorest majority" or the "poorest of the poor." It concentrated assistance into many categories such as food and nutrition, health and family planning, education, and human development.[4]

In 1978, President Jimmy Carter created a new organization, known as the International Development Cooperation Agency, which was supposed to coordinate all the assistance being provided by the U.S. This organization existed mostly on paper, did not have much authority, and did not survive. It was quietly abolished in 1998.

USAID partners to end extreme poverty and promote resilient, democratic societies while advancing our security and prosperity.

As seen by the above chart, USAID is complex. It is directed by the USAID Administrator, two Deputy Administrators, and supported by a series of offices, regional bureaus, departments, and technical offices. The regional bureaus are represented by field offices located in many countries of the world.

The above chart shows the Office of the Inspector General, for which I served for many years, as a separate entity. As a result of the Inspector General Act of 1978, it is now entirely independent of USAID. Moreover, responsibilities of the Inspector General has been expanded; in effect, the Office of I.G. now has oversight responsibilities for the following separate organization: (a) USAID; (b) Millennium Challenge Corporation; (c) U.S. African Development Foundation; (d) Inter-American Foundation; (e) Overseas Private Investment Corporation. The scope of this book does not include the most current functions of the Office of Inspector General.

---

[3] Foreign Assistance Act of 1961 and own experience.
[4] An Internet Document called "Overview of the US Foreign Assistance Acts, p2

PART E. PROFILES OF ASSISTANCE PER AID/W DOCUMENTS[5]

Per the website (www.USAID.gov/about_USAID/primer.html),[6] USAID "…plays a vital role in promoting U.S. national security, foreign policy, and the War on Terrorism…." It aids "…in Pakistan, Africa, Asia, Near East, Latin America and the Caribbean, Europe and Eurasia…" and the types of assistance that it provided during the writing of this book include:

- Agriculture and Food Security
- Democracy and Government
- Economic Growth
- Technical assistance and capacity building.
- Education, Training, and scholarships.
- Food aid and disaster relief.
- Health.
- Ending Extreme Poverty.
- Environment.
- Infrastructure construction.
- Small-enterprise loans.
- Budget support.
- Enterprise funds.

Just for information purposes only, here is what USAID will do beginning with the reorganization of 2021:

- Agriculture and Food Security.
- Anti-Corruption.
- Climate Change.
- Democracy, Human Rights, and Governance.
- Economic Growth and Trade.

---

[5] Based on Attachment B of an Audit Plan For The Office of Contracts and Grant Management, dated April 20, 1977

[6] Web site of U.S. Agency For International Development, different parts.

- Education.
- Environment, Energy, and Infrastructure.
- Gender Equality and Women's Empowerment.
- Global Health.
- Humanitarian Assistance.
- Innovation, Technology, and Research.
- Nutrition.
- Transformation at USAID.
- Water and Sanitation.
- Working in Crises and Conflict.

To sum it up, USAID's future responsibilities have been significantly expanded.

Looking at the Past. During one of my assignments in the Washington Office, I was asked to prepare a comprehensive review plan to evaluate USAID's Office of Contracts and Grants. One other person helped me. Back in 1978, this huge office was then in charge of receiving requests from the technical offices, advertising for the services, identifying the best supplier to do the work, negotiating with that company or organization, and writing the required legal document (contract, grant, Indefinite Quantity Contract or IQC, or other). (Note: As described in this part, the Office of Contracts and Grants was a most important one back then; however, its importance is no longer prominent – according to the previously shown organizational chart).

One of the first things we did was to determine the number of active documents (1,908) at the time and their total value ($635,407,000). These were the total active contracts, grants, and documents that the AID/W Office of Contracts and Grants had generated for the AID/W technical offices alone; it did not include multiple and bilateral agreements with the different countries, administrative costs, salaries, Public Law 480 Food for Peace assistance or Commodity Import Programs, Cash Grants, and others. However, the statistics give a feel for magnitudes and other interesting information.

Anyway, our cut-off date was in 1978. The information of the active documents and total value were then reassembled into 12 different profiles to analyze the statistics from different perspectives. Here is the way that four profiles – that I chose to include in this book -- looked at the time:

The first Profile is by type of document. It shows that at that time, documents were basically divided between grants and contracts.

		Number of Agreements	US $000	Percent
By Type of Document:				
1.1	Grants	374	$ 277,963	43.7%
1.2	Contracts	956	$ 273,166	43.0%
1.3	Other -- IQC, W.O., D.O. others	578	$ 84,278	13.3%
	Total	**1908**	**$ 635,407**	**100.0%**

The work order and delivery orders were the type of documents used at the time but were not the preferred type of documents. The Indefinite Quantity Contracts[7] were beginning to gain importance and became a very popular form of contracting for services. These IQC were essentially time and material types of contracts. Under an IQC, USAID negotiated predetermined labor rates with various contractors. The predetermined labor rates contained several factors: direct labor, indirect costs, administrative fees, and a certain percent for profit. After I completed the Audit Plan, the IQC types of contracts were reviewed, and many abuses were found. ***Even at the time when I retired, Contractors were still abusing the system by charging USAID all the IQC factors and a separate "Indirect Costs" and fees -- I hope the current IG monitors these types of abuses very carefully.***

The second Profile is by type of documents. Most were reimbursable contracts. The second form was "Other types of contracts," and the third was grants.

Number of Agreements	US $000	Percent

[7] Audit Report No. 77-70, May 18, 1977, entitled "Survey of AID Policies and Procedures for Indefinite Quantity Contracts. Filed in w/p of Chapter 3 files.

By Type of Specific Document				
2.1	Fixed Price Contracts	263	$ 28,036	4.4%
2.2	Cost Reimbursement	710	$ 244,035	38.4%
2.3	Cooperative Agreement	11	$ 4,006	1.0%
2.4	Grants	374	$ 277,963	43.8%
2.5	PASA	0	$ -	0.0%
2.6	Other -- IQC, D.O., and others.	550	$ 81,367	12.4%
	Total	**1908**	**$ 635,407**	**100.0%**

The third Profile is by Purpose or Objectives. It showed that the amounts of documents written by the Contracts Office were mostly for Technical Assistance, research, and different technical services needed by AID.

By Purpose or Objectives		Number of Agreements	US $000	Percent
3.1	Training	120	$ 27,179	4.3%
3.2	Technical Assistance	791	$ 311,873	49.1%
3.3	Architectural and Engineering	49	$ 7,881	1.2%
3.4	Construction	15	$ 5,893	0.9%
3.5	Voluntary Funds	15	$ 6,212	1.0%
3.6	Research	145	$ 98,132	15.4%
3.7	Technical Services to AID	506	$ 60,502	9.5%
3.8	Training and Technical Assistance	66	$ 19,428	3.1%
3.9	Commodities	45	$ 4,394	0.7%
3.1	Other	156	$ 93,913	14.8%
		1908	**$ 635,407**	**100.0 %**

The fourth Profile was by geographical areas. It clearly showed that documents written in Washington affected worldwide areas, Middle East, Latin America, and Africa.

By Geographical Areas		Number of Agreements	US $000	Percent
4.1	World-Wide	714	$ 316,048	49.7%
4.2	Asia	281	$ 44,265	7.0%
4.3	Near East	198	$ 77,146	12.1%
4.4	Latin America	378	$ 79,416	12.5%
4.5	Europe	11	$ 6,717	1.1%
4.6	Africa	311	$ 106,553	16.8%
4.7	Miscellaneous	15	$ 5,262	0.8%
	Total	**1908**	**$ 635,407**	**100.0 %**

Of course, the 1978 statistics shown in the above four profiles are no longer representative of a picture taken in today's world conditions. They certainly do not consider the bilateral assistance to the individual countries around the world. But they give a feel for how USAID assistance documents awarded through the central office looked at the time. In today's world, probably a great deal would go to Israel, Egypt, Iraq, the rest of the Middle East, and Africa.

PART F. HERE IS A DISTINCTION BETWEEN PROJECT AND NON-PROJECT ASSISTANCE AT FIELD LEVELS

We now go to field offices. A field USAID Mission usually consists of a Mission Director, a Deputy, Directors for the various Departments (agriculture, health, and others.), and their respective Project Officers.

The Missions usually operate using three types of modalities. The principal ways this is done in the field is through Projects and Non-Projects. Here is the differentiation guidance (called Paradigm) in a handbook (HB 3 of that time). USAID sets the parameters of when an activity should be a Project or a Non-Project activity. The Paradigm follows:

	Project Assistance	**Non-Project Assistance**
Objective	To increase the well being of a specified, identifiable portion of the population through the creation or transfer of knowledge creation or modification of facilities or institutions, or modification of policies and programs.	To increase the supply of resources. The volume of assistance is dependent upon the adequacy of supply and economic variables, rather than impact upon specified beneficiaries. .
Measurable Results	Generally, a long-range change in the condition of The target population occurs.	Generally, a short-term relief from macro-constraints and changes in the general economy takes place.
Analysis	Depends upon demonstrated linkages between the project inputs and the target group; Essentially by micro-economics analysis.	Depends upon the linkage between the resource supply and the inputs; essentially by macro--economics.

In sum, the above paradigm provides excellent parameters for projects and non-program assistance. Simply put:

- If the activity is to affect a definite or identifiable part of the population (say a grain silo) and the economic effects will be over a long-term basis, it should be a project.
- If the activity is to increase resources (say food) that are in short supply in that country and the economic effect will be for a short duration, then the proposed activity must be financed as a Non-Program Assistance.

There have been times when these instructions were not followed. The consequences were terrible. In fact, as will be explained in Chapter13 covering my tour in Egypt, my team and I did a review of over $1.0 billion of the Commodity Import Program and found some very complex type of problems which had quickly developed when USAID/Egypt officials attempted to misuse this theory to accomplish "Project-Like Activities" or to purchase "Durable Commodities" using a non-project approach.

PART G. TYPES OF PROJECTS CONDUCTED AT FIELD LEVELS

This part shows examples of the types of projects conducted at the country or field level. My information dates from my first assignment (to Peru, in January 1962) to my last assignment (to Kenya in 1988).

PART G1. TWO ICA PREFERRED ASSISTANCE CONDUITS INHERITED BY USAID

Servicios: When I joined the organization, a great many activities in the Caribbean and Central and South America centered on joint-ventures – called "Servicios" -- between USAID and the respective host governments (a "host government" means the government of any given country such as Peru, Ecuador, Vietnam, Colombia, and others.). There were separate Servicios – in each country -- for Agriculture, Labor, Health, Education, Rural Development, and Regional Development Plans.

These Servicios were huge organizations and normally had two joint directors – one representing USAID (which took over ICA functions) and one representing the host government. Most times, funds were assigned equally by both USAID and the host government. Every Servicio had its own "Controller," and each had a slew of administrative and technical people who implemented projects within their field of specialty. This concept for programs implementation had been in place during the time when USAID was known as the ICA. When USAID took over the ICA's functions and the "Alianza Para El Progreso," (Alliance for Progress) was conceived, the concept lost favor. After that, the Servicios began to phase out and were all closed in the late 1960s.

PART G2. ESTABLISHMENT OF MUTUAL ASSOCIATION SYSTEMS

The establishment of a Mutual Association System in Ecuador had Serious Problems: At the time I arrived in Ecuador, the USAID was helping the Central Housing Bank of Ecuador establish and guide the organization and operations of an entire Mutual Association Banking System. As shown in Chapter 6 of this book, my review – dating back over 50 years ago -- showed a program with numerous problems, at all levels and of all nature. It was a program that seemed afflicted by Murphy's Law... "Whatever could go wrong…went…" This Program -- that because of its multiple levels, its separate locations, its different complexions, the requirements and following of strict rules and regulations, and in need of constant guidance and monitoring – had not been properly designed, did not have the right number of people to implement it and needed radical improvement. Twelve different Mutual Associations were chartered and had haphazardly begun to operate in different cities -- like Quito (2), Loja (1), Ambato (1), Cuenca (1), Esmeraldas (1), Guayaquil (3), Ibarra (1), Riobamba (1), and Quevedo (1).[8] However, our 102-page final report showed a nightmare of problems and – some very serious abuses. Charters, rules, procedures, and monitor were not in place, and each association was observing different rules and operations were "…every which way…"

After completion of my review, I helped complete a study where there was embezzlement in the Civic Action Project, and I was subsequently transferred to South Vietnam. I had not revisited this area until I began writing this book. My recent review of the Internet showed that only five (of 12) Ecuadorean Mutual Associations established during my time (Pichincha, Azuay, Ambato, Cuenca, and Imbabura), that I reviewed are still in existence

[8] Basic information came from Audit Report 65-38 entitled AID Loan 518-A-012, Ecuador: Central Housing Bank Program., Chapter 3 file

and growing. The others probably did not survive. In sum, this program was only partially successful.

PART G3. PROJECT, LOANS, AND GRANTS AGREEMENTS REPLACED ICA ASSISTANCE CONCEPTS

Project Agreements: Once it took over, USAID began to sign separate bilateral project agreements" with the host governments. Since activities may have different objectives, project agreements are signed for each individual activity, i.e., Agriculture, Private Enterprise, Transportation, Labor, Health, Education, Public Safety, Community Development, Women in Development, Civic Action, Drug Enforcement, and others. Each project agreement describes how it will achieve the objectives of the agreed activity. This plan usually shows the required inputs (like technical services, commodities, participant training, and others.). Here is a brief description:

- Technical services are provided through a (Project Implementation Order for Technical Services or, in USAID's terms, a "PIO/T." Technical service contracts were and are signed, usually with a U.S. firm, organization, and/or individual, to provide the needed type of technician or technical help (engineering, architectural, agricultural, education, and others.).
- Commodities are provided through a Project Implementation Order for Commodities (known as a PIO/C) and can be any items needed to implement the project activity (tractors, fertilizer, seeds, irrigation pumps, computers, electrical generators, condoms, pills, and others.). Normally, the commodities must be purchased in the U.S.
- Participant Training (training of people) is done through a Project Implementation Order for Participants (PIO/P). Although the individual signs an agreement to return to the country of origin after completion of the studies, however, many stay in the U.S. or go to other countries. I*n other words, if the participant training program is to achieve its objectives, its implementation needs to be improved.*

The agreements also provide the terms under which the funds are disbursed -- usually in step with the progress of the activity. In this connection, funds provided by USAID may be either grants or loans:

- Grants do not have to be repaid by the host country.
- Loans must be repaid by the host country. These are soft term and long-term types of loans. They may be repaid in either U.S. dollars or local currency.
- One other condition is that it is USAID policy that whenever possible, commodities and services have their origin in the United States. This is an excellent policy because most funds that originate in the U.S. return to help the U.S. economy.

Development or Capital Development Loans: There were also several types of development loans that had been inherited – and basically "renamed" -- from the newly eliminated Development Loan Fund. USAID refined these types of loans and, to my knowledge, continue even today. These loans cover the gamut of needed activities and country requirements. Aside from financial parameters, the objectives of USAID loan programs have no discernible limits. They can be for anything. Here are some examples:

- Peru was provided loans for the Puno Emergency, the Lima Water Authority, feasibility studies, the Pucallpa Road, Mutual Savings Association, Central Homes, and others.
- Ecuador had a number of loans. One was to establish an entire Mutual Association Program (discussed earlier); another was to achieve an Integrated Rural Development Program (also discussed later on);
- Egypt had a massive number of projects and loans. One loan was for the construction of Grain Silos. A great many were for procurement of durable and non-durable commodities and to implement "project-like" activities.

Two-Step Loans:[9] Some of the loans made by USAID are two-step types of financing mechanisms. Colombia is a good example. Under a two-step loan

---

[9] Information obtained from an Audit Report (No. 1-514-71-96) I did in March 15, 1971 entitled "Eleven Two-Step Loans of Colombia," P.2 and Exhibit A.

arrangement, from 1968 to 1972, Colombia borrowed $55 million to achieve nine different projects through local organizations.

Since the projects were to be achieved by semi-private organizations, the USAID signed the Loans through the Government of Colombia (GOC). In turn, the GOC signed individual sub-loans, contracts, or agreements with nine organizations. Here is a partial list: the Cali Sewerage ($3.7 million), the Rural Electric Cooperatives ($1.3 million), Medellin Sewerage ($.2 million), Bogota Sewerage ($.4 million), a livestock bank ($6.1 million), and a Private Investment Fund ($10. million).

Repayments between the two levels of participants had different arrangements for (a) Interest rates, (b) grace periods, and (c) repayment terms. In effect:

- The GOC was to repay USAID in U.S. Dollars. The rate of interest ranged between 75 to 2.0%. It had a 10-year grace period. The Government was to repay the complete loan for 30-40 Years.
- The Semi-Autonomous Organizations were to repay the GOC in Local Currency. Their rate of interest was between 2.0 to 9.5%. They had a grace period of 5 to 10 years. And, they had to repay the loan between 10 to 20 Years. The Local Currency repayments were deposited in certain Special Accounts.

In sum, there were financial benefits accruing to the GOC through the differences between rates of interest, grace periods, and repayment terms. These were referred to as (a) Interest Differentials, (b) Grace Differentials, and (c) Principal Differentials. The accrued amounts of the Local Currency in the Special Accounts could then be either reused for other sub-programs, re-loaned to other entities, and/or sometimes used to subsidize the Government's budget. *Because of the five-country benefit, the two-step approach is, in my opinion, an excellent assistance approach; I discuss the five benefits to host countries in Chapter 19.*

PART G4. IN 1973, CONGRESS DESIRE TO REACH POOREST OF POOR INITIATED CONCEPT OF DESIGNING VERY COMPLEX LOANS AND GRANTS

Complex Loan or Grant Programs: By the middle of 1970s, as Congress issued its 1973 mandate to try to reach the poorest of the poor and both USAID and Host Governments became comfortable with the Project and Program concept, USAID began to design greatly complicated integrated programs which could be financed with grant or loan funds – depending on the country. Although each country had specific goals that were in of addressing, there were great similarities between programs. Here is one example which might very well be representative of those being implemented in other similar countries where the complex type of programs is in place.

In the 1980s, the "Integrated Rural Development Program for Agriculture of Ecuador (Project 518-0012)"[10] represented a national (Ecuadorean) policy that t pursued two broad objectives: (a) to reduce the isolation of rural areas; and (b) to curtail massive migrations by Campesinos into the cities. The overall program was designed to create and support an implementing organization – as a Secretariat very near the Presidential level – to be called "The Rural Development Secretariat (SEDRI)." This secretariat was to implement activities in seventeen different areas of Ecuador and involve activities in agriculture, health, forestry, energy, rural technology, community development, and training.

To finance such a complex program, Ecuador received financial assistance from a slew of international organizations such as USAID, Inter-American Development Bank, World Bank, United Nations, Organization of American States, Germany, and others.

Aside from establishing SEDRI, USAID was to finance and implement two "multidimensional interventions" in two areas of Ecuador (the Salcedo and Quimiag-Penipe area). These areas were extremely difficult to work in because they were near the top of the Cotopaxi and Chimborazo Volcanoes.

---

[10] Basic information came from a draft audit report I wrote in December 7, 1983 entitled "Draft Audit Report for the Integrated Rural Development Program for Agriculture (Project 518-0012, Loan No. 518-T-038).

In any event, each intervention contained the following features:

1. Two irrigations systems and several tertiary canals.
2. Short and Long-Term credit for farms, commodities, and technical assistance.
3. Financial and technical assistance.
4. Marketing inputs such as tree nurseries, animal reproduction centers, and road improvements.
5. Land tenure assistance (titling, legal aid, and studies.
6. Forestry and resources conservation.
7. Community participation centers.
8. Health, nutrition, and potable water.
9. Other employment opportunities.

As the reader might observe, these programs were "masters of complexity," planning was most complex, progress usually slow, and an evaluation of achievements extremely difficult to determine. **I saw and evaluated these types of assistance, or broad sector approaches in Ecuador, Honduras, Costa Rica, Jamaica, Haiti, Botswana, and Yemen.** *In each area, I was able to show some commendable degrees of progress, different types of program implementation problems, and recommend ways in which improvements could be made.* ***(Note: If a broad base type of an evaluation were to be done today, I wonder whether all the work was completed and whether the principal project objectives – of curtailing Campesinos from migrating into the Urban areas -- were achieved??).***

G5. A Unique Way USAID Reaches The Poorest Of The Poor

Shift to Poorest of Poor: When I first joined, USAID assistance was granted using the "trickle-down economic theory," meaning that most funds were granted through governments and expected to gradually cascade to the different strata of the country socio-economic structure.

As I stated previously, this concept was changed beginning in 1973 when the U.S. Congress passed a congressional mandate requiring USAID to redirect its efforts and emphasize the rural and the poorest of the poor. This new direction became a great implementation challenge because many countries did not have a good handle on the number of people in rural towns and villages. Planning and implementation for such types of activities were difficult.

The result was the development of overly complex types of projects – like the Integrated Rural Development Projects in different countries – were designed primarily to attempt to help or affect some of those classified as the so-called "poorest of the poor."

Despite the complex concepts used in the early beginning of the 1973 Congressional Mandate, it came down to a simpler change in lending philosophy. As explained below, changes to the way loans were made has been a huge difference for one segment of the poorest population. There is uncertainty on the origins of the concept. Some say that the first person to use the theory was Muhammad Yunis, from Bangladesh, who established the Grameen Bank[11]. Others attribute the first use to John Hatch, who while serving as a consultant for USAID and based in Bolivia, began to use the concept in the Bolivian Villages. *Regardless of who first started it, the concept has been fantastic in addressing segments of the poorest of the poor.* It works in this manner:

- USAID signs a project agreement with the host country to implement a microloan or credit financing program.
- It contracts organizations like the Foundation for International Community Assistance (FINCA International) to implement a village lending program in each country. FINCA was founded in 1984 by John Hatch, who started the program in Bolivia. FINCA now has programs in many countries around the world.
- FINCA International (and other similar organizations) then goes to the country, selects the villages, begins an uncomplicated training program (in accounting, design, marketing, and others.), and makes small financial loans, mostly to women (men seem too unreliable) for any small project that the women may think about. They may buy a small

---

[11] Yunus and the Grameen Bank won the Nobel Peace Prize in 2006 for the efforts to further social and economic development. The Grameen Bank is a community development bank founded in Bangladesh that makes small loans to the poor without requiring collateral.

refrigerator and set up a small stand to sell soft drinks or beers. They may increase their inventory of chickens to sell. They may buy a cow to sell milk. In other words, the microcredit can be for anything small.

- The participants (women and/or men) in the project are charged a very small amount of interest but must repay their loans in a timely manner. Here is a happy note: The vast majority is prompt with their repayment.
- With the help of FINCA, the participants establish a working "village bank."
- The amounts which are repaid are deposited in the "village bank" and recycled by loans for other purposes.

One article in a newspaper said that over 100 million of the "poorest of the poor" families have benefited from these types of programs. Another article in the Nature Conservatory for August/September 2014, says that the micro-lending concept is highly effective in the Samburu area of Kenya. According to the article, 2,225 women in 12 "conservancies" (areas being helped by the Nature's Conservancy Organization) are receiving micro-loans and training in accounting and marketing.[12] *The article does not say whether USAID is contributing funds or effort in this activity. Nevertheless, and not surprisingly, the women tend to repay their loans promptly, and the delinquency rate is only a minimal 1%. In sum, this is a fabulous program which provides an exceptional return on investment. I hope the concept is widened and adopted on a worldwide basis.*

PART H. NON-PROGRAM TYPE OF ASSISTANCE

Non-Program Assistance: There are three basic types of non-program assistance: Cash Grants, Commodity Import Programs, and P.L. 480 Programs. Massive Cash Transfer Grants are made to certain countries like Israel; these types are purely political and are not normally subject to review,

[12] The Nature Conservancy, August/September 2014, p. 42.

and I do not include any discussion about these programs in this book. The next is the Commodity Import Programs (CIP). The theory of the Non-Program Assistance such as Cash Transfer Grants and Commodity Import Programs (CIP) and the P.L. 480 Programs are the same. They are short-term and Balance of Payment techniques. However, the P.L. 480 Programs are limited to agricultural commodities. In contrast, the CIP funds can be used to import a great deal of other types of commodities (tallow – used to make soap, tin plate, coking coal, wood pulp, fishmeal, soybean, seed, oil, cement, clinker, minerals, radios, ampule tubing, and others.).[13]

PART H1. EXAMPLES OF COMMODITY IMPORT PROGRAMS

The reader will find extraordinary examples of the many problems we found during our audits of the CIP in Egypt. These examples also include instances when the Mission tried to bypass the Paradigm distinction on Project and non-Project type of activity. Therefore, I defer discussion of them until Chapter 13.

PART H2. THREE OBJECTIVES OF PUBLIC LAW 480 PROGRAMS

Public Law 480 Programs: USAID also carries out a huge Public Law 480 Program – under Title I, II, and III. Because of the fast-moving nature of these programs, they usually are meant for short-term humanitarian and quick balance of payment effects. Under these programs, USAID buys commodities (bulgur, vegetable oils, corn, nonfat dry milk, wheat, wheat flour, tobacco, and others) from the Commodity Credit Corporation. Depending on the agreement with the host government, the commodities are sold, or granted through governmental organizations, and/or given to people in different countries through Non-Government Organizations (NGOs or charitable organizations). Each Title has a different purpose:

- Title I program commodities are usually sold to the Host Country. The country repays the loan in Local Currency which is deposited in

[13] Information obtained from audit reports issued while in Vietnam and Egypt

Special Accounts. These Local Currency Generations can be used for budgetary support of new or old projects.

- Title II commodities are flexible assets of USAID. Depending on the country, commodities provided under PL 480 Title II Provisions may be either sold or donated to the Host Country. In Vietnam, for instance, we evaluated a repetitive grant program where USAID provided 130,000 metric tons of Title II commodities, valued at $28.0 million and which benefited 4.6 million recipients who were in refugee relief camps, self-help projects, relocation activities, Montagnard relief, militias, civil guard, and others.[14]
- Title III (Food for Peace) is a huge program where the People of the United States donate food stuff (wheat, milk, others) to needy people and in emergencies. These types of food donations are through NGOs like Catholic Relief Services, Caritas, United Nations, UNICEF, local organizations, and others.

During my time with USAID, I saw and evaluated many programs under the above three different titles. Although I found different problems, the foodstuff was reaching its destinations.

PART I. SAMPLES OF OTHER TYPES OF USAID ASSISTANCE

Other Type of Program Assistance: As mentioned earlier, USAID, throughout the years, has provided all kinds of construction and other types of programs. For instance, USAID funded: (a) the development of the Hamlet Radio Telecommunication System in Vietnam; (b) a television education program in El Salvador; (c) the construction of grain silos in Egypt; (d) the construction of barges; (e) a donation of an entire ship to be used to generate pure water and electricity in Colombia; and (f) many others. This part includes some examples:

[14] Information came from an audit report the author helped issue called "Report on Examination of the Public Law 480, Title II (Section 201) Program in Vietnam, as of December 31, 1965, A/R 67-71."

PART I1. CREATION AND ASSISTANCE TO BANKS

Creation and/or Assistance To Banks: USAID has been instrumental in creating and/or supporting banks in Less Developed Countries. Some examples are: The Central American Bank for Economic Integration (CABEI); Commodity Import Program (CIP) of National Bank of Vietnam; Mutual Associations or Savings Banks in different countries. Here is CABEI as an example:

The Central American Bank for Economic Integration (CABEI) is one of those lasting success stories.[15] The concept for such a bank was first proposed by a group of Latin American economists in 1948. The actual development of the idea began to take shape in the 1950s when the five Central American countries (Guatemala, Nicaragua, Costa Rica, El Salvador, and Honduras) began to negotiate the needed International Treaty.

CABEI was finally established on May 8, 1961, and had two initial basic objectives: (a) to promote balanced economic development within each Central American country and (b) to promote Central American economic integration.

When our evaluation team (me included) visited CABEI, it had been operational for 10 years. During this time, the USAID had been providing over $150 million in assistance, the Inter-American Development Bank was next with $61.0 million, and the bank had established lines of credit with a number of other nations.

In all, CABEI had availability of funds amounting to over $328.5 million. The Bank had three distinct types of funds which were used in the following manner:

- The Ordinary Fund was used to finance industrial projects and projects related to exports and Balance of Payments purposes.
- The Integration Fund was used to finance economic infrastructure projects.

---

[15] Information came from A/R 1-596-72-57, a Review of "The Central American Bank for Economic Integration through the AID Rgional Office for Central Americn and Panama (ROCAP), various pages, filed in File on Chapter 3.

- The Housing Fund was used to create and sustain a regional secondary mortgage market for medium-priced houses.

<u>Here was our conclusion of our review.</u> *Our evaluation concluded that "...CABEI was achieving the objectives for which it was organized and that it was a viable and effective force in the accomplishment of economic integration in Central America...."[16] These objectives were being fulfilled by financing regional projects geared to the economic infrastructure, the balance of payments, and urban development requirements of each country. However, we did find at least 19 different areas where improvements could be made.*

Here is the image of CABEI as of the time this chapter was written. According to the Internet, CABEI – now over 50 years old -- is now an established international institution. It still has its founding member countries (Guatemala, El Salvador, Honduras, Nicaragua, and Costa Rica). In addition, it has added non-regional members such as Mexico, Taiwan, Argentina, Colombia, Spain, Panama, Dominican Republic, and Belize. The Internet does not say whether the U.S. is a member and/or USAID is still assisting CABEI.

CABEI's strategic objectives are changing. The bank is now addressing Poverty – the Poorest of the Poor – tourism, globalization, and integration. The Financial Statements as of December 2020 and December 2008 show the following broad amounts (in Billions of U.S. Dollars):

	Year 2020	Year 2008	Growth in 12 Years
Assets	13.2	5.5	7.7
Liabilities	9.6	3.7	5.9
Equity	3.6	1.8	1.8

In sum, the growth of CABEI is most impressive. Certain facts are evident. In its initial stages, CABEI received help from the four or five Central American Countries, USAID, IDB, and others. It certainly seems like a healthy-going concern. Its success should rightfully be attributed to the forward visions of the Central American Countries, USAID, IDB, and others.

---

[16] Ibid

The Autonomous Municipal Development Bank of Honduras: In another example, USAID helped establish the Banco Municipal Autonomo or the Autonomous Municipal Development Bank in Honduras, which had two objectives (a) to increase financing of infrastructure improvements (potable water systems, sewage systems, markets, slaughterhouses, transport terminals, electrical systems, and others.) in different cities; and, (b) to improve the ability of municipalities to generate revenues and manage those projects.[17] I could not find the most current Financial Statement on the Internet for this bank.

PART 12. DONATION OF EXCESS PROPERTY PROGRAMS

Excess Property Programs: Whenever the U.S. Government has a property that it no longer needs, the USAID is authorized by Sections 607 and 608 of the Foreign Assistance Act of 1961, as amended, to donate limited numbers of "Excess Property" to host governments to help in certain weak areas.

I saw a great many such types of donations. Here is one example. In the 1960s, USAID donated Excess Property amounting to $23 million to Colombia. This Property included (a) three APD vessels[18] to furnish auxiliary water and electrical power to two cities; (b) four harbor tugs to improve the capacity of several Colombian ports; (c) two revolving cranes to expedite unloading of ships; (d) eight aircraft to fly cargo and personnel to and from remote areas; (e) two locomotives and a crane to help complete a dike in Boca de Cenisa; (f) and others.[19] The APD vessels had been pilfered of most electronic equipment. However, the other donated items were fulfilling their planned objectives.

During the Vietnam War, USAID had a very bad experience when the U.S. Army donated to USAID numerous trailer homes which were to be used as employee homes or as offices. During the shipment from Europe to South Vietnam, the vast majority of the trailer homes were broken into, stripped of

---

[17] Based on Audit Report 69-09, that I did on Results of Examination of Excess Property to Colombia, see File for Chapter 3.

[18] APD vessels were converted U.S. Navy destroyers and destroyer escorts used for amphibious operations during World War II and afterward.

[19] Ibid

almost everything, and many had to be abandoned (See Chapter 7 for more details).

PART I3. USAID HELPED THE GREEN REVOLUTION AND ACHIEVES EXCEPTIONAL CONTRIBUTIONS TO VARIOUS SECTORIAL RESEARCH.

Research By Universities And Institutions: USAID also finances a great deal of research done by many U.S. and international universities and/or international institutions. USAID always provides funding for research in the agri-business and population fields. *As my knowledge of USAID increased, I kept hearing that the rationale for this emphasis was the "Malthusian Syndrome." This theory is based on an essay written long ago by Thomas Robert Malthus, a priest and mathematician who analyzed the interrelationship between population and food. His conclusions were that while the population grew geometrically and doubled every 25 years, food and/or agricultural production grew arithmetically. Therefore, the population would eventually outpace production, and there could be starvation.*[20]

In the 1960s, the population explosion in India nearly proved the "Malthusian Syndrome" to be real. India experienced extreme problems with its agricultural production and could not produce enough wheat to feed its exploding population. Fortunately, the research of Norman Borlaug, a U.S. agronomist, paid off dramatically. At the time, Borlaug was employed by the Ford and Rockefeller foundations and working at the International Maize and Wheat Improvement Center in Mexico (CIMMYT) to improve wheat production. In addition to receiving support from the Ford and Rockefeller foundations, CIMMYT also received financing from USAID. Borlaug developed a type of wheat that could be harvested twice a year instead of once a year but needed intensive fertilization and adequate irrigation. At the time, these research findings were a Godsend, helping India avoid massive starvation. It is known as the "Green Revolution." Although there are now complicated problems in India (mostly due to the overuse of pesticides), the Green Revolution is being attempted in Africa. Norman Borlaug won the

[20] An article entitled "The End of Plenty" (Page 39) of the National Geographic Magazine of June 2009.

Nobel Peace Prize in 1970 for his extraordinary contribution to alleviating world hunger. [21]

In any event, USAID does a lot to help agricultural research done by many universities and international organizations such as CIMMYT, International Center for Tropical Agriculture (CIAT), International Potato Center (CIP), International Food Policy Research Institute (IFPRI), International Livestock Research Institute (ILR), and many others.

PART I3. KEENLY AWARE, USAID FULLY SUPPORTS THE CURBING OF UNCHECKED DEMOGRAPHIC GROWTH

Demographic Assistance: In equal importance is USAID's support towards the tremendous population growth problem. A quick study of the U.S. Census Bureau International Data Base[22] shows the following trend:

YEAR	WORLD POPULATION: ACTUAL AND PROJECTED
1950	2.7 billion
1970	4.0 billion
1990	5.5 billion
2010	7.5 billion
2030	8.5 billion
2050	9.7 billion

In other words, unless something is done, the population growth in only one hundred years (1950 to 2050) will be about 359% or 4 times as much as in 1950. The Census Bureau database also provides a tremendous number of

[21] IBID, National Geographic of June 2009 Pages 26 to 59
[22] U.S. Census Bureau, International Data Base Internet www.census.gov/ipc/www/idb/worldpopgraph.html

statistical profiles. Some quick statistics on the five most populated countries follow:

Country	Year 2009	Year 2050	Growth
China	1,339	1,424	1.06%
India	1,167	1,807	1.55
USA	307	439	1.42
Indonesia	240	313	1.30
Brazil	199	295	1.48

As the Census estimate shows India's population – with a 155 percent increase in population and a potential prior history of massive starvation – will, by 2050, surpass China's population with its population growth rate of 106 percent.[23] The remaining profiles of these statistics are most troubling for less developed countries. How will the world feed an ever-increasing population? As the population growth expands into suburbs and reduces the agricultural areas, will the world be able to sustain food production? Will the "Malthusian Syndrome" come true, and will there be massive starvation?

The point is that USAID's support in the demographic area is well-founded. In effect, USAID has aided demographic groups, such as the International Planned Parenthood Federation (IPPF), the Pan American Health Organization (PAHO), other similarly inclined international organizations, and, of course, any of the local ones that can be organized.

For instance, all the above three (USAID, IPPF, PAHO), World Education Inc., and the Swedish Government have supported the Costa Rican Demographic Association (CRDA). In 19XX, I did a review of this organization. CRDA had been operating for about 4 years by then. Thinking in terms of the way that the country population was growing – fast and

[23] In the late 1970s and early 1980s, the Chinese government initiated a "one child policy" to limit China's population growth. In 2015, the Chinese government announced it would end this policy in 2016.

uncontrolled -- a number of doctors organized CRDA with a number of objectives in mind: (a) to make the public aware of the population problem, (b) to get women and people to join the organization, (c) encourage studies, and (d) provide needed commodities (condoms, pills, IUDs, and others.) to needy women.

As planned in the objectives, the right type of publicity directed to the right type of population and availability of needed commodities and services were essential. Thus, the CRDA undertook the following unique advertising radio campaign to transmit messages to the population:

- The radio broadcasts were initially directed towards the general motivation of the middle and upper classes
- The second step was to direct radio broadcasts at the middle and lower classes using messages that emphasized home and general comforts.
- During the third step, the radio broadcasts tried to reach men, women, teenagers, and professionals.
- At the same time, CRDA helped provide the needed information, services, and commodities, such as birth control pills, injections, condoms, intra uterine devices, and foams.

During my study, I did find areas in need of improvements. However, the organization was achieving its objectives, and the Costa Rican population growth rate had decreased over a 10-year period from 3.85 to 2.60. Thus, the massive and carefully focused, and multi-level publicity campaign was paying huge dividends. And USAID's assistance was providing exceptional help in this area.[24] Hopefully, USAID will continue to establish and support organizations, like the CRDA, to promote directed publicity and commodity availability in the 134 countries that it now helps.

PART I4. ASSISTANCE DURING HEALTH PANDEMICS

HIV/AIDs Pandemic: After the HIV/AIDs pandemic began appearing in the late 1970 and early 1980s, USAID refocused its assistance to help identify

---

[24] Based on A/T 1-512-72-113, USAID/Costa Rica, The Costa Rican Demographic Association, in Chapter 3 File.

those who were infected and try to prevent the disease from spreading. According to some statistics, USAID has provided over $7.0 billion to fight this terrible disease.[25]

In the case of the HIV/AIDs Pandemic: *I believe that USAID's challenges in this area are only being partially met.* Here is why, USAID's assistance began to make inroads in 1986. At that time, I was close to retiring, but we were all aware of the damage caused by HIV/AIDs. As part of a team, one of my best friends participated in a USAID Inspector General (USAID IG) reviewing USAID HIV/AIDs programs. As part of this review, the team conducted fieldwork in several countries, including Mexico, Brazil, Jamaica, Thailand, and Pakistan, to evaluate education programs, as well as the distribution and efficacy of condoms and other protective products. The review included fieldwork at participating Non-governmental Organizations (NGOs) which usually are working to curb human trafficking, provide sexual education, as well as supplies. As part of the team's fieldwork, the team traveled to a few brothels in Brazil and other countries to see the extent of protection that condoms afforded and as well as efforts by sex workers to protect themselves. The team found a dismal picture. Condoms were often defective, tore easily, and did not offer protection. Infected persons were identified; however, once identified, they got no further help. Some infected people had purposely reverted to unsafe sex practices with the intention of "getting even" with a society that was not providing any help.[26]

From the time that we made our study, USAID has made certain changes in its plans. It now directs most of its assistance to HIV/AIDs afflicted countries in "Africa and the Caribbean, Botswana, Cote of Ivories, Ethiopia, Guyana, Haiti, Kenya, Mozambique, Namibia, Nigeria, Rwanda, South Africa, Tanzania, Uganda, and Zambia…. where nearly 20 million people – men, women, and children – are infected…." [27]

---

[25] USAID Health HIV/AIDS, Overview, Internet www.USAID.gov/our_work/global-health/aids/

[26] Verbal corroboration with colleagues and friends who participated in the review.

[27] An Internet Article called "USAID Combatting Trafficking in Persons," www.USAID.gov/our_work/cross-cutting_programs/trafficking/

PART I5 TRAFFICKING OF VICTIMS (PERSONS) PROTECTION ACT OF 2000

I bring this up because USAID's rules on assistance to the HIV/AID Pandemic have further changed – because of the "Trafficking Victims Protection Act of 2000" and the "U.S. Leadership Against HIV/AIDS, Tuberculosis and Malaria Act of 2003," as well as the "President's Emergency Plan for AIDS Relief (PEPFAR)." The problem of victim trafficking is most complex and affects men, women, and children. "…Annually, between 700,000 and 4 million people are bought and sold as prostitutes, domestic workers, sex slaves, child laborers, and child soldiers…."[28]

Background on what I wrote in my first draft in 2010:

- Begin Quote: "I feel that USAID might not be able to fulfill its objectives under the current Trafficking of Victims Act of 2000 because…. USAID no longer provides assistance to just any organization that may be involved with the HIV/AID pandemic. For an organization to receive USAID's funds, it must have "… (1) a policy explicitly opposing prostitution and sex trafficking, and (2) certification of compliance with the "Prohibition on the Promotion and Advocacy of the Legalization of Practice of Prostitution or Sex Trafficking" which applies to all organization activities, including those with funding from private grants…." These provisions are called "the Prostitution Pledge Requirement." [29]
- "This legal requirement was most controversial. Some countries – like Brazil (with its many brothels and volunteer sex workers) – have refused any further HIV/AID assistance. Total assistance since 19xx to Brazil would have amounted to over $40.0 million.[30] Moreover, since 2003, many organizations have been challenging USAID through the courts. Some of these challenging organizations include the DKT

---

[28] An Internet Article called "USAID Combatting Trafficking in Persons," www.USAID.gov/our_work/cross-cutting_programs/trafficking/

[29] An Internet Article entitled "The US Anti-Prostitution Pledge: First Amendment Challenges and Public Health Priorities, www.medscape.com/viewarticle/560914_print

[30] Ibid

[31]International, Alliance for Open Society International,[32] the Open Society Institute, Pathfinder International, The Brennan Institute, and others. *Their basis is that the Prostitution Pledge Requirements violates the First Amendment – or freedom of expression part -- of our constitution.* [33]

- *"In the above connection, all of the participants of the HIV/AIDs pandemic program agree that "trafficking" in human beings, forced prostitution of women and children, and (supplying people) to the sex industry is a universal criminal and a human rights offense.*[34] *However, the "...core of the debate is that for many stakeholders, the category "sex workers" includes consenting adults who sell sex of their own volition; these people are not trafficking victims and have called for recognition of their rights as workers, in settings that include Bangladesh, India, Thailand, Brazil, Dominican Republic...and others...."* [35] *In other words, many males and females, the world over, voluntarily exercise their First Amendment Rights – or freedom of their expression -- and choose to practice the oldest profession. They are not trafficking in human beings, and those participants might want to unionize.*
- "The legal challenges were in the courts since 2003. Instead of clearing up the confusion, Courts made things more confusing. Their ruling was that the "Prostitution Law" is unconstitutional, but they have also made other rulings that have only added more misunderstanding to this prominent issue. For example, in 2006, two judges once again ruled that the "Anti-Prostitution Law" to be unconstitutional. Over the years, USAID has attempted to clarify the intent of the "Prostitution Pledge," yet, as of this writing (in 2010),

---

[31] DKT stands for the Drammen Kommunale Trikk, it is a charitable International Organization created in 1989 and promotes Family Planning and HIV Prevention. See Internet for more details.

[32] Ibid

[33] ibid

[34] ibid

[35] An Internet Article entitled "The US Anti-Prostitution Pledge: First Amendment Challenges and Public Health Priorities, www.medscape.com/viewarticle/560914_print

confusing terms continue to plague the effective implementation of this program.[36]

- "As an informed outsider, it is my opinion that while the legal desire to eradicate the oldest profession and save true victims might be a commendable effort, it is a challenge that may fail. *Moreover, the mingling of the Prostitution Pledge Requirement together with the HIV/AIDs Pandemic problem is a messy – and unwarranted -- mixture of laws and assistance concepts. In the end, the application of this requirement will adversely affect the true victims and voluntary sex workers in several ways that the HIV/AIDs assistance was meant to help. In the first place, the HIV/AIDs assistance will not reach all people – whether victims or volunteer sex workers – that the assistance is supposed to help. Secondly, because those infected are not being reached, the cycle of infection will continue to infect others. Thus, the cyclical nature of the disease will continue without abatement.*
- *"To me, these laws need changing. Otherwise, the participants (USAID, NGOs, International organizations, host countries, and others.) and the courts will be forever wasting time and effort trying to balance the Prostitution Prohibition Pledge, the First Amendment Rights, and the unconstitutional aspects of the Prostitution Pledge.*[37] [38] *In sum, the legal restrictions placed by the "Anti-Prostitution Pledge" are not realistic, and the actual and potential HIV/AIDs victims will not receive the needed help. The laws need reassessment and, to be issued to more clearly encompass the true dimensions of the HIV/AIDs affected population and problem." End of my Quotation*

As noted above, the U.S. Trafficking of Victims Protective Act (TVPA) of 2000 was, indeed, extremely strict, restrictive, and controversial. It also conflicted -- or left out -- numerous – factors, situations, terminology, victims'

---

[36] Articles in the Internet called "Decision rendered on the Prostitution Pledge," and "An Analysis of the Implementation of PEPFAR's anti-prostitution pledge and its implication for successful HIV prevention among organizations who work with sex workers.
[37] An Internet Article entitled "The US Anti-Prostitution Pledge: First Amendment Challenges and Public Health Priorities, www.medscape.com/viewarticle/560914_print
[38] Conclusion based on the Article entitled "The US Anti-Prostitution Pledge First Amendment Challenges and Public Health Priorities (Page 3).

ages, social conditions, and others. -- encountered in the U.S. and those that offended other countries and on a worldwide basis. These factors include contradictions or complications with constitutions, beliefs, habits, voluntary practices, victims' age, countries' laws, personal liberties, social behaviors, child marriages, child soldiers, partnerships, severities, coercions, recourses to victims, and numerous other types of cases.

Evolutions to the Laws: Between the passage of the TVPA 2000 and the year 2017, there have been five amendments to the original law and a final 2017 codification in the 22 U.S. Code and incorporated as Chapter 78 of that law. The amendments include cases found and needed evolutions, as found over the years, and are known as the Trafficking Victims Protection Reauthorization Acts (TVPRA), TVPRA's 2001, TVPRA's 2003, TVPRA's 2005, TVPRA2008; and TVPRA2013. And finally, all the amendments and changes have now been incorporated into a most complicated law, i.e., the "22 U.S. Code Chapter 78 – Trafficking Victims Protection Act…."

Divided into fourteen parts, this law incorporates many legal terms which are used to define prohibition, prevention, identification, sanctions, and prosecutions against perpetrators or traffickers of victims. Victims are those identified as such by the 5 TVPRA's. Over the many years, the U.S. and the many countries met and eventually signed a protocol, known as the Palermo Protocol, to curb and/or eradicate prostitution and trafficking of human victims. This gave rise to the codification of 22 U.S. Code Chapter 78 – Trafficking Victims Protection Act which was passed by the U.S. Congress and signed by the President. According to the excellent descriptions stated by the Internet and listed in the U.S. Code Title 22 Foreign Relations and Intercourse, I Find Law, the following are some important aspects of Chapter 78:

- Quote: The purposes of this chapter are to combat trafficking in persons, a contemporary manifestation of slavery whose victims are predominantly women and children, to ensure just and effective punishment of traffickers, and to protect their victims. End of Quote.
- According to Chapter 78, the U.S. Congress found – and lists – over 24 ways that trafficking of victims and other ways which equaling l "modern-day slavery –takes place and is affecting the United States and the world. It also lists about 32 different terms which are included

in the "Definitions" section (Both the Findings and Definitions are too long and complicated to list or describe).

- Chapter 78 also authorizes the U. S President to establish an "Interagency Task Force," which is composed of high officials appointed by the President. In effect, this is what Chapter 78 says: Begin Quote: The President shall appoint the members of the Task Force, which shall include the Secretary of State, the Administrator of the United States Agency for International Development, the Attorney General, the Secretary of Labor, the Secretary of Health and Human Services, the Director of National Intelligence, the Secretary of Defense, the Secretary of Homeland Security, the Secretary of Education, and such other officials as may be designated by the President. End of Quote. Here, it is assumed that these high officials will be adequately staffed by personnel from their respective offices)
- The remaining portions of Chapter 78 describe, in 14 divisions, the "Four P's" (Prohibition, Protection, Partnership, and Prosecutions) – and more—of the law)
- U.S. Code 22 Chapter 83 contains the details of the "U.S. Leadership Against HIV/AIDS, Tuberculosis and Malaria Act of 2003." It deals mostly with diseases, and I will not elaborate on it in this book).

As the reader might well imagine, the TVPA's, the TVPRA's, and codification of 22 U.S. Code Chapter 78 – Trafficking Victims Protection Act represent factors, legal cases, discussions, meetings, and items encountered over a number of years and are stated in the Law. The Law is being worked on by a formidable group of talented and prestigious officials. Chapters 78 and 83 are the most complex legal documents, and therefore, they are way beyond the limited scope of this book. If the reader needs or wants more details on the above acts and laws, a good start will be on the Internet. The reader will find particularly helpful, the descriptions given by Internet Section called "U.S. Code Title 22, Foreign Relations and Intercourse/ Find Laws (Click on Chapter 78 and/or 83 and read the abbreviated language of each section). After this, the reader can make sense by reading the "Summary of the Trafficking Victims Protection Act…which describes TVPACT and the TVPRA 2001 to 2013. Then, there is the 22 U.S.

Code Chapter 78=Trafficking Victims Protection… which consist of 14 U.S. Code and notes.

Part I6 Other Types Of USAID Assistance

Miscellaneous Help: USAID also provided financial resources to other international organizations, like the Pan American Health Organization (PAHO), International Planned Parenthood Federation, Asia Foundation, The Regional Technical AIDS Center, and many others.

In addition, the Regional Technical AIDS Center started in 1957 and used to be based in Mexico. It was a low-cost operation, costing about $2.0 million, and did business in 18 Latin American countries. Its activities ranged from research to production of original films, translation, and distribution of books and other materials. In effect, its main goals were the transfer of technology to other countries. [39] This center has now been closed. Its functions were transferred to the Centro Interamericano de Adiestramiento en Comunicaciones para Población (Inter-American Training and Community Center for Population) or (CIACOP) – which also is a part of the previously mentioned Costa Rican Demographic Association (CRDA) – of Costa Rica.

Part J. Assistance Highlights From The "Front Lines."

Background: USAID used to produce a monthly newspaper called "Front Lines." This periodical was distributed to employees, retirees, host countries, throughout the U.S. Government, and interested people. This monthly newspaper provided a wealth of information and articles which would give a reader a good "feel" for the types of assistance that USAID provides in any given month. Unfortunately, USAID discontinued the (paper) "Front Lines" around the Year 2010. Nevertheless, I had written this section of my book before I found out that, without telling the retirees anything, USAID had renewed the USAID Front Lines sometime in the year 2012 or thereabout. I

[39] Information obtained from A/R 1-74-53, January 1974, entitled "Report of Audit Regional Technical AIDS Center of Mexico City.

will try to give the reader a minor portion of things and places that USAID is currently working on as of May 2021 towards the end of this Part.

In any event, so that the reader can get a “feel” for the type of assistance being provided in the years 2009 and 2010, I am including the following samples of headlines and information contained in the Front Lines for those years:[40]

***Agricultural Assistance*:** USAID provided: (a) help to farmers in Honduras to diversify its crop production; (b) financial assistance to connect new roads to isolated West Bank Villages; (c) help to the Indigenous mountain people of Peru to plant legal crops instead of Coca; (d) help to Ethiopia branch out its agricultural production to meet a delicate balance of population, food, and enterprise; and, (e) a $3.5 Billion in several countries to introduce a “Feed the Future Initiative” designed to address a 40 million growing population and the decreasing food supply.

***Health Assistance*:** USAID provided: (a) nearly $1.0 billion to combat the H1N1 Avian Flu in various parts of the world; (b) deworming tablets to treat over 10,000 Sudanese children in the villages; (c) research financial assistance to find HIV antibodies; (d) a project to create awareness, in Cambodia, of the HIV pandemic; (e) technical services and commodities to Tanzania to combat its perennial Malaria and Maternal Health problems; (f) help to Senegal to protect women through its Family Planning assistance; (g) programs, in Burundi, on child nutrition; (h) technical and commodity assistance to Afghanistan to carry out a vaccination campaign against a polio epidemic; (i) assistance to Ukraine in its efforts to modernize mother and children’s hospitals and child birthing practices; and, (j) assistance to a number of African countries on their effort of cut Malaria infections by 50% by the year 2015.

***Education Assistance*:** USAID: (a) introduced new training methods to teach standard Arabic and was helping boost women’s literacy in Morocco and Middle Eastern countries; (b) carried out seminars for leaders integrating education and religion; (c) established an education training program to help Yemeni women get a chance to improve their literacy; and, (d) designed and

---

[40] The Front Lines is a monthly newspaper produced by USAID. See https://medium.com/USAID-frontlines for the latest copy of *Frontlines* .

was implementing a teacher's training program to help them observe and analyze unique learning behaviors of children.

Renewal Energy Assistance**:** USAID provided: (a) technical services and commodities to install Solar Energy systems in Liberia and other countries, which were to be used in isolated communities to power lights for night training schools and refrigerators used to preserve vaccines; (b) education to different countries on the need to develop clean energy processes so as not to affect the environment; (c) and was implementing a new $125 million energy program, in Pakistan, to boost and keep antiquated factories running at top performance; and, (d) a program in Brazil designed to train students in assembling, installing, and maintaining solar panels.

HIV/AID Pandemic Assistance**:** USAID (a) financed the costs of making populations in foreign countries, become aware of the human trafficking problem; and (b) had opened a safe house, Theodora's Place in Jamaica, to protect girls from becoming victims of sex trafficking.

Disaster Relief Assistance**:** Over several natural disasters, USAID has provided: (a) assistance to Indonesia in the wake of different earthquakes; (b) help to Vietnam after its typhoon tragedies; (c) help to the indigenous Brazilian population in isolated jungle places so as to map their areas and join them to our modern world; (d) about $9.9 billion in urgent disaster relief – in different forms (food, shelter, and others.) -- to Haiti after the January 12, 2010 earthquake that killed over 212,000 people and left hundreds of thousands of homeless; (e) help to Chile after the massive earthquake of February 27, 2010, and Tsunami disaster; and, (f) assistance to Mozambique after its disastrous flooding.

War on Poverty Assistance**:** USAID has been (a) helping Mozambique and other African countries begin inroads – in different ways and with different assistance programs -- to climb their way out of poverty; (b) trying to establish several outreach centers in El Salvador to attempt to enable young people to break the pull of gang life; and, (c) implementing a $22.5 million program, in Pakistan, to help feed the country's children and women after the recession discouraged them from attending education centers.

Informal Sector Assistance**:** USAID (a) had established a new Real Estate Office in the Cairo, Egypt Office and was helping the Government of Egypt institute real estate reforms to enable Egyptians to own homes; and (b) was working with social media to develop digital and social media tools – such as blogs, Facebook, and Twitter – to help reduce conflict and empower youth in Lebanon.

Miscellaneous Assistance**:** USAID was (a) funding the ASEAN Wildlife Enforcement Network Support Program and the FREELAND Foundation, both of which were conducting operations to catch elephant and rhino poachers and thereby curb ivory trafficking; (b) helping Ukraine to develop market economies throughout the country; and (c) helping Kazakhstan install and operate water pumps that now provide clean water for its population.

Conclusion as shown by the "Front Lines:" In sum, in the years of 2009 to 2010, USAID was providing several types of assistance to more than 30 different countries. Some of the programs that USAID is financing and/or implementing are very far-reaching and go to the heart of perennial problems. Here are some examples:

a) A program called "Feed the Future Initiative" will hopefully prevent the Malthusian Theory from coming true.
b) The attempt to integrate religion and education through seminars, if successful, will be extremely beneficial to women and children where, in many Middle Eastern countries, women and children are illiterate.
c) Programs that provide training and basic education to women – in countries like Pakistan, Afghanistan, and other Middle Eastern Countries –will be extremely beneficial. Children's educational methodologies leave a great deal to be desired, and religious extremists in these countries prohibit women and female children from attending school.
d) Programs to provide solar electricity to villages in order to facilitate the development of night education programs and provide refrigeration for the vaccination campaigns. As a former director of a health program in Guatemala, I have personal and professional experience with these types of problems. Many villages – and I have been to many -- often do not have electricity, refrigeration, clean water, and/or reliable communications. Mounting a vaccination campaign without the support of a "Cold Chain System" (for refrigerating vaccines) can

lead to multiple problems – vaccine spoilage, lack of coverage, increased illnesses among the population, and others.

e) As discussed in a previous part of this Chapter, forced human trafficking is a great problem. Thus, integrating education and forced human trafficking is a good strategy to curve this problem.

f) Real estate reform in Egypt is timely and urgently needed. During my tour in Egypt, I was amazed at the number of homes that always seemed unfinished. Often the first and second floors seemed to be finished, but most homes appeared to otherwise be unfinished, with steel bars sticking out in different places. The explanation was that the Egyptian Government's tax and real estate laws discouraged owners from ever "finishing" a home.

g) The poaching of elephants and rhinos and the related ivory trafficking are huge problems in Africa. According to the October/November Issue of the *Nature Conservancy*, there was a time when there were over 1.2 million Elephants in Africa. There are fewer than 500,000 now. Poachers have killed about 100,000 elephants in the past three years and many others over the course of 34 years. Also, when I served a tour in Kenya, I visited a rhino sanctuary where I saw – and touched – three (of five) tamed Rhinos. A guard with a rifle was assigned to protect each rhino. Note: rhino's precious horns are ground down and sold in Middle Eastern countries and Hong Kong as aphrodisiacs.) Shortly after my visit, poachers killed all five rhinos. My angry question is "And where were the guards who were supposed to protect them?"

h) USAID continues to provide needed relief help -- when needed, in the right amount, in the right kind, and properly controlled – when natural disasters or famine strikes countries and places around the world.

In the years 2015, 2016, and 2017, for example, USAID was providing help at the beginning Pandemic of COVID-19:

a) **Assistance Against COVID-19:** As mentioned, USAID is a highly active organization and attempts to address Pandemics as they begin to take place. In this vein, as of September 22, 2021, for instance, USAID was (a) investing $345 Million to accelerate Global Fight against COVID-19; (b) providing $2.8 million in assistance to Tajikistan; (c) providing $2.0 million go UNICEF and WHO to support against the Pandemic; (d) providing $1.0 million assistance to Timor-Leste to extend the reach of vaccination program; and, (e) providing both financial and informational support about the COVI-19 to about 120 different countries.

b) **Some other samples covering 2015, 2016, and 2017**: USAID was providing different types of assistance projects: (a) one in Sri Lanka established locally made prosthetics to help amputees; (b) contraception education was being made in the Congo; (c) one project in Northern Ghana was using soy cows to boost Protein in children; (d) in Jordan females were paving the way for the future; (e) a health activity monitors recovery efforts of EBOLA; (f) In Indonesian Coastal communities mangrove conservation is now boosting income by nearly 60%; (g) in Kosovo, work was helping a new generational democracy; (g) In the Kyrgyz Republic, USAID provided health tools to fight Tuberculosis; and, (h) in Sri Lanka, USAID is helping small businesses to recuperate from its war-weary status.

And there are many more projects and activities. If the reader wants to read USAID events, information can be found at the following website: https://www.USAID.gov/news-information/frontlines/july-august-2017 or simply type USAID Front Lines for 2017.

PART K. "EL OTRO SENDERO (THE OTHER PATH)" IS AN EXCELLENT TREATISE ON HOW TO HELP THE UNDER-SERVED INFORMAL SECTOR [41]

The Rest of the Informal Sector: As discussed in the preceding part, USAID has been making in-roads with the poorest populations through micro-lending programs. Yet, one segment of the population that remained elusive and, in fact, had not been either reached or was in any event under-served -- during my time in USAID -- was the informal sector. In Less Developed Countries,

---

[41] A Paper called Constraints On People: The Original of Underground Economies and Limits to Their Growth, written by Hernando De Soto.

the informal sector is usually "…composed of people, who, although pursuing legal ends, such as building a house …"[42] or operating a business, have not met all the legal requirements. *In other words, these are private persons who work for themselves, often without a social safety net, such as street vendors, bus/truck/taxi drivers, transportation carriers, carpenters, hairdressers, barbers, bricklayers, seamstress electricians, gardeners, garbage collectors, and others. Countries, such as Peru, have large informal sectors. As can be noted in this section, the informal sector has numerous complex problems and challenges stemming from the lack of recognition of their work by the country's legal system.*

Near the end of my career at USAID, the Agency hosted a seminar to discuss critical issues facing "third world" development. The seminar's moderator was Dr. Hernando de Soto, an economist and director of the Institute for Liberty and Democracy (hereafter referred to as ILD) in Lima, Peru). ILD is a "Think Tank" private organization. During this conference, Dr. de Soto presented a very provocative dissertation and then authored a book[43]on the causes of Latin American underdevelopment and how the situation could be resolved. The title of the paper was "El Otro Sendero" (The Other Path). (Note: At the time of the presentation, there was a terrorist group called "Sendero Luminoso (Shining Path)," which was Marxist-Leninist and advocated a radical change in Peru through violence and terrorism). *Thus "El Otro Sendero," espoused by ILD, offered an alternative to the violent one of the Shining Path. The ILD recommended solutions that seemed like a path that USAID could follow in its help to third countries.*

Dr. de Soto, hereafter also referred to as ILD, based its conclusion on a five-year study in Peru. The ILD paper and book presented very complex economic concepts, theories, and findings that cannot be presented in detail in this short section. These are a few of the salient conclusions:

a) At the time of the ILD study, Peru's informal sector: (a) constituted 50% of the country's population; (b) accounted for 61.2% of all man-

[42] A Paper called Constraints On People: The Original of Underground Economies and Limits to Their Growth, written by Hernando De Soto.
[43] The Book is called (in Spanish) "El Otro Sendero," and (in English) "The Other Path" by Hernando de Soto.

hours worked in a year; and (c) produced 38.9% of the country's Gross Domestic Product.

b) Laws in Latin America were antiquated, discouraged entrepreneurship, and did not allow popular participation in government. Thus, the ILD equated the current economic system to those that existed in European "mercantilism" of the 16th to the 18th centuries; in modern times, these eventually decayed and have modified.[44]

c) As a result, the ILD found the informal sector in Peru in a sad situation and in need of urgent help. In the ILD view, the informal sector was in sad condition because Peruvian governmental institutions were dysfunctional, and the legal system had lost its legitimacy. This conclusion seems valid. In Peru, for instance, about 99% of 27,400 laws, rules, and regulations were, at the time, instituted each year by the "elite;" for their own special interests; the common people were not consulted or given a voice in the process; and they represented a labyrinth of rules and regulations – which the common people found virtually impossible to comply. Thus, people working in the informal sector remained on the periphery and operated outside the law. In effect, most of them: (a) paid no taxes; (b) did not observe regulatory safety processes; (c) did not own property; (d) were not protected by contracts; and (e) did not have enforcement power on verbal contracts.[45]

d) The clearest conclusion was that there was an obvious need for transparency, honesty, accountability, administrative reforms, simplifications, and decentralization of government, laws, rules, and regulations. The ILD presented a series of examples.

e) One glaring example was the housing situation in Peru. For instance, in 1985, there were 282 invasions of private and public lands by

---

[44] Mercantilism was an economic theory and practice common in Europe during the 16th through the 18th centuries that governmental regulation of a nation's economy.

[45] As of September 2020, despite a mandate requiring people to wear masks and practice social distancing while in public areas, and a periodic dawn-to-dusk curfew, Peru had one of the highest numbers of COVID-19 cases in the world. One factor that may have contributed to the high prevalence of COVID-19 in Peru is the existence of the large informal sector. People working in the informal sector have little savings and must venture out each day to buy food and work instead of staying home.

groups of between 10 and 40,000 people from the Peruvian informal sector. In its study, ILD asked why this phenomenon was taking place. Its findings were most revealing. High property costs in Peru's urban areas prevented the informal population from buying property within city limits. *Their only option was to buy undeveloped land in the desert. However, even after qualifying for such purchases, there were a series of hurdles and obstacles that these prospective buyers had to clear. The process involved (a) following and completing 207 administrative steps; (b) meeting regulations of 48 different government offices; (c) immediately paying the cost of the land; (d) incurring about $2,156 per family in additional costs; (e) following the labyrinth of the governmental red-tape for 27 months; (f) incurring 56 months of human effort to learn and pursue the various rules and regulations; and, (g) waiting – an interminable 7 years -- to receive the title to his/her land and home. In sum, because of all the obstacles to comply with the land titling laws, the time and costs were prohibitive. Thus, the informal population saw the invasion of public and private lands as a much easier alternative. But, surprise, surprise! As the "invaders of Public Lands" soon found out, it would take 20 years for the government to recognize their ownership and accord them title to the land. Without a doubt, there was an urgent need for a wide range of governmental and administrative reforms.*[46]

f) Another glaring example related to Peru's industrial sector. The ILD designed and went through the motions of establishing a small garment factory in an industrial area consisting of a small sewing machine company consisting of 2 sewing machines. Using university students and a lawyer, the ILD then followed all rules, regulations, and laws to fill out forms, obtain licenses, and walk the application from office to office to formally establish the company. The results were that it took 289 days to establish the company at the cost of about $1,231, as well as requests for "mordidas" (bribes) from 10 different officials – which the ILD paid on two occasions.

---

[46] These land invasions have also had the unfortunate effect of making the job of protecting Peru's antiquities more difficult, particularly in Peru's capital, Lima.

g) The street vendors had even greater difficulties. It took them 12 years from the time they started to organize themselves to the completion of a formal market.

h) The government's debt and availability of credit also made it difficult to pay for needed infrastructure. In 19XX, the Peruvian government owed a great deal of money to foreign banks and organizations and was finding it hard to meet its debts, which forced interest rates higher. As a result, the potential Peruvian investors had to: (a) pay higher interest charges; (b) receive shorter term repayment times on all credit; (c) expect lower (only 23%) profits; and (d) pay a greater percentage of the investor's income (76.7%) to the government. Thus, needed investments within the country were too costly and there was no incentive for prospective financiers to invest in needed infrastructure.

i) On the other hand, ILD found that there was a need for the establishment of certain laws and regulations to guide the informal sector. For instance, laws and regulations were needed to help the informal sector in the areas of contracts, property titling, and rights, torts, finance, loans, credit, and safety.

j) After publishing its book *El Otro Sendero*, ILD created a newspaper sounding board called "Everyone's Balcony," where anyone could register complaints. In the first month alone, the ILD received 300,000 complaints from people in the informal sector. The high number of complaints were not lost on the politicians of Peru. For instance, President Alberto Fujimori immediately introduced "Land Titling" laws, which were like those espoused by ILD. Peru's Congress passed it. Even the Communists got on the bandwagon and introduced similar types of reforms to title properties. In sum, the political environment began to be more responsive to the needs of the informal sector.

k) Noting that the Shining Path had been offering the Peruvian country political change through terrorism and violence and now was enthusiastically pursuing change through peaceful means, *the ILD drew two conclusions: "...First is that, ideologically, much of the left appears to be soft; they are less committed to the tenets of Marxism-Leninism than they are to achieving change that is popular with their constituency. Second, the use of a private ombudsman system, (like) Everyone's Balcony, is an effective mechanism not only for demonstrating how democratic participation works but for achieving reform.*"[47]

l) As mentioned earlier, *El Otro Sendero* presents an excellent analysis, economic theories, and concepts that cannot be discussed in such a brief section of this book. Its basic recommendations, in brief, fall into four basic categories: "…(a) opening up economic participation, (b) creation of an institution to decentralize and deregulate government power; (c) creation of institutions to control and make accountable the monopolistic exercise of government power, and (d) public education to mobilize support for change…."

In sum, during my time with USAID, our efforts to help the poorest of the poor had not yet reached the great majority of the population, which made up the informal sector. Looking at the conditions now, I still see tremendous lessons that USAID could learn from *El Otro Sendero* and other studies that have been made by organizations like the ILD.

However, as the reader can well imagine, helping the informal sector is a most difficult and complex area. But the Study by ILD shows some potential ways:

- One important lesson is that some governments, particularly in Latin America, may need a great deal of technical support, particularly in the areas of transparency, honesty, accountability, administrative reforms, decentralization of government, and simplification of laws, rules, and regulations.
- Moreover, to influence and affect needed governmental reforms in Less Developed Countries, maybe USAID could help create, organize, support, and replicate (a) organizations, like ILD in the different countries, and (b) programs designed towards introducing sounding boards, like the "Everyone's Balcony." If the governments can be motivated to correct their defects, the benefits to the informal sector and those countries will be immeasurable.

---

[47] Paper on El Otro Sendero, by Dr. Hernando de Soto, p20.

PART L. CONCLUDING REMARKS

Since its inception in 1962, USAID has worked in many different areas. These include agriculture and food security; democracy and government; economic growth; technical assistance and capacity building; education; training, including scholarships; food aid and disaster relief; ending extreme poverty; protecting the environment; infrastructure construction; small-enterprise loans; budget support; enterprise funds; credit guarantees; climate changes; health problems; HIV Pandemics; and is currently very active addressing the problems created by COVID-19.

During my career, I reviewed numerous Projects and Non-Projects such as the ones listed above. I authored numerous reports detailing the numerous areas that were really working in a perfect manner and many which needed improvements. However, the emphasis in this book is on looking back, reminiscing, writing mostly about the experiences I had, and giving examples of interesting research, situations, things, and experiences – and certainly some rough situations -- that my family and I encountered during my twenty-eight plus years in the Foreign Service and my numerous years as an International Financial Consultant. This will be my emphasis for the rest of this book and, I sincerely hope that I achieve the six objectives that were listed in the prologue.

In ending this chapter, let me suggest that the reader -- and especially the high-level echelon of USAID, CIGIE, Inspector General, and OAS -- review carefully the "Memories of the Past with Visions Toward the Future as stated in Chapters 19 and 22. In those sections, I recount projects and techniques which have worked well in past and those that have not; I also provide suggestions, recommendations, theories, and ideas which should be carefully reviewed for a possible future adaptations.

CHAPTER FOUR
MY PROFESSIONAL BIO DATA: EXCEPTIONAL CAREERS IN FOREIGN SERVICE

U.S. Agency for International Development: As discussed in the previous chapter, I was employed by USAID for 28 years (about 40 years total with the U.S. Government and as an International Financial Consultant). Since USAID assistance covers the gamut of disciplines -- from agriculture, education, industry, health, family planning, emergency relief, informal sector, commodity import programs, housing, and others. – I had the privilege and the extraordinary opportunity to become -- and became -- a highly skilled and multi-faceted professional in audit, programmatic evaluations, and special studies. I served with the following offices:

- Between 1962 and 1972, I was part of USAID's Office of The Controller, serving in positions, including Chief Auditor, Deputy Chief Auditor, Deputy Unit Chief, Audit Manager, and Acting Controller.
- In 1972, USAID formed a separate Office of the Auditor General (AG). Accordingly, the audit and investigative staff from the Office of the Controller – and me (because of my skills – were transferred to this new AG Office.
- The Inspector General Act of 1978 transferred all audits, investigations, and special units into an independent Office of the Inspector General. I served the remainder of my career in that office.

In all, I was posted and lived in over nine different countries and served on temporary duty assignments (TDY) to about twenty-six others. While on vacation, my family and I also visited numerous other countries. Here is a list of my different postings, TDY assignments, or work and vacation abroad (times are approximations):

- More than one year: Guatemala (2.0 Years), Kenya (4.0), Regional Latin America (2.0), Egypt (3.5), Pakistan (1.5), Panama (2.5),

Colombia (3.5), Vietnam (2.0), Ecuador (2.0), Peru (2.5), AID/Washington (4.5), and, I served, during my U.S. Air Force Years, in for Japan (2.0).

- TDYs of between 15 to 120 days: Guatemala; El Salvador; Honduras, Nicaragua; Costa Rica; Mexico; Dominican Republic, Haiti, Ecuador, Peru, Jamaica, Bangladesh, Afghanistan, Yemen, Botswana, Sudan, Zaire, Senegal, Tanzania, Burundi, Zimbabwe, and South Africa.
- With my family: Mexico; Spain; Israel; Italy; France; Germany; the Netherlands; and Austria.

In order of importance, here are the positions I served with USAID: **(Note: I am proud to say that I was the first -- and as far as I know -- the only Mexican American to serve six years as a Regional Deputy and Acting Regional Inspector General for USAID.):**

- Acting Regional Inspector General for Latin America (and Egypt), one year.
- Deputy Regional Inspector General/Latin America, two years.
- Deputy Regional Inspector General, in Egypt, three years.
- Audit Manager for Federal Audit Programs, six years.
- Chief Resident Auditor, seven years.
- Deputy Resident, Deputy Chief Auditor, Auditor, or Acting controller seven years.

These are the education, certificates, and awards I have gotten throughout the years:

- Bachelor of Business Administration, University of Texas, June 1958
- Many courses in evaluation, writing, contracts, management, and computers
- Certified Government Financial Manager (CGFM).
- Certified Internal Auditor (C.I.A.).
- Medal for Civilian Service in Vietnam.

- Various USAID Awards for "Significant" Discoveries of Fraud. Embezzlements, Collusions, and others.
- Departmental Diploma De Honor "Al Merito" (Merit Diploma) from Guatemala.
- Phi Theta Kappa in Junior College.
- Martin High School Tiger Legend Award
- Meritorious Honor Award from USAID.

During my career, I have been Director of a Health Project in Guatemala and employed and supervised efforts of over 50 people, Director of Audit Offices where I supervised, planned, participated, and done fieldwork and written and edited and published many reports and studies covering the multiple disciplines. Examples follow:

Agriculture	*Costa Rican Agriculture Sector, Honduras Agriculture Sector; Integrated Rural Development Programs of (Jamaica), (Ecuador), (Haiti), and (Botswana), Yemen Agricultural Development Support Program.*
Banks	Central American Bank for Economic Integration; Commodity Import Program of National Bank of Vietnam.
Computers	Scheduling and Ordering System General Dynamics; Payroll System at General Dynamics; Commodity Import Program of USAID/Egypt; Participant Training System in Egypt; Survey of A.I.D. Accounting System; Financial and Payment Procedures and Controls; Asset and Spare Parts Inventory System of Afghan Construction and Logistics Project, OAS's Internet Connection.
Education	El Salvador Education Sector and Instructional Television Program, Honduras Primary Rural Education Program, and Jamaica Rural Education.

System Evaluations	Financial Systems? in Sudan and Pakistan, Personnel and Payroll, Payment Procedures, Procurement Systems in the OAS, Human Resources Mechanisms.
Health	Chief of Party (Director) for a Child Survival Project in Guatemala. (Major achievements explained later).
Land Mines	An OAS review of the Land Mine Problem of Central America.
Non-Program	Commodity Import Program and Cash Transfer Grants of Egypt, Colombia, El Salvador, Jamaica, and Sudan.
Population And Others	Costa Rican Demographic Association, Panama Population Program, Population Commodities of Pakistan and Bangladesh, Costa Rican Urban Development, Program Review of Employment Contracts, Risk Property Loss, Electoral Observation in Haiti, Trade Programs, and others.

I have had the privilege and an extraordinary opportunity to conduct numerous studies covering the gamut of disciplines. These reviews were comprehensive and evaluative in nature. The reports covered all aspects of a project (managerial, program design, implementation, financial, USAID internal controls, and others.). After analyzing legal documents and background material and obtaining a working background, I made an assessment on whether: (a) the development activity (program, project, function, and others.) was achieving desired objectives; (b) management was using resources in an effective manner; (c) the project was being implemented in an efficient and economical manner; (d) there was any evidence of misuse, waste, mismanagement, or fraud; (e) procedures and internal controls were adequate; (f) the organization was in compliance with laws and regulations; and (g) any aspect of the development activity, procedures, or functions were in need of improvement or change. I reviewed and used such documents as loans, grants, project agreements, contracts, project design papers, implementation letters, handbooks, evaluation reports, host country budgets, decrees, laws, procedures, and others., to analyze each program or project and then prepared and published a comprehensive report. Some complicated activities required me to prepare comprehensive audit programs, which included phasing in and out different types of disciplines.

International Financial and Management Consultant: After I retired from USAID, I traveled to different parts of the U.S. for a year. I then began doing short-term consulting work from June 15, 1990, to June 1992 with two companies.

The Support Services Construction Corporation contracted me to do a review of an Adventist Development Relief Agency project (ADRA) in Sudan. This was a short contract where I was asked to determine if ADRA was using an acceptable accounting system. I found that although the system was rudimentary and was not documented, it was serving a satisfactory purpose. I recommended that the system be documented. Because it was such a short assignment and my stay in Sudan was routine, I have no further comment.

Chief Administrative Officer of ACLU: After that assignment, the Construction Control Service Corporation gave me a contract as Chief Administrative Officer to help implement the Afghan Construction and Logistics Unit Project (ACLU) in Peshawar, Pakistan. The ACLU Project was financed by USAID and other "very special" organizations. The objectives were to build roads and bridges from Pakistan to Kabul. Also, this project helped the Mujahedeen in their efforts to get the Russians out of Afghanistan. As Chief Administrative Officer, I made disbursements, vulnerability and risk assessments, developed computer systems for use on inventories, and advised and/or resolved problems related to a special type of "accident protection fund" (a sort of insurance – to cover injuries and/or deaths during construction and activities in Afghanistan -- called the Solatium Fund), risk of loss, employment contracts, organizational structure, and many others.

This assignment was a hairy one and felt more dangerous than the two years I spent in Vietnam. With all the warring separate Mujahedeen warlords and factions, Peshawar was a cauldron. I was there six months and was politely "requested" (really ordered) to leave because my life was in danger, and my safety could not be guaranteed. (see Chapter 20 for more details).

Health Director: Between June 1992 and November 1993, I worked under a contract with "Clapp and Mayne, Inc." a private organization. Based in Guatemala, I was the Chief of Party (Director) responsible for re-starting, directing, and managing a Child Survival Project for the Ministry of Health financed by the USAID (See Chapter 21 for more details).

Organization of American States (OAS): Between April 1994 to 1998, I was contracted by the Office of the OAS Inspector General (as an International Financial and Management Consultant) to work under a series of Personal Services Contracts. During this time, I did evaluations, audits, risk assessments, and studies covering: The Land Mine Problem in Central America, Employment Mechanisms, Trade Programs, Flow of Funds, Payment Procedures, Payroll, Inventories, the Internet, several Special Reviews, Procurement System, and Electoral Observations; some studies resulted in changes in the way OAS conducted some of its operational and developmental affairs.

OAS is an extremely important, but highly political organization. As such, appointed high-level officials are not amenable to strong criticism. Working under two "strong" Inspectors General during this four-year period, I called attention to numerous weaknesses that OAS management needed to correct. When these two fine Inspectors General retired, people up high whom I may have alienated – including the newly appointed Inspector General and the Director of Management -- probably no longer wanted me to make those types of waves. Once the "strong Inspector General" retired, political considerations and retaliation came fast and furious. Contracts ceased to come my way, and I was – for all intent and purposes – declared a "Persona-Non-Grata," and I never again worked for OAS (See Chapter 22 for more discussion).

However, I have been happy in my retirement. I have done the research, authored a historical book entitled *Inherit the Dust from the Four Winds of Revilla*) and this book, given lectures to discuss my book and the "The Battle of Medina," written a number of articles, and am now completing this book.

In sum, I have (a) made numerous studies covering different disciplines; (b) made all kinds of analyses; (c) written reports amounting to over 2,800 pages; (b) made more than 800 recommendations to improve programs or procedures; and (c) examined programs amounting to way over the U.S. $6.0 Billion.

It has now been over 30 years since I left USAID; yet, as noted in various chapters; and my professional life has been tremendously educational and challenging. I continue to believe that USAID, as an organization, is truly first-rate and exceptional.

However, as will be noted in later chapters, there were some rough parts along the way. In effect, my experience with the USAID Office of the Inspector General -- of that time -- showed a mixed picture where some parts were exceptional, and others where the office could have (a) made a better selection of people who came from other U.S. Government agencies-- without the experience of overseas assignments or having lived in less developed countries -- they were appointed as "managers," (b) had a more discernible career ladder, (c) had a better educational philosophy geared towards human capital improvement, and (d) made better use of investigative authority and personnel. Although now slipping into the recesses of my 90-year-old mind, these rough aspects of my experience still weigh negatively in my mind; I will try to discuss some of these negative periods -- in the form of telling my side of the story -- in later chapters (number 16 to 19) so as to leave a complete closure to my life.

CHAPTER FIVE
IN PERU, CHIEF RESIDENT AUDITOR, EXCEPTIONAL LEARNING EXPERIENCE TOUR, COUPS, AND LASTING FRIENDSHIPS

PART A. INTRODUCTORY REMARKS

Introduction: This chapter discusses our assignment to Lima, Peru. This was our first post, and it was a beautiful assignment. The assignment brought a very nice change in lifestyle, the birth of a beautiful daughter, excellent friendships, diplomatic cocktails galore, beautiful music, excellent food, a few earthquakes, exposure to Peruvian History and Politics, experiences during two coup d'états, a total immersion in USAID Programs, relations with the Peace Corps, a visit to the Altiplano (mountains) and Machu Picchu, questions about the "Informal Sector," an introduction to the rough USAID Personnel Evaluation and Appraisal Report System, a threat by the "Tupamaros," and a lasting learning experience. Because of the many topics discussed, this Chapter is divided into 13 Parts:

- Part A Introductory Remarks.
- Part B Life in Lima.
- Part C Country History and Diplomatic Situation.
- Part D Work at the Office.
- Part E. USAID Programs in Peru.
- Part F Acting Controller.
- Part G the Peace Corps Arrived in Peru.
- Part H My Visit to the Altiplano and Machu Picchu.
- Part I The Informal Sector.

- Part J. The Personnel Evaluation and Appraisal System.
- Part K Death of President Kennedy.
- Part L The Threat of the Tupamaros.
- Part M Transfer to Ecuador and Concluding Remarks.

PART B. LIFE IN LIMA

Nice Change to Lifestyle: At the time of our assignment to Lima, in early 1962, the family consisted of my wife, two sons (Joe and Jerry), and me. The following year our third child was born. Linda Marisol was born on September 4, 1963. She grew up to be a fabulous, fiery redhead with a beautiful personality, above-average intelligence, and highly creative skills. She married young, had a baby girl (Lauren), divorced, had a few human problems, and died at an early age. Her ex-husband also died young. We miss her terribly. Lauren, my granddaughter, lived with me for 10 years and is now 26 years old, married, and recently had a baby girl. Lauren is, like her mom, red-head, extremely intelligent, beautiful, fiery, and very personable. She is now married to an exceptionally intelligent person – her husband's name is Andrew Delaney. They now have a baby girl (Natalie Marisol De Laney). She is fabulous.

In any event, the family enjoyed Lima tremendously. Lima is a beautiful modern city, and the country itself is just fantastic. Points of great interest are Lima, Callao, Ayacucho, Arequipa, Puno, Cuzco, Pasto, Machu Picchu, Piura, Chacaclayo, Chimbote, Trujillo, Pucallpa, and the jungle area. Although there is a definite class distinction – the rich, poor, and over 11.0 million "Cholitos" (mostly illiterate and living in the mountains) – the socio-economic conditions easily accommodate foreigners.

Cultural Lessons: When we first arrived, we lived in a three-bedroom apartment on the second floor of a nice building. My wife and I learned a most interesting cultural lesson very early in the assignment:

- Day after day, I would come from work, and my wife would complain that the stove and the refrigerator were not working right. She had talked a number of times with the building handyman, but he would not come to fix the appliances. She was upset and took me to the window: "Just look at him there on the grass, laying down, talking, and flirting with those maids (the maids always wore a blue uniform); that is all he does all day. He lies there, doing nothing, and talks and flirts with all the maids that come out...." So, I kept watching him....and he was an operator. He would lay there on his belly, legs folded upward, and flirted with all the young girls. The girls obviously liked it. He would tease them, touch their legs, or get up and pat them on their fanny, and the girls laughed and giggled and played hard to get. Anyway, my wife and I went out to scold him.

- While I used strong words of encouragement for him to come and fix the appliances, he would stare at my wife and me, shift his eyes, not saying anything, and be as calm as if we were not there. When I got through, and without moving from his position, he told us in a very deliberate manner: "You people from the United States are always in a rush to get everything done right away. But you need to remember that we are in Peru. We do things differently. I will come over to fix the appliances – mañana. End of conversation.

The above talks much about the laid-back Peruvian culture. And I don't remember the appliances ever getting fixed.

Settling Down: Soon after that incident, we got our brand new 1961 Dodge Dart. This car was a long one with fins. Instead of a gearshift, as we know it, the car had buttons, i.e., you pressed one button for the park, another for neutral, another for the drive, and another for reverse. In other words, the system was ahead of its time, but Chrysler discontinued the shifting feature soon after. The car did have a powerful V8 Engine. It drove nicely in Lima but got hot one time climbing the mountains to Chacaclayo.

We also quickly found (and leased) a real nice house; it was a green-colored-all-brick home that was located at "Daniel Hernandez # 230 in the middle of San Isidro – a very plush area of Lima. The house belonged to one of the richest men in Peru – a lawyer and politician. At about $1,500 a month, rent was about the average paid by any diplomat. *The funny part of it was that I would take a personal check to the guy's plush office, and he would not cash it; in fact, he did not cash any of my checks for nearly 15 to 17 months (over* *the U.S. $22,500). My "inflated and unrealistic" bank balances were driving me up a wall. Repeatedly, I had long conversations with him, asked him to cash the checks, and I finally warned him that I could be transferred. He finally began to cash my checks. I never knew why he would not cash them – maybe he just did not need the money, or maybe he was waiting for the Peruvian currency to depreciate – it did.*

Friends and Diplomatic Parties: Peru was a friendly and fun assignment. The house witnessed many office and community parties. We quickly developed many friendships – Bill and Gladys C., Julio and Chela T., Gerardo and Betty, Ramon, Juan, Adela, Carola, Leonor, Clarita, and others. Even after close to 60 years, some remained my friends; many have passed on. I remember two with great fondness:

- Gerardo and Betty baptized Linda Marisol and became our "Compadres." The two were fabulous friends. Gerardo developed cancer and died a few years back. Betty settled with her daughter, a doctor, in Florida, and we lost contact with her about 14 years ago.
- Julio and Chela T. were friends of ours until both passed on a few years back. Julio had worked for the Office of USAID Controller, as a budget officer, for a long time. He was an exceptional friend. Whenever we had a dance – at our house or any other place -- Julio would get his handkerchief out, dance, and waive it to the tune of Marinera or the guaynito; he was a terrific man, a good dancer, and a good friend. They lived in Washington D.C. with their daughter for many years. Chela died of cancer; Julio developed Parkinson's disease and passed on about 15 years ago. His daughter, Chela, and I still communicate with each other, although we have now lost contact.

And we were constantly being invited to many U.S. Embassy and USAID cocktails and parties. We met the elite of the country and diplomatic corps assigned to Peru. Diplomatic cocktails are always plush affairs. People normally makes them very nicely dressed, lots of drinks, great mixing by people, making contacts and friends, exchanging of information, and eating nice meals. Aside from the usual alcoholic drinks (like Scotch, Bourbon, Vodka, Rum), the popular drink was "Pisco Sour" and the favorite food was the "Anticuchos" (pieces of steak, heart, chicken, and others.) marinated in special Peruvian sauce and dipped in a especially delightful Picante sauce. The memories make my mouth water.

Servants and The Evil Men: For some reason, servants were hard to keep. We usually had two or three servants; one was the cook and house cleaner; the other took care of the children. The house had enough servants' quarters for four people.

- I remember one girl (Rosa) that was extremely good. My wife used to tell me that her "primo" (cousin) would sometime come and visit her. After being with us for about six months, Rosa told us that she was going home, to the Altiplano, for a week. Since we had two other house cleaners, we did not mind. When she did not return for two months, we hired someone else. Rosa finally came back about eight months later and wanted her job back. My wife discussed the situation with her: "But, Rosa, why didn't you return in time?" Rosa explained: "Señora, di un mal paso. (I made a wrong step.)" My wife, naively: "What happened? Did you fall down???" Rosa: "No, Señora, "un mal hombre me engaño" (a bad man lied to me); he promised to marry me, got me pregnant, and then left when he found out I was expecting a baby."

We hired her back. But, throughout our work in Latin America, we had a few servants – and friends – who became pregnant, and the reason was always a variation of the above story, i.e., the evil man lied, promised to marry, conquered the girl, and quickly took off after doing the damage.

Food, Restaurants, and Music: Peru is famous for its food and restaurants. I talked about Anticuchos earlier. However, equally tasty are the Ceviche's (raw fish cooked only with lemon, onion, and spicy peppers), the Pariguelas (sea food combinations soups that are excellent for hangovers), Papa a La Huancaina (potatoes with special sauce), Callus a la Italiana (cow's intestines cooked a certain way), Chicha Morada (the drinks of the Incas – made out of purple corn), the "Algarrobina" (a potent drink said to increase sexual powers), and many others. We liked going to a restaurant that was called "La Querencia." This was an Argentine restaurant that specialized in charcoal-grilled steaks, cooked to perfection, and dipped in a special sauce called

"Chimichurri." Our preference was for "La Marucha," a sirloin steak so big that we seldom finished our portions.

Peruvian music is just fabulous. During the time we were in Peru, there were some beautiful songs on the radio. Chabuca Granda was the favorite composer, and her songs were listened everywhere: "La Flor De la Canela," "Fina Estampa" and others. As you go into the Barrios and lower-class areas, you hear the melodious sounds of the "Flautas (flutes)" and the happy sounds of the Altiplano huaynitos. These are just beautiful sounds.

Earthquakes: Earthquakes in Peru are frequent, and some are violent. We experienced about 5 of them. Most of them happened at night. All were memorable. Here are two examples:

The first one came soon after we moved into permanent housing. It was the middle of the night, and suddenly, the walls started creaking; things began falling all over; the whole room started shaking terribly; and the rumbling noises from inside the earth were horrendous. My wife, in her nightgown, me, in my shorts and looking for my pants, jumped out of bed, ran to our two tiny son's bedrooms, grabbed them, managed the stairways in the dark, and got outside the house – in less than ½ minute flat. All the neighbors were on the street in various stages of undress, disheveled, without shoes, and most praying to every saint they knew. A voyeur would have had a field day. We must have stayed on the streets for a few hours. The houses held. Then the aftershocks kept us on edge the remainder of the night; I don't think we slept at all the rest of the night.

That first earthquake taught us to be prepared, and from then on, I slept with my bottom pajamas. One earthquake came when my wife was about six months pregnant. Once again, the walls creaked like crazy, moved and shook, things fell, and the rumbling noise from the center of the earth was horrendous. While my poor wife waddled down the flight of stairs, I went to Joe's and Jerry's room somehow picked them up and managed to catch up with my wife on the stairs. We were out the door in less than a minute. Once again, all our neighbors were on the streets, again in various stages of undress, scared stiff, praying, talking, and strategizing. Once again, the aftershocks were scary, and it seemed like we were running outside every few minutes.

Make no mistake; earthquakes are terrible experiences for any person to go through. We heard that in one of the Peruvian villages, there had been about 3,500 fatalities. Aside from those in Peru, I have felt the earth move several times more in Ecuador and Colombia. As I will explain later, the office sent me to Managua, Nicaragua, right after its earthquake of December 23, 1972. Also, on January 17, 1994, I was visiting my daughter and her husband in Palos Verdes (California) when the harsh 6.8 earthquakes in Northridge (Los Angeles), California, destroyed many buildings and killed at least fifty-seven people. You never get used to the scary feeling.

Family Illnesses and Accidents: Our assignment to Peru was not without incidents related to health and accidents.

- Shortly after moving into the permanent house, two-year-old Jerry was trying to climb to the Medicine cabinet in the bathroom and fell down. He hit his head on a ledge so hard that blood was all over the place. We took him to the closest hospital. The doctors were extremely professional, stopped the bleeding, and sewed about eight stitches on Jerry's head. We were extremely worried about a concussion. But he came through with flying colors.
- The climate in Lima is very humid and lends itself to frequent colds and illnesses. Three-year-old Joe was constantly having colds and throat problems. Eventually, the doctors recommended and did a surgical removal of his tonsils.
- Of course, the birth of Linda Marisol on September 4, 1963, was a most joyous event.

PART C. COUNTRY HISTORY AND DIPLOMATIC SITUATION

The Peruvian History is fabulous and worthy of a separate book. Therefore, this section presents only a very brief review. As the reader might know, the Incas were the first settlers of the country and inhabited Puno, Cuzco, Arequipa, the Altiplano and conquered Ecuador for a time. Inca leaders of the time were Huayna Capac, Huascar, Atahualpa, others. The Inca People were conquered by the Spanish Conquistador, Francisco Pizarro, in

1533. The country was under Colonial Spaniard rule until it became independent on July 28, 1821. Since that date, Peru has been governed and ruled by well over ninety-eight personalities – variously called a Protector, Liberator, Interim President, President, Supreme Delegate, Provisional Ruler, Supreme Legislator, Supreme Leader of the Nation, Constitutional President, and others. Here are some telling facts:

- There have been ten dictators.
- Twenty-two (22) other rulers (dictators) have come by way of a coup d'état.
- Eighteen (18) have been interim presidents, most lasting 1 to 5 days.
- Ten (10) "Presidents" were appointed by Congressional Edict.
- Twenty-nine (29) have been elected through a direct vote.
- Four were appointed by Chile during its occupation of Peru.

In sum, until recently, historical events do not show a very stable political situation for Peru, and corruption has abounded. When we first got to Peru, the country was in a state of flux. It had a coup d'état in 1948, been ruled by General Manuel Odria from 1948 to June 1950, then had an Interim President (Zenon Noriega Aguero) for two months, "elected" General Manuel Odria all over again for six years, and then elected Manuel Prado Y Ugarteche for six years.

One Coup De' Etat: Although General Manuel Odria remained in the background as the powerhouse, Manuel Prado Ugarteche was the President at the time of our arrival. But this was not for long. New elections were scheduled, and there were six candidates running – three of whom were the leaders:

- Raul Haya De La Torre, who represented the American Revolutionary Popular Alliance (APRA) Party. He had been a very popular leader whom people liked, but the Military (the Oligarchs and the Church) did not. The U.S. favored him.
- He was opposed by Fernando Belaunde Terry, a Socialist Democrat, running under the Popular Alliance Party. Wanting a change, the great majority of Peruvians seemed to prefer this candidate.

- General Manuel Odria was the third candidate. As recalled, he had directed a government takeover, been president once, ruled behind the scenes, and now wanted to regain the Presidency in an official election.

The elections never took place.

- On Wednesday, July 18, 1962, I got up at my regular time, dressed up, ate breakfast, got in the car, and left for the office. I noted that for some reason, all the streets were empty. Frequently, I would see a tank or military vehicle running around the streets. Not knowing better, I continued to the U.S. Embassy and parked. As I was about to enter, the U.S. Ambassador (James Loeb) was almost at the door. I opened the door for him and made my usual greeting, "Hi, Mr. Ambassador, how are you?" He knew me by then, and asked me: "Joe, what are you doing here today? Haven't you heard that there has been a coup d'état? Go home……we are breaking relations with Peru….do not show up until we say so…" My introduction to a Military coup d'état had been unplanned, and my instructions, on what to do, had come straight from the Country Boss. I quickly turned around and, on my way, picked up more food and supplies and went home as fast as I could. We stayed home until people began to venture out to get food and other needed things. Later, we learned that General Ricardo Perez Godoy, favoring Odria but expecting either Belaunde Terry or Haya de La Torre to win, had taken over the country through a Military Junta. With a few hundred shots fired, the coup had been an easy take-over. Ambassador Loeb was immediately recalled and returned to the U.S. within a few days.

- Since the people began to object to the coup and wanted fair elections, they began to demonstrate on the streets. For this reason, General Ricardo Perez Godoy only ruled for about nine months. By then, a new Ambassador, J. Wesley Jones, had been appointed on February 6, 1963. One month after his appointment (a nicely, convenient, and managed -- coincidence), there was another coup. On March 3, 1963, General Nicolas Lindley took over the country. His rule lasted five months. He held free elections, and Fernando Belaunde Terry became the Constitutional President of Peru on July 28, 1963. He was the

President until 1968. He stayed away from power until 1985 when he was reelected. He died at age 89 in the Year 2002.

As shown above, the coup d'états and elections in Peru were not terribly violent. Until the political situations were clarified, and the U.S. Government was able to sort out the personalities and direction of the new governments, there usually would be a break in diplomatic relations. Breaks normally lasted 15 to 20 days, and normal relations would be renewed. I was in several countries when government take-over and coup d'états took place.

Part D. Work At The Office

After my arrival in Peru and my first walk into the office, Bill Chevoor. (USAID/Peru Controller) took me around his office (consisting of a staff of about 30 Peruvian men and women) and all over the Mission. I met many people: Robert C – (Director), James B (Deputy), Rudy F (Executive Officer), and Technical Program Directors galore. I was introduced as the new Chief Auditor. Aside from other duties, which was the official title and position I held for the next 2 ½ years.

My initial instructions were to get ten completed draft reports finalized and issued, lead the efforts of nine people in my office, and design an index and filing system for the huge inventory of Office documents.

Boy, what a fiasco those first two to three months were. Neither my university education nor my previous audit experience had prepared me for either the current position or the type of reviews that needed to be made. As I found out, reviews needed by USAID (Peru and in General) were a balanced approach (Financial Reviews combined with Programmatic Evaluations).

All the completed reviews and draft reports had an extremely limited financial focus, and all were in Spanish. Like me, the staff had no formal training in doing "Programmatic Evaluations." The staff had been trained and educated to do financial audits and studies, and there were no standard reporting formats. Written in different styles and formats, the reports all contained enormously long and very flowery prose and sentences. With such a flowery and long-winded style of writing, important problems, which should have been highlighted, were nor clearly stated and delegated into insignificance.

My first four tries were to simply translate the reports. Bill C., the Controller, turned out to be a terrific taskmaster and the best teacher I could possibly ever have.

I remember my first few discussions of those reports even today. Bill C was rough and would critique me sentence by sentence: "…did the staff analyze the (Project, Loan, Grant, P.L. 480, or International agreement) …did they have a plan…the emphasis on this report is purely financial, what about the program…how is it doing…have you read the agreement……what did the agreement say the Project was to achieve….are the objectives being achieved…. did you look at the workpapers… Exactly, what did this guy do… where did he go…what did he study…did he see the activity…did he do field trips…I can't believe this….how do you interpret those statements… what are you saying here….why go in circles? Why not just say it like this…did he talk to any of the indigenous people… (on and on and on)? "

Every time we reviewed a report, I walked out of there with my tail between my legs, completely exhausted and demoralized, angry at myself, and full of determination to do better next time. But it seemed like – until I learned my job -- I seemed to repeat the same type of mistakes time and again. After the fourth report, I suspended the remaining six. I sat with the staff, explained the analytical criticisms and the revised programmatic emphasis. However, I had a couple of dissents -- particularly from the older, more traditionalist people, the staff – and I – fast turned around the thrust of our studies. From then on, we developed a protocol: all reviews were started by analyzing the Agreements, developing a work plan, balancing the studies using a financial and programmatic approach, visiting the field, talking to people, and doing other technical steps. We redid the work on the remaining 6 reviews with much more emphasis on the programmatic aspects.

As noted, I learned fast. I had to. Although Bill C was rough, he was an exceptional teacher to an inexperienced Chief Auditor. Each literate slap on the face Bill C gave me, and every kick in the rear I experienced from him were exceptional lessons that I learned. This training, although

rough, lasted me for a lifetime. I heard that Bill and his wife (Gladys) had passed away a few years ago. So, Bill C., wherever you are today, a big hug and thanks.

Having said the above, let me say that most Universities – of my time – did an exceptional job of preparing an accounting or auditing student for a financial, accounting, and CPA financial type of jobs. However, for the future, I wish the universities would restructure their curriculum to prepare top-notch students in Programmatic Evaluations.

Cultural Fridays: Let me quickly add that our office experience was not all work:

- The Office was a fun group. Every Friday was "Viernes Cultural" (Cultural Friday), which meant that the entire office (mostly men but some venturous office ladies) would gather in a bar, drink up a few Pilsen Beers, shoot the bull, and often wind up going to my house to end the night. Whenever I brought a large group, my wife would have fits. She liked to plan for events very carefully, and these types of group gatherings were so spontaneous and lacked preparations. But we had fun.
- With so many people in the whole office, there were, it seemed, birthdays every other day. A birthday called for the entire office going to a restaurant for a couple of hours and having a feast. We listened to good music, did our best at dancing, chatted, had a couple of drinks, sang the Happy Birthday songs, ate, and returned to the office in proper form – to whiz through our designated work.
- The Peruvian women who worked in the Office were just fabulous. They were sexy, jovial, funny, highly intelligent, congenial, and just plain great. One of my secretaries was a funny lady. In her late 30's, slightly on the heavy side, homely, and single, Ines (her name) had a nice pair of legs. She would cross them or raise her skirt in a way that her nice thighs, and more, would be showing. Many times, my men would stare at them. One or another secretary would tell Ines: "…Ines, Ramon te esta viendo las piernas; parece ver hasta tu alma (Ines, Ramon is looking at your legs; he seems to see even your soul..)…" Invariably and unflustered, Ines would respond: "…Dejalo, lo que se

van a comer los guzanos, que lo gocen los humanos (Let him…let the humans enjoy what the worms will eat when I am dead and gone)." We would all burst out laughing.

PART E. USAID PROGRAMS IN PERU

At the cost of long hours and lots of homework, I began -- within a few months -- to be totally immersed in the programs that were being implemented by USAID/Peru and assume the functions of the Acting USAID/Peru Controller (when Bill C went on Home Leave, was sick, or on special assignments elsewhere).

One thing that helped me learn about the programs was the Index to Office Documents that I developed. In 1962, there were no personal computers or word processors, so developing a flexible system had been attempted but had always resulted in failure. In my unorthodox manner, I made use of "Ditto Reproduction Paper" and a numbering system. The Typist would give a series of numbers to each file. If there were additions to the file, later, the Typist would simply cut the Ditto Paper, type the new information, make a copy, and presto the change had been made. Word got around, and other offices sent secretaries to learn the system.

Chapter 3 of this book dealt with the many types of programs that USAID implements throughout the world. In Peru, we had the usual Servicios for Agriculture, Labor, Health, and others. They began to phase out around the time I got there.

In turn, USAID began to sign separate "Project Agreements" for Agriculture (6 projects), Private Enterprise (3), Transportation (2), Labor (1), Health (1) Education (3), Public Safety (2), Community Development (2) and others.

There were also 8 different development loans that had been inherited from the newly eliminated Development Loan Fund. These loans were for Puno Emergency, Lima Water, Feasibility Studies, Pucallpa Road, Mutual Savings Association, Central Homes, and others.

Latifundios (large farms) Versus Minifundios (smaller tracts of lands) was a major problem that was extremely hard to solve. During my time in

Peru, there was a great deal of emphasis on trying to help the government achieve its Agrarian or Land Reform Law of 1964. There was talk about how to break the big farms (Latifundios) and how to title land and support the smaller plots (minifundios). This whole subject was most complex, and there were studies after studies all with contradicting conclusions. The need for land reform and the breaking of the huge Latifundios was never in question. What seemed to be most confusing was the degree of multiplication of problems that took place afterwards. For instance, when large tracts of land were further divided up and redistributed to the smaller farmers, they became minifundios. **At that point, titling began to be most difficult because when the new owner died, the minifundios were further divided down according to the number of children. This exponential redistribution of minifundios lands could really become a nightmare. I do not think the problem was solved. The subject of Land Reform is most complex**.

USAID/Peru also had a huge Public Law 480 Program – under Title I, II, and III. Title I programs were designed to generate Local Currency to be used on new projects or the Servicios. Under Title II, certain types of commodities were also sold to generate local currency. And Title III was a huge program where the People of the United States donated foodstuff (wheat, milk, others) to needy people and in emergencies. These types of food donations were granted through organizations like Catholic Relief Services, UNICEF, local organizations, and others.

PART F. ACTING CONTROLLER

When Bill C went on Home Leave, I took over as Acting Controller. We had an excellent staff, and accounting books – divided by categories of disciplines (i.e., education, agriculture, and others.) -- were routinely reconciled and reports sent to Washington.

- One guy (Danilo) was always the first to reconcile his accounts, and he had been given several awards for doing so. One day, he came to me and told me that he wanted to terminate his employment and asked me for a Recommendation Letter so he could find a job in USAID/Uruguay or Argentina – where he was going. The Chief Accountant (Juan) and I composed a beautiful letter for him. And he left. A month passed, and the accountant that took over Danilo's Subsidiary could not reconcile his accounts. We began to be late. Perturbed, I assigned one of my best Auditors to make a study of that subsidiary. As soon as he began, he uncovered that Danilo had been "cooking the books." There were errors galore, and he would pencil in "…I am missing .50 centavos here… I am missing $3 Here, and others." When that information came to me, I immediately informed the Controllers of USAID/Uruguay and Argentina so they would not hire the guy. Also, I announced that other subsidiaries would be examined. Very quickly, another accountant quit. I was not surprised that my statements were enough of a scare to people to make another person quit so quickly.

The experience taught me a few lessons; for instance, (a) to be careful in evaluating prospective employees; (b) to be careful with my evaluation of personal; and (c) to draft Letters of Recommendation with great care.

PART G. THE PEACE CORPS

As will be recalled, President John F. Kennedy initiated the concept of the Peace Corps – where people of all ages would go to a country and teach the locals how to do certain things. Peru was one of the first countries to receive a Country Director and a contingent of "Peace Corps Volunteers."

The USAID Office of Controller was assigned the responsibility to manage the funds assigned to the Peace Corps. Frank M. – a person who had managed the candidacy of John F. Kennedy – was appointed as the Peace Corps Director in Peru. When we first met the guy, he quickly showed his arrogance and tried to intimidate us into letting him do anything he wanted with the funds. I was glad Bill C. had not yet gone on Home Leave. Bill C let him know that he had to use funds according to U.S. Government rules and regulations.

Undeterred, Frank M. would try different angles to use funds in unauthorized ways. We played the game and blocked his many weird attempts.

- But, in all fairness, the Peace Corps had strange needs, and many things were either unplanned or unanticipated. Therefore, we frequently had to improvise on rules. For instance, the Country Peace Corps Director did not have a "Representation Allowance;" the Peace Corps had to be advised to develop one. The poor Peace Corps Volunteer came to the country, was assigned to the boondocks, and had to look for their own shacks or rooms. Since they received only a minor stipend (about $100 a month), no furniture, and no housing allowance, we had to bend the rules to pay them the $30 or $50 needed to rent a place. Sometimes girls rented a shack, caught men peeping through the walls as they were bathing; we had to find ways of financing security measures. A few girls were raped, and we needed to find ways to get them to hospitals and evacuate them. Some "projects (fishery, aviaries, agriculture) needed "seed capital;" we produced amounts needed.
- **(Note: Many years later, my son, Joe III, became a Peace Corps Volunteer and served in Costa Rica and Ecuador. Like other volunteers, he suffered immensely – lived in a shack, walked ten miles each way to take a bus, taught people agriculture, and suffered many stomach problems. As a result of the experience, Joe is an exceptionally strong and beautiful "people's person."** He is married to Lucy -- a beautiful Peruvian-born but U.S. Citizen, professional who worked for – and recently retired from – the Inter-American Development Bank. My granddaughter, Estela, is now a fabulous 29 year-old beauty).

PART H. VISIT TO THE ALTIPLANO AND MACHU PICCHU

Since I was multi-tasking assignments to the other people, I accompanied one person (Jorge) on a trip that would take us to Pasco, Ica, Arequipa, Puno, Lake Titicaca, Cuzco (and Machu Picchu). This way, we would see a variety of programs, including Food for Peace (PL 480 Title III). We went by a rented leased car or "Collectivo (a shared taxi)"

- The leg of the trip from Lima to Pasco, to Ica, to Arequipa was fantastic. I saw the country, talked to the people, saw the programs in action, and others. Arequipa was a beautiful city with an exceptional hotel. Problems began the minute we left Arequipa and began to climb to the Altiplano. As we climbed up the 19,000 ft. high mountain (called either Crucero Alto or Lagunilla), I began experiencing the worst "Soroche (Altitude Sickness)" you can ever have. I was sure that this was my last day on this earth – my head was splitting; I was vomiting, and my diarrhea had the driver stopping every 10 minutes. Somehow, we got to Puno. I went to my room. *Jorge told them to bring me "Mate De Coca (Tea made out of Coca Leaves)." Within one or two hours, I was perfect.* ***Coca Tea must have some terrific medicinal qualities; in effect, the Cholitos (Peruvian Indians) are very consistent in having with them and chewing (the Altiplano Peruvians call it "cha-cha la Coca" leaves as they walk or run. This protects them from illnesses and delays exertion. I have often wondered why the U.S. does not explore its medical use.***

- We visited the projects in Puno and headed to Cuzco via train. I will always remember that train ride on the Altiplano. You see the llamas and alpacas roaming in herds and the Inca peasants, with their colorful dresses, walking, chewing the Coca leaves, and spinning their yarns. We finally got to Cuzco and stayed in one of the best hotels. **As we were checking in, the Clerk asked me: "How many Cholitas (word for an Indian woman) do you want?" I saw Jorge smiling, and I did not know how to answer that one. My imagination and thoughts were running wild; I kept thinking, what am I going to do with two women? So, hedging, I asked him how many he would recommend. He told me, "Two because it does get cold at night." So, I said, ok. When I went to my room, my first observation was that the bed was extremely narrow, and my mind was really playing weird tricks on me. I kept asking myself: "...how can three of us people fit in this bed…and just what am I going to do with two women in bed…" When I was almost ready to turn in, the bed clerk walked in. True to his words, he brought in the "two Cholitas;" -- the Cholitas turned out to be two hot water bottles.**

What a bummer! However, it did get cold, and the two Cholitas kept me nice and warm.

- After a few days visiting the projects and food distribution centers, I was on my way, once again by train, to Machu Picchu. Machu Picchu is a fantastic place, and I will not try to even describe it. It is truly "a place for the Gods…" Anyway, I left Cuzco early in the morning, and I think I came back the same day. During the trip, I met a Priest and a guy who said he was a Communist. Up the zig-zag road, we went on the bus all the way to the center of the "Inca City." After we walked around and had taken a guided tour, the three of us began to talk about politics and religion. I was caught in between a highly religious person and an avowed atheist. One talked about Christianity and God, the other about infinity and the non-existence of such a being. Two talked about the democratic rule and the other about mass benefits and rulings. The three of us talked and talked, and we almost did not make the last bus back down. It was a most memorable discussion.

Jorge and I made it back to Lima. But I will always remember this trip, the Soroche, the Mate de Coca, the views of the Altiplano, the two Cholitas, Cuzco, Machu Picchu, and the conversation with the Priest and the Communist.

PART I. THE INFORMAL SECTOR

The "Informal Sector" was and is a giant sleeping problem in every country that is difficult to address (See a more detailed discussion of the Informal Sector in Chapter 3K).

As we adjusted to our new way of life, I saw many examples of people not being incorporated into the formal economic system of Peru. There were numerous female servants, gardeners, street vendors of all types (vegetables, milk, food, taxi drivers, and others.). During my trip to the Altiplano, I saw more obvious exclusions from the formal economic sector, such as women and children keeping llama herds, tilling their farm, walking, and twirling the yarn that eventually resulted in quilts, and many others. These people obviously did not pay taxes, kept their earnings, did subsistence types of living, and did not receive direct economic benefits.

In my naïve questions, I would constantly be asking how all this mass of humanity and economic efforts fit into the scheme of assistance. At that time, nothing much was known about the "Informal Sector," and responses were most ambiguous, and I was discouraged from focusing or asking further questions on this subject.

As I went from country to country, in my later assignments, I frequently saw the same phenomena everywhere. However, by then -- and with so much exposure to identical conditions in many countries -- I had become "conditioned" or desensitized to this economic disorder, accepted it as a fact, and was no longer affected by it.

As mentioned in Chapter 3 Part K, it was not until 1986 that one author (Hernando de Soto) authored an excellent paper (El Otro Sendero) that the Informal Sector was finally recognized as an existing, but unacknowledged, huge problem. He pointed out that there were about 91,000 street vendors (women, children, and men) who produced 38.9 percent of the national income. Yet, they are not incorporated into the formal sector, do not pay taxes, do not own property, and most do not receive benefit from the Government.

In retrospect, I wish that I had persisted more in my questions. Maybe, USAID could have focused on the problem – related to the "Informal Sector" -- much earlier.

PART J. PERSONNEL EVALUATION AND APPRAISAL REPORT SYSTEM

Boy, was I shocked when I received my first Personnel Evaluation and Appraisal Report (PER). The PER shown to me was not all that bad; it was balanced. However, I found out that USAID had two types of documents that would be written on an employee. These documents were very complex; they were not just check marks on a one-page standard document as used elsewhere in the Government. The documents were page after page of carefully worded sentences describing the work done by the employee during the year and carefully rating each phase.

More importantly, was that only the PER was shown to the employee; in essence, this one could say flowery things. However, there was the second document, the Personnel Appraisal Report (PAR) that was secret and could not be seen by the employee. The PAR was really a dangerous double-edged tool; an unhappy or vindictive supervisor could say pleasant things on the PER and then blast the employee in the PAR. Both the PER and PAR were evaluated in Washington, and some employees got their walking papers based mostly on the PAR. And the poor employee could not even see that secret document. Therefore, he/she had no recourse or was able to file a grievance either against the supervisor or USAID.

It was indeed an awful personnel evaluation system. I certainly felt extremely uncomfortable with the PAR system. In any event, I lived with these duplicitous and possible contradictory systems for about 5 years. After employees, including myself, objected to its unfairness and the tremendous personnel needs of Vietnam, the PAR part of the system was eventually eliminated.

Years later, I was finally permitted to see my PAR's. I was happy to see that my fears were unfounded. All my PARs were honest and fair evaluations. But I was happy that this secretive part of the evaluation system was eliminated.

PART K. DEATH OF PRESIDENT KENNEDY

November 22, 1963, was an extremely sad day in Peru. It was about 11:00 AM, local time when one of the Secretaries came through all the offices saying that they had just heard on the radio that President John F. Kennedy had been shot and was dead.

The local staff and all of us were in shock, and many of us were crying. Almost immediately, everyone was called to a meeting at the yard of the Embassy. The U.S. Ambassador gave the official notification. He announced that the Nation was in mourning and told everyone to go home for the rest of the day and stay home on the day of the burial.

There is no doubt that President John F. Kennedy was loved very much in that country.

PART L. THREATS BY THE TUPAMAROS

Early after my arrival in Peru, a terrorist organization called as the Movimiento de Liberacion Nacional (National Liberation Movement) was organized in Uruguay. It became better known as the "Tupamaros." Although they used normal terrorist tactics -- like robbing banks, gun shops, businesses, and others. – their main threatening strategy was the kidnapping of political personnel. We were warned about them and to be careful.

It was not until 1964, nearing my end of the first tour, that some Communist group and/or the Tupamaros came out with a pamphlet called "Who is who in the CIA," which listed many of the CIA operatives in Central and South America and marked them for kidnapping or murder. *My name was in* the pamphlet. I understand this document was later published in the form of a book.

PART M. TRANSFER TO ECUADOR AND CONCLUDING REMARKS

Anyway, when I saw the pamphlet, two things happened. First, I signed a document saying that if I was kidnapped by a terrorist – probably by the Tupamaros – the U.S. Government was not to pay ransom for me or attempt to rescue me. The second was that an opening came up in Quito, Ecuador, and my family and I were transferred there at the end of my tour.

The 1961 Dodge Dart went fast; a friend paid us the full purchase price of the car. As usual, packing and the transfer were a real hassle but manageable. We were given farewell parties to no end.

All of us hated to leave Lima, Peru. We really loved the people and the country. Being the first assignment, it was a fabulous learning experience that lasted me a lifetime. During my assignment in Peru, we did over 50 studies covering the gamut of all USAID programs – Servicios, P.L. 480 Title I, III, irrigation projects, agricultural projects, education, Puno Emergency. Here are some statistics:

Programs or Functional Areas	Reports Issued	Reports In Draft	Work In Progress
Projects Agreements	8	5	3
Servicios	12	1	1
Development Loan Funds	2	0	1
Food Distribution			
P.L. 480, Title II	1	2	1
P.L. 480, Title III	7	1	6
Foreign Owned U.S. Currency	6	0	0
Local Owned Currency	0	0	1
Other	12	1	2
Totals	**48**	**10**	**15**

During our tour in Ecuador, we, as a family, took a ship tour from Guayaquil to Callao; we met old friends, did some nice shopping, and had a real enjoyable time. By myself, I returned to Lima several times during the next 25 years. A return to Lima was always like coming home, being welcomed by friends, and feeling that warmth and affection that only the Peruvians seem to be able to give.

CHAPTER SIX
IN ECUADOR, CHIEF RESIDENT AUDITOR, A TROUBLED PROGRAM, A SIZEABLE EMBEZZLEMENT, MY AUDITION AS A TOREADOR, AND TRANSFER TO SOUTH VIETNAM

PART A. INTRODUCTORY REMARKS

Introduction: Once we left Lima, we returned to the United States on home leave for 30 days. We rented an apartment and visited our families in Austin, Laredo, and Monterrey, Mexico. We also went to Washington, D.C. for two weeks of "consultation" with USAID officials. After this, our family of five then proceeded to Quito, Ecuador. Once again, there are some complicated information and issues discussed. For these reasons, this chapter is presented in nine Parts:

- Part A. Introductory Remarks.
- Part B. An Ecuadorean History.
- Part C. The Death of My Sister.
- Part D. Life in Quito.
- Part E. Auditioning as a Toreador.
- Part F. The Technical Side of Work.
- Part G. The Mutual Savings Association Program administered By Ecuadorean Central Housing Bank Program (EHB).
- Part H. A Civic Action Project Embezzlement.
- Part I. My Transfer to South Vietnam and My Concluding Remarks.

PART B. THE ECUADOREAN HISTORY

Ecuador is a land of many contrasts: The assignment brought a continuing nice lifestyle, exposure to Ecuadorian history, new friendships, diplomatic cocktails, beautiful music, visits to many places in Ecuador, more experiences with coup d'états. It also brought difficult challenges with a poorly planned program, discovery of my first embezzlement case, an audition to be a "Toreador" (bullfighter), and my conversion from a "limited" Foreign Service employee to being a permanent Foreign Service Officer. In the middle of my tour in Ecuador, USAID also needed my capabilities to work in the Republic of South Vietnam and transferred me there.

Ecuadorian History and Government: Ecuador is situated on the west coast of South America, about 3,000 miles south of New York, and includes an area measuring about 116,270 square miles. Ecuador's geography is divided into three main areas: a coastal region, the Sierra or Ecuadorian highlands, and an Eastern or jungle area.[48] Because it straddles the Equator, the Spaniards named the region Ecuador.

Once again, books exist that cover the history of Ecuador. My book is not meant to be all-inclusive. Briefly, Ecuador had its Pre-Columbian period, the period of the Spanish Conquest, the Spanish Colonial era, Ecuadorian Independence, and Ecuador as a Republic.[49]

Ecuador's Pre-Columbian Period was marked by the emergence of many Indigenous cultures such as: the Vegas, El Inga, Valdivia, Machallila, Chorrera, La Bahia, La Tolita, Los Manteños, Los Huancavelica, Los Shiras, the Kingdom of Quito, and the Incas. Briefly, the Kingdom of Quito was formed by a series of cultures – Quitus, Puruhaes, Cañares, who inhabited the area that is now Ecuador. This Kingdom was defeated by the Shyris, the predominant indigenous group for 700 years. The Incas, whose capital was in Cuzco, Peru, eventually conquered most, although not all, of Ecuador. Under Huayna Capac, the Inca Empire reached its apogee, but his death in Quito in

---

[48] A Department of State Post Report called "Welcome to Quito" dated 1961, P. 5

[49] The historical synopsis was obtained from different documents – Post Report on Quito, Internet Articles called "History of Ecuador" found at http://en.wikipedia.org/wiki/History_of_Ecuador

the year1524 resulted in a civil war involving his sons Huascar and Atahualpa. Atahualpa eventually won the civil war, just in time for the Spanish Conquest.

Francisco Pizarro, the Spanish Conquistador, defeated Atahualpa in 1532. In 1534, after defeating Inca general Rumiñahui's in battle, Diego de Almagro and Sebastian de Belacazar established the City of Quito in 1534. Ecuador remained under colonial rule from 1534 until May 24, 1822, when revolutionaries -- including Simon Bolivar and Antonio Jose de Sucre, -- helped Ecuador gain its Independence. After independence, Ecuador, Colombia, and Venezuela formed the Confederation of Grand Colombia; this union lasted for 8 years and was dissolved. The country became the Republic of Ecuador in mid-1830.

In its close to 200 years as a Republic, Ecuador has had a very unstable existence. It has had 20 different Constitutions and has been led by nearly 90 leaders of various capacities – Presidents, Interim Presidents, acting, Juntas, and others. Some have lasted only 3 days; others have been disqualified; some resigned from office, and at least three have died or been assassinated while in office. Peru has invaded Ecuador three times. At various times, Ecuador has been led by conservatives, liberals, social democrats, and others – not always in a peaceful manner. [50]

Even slavery and religion have been the subject of Constitutional changes. For instance:

- Slavery was abolished in March 1854, giving liberty to over sixty thousand Black slaves (the books I used for research, call them "Negroes").
- When President Gabriel Garcia Moreno came into power, he changed the Constitution in 1869 whereby only practicing Roman Catholics could be Ecuadorian citizens. These provisions were eliminated by another president (General Eloy Alfaro) during the Constitutional changes of 1897 and 1906. [51]

Until 2008, all Presidents served only one four-year term. The Constitution has now been changed, and the current President Guillermo

[50] Statistics obtained from Internet http://www.ecuaworld.com/discover/president.htm
[51] The U.S. State Department Post Report for Ecuador, p2 and p3

Lasso, who was elected in May 2021, might be able to serve for two consecutive terms for a total of 8 years. Nevertheless, even with such a checkered history, it is interesting that the following Presidents have been able to serve more than one time (not necessarily consecutive terms):

- Juan Jose Flores served three times.
- Gabriel Garcia Moreno served three times.
- Eloy Alfaro served two terms.
- Jose Maria Velasco served five times

At the time of our arrival in Ecuador in 1964, a Military Junta composed of four Generals (Castro/Cabrera/Gandara/ and Freile) ruled the country. They ruled from 1963 to 1966. There was an attempted coup against the ruling junta, but as such things go in Ecuador, it was peaceful. During this attempted coup, I was visiting a friend and had to stay inside a middle (and thus "safe") room within his house because soldiers on horseback were firing a series of shots around the house. However, most of the Generals remained united, kicking out the rebellious faction. Clemente Yaravi Imbabura took over provisionally in March 1966 and was replaced by Otto Arosemena Gomez as interim president in November 1966. Arosemena remained as president from November 1966 to August 1968. We had left the country by then.

PART C. DEATH OF MY SISTER

Death of My Sister: Shortly after our arrival in Quito, I got a call from my parents. They told me that my older sister – Maria Estela Peña Martinez – was extremely sick with a major kidney infection which was further complicated by pregnancy. My sister Estela was born on May 30, 1931. She had beautiful green eyes and was married and had a little girl. She could no longer be helped and died on March 3, 1965. Because I had just arrived in Quito and the workload was just too heavy, I was not able to return to Laredo to attend her funeral. She left a husband (Alonzo) and a small daughter (Leticia). Alonzo later remarried and died some years later from Cancer. My parents reared Leticia (or Letty) from my sister's death until she got married. Letty graduated from Laredo State University, divorced after several married years, taught school for over 23 years, and finally retired after working as a teacher in the

Laredo public school system. At this writing, and because of her extraordinary qualifications, Letty was hired – and worked – as a secretary for an extremely popular Law Office. She is now completely retired.

PART D. LIFE IN ECUADOR

When we arrived in Quito, we were put in a small two-bedroom apartment within the Hotel Quito, a new hotel with a spectacular view of the valley below. The apartment faced the pool and featured a stunning view of Pichincha, which is an active volcano. It was a nice arrangement where we would sometimes cook in the apartment or eat in the hotel restaurant. The food was outstanding.

At the time of our stay, Quito – a most picturesque city -- sat in a corridor that was no more than 10 miles long and three miles wide. The (still active) Pichincha volcano prevented further width extension. Since Quito is about 9,500 ft high, the temperature and days seem to be very consistent. On any given day, the temperature ranged between 35 degrees at night to a maximum of 75 degrees during the day. During the time we were in Ecuador, it rained about every day, and the scenery was always green.

Quito is, in fact, a beautiful city. However -- and maybe because it is cold at night -- the people tend to be much more conservative and aloof than in lively Lima environment. At the time, there was a great class distinction, in Quito, between those that have and the ones that are poor.

We soon got a "niñera"– a caretaker for our children. Her name was Maria, and she was the best maid we ever had. She remained with us for the two years that we were there, and we made every effort to bring her to the U.S. with us, but we could not get her either a U.S. visa or an Ecuadorian passport.

Although it took us a while, we located a newly built house in an area of Quito close to the airport that was just being constructed. So, the place seemed a little isolated. Both sides of the house were vacant lots. The lots were occupied by two extremely poor Indigenous families who lived in haphazardly made shacks.

The neighbors frequently became drunk with aguardiente (a homemade moonshine) and got a little noisy. In addition, when we got the children some rabbits, we would leave the rabbits in the backyard because they liked to dig holes and hide in them. The rabbits began to multiply, but they never got beyond 3 or 4; the neighbors would jump the fence at night and steal them for food.

The Great Patojo: To curb the theft of rabbits that were taking place, we finally decided to get a dog. We bought a puppy, who was later run down by a car. However, to give time for the puppy to grow, we also decided to rent a dog. His name was "Patojo."

- Ah, yes, the great Patojo. Let me tell you quickly about Patojo because he is a story all by its own. He was a half-breed German Shepard that had one leg shorter than the rest and always limped (that is why someone gave him the name Patojo), and he was technically not our dog. Like I said, we had bought a nice puppy that we intended to keep (unfortunately, he was later killed by a car), and we "rented" Patojo from an Ecuadorian Pet Farm to protect us – while the puppy grew -- from robbers and thieves that seemed to frequently mill around our half-isolated home. The only problems with Patojo were that he was a tired old dog, ate like a hog, slept all the time, feared his shadow, howled at the moon, barked at nothing, and scared the wits out of us when he barked at nothing in the middle of the night. The most annoying thing was that he never seemed to bark at the bad guys. To this day, I have always believed that he must have been one of the co-conspirators. Since he was always sleeping at the wheel, we had taken him back to the Pet Farm several times. But time and again, Patojo kept escaping – more likely, the escapes were arranged by the Pet Farm owner -- and returning to our home. So, we kept him until we left.

Children's School: Our two sons were quickly enrolled in school – Joe, the oldest, went to Colegio Cotopaxi. Jerry, the second son, went to Escuela Americana. Linda, the baby, stayed home. The school buses from the respective schools would pick up Joe and Jerry, take them to school and return them home. There were a few times when some little friend would invite Jerry to come play at home; without telling anyone, Jerry would get off the bus, and we would wind up – crazily -- searching for him all over.

Our New Car: We also got a brand new 1964 Chevrolet Bel-Air that we had ordered. It was an exceptional car. However, towards the end of my tour, my wife and kids were driving it. A careless bus driver failed to signal that he was turning, and my wife hit the bus. The accident did a great deal of damage to the car. At the time the accident happened, I was being transferred to Vietnam. So, there were some complications in selling it. A buyer and I agreed on a discounted price. We left Ecuador as the car was being fixed. The buyer paid me when he took possession of it. We lost a great deal of money selling it.

Family Trips: We made many trips around the country – to Ambato, Otavalo, Santo Domingo de los Colorados, Guayaquil, and other towns. We saw Cotopaxi (the active volcano) from a distance many times; it is a fabulous sight. We saw other active volcanoes, as they were erupting, a couple of times. On some of these trips, we bought some beautiful wooden carvings and carpets, which we still have. We also made a trip, via a cruise ship, from Guayaquil back to Lima, Peru, and a car trip with another couple to Tulcan and nearby Colombia.

- Our cruise back to Peru was just beautiful. Two problems occurred. The first occurred at the airport when the old DC-3 propeller-driven plane that we were scheduled to fly was rolled out twice. First, one engine would not turn over, and then after they repaired the first engine, the second engine would not turn over. Pauline finally decided that this was not a smart thing to do since the airplane was clearly not safe to fly, and we ended up driving from Quito down the winding mountainous road to Santo Domingo de los Colorado's and onto Guayaquil, on the coast of Ecuador. Also, Pauline got seasick, and there were a few times that the three children wanted to go every way, and it was hard trying to please all of them. When we got to Callao and Lima, it was just like coming home. We visited old friends and went to places that we had not been. We even went to a table factory where the workers were hearing impaired, i.e., they were deaf and mute. We bought a beautiful round table, made of carved leather, which shows the Inca Calendar. We still have the table. It was just a beautiful visit.

- My wife and I made the trip to Tulcan and Pasto, Colombia, together with a colleague (Chuck) and his wife (Pilar). This trip was quite interesting for two reasons. As we passed the town of Ibarra in northern Ecuador and began climbing the mountain towards the border with Colombia, the houses in the villages seemed as those in Africa. Obviously, the people had been Black Slaves, and their little houses resembled those that we later saw in Africa. The other interesting part was that we could not find any decent hotels in Tulcan or on the other side in Colombia. So, the four of us stayed in a one-room shack that we were somehow able to rent. The shack had two narrow beds. The shack had a burlap curtain that divided the toilet. So, the sounds in the toilet could be heard any time one of us went in there. We were all embarrassed to hear each other's toilet and snoring sounds. So, we returned the following day to Quito.

PART E. AUDITIONING AS A TOREADOR

Let me now turn to the time when I can claim that I auditioned for and became an instant Bullfighter. Oh, I do not mean to brag or anything like that. But, as an adaptive learner and, in my unbiased assessment, I demonstrated the serenity, temerity, courage, and majesty of a possible future great of the blood and sand arena.

Yes, I can now claim that I could have been as great as or greater than the likes of Manuel Benitez Perez. He is best known as "El Cordobes." El Cordobes, from Palma Del Rio, Cordoba, Spain, was, in fact, one of the greatest bullfighters of any era. I saw this "Maestro De La Faena" several times at the bull rings in Lima and Quito. He could do things with a bull (like that on the left) that only the greatest would have the courage to attempt. I remember that a few times, just before the bull was sent into the arena, "El Cordobes" would go to the center of the ring, kneel, his legs half open and planted on the sand. The spectators, including myself, would be transfixed and quiet, for we knew a decisive moment was at hand. One slight turn in the wrong direction by the bull, and this great man would be dead. The gates would open. Blinded by the sun and without getting his bearing, the angry bull would charge the statuesque figure in the center, yet El Cordobes stayed on the ground, waived the cape, and just by a miracle -- the bull attacked the cape. In my book, that was the gift of a great matador. Yes, I might have probably been in that class. Well, you be the judge.

It happened like this: a friend of mine (Alonzo P.) and I heard about a "Corrida de Pueblo" (community bullfight) that took place in some of the villages in rural Ecuador during certain religious holidays.[52] So, we decided to go. We took my brand new 1964 Chevrolet Bel-Air and headed on to the village about 20 miles away on an unpaved, bumpy, and dilapidated road.

When we got there, we found the "bull-ring," – well, it was a bullring in a sort of fashion. The central "arena" was a clearing in the village with two trees near the center and the surrounding fence made of haphazardly placed pieces of wood. For a time, Alonzo and I went around taking in the sights -- we saw huge crowds of Campesinos milling around, drinking homemade aguardiente, and eating the local delicacy -- Cui (Guinea Pig), which looks like a rat. Since we were the only foreigners, the locals, in their friendly manner, came over to talk to us. They also offered us a drink of their aguardiente, rot-gut moonshine. It was a "shared arrangement" where everyone drank from the same bottle, container, glass, or whatever (germs and all). Not wanting to make them feel bad, and being the consummate diplomats, we drank the moonshine.

Let me tell you, the Ecuadorian homemade aguardiente was not nearly as smooth as Tennessee Whisky or the Colombian aguardiente (which tastes like

---

[52] I am referring to my friend Alonzo Perales who is married to Alicia. In Ecuador, they had 4 children and were working with the Fulbright Commission.

anisette); there is a definite difference. The homemade Ecuadorian aguardiente – of that village -- tasted like kerosene, gasoline, ethanol alcohol, and castor oil mixed together. It might have contained a little or a lot of each. It is a memorable drink that, even after so many years, I still seem to taste, in my mind anyway, now, and then. It can be deadly, and it certainly does not take long for you to get zonked.

So, half zonked, we ate the grilled cui (Guinea Pig), which was not bad but was greasy. Subsequently, I ate cui, but only when I was on the road, and there was nothing else to eat. And we kept accepting the aguardiente offered to us.

The bullfight then began. If you want to experience the environment of a "Corrida de Pueblo," go to the following website and click on "Corrida de Toros in Chupan."

http://www.youtube.com/watch?v=rwAUOICEIII&NR=1

The only problem was that it was not a small bull but a mean-spirited medium-aged **cow**. Why it was so angry, so mean, and with so much energy, I will never know. It charged into the makeshift arena with an eye to destroying everything in sight. Pandemonium broke. The dogs began barking like crazy and chased after the cow. The noise got the cow angrier, and it chased after the dogs. Encouraged by the aguardiente, the Campesinos began to jump into the arena, taking turns with the capes -- well, ok, they were really rags, sheets, burlap sacks, or whatever. They say cows are more dangerous than bulls because they charge with their eyes open. This one was no exception. People were thrown into the air with the greatest of ease, but they got back up and continued.

Someone gave me one of the "capes" and challenged me to go into the arena. With the false courage that a drink too many gives you, I rushed into the arena, headed straight for the trees, and saw the cow eye me with curiosity and charge towards me. With the grace of a true Matador, I went behind one tree (well, I said that I was half drunk, but I was not stupid), waived the cape, and made a pass at the cow. She went past me, threw one guy up in the air, came back at me, I got on the other side of the tree, made another pass. This time, the cow took the so-called Cape. Having done my "Faena," I rushed back to the fence.

Stay with me! The story continues. A young Campesino, drunk as a skunk, walked slowly, with great flair, majesty, and courage of a man with a cape. He kept looking at the cow, and the cow kept looking at him. Near the center of the arena, he knelt -- in the style of El Cordobes -- brave as they come. He yelled at the cow: "Eh, toro," "eh, toro." And I made a note to myself: "…that guy made a mistake; he does not know a male bull from a cow…." Then, the people gasped and recognized greatness (or stupidity). That cow charged, eyes wide open, drove its horn through the Campesino's left arm -- close to the armpit-- lifted him up, and threw him 10-feet up in the air. As he fell on the ground, the cow continued to try to gore him some more. It was distracted by some other Campesinos and took off somewhere else. Since the Campesino was close to us, we jumped in to pull him to one side. He was bleeding profusely. Although half-drunk, I still was lucid enough to fashion a tourniquet from a piece of the cape. Two of his friends and my friend and I began carrying him out of the arena. That temperamental cow saw us and charged our way. Courageously and fast as supermen, we dropped the poor guy and ran for the fence. That cow was again distracted and went a separate way. We picked him up, and three more times, that cow charged the group, and we -- full of grace and courage -- dropped the poor guy and rushed to the fence. As we were getting out of the arena, I looked behind me and saw that the cow, with no semblance of ever stopping, continued to grace the sky with the heavenly bodies of aguardiente drunks -- and fun-loving village people.

The kid needed a hospital. There was none in the village. So, Alonzo, two of the kid's friends, and I climbed in my car and drove to Quito. Everyone bounced around to the rhythm of the road. Still drunk but now delirious, the kid kept asking if he was going to die. I drove him to a hospital, and we all stayed there until the doctors patched him up and said that he would live. Then, I went to my home -- to my wife, three beautiful children, a house cleaner, and "Patojo" (the dog I discussed earlier). Having seen some bullfighting before, my wife was angry with me for having "auditioned as a Toreador" and understanding for helping the poor campesino that got gored.

When I visited the hospital the following day, the hospital director called me. We went back and forth: (He) You owe the hospital Sucres 1,000 (something in that order) because we helped the young man. (Me) But I do not even know him. (He): You brought him in. (Me) But he was bleeding and would have died. (He) You still brought him in. (Me) Collect from him or his friends. (He) The others do not have any work or money. From then on, it was high-level negotiations between the hospital director and me. To make the story short: I wound up paying about five hundred Sucres (or something like that). At the time, the Ecuadorian currency was known as the Sucre in honor of Jose Antonio de Sucre, who liberated Ecuador. Ecuador in 2000 switched to using the U.S. dollar as its currency.

The above story of the hospital collecting from an innocent bystander for the costs of an accident may sound amazing. However, many countries do exactly that. After reading the above, a good friend of mine told me: Begin Quote: …When (I lived in Venezuela for a time), stories of people in car wrecks being left abandoned by the side of the road abounded, and we were horrified at the lack of Good Samaritan attitude. But anybody who WAS a Good Samaritan got stuck with whatever the bill was because "You were the one who brought him in," just as you said…. End of Quote. This is sad but true. I wonder if it's still that way (in some of the other countries). Also, Joe, my son, who was in the Peace Corps in Costa Rica and Ecuador, tells me the same stories – anyone taking an injured party to the hospital is responsible for the bill.

In sum, I learned a few things from my audition as a toreador. First of all, keep away from old and angry cows and aguardiente. Experienced middle-aged cows can be tricky and mean, and the aguardiente hangovers can be brutal and costly. And finally, looking back -- and after an unbiased evaluation of my performance -- as a toreador, I concluded that I was just too much of a competition for the Great Cordobes. So, it was at that moment that I retired from the field of "Matadores" – see, I have you roaring with laughter now. All kidding aside, that cow fight was a great experience.

First Place in a Golf Tournament: Shortly after our arrival in Ecuador, I began to take up golf to pass my time. I was never very good at it, but I kept at it, and gradually I got better. One lady was selling her clubs, and I bought them. She gave me the clubs, but no golf bag. The Diplomats of Quito formed a tournament which was divided into (a) Learners; (b) Medium Proficient; and (c) "Exceptional." Knowing that I did not have a chance to win, I entered the "Learners," where about seven other participants would play. Throughout the one- or two-day tournament, the "Learners" were all very nervous and made mistakes. Was I nervous? Not me! I had the five- or six-women's clubs and remained unflustered and just continued to forge ahead. Huge surprise! Like I said, all the people in the lowest category of players kept making mistakes and getting very nervous. And then, to my surprise--as well as to the surprise of virtually everyone else--I won the "Learners' class part of the tournament. Unfortunately, that was my high-water mark, at least as far as my golf playing goes.

PART F. THE TECHNICAL SIDE OF WORK

Work in the Office: The Office of the Controller was a large division of USAID/Ecuador. Joe M. was the Controller; there was his deputy, and Bill J was the Chief Auditor. All were excellent people and co-workers. Joe M. was a good manager; he was an exceptional politician who delegated most work and dealt with current problems and issues. Bill J. was soon transferred, and I became the Chief Auditor.

Work was heavy. My first assignment was two-fold:

a) To make a quick survey of all active projects and see if there were any salient problems, with any USAID financed Projects, that needed to be urgently addressed; and,

b) To do an urgently needed review of the Ecuadorean Central Housing Bank (EHB) who was implementing the USAID financed Ecuadorean Mutual Savings and Loan System. (Note: There was a feeling among all the high officials of USAID - (these included the USAID Director, Program Officer, Project Manager, USAID Controller, and others) that the program implementation might be behind schedule and there could be some other more serious problems.

My survey quickly identified one activity – the Civic Action Project – where the procedures and internal controls over funds and commodities seemed so loose that I felt there could be a serious chance for a "diversion of assets." In other words, my probes, and tests in the areas of supply and material disclosed that there could be major embezzlement problems.

(Note: Aside from the EHB Program and the Civic Action Project, all other USAID programs showed semblances of various programmatic types of problems – but none showed the glaring defects as those two.

We discussed the results of my survey among our top officers. Although the Civic Action Project had profoundly serious defects, we decided that I was to still do the EHB Program first. At the same time, I was to take over as Chief Auditor when Bill left and guide the experience growth of the new U.S. auditor when he arrived. So, until Charles U., the new Auditor, arrived, we worked on the audit of the Housing Project and did other jobs.

Part G. Our Review Of The Mutual Savings And Loan Program As Administered By The Ecuadorean Central Housing Bank Program (EHB)

Some Background: The objective of the EHB program was to establish a Mutual Savings and Loans Association System like the one the U.S. has.

Program plans – for a US$10 million program -- had been designed by ICA, and the development loan (No. 518-A-012) had been awarded to the Government of Ecuador (GOE) on October 31, 1961. Under the terms of the agreement, (a) the DLF/USAID Loan was to be US$5.0 million, and (b) the GOE share was to be the equivalent of US$5.0 Million.

Contributions were stated in a USAID Loan Agreement, a GOE Guaranty Agreement, an agreement between the GOE and its Instituto de Seguridad Social (Social Security Institute, hereafter called ESSI). This program was transferred to USAID when it came into existence. In short, USAID was to Loan US$5.0 Million, and the GOE was to contribute the equivalent of US$5.0 Million through the ESSI.

The objectives of the program were to establish, guide (through rules and regulations), manage, and monitor a system of Mutual Savings and Loan Associations. These Associations were to operate similarly to the way the U.S. Savings and Loan Banks operate. In essence, the Associations normally: (a) receive deposits from private persons; (b) make loans for affordable housing;

(c) write and monitor mortgage documents; (d) collect interest, and principal payments from the housing loans; (d) make needed investments; (e) account for every individual transaction and source of funds; and (f) perform other similar functions.

At our cut-off, USAID, and the Government of Ecuador (GOE) had signed seven Implementation Letters that described the formulas to be used to determine the amount of each contribution and the method of disbursing the funds. The formulas were very complicated; they contained conflicting and confusing provisions; as a result, these formulas were, by themselves, part of the problems later found in our audit.

My audit team consisted of 2 people from my staff, 2 people from the Ecuadorean Central Housing Bank, and myself as supervisor. At our cut-off date, there had been 12 mutual associations established. There were 10,927 members who had deposited the equivalent of about US$1.5 million. The Associations had made 1,754 Mortgages amounting to about US $6.9 million.

Here is a Short Preview of Our Findings: Our review showed a program that was experiencing the "classic "Murphy's Law" (everything that could go wrong -- went wrong). In effect, this program was filled with a nightmare of serious problems. Almost every program level and area we touched had problems.

The biggest problem with the program was that it was not properly planned. Implementation letters were written in a very poor, contradictory, and defective manner. With only one U.S. Technician assigned to this complex Program, supervision, monitoring, guidance, and periodic assessments were generally not found by us. The desired sustainability of the individual associations was not carefully researched, designed, or envisioned. Ambiguity in the way the Standard Regulations were written gave rise to a variety of interpretations which resulted in control, by the few families, of some associations in some areas. In addition, there were other uncontrolled and adverse contributions. For instance, the Government of Ecuador (through its Instituto de Seguridad Social), EHB, and the Inter-American Development Bank (IDB) had signed the separate US $10.6 million agreement for the direct construction of housing units throughout the country. As a result – rather than supervise and implement the development of mutual savings and loan associations -- EHB became more interested in constructing housing units all over the country. Consequently, EHB: (a) switched its emphasis from the USAID savings and loan project to the construction of the housing units funded by IDB; and (b) equally bad, it began comingling the different funds (AID, IDB, ISSC, and counterpart funds (i.e., generated repayments of principal and interest), and others into one account.

Reconstructing Funding Sources and Their Application: Because the EHB had been commingling the funds for the different programs and non-programs, we had to reconstruct the funding sources and their application. This was an extremely challenging phase. During our audit, we had to review all the accounting transactions -- separate identifiable costs, estimate some and prorate some according to different formulas. Based on our review, the financial picture of the several programs was as follows:

	In Millions	Of	Ecuadorean	Sucres
Source of Funding	AID	IDB	Other	Total
USAID	56.7			56.7
ISSC	43.3	8.6		51.9
IDB		44.7		44.7
GOE		34	1.6	35.6
EHB			7.7	7.7
Total	**100**	**87.3**	**9.3**	**196.6**
Equals to Millions of				
U.S. $ Dollars	**5.5**	**4.8**	**0.5**	**10.8**

The above table shows these conclusions: (a) USAID and ICCS had contributed about 100 Million Sucres (or about US $5.5 million) towards the Savings and Loans Program; (b) the ICCS, IDB, and GOE (own funds) had contributed about 87.3 million Sucres (about US$4.8 million) towards the IDB

Housing Construction Project; and, (c) there had been comingling of GOE and EHB Program funds, amounting to 9.3 million Sucres (about US $500,000) and used for undetermined purposes.

Contents of Our Report: In the end, we prepared a 102-page report detailing the different problems that we found and the many recommendations for improvements. Here is a brief synopsis of what we found:

1. The program had not been well designed, and the implementation letters were confusing and contradictory. As a result, the Special regulations -- which were to provide standard policies, rules, and regulations so that all EHB Savings and Loans Associations functioned in an identical manner -- had been loosely written and had been changed a number of times. These program defects and confusion gave the Associations the undesired opportunity to interpret and use them every which way -- to their maximum advantage and detriment.
2. Only one U.S. technician had been assigned to supervise such a complicated program. As a result, USAID's and EHB's program management and monitoring were, to say the least, loose.
3. As noted above, the EHB and the (IDB had signed the separate US $10.6 million agreement for the direct construction of housing units throughout the country. Rather than supervise the development of the Associations, EHB (a) switched its emphasis from the USAID program to the construction of the IDB-funded housing units, and (b) began comingling the different funds. As such, the EHB was not a good Program Administrator.
4. As noted above, reconstruction and assignment of disbursements and costs was an extreme challenge.
5. As prescribed by Program Plans, the interest charged on loans made by the Associations proved to be unrealistically low. For instance, the Associations charged a 4% to 6% rate on its loans. By comparison: (a) commercial banks charged 10% Interest; and (b) the interest rate charged by USAID on loan made to the EHB was too high. As a result, the Program never contemplated an accurate program's sustainability factors for the Savings and Loans Associations.

6. With respect to USAID, EHB, and IDB, we found that: (a) the Letters of Implementation prescribed ambiguous guidance; (b) certain loan terms were unenforceable; (c) the voting provisions of the Special Regulations led a group of families, of one area, to unite and to legally take-over one Association; (f) EHB and the 12 Associations did not have a good relationship, which led to a lack of communication among themselves; (e) the way the Associations implemented the loans could not create cyclical characteristics of the desired system; (f) EHB needed to establish a uniform accounting and reporting system for the 12 Associations; (g) EHB rulings related to retaining insurance premiums hurt the Associations; (h) a construction project, called North Quito ran over the budget and adversely affected two Associations; (i) EHB, without due compensation, was using the services of one Association to collect IDB-related program collections; and (j) the IDB program had some serious problems that needed coordination with USAID and correction.
7. Problems related to the 12 Associations were very extensive and complicated. The major ones: (a) the financial situations of some of the Associations were precarious; (b) some Associations were engaging in contracts that were not of benefit to them; (c) some Associations were making loans that were in contradiction with the Special Regulations; (d) the Associations' idle funds were not deposited in income-producing investments; (e) the EHB intervened in one Association without basis; (f) the lack of growth by some Associations warranted serious concerns; and (g) others.
8. One Association based in Guayaquil was controlled by 9 depositors. All 9 depositors were "Family Related." The 9 depositors had made 69.8% of all deposits. Moreover, 82.3% of all mortgages made by this Association were concentrated in the El Paraiso area of Guayaquil. All home construction in this area had been done by a company owned by one of the 9 depositors.

General Summary of Audit: In sum, the Ecuadorean Mutual Savings and Loan Association had numerous serious problems duc primarily to (a) poor initial planning; (b) a lack of clear language and guidance written in the Loan, Implementation Letters, and the Standard Regulations; (c) as the Program

Administrator, the EHB lacked a single solid commitment to establish and monitor a national savings and loan system and should not have branched off towards constructing activities; (d) the system was formed by groups of people who quickly learned how to manipulate the system to their advantage; (e) a lack of knowledgeable U.S. technicians to guide and monitor the program; and (e) other causes.

Soon after completing the review, I was transferred to South Vietnam. As such, I was never able to follow up to see if our recommendations had been implemented. However, recently (over 55 years after our review), I checked the Internet to see which of the 12 Mutual Savings and Loans Associations still existed. I was happy to see that five or six of them still survived. The Association based in Pichincha seems to be the strongest one and has taken over the Associations in Ambato, Quevedo, and Rio Frio. The Association based in Cuenca, an Andean city in the south of Ecuador – which I visited during the review -- also seems to be strong. Unfortunately, others did not survive.

PART H. THE CIVIC ACTION EMBEZZLEMENT

As mentioned earlier, my review also showed evidence of profoundly serious problems with the Ecuadorean Civic Action Program.

Charles U. (Chuck), the second U.S. auditor, arrived about six months after I did. Married to a beautiful (and temperamental) Spaniard lady (Pilar), he turned out to be an exceptional analyst and a quick learner. I gave him two reports to review and assigned him small minor jobs so he could get his feet wet. After he had completed his work on these two reviews, I assigned him the complicated Civic Action Program.

The Civic Action Program represented a triple effort on the part of the USAID/Ecuador: the U.S. Department of Army (Army); and the Ecuadorian Army. USAID/Ecuador provided the funding for the program; the U.S. Army supplied the technical guidance, and the Ecuadorian Army executed the program. The design of the program was conceived in this way for two reasons. First, it was to improve public confidence in the military. Second, it was to use the capacities of the Ecuadorian military to raise social and economic living standards throughout the country.

Chuck quickly ran into the same problems that I had detected. He noticed that commodities had been bought that could not be used on the project. These included the purchase of white cement, normally used in the construction of homes and buildings for use on road projects as well as the purchase of 350 doors and locks for a project that only required seventy-five. There were other anomalies as well. When he visited the various projects, he found that items had either never been delivered or had been delivered in insufficient numbers, and suspicious credits had been given as a donation to a certain employee.

After we exchanged ideas and Chuck explored different avenues, he was able to produce unmistakable evidence of collusion between four people: (a) A U.S. Army local employee, (b) our own local USAID/Ecuador Chief Accountant, (c) our own Assistant USAID/Ecuador Accountant, and (d) a Supply Company. These people used several embezzlement methods – forgery, payment to non-existent companies or persons, non-delivery of commodities, and other devious techniques. These crooks had embezzled about $100,000, which was a hefty sum in those days.

What was most troubling was those two USAID/Ecuador local employees--the Chief Accountant and his assistant--were involved. They had worked with USAID for many years. The Chief Accountant (Raul) had a wife, six children, and a mistress who also worked for USAID. Once the review got underway and we had found evidence of the fraud, Raul would frequently come to my office and try to influence our activities by saying that he had a family, and our review should consider his years of service. Without showing our cards, I would act as if we had not yet found anything of significance. However, the various meetings showed that the crooks knew that we knew of the embezzlement.

Once we found the incriminating evidence, we had no option but to call in another USAID Special (Investigative) Office and the Ecuadorian Prosecutors. We gave them the facts, and at that point, our participation ended. They took over the lead in the investigation.

After they had concluded their investigation, the USAID Investigator and the Ecuadorian Prosecutor's Office made a huge mistake. They called the four culprits into the offices and told them of the pending charges. The four culprits then said that they would turn themselves into the police the following day. That night, the U.S. Army local employee, the USAID/Ecuador local Assistant Accountant, and the Director of the company escaped from the country.

Only the local Chief Accountant (Raul) was jailed. Over the following months, the U.S. Ambassador would call us in, tell us that Raul – who had a wife and six children -- was very depressed, was requesting freedom, and was threatening suicide. The U.S. Ambassador never wavered. He asked us to draft a speech for his delivery just in case that Raul made good on his suicide threat. In the statement, the Ambassador would explain why Raul had been in jail and express our country's regret that Raul had chosen to kill himself. We then described the embezzlement that the group had done. To my knowledge, the other three culprits were never caught.

PART I. TRANSFER TO VIETNAM AND CONCLUDING REMARKS

As I was getting close to the end of my two-year assignment in Ecuador, USAID sent me a proposal asking if I would be willing to become a permanent Foreign Service Officer. That was a nice offer, but it came with a fine print; if I accepted, it meant that I could be assigned anywhere in the world.

By then, I liked my job very much, had been promoted to the next higher level, and liked Foreign Service very much. So, I accepted. Not a month went by, and I was transferred to South Vietnam. My family and I liked Ecuador very much and have many good memories of the time spent there. I also left in place an excellent team and made some exceptional friends.

Chapter Seven
In South Vietnam, Deputy Unit Chief, Lifelong Friendships, Dangerous Situation, Shook Hands With Vietcong And Was In Tet Offensive

Part A. Introductory Remarks

Introduction. This Chapter is divided into ten Parts.

- Part A Introductory Remarks.
- Part B Home Leave and related activities.
- Part C Brief History of Vietnam.
- Part D. My Arrival in South Vietnam.
- Part E. Life in Vietnam.
- Part F. Description of Some Office Staff.
- Part G. Technical Side of Work in Vietnam.
- Part H Transfer of Carlos.
- Part I. The Tet Offensive.
- Part J. Concluding Remarks.

Part B. Home Leave And Related Activities

We left Quito in mid-May 1966 and went back to Austin on home leave for about 20 days. Since I was going to Vietnam – a country in turmoil and war -- I could not take my family to that post. The alternatives were to leave them in Austin or move them to the Philippines. Pauline's family was in Austin, so we decided that she, Joe, Jerry, and Linda, would stay in Austin. So, we made plans to buy a house there. We also decided that if I came back, alive, from Vietnam, this would eventually be our retirement home sometime in the future.

When we got to Austin, we rented an apartment and bought a used yellow Buick. We could not buy a new car because the one in Ecuador was still being repaired, and the buyer would not pay us until the work was completed. Once again, we visited our families in Austin, Laredo, and Monterrey, Mexico. Our visit to Laredo was a sad one. My father had been suffering from prostate cancer for a few years and was now in the last stages of his illness.

Finding A House In Austin. In Austin, we shopped around for a house. Finding a house close to Pauline's relatives was essential for the support she and the three children (Joe, Jerry, and Linda) were going to need during the time I was gone and perhaps -- if I did not come back. Back in 1966, Austin was a small city of perhaps 200,000 people, and we soon found a nice house – in what was then the outskirts of the city in an area known as South Congress or South Congress (SOCO) for those inclined to call it that. It is a nice two-story four-bedroom house. Buying this house was the best investment we ever made. We paid about $37,500, have lived in it off/on, and rented it off and on. We paid off the mortgage on the house years ago and I recently sold it. The house multiplied in value. If we can paraphrase the Malthusian Theory, while the supply of housing in Austin has, throughout the years, significantly decreased in relation to the need, Austin's population has multiplied astronomically as it became the "Live Music Capital of the World." On the negative side, as property values have increased, the City of Austin has had fun increasing our Property Taxes.

Death of My Father. After settling my family in the newly purchased home, I was ready to go to Vietnam. Two days before I was to leave, I got a call from my cousin (Joe Jacobs.), who lives in Laredo. He told me that my father was gravely ill and was not expected to last more than one week. He urged me not to leave the country.

I immediately called the USAID Executive Officer in Washington, explained the situation, and was given a two-week assignment in Washington. Two days after my arrival in Washington, I got the expected call informing me that my father had passed away.

I returned to Austin and went to Laredo. My mother and brother were grieving. With my father's small life insurance and my help, I bought four cemetery plots for my father, mother, and brother and made the funeral arrangements. Saying goodbye to such a good, honest, and hard-working, man was extremely sad. There were many people who attended both the funeral home and the burial. My father was born on June 22, 1892. He died on July 9, 1966. He was 74 years old at the time he passed away. I will always remember him with immense pride and know him as a great man.

PART C. BRIEF HISTORY OF VIETNAM

Once again, a great number of books have been written on the history of Vietnam. This section will only show the highlights of Vietnam's long history:

- Just before the Christian era, in 221 BC, the Kingdom of au Lac was founded near the Red River.
- This kingdom was conquered by the Chin Dynasty who sent a Chinese Emissary to rule it.
- After the death of the Chin Emperor, the local Chinese Emissary created his own kingdom and ruled Nam Viet (South Vietnam) for a time.
- The Chinese tried to impose their rules, their Confucian philosophy, and their customs to integrate Vietnam into the Han Empire.
- The Chinese ruled Vietnam for 1,000 years. Over the years, a series of revolts took place. It was during the Ly dynasty when the Chinese gave up their conquering efforts in Vietnam.
- Afterward, the Vietnamese were invaded by the Mongol Dynasty; Vietnam defeated the Mongols and expanded its territory.
- France came into the picture. Vietnam and its neighboring territory became known as Indochina.

- During World War II, the Japanese claimed Vietnam as a territory. When the Japanese surrendered in 1945, Hanoi was established as the capital of Vietnam.
- After World War II, the French refused to grant the Vietnamese their independence. Negotiations between France and the Vietminh failed. Vietnam was divided along the 35th parallel into a North and a South Vietnam. The Vietminh under Ho Chi Minh controlled the North, the French the south. The first Indo-Chinese War broke out in 1946. The conflict lasted for approximately 8 years.
- In 1953 -1954, the Vietminh gave the French its greatest defeat at the "fortified last stand" base of Diem-Bien-Phou.
- The War between France and Vietminh ended. A compromise was reached dividing Vietnam at the 17th parallel into North and South Vietnam.
- While the Vietminh formed their part of the country as a communist nation, South Vietnam went through a series of government coups and take-overs.
- With a desire to establish a democratic system, the Kennedy Administration began supporting the staunch anti-communist government presided by Ngo Din Diem.
- Diem refused to hold free elections, opposed domestic opposition, favored Catholics, and began to alienate the civilian population seriously. As a result, Diem was overthrown in 1963 and killed during a coup.
- To prevent the collapse of the Saigon regime, Lyndon Johnson, the U.S. President, in 1965, approved the commitment of U.S. troops to the defense of South Vietnam. He also began an extensive bombing of the North in an operation known as Rolling Thunder. Major increases in troops and financial and economic assistance followed. USAID became a major player in providing economic support for Vietnam.
- Although the U.S. military effort disrupted significant advances by the North Vietnamese, the Viet-Cong planned an exceptional attack

throughout the country during the season of Tet -- known as the Tet Offensive. The Tet Offensive began on January 31, 1968. Being there myself, I remember the havoc that the attack created for the then South Vietnamese regime of President Nguyen Van Thieu.

- After the war began, the U.S. population began to turn against the war, and there were huge demonstrations against the war. Despite the protests, President Richard Nixon continued to support a failing effort. The turning point of the war came in February 1975. In that month, the North Vietnamese made a major military offensive. The U.S. was forced to leave the country, and South Vietnam ceased to exist. Hanoi became the capital of the re-unified Vietnam, and Saigon (was renamed Ho Chi Minh City but I will, in this book call it Saigon).

The country is now known as the Socialist Republic of Vietnam, and the U.S. and Vietnam established diplomatic relations.

Part D. My Arrival In South Vietnam

My trip to South Vietnam was long. We stopped in Hawaii, Korea, Hong Kong, and the Philippines, and we finally got to the airport at the Tan Son Nhut Air Base in South Vietnam on July 22, 1966. By then, I was a bundle of nerves, not knowing what to expect in that country.

I knew someone from USAID would be there to receive me but did not know who. As is usual at airports in foreign countries, numerous people congregate; they push, shove, and yell to attract the attention of the incoming passengers. The reception area, in this case, was no exception. It was full of boisterous people, milling, yelling, and carrying on loud conversations. As I came down the ramp, I saw a massive amount of humanity. In the very back of the crowd was a man jumping up and down, up, and down, up, and down. I thought that was funny. As I passed through the crowd, that man in the back yelled at me – with a clear Spanish accent – "Are you José Peña?"

After I had said "yes" and he had told me his name was Carlos, I tried to say a few words in Spanish. With an urgent sense of appeal, he told me "Please speak to me in English because I am trying to perfect my English...."

This is how I was first introduced to Carlos Rau Cabrera., and this is how a lifelong friendship with a great person began.

- Ever since that July 1966 day, I have considered Carlos as my brother and his wife Carmencita as my sister. Both Carlos and Carmencita were born in Puerto Rico. Carlos was an excellent professional, extremely analytical, extrovert, jovial, friendly, and highly charismatic. People instantly liked him. Sad to say, Carlos died recently. His family consists of 7 children, some of whom border on geniuses. One (Raul) is a Doctor in Chemistry. Another (Gina) speaks four or five languages, is in the U.S. Foreign Service, has two children, and, after a tour in Iraq, is now posted in Kenya. Goldie is extremely tall, handsome, personable, gregarious, funny, and charismatic. Tessie and her family live in Puerto Rico. Tessie, Edna, Carlos Julio, Christie, and remaining many grandchildren are equally bright and extroverts.

Yes, my good friends Carlos and Carmencita go back 55 years. Anyway, Carlos gave me a quick briefing on the situation in Vietnam, the office, and took me to a one-bedroom apartment that I would share with a person of Chinese descent. The apartment was small. It had a living area, kitchen, and one bedroom, which fit only two single beds. For a person who had lived in houses with my family, the arrangement was very awkward.

Change of Apartments. From that day on, Carlos and I seemed inseparable. He lived with John Ky, who was also of Chinese descent. Since we were getting along together well, I arranged with John Ky. So, he could go (and went) to live with my roommate, and I went to live with Carlos. Once again, it was a small apartment – a living area, kitchen, and one bedroom with two small beds.

Living In Separate Apartments. Later, Carlos and I moved to separate single apartments in a building that was in downtown Saigon. Since all occupants of the building were U.S. Government employees (U.S. Embassy, USAID, CIA.), a squad of Vietnamese soldiers guarded the building. They sat in front of our building, behind a high pile of sandbags, and each had a machine gun, grenades, and other types of rifles and ammunition.

Thus, the only thing that changed in our arrangement was that each of us had a USAID- furnished single apartment – a living area, kitchen, and a nice sized bedroom with a "plush" full bed. Since the apartments were in the same location – Carlos on the second floor and me on the third -- we continued to share in all arrangements – a motorcycle that I bought, the maid (Cse), and the food. Eventually, the office gave me a 1946 Jeep which the U.S. Army had declared surplus; Carlos and I shared it. I eventually sold the motorcycle to another USAID colleague.

PART E. LIFE IN VIETNAM

Most of my tour in Vietnam was very tolerable, and I could even describe it as very nice. Saigon (now Ho Chi Minh City) was then a bustling metropolis. The Vietnamese are very industrious and bright people. Because of the way they eat and exercise, people tend to be slim, and their oriental features are extremely pretty. Back then, we would see the people – mostly on bicycles, scooters, and motorcycles – riding in many directions. Traffic was always heavy.

The women and girls have beautiful faces, lovely figures, and with their flowing "Au Dais" (Vietnamese dress) have a very sexy look. The Au Dai is a very sexy combination of silk pants, a flowing top, and a very pronounced "VPL" (Visible Panty Line). I enjoyed and missed those sights very much. Since the country was at war and the needs of the Vietnamese families were restricted, there tended to be a great deal of liaisons and inter-relationships between Americans and the local girls in different forms – boy/girlfriend, friends with two-way benefits, living arrangements, and there was also open prostitution.

In any event, the usual sounds of a bustling metropolis were always present. In addition, all of us could hear – and feel -- the U.S. jets fly by and feel the thuds, thunder, and the rumble of the earth as the bombs hit the ground in the outlying jungle near Saigon. We got an excellent maid. Her name was Cse. She cooked for us almost every day. On weekends, Carlos, friends, and I would buy some nice steaks and have a barbeque on the roof of the apartment building as well as a few beers. With time, we almost became immune to the trembling and shaking of the earth caused by the U.S. bombing right outside Saigon. We alternated where we would eat. Sometimes we would eat at the apartment, sometimes we would eat on the roof, and sometimes we would eat in the excellent Vietnamese restaurants that existed nearby. We liked going to a restaurant that specialized in spicy crabs. At that time, Carlos was not used to eating hot and spicy food; whenever he would eat hot, spicy food, he would make funny noises and say, "HAAAA! Ola Cheetah, this is too spicy and hot…." Of course, because I had lived on the border with Mexico and was used to eating hot, spicy food, I especially loved this restaurant. Years later, after we had left Vietnam, our roles became reversed: He was the one that ate very hot peppers like the "Habaneros," an especially nasty pepper, and I was the one making funny noises and saying, "ola Cheetah, these are hot…". Those were good times. Even now, I can still taste those hot, spicy, and tasty crabs.

As mentioned earlier, Cse was an excellent maid/cook. Cse spoke little English. Nevertheless, we would give her money; she would buy the food in the local market and cook – and every day was a different feast. One dish that we liked resembled "chicken-a-la-king." Cse would prepare it with crab meat rather than chicken. She would cook the crab meat in a distinct way and place it on top of toast. Wow! What a treat!

While Cse worked for us, one of her children had a strange accident or illness and lost one of his eyes. Carlos and I financed his medical costs, which involved the implant of an artificial eye. Cse was eternally grateful.

We bought beer, sodas, and other items and did a lot of our shopping in the PX at the Tan Son Knut Air Base. We seldom drank the local "Bam-i-Bam (33)" beer of Vietnam because it gave terrible hangovers.

We frequently went to downtown Saigon (now called Ho Chi Minh City) but had to be extremely careful when we went. Several USAID people – and some of our friends – were shot in downtown Saigon by motorcycle-riding Viet Cong. There were also a few times when the Vietcong would go to restaurants, eat, place, and leave timed bombs and kill a great many people – Vietnamese and foreigners alike. I remember three events where Carlos and I felt were in danger:

- The first occurred while we were driving in the jeep towards the PX in Chalon, which is part of Saigon. While driving in the jeep, we made a mistake and took the wrong road. We wound up getting lost among a series of Vietnamese villages. The scenery was just fantastic – the people with their straw hats toiling in the rice paddies close to their bungalows. However, we were so completely lost that we were going around and around the same places. That was the only time I saw Carlos get angry with me: "Ola Cheetah, we are lost; why don't you watch where you are driving…." We finally asked some farmers for direction in our very limited Vietnamese and pointing: "Saigon?" "Chalon?" "Saigon?" We eventually got back safe and sound.

- A second time occurred when we were eating in a Saigon restaurant. Three young men, dressed in South Vietnamese Army uniforms, with guns, and a briefcase, came into the restaurant. Without asking, they sat down with us at our table. Being in the middle of our meal, we looked at each other and just froze. They ordered beers, and food, and chatted with us in Vietnamese (which we did not understand but interacted with signs and smiles). Nervous, Carlos and I conversed in Spanish and jabbered, in our limited Vietnamese, with the three "invitees." We figured they were Viet Cong, and we were in danger. Carlos said in Spanish: "Ola Cheetah if they get up to leave, we run for our lives…" We invited them to more beers. Calmly, we ate our meal and paid everyone's bill. As we were getting ready to leave, we bought them an extra beer and left. In the end, it cost us 3 unplanned meals and 9 beers. But the cost was worth it. To this day, we still think that the 3 were Viet Cong and that we could have been seriously hurt or killed.

- The third time I felt extreme danger was very near the Tet Offensive. I will discuss this event in detail at a later point.

Part F. Description Of Some Office Staff Members

Because of the war, the amount of economic assistance that the U.S. provided to South Vietnam was enormous, both from the standpoint of the type of assistance provided and the level of the manpower devoted to administering and monitoring it. All USAID offices in the country were "humongous." The Office of Controller – which was known as the Office of

The Assistant Director for Financial Management and was headed by David C. -- and the Audit Office were no exceptions. We had a huge staff in the Accounting Branch, the Budgeting Branch, and the Audit Branch.

I was part of the audit office. Because of its size, the audit office was headed by the Chief of the Audit Branch (Frank K). Under him was the Deputy Chief of Audit Branch (Robert H.). The Audit Branch was divided into sections that corresponded to the many components of USAID's assistance programs in Vietnam, such as the Commodity Import Program; (CIP), the contracting branch; the agriculture; education, etc.). . We also had representatives in "Regional Posts" in different geographic areas of Vietnam – like Da Nang, Kon Tum, Pelkie, Naha Trang, Ben Tre, and others.

Because so much assistance was being provided through the Commodity Import Program and the P.L. 480 programs, I was assigned as Assistant Section Chief to Section B (headed by Robert G.) -- 1 of 3 commodity import programs sections. We might have had about 15 to 20 people assigned to our section alone – some of whom were assigned to the regional offices outside Saigon.

You name a type of personality, level of intelligence, education, and/or attitude – and our office had it. Here is a description of some that come to my mind.

- Frank K, the Branch Chief, was a USAID old-timer. Normally based in AID/Washington, he had come to Peru one time to do a "mission-wide review," so I knew him well. He was a loner and had never married. He was a real good technician but not the best administrator. His way of directing the office was to try to micro-manage all reviews.
- In his early 50's, Robert H was new to USAID. When his marriage had ended, he had joined USAID and was immediately assigned to Vietnam. A gentle person, he was a good administrator, handled the office administrative aspects, and tried to learn the intricacies and programs that USAID had in Vietnam. In Vietnam, he met an American woman and eventually married her.

- Robert G., my Section Chief, had been with USAID for some time. He was knowledgeable, jovial, and easy to get along with. He and I shared the same office, and I acted as Section Chief when he was not there.

- Eugene T. had a strong personality but was an excellent person. He was new to USAID. He had undergone a messy divorce. He had a daughter in the U.S. In Vietnam, he found a beautiful Vietnamese girlfriend, whose name was Thu Lan, whom he later married. During the Tet Offensive, Gene and Thu Lan fed me because I was close to being transferred to Colombia and did not have much food. We became good friends. Gene retired from USAID and died about 6 years ago. Even at this writing, Thu Lan and I continue to be good friends.

- Bill S. knew a great deal about investing; he invested a great deal of money in IBM. He had a strong personality and sometimes could be difficult to work with. He married Mimi, a Vietnamese woman. Bill worked under me when I was the Deputy Regional Inspector General for Latin America. He died a few years ago. Mimi S. is still a good friend of mine.

- John KY, mentioned earlier, was probably a very wealthy person. He was funny in a few ways. For instance, when Carlos and I asked him if he would trade apartments with me, he readily said "yes." He then went on to prepare a detailed list of all the food that he and Carlos had bought. He divided bean by bean into packets and told Carlos: "You owe me so much…." John KY would commute from his apartment and be exactly on time at the office. He would then get his sweater from the left lower drawer of his desk, put it on, be at his desk all day long (he never traveled outside Saigon), and leave exactly on time. He never got a Vietnamese girlfriend or took chances by going downtown. One time, I asked him why he did not enjoy life a little more. He then proceeded to give me a lecture on his philosophy of life. He; said: "You know, the earth is round and always rotates in the same manner; the sun always rises in the East and settles in the West; there is a summer and there is a winter; and life follows an identical manner you are born, live your life, and you die…." That is the reason why I am the way I am. A few years later, I met John KY in Bangladesh. He had married an American lady. He invited me for dinner a couple of times. I found that he had changed a lot.

- One person -- I will call Guy One -- was in Vietnam for about six to eight months. Guy One was a handsome person. He was brand new to USAID and was assigned as our representative in an outlying USAID post near the border with Thailand border where the Viet Cong were very active. His duties were to stay in that post; do assign field visits in his region; come to Saigon every 15 days to tender his time and cost sheets; brief us on his observations; and return to his assigned post. He seemed most convincing for a few months. However, one day, Frank K., the Branch Chief, got a call from the Director of the Regional Office. The Regional Director seemed upset that our Audit Office had not sent a representative to that region. When Frank K called us (Robert and I) in and asked what was going on, we were very confused. After talking with the Regional Director once again, Frank K. requested the Special Investigations Group to check the alleged absence. **Surprise! Surprise**! The investigative team found that Guy One had come into Vietnam, gone to the regional post for one or two weeks, and then established the following pattern: (a) He would come to Saigon, (b) tender his time and cost sheets, (c) give us a cursory briefing, (d) buy a round trip to Bangkok (Thailand), (e) stay in a nice hotel, (f) have girlfriend galore, live a good life, (g) stay out of danger, (h) return to Saigon every 15 days, (i) tender his fictitious time sheet, (j) return to Thailand, and (k) start the cycle all over again. (Note: In Vietnam, we were paid our salaries, plus 25% danger pay, plus a daily per-diem if assigned outside Saigon). So, Guy One was collecting a huge amount of money. He was collecting not just his salary and the 25 % danger pay differential; he was also collecting the additional per-diem for staff assigned to locations outside Saigon, plus the cost of the air fare for traveling to and from Saigon (as miscellaneous costs). He lived a nice life in Thailand, had girlfriends galore, and stayed out of danger. Neat employment assignment, huh! Because *the Agency did not want to pursue a costly legal process of prosecution, the guy's employment was immediately terminated, and he was quietly flown back to the U.S.*

As I said before, there are just too many people and too many interesting stories – like Domenic N., Frank D., Richard B., Carl K, and others -- that I could talk about of people I met in Vietnam. But the above will give a general feel for the different personalities that I remember.

Let me now turn to the Vietnamese in our section. Most were top-notch. In my mind, I still see their faces but do not remember their names.

Of all the secretaries and assistants in the office, I remember my Vietnamese secretary with great fondness. Van Nguyen was her name. Invariably, Van always wore different Au dais. She was beautiful, sweet, and top-notch. She always did her best at everything she did. I sincerely hope that she, her mom, sister, rest of the family left Vietnam and are safely living in the U.S.

I also remember Mr. Huong. Mr. Huong must have been in his mid-40 – but looked older. He usually accompanied me on my trips whenever I went to the outlying areas of Saigon or the boondocks. During these trips, we discussed differences in our cultures and philosophies of life:

- One time, we visited a little village and saw a tomb that may have been between 500 to 1,000 years old. I gave Mr. Huong the camera, and he took my picture in front of the tomb. Once this was done, I told him to pose for me, and I would take his picture. Taking his time to respond, he looked at me very strangely and, in a very deliberate and measured manner, said: "I cannot pose in front of this tomb; this person is not my relative or my ancestor." He added, "When you and I visit my ancestral village, I will pose in front of my ancestors. They span thousands of years…." With those words, he was emphasizing the love, respect, and reverence that the Vietnamese – and Asians – have for their dead relatives and ancestors. These are feelings and traditions which we, as Americans, do not usually demonstrate.
- Another time, Mr. Huong and I were discussing religion, marriages, and relationships. Mr. Huong, a Buddhist, or Muslim had 4 wives. He defended the arrangement by telling me: "You know, Mr. Peña, you Americans can only marry onc time; yet you go behind your sacred vows and get several girlfriends. Over time, your wife and girlfriends fight and make your life miserable whereas, here in Vietnam, we can

marry as many as 4 wives; each wife knows each other; they all live in one house; they share in home duties; they have their nights assigned for sex; and they don't make our lives miserable. I tell you, Mr. Peña, for a man, life is much better in Vietnam…." I certainly could not quarrel with such logic.

Pauline's Illness. I had been in Vietnam for about six months when I got an emergency call that Pauline, my wife, had been hospitalized with a kidney infection. I used one of my emergency leaves, known as "visitation benefits," to return to the U.S. Visitation benefits were earned by those of us that were married and did not have our families at post (none of us did). Anyway, I got home to see that Pauline had surgery and had an almost full recovery. At the end of two weeks, I was on my way back to Vietnam.[53] Pauline died on July 14, 2019, of several complications. We all love her dearly and miss her terribly.

PART G. TECHNICAL SIDE OF WORK IN VIETNAM

Work in the Office. Because of its fast cycle time and quick economic impact, the Government of Vietnam (GVN) were extensively importing goods furnished through the CIP Program. Some of the items being imported and financed through the CIP were: tin plates, petroleum products, non-metallic minerals such as cement with clinker, and others, ampule tubing, metallic minerals, printing presses.[54] Oh, yes! How can I forget one of the highest costs: demurrage? I will explain this later in this chapter.

As soon as I settled in the CIP Section B, I was asked to review the work and draft reports covering 3 contract reviews. The draft reports needed a great deal of work. I was able to finalize two reports. The fieldwork for the third review

---

[53] Also, during the time I was in Vietnam, on August 1, 1966, some nut, named Charles Whitman, a former marine and student at the University of Texas at Austin climbed the university tower, and started shooting at innocent people. He, killed 14 innocent people and wounded many others. The incident worried me a great deal because my family was living in Austin.

[54] Clinker, which consists of .pieces of rock that are mixed with cement mix to make the cement stronger... Tinplate, which is used for, among other things, roofing and other uses, consists of steel that coated with a thin layer of tin, hence its name.

was very poorly done, and I returned it to the person who had done the work; he was most upset but re-did the work. As a result, we were finally able to issue the three reports.

From then on, I was busy supervising, doing, participating, writing, editing, and consulting with auditors or audit teams. Here are just a few examples of reviews that the office did during my time in Vietnam:

A Standard Program. Although the CIP normally has a uniform cycle and distinct pattern, the audit staff had not developed a uniform basic methodology for conducting individual audits. Each auditor developed a distinct program or method for conducting an audit, worked independently, and checked items in a haphazard manner. When commodities were being sent beyond the boundaries of Saigon -- where there was danger -- auditors often did not do any end-use checks to determine that the goods were being used for their intended purpose." As a result, we could never be sure if the items ordered had been received in the country and were being used at the destination as intended.

I was asked to write – and wrote – a basic uniform audit program that everyone in our section would follow. The end-use checks (for cement, iron bars,.) continued to be sporadic and limited because exposing our staff to the dangers of the war was out of the question. The supervisors agreed that we would only do detailed end-checks in areas that were close-by Saigon or the Regional Office areas.

Procedures of USAID and the Bank of Vietnam (Audit Report (A/R) 67-55). I did a survey of procedures used by the USAID Commercial Import Division and the Bank of Vietnam to import goods through the CIP. The review showed that (a) $5.1 million could be "de-obligated" and used for other purposes; (b) records of USAID and GVN needed to be reconciled; (c) the GVN needed to file prescribed reports with USAID in a timely manner, and (d) items that had been transferred from USAID/Cambodia -- and no longer needed there -- needed to be accounted for and sold.

Survey of Regional Offices (A/R 67-73). Since Vietnam was divided into several regions covering Vietnam's many provinces, we made a survey of region 3 to study the procedures used in all phases of commodity importations, such as: (a) controls over the use of commodities, (b) inventory,

(c) record keeping, (d) warehousing, (e) transportation to the final destination and (f) final end-use. We found several problem areas.

Demurrage Costs. Because of the size of the USAID assistance program to Vietnam, and the competing requirements of the U.S. military, ship after ship would come into the port area of Saigon and remain unloaded for extended periods of time. Ships are supposed to be unloaded within a specified period; any additional time needed to unload can result in additional costs during what is known as – *the "Demurrage Period."* The party that charters the shipment typically incurs the Demurrage and must pay for it. Because the U.S. military had priority in unloading all arriving shipments, USAID was the one that was charged with most of the Demurrage Costs. As one can just imagine, there were ships galore in the port of Saigon, and USAID was incurring exorbitant amounts of demurrage costs.

Finding a solution to this huge problem was an urgent matter because the costs were now very substantial. All of us were encouraged to submit ideas about how to resolve this problem. Although I submitted three ideas, they proved impractical to implement. Without success, teams and committees were assigned the task of finding a resolution.

- In comes a person that I will call Guy Two. Guy Two – a person in his late forty's, handsome, very intelligent, and with business and shipping experience -- arrived in Vietnam. He was assigned to/or took upon himself the task of finding a solution to our o Demurrage Cost problem. After a month, Guy Two told me (and Bob G.) that he wanted to talk to Frank K. I asked him what it was all about. In a very authoritative manner, Guy Two said that he had found a solution to the Demurrage Cost problem. He told me that his plan was Top Secret and that he would only discuss it with Frank K. Thus, Frank K and Guy Two met. After the meeting was over, Frank K called Bob G and me, showed us the plan, and, chuckling, asked us for our thoughts.
- We looked at it and just shook our heads. The plan was all laid out incredibly detailed and contained some pencil drawings. It called for the construction of a gigantic crane. As the ships came into the port of Saigon, they would immediately go for unloading. The huge crane would lift the entire ship out of the water, turn it upside down, shake it,

dump the shipments on the port, return the ship to its rightful position, send the empty ship on its way back, and begin the cycle all over. All the dumped shipments would then be separated and hauled in trucks and tractors. Pretty wild, huh!

Due to the dangers of Vietnam, Guy Two seemed to have cracked in the short time that he had been in Vietnam. He was flown back to a U.S. hospital, and his employment ended afterward. I don't think we ever found an easy solution to the Demurrage Cost Problem. If this type of cost has continued at the present time, I would suggest that USAID conduct special study involving the military and shipping companies to find a more equitable solution.

Trailer Homes (A/R 68-13). With the tremendous influx of USAID economic assistance and the proportionate increase in technicians coming into the country, there was a shortage of housing facilities in Saigon as well as in the different regions of the country. After France ordered all NATO forces out of the country, in mid-1967, the U.S. military in France declared 345 house trailers as "Excess Property." Since we could use the trailers in Vietnam, USAID accepted the Excess Property and arranged – through Procurement Actions -- to import all 345 of the trailers.

The importation of the trailers turned out to be a nightmare -- full of pilferages, complicated problems, and unplanned costs. Here were some of the problems:

a) When USAID inspected the 345 in France, they were being occupied by the U.S. military and therefore were in an almost perfect state.

b) The 345 trailers were to be subsequently transported, by rail and/or trucks, via Frankfurt, Germany, to the port of Antwerp, Belgium, for shipment to Vietnam.

c) By the time the trailers arrived in Frankfurt, almost all had been stripped. They did not have refrigerators, toilets, beds, sinks, floors, windows.).

d) Of the 345 trailers shipped, forty-five were deemed to be a total loss in Europe. Some were cannibalized, and the remainder were scrapped.

e) The first shipment of 106 house trailers arrived in Vietnam. Once again, they were vandalized. Their windows had been broken, and the insides were once again stripped.

f) Of the 106 trailers that had arrived, 25 remained on the ship and were sent to one of the regions. Another 10 were placed on barges waiting to be unloaded.

g) The 10 house trailers that were placed on barges were lost for a few days. They were later found near a village about 3 miles down the Saigon River. You guessed it: The door locks had been broken, and the insides had been completely ransacked.

In sum, USAID wound up expending over $1.3 million in shipping and refurbishing costs. There had been pilferages in all phases of the shipments. Forty-five house trailers were declared a total loss in Germany. Many others arrived in Vietnam pilferage, extensively damaged, and damaged beyond repair. The furniture in the 10 house trailers in the barges probably wound up in homes or tunnels of the Viet Cong.

Petroleum Products (A/R 67-39). The GVN had imported $47.5 million in petroleum products under the CIP. The petroleum products had been licensed to three oil companies: Shell, ESSO (now known as EXXON), and Caltex. We found that USAID had no policy for claiming transportation losses. For sure, there were a number of losses; however, we found that not surprising, the companies were not filing any loss claims against their own companies. The companies might have filed the losses against their own insurances; however, because these were private losses, our audit did not cover this phase of losses.

Cement and Clinker (A/R 67-72). The GVN was importing about $40.5 million in non-metallic minerals and products. The type of commodities imported included (a) Cement ($29.4 million), (b) Clinker ($2.3 million), and (c) other non-metallic products ($8.8 million). [55] We found a number of

---

[55] (Note: Per the internet, here is a definition of **Cement clinker. Clinker is a bonding agent used together with cement. It is a solid material produced in the manufacture of Portland cement as an intermediary product. Clinker occurs as lumps or nodules, usually 3 millimeters to 25 millimeters in diameter. It is produced by sintering limestone and alumina silicate materials such as clay during the cement kiln stage. It is used as a bonding element.**)

problems. For example, we found that cement importers were claiming very high losses because their records were defective and inaccurate. One importer alone claimed to have lost 34,180 bags of cement. Thus, "…there was no assurance that importers were not understating receipts of cement and disposing of concealed receipts of cement through black market channels…."

Tinplate Importations (A/R 67-68). The GVN had imported about $3.5 million of tinplate, which was to be used in roofing construction and building partitions and walls, as well as for the manufacturing of toys, cans, and containers. We found a few problems. One was especially troubling because a number of importers were not listing the end-buyers; thus, the final use of those products could never be verified.

Printing Presses (A/R 67-69). The GVN had imported about $2.1 million in printing presses and related equipment and parts; these had been licensed to 5 importers. We found no problems with this program: The items had come in and were being used by the five importers.

I could provide more examples. However, the above gives a feel for the type of complications that can be found in a country at war.

PART H. TRANSFER OF CARLOS

A Personnel Officer Comes To Vietnam. A team from the USAID Personnel Office came to Vietnam to do some sort of study. Among the team was a good friend of mine. Her name was Barbara illiams. (and her team) met with Carlos and me. The team questioned the wisdom of assigning people like Carlos and me -- who were fluent in Spanish – to a country where our language skills could not be maximized. Barbara asked us if we wanted to get a transfer back to Latin America. We readily said yes. The personnel team left.

About a month went by, and Frank K called both Carlos and me into his office. He was upset. We soon found out why. He had received a formal communication known as a "cable" advising him that USAID was transferring Carlos to the Dominican Republic and me to Colombia.

Frank K was really upset. In a paranoiac manner, he repeatedly questioned the "strange coincidence" of both transfers. We kept defending the agency's logic of re-assigning us to countries where – with our Spanish capabilities – we could do the best.

Angrily, Frank K. finally told us. "I am only going to transfer one of you…the other one will stay here, which of you wants to let the other one transfer…." Since my family was safe in the U.S. and Carlos' family was in the Philippines, and he and his wife were beginning to have problems, I agreed to remain in Vietnam.

On the day that Carlos was to leave, ten of us gave him a big party. We were all drunk. We took Carlos to the airport and "poured" him into the plane….and he was gone. For me, it was a sad parting.

PART I. THE TET OFFENSIVE

My Transfer to Colombia Remained Pending. USAID's personnel office never withdrew my transfer from Vietnam to Colombia; they just delayed it for about six months. So, between the time Carlos left and my own transfer (maybe 6 months), I worked on different CIP reviews and finalized different reports. I kept Cse as my maid and cook. I would frequently have my many friends come over and visit. One of my friends was Guadalupe (Lupe) Rocha. Like me, Lupe was born in Laredo, a few houses from my own, so he was a longtime friend. At the time, Lupe was in the Air Force and based at Ton San Nhut Air Base. He liked to visit me, eat my food, drink my beer, and chat. I liked Lupe very much. He retired from the Air Force, and I heard he had passed on a few years ago.

Viet Cong Were Quietly Planning Before Tet Offensive. Just before the 1968 Tet Offensive, the situation in Vietnam had been very quiet for at least 3 or 4 months. The Viet Cong did not seem to be making any sizeable incursions or attacks anywhere in the country. Their lack of attacks or incursions seemed extremely odd. Thus, inside the country, we got mixed information on the progress of the war.

- On the one hand, the armed forces radio announcer, in Vietnam, would give very optimistic statements on the progress of the war; according to our military, the Viet Cong was experiencing extremely high casualties and losing the war. This seemed to account for the "lull" in the war.

- On the other hand, news coming from informational sources in the U.S. gave a different picture. This source said that the U.S. casualties were high and rising; Muhammad Ali (the heavyweight boxer and champion of the world) did not support the war and had refused to be inducted into the U.S. Army. According to this information, demonstrations against the war were mounting; and there were rumors that Robert McNamara was on the way out (he quit February 29, 1968).

In any event, the U.S. bombing campaign known as Operation Rolling Thunder continued, and the Viet Cong remained very silent.

Because of my pending transfer in February 1968, I was deliberately running low on food. I did have plenty of beer and sodas.

Shaking The Hands of Viet Cong. Around January 25, 1968, I was doing a review to determine why there was such a heavy importation and loss of cement and iron under the CIP, especially in certain villages. I checked with the U.S. Embassy's Security Office to see if I could go to 3 to 5 villages about 10 to 15 miles outside Saigon to do the "end-use check." These villages seemed to be getting a great deal of cement. The Security Office gave me the go-ahead and the necessary documents.

Mr. Huong, a driver from the Embassy's motor pool, and I – all unarmed -- drove towards the five villages. Although the unpaved road was dusty and rough, the scenery was just beautiful. The industrious Vietnamese, in their usual dress and bamboo hat, were busy planting their rice paddies. Our first village was about 5 miles from Saigon. Its location was about 1/2 mile off the main road. We found that it had received some but not all the shipments of cement. The Village Elder showed their cement storage area, which consisted of two bamboo shacks, the sides of which were covered with plastic to protect them against the rain.

We then proceeded to the next village. Once again, the village was located about one-half mile off the main road. The jungle covering felt eerie. It was an exceedingly small village. The Village Elder met us in the center of the village. Since there were no chairs, our meeting took place standing up. We began talking to the village elder; he seemed quite nervous that we were asking questions about the cement. He said that the shipments were getting there but that the warehouse was about 3 or 4 kilometers into the jungle. Since the story sounded fishy, I continued -- in a very nice and friendly manner -- to ask questions, and Mr. Huong continued to translate.

Suddenly, three young Vietnamese men came out of nowhere and squatted behind us. I said to myself: "Oh wow, what is this?" While one side of my brain kept asking questions of the Elder, my other side was ticking off the odd and troubling aspects that I had seen of the three men.

- For example, all were young (no more than 25). They seemed well-built and very sharp; were clean-shaven; wore clean clothes; certainly, they had not been working in the rice paddies. In addition, all walked (or maybe "marched" is a better term) one by one, as if observing spaces and a sense of order; were not the submissive types normally seen in farmers; and were circling us and their squatting seemed very ominous.

The back of my hair began to rise. Just a minute later, three more young men came into the picture, and once again, they squatted behind us. Once again, I noted the same thing of the group – age, sharp, shaven, clean, and orderly walk. One of the squatters asked a few questions of the Elder; the Elder answered. The tone of the Elder changed, and he became quite authoritative. Mr. Huong's body language told me he was nervous.

The back of my hair continued to rise. Now incredibly nervous, Mr. Huong began giving me desperate hints that we should leave. Then another group of three men came, and we were now surrounded.

By then, the back of my hair was really standing up. I knew we had to leave fast. Full of false smiles, I told Mr. Huong to thank the Elder and the others for their full cooperation, that the Elder had answered all the questions in a satisfactory manner, and that I appreciated his help. I saw the driver get into the Jeep and start it. I then shook the Elder's hand and the hands of most of the surrounding Vietnamese men – and we RUSHED from the area. So, we skipped the three other villages.

Pale with fear, Mr. Huong and the driver told me that those men were Viet Cong and we had been in real danger. When we got back to Saigon that afternoon, I gave a briefing to our office and to the security office. They asked a few questions. They thanked me, and that was the last I heard about my encounter with the nine young people.

As we were to find out on January 31, 1968, the Viet Cong had been quiet for a few months. In effect, they had been very actively planning the 1968 surprise Tet Offensive. During this "quiet time," they had been gradually amassing soldiers, arms, ammunition, and equipment around key cities. I believe that this is the reason why we -- Mr. Huong, the driver, and me -- were not captured or killed in that village. The Viet Cong did not want to tip their plans.

The Tet celebrations, in honor of the Vietnamese New Year, are great affairs. There are fireworks, dancing, firecrackers galore. So, it was not surprising to me that the celebrations would start on the night before Tet, which that year was to occur on January 31. With Gene and Thu Lan, I had a few beers and went to sleep somewhat early.

Firecrackers began to pop all around. They were loud and close to us. Then, the rattling of what seemed like machine guns sounded. Some things seemed to be hitting our building. I finally went to sleep.

Since it was a holiday and, I did not have much food, I got up in the morning, got dressed, got into the 1946 jeep, backed up from the garage, and drove maybe half a block towards a U.S- operated cafeteria. I got stopped by a U.S. military policeman who asked me: "Where do you think you are going?" Annoyed that he, a soldier, was questioning a civilian like me, my response was curt and snotty: "If you don't mind, I am on my way to eat breakfast." He said, "Don't you know that Saigon is under attack by the Viet Cong? There is shooting and killings all over! Please return to your apartment and stay there." That was my introduction to the "Tet Offensive."

You have never seen a person so thankful. I drove as fast as I could, back to the apartment. I went to the many apartments occupied by USAID and other U.S. staff and warned all the occupants. By then, we could hear the different explosions and shootings that were taking place.

As mentioned earlier, we had a squad of Vietnamese soldiers who guarded our building. They were behind sandbags and had machine guns. They were there all the time. Nevertheless, that afternoon, some U.S. military people came over to the apartment building to give us a few old rifles. They also organized us so that each of us – supported by a Vietnamese soldier -- would stand guard duty near the entrance of the building for four hours at a time. At the end of the four hours, we would be relieved by another civilian.

My tour of guard duty came around 7 or 8 PM. Per instructions, the entire building was dark. The shooting rampage on the outside continued. We placed a sofa in front of the front door. The young Vietnamese soldier, with his pistol, lay down on the sofa. Since I did not know if I could trust him, I sat with my rifle on a comfortable chair in front of him. He seemed to have gone to sleep – and I kept watching him (and the damned door). He shifted positions – and I watched him. He seemed to snore – and I watched him. He yawned and stretched – and I kept watching every move (and the damn door).

Suddenly, there was an explosion like a grenade, and the Vietnamese guards behind the sandbags began firing the machine gun. In turn, a few shots hit the building and seemed to have hit the front door. The Vietnamese soldier who had been lying on the couch jumped up and took off into the darker areas of the building. So, there I was all alone to defend that damn front door. I got behind a cement pillar, took the safety pin off the rifle, and pointed it at the front door. I made up my mind that anyone that tried to come in was going to get shot.

The shooting on the outside continued for a short while, and then it subsided. At around 11 or 12 PM, it was my time to be relieved as the front-door guard. As I arrived at my apartment, the shooting started up again, and I got away from the window, went to the kitchen (the safest place in the apartment), sat on the floor, and drank a couple of beers.

During the entire offensive, Gene and Thu Lan fed me – and I am grateful for what they did. During the day and sometimes at night, we would go to the roof of the apartment and see the aircraft bombing targets close by, as well as the tracer bullets. We also saw some dead bodies close to our building.

After several days, we finally got the all-clear sign. Once the situation in Saigon had been stabilized, Cse, Van, and others came to see if we were all right. They asked when they could go back to work. I visited the Air Base at Tan Son Nhut to check on my friend Lupe. He was alright. He told me that a few U.S. airmen had been killed. I also went around and took some pictures.

A few weeks later, Vice President Hubert Humphrey arrived in the country, and he and General William Westmoreland gave us a nice talk.[56] Here are some pictures:

The first picture shows the bombing and fire that took place near the apartment. The second picture shows a destroyed car near the U.S. Embassy.

The third picture shows the way a building, like the one we lived in, were left after the Tet Offensive. The fourth picture shows Vice President Hubert Humphrey, General Westmoreland, U.S. Ambassador to South Vietnam Ellsworth Bunker, and other high officials giving us a pep talk after the Tet Offensive.

PART J. CONCLUDING REMARKS

I left Vietnam in February 1968, grateful for the experience, happy to be alive and well, sad to leave both my American and Vietnamese friends. I also left looking forward to picking up my family in Austin and to serving some nice few tours in a "peaceful" country like Colombia.

---

[56] At the time, General Westmoreland was the commander of U.S. forces in South Vietnam.

As I said before, from the standpoint of a Foreign Service Career and my own personal point-of-view, my assignment to Vietnam was very decent, and I could say nice. I learned about Vietnamese history, and culture, made many nice American and Vietnamese friends, ate good food, and saw parts of a beautiful country. On the other hand, having to be away from my family was very difficult. This later contributed to long-lasting marital problems.

From a professional (technical) point of view, Vietnam was probably not the most satisfying assignment of my career for several reasons. First: the U.S. was in a losing, unpopular, protracted guerilla war, which limited free travel throughout the country. Second, I did not know Vietnamese well, and my language limitations prevented me from freely communicating for professional purposes and from making friends with the Vietnamese. Third, communications with people and other officials were most difficult because of the danger, size, and a few places throughout the country where U.S. officials were posted. Fourth, my assignment to only one section – the CIP -- limited my exposure and understanding of the USAID assistance program to a very narrow segment of the assistance program. Finally, my assignment to conduct audits of just the CIP prevented me from making possible contributions and affecting broader policy issues.

CHAPTER EIGHT
IN COLOMBIA, CHIEF RESIDENT AUDITOR, EXCELLENT STAFF, EXCEPTIONAL AUDITS, AND ROUGH TRANSITION TO NEWLY CREATED OFFICE OF THE AUDITOR GENERAL

PART A. INTRODUCTORY COMMENTS

Introduction. This Chapter is divided into seventeen (17) Parts:

- Part A Introductory Remarks.
- Part B Home Leave.
- Part C. Brief History of Colombia.
- Part D. Life in Bogota and Colombia.
- Part E. Family Returns to the United States.
- Part F. Personnel in Office of USAID Controller.
- Part G. Our Audit Staff Under USAID Controller.
- Part H. Some of the Audits Done in Colombia.
- Part I. Review of the University of Nebraska project.
- Part J. Two-Step Loans. [57]
- Part K. The Private Investment Fund (PIF).
- Part L. The Cali Sewerage Program.
- Part M. Excess Property Programs.[58]
- Part N. Conduct of Reviews.

---

[57] Information obtained from an Audit Report (No. 1-514-71-96) I did in March 15, 1971 entitled "Eleven Two-Step Loans of Colombia," P.2 and Exhibit A.
[58] A.R. 69-09, Review of Excess Property Awarded by USAID to Colombia.

- Part O. The Report Clearance Process.
- Part P. Creation of Office of Auditor General.
- Part Q. Concluding Remarks.

PART B. HOME LEAVE

From Saigon, I proceeded directly to Austin, Texas. A short period of home leave followed. During this time, I got reacquainted with my three children, Joe, Jerry, and Linda. They were just beautiful, and their love for me was most evident. Somehow, I did note some "territorial" rough spots between Pauline and me. During my stay in Austin, I also visited my mother and brother in Laredo. Although I had noted the rough spots with my wife, we proceeded to put some furniture in storage; pack up, buy a new 1968 Chevrolet Impala, and headed for Bogota, Colombia. By then, it was evident that the nearly two-year separation from Pauline and my family had some undesirable effects on our family life. We were met at the El Dorado Airport outside Bogota and taken to our temporary quarters. Let me first give a brief history of Colombia.

PART C. BRIEF HISTORY OF COLOMBIA

The country was settled nearly 10,000 years before Christ (BC). At that time, groups of hunters, and their respective cultures, called the "Tairona's," lived and traded along what is called the "Tequendama." Another group, called the "Muisca," lived and traded along the Magdalena River Valley. Even by then, both groups had a highly organized political structure since they were ruled by an organization in the form of a pyramid called the "Casciaro," with a "Cacique" or chief at the top. Because the history of Colombia is too extensive and complex to try to summarize in this book, I am just including a brief timeline of its history as well as a brief description of important events. I urge interested readers to read the extensive material about Colombia's history on the Internet. Here is an abbreviated historical timeline:

Timeline of Colombian History[60]

Period	From	To
Pre-Colombian Period		1499
Spanish Colonization	1499	1550
New Kingdom of Granada	1550	1717
Viceroyalty of New Granada	1717	1813
United Provinces of New Granada	1810	1816
Gran Colombia	1816	1831
Republic of New Granada	1831	1858
Granada Confederation	1858	1863
United States of Colombia	1863	1886
Republic of Colombia	1886	Present

There have been many important events in the history of Colombia, like the following: (a) the thousand-day war which took place between 1899 to 1902; (b) Panama, which had been part of Colombia, separated from it in 1903; (c) Colombia and Peru which had a war that lasted from 1932 to 1933; (d) Colombia helped the allies during the World War of 1939 to 1945; (e) there was a great deal of violence in Colombia during the period of 1948 to 1958; and, (f) a rebellious group, known as the National Front, challenged the legitimacy of the elected government during the period 1958 to 1968. Back in 1968, Bogota and the rest of the Colombian country were still developing; this is to say that it was not yet modernized, and it lacked many commodities. Nevertheless, our arrival in Bogota took place during a reasonably peaceful time in the country. This gave us a chance to see some of the country. Once we left Colombia in 1972, the country took a turn for the worse; over the past

50 years, Colombia has waged an internecine war against a movement, variously called: The Revolutionary Armed Forces of Colombia—People's Army (Spanish: "EP," for "Ejército del Pueblo" or "People's Army." It also became involved in drugs, kidnapping, and human trafficking. In other words, Colombia was not the best country to visit at that time.

PART D. LIFE IN BOGOTA AND COLOMBIA

In any event, since Colombia was peaceful at the time, we enjoyed the assignment. Our base and the home city were Bogota. Here is its description.

The City of Bogota. Even then, Bogota was a beautiful city. It sat at the base of a 10,000-foot-tall mountain known as Montserrat and was divided into north and south Bogota. The Southside contains the colonial part of Bogota. It was not the best part to live in. The northern part of Bogota is the most modern, and it is where we eventually located our permanent house. At the time, the U.S. embassy was in the southern part of Bogota.

Temporary Quarters. As stated earlier, after arriving in Bogota, we were taken to our temporary quarters. It was a huge apartment in the center of the city, with all the trimmings. That first night, the children were somewhat insecure, and the five of us crowded into one bed. We stayed in that apartment for close to two months until we finally found a house in the northern part of the city. And, just by coincidence, our house was located close to some friends (Manuel and Isabel, Judy, and Paul)) whom we had met in Ecuador. It made our lives extremely comfortable, and we had many parties from then on.

Birth of My Youngest Daughter. Soon after our arrival in Colombia, we were happily surprised to find out that Pauline was pregnant. Melissa Gisela Pena was born on October 26, 1968. She has grown to be a beautiful person – she has not married up to now and is extremely religious.

PART E. FAMILY RETURNS TO THE UNITED STATES

Family Remained in Colombia A Short Time and Returned to the U.S. As mentioned before, the two-year separation during the time I was in Vietnam caused serious marital problems between Pauline and me. After finding a permanent housing arrangement and after Melissa was born, Pauline and my children remained in Colombia for close to two years. During this time, we would often take road trips to several nearby locations such as Melgar, Girardot, Rio Hondo, and other parts.

- We liked going on weekend trips to Melgar and Girardot because both were relatively close by and were located at a lower altitude than that Bogota. They were, therefore, far warmer. At Melgar, we would go to a restaurant near the river where they made a delicious soup known as "Caldo de Bagre" (Catfish Soup). On one such trip -- while Pauline decided to stay home to take care of Melissa-- I took Joe, Jerry, and Linda to Girardot by myself. The road was a little rough – zigzagging, precipices, and tight turns all the way. Things went well going down. The kids and I ate some of the soup, and things were just fine. But on the return trip, one of the kids (most likely Linda) became nauseous and began vomiting. Pandemonium broke out; the other two got sick too and started blaming each other and fighting with each other. Boy, I was happy to get home.
- We liked to take day trips to the Catedral de Sal (Salt Cathedral) located outside of Bogota. At the time, you could drive your car into the Cathedral, park, and go into the church on foot. Since then, they closed that Cathedral due to its having become unstable and dangerous. The Colombians have opened another, much larger Salt Cathedral. While the new Cathedral is beautiful, you can no longer drive your car into that cathedral.
- In addition, we liked to take day trips to some falls known as the Tequendama Falls outside of Bogota. At the time, the falls were big and beautiful; the cascade of water was something to see. Now, the falls have dried up because of overdevelopment. Near the falls, we would visit a lake that contains the remains of a little village composed of whitewashed buildings that was inundated as a result of the development of a nearby dam. The old village, which could still be seen underwater in 1968, was known as "Guatavita la Vieja." (Old Guatavita). The village's inhabitants had been moved to a new town, known as "Guatavita la Nueva" (New Guatavita). Guatavita la Nueva

was beautiful, but it was still sad to see the remains of Old Guatavita underwater.

- Melissa was baptized by our good friends – Manuel (Manolo) and Isabel. Manolo had been born in Spain and Isabel in Peru. They were beautiful people. We often had parties at their house. Both were exceptional cooks. Manolo would always cook "Gambas al Ajillo (Shrimp in Garlic Sauce). " He would cook the Shrimp in a ½ cup of Olive Oil, put garlic, salt, black pepper, and small amounts of green (hot) chiles. He would let the combination simmer and then put the huge shrimp. Fantastic! Afterward, he would place a steak for each one on the grill and ask everyone: "Como quieres tu bissteak? (How do you like your steak?) We would tell him "Medium rare, rare, well done, etc." Then, he would turn to me and say: "Estos cabrones se comen como salgan los Steaks…." (These dummies will eat the steaks anyway I cook them). Manolo was a funny person. He worked for an oil company, got "dengue fever" while in the field, which affected his liver and other systems. He died of complications from the fever many years ago. We also lost track of Isabel and the family. They were exceptional friends, and I miss them.

By August 1970, my marital problems continued, and things deteriorated in Colombia. Therefore, Pauline decided to return to the U.S. with the four children. They moved back into our house in Austin, Texas, for the remainder of my tour in Colombia. I was left by myself in Colombia for the remaining 2 years. I moved from the north side house to a very nice three-bedroom apartment downtown. Although I acquired good friends and continued to have nice parties, I cannot say it was a real happy time for me.

- In fact, there were a few months when I was somewhat depressed. This time was when Linda, my daughter, got very sick with Rheumatic Fever and was in the hospital for one month. By then, I had become Chief Auditor and had teams in Cali and Medellin. My workload was so heavy that although I frequently called Pauline, I was not able to go to Austin to see my little girl. That month was one of the lowest times in my life. Linda grew up to be a beautiful red head, smart, independent, and close to me. She married the love of her life (Kendall), had a beautiful daughter (Lauren), and then divorced. Linda died in 2003, and Kendall also died 4 years later. Lauren lived with me for eight to ten years and married her High School sweetheart (Andrew De Laney). I miss Linda greatly, and Lauren and I continue to love each other very much.

PART F. PERSONNEL IN OFFICE OF USAID CONTROLLER

At the time I arrived, "Missions" to Colombia were a large. Although I was never told why the many organizations were so large, I believe that the way the Guerilla "Che" Guevara was killed on October 9, 1967, in Bolivia, influenced the growth of Missions in South America; perhaps the U.S. wanted to prevent an influx of guerilla type of operations throughout the continent. In any event, there was a large staff from the Embassy (State Department), U.S. Information Agency, military attaches, USAID, and other staff. I spent most of my work in USAID, and my association with other U.S. Organizations was very limited; this is to say that the remaining parts of this chapter are about my work in USAID.

Anyway, USAID was headed by a director and had many different offices – agriculture, health, education, engineering etc. There was also an Office of the Controller, headed by Albert K. a Deputy Controller (Pat P.), and the Office of Audit, which was then under the Controller and was headed by Dudley St. I was assigned as the Deputy Chief Auditor. Both Albert and Dudley and their wives were just great people, and we all worked well together. Later, while I was still there, Albert was transferred and replaced by Rob B. (as Controller) and Bill M (as a Deputy Controller). Bill, a single person, and I became good friends.

PART G. OUR AUDIT STAFF UNDER USAID CONTROLLER

Description of Audit Staff. When I was originally named to transfer from Vietnam to Colombia, I had been proposed for the Chief Auditor's position. However, since my transfer was delayed for six months, a new Chief Auditor

(Dudley St.) was named. When Dudley left, somewhere in 1970, I became the Chief Auditor. In 1972, I was promoted to an FS 1 level.

The Office of Audit was composed of Dudley, and about 8 local auditors and one U.S. citizen (Marc B) were recruited as local auditors. Once we began to issue reports and Washington realized how sophisticated the Colombian programs 5 other U.S. personnel joined us. This is to say, and the office was an exceptionally large one. Most of the Colombian staff were young, nice looking, and very sharp.

When I got to Colombia, all the staff had been working on a very large project related to a review of The U.S. University of Nebraska. But it seemed like they could not finish the job. Here is a very brief description of a few of our people.

- Marc B. was a U.S. citizen and had a very unusual history. He was not originally a professional auditor. He had been a boxer, a wrestler, a painter (had exceptional art pieces of his own), a sculptor, and a translator. A highly temperamental person, he was married to a Colombian lady, and they had two extremely intelligent daughters. He lived in Bogota and had been recruited there as a local auditor. Eventually, Marc became an FSO himself and was later assigned to Panama and Washington D.C. I would see him again in Washington D.C. (Note: It was during a future assignment to Panama that Marc, in one of his temperamental moments, is said to have picked up a desk and flipped it to a supervisor.)
- Antonio Del C. was a real bright Colombian auditor. He had graduated with a master's degree, was a quick learner, and had a strong personality. He spoke his piece whenever he thought things were not right. He was new to USAID and eventually quit the organization. He became a CEO of a Certified Public Accounting Office and a trash collection agency – and, with the growth of the Colombian population--is now probably a multi- millionaire.
- Alfonso C. and his wife, Crystal, were my good friends. Back in 1968, he had recently joined USAID, was bright as they come, a fast learner, and a hard worker. After the Office of Audit became part of the USAID Auditor General, Alfonso went to the U.S. and began working for the Organization of American States (OAS). When I retired from

USAID and became the Chief of Party of a Guatemalan Health Project, Alfonso had become "Acting Inspector General of OAS." After I left that position, he asked me to come and work for him – and I did. Isn't it ironic? During my time in USAID/Colombia, Alfonso worked for me. I worked for him under contract for nearly four years. This just shows how the world is so small, and "What goes around, comes around…." When Alfonso retired, he was replaced by Guillermo B – who also served as the OAS Acting Inspector General for a period. As I will later discuss, I worked for Guillermo as well. The three of us continue to be good friends -- and to stay in touch.

- Marcus C. was a U. S. Auditor and a most unusual personality. Born into a Filipino family, Marcus had had two heart surgeries, was married to a real fine person, and had two children. Marcus lived burning "…his candles at both ends…" I sponsored him when he first arrived in Bogota. When he arrived -- at "…let's say 11:00 AM… on a certain day…" – he arrived by himself. His family came later. I took him to the temporary apartment and then to the office. I introduced him all around. At 4:00 PM that same day, I invited him to have dinner with me. His response: "Sorry, Joe, I can't have dinner with you…I already have a date with a girl who was introduced to me, by phone, by a friend…." Marcus was a funny guy but a good worker. He did all kinds of crazy things and eventually died of a heart attack.
- William M. was another U.S. auditor. He and I had met each other in Vietnam. He found a house on the north side of the city. The water reservoir on top of his house was round. So, he painted it black with the white number "8" just like on a billiard ball. Anyone that wanted directions would say: "You turn left or right from the house that has the "black 8 ball." William M. did not like to work too hard. He eventually quit USAID, and I really suffered trying to write an "Employee Evaluation Report" that talked about his good qualities. The last time I heard from him, he was studying at a university to become the administrator of a hospital.
- Rafael Z. was another U.S. auditor. He was married to a fine lady (Ligia) from El Salvador. Rafael was a real good asset to our office because he was fluent in both Spanish and English, which was not true for most of the U.S. direct hires. He had been born in El Salvador but

was a U.S. citizen. He was young and needed some training. Ligia and Rafael had two sons. Eventually, they divorced. I recently heard that Rafael had passed on. I sometimes still communicate with Ligia by e-mail.

- Having been a Colonel in the Colombian Army, one of the other local auditors (HP) was a good professional. However, he tended to invite us, during "cultural Fridays," to secret houses of ill repute. The only time I went, my wife was still in Colombia, so mine was a very benign short visit; that is to say, I had one drink and rushed home. Houses of Ill repute are not part of my style. I did learn, however, that after one or two drinks, the retired Colonel tended to invite all the people – including the "Ladies of the Night" -- to drink "champagne." That short visit cost me over $100. So, I shied away from future invitations.
- As mentioned earlier, Bill M, the Deputy Controller, and I became good friends and frequently drove my car to different places. Bill liked to drink and had a drinking problem. One time, when we went to Villa de Leyva, he asked if he could drive. Villa de Leyva is a colonial town about two and half hours by road from Bogota that features the largest entirely cobbled square in Latin America. He drove for a while, but I became frightened because he wanted to "play chicken" with people driving in the opposite direction. Nevertheless, Bill M was a nice person. During one of my parties at the apartment, I introduced him to several women friends who lived in the same apartment complex. One of them was Marina, a lovely brunette with a beautiful personality. They seemed to get along fine. As I will explain in a later chapter, after leaving Colombia, I was transferred from Panama and then – through a gross misjudgment of the then Inspector General – to Miami and on to Washington D.C. During my tour of duty in Washington D. C., Bill showed up in my office and said: "Joe, come with me, two people want to see you." When we got to the motel, there was Marina and their baby. Marina and Bill had gotten married. Later, they divorced. After their divorce, he was assigned to South Africa, where he was killed in a motorcycle accident. (Incidentally, Rob B, the Controller in USAID Colombia, was also killed in another motorcycle accident in South Africa.)

The remaining people on the staff were great – young, smart, fast learners, good analytically, and hard-working. The Controller's Staff and many other friends were mostly composed of pretty people: Carmencita (our secretary), Mari Carmen (accountant), Estela (accountant), Esther, Marina, Luz, Virginia, Yvonne, and several others whose names I cannot recall.

PART H. SOME OF THE AUDITS DONE IN COLOMBIA

Introductory Remarks. My assignment in Colombia lasted 3 ½ years. As I will discuss further later, I quickly found that the USAID and the GOC had been implementing some highly sophisticated programs. As such, reviewing such programs took a long time.

During my tour in Colombia, I supervised and participated in numerous types of reviews, special studies, editing, writing, supervising, etc. I will not discuss all the work that I did there; time, space, and the limited nature of my book would not permit this. For this reason, I will only include five examples:

a) Our review of the University of Nebraska.
b) A review of "two-step" loans made by USAID to the GOC.
c) A review of the Private Investment Fund – a very sophisticated and complex financial arrangements.
d) A review of the Cali Sewerage Project -- where we found a project that seemed to have been afflicted by "Murphy's Law," i.e., everything seemed to be going wrong.
e) A review of the "Excess Property" donated to Colombia.

PART I. OUR REVIEW OF THE UNIVERSITY OF NEBRASKA PROJECT

Background Information. As previously noted, when I arrived in Colombia, almost the entire USAID audit staff was involved in a large and somewhat complicated review of an agricultural project being implemented by the

University of Nebraska. [59] Both the Controller and the Chief Auditor were worried about the time spent on it and the lack of tangible results. So, I was assigned to take over the study and complete it. After talking with each of the participants, I quickly found out why the study was taking so long. Without an experienced person at the helm, the staff seemed to be going in circles. To provide the needed direction, I met with each of my staff, asked questions, provided positive encouragement of the person's work, and gave the necessary instructions based on my understanding of what the official's scope of work entailed. We concluded the review within two months and came up with a very informative report.

Here is a summary of what we found:

- On the positive side, Nebraska was providing good training to the host government. Moreover, Nebraska, and the Government of Colombia (GOC) were working closely as a team. In terms of achievements, Nebraska had or was providing twenty-two full-time U.S. agricultural professionals, 17 short-term technicians, and 207 man-months of technical assistance in support of the project. It had also identified and sent 16 people to train in the United States. In short, the project was in the process of achieving most of its objectives.
- On the negative side, Nebraska was not going to provide enough training. The contract called for Nebraska to provide 641 man-months of technical assistance; however, our calculations showed there would be a significant shortfall of 180.7 man-months by the end of the contract. Furthermore, while the value of the contract was about $2.0 million, our projections showed that about $80,000 might need to be de-obligated. A major problem that adversely affected our work was that the original accounts and records were in the U.S. Since these records were not available in Colombia – and a coordinated audit approach had not yet been devised – there would be limitations to our study. i.e., we could not make a certification that all U.S. Financial data was accurate.

---

[59] A.R. No. 68-08, dated June 28, 1968, Review of the University of Nebraska

In the report, we made 8 recommendations. After completing this study, the Chief Auditor, the Controller, and the staff were all highly motivated and eager to undertake more complicated evaluations.

PART J. TWO-STEP LOANS [60]

Introduction: As explained in an earlier part of this book, many of the loans made by USAID were two-step types of financing mechanisms. Colombia was a good example. For example, under a two-step loan arrangement, the Government of Colombia (GOC) borrowed $55 million to achieve nine different projects through local organizations. Here is a partial list: (a) the Private Investment Fund ($10.0 in millions and objectives are later explained); (b), the Cali Sewerage ($3.7); (c) the Rural Electric Cooperatives ($1.3); (d) Medellin Sewerage ($.2); (e) Bogota Sewerage ($.4); and (f) livestock bank ($6.1).

Since the projects were to be achieved by semi-private organizations, the USAID signed the Loans through the Government of Colombia (GOC). In turn, the GOC signed individual sub-loans, contracts, or agreements with the nine organizations.

Repayments between the two levels of participants had different arrangements as to (a) Interest rates, (b) grace periods, and (c) repayment terms. In effect:

- The GOC was to repay USAID in U.S. Dollars. The rate of interest ranged between .75 to 2.0%. The bilateral loan had a 10-year grace period. The Government was to repay the complete loan over a period of 30-40 Years.
- The Semi-Autonomous Organizations were to repay the GOC in Local Currency. Their rate of interest was between 2.0 to 9.5%. They had a grace period of 5 to 10 years. And they were to repay the loan between 10 to 20 Years. The Local Currency repayments were deposited in certain Special Accounts.

---

[60] Information obtained from an Audit Report (No. 1-514-71-96) I did in March 15, 1971 entitled "Eleven Two-Step Loans of Colombia," P.2 and Exhibit A.

In sum, the beauty of the Two-Step Loans was/is the financial benefits accruing to the Colombian Government through the differences between rates of interest, grace periods, and repayment terms. These were referred to as (a) Interest Differentials, (b) Grace Differentials, and (c) Principal Repayment Differentials. The accrued amounts of the Special Accounts could then be either reused for other programs, re-loaned to other entities, and/or sometimes used to subsidize the Government's budget. **Because of the five-country benefit (itemized later in this book), the two-step approach is an excellent assistance approach. However, some fine-tuning may be needed in several areas.**

PART K. THE PRIVATE INVESTMENT FUND (PIF)

Introduction: Created on February 28, 1963, PIF was administered by the Bank of the Republic of Colombia (BORC). [61] Our review of PIF showed the degree of sophistication that we encountered in some of our reviews during my assignment in Colombia. Although PIF was administered by the BOR, it was receiving funds (converted in Millions of U.S. Dollars) from (a) three USAID Loans -- some of the funding was through the "two-step" loan mentioned previously – ($11.6 million); (b) a number of local currency generated programs (like P.L. 480 and counterpart funds -- $60.); (c) Interest differential (.5); (d) the Government of the Netherlands ($1.4); (e) the Inter-American Development Bank ($3.0); (f) The Government of West Germany ($5.0); (g) the World Bank ($37.5), (h) the Colombian Social Security Ministry ($4.8), and (g) others.

In other words, the total amount of the different contributions was about $123 million. Of this amount, about $86 million had been released to PIF. Although our reviews were supposed to be limited to USAID loans and their generations to local currency, we had to examine parts of the other contributors – primarily because the Bank of Republic did not keep its accounting records separately for each contributor.

---

[61] A.R. 69-08, Results of Examination of the Private Investment Fund of the Bank of the Republic, Project 514-56-920-115.

The result of the examination was exceptional. Most of the funds were converted to local currency and used to make sub-loans towards achieving different objectives: (a) diversification and export promotion; (b) elimination of shortages in the production of goods; and (c) Import substitution.

Here are the positive achievements. Briefly, our 70-plus pages of the report showed the many statistical profiles of the numerous sub-loans. Sub-loans were having a positive impact on almost every department (U.S. equivalent to States) of Colombia (Antioquia, Boyacá, Bolivar, Mata, Valle, etc.). Almost all segments of the Colombian economy were being affected, i.e., sub-loans were being made for: (a) agriculture (banana, sugar, cacao, etc.); (b) manufacturing and processing (textiles, clothing, etc.); (c) industrial groups (metal, machinery, electrical, etc.). Our sample included 70 sub-loans; these borrowers had increased exports, during a four-year period, from $4.0 to $20.0 million.

These are the major negative observations noted in our report:

- Neither the GOC nor the Bank of the Republic (BOR) was maintaining separate accounting books or records to correlate sub-loans with the funding contributors. The root problem was that the USAID lending documents did not specify who was to do this type of accounting. Finer tuning to the "two-step" loans, in this aspect, was needed.

- Due to the size, complexity, purpose, and different financial obligations of sub-loans being made by the PIF, the BOR needed to establish PIF as a separate department and empower it to fulfill its contractual responsibilities for the various phases of the programs.

- Although the BOR had committed about Peso 128.9 (about the U.S. $12.8) for several sub-loans, the GOC had not transferred these funds to the bank. This delinquency was 3 years old. For this reason, the BOR could not implement the sub-loans. The solution was for the GOC to urgently transfer this amount (Peso 128.9 million) to the BOR.

- Although the USAID loans specified that the BOR could retain 2% as administrative costs, the BOR substituted a different formula. However, the BOR formula was the most favorable to the sub-borrowers. Therefore, the USAID loans needed to be changed.

- Although USAID Loans required the sub-loans to display the AID Emblem, the BOR failed to include such a clause, and sub-borrowers were not complying with this requirement. (These were common findings. We usually found these types of observations in most of our reviews).

There were other types of findings. However, the main purpose of including the above is to show how sophisticated and complicated the reviews were.

PART L. THE CALI SEWERAGE PROGRAM

Introduction: Our review of the Cali Sewerage Program showed a project that seemed to have been afflicted by "Murphy's Law," i.e., whatever could go wrong, went....

The project had its beginning back to 1956 when a U.S. Consulting Firm made a study and determined that the Municipality of Cali needed the sewerage. The Corporacion Autonoma Regional del Cauca (CVC) updated this study. Although the updated version was not the final program design, the study was used to justify the USAID Loan. Based on this preliminary design, the Cali Sewerage was to cost the equivalent of $5.5 million and be financed by (a) a $3.7 million loan from USAID and (b) $1.8 million from EMCALI. CVC estimated that the project could be completed in 20 months. Estimates proved wrong.

Using the "Two-Step Loan" procedures, USAID granted the loan on September 16, 1963. As of October 31, 1969 (6 years later), the agreement had been amended once and 11 Letters of Implementation had been issued.

Our Audit Findings: To make my story short, we found problems in just about every phase of this project, and it seemed like the program was affected by a multitude of factors. Brief descriptions of some of the problems follow.

- When the 1956 engineering study was made, the U.S. Consulting Study recommended "...a sewerage system that would consist of a separate sanitary sewerage system and a separate storm drain system...However, the Municipality of Cali did not comply with the recommendations. Between 1954 and 1961, Cali began to install a combined sewerage and storm drain system in certain parts of the city...."[62] Of course, this created a more costly program.

- Also, between 1954 and our cut-off, the geographical population of Cali shifted, and changes to the program were needed.
- The original project ceiling ($5.5 million) had been based on the Prevailing Rate of Exchange of Peso 10 to the U.S. $1.00. After the loan was approved, the GOC devalued its currency, and the Rate of Exchange gradually went from Pesos 10 to Peso 17.71 to the U.S. $1.00. The devaluation of the currency created a few problems: (a) there were less U.S. Dollars program requirements in some areas and more in others, i.e., depending on whether the U.S. Dollars were converted to Peso or the other way around; (b) Local Currency program costs increased, and (c) there was a radical increase in the Counterpart Funds generated and project requirements.
- The services of a Local Engineering Consulting Firm were contracted to finalize the program plans and design. One problem with this contract was that this firm was contracted one year retroactively to the signing of the loan. For some reason, EMCALI kept extending the contract for this firm – even when USAID requested that the Contractor be dismissed.
- This Consulting Firm was to produce the final design within 10 months from the beginning of the contract. However, for unknown reasons, it took this firm a total of 30 months to produce a final design of the Cali Sewerage at the cost of over U.S. $611,000.
- In the Loan Agreement, the Cali Sewerage was described as consisting of 8 different sections: (a) construction of the final 1.7 kilometers of the Eastern Interceptor; (b) construction of a second 4.14 kilometer Eastern Interceptor; (c) construction of 7.8-kilometer Cañaveralejo Collector; (d) construction of the Cañaveralejo Pumping Station; (e) reshaping the concrete lining of 9.9-kilometer of existing canals; (f) construction of 14.1 kilometers of new concrete-lined canals; (g) construction of 20 separation structures; and, (h) the procurement of

[62] A.R. 70-08-C A Review of the Cali Sewerage Program, Page 10

equipment and services. However, sometime after the USAID Loan was approved, it was found that CVC had merely "projected" the original study. Thus, the implementation plans had to be radically changed to accommodate population growth, geographical migrations, currency devaluation, cost estimates, time estimates, and other assumptions.

The following table shows how the Cali Sewerage was being constructed at the time of our study. The table combines the different program sections with expected and actual Percentage of Completion:

Section	Brief Construction Description	Completion Percent Expected	Actual
A	Sewerage Pipe Construction	100%	100%
B	Collectors, canals in North of South expressway	95	38.3
C-1	Collectors, canals, structures on west of the South expressway	90	66.0
C-2	Collectors, canals, structures, North of the South expressway and West of the Simon Bolivar Expressway	100	75.6
D	Collectors, canals, structures, South of the South Expressway	80	53

E	The Pumping Station		
F	Excavation of Stabilizing Pond	30	24.5

Sections B, C-1, C-2, and D consisted of 10 sub-sections each. The subsections were for sewers, manholes, special structures, canals, bridges, sheeting places, excavations, and others. Each subsection had different Percentages of Completion (from 0 to 100%). To simplify my analysis, the above table shows the composite Percentage of Completion for the individual sub-sections.

Section E consisted of 8 separate sub-sections: mechanical trash racks (E-1); sewage pumps (E-2); crane and accessories (E-3); silt basin equipment (E-4); pipe and fitting (E-5); miscellaneous equipment (E-6); electrical equipment (E-7); and construction of the pumping station (E-8). This section was just beginning at the time of our review.

Here is our overall conclusion on the Cali Sewerage. In sum, at our review cut-off, only one section (A) had been completed. The above table shows that even after 6 years, the program was significantly behind the planned construction schedule because of the number of above-mentioned problems.

Our final conclusions were that the program plans did not seem to have followed the best "Critical Path" in the construction of this sewerage; in fact, the planned components seemed to be constructed in a haphazard manner. In our opinion, this program would, most likely, not be completed by the Terminal Date for Request for Disbursement (July 31, 1970). Moreover, the cost would probably exceed the new program estimate of $7.7 million. I sincerely hope that this project was eventually completed. However, we were not able to follow this project, after the issuance of our report, due to our heavy audit workload.

PART M. EXCESS PROPERTY PROGRAMS.[63]

As explained in an earlier part of the book, whenever the U.S. Government has the property that it no longer needs, the USAID is authorized by Sections 607 and 608 of the Foreign Assistance Act of 1961, as amended, to donate such "Excess Property" to Host Governments to help out in certain weak areas.

During my work with USAID, I saw a great many such types of donations. Here is one example. USAID donated Excess Property, amounting to $23 million, to Colombia; this Excess Property included (a) three APD vessels to furnish auxiliary water and electrical power to two cities; (b) four harbor tugs to improve the capacity of several Colombian ports; (c) two revolving cranes to expedite unloading of ships; (d) eight aircraft to fly cargo and personnel to and from remote areas; (e) two locomotives and a crane to help complete a dike in Boca de Ceniza; (f) and others.[64]

While the staff was doing the Cali Sewerage and other reviews, I (and a Colombian Assistant) combined my supervisory trips and visited the audit teams and the Excess Property. My trip took me from Bogota to Cali, to Medellin, to Cartagena, to Barranquilla, to Santa Marta, and back to Bogota. Part of the trip was flown in a small version of the Fokker 50 plane. The passengers sat below the wings, propellers, and tires. Back in the 1970s, the planes did not have a GPS, and the pilots and passengers flew by "the seat of our pants" – in a narrow flight corridor, and we saw the mountains near each of the wings (pretty darn scary).

- A funny incident also took place during my arrival in Santa Marta. When I got to the Port City and checked in the "best hotel in the city," the other auditor and I went to the beach, and we, each, ate a Red Snapper cooked in the local format – it was the best fish I have ever eaten. Anyway, the hotel did not have air conditioning. So, I got a room on the third floor. That night, I slept with the window open. It was in the middle of the night when I began hearing a strange "tap and scratch" type of noise. I got up and walked to the open window. As I

---

[63] A.R. 69-09, Review of Excess Property Awarded by USAID to Colombia.
[64] Ibid

got near the window, a hook and a rope came flying in. This time, the hook held. I looked out of the window and saw one guy standing on the ledge of the second floor. It was a thief trying to get into my room. I got the hook and threw it out to him. Then, I asked him what he was doing. He said: "Yo siempre duermo aqui en el balcon del Segundo piso.." (I always sleep here on the ledge of the second floor…). So, I then told him to go sleep with his mother. He meekly began to go down; I shut the window and went down and told the hotel manager. Although they could not believe it, they called the police. But, alas, the thief was gone.

During this trip, we saw tugboats, cranes, train locomotives, cargo vessels, and several other things. We took a great many pictures of the donated property and presented them in our final report. The donated property was providing water and electricity as planned. However, the ships had been ransacked (perhaps by the Military) of most of the electronic equipment and gears. Also, the ship in Santa Marta was listed, and it was in danger of sinking.

PART N. CONDUCT OF REVIEWS

Introduction: I could have included many other reports that I did during my stays in Colombia – such as our reviews of Colombia's Rural Electric Program; the National Agricultural Planning Program; the Industrial and Export Development Program, and the Supervised Agricultural Credit Program, my main reason for selecting the projects that I write about and not the other ones was to show the following:

a) Exceptional Colombian Auditors primarily conducted the reviews. Once the other U.S. Audit Staff began to arrive, they were paired with this fine Colombian staff.
b) Most of the auditors had been schooled in the traditional "financial reviews," but with my tutoring," they quickly shifted to "evaluative reviews."
c) **Since each review might cover a range of disciplines, the audit staff and I developed and observed an established protocol.** We would inform the program or project director that we were beginning a

review of the project or program. After that, the reviews were comprehensive and evaluative in nature. The review would include all phases (managerial, program design, implementation, internal controls, financial, usage, etc.) of the specific development activity. After analyzing legal documents and background material and obtaining a working background, we got a background briefing from the project manager. We then would develop an audit program. Once developed, the intensive program assessment based on the audit program would begin. As part of our review, we would determine whether: (a) the development activity (program, project, function, etc.) was achieving its desired objectives; (b) management was using resources in an effective manner; (c) the project was being implemented in an efficient and economical manner; (d) there was any evidence of misuse, waste, mismanagement, or fraud; (e) procedures and internal controls were adequate; (f) the organization was in compliance with laws and regulations; and (g) any aspect of the development activity, procedures, or functions were in need of improvement or change. I was briefed on the progress of the reviews every other day. As needed, I helped the staff analyze, interpret, and use such documents as loans, grants, project agreements, contracts, project design papers, implementation letters, handbooks, evaluation reports, host country budgets, decrees, laws, procedures, etc. We sampled components of the program, i.e., we visited sub-borrowers, the construction parts, etc.

d) Since we held regular (normally every two weeks) meetings, there was always normal feedback on ideas and the status of the audit jobs.

e) Whenever we developed a "negative finding," we vetted, verified and/or coordinated the finding with the project manager to determine the validity of the finding and the reasons for it. In later years, this practice became the basis for a formal procedure called the "Report of Audit Finding (RAF), that was developed under the auspices of the Inspector General.

Once the review was completed, the team and I prepared a working "Draft Audit Report," which we submitted to the Controller and the Deputy

Controller of the mission. They would comment on the report, and we would make any needed modifications. We then prepared the draft of what we considered our "final draft."

PART O. THE REPORT CLEARANCE PROCESS

Once the draft report was in the report clearance stage, we would meet with the program or project manager to get their feedback and comments. We would then discuss the report with the Mission committee that reviewed each audit report. Normally presided by the USAID Mission Director or his deputy, the committee was typically composed of 8 to 12 agency officials. The questions they would ask about the report could be extremely incisive. So, until I got used to this in-depth questioning, this phase could be extremely intimidating.

If anyone presented persuasive evidence that our facts were faulty, we could amend the draft report, but in each case, we were careful about presenting the facts correctly, and our recommendations were always appropriate and implementable. We were often congratulated on "a work well done."

Hurrah! The final Audit Report was published, issued, and distributed. The above-described procedures are important to remember because of the changes that came about. In effect -- with the creation of a newly established "Office of The Auditor General's Office" and separation from the Office of Controller – the clearances of reports became very complicated, and the issues merited deep discussion and resolutions.

PART P. CREATION OF THE OFFICE OF THE AUDITOR GENERAL

As noted before, during my tours of duty in Peru, Ecuador, South Vietnam, and part of my tour of duty in Colombia, I was assigned to the Office of the Controller, serving in a number of positions, including Chief Auditor, Deputy Chief Auditor, Deputy Unit Chief, Audit Manager, and

Acting Controller. Throughout the years, I had assumed positions of increasing authority and had been promoted from an FS-4 to an FS-1. [65]

On December 12, 1969, USAID created the Office of the Auditor-General. A few days after its creation, USAID also established the Area Auditor General Office for Latin America (north) in Guatemala City, Guatemala. Richard S. was appointed as the Area Auditor General, and Jim G. was named his Deputy. The agency transferred a few USAID staff into the new office based on their skills. Audit and investigations personnel were transferred from the Controller's Office to the new office. Because of my skills, the agency transferred me – on paper only -- to the Area Office of The Auditor General for Latin America. Although we were now part of the Auditor General, my audit staff and I remained in Colombia and continued to work in the usual manner.

For about two years, FSO staff assigned to the Auditor General continued to work in their respective countries in the usual manner. However, towards the middle of 1971, the Office of the Regional Auditor General was moved from Guatemala and re-established in Panama City, Panama. Let me say that this move was somewhat confusing. As I remember it, Jim G. (the Deputy) was left to close out the Guatemala Office. Richard S. (a long-time USAID Controller) was transferred from Guatemala to Panama and became the Regional Auditor General there. A person (Walter K.) that I did not know became his Deputy or "Acting Deputy." At some later date, Walter K. was replaced, as Deputy A.G., again by Jim G. In any event, three new positions of "Audit Managers" were established. Larry I. – and maybe 2 others – was named as Audit Managers.

Not long after the establishment of the Panama regional office, around March 1971, Larry came for his first official visit to Colombia. Larry and I might have met once or twice, but we had never worked together, and we did not know each other well. Without getting into too much detail, let me say that his visit was not the most constructive one. He certainly was not the smoothest or most diplomatic type of manager. We held courtesy meetings with several Mission Offices (the USAID Director, the Controller, program officers and,

---

[65] At the time in the USAID Foreign Service, Foreign Service officers were called "Foreign Service Reserve Officers. However, I use the term Foreign Service Officer because we had all the ranks and privileges of a regular FSO.

others) but these were somewhat awkward. Larry's tenor during these sessions seemed condescending and stilted to emphasize the importance of the separation, independence, and powers vested on the new AG Office and himself; and inject – in a not too subtle manner – negative comments about past audit reviews done by my audit staff and I had done.

When we met to discuss office matters, Larry's constant theme was to repeat his position in the new office and re-emphasize that he was our supervisor. At some point during our meeting, we reviewed one draft report that had just been cleared by everyone in the Mission and was ready for issuance. After browsing through it, he expressed disappointment with the report and wanted to make radical changes. Since I had participated in all phases of the review and the audit team had done a great job, I thought it was an excellent report. For this reason, I was not going to let Larry make radical changes – and, so, Larry and I "tangled." After a few heated exchanges, I told him that the review had been done observing an established protocol and that the findings, recommendations, and the report had been completely vetted and cleared by everyone. I told him that he could make only minor editorial changes but no more. If he decided to make radical changes, I told him that I would write a memo to Richard S. (the Regional Auditor General). That got his attention. Larry obviously did not want Richard S. to know any facts or that he was going beyond his authority on his Colombian visit.

To make the story short, he made only *very minor editorial changes*. He left shortly after that but etched in his mind were only bad impressions of me and parts of the office. There was a sequel to his visit:

- Shortly after Larry's departure, the Controller, Bill M., and I met – at his request. There was some bantering about "your new supervisor…and some other derogatory descriptions of him…." However, the important thing they wanted to discuss was whether I was going to change the way we conducted our reviews and the clearance procedures. I told them that I would add a step where the draft reports would be sent to Panama just before submission to the Mission for final clearance – I did not anticipate other changes. That is the way we operated until my departure from Colombia.

- As noted, this was the first time I had worked with Larry, and the meeting had lasted no more than 2 or three days. Yet, Larry wrote my Employee Evaluation Report (EER), also known as Personal Evaluation Report (PER), **for the year**. In my view, the EER was not a fair assessment of my work. In his report, he said that I was not "synergistic" (his word – meaning that I was inflexible). He also used other negative words.
- Although the information in the EER is supposed to be confidential -- only the Rating Officer, the Reviewing Officer, the Rated Officer, and the review panel (in Missions and/or USAID in Washington) are supposed to know the EER's content -- I later found that people in Panama were describing me as a bad apple. In fact, when I first met people from the AG Panama Office, they were somewhat reluctant to be colleagues and friends. Within days, these colleagues were the best of my friends, and we were working as a team. But this was not the type of reception an FS-1 Career Officer should have gotten.
- Somewhere around this time, I was proposed for a transfer to the Congo (in Africa). I don't know if the EER and proposed transfer were related or not. However, according to what I heard, the justification for the transfer was that "…Joe speaks, reads, and writes Spanish; he can study and learn French…." After I exchanged correspondence with USAID Washington – requesting a transfer to the Office of Controller and posting to USAID headquarters in Washington, or a transfer to another Central or South American Country -- the proposal was canceled.

What was the outcome at the end of my exceptional tour in Colombia? I was transferred to the Office of the Auditor-General in Panama – as just a common or regular Auditor. In other words, the newly created Office of the Area Auditor General did not take advantage of my experience.

And where was Larry assigned? He was transferred from Panama and took my place in Colombia. Nice move, huh! Was Larry's visit to Colombia a prearranged agreement to his possible transfer to Colombia? Did his visit to Colombia constitute a conflict of interest? Was it fair for him to write my

EER? I will let the reader make his/her own mind. In any event, Larry and I never worked together again – thank goodness.

PART Q. CONCLUDING REMARKS

I left Colombia around July or August 1972. My tour of duty in Colombia was great. We completed some fabulous evaluative reviews and issued extremely important reports. All these fabulous achievements were possible because the USAID Mission to Colombia had some fabulously professional people. In particular, the Colombian auditors were extraordinarily professional; they were flexible and quick studies, and they quickly adapted to the new audit philosophy of doing comprehensive evaluative reviews. With the help of this fine staff, we were able to produce numerous exceptional reports. It is sad to note that when the Office of the Auditor-General became the Office of the Inspector General (OIG), the employment of most local audit employees was ended. These extremely valuable personnel resources were either fired or transferred to other parts of the Mission. We certainly had extremely valuable local audit staff. Most certainly, I wish the OIG had found a way to keep them.

I left very good friends and colleagues in Colombia. I only wish my transition from the Colombian assignment to the Office of the Auditor-General in Panama would have been a smoother and more respectful one – for the Colombian audit team and of my own performance. My past employment history with the Agency and our work in Colombia and other previous country assignments warranted no less. So, why was I treated, by Larry and then by the Office of the Panama Regional Office in such an unprofessional and disrespectful manner? Let me explain that this was not the last time that I got harsh treatment during my career with the Auditor and Inspector General. Here is a very brief preview of the harsh treatments I will be talking about later in Chapters 16, 17, 18, and 19:

When I transferred from Panama to Washington, the assignment was to be a "Rotation Assignment," which meant that I could study and improve my skills. However, I was placed on constant traveling status and never given a chance to study or get my "Master's Degree." When I talked to the then

Auditor General, he did not like what I was saying, and within a month, I was "exiled" to Pakistan (See Chapter 11 for details).

After serving as Deputy Regional Inspector in Egypt and Latin America and being the Acting Regional Inspector General in both countries, the then Inspector General hired 8 people from the U.S. General Accounting Office (GAO), gave them high FS ranks, and placed them in key positions. Most probably, with the authorization of the IG, these people tried to institute impractical policies. These were all wrong and impractical, and I dissented. The IG, using the GAO/FSO people, retaliated against me. Despite fabulous achievements, my tour as Deputy Regional Inspector General for Latin America was terminated, and there were other extremely serious false allegations and accusations against me. Over a period of three years, I was investigated and persecuted for 3 years. The investigation was concluded nearly 1 and 1/2 years after my retirement. See Chapters 16, 17, 18, and 19 for all details.

Center: Jose M. Pena, Author, and Pauline A.
Two on Right Side: Jose M. Pena III and Melissa G. Pena
Three on Left Side: Kendall Bucher, Linda Pena Bucher, and Jerry Pena
Pauline, Kendall, Linda, and Jerry have passed away

Lucy, Estela, and Jose M. Pena III
on a California vacation

Jose is graduate of William and Mary University, Kentucky University, served in Peace Corps, and now works for the U.S. General Accountability Office

Lucy graduated from San Marcos University of Peru and just retired from The Inter-American Development Bank

Estela (my granddaughter) recently graduated with a bachelor's degree in Linguistics and Psychology and is currently attending the California State Long Beach University studying Towards Her master's degree

Lauren Marie Bucher Delaney (My Granddaughter)
and Her Husband Andrew Delaney
At Their Beautiful Modern Wedding

Jerry, me, and Jose M. Pena III
In Happier Days of the1970
Jerry Died as a Result of Nurse's Terrible Medical Mistake

THESE PHOTOS ARE DEDICATED TO CARLOS R. CABRERA AND HIS WIFE CARMENCITA

THESE WERE BETTER TIMES. OUR GOOD FRIENDSHIP DATED BACK TO VIETNAM.

WE RECENTLY LOST CARLOS; MAY HE REST IN PEACE

Chapter Nine
In Panama, Family Reunification, Audit Manager, TDY's In Honduras, Earthquake In Nicaragua, Exceptional Audits, Heavy Travel In Central And South America

Part A. Introductory Comments

Background Information. After I left Colombia, I went directly to Austin, started my Home Leave, and tried to find a peaceful solution to my marital problems. About three weeks into my leave, I got a letter, from the AAG/LA, telling me not to go to Panama directly but to go on Temporary Duty (TDY), without the family, to Honduras to help on a complex audit of a bank. That is how the sequence of my transfer to Panama took place and the reason why this chapter is divided into 11 parts:

- Part A. Introductory Comments.
- Part B. Home Leave and Family Reunification.
- Part C. My TDY to Honduras.
- Part D. Short History of Panama.
- Part E. Life in Panama.
- Part F. Some Staff in Panama who participated in the Honduras TDY.
- Part G. Three (of many issued) AAG/LA Audits Analyzed as Examples.
- Part H. The CABEI Review in Honduras.
- Part I. Review of a USAID Family Planning Project in Costa Rica.
- Part J. Review of USAID disaster Relief On the 1972 Earthquake in Nicaragua.
- Part K. My Concluding Remarks.

My concluding remarks are favorable to the Panama AAG/LA Office and extremely critical of the crazy logic and the costly effects incurred – by a new Auditor General when he closed the Panama Office and moved its operations to MIAMI, FLORIDA. That decision was really "out of this world." My next chapter shows details of this illogical closing of the Panama Regional Office.

PART B. HOME LEAVE AND FAMILY REUNIFICATION

As the reader might remember, my wife and four children had left me alone in Colombia primarily because my assignment to Vietnam had not been too beneficial to our marriage. For this reason, Pauline and I wanted some space to determine what the future held for us.

Upon my arrival in Austin, this marital condition weighed heavily on my mind. I had long conversations with Joe, Jerry, Linda, and baby talks with Melissa. I kept marveling at how grown and beautiful my four children had become. Joe and Jerry were so tall and handsome. I had bought them jungle uniforms like the ones used in Vietnam for them to wear; it was obvious that the uniforms I had sent them from Vietnam no longer fit them, and in any event, the times had changed profoundly, with the sentiment against the war in Vietnam. Linda, with her flaming red hair, no longer could use the "Au Dai" dress that I had also sent to her. And Melissa, now about 3 years old, clung to her mom – and hardly recognized me.

Joe, an awfully bright person – even in childhood -- seemed very mature for his age and always spoke very frankly with me. Jerry, with the tremendous musical ability he had since childhood, told me about the things that were taking place in his Catholic school. Years later, he told me the following story that took place:

- The school classes were composed of both little girls and boys. The teacher was a cranky middle-aged Nun. One day, the kids began to jostle each other and misbehave, as kids often do. The teacher got very upset and began to chastise all the kids: "…You children are a bunch of very ungrateful persons. You are constantly misbehaving. When you are acting in that manner, I think you were the ones that placed Jesus Christ on the Cross and sacrificed him…." There was a strange

> moment of silence. Then one kid said, "…Sister, we did not sacrifice or kill Jesus Christ…. We are just kids…." I thought this was a fabulous response to an unfounded allegation.

In turn, Pauline and I also had long discussions. She told me about the death of Gilbert O. (her brother-in-law) and how lonely his wife and the children (Arthur, Rose Ellen, and Robert) were. She told me about the hardships that Linda had gone through while battling a rheumatic fever in the hospital. And she told me that she wished we could get together again for the sake of the children.

I visited my mother in Laredo, and the above scene played in my mind. My mother -- a very perceptive person – quickly captured my dilemma and counseled me on how to approach the type of decision that needed to be made. In her very quiet manner, and between tears, my mother told me that perhaps errors might have been made in the way Pauline and I had elected to marry each other and that perhaps we should have made sure that we knew each other well. That was now history. At this point in our lives, we no longer could make isolated decisions because they also affected the children. The decision had to be based on the four children in our equation. When I returned to Austin from Laredo, Pauline and I made the decision to stay together and reunite the family.

Right about this time, I got a letter from the Area Auditor General in Panama telling me to alter my travel plans to Panama. Instead of going directly from Austin to Panama, I was to proceed directly on a TDY assignment for about 3 months to Honduras to help with an audit of the Central American Bank for Economic Integration (CABEI). By then, I had already bought a car -- a beautiful orange and black 1971 Ford Torino. It was for this reason that I went first by road from Austin to Honduras and from there to Panama. So, my family finally joined me in Panama six months later.

Part C. My Temporary Assignment In Honduras

As ordered by the AAG in Panama, I altered my travel routes and travelled; I travelled in my Ford Torino from Austin to Laredo (visited my mom again for two days), then drove to Mexico City, and passed through Guatemala, arriving in Honduras on a Friday night. Although I did not know any of the Audit Team that was doing the review, I stayed in the same hotel where they were staying.

Since there were governmental restrictions on currency exchanges, the hotel would not exchange any of my U.S. Dollars for Lempiras (the Honduras Currency). I asked the hotel manager if I could see Charles C. (the Team Leader); the manager told me that the team had gone to visit some office (it turned out to be ROCAP), in Guatemala, for a few days and that they would be back on Sunday. Boy, without local currency in a strange country, I was in real "deep Kimchee."

That night, I went to bed hungry. The next morning, I walked outside the hotel and found a small restaurant. I met with the owner; her name, if my memory is correct, was Olivia. I flashed a $100 bill, and I told her about my problem with the currency exchange. I told her that I would leave that money with her if I could eat my different meals at her restaurant until Monday. Olivia was a real pretty lady, about 28 years of age. She sized me up and laughed out loud. Without taking my $100, she told the waitress to serve me anything I wanted for the next three or four days. So, I ate there many times from then on. Once after she had attended to some customers, Olivia joined me at the table. She started asking questions: (a) my name, (b) where I was from; (c) what I was doing in Honduras; (d) how long I was going to be in Honduras; and (d) how I had gotten to Honduras. When I told her that I had driven all the way from the U.S., she asked me if I had encountered any bandits or thieves. I said that the trip was uneventful. She burst out laughing and told me, "…O, tu estas loco o fumas café tostaditas…" (Either you are crazy or you are smoking)..then – after I asked -- she defined "café tostaditas" for me.) We laughed. Very subtly, she told me she had a boyfriend (in other words, she told me "…we could only be friends." which was fine with me.) From then on, and when I was getting ready to leave, she gave me a big hug and told me, "…Bienvenido a Honduras." So, this became "my favorite restaurant," and from then on, we were good friends. By Sunday night, I owed for meals and beers that I had drank; I paid my debt the following day. More importantly, from then on, both the Audit Team and I ate there frequently.

Anyway, the weekend and Sunday came around fast. When I saw Chuck C., Luis P., Miles S, and another Panamanian auditor (I don't recall his name) coming into the Hotel, I went over and introduced myself. I noticed that they seemed to shy away from me as if I had Leprosy. We talked a little, and Chuck C. exchanged my $100 for Lempiras. I then invited them to a beer in the hotel bar. We had a couple of beers. By the way, our conversation went; I knew they were sizing me up. But that was Ok. I was also sizing them up myself. By night's end, I had them laughing at how I still owed my friend Olivia (the restaurant owner) for the meals. The next morning, we went to eat at my favorite restaurant; Olivia and I greeted each other with a big hug – and I even planted a kiss on her cheek. From that point on, the team was in my pocket. I immediately paid my debt to Olivia. After breakfast on that day, we went to work as a Team. Chuck and I met, and he gave me background information, and we discussed the tentative audit approach that they were planning to take. A few days after getting "my feet wet," I was able to suggest a firmer course of action. Once Chuck realized that I was going to help – not hurt or fight with – him, he told me that rumors persisted in Panama that I was a real "rotten apple." That was the reason the four of them were somewhat hesitant to become close friends of mine. I guess Larry had done some damage to my reputation.

PART D. BRIEF DESCRIPTION OF AAG/LA AUDIT TEAM IN HONDURAS

- Let me briefly describe the Audit Team. Richard S. was an exceptional Auditor General. He was a long-time Controller, diplomatic and smooth as they come. He knew how USAID Missions operated, knew how to deal with – U.S. Ambassador, USAID Mission Directors, operational managers, etc. And he was an excellent manager of people. He and I got along extremely well. He reviewed the final audit report. When Richard S. decided to retire, he was replaced by Fred S. in 1973. Fred S. was equally exceptional.
- Walt K., the Deputy Auditor General, was a bright person but was somewhat narcissistic. He and I were not the best of friends. He tended to speak down to people. One time, he began to ask questions about

how I did audits. When I gave him a dissertation on how we developed the protocol and did the reviews in Colombia, he looked at me and told me I had copied his audit concepts. He then finished up by telling me: "Joe, you are not in my league." That comment was most insulting. So, as smoothly as I could, I reiterated that I did not know him when I was in Colombia; the audit protocol was mine, which I had developed during my 15 years in USAID. He did not like my rebuttal.

- Nevertheless, from my dealings with him, I had the feeling that Walt had a bi-Polar personality." For example, when the pressure mounted in the office, Walt would often go home and stay in bed for a few days. Although he tended to be a little too verbose in changing our original reports, he was a decent writer. He came to Honduras once, helped or guided us in writing the report, and went to the exit conference with USAID officials in Guatemala[66]. He was eventually replaced by Jim Gr. – a fine person.

- Chuck C. was one of those beautiful personalities you rarely meet in a lifetime. A blond person with a cropped hairdo, Chuck was married to Carmen; they had two sons whom I met after I eventually got to Panama. This was a beautiful family. In childhood, Chuck had suffered paralytic polio during the Polio epidemic and was left with a slight limp. Although Chuck had recently joined USAID and did not speak Spanish, he was a fabulous professional, and we made an exceptional team. We were best friends until he decided to resign from USAID about three years after the CABEI review. I hope he reads my book. I still think of him and Carmen.

- Luis P. was/is a Panamanian "local" Auditor, was also a fabulous person. We quickly made friends. He was most intelligent and had a very interesting past. During one of our talks, he told me that when one of the Panamanian Juntas took over, he was arrested, made to completely strip and stand at attention for 7 hours. He was incarcerated for a few days and eventually released. He had joined USAID/Panama

---

[66] An Exit Conference typically occurs at the end of the audit work , after the team has developed the report's main findings and conclusions. It is a key stage in the audit process and is done to enable agency officials to discuss the facts in the report, as well as the report's findings and conclusions.

as an accountant but had recently transferred to the Office of the Auditor General. He was a fast adaptive person, and he enjoyed collaborating with me. I still think of him and talk about him with my friend Carlos.

- Also, a U.S. Auditor, M.S. was a tall gentleman who was "Gay." M.S. was highly intelligent. Although he did not speak Spanish, he was a good financial auditor and did his work well. (Note: Sadly, during one future trip to either Puerto Rico or the Dominican Republic, M.S. was brutally murdered; may he Rest in Peace).
- I don't recall the name of the other Panamanian Local Auditor. All I remember is that he was used as a translator to interpret financial transactions and in the visits made by either Chuck or M.S. to sub-borrowers or other countries.

Let me conclude by saying that Chuck C., Luis P., and I became the best of friends. Whenever I was assigned a job outside of Panama, Luis P. always volunteered to accompany me…." because I learn a lot from you, and you treat people with a great deal of respect…." Anyway, we all worked well together and did an exceptional job. I will discuss our audit (of CABEI) results in Part G later. So, for now, I will jump ahead to a brief history of Panama.

PART E. SOME HISTORY OF PANAMA

A Brief History of Panama. Briefly, Panama was discovered in 1501 by Rodrigo de Bastides, a Spanish explorer. Panama joined Colombia when the latter declared its independence in 1821. It remained a part of Colombia until November 3, 1903, when, with U.S. support, it became independent. The U.S. wanted to build a canal across the Isthmus that would connect the Pacific Ocean with the Atlantic Ocean. Thus, almost immediately, on November 06, 1903, the U.S. recognized the Republic of Panama, signing12 months later the Hay-Bunau-Varilla Treaty, which gave the U.S. permanent and exclusive possession over a Panama Canal Zone. Panama agreed to let the U.S. build the Panama Canal and received $10 Million and an annuity of $250,000. On August 15, 1914, the Panama Canal was inaugurated with the passage of a cargo and passenger ship called "the *Ancon*."[67] In 1964, the Panamanians rioted over the sovereignty of the Canal Zone. Consequently, President Carter and Dictator Omar Torrijos signed an agreement in 1977 to turn over the Panama Canal to the Republic of Panama at the turn of the century; this agreement was fulfilled. In sum, the cost of building the Panama Canal was over $350 million of U.S. Dollars. However, and without a doubt, the Panama Canal has been a fabulous investment for the United States and many countries in the world.

Panama is a beautiful country. It also turned out to be a good family post; we were able to visit some beautiful locations and travel by road to Costa Rica and other Central American countries. At the time of our tour, the U.S. military had a few bases in the Canal Zone with PX's where we could shop; movie theaters where we could see current movies; and fantastic officers' clubs and restaurants where we could eat. In addition, there were also a few first-class golf courses on the military bases and not-to-mention; the beaches of Panama were world-class and beautiful.

PART F. LIFE IN PANAMA

After my TDY to Honduras, I proceeded to Panama and arranged my family's stay in Panama. Knowing that I was coming by myself, the USAID Logistics Office located a two-bedroom apartment about two blocks from the office. In this way, I was able to move furniture and other items coming in from Colombia into my apartment right away.

- But…I got the surprise of my life when I walked into my apartment after going to work three days after my arrival. I opened the door at 6:00 PM and had a real strange feeling. As I closed the door, I looked around, and my apartment had been ransacked. Gone were my television, typewriter, dishes, some adornments, and other items. Although the Security Office came, none of the stolen items were found. The only thing I could do was change the locks and never again loan the key to anyone. Sometimes, I would forget and leave on my desk some change or a gold coin I had gotten; these were also stolen.

---

[67] The Internet, articles called History of the Republic of Panama

So, I learned to be careful and take care of my things. Those were the "welcoming" bad experiences that I had in Panama. Cesc Le Vie.

By the time my family arrived in Panama, I had developed nice friendships with colleagues and workers. Because we would need two cars, I had also bought an old 1965 Volkswagen Beetle from a colleague (John D.) that was leaving Panama. So, we had two cars; Pauline would drive the Ford, and I would drive the VW Beetle. So, the only thing that was needed was to find a maid and permanent housing. In other words, we were up and running with the assignment in Panama.

We liked our assignment to Panama very much. After some searching, we got a real nice house very close to the center of town in an area called "Punta Paitilla" and a nice maid. Later, Melissa told me that the maid would often smoke a "Cigar" in front of her – but she was a good maid anyway. We got a large German Shepard puppy, which my children christened "Sarge" because of the way he stood--as if he were a drill sergeant in front of a platoon. As I also previously mentioned, the U.S. military had a few bases -- there was Fort Clayton, Howard Air Force Base, Rodman Naval Base, and Fort Amador, among others-- where there were PX's, movies, restaurants, and every week we would go into the Canal Zone to shop, watch a movie and eat. Although I traveled extensively, Pauline and I would go to the nice restaurants during the times when I was in Panama. One of the bases had a nice golf course called Hiroko that Joe, Jerry, and I frequented. In fact, to our utter astonishment, Jerry made a hole in one on one of the outings. Hiroko was not an easy golf course to navigate, yet somehow, he managed to do it

The kids were happy that I had the old 1965 Volkswagen Beetle. The VW was an exceptional car--not fast or flashy, but very reliable. It took us every place. Because of the shape of the car and because it was so small, I remember my sons had to scrunch down while in the back seat. Also, because the engine was so small, sometimes, when crossing the Bridge of the Americas that connected both sides on the Pacific part of the Canal, the car would struggle, and the kids would grimace and grunt, trying to give additional power to the small VW motor. We'd start chanting, "Come on, car, you can make it!" Fortunately, we would soon reach the crest of the bridge and begin going downhill. Since the beaches in Panama are just beautiful, we took numerous trips to them. Because Kobe Beach was nearby and had a shark net, we often went to that beach on weekends. Frequently, we would get buckets full of huge sea shrimp, crabs, lobsters, and clams, bake them, and have a feast. At first, we were so dumb that we would try to catch the crabs barehanded – and got our hands pinched many times. Here is where Jerry proved to be the smartest one; he decided he did not want to get pinched anymore and found that a pair of Barbeque prongs would do the trick. The rest of us quickly picked up on his insight and began using tongs as well.

Joe and Jerry attended Corundum Junior High School in the Canal Zone. On the Pacific side of the Canal Zone, there was one high school and one junior high school. Football and basketball games pitted players from these two schools against each other and the schools on the Atlantic side of the Canal Zone.

We went across the Panamanian isthmus a couple of times. Of course, we visited and saw the Panama Canal and how the ships crossed from one ocean to the other. One time, all of us got in the Ford and drove to see the Poas Volcano near San Jose, Costa Rica. I was extremely leery about letting the kids loose – for fear they might get too close or fall into the extremely deep crater. It turned out that the return trip down the mountain was a bit of a hair-raiser, as the car stalled and for a short period of time, we had to steer and brake the car without support from the hydraulic system. We took some exceptional pictures of the volcanoes and had a grand time in San José.

My sons and I especially had a chance to bond. In addition to playing golf together, we often went fishing. Of course, just because we would often go fishing, that did not mean we would often catch anything. I remember once we caught a fish, but when we ate it, it was oily, we had to throw it out. In addition to going fishing, we would often watch boxing matches together. I remember one night we went to National Stadium in Panama City to watch on a big projection screen the second 1974 boxing match between Muhammad Ali and Joe Frazier held at the Madison Square Garden in New York City. The match was televised via satellite throughout the world. Because I was a huge fan of Ali--I had supported him even during the period his license had been taken away--my sons also were huge fans of him. Frazier won that boxing match by a decision.

As I will mention later, Chuck C., his wife Carmen, two boys, Luis P., Beverly B., and I had become extremely good friends. In Panama, we would have many parties, go on picnics, and go to the beaches together. In sum, our tour in Panama was just great.

PART G. THREE AAG/LA AUDITS DISCUSSED AS EXAMPLES

Although the AAG/LA Office and I did a great many audits in Panama and Latin America, I will now discuss only the following three examples of the work we did in Honduras, Costa Rica, and Nicaragua:

- Part H The CABEI Review in Honduras.
- Part I Review of a USAID Family Planning Project in Costa Rica.
- Part J Review of USAID disaster Relief On the 1972 Earthquake in Nicaragua.

PART H. AUDIT OF USAID SUPPORT FOR CABEI.

As mentioned earlier in this book, USAID's support for the CABEI is one of those remarkable success stories. [68] CABEI is based in Tegucigalpa, the capital of Honduras. The concept for such a bank was first proposed by a group of Latin American economists in 1948, but really began to take shape in the 1950's after the five Central American countries--Guatemala, Nicaragua, Costa Rica, El Salvador, and Honduras--signed an agreement creating the Organization of Central American States.

CABEI was finally established on May 8, 1961. It had two initial basic objectives – to promote: (a) a balanced economic development within each Central American country and (b) a Central American economic integration.

---

[68] A/R 1-596-72-57, a Review of "The Central American Bank for Economic Integration through the AID Regional Office for Central American and Panama (ROCAP), various pages, filed in File on Chapter 3.

At the time of our evaluation, CABEI had been operational for 10 years. During this time, the USAID had provided over $150 million in assistance. The IDB was next with $61.0 million. In addition, CABEI had established lines of credit with a few other nations.

In all, at the time of our review, CABEI had a total of over $328.5 million in funding. CABEI had three different types of funds:

- The Ordinary Fund was used to finance industrial projects as well as export and balance of payments projects.
- The Integration Fund was used to finance economic infrastructure projects.
- The Housing Fund was used to create and sustain a regional secondary mortgage market for medium-priced houses.

The scope of our three-month (August to November 1972) review was formidable. It covered a 10-year period – from CABEI's inception to October 31, 1972. We reviewed CABEI's three funds as well as its operations. We also examined documents, financial information, and sub-borrower records in Honduras, Guatemala, Costa Rica, El Salvador, and Nicaragua. In addition, we sampled 77 sub-loans and visited 39 project sites.

We concluded that "…CABEI was achieving the objectives for which it was organized" and that "…it was a viable and effective force in the accomplishment of economic integration in Central America…."[69] These objectives were being fulfilled by financing regional projects geared to the economic infrastructure, the balance of payments, and urban development requirements of each country. However, we did find at least 19 different areas where improvements could be made. CABEI appears to have corrected all 19 problem areas; for this reason, I will not itemize them.

As of the time of this writing, CABEI – now over 70 years old -- is an established international institution. It still serves its founding member countries (Guatemala, El Salvador, Honduras, Nicaragua, and Costa Rica) but now also serves several non-regional members such as Mexico, Taiwan, Argentina, Colombia, Spain, Panama, Dominican Republic, and Belize. While

---

[69] Ibid

the United States is not a member of CABEI, it does partner with CABEI to help fund projects in Central America. For example, USAID is partnering with CABEI and others in an Alliance for the Dry Corridor of Honduras, designed to enable low-income families in a region of southwestern Honduras to move out of extreme poverty.

Since the time of our review, CABEI's strategic objectives have changed. For instance, CABEI is now addressing poverty; it is also promoting – tourism, globalization, and integration. As of December 2018, its assets were valued at about $11 Billion; its liabilities were about $8 Billion; and its equity was about $3 Billion.[70]

In short, CABEI was helped in its initial stages by USAID, IDB, and others. It certainly seems like a healthy-going concern. Its success should rightfully be attributed to USAID, IDB, and others.

The five of us, as an audit team, spent three months doing the CABEI review. We completed our work o/a November 24, 1972. Chuck and the three others went by plane to Panama, and I drove my car from Honduras to Panama. Because of the expiration of the A.I.D. Continuing Resolution, the Office of AG had funding limitations, and we did not have the Exit Conference, in Guatemala, until January 13, 1973.

With some help and guidance from Deputy A.G., we produced such a fabulous 90-page final report that Richard L. S., the AAG/LA, gave each of us a Letter of Commendation, which was placed in our files. In part, it states, "….I wish to take this opportunity to commend you on your excellent performance during the audit….I am aware of the extended hours beyond the normal work period that you contributed to the audit…This effort attests to your dedication to a job well-done…"

The three months in Honduras gave Chuck C. and me a great deal of time to know each other. We became the best of friends. In Honduras, we drove together, in my car, to different places – San Pedro Sula, El Copan, El Picacho, and others. We frequently ate at my favorite restaurant in Tegucigalpa, and Olivia would always tease us by saying "…No quieren

[70] Central American Bank for Economic Integration 2018 Annual Report at. https://www.bcie.org/fileadmin/bcie/english/files/news-and-media/publications/annual_reports/CABEI-AnnualReport-2018.pdf

fumar café tostadito?" These was her code words for asking us if we wanted a little marijuana. We would say: "No, Gracias...." We all then would laugh.

PART I. REVIEW OF USAID ASSISTANCE FOR THE COSTA RICAN DEMOGRAPHIC ASSOCIATION

I have already briefly discussed the CRDA earlier in this book; this will be a brief discussion. Several organizations, including USAID, the International Planned Parenthood Federation (IPPF), the Pan American Health Organization the World Education Inc., and the Swedish Government, have supported the Costa Rican Demographic Association (CRDA) for a long time.

Shortly after I got to Panama from Honduras, USAID/Costa Rica received some allegations that the CRDA, somehow, had accumulated a great deal of funds. They could not understand where it was coming from or how CRDA was going to use it. So, the Auditor General sent me to make a special review of the organization.

When I got to Costa Rica, I called on the Ambassador, the USAID Director, the Controller, and the accounting people. I also received a briefing from the USAID Populations Officer. The Controller and his people were fabulous; they were informative and very helpful. The Chief Accountant (Rafael or "Rafito," his nickname), the Project Accountant (Cecilia C.edeno), and I became good friends. Every time USAID sent me to Costa Rica, we would eat together and have a few nightcaps. Cecilia wrote Xmas cards to my family and me for many years.

After my visit to the USAID mission in Costa Rica, I went to CRDA's office and met with the Director and a great many of the workers – most were beautiful women. The Director assigned Julia Alvarez. to escort me around and show me what CRDA was all about. In a word, all treated me nicely.

I quickly determined that the source of the new funding was the IPPF and that everything was fine. So, I continued my review into the other parts of the organization. CRDA showed me the different areas of operations.

Here is some background on the organization and what I saw. At the time of my visit, CRDA had only been created about 4 years earlier. As an organization, its primary focus was to address the fast and uncontrolled growth of the Costa Rican population. Looking at these facts, some doctors organized CRDA with several objectives in mind: (a) to make the public aware of the population problem; (b) to get women and people to join the organization; (c) to encourage studies about population profiles and growth; and (d) to provide needed commodities (condoms, pills, IUDs, etc.) and services to needy women.

I found that CRDA was well planned from its beginning. CRDA had three sets of integrated strategies to (a) direct the right type of publicity; (b) direct the publicity to the right type of population; and (c) have (and make) available needed commodities and services at the proper time and when needed. Thus, the CRDA undertook the phased approach to convince Costa Rican families to plan their families using a radio campaign to transmit very explicitly directed messages:

- The first step was to direct radio messages to motivate the middle and upper population class levels.
- The second step was to direct radio messages at the middle- and lower-class levels using themes that emphasized home and general comforts.
- During the third step, the radio messages were designed to reach men, women, teenagers, and professionals.
- The fourth and last step was to provide the needed information services and commodities (pills, injections, condoms, IUDs, Foams, etc.).

With Julia help, I interviewed numerous women who had come to get commodities or services from CRDA. Here is what I remember some of them telling me:

a) Most women were well informed on the different Family Planning methods.

b) Most women were there, voluntarily, to get birth control pills.

c) A few were there to have an IUD inserted (they seemed unashamed).

d) Very few were there to be injected with a birth control medicine called "Depo Provera;" their fear was due to unwanted side effects, including sterilization of a woman – when received too many times.

e) I did not see any woman who was there for tubal ligation (I was told that CRDA merely referred women desiring this procedure to another clinic).

f) CRDA provided services and commodities free of charge or through a coupon system.

In sum, the organization was achieving its objectives, and the Costa Rican population rate had decreased over 10-years period, from 3.85 to 2.60. Thus, the massive, carefully focused, multi-level publicity campaign was paying huge dividends. And USAID assistance was providing exceptional help in this area. [71]

Hopefully, USAID has continued to establish and support organizations, like the CRDA, to promote directed publicity and commodity availability in the different parts of the world.

PART J. REVIEW OF USAID ASSISTANCE PROVIDED FOR THE 1972 EARTHQUAKE OF NICARAGUA.72

On December 23, 1972, the city of Managua, Nicaragua, suffered a devastating earthquake that took an estimated 10,000 to 12,000 lives and caused widespread property damage (destroyed over 40,000 homes) and left about 200,000 people homeless. On January 2, 1973, the Government of Nicaragua (GON) – then headed by Anastasio Somoza -- requested assistance from USAID for the purpose of constructing an estimated 13,000 to 15,000 temporary shelters. USAID and the GON signed a grant agreement on January 15, 1973, through which USAID made available $3.0 million to construct the

[71] A/R 1-512-72-113, USAID/Costa Rica, The Costa Rican Demographic Association, in Chapter 3 File.

[72] A/R. 1-524-73-126, Audit Report of USAID/Nicaragua, Temporary Shelter Program, Grant No. CF-524-01

shelters, and the Organization of American States made available about $300,000 to place roofs over 3,120 of the shelters.[73]

Since "…time was of the essence…" and construction and occupations of the temporary shelters needed urgent attention, the Banco de la Vivienda de Nicaragua (BAVINIC) was to (and did) administer (provided the land, designed the shelters, contracted builders' services, provided engineering services, etc.) and USAID agreed to assign two officers to monitor the progress and disburse the needed funds in a prompt manner.

Due to the urgency of the situation, the Office of Controller provided a Special Controller (Richard H.), and the Office of the Area Auditor General in Panama assigned me to monitor the progress of construction.

When Richard H. and I got to Nicaragua, we could still, at times, feel (or think we felt) some aftershocks. We also saw rows and rows of houses that had been flattened like pancakes by **the earthquake. The petrifying scent of death seemed to be everywhere**. Since all the city's hotels were either destroyed, damaged, or completely full, USAID/Nicaragua rented – for Richard H., I, and others -- some "Chalets" behind a house that had not been destroyed by the earthquake. We slept in cots and bunked in those chalets for nearly 4 months. Nights were eerie. Some nights, we would run out when we merely perceived that the earth was shaking. (Note: To see the 1972 Managua destruction, visit the website: **https://www.youtube.com/watch?v=fuzSoW2A5MY**)

- Anyway, Richard H. was a young USAID Controller (in his mid-30's). Although he and I had not previously worked together, we quickly became the best of friends and colleagues. Richard planned to retire in Florida and pursue his great interest in buying old cars and renewing them. He had a slight limp as he walked. So, one time while we ate, I asked him why he limped. Here is the story he told me. A few years back, he bought an old convertible car and began to renew it. He unscrewed the steering wheel and took it off. After a while, he put the steering wheel back in the car – but forgot to secure it tightly. He then fixed the motor and the dents in the body of the car. He also painted it. That car looked perfect. He decided to see how the car ran. Pushing

[73] Ibid.

the pedal to seventy miles (or more), he made the mistake of pulling out the steering wheel. He lost complete control over the car and crashed into an old tree, and first responders found him badly hurt on top of one of the branches. As a result of the accident, he had one leg shorter than the other.

- Richard had a fun type of personality. I do not remember why, but Richard H. had his own car in Nicaragua (a brown Toyota with no air conditioning). On the other hand, USAID/Nicaragua loaned me one of their motor pool cars so I could monitor the projects. Since there were no restaurants where we could eat, we arranged with the maid who lived in the main house to make us breakfast each morning (it seemed like our breakfast was always coffee, eggs, and tortilla or toast); we ate that every day and it got a little boring. At night, Richard and I would climb in his car; he would keep all windows up (to minimize the outside smells); and we'd begin to sweat. I would ask him: "…Richard, why don't we roll down the car windows?" He would look at me, in his mischievous smile, and then say: "…why are you asking that question? Do you want the Nicaraguans to know that I don't have an air conditioner in my car…"? We would burst out laughing. Most nights, we would drive over to a "Nicaraguan Cantina" near the chalet and have a few "Flor De Caña" rum and cokes. We would eat, hear some music, and watch the Nicaraguans dance to the beat of their beautiful rhythmic songs. On our way home, we often discussed the incongruent lives he and I were living in Nicaragua. To both of us, it seemed so odd that, on the one hand, we could smell death everywhere and see the flattened structures where people had died and were still buried. On the other, we had just been in a place where people might have been grieving; but they – like us -- were alive, having fun, and saying to themselves: "…life goes on…." These two aspects – death and life – did not seem to be in sync with the current situation in Nicaragua. The whole thing seemed so unreal.

- In short, Richard and I made a good match, and we did a good job of monitoring the implementation of the Temporary Shelter program. Since the shelters were being constructed in four different locations (called America 1, 2, 3, and 4) in Nicaragua, Richard and I would alternate our visits to do our monitoring. On days that Richard would visit a given location (say America 1), I would visit America 2. And, when I visited America 3, Richard would visit America 4. At night, we would coordinate our observations. We would provide briefings to the USAID Director (Peter H.??) once a week and to Ambassador (Turner S.) at the Ambassador's residence about once every two to three weeks. Briefings for the Ambassador were always -- for me -- mental torture, primarily because the Ambassador's wife had, to say it mildly, a "mean streak." Even when over 60-70% of the population in Managua was homeless, she wanted to dictate rules for everything. For instance, she made us wait outside the residence – a beautiful multi-level home that had not been damaged by the earthquake -- until the Ambassador was ready to receive us; we could not walk or sit on the outside grass; once inside the residence, we were prohibited from sitting on any chairs of the living room; and, if we were in urgent need to use the toilet, she (or her servants) would instruct us to use the portable toilets outside the home. Visits to the Residence always reminded me of an old book called "The Ugly American."

- The rainy season in Nicaragua, which normally starts in April, can create serious problems because of the layout and absorptive capacity of the land. I experienced one such a serious problem on May 17, 1973. Here is what happened. I drove to one of America's Temporary Shelters. To enter the area of the shelter, one had to cross a riverbed gorge that measured about 25 feet wide and about 2 feet deep; it slanted at the car crossing. When I arrived at the shelters, the riverbed was completely dry, and the hills were on my left side. On my return trip to the "Chalet," I could see thunder and lightning on my right up in the hills, but it was not yet raining on the road. I reached the bank of the riverbed and saw that it was dry. So, I began to cross it. When I was halfway, I looked to my right side and saw a deluge of water and mud coming my way; I guess the storm had already taken place on the top of the hill. I stepped on the accelerator, but the strong current dragged the car (and me) sideways for about a quarter or half a block. Mud and water began to slip into the car. However, "Someone up there" took care of me, and the car stopped floating when it hit some

> dunes. With a dead motor and scared, I quickly decided to get out through my driver's window. Luckily, the bank was near, and I was out of the gorge in no time. Although I was all wet, I got home alright. The next day, someone, maybe Richard, drove me to the location of my car. Although the car was soaked and muddy inside, I was able to start it. I went to the motor pool and exchanged it for another. That was one of the scariest times of my life. However, as I later found out, that storm also gravely affected many of the Temporary Shelters; I will explain this in a brief time.

By the conclusion of our visit, which occurred on June 10, 1973, USAID had disbursed about $2.8 million, and the shelters had been constructed. Much was accomplished in a short period of time. Here is a brief profile of the Temporary Shelter Program that was accomplished: (a) BAVINIC contracted 15 different Construction Companies to build the shelters; (b) these 15 builders – in record time -- constructed 11,135 Temporary Shelters (down from the 13,000 to 15,000 originally planned) in 4 different locations of Managua. ; (c) as mentioned earlier, the locations were named America 1, 2, 3, and 4; (d) of the 11,135 shelters built, 5,566 were duplexes and the remainder were individual homes; (e) the individual shelters were about 19.50 square meters in size; (f) and their floors were made out of dirt; (g) as planned, the shelters were to have electrical lights, water taps, one latrine, and a communal shower; (h) certain criteria and rules were placed in effect to ensure equitable occupation by lower strata population and those that had not previously owned a home; (l) BAVINIC could collect a certain specified amount to cover such costs as rent, garbage collection, etc. (ranging between $5. to $8.50); and (m) since these were temporary shelters, they were expected to be either destroyed or upgraded sometime in the future. By June 10, BAVINIC had signed rental contracts for only 2,579 units. According to our calculations, the statistics meant that about 11,600 people were living in the shelters.

Unfortunately, the original plans did not contemplate an elaborate storm sewerage system. As a result, a storm that occurred on May 17, 1973 (and others) affected 45 (and maybe more) families who were inundated inside their houses and had to tear wood planks to permit the water to flow. They lost their belongings and had to vacate their homes to survive. Because of this and due to their wanting to stay close to other relatives, there had been a significant reduction in demand for the shelters. BAVINIC initiated plans to construct an adequate sewerage system.

My visits and review noted many problems. Many were corrected immediately. Here is a list of some: (a) the houses needed cement floors; (b) many occupants were building unrestricted and unauthorized extensions to their properties; (c) an excessive number of occupants (11 in number) were living together in the same houses; (d) none of the locations had medical clinics; (e) the roads to the shelters were made of dirt and driving on them was hazardous; (f) a few stores had been established in the four communities; and, (g) three schools were in the process of being built.

Our conversations with the occupants showed that (a) some were already delinquent in the payment of their rents – some said the distance to BAVINIC was too far-- and (b) all occupants had the intention of making the shelters their permanent home. Thus, BAVINIC needed to: (a) make the shelters more durable; (b) facilitate rental payments on the part of occupants; (c) facilitate easier procedures for occupants to purchase their home; and (d) establish standards for adding rooms, galleries, etc.

I also found problems with the way BAVINIC administered the program, among them: (a) processing of contracts was slow; (b) contracts contained a number of errors; (c) records did not separate collections for trash, maintenance, land rental, etc.; (d) BAVINC was not submitting any periodic reports to USAID; and, (e) with only 2,579 rental contracts signed, there was no realistic probabilities that all the 11,135 could be occupied by the August 1973 date the grant terminated. In our audit report, we gave the GON 3 different alternatives to resolve this problem. However, the best option was to: "…Maintain the present occupancy requirements…..expand and accelerate completion of duplexes instead of individual units….reduce population density (by reducing numbers of shelters)… and eliminate the creation of slum areas…."[74]

We issued our Area Auditor General for Latin America audit (no. 1-524-73-126) on June 29, 1973. Although this was to be an "Interim Audit," I got assigned to other priority reviews, and I never did a follow-up review of the

[74] IBID, page 6.

Temporary Shelters. Richard and I parted Nicaragua as excellent friends. We knew we had done a good job. We also knew that a few shelters needed to be destroyed for various reasons – some had been damaged by the rains; some needed to be consolidated or made into duplexes, etc. Eight years after our Nicaragua TDY, in 1980, Richard and I once again served together; this time, we were assigned to sit on the 1980 Employee Evaluation Panel and evaluate numerous (258) Foreign Services Officers. I will discuss this later in another chapter.

As noted in our Interim Report, we noted that BAVINIC urgently needed T/A for its operations. For instance, we noted that BAVINIC was delinquent in the collection of contracted rent and was not maintaining adequate records of the Trust Fund accumulations. In addition, BAVINIC's planning for the 11,135 constructed Temporary Shelters did not contemplate a sewerage system; this created major problems during the rainy season. And when the system was built, it was not well designed and needed modifications. Thus, the problem is clear: BAVINIC needed T/A in its operations. Yet, BAVINIC seemed reluctant to get the T/A from U.S. Sources. From what we gathered; the hesitancy was due to the following:

- The reason, as explained by BAVINIC, is that the salary and benefits of U.S. Consultants are extremely high – and they all come out of a loan that will eventually be repaid to the U.S. The GON and BAVINIC's position is, to me, clear. Much like the GON and BAVINIC, other Recipient Nations are probably equally reluctant to use **loan funds** to reimburse the high salary and benefits that a U.S. Consultants is usually paid -- especially if the financing is to be with a repayable loan.

If we were to hypothesize that the T/A to be provided was to be financed in the form of a Grant or that the Recipient Nation could obtain the T/A at a lower cost from any other source (Colombia, Costa Rica, CABEI, etc.) --- then, we would probably conclude that the Technical Assistance would be more expeditiously accepted and used. To me, U.S. Consultants of 1977 were not competing on a level field, and USAID needs to look at this – If it has not done so yet -- as an Agency-wide problem.

- In my opinion -- if this problem has not yet been addressed – then either the appropriate USAID Office or the USAID Inspector General should undertake an Agency-wide study (a) to determine whether other Recipient Governments are also reluctant to pay the salary and benefits of U.S. Consultants when financing is with Loans; and (b) whether the U.S. Congress and/or the USAID need to change laws or policies so that T/A – which is available from U.S. Consultants – can be financed, or even obtained from other source places, under a more competitive mode.

PART K. MY CONCLUDING REMARKS

As noted in this chapter, Panama was an exceptional family post. Education, recreation, sightseeing, and shopping facilities could not have been better. From a professional point of view, my travels were heavy, but I kept the family together; I learned a great deal; I made many friends; visited many parts of the various Central and South American Countries; and wrote some valuable reports and recommendations.

The Office of the AAG/LA had excellent U.S. and Local Audit Staff. As a whole and looking at performance in hindsight, the AAG/LA Office did many exceptional audits, and most were very complex reviews. In fact, some covered complete sectors of Central American countries. Besides the above 3 detailed examples, here is a very short list of some other reviews that were done during my time in Panama:

- The Agricultural Development Program of Costa Rica; the Agricultural Sector Loan of Costa Rica; the Agricultural Technical School in Costa Rica; The Educational Program and Televised System of El Salvador; the USAID Administrative Office of Panama; The Health and Population Program of Panama; the Rural Mobile Health Program of Panama; the Health and Population Program of Panama; and many others.

Without a doubt, this was an exceptional post, and everyone assigned to it was doing excellent work. And yet, the Office of the AAG/LA – including all related AAG/LA Mission-Base Office -- was closed in its entirety, and all of us were transferred to Miami, Florida. Yes, I did say Miami, Florida. Why? This is an excellent question. Let me give the reader a very quick and short response: the closure of the Regional AAG/LA Office in Panama represents one of the most irrational decisions that could only be made by a newly appointed –and very ill-informed -- USAID Auditor General. I provide more details of my harsh opinion in my next chapter (Chapter 10).

CHAPTER TEN
IRRATIONAL AUDITOR GENERAL JOINS USAID, MAKES ERRONEOUS POLICY DECISION TO CLOSE THE PANAMA OFFICE AND MIAMI BASE EXPERIMENT FAILS

PART A. INTRODUCTORY COMMENTS

Introduction. This chapter is divided into the following 6 parts:

- Part A. Introductory Comments.
- Part B. The Appointment of New USAID Auditor General and his decision to close the AAG/LA Panama Office.
- Part C. We Draft Dissenting Letter.
- Part D. My Assignment to Home Leave and Transfer to Miami Office.
- Part E. My Reassignment to A.G Washington Office.
- Part F. My Concluding Remarks.

PART B. APPOINTMENT OF NEW USAID AUDITOR GENERAL AND HIS DECISION TO CLOSE THE AAG/LA PANAMA OFFICE

Towards the end of my 2 ½ year tour in Panama, a new Auditor General (R. Ganl) was appointed and took over the USAID Office of the Auditor General in Washington.

Decision to Close AAG/LA Panama. Almost immediately after assuming his office, this political appointee made the decision that operating a Regional Office from Panama was just too costly because it entailed assigning technical personal and their families, and paying the rent on our homes, as well as the education costs for our children, etc. So, he made the decision to close the

Regional Office in Panama and move it to Miami, Florida. Yes, you read right. His idea was that USAID would rent a space for the Office of the AAG/LA close to the Miami Airport, and staff assigned to that office would spend almost 95 - 98% of their time on travel. His rationale was that the staff -- mostly U.S. Auditors who were not bilingual in Spanish would cover the same huge area – Central, South America, and the Caribbean from Miami. The assignment to Miami would be considered a "Rotation Assignment" since the U.S. staff in Panama were career FSOs.

In Panama, rumors of R. Ganl's proposal spread like wildfire. Thus, we had a little preparation time. Ganl came to Panama together with the Director of USAID/Washington Audit Office (R. Des). He met first with Fred S. and Jim Gr. He then assembled all of us, and, with his odd beady-eyed look (he did have "beady-eyes"), he gave us his decision. He described his reasons for moving the office to Miami (the high housing and education costs) as well as his plans to place the office close to the airport. Most of us thought his decision was ludicrous. In fact, it was crazy and made no sense from any angle that you looked. As the meeting progressed, all the staff kept looking at each other – and asking, with our eyes – "…who will be first to dispute this dumb-ass reasoning…" Since we were all long-time professionals who were outspoken, not shy, and had the courage of our convictions, all of us (of course, me included) had the temerity of pointing out all the faults in his reasoning. We disputed his rationale and told him many facts:

- In Panama, the AAG/LA enjoyed free office space. By contrast, the AAG/LA would have to pay for office costs, and the costs would be substantial. What we saved in housing and education costs would be eaten by costlier airfares and the per-diem costs associated with hotel stays and food. All the U.S. staff were FSOs, and, as such, we were to serve in different overseas countries; being assigned to Miami broke the rules of our employment. We told him that the travel factor, at 95 - 98%, would be intolerable to ourselves and our families. People could have nervous breakdowns or would be quitting left and right. The marital situation would be untenable, and personnel morale would be disastrous.

He flatly told us that he did not give a damn (his words) about personnel and family hardships. He said that the options for us were clear – his implications were "…either you go or resign…." In other words, this political-self-righteous-beady-eyed nincompoop had already made up his mind, and no one was going to change it. He told us the Regional Auditor General of the Panama Office (Fred S.) would be leaving within the month and opening the Miami Office. The Deputy (Jim Gr) would be leaving in three months. The Panama office would be closed as soon as the school year was over.

PART C. WE DRAFT DISSENTING LETTER

After R. Ganl left, all the staff got together. We excluded Fred S. and Jim Gr. from the meeting because we did not want to get them in trouble. Of course, all of us were extremely angry and concerned that we were being transferred from Panama to a U.S. location without the benefits accorded to FSOs. We were also concerned about the amount of travel that would be associated with the move. Two or three colleagues (including my friend Chuck C.) said they would be resigning.

In any event, we decided to write a letter, to the USAID Administrator, dissenting with the newly appointed Auditor General. The letter disputed the Auditor General's irrationality on a point-by-point basis. We signed it and sent it. We don't know if it changed anyone's mind, but to our surprise, something did!

PART D. ASSIGNMENT TO MIAMI

No Choice, But Serve in Miami. In my case, I had been in Panama for 2 ½ years. Because I had never served in Washington, I requested to be transferred to the Auditor General's Washington D.C. office. However, when I got my transfer orders, I was ordered to go on Home Leave and be transferred to Miami. Since I already had 15 years invested as an FSO and over 20-years with the U.S. Government, I had no choice but to go to Miami.

We sold the two cars. Then my family (wife, four children, plus Sarge the German Shepard packed up and went on home leave for a period of time to Austin, Texas.

We had had such good luck with the old beat-up 1965 Volkswagen that we searched for and got a green Volkswagen station wagon in Austin. As some of you remember, these vehicles had the motor in the back, and you could hardly fit any luggage there. For that reason, we bought a luggage rack for use on the top of the station wagon.

We had a ball in Austin. Since we owned a home in Austin, there was no problem. We stayed there for a full month, traveled throughout Texas and to Laredo to see my mother and Monterrey to see Pauline's dad and family.

Time to go to Miami. Our vacation time in Austin went fast, but this gave us time to plan our stay in Miami. We decided we would buy a house when we got there. When it was time to go to Miami, we loaded up the Volkswagen. I drove my wife sat in front with my youngest daughter (Melissa), and the other three (Joe, Jerry, and Linda) sat in the back seat. We decided Sarge would fit nicely on top of the motor part of the car just behind the back seat. We put all the bags in the luggage rack on top of the car. Sarge was an obedient and noble dog. He laid in the back very quietly – at first.

- We had traveled no more than a hundred miles towards Houston, and different problems began. Old Sarge got too hot on top of the motor, so he jumped in the back seat with the kids. The back seat got too crowded, the kids started fighting with each other, and the disruptions got heated. We would stop at every rest stop, kids would let out some of the pent-up energy, and Sarge would stretch. Back into the car once again we went, and the fighting would start up all over again. Finally, Joe, the oldest, decided he give Sarge his space and move to the space on top of the motor. How he stood that hot motor, I will never know.

Our trip from Austin by road was fun. We stopped in New Orleans and saw the French Quarter. Nonetheless, stopping for breaks at night was a blissful time. When we would stop for the night, everybody (except Sarge) would jump into swimming pools and cool down. We finally got to Orlando, Florida. As planned, the following two days were delightful. We stayed in a nice motel, went to Disney World, and relaxed.

Part E. Reassignment To Washington AAG Office

Miami AAG/LA Closed. On the third day in Orlando, I called Jim Gr., Deputy in Miami, and was about to tell him that we were arriving in Miami the following day. He gave me a big surprise. Auditor General (R. Ganl) had either quit or been fired – we were later told that he was fired. The newly appointed Auditor General (Harry Cr), another political appointee, had now closed the Miami Regional Office. Since going back to Panama would be an embarrassment to the Office of the Auditor General and would admit a huge mistake, he had decided that the Latin American Regional Office would now be based in Washington D.C. The Miami experiment had lasted no more than three months – a monumental waste of human and financial resources for the U.S. government. In sum, R. Ganl made one of the most idiotic decisions a manager could make when he decided – against all our advice – to close the Panama Office and move it to Miami, Florida.

Jim Gr. told me: "Do not come here. This Office is now closed. Turn right around and go into Washington." Torn between happiness and confusion, we loaded up the station wagon the following day and proceeded to Washington D.C. Again, we took in the sights. For example, we saw the U.S.S. North Carolina, which is moored at Wilmington.

It was in North Carolina that we had a problem with the car. As mentioned before, Old Sarge did not like being on top of the hot motor, so he would jump in the back seat with the kids, and Joe, being the oldest, would wind up taking Sarge's place on top of the hot motor.

- Clipping along at 60 miles an hour, suddenly, I felt the steering wheel radically different. Just about the same time, I saw our front left tire next to my side window. While the car moved forward, that tire was racing backward – and fast. I saw the back car try to avoid the tire, but it hit the car and bounced all around. That sight – of the front tire being at the same speed level as the driver – was the weirdest feeling I had ever had. Because of the weight on the car, the little gadgets that held the tire, and the car busted, and the front of the car no longer had a tire. At the same time, our left front of the car dipped down, and somehow

– a miracle of God – we did not overturn. Somehow, I maneuvered the car to a stop. How, even to this day, I don't know. You have never seen a man so grateful that all of us, including the people in the car behind, were safe and sound. Later, I was told that it was fortunate that I had not aggressively braked because that would have resulted in the car's having overturned.

Getting the car fixed took one whole day. And we finally got to Washington D.C. a few days afterward.

PART F. MY CONCLUDING REMARKS

Yes, the Miami experiment was a disastrous failure. The closure of the AAG/LA Office in Panama – and the attempt to set up the Regional Office in Miami -- will probably go down in the USAID history as one of the most irrational decisions that could only be made by a very ill-informed and ignorant person who should never have been appointed as a USAID Auditor General.

In effect, this erroneous decision was costly to the U.S. Government in several ways. It certainly was unwise and costly. For instance, the rules of all FSO's employment were broken. All the local personnel were terminated or transferred to other U.S. organizations; these personnel were highly trained and a formidable asset to the Auditor General. All U.S. personnel and their family were adversely affected – children were withdrawn from schools and created emotional problems for some. Home rental contracts were broken, and costly terminations took place. We also lost a few of our best U.S. people, like Chuck C. and others; they resigned instead of going to Miami. All Office work was stopped and/or interrupted. Staff personnel doing work in other countries had to return to Panama to pack up so they could transfer to Miami. There were other types of costs – emotional, economic, and U.S. Government -- which can only be imagined.

Indeed, this was an idiotic decision which should never have taken place.

Chapter Eleven
In Washington, As A.I.C. Assigned Tough Jobs, Caused Change To CPA Ruling, Affecting Several U.S. Government Agencies, Questioned A.G. On Education Policy, Exiled To Pakistan

Part A. Introduction And Settling The Family In Washington

Introduction. This chapter is divided into 13 parts:

- Part A Introductory Comments and the Settling of Family in Washington.
- Part B. Reunification with my Friends.
- Part C. My New Friend Rudy.
- Part D. Lamenting Resignation of Some Friends.
- Part E. A Gullible and Scamming Person.
- Part F. Existing Alcoholism Problems in the A.G Office.
- Part G. A 1976 Futuristic Vision About the Enforcement of Drug Programs.
- Part H. A Special Review of the Opportunities Industrialization Centers International (OICI).
- Part I. Audit of The Asia Foundation and AICPA Erroneous Ruling.
- Part J. An Audit Plan of Contracts' Office.
- Part K. My Discussion on Education Policy of Auditor General.
- Part L. My Exile to Pakistan.
- Part M. My Concluding Remarks.

A detailed presentation of the chapter follows.

Settling Family in Washington D.C. When we arrived in Washington, we first moved to a temporary apartment in Silver Spring, Maryland. Once we had decided to live in Virginia, we moved from that apartment to another in the Arlanda section of Alexandria. We quickly found that locating and buying a house was something else. After considerable searching, we finally located a nice four-bedroom house in Fairfax County. We signed a contract to the house located at 4207 Duvawn Street in Alexandria, Virginia; however, the real estate agent helping us forgot to write in the agreement five key important words "…Time is of the essence…." Those five words created nearly two months of procrastination on the part of the previous homeowners, i.e., they would not move. Initially, Pauline had to drive the kids a considerable distance in the morning and pick them up in the afternoon, and for that reason, we bought a second car, a 1972 Chevrolet Impala.

Once the previous homeowners had moved out and we settled in, things began to fall in place. Joe started senior high school, and Jerry and Linda began attending middle. And little Melissa began going to kindergarten where almost immediately, they diagnosed a learning disability, which resulted in major complications to a later assignment to Kenya. Briefly, the USAID Inspector General (IG) inappropriately used this diagnosis to *investigate me (see Chapter 17) for a false accusation of committing fraud.*

In any event, the 3 ½ years that I was in Washington were good for us. We decided to increase the size of the house; so, we reduced the size of the basement area and make part of it into a combination bedroom and my small office. In the summer of 1976, we took a 15-day vacation to look for a place for Joe and Jerry's university studies. We visited 7 different universities, including William and Mary, the University of Texas at Austin, Southern Methodist University in Dallas, Rice University in Houston, and others.

By the time Joe III graduated from high school in 1977, he had applied (and had been accepted) by all the universities we visited. He chose William and Mary and graduated four years later with honors.

During his years in Virginia high school, Jerry played the guitar and sang in various school shows.

Linda graduated from high school in 1981. Since Linda was very intelligent and creative, I encouraged her to go to college. However, she did not want to do it. She worked in a couple of banks and restaurants and fell in love with a young man named Kendall Bucher and later followed him to California. They got married in Alexandria, Va. They had a daughter (Lauren). Sadly, when both Linda and Kendall passed on, Lauren lived with me for eight to ten years. At this writing, she is already married to Andrew De Laney, who is a fine person; they had their first child, a daughter, named Natalie Marisol De Laney), and born on February 23, 2022. She is just beautiful.

Despite her Learning Disabilities, Melissa went on to graduate and get a diploma from the Brush Ranch High School in New Mexico.

In sum, from a family point of view, things went well during the time we were on rotation assignment in Washington, D.C. I will now discuss work during the Washington assignment.

Part B. Reunification With Old Friends

When I got to the office in mid-1974, I was placed in a "Rotation Assignment" to the Assistant Auditor General/Washington D.C. office (AAG/W). The AAG/W was huge; there were over 30 people assigned to this office. I was happy to be reunited with my old friends from Vietnam, Panama, and other places. At that time, there were only about five Latinos in the Auditor General's Office. Carlos Cabrera Morales. Carlos and his wife (Carmencita) have always been like my brother and sister. Other Latino friends included Rudy C., Joe V., and Roberto F.

Part C. My New Friend Rudy

Carlos C and Rudy C were highly qualified professionals. Rudy C., an exceptional person, had excellent technical, administrative, and managerial skills. He could have easily been a Regional Auditor General anywhere in the world; however, he – like me and others -- was Latino, and there was some discrimination against us. He retired in Florida.

PART D. LAMENTING RESIGNATION OF SOME FRIENDS

Some of my friends chose to resign or retire from USAID – primarily because they were tired of traveling so extensively and of the irrational decisions that the big wheels were making regarding the closure of posts (like Panama, Colombia, etc). I was sad to see my friends, Chuck C., Fred S., and Jim Gr, leave the USAID; they were exceptional people.

PART E. A GULLIBLE AND A SCAMMING PERSON

The office had some people who were not too smart and did not want to respect employment rules. Let me tell you about one good example. Carlos RC often played pranks on some of the gullible people. Hank L. sat at the desk in front of me. He was odd and not the brightest. He would come early in the morning, pick up some work papers, tell me he was off somewhere, return in the afternoon, leave the workpapers and quit work. One day, Carlos came over and wrote on a piece of paper, "You were called by Mr. Lyon, please call him. If he is not there, please talk to Mr. Bare. Tel. 202-xxx-xxxx). Hank came, picked up the note, and dialed the number. I heard him say: "May I speak with Mr. Lyon? He is not there…May I speak with Mr. Bare? (a long pause). What? You say this is **the Washington Zoo,** and someone is pulling my leg…." All hell broke loose. With murder in his eyes, he was looking for the person who had left the note. Although I burst out laughing, I claimed not to have known. (Note: Later, Hank was caught in a scam, where he had two jobs. That is why he would come in the morning, pick up his work papers, distribute newspapers, run errands for another company all day, and then come back and leave for home – giving the impression he had been working for the Agency all day. He was immediately terminated. This guy's 5-cylinder brain was really running on a minus 5 cylinder mind; his greed sacrificed a good-paying job).

Because of the good-natured pranks that Carlos played, Gino P would frequently ask him, "Carlos, what are you going to be when you grow up….." The answer would always be ridiculously funny, and Gino P would laugh in short garrulous spurts and chomp on his cigar. Gino P. was later transferred to Pakistan, and he and I worked there and continued to be good friends.

PART F. EXISTING ALCOHOLISM PROBLEMS IN OFFICE

One of my friends had a serious drinking problem. All it would take was one drink (of Vodka). He would not come to the office and be "lost" for a week. Carlos C. knew his habits well and would consistently be the assigned person to go pick him up, get him into a hospital, and have him return to a productive life. One time, while posted in Panama, my friend was assigned to go on TDY and do a special assignment in Honduras. My friend went missing for a week. Frantic, the office sent Carlos C to find him. He found him at the beach in San Pedro Sula (Honduras). He had gone native -- no shirt, no shoes, and zonked completely out of his mind. To cajole him, Carlos gave him more liquor, convinced the airlines to accept him, carried him on the plane, and got him to the hospital in Panama, where he spent 20 days. There were a few similar instances where even his wife would get involved. She would call the police, have him thrown in jail, and then have him hospitalized. Yet, he was a fabulous man, an excellent professional, and a good friend.

It was the nature and pressure of our work, but alcoholism was unusually high within the Agency. I just do not know. But my friend was not the only one to suffer from such an illness. There were at least twenty others, including myself. I was a "Maintenance Drinker," which means that I would go to work each day, return home, eat dinner, drink four or five scotch and water, go to sleep, and be ready for work the following day. At parties and cocktails, I would get zonked. I did this type of drinking for over 25 years until I quit in 1988. I haven't touched a drink since.

PART G. A 1976 FUTURISTIC VISION ABOUT THE DRUG ENFORCEMENT PROGRAMS

For a long time, I have had a special interest in the use of the "weed," as well as the conversion of "coca leaves" into a form of medicine. My interest dates to the time when I was assigned to Peru, went to its Altiplano (high mountains), got sick with altitude sickness, and was given and drank two cups of tea from coca leaves. The tea cured me within two to three hours. Therefore, this part is particularly interesting to me.

Here is some background. On/about June 18, 1971 – and using The Controlled Substance Act of 1970 as a basis -- President Nixon declared a policy known as the "War on Drugs." The policy, which continues as of this writing, was designed to serve as a deterrent and massive attempt at curbing, the flow of illicit drugs into the United States. Thus, there was a big emphasis on assisting less developed countries to eradicate narcotic-related crops, like coca, poppy, and marijuana. (Note: These drugs are listed on Schedule 1 of The Controlled Substance Act.). There has also been an effort to implement "crop substitutions" and encourage farmers and others to stop growing these crops and start growing other types of products, like coffee and cocoa. [75]

- (Note: Briefly, The Controlled Substance Act of 1970 contains five Schedules listing distinct types of drugs and categorizing them in diminishing order according to their dangerous effect. Schedule 1, which lists the most dangerous drugs, contains a long list of drugs (including Marijuana or Cannabis, cocaine, opium, etc.) under three types of sub-categories: "…(a) the drug or other substance has a high potential for abuse; (b) the drug or other substance has no currently accepted medical use in treatment in the United States; and, (c) there is a lack of accepted safety for the use of the drug or other substance under medical supervision…")

Based on the Controlled Substance Act, a high USAID official requested a worldwide study of drug control programs. The question being asked was whether restrictive drug programs, and a desired related "crop substitution" programs were, in actual practice, effective and made good economic sense for use in developing countries.

As a result, sometime in 1975 or 1976, Carlos C and Frank A. were assigned to do a worldwide study of the "Drug Enforcement Assistance Programs." Their task was to determine the practicality of assistance programs and related policies applied to the different countries.

---

[75] These programs are now called "alternative development" programs.

Being the best of friends, Carlos and I would frequently talk and interchange ideas about his study and I help him in drafting their draft report. After visiting a series of different countries, in South America and the Far East, including Bolivia, Peru, Colombia, and Thailand, the team, with my help, authored **a report that argued against continuing the U.S. drug control policy.** The team's analysis showed that Farmers in Bolivia and other countries would not be receptive to having their coca or cannabis eradicated and would not accept a crop substitution approach. Why should they? The base product (coca leaves) is their livelihood. Farmers in the Altiplano (high altitude places like Bolivia) use it to ward off hunger, and altitude sickness and drink tea made from coca for medicinal purposes and even as soft drinks.

In fact, I can personally attest that coca leaves have some sort of medicinal properties. My experience with coca leaves dates to 1963, when I was assigned in Peru to review the PL 480 Food Assistance Program. To do the study, a local person on my staff, a chauffeur, and I traveled by car from Lima to Arequipa, and from there to Puno and Cusco. I got extremely sick from what the locals call "soroche" (altitude sickness) crossing the 19,000-foot mountain range from Arequipa to Puno. I was going every which way – extreme headaches, vomiting, diarrhea, the works. At those altitudes, you can become dehydrated real fast. By the time we got to Puno, I was so sick that I thought death was near. As soon as I got to the hotel, the hotel manager said, "I will fix you really quick." They gave me "Mate de Coca" -- a tea made of Coca Leaves. All it took to fix me up was two or three cups of that tea. I was good as I could be within three hours. So, I can attest that coca leaves can serve a great medicinal purpose.

The Audit Team concluded that demand for the drug in the U.S. would continue to grow. They also felt that the production of the illegal crops helped improve economic conditions, as well as improving living conditions at the source. For that reason, attempting to stop or curb the flow of drugs in the United States seemed like a lost cause. Most importantly, they found that there was too much profit being made at every step of the way -- from the farmer to the end consumer. In short, they recommended a three-prong approach that would eliminate the systemic profit factor by taking the following steps:

a) Except for highly addictive drugs, legalizing most drugs.

b) Instituting required regulations so that the U.S. could obtain revenues through the taxation of the sales of illegal drugs.

c) Establishing drug addiction clinics in the U.S to treat addicts in the same way that the U.S. treats alcoholism. The proceeds of the U.S. taxation on drugs would pay for the drug addiction clinics.

When I reviewed and helped rewrite the draft report and the recommended solutions, I thought their points were correct. Their recommendations had a futuristic vision but did not address either the past or the present of the condition. I also felt that the top people would not accept such radical expression of opinions.

When the Office Big Wheels and Agency politicians saw the team's conclusions, they were all rattled, and they were not about to change courses. Probably, they began to consider Carlos C and Frank A to be completely off their rocker. As a result, a good study never became exposed. The report was changed or canceled by either someone in the Audit Office or elsewhere in a high USAID Auditor General's Offices. In short, the failing drug policies were allowed to continue.

Were the team and their conclusions wrong? Look at what has happened in the past 56-plus years.

Since 1976, the U.S. has tried every conceivable enforcement avenue -- alternative development; crop eradication using aerial spraying and manual eradication; military support, including helicopters, arms, ships, etc.), as well as fences, the use of canines, and incarcerating people for even minor drug peddling or possession of small amounts of illegal drugs. This has been done to curb the growth or flow of Marijuana, cocaine, heroin, crack, etc. And yet, the supplying countries have not stopped producing drugs or manufacturing dangerous imitations. Why? Just as the team concluded in 1976, our country is the largest market for their products. In fact, since the 1970s, drug consumption in the U.S. has grown and evolved. There are now synthetic variations of drugs, including Crack, ecstasy, Molly, and others. If the U.S. demand for illegal drugs continues, and if profit continues to be high at every point of the system, the problem will persist and continue to grow. Just look at production statistics in Bolivia and Afghanistan. And just look at the constant newspaper headlines showing the ways drug traffickers avoid being caught.

Illegal drugs are made available in the U.S -- among them human mules, tunnels, submarines, and airplanes.... in addition, consider how the production of some illegal drugs, such as cannabis, has shifted to the U.S. using hydroponics and clandestine farms. The prison population continues to be increased when non-violent people are incarcerated for possession of minor amounts of illegal drugs or when someone smokes a reefer or is pictured puffing Mary Jane on a bong. Meanwhile, the drug trafficking cartels in Mexico and other places have expanded their operations to include gunrunning, kidnapping, murder for hire, etc.

From a medical perspective, were my friends and their conclusions in 1976, wrong? Not by a long shot. We have since found that using Tetra Hydro Cannabin (THC) in Marijuana for medicinal purposes can help tremendously to alleviate the symptoms of some diseases and conditions. In fact, as of today, twenty-seven states in the United States have either now legalized or decriminalized the use of cannabis for recreational purposes. Also, in 2013, Uruguay was the first in the Americas to legalize Marijuana throughout the country. From the CNN series on "The Weed," I understand that Israel is now researching and allowing the use of Marijuana, together with "coca leaves," for different medicinal purposes. Thus, the time has come for the remaining U.S. states to reassess this perennial problem and find more practical solutions. It seems to me that the recommendations made in that ancient USAID draft report, combined with more recommendations made by the Latin American Commission on Drugs and Democracy, are still valid and merit reconsideration. The recommendations need some minor modifications; for instance, the U.S. might want to adopt a high-profile publicity campaign – like the one on cigarettes – against the use of drugs. It is estimated that if drugs were legally sold and taxed at a comparable tax as alcohol or cigarettes, the tax revenue to the U.S. Treasury would be over $34.3 billion annually.

States Legalize Marijuana. It is most interesting that as I was writing and/or editing this section, many U.S. states have now legalized Marijuana; and a group of Regional Leaders – Former Presidents of Latin America (Brazilian Fernando Henrique Cardoso, Columbian Cesar Gaviria, Mexican Ernesto Zedillo) – presided, o/a February 13, 2009, over the Latin American Commission on Drugs and Democracy. They issued a report which encouraged the adoption of several policies:

a) the need to legalize certain types of drugs.

b) the need to find alternatives to eradication, interdiction, and penalizing drug use.

c) the need to treat drug users as patients and not criminals.

d) the needs to encourage drug debate within the U.S. (to find more realistic solutions to the drug problems.

Don't the above suggestions resemble the recommendations made by our audit team? In effect, the legal enforcement seems overloaded, and the U.S. policy goes counter to the philosophical nature (an illness) of the problem. Thus, if we were to hypothesize the outcome of finding a sensible resolution (to the drug problem) -- back in 1976 or today -- we probably would reach the same conclusion: not to throw good money into a wide spectrum of drugs.

- We should funnel resources against the interrelated problems: (a) drug addiction; (b) drug demand in the U.S.; (c) jail incarceration of addictive and sick persons; and (d) the pervasive Profit Factor that exists at every point in the system.

The findings of my friends at the time, were certainly "…a great view of the way the drug problem would look 50 years into the future…" It is now time for the U.S. to have more debate on this perennial problem to find more practical solutions. Just as in 1976, I still think the recommendations of my friends – combined with the recommendations made by the Latin American Commission on Drugs and Democracy -- make sense today.

A final note on my two friends: about five years after the study, Frank A. – a very young man in his 50s -- developed Alzheimer's disease, was hospitalized for many years, and passed away. Moreover, I recently learned that my good friend Carlos C. also had Alzheimer and has passed on. Carmen, his wife is also very sick. I hope that researchers urgently find a cure for Alzheimer's, Cancer, and Parkinson's, and all other diseases.

Finally, let me make one thing clear. I have never done, possessed, or dealt in drugs in my life, and I gave up alcohol over 33 years ago. So, I have no conflict of interest. My position only comes from professional analysis, hindsight, intuition, and old age ... I certainly believe in the Spanish

"dicho" (saying) that says "Mas sabe el Diablo por Viejo que por Diablo..." (...The devil knows more because of age, then because he is the devil...)

PART H. A SPECIAL REVIEW OF THE OPPORTUNITIES INDUSTRIALIZATION CENTERS INTERNATIONAL (OICI)

Work in Washington was heavy and very analytical in nature. Back in the early-to-mid 1970s, there were no Word Processors or computers with word processing software; so, report writing consisted of a lot of writing, and rewriting, and typing, and retyping.

As might be remembered, I was assigned to USAID/Washington on rotation, partly to acquiesce to my complaining about the need to upgrade my university education) and partly so I could be on non-traveling status. I really wanted to go back to a university to get my master's degree.

But.... surprise! Instead, I was once again placed on constant traveling jobs that required the skills I had. The jobs that were assigned to me were real "jewels." They were very complex jobs that only a foolhardy man either wanted or would voluntarily do. In reality, no one wanted to tackle them. Following are some brief examples:

One Friday afternoon, around 4:00 PM, in August 1975, I was called into the head office of the Regional Auditor General for Washington. Seated there was the AAG for Washington, the Deputy AAG, and my immediate supervisor (Billy Ab.). Without fanfare, I was given a thick "Highly Classified" file with 78 civil and criminal allegations and told that I needed to be in Philadelphia, Pennsylvania, by the following Monday morning to supervise a team composed of myself, one assistant (Jon), and a team of five Filipinos contracted from a Certified Public Accounting (CPA) firm. Without ever working with this team or having seen the allegations, our responsibilities were to investigate all the financial records and allegations made against a Black Organization called Opportunities Industrialization Centers International (OICI). This organization was founded by a well-known Reverend Leon S. and had technical programs in a few African countries. USAID was providing 99% of all funds for this organization.

My jaws just fell, and my blood pressure went sky high. I kept asking many questions. "Why the urgency?" “How long had they known about the allegations? I also asked them why someone else had not been sent to do the job and why they had waited until this afternoon to foist such a complex investigation on me. I noted that the investigation should be assigned to the Investigations Office of the AG. I told them I needed time to do research and prepare myself. No one would answer. I left the meeting with the package that they had provided and with a great deal of frustration and anger. I just had that certain feeling that all three (especially Billy Ab.) had known about the investigation– and “sat” on -- the case for quite a long time. Billy Ab. was an operator, who was a smooth talker, and knew how to “talk a good game (meaning B.S. his way out of anything.)”

After working, at my home, all Friday night and all day, and all night on Saturday, I found that the allegations had been made in April 1975 and were five months old. No office wanted any part of them. The Office of Investigations of the USAID Auditor General said they were overloaded (that was nonsense); and no “Anglo” wanted to do the study because the head office in Philadelphia was in a black neighborhood. There was fear of reprisals by the Black community. This is the reason why the team was composed of a Mexican American (me), the Filipinos, and one non-senior Anglo (Jon). There were seventy-eight different allegations; over 35 of them were against the director (his name was Dia), and he was second in command to the Reverend). The remaining forty-three allegations were of systemic and procedural violations. Some allegations were juicy, involving sex in the office and sexual harassment. The organization's bookkeeper had made many of the allegations, and he had been promptly terminated.

To help my wife, I took my two sons (Joe and Jerry) to Philadelphia with me – and during the subsequent free weekends, we visited New York City, including the Empire State Building, Times Square, and the Statue of Liberty. I remember Times Square was seedy at the time.

Anyway, by the time I got to Philadelphia on Sunday afternoon, I had sorted, organized, and separated the duties and responsibilities of all the team members. Early on Monday morning, the team got to know each other, and we met with the Reverend. With a great deal of sincerity and professionalism, the Reverend told us that he knew of the allegations, saw the need for our study, and opened the doors of his organization to us. In other words, he was fully cooperative. While I assigned the CPA firm to review the financial records and my assistant, Jon, to research the non-controversial items, I took the 35 most sensitive issues.

A few days later, Jon and I met with the former bookkeeper in the restaurant of a hotel. I bought lunch for the three of us. He gave us a nice briefing and confirmed most of the allegations. I let Jon write up the notes from the meeting and I gave pertinent financial leads to our CPA team.

As I said, the controversial items were jewels. **Several ladies had submitted allegations of sexual harassment. I met with them on an individual basis. The first lady that volunteered to meet with me was a very light-skinned-freckle-faced young Black woman, maybe in her late 20s, friendly, direct, and outspoken. Her name was Millie. She answered my questions bluntly and without a semblance of embarrassment or compunction. Me: "Millie, you say in your letter that Mr. Dia… would not give you a job unless you slept with him. Is that right?" (Millie) "Of course it is right. I actually had to f..k (her words) the bastard a few times to get the job (there was a small pause), and then she continued "…actually, he was not a bad lay…but his f…king is not the issue,.." And she would raise her head slightly towards me, flash a big smile, size me up to see my reaction, and continue to give me further details and explanations.** There were other juicy responses from her. She confirmed some of the other allegations about other women. So, when I talked to the other ladies, and they gave similar answers, I knew the information could be relied on. The other ladies were not as descriptive, but they sometimes used the same type of "Millie's" distinctive language.

There were also allegations of high personnel turnover; we reviewed 57 files of people who had quit and talked with a few of them. Most were due to personality conflicts with the Director, and **the letters minced no words, calling him ignorant, a mother f..ker, other choice words, and challenging him to duels**. Other allegations said there was reverse discrimination because no Whites worked in the organization; they were all true. The Director often deviated on trips to Africa to different countries to visit girlfriends. I analyzed his passport and determined who paid for tickets. And so on, the review went. The review took a month, but most of the allegations were correct. In fact, the financial situation of the Organization was most precarious, and it was not being managed in an efficient manner.

In the end, I (we) confronted the Director, in front of, the Reverend at our exit conference. When confronted, the Director flinched a few times – especially about his affairs with women as a pre-condition to employment. The Reverend was very quiet during our entire presentation. We had the facts, and it was an easy confirmation of our conclusions. We had a very successful and uneventful stay. The Reverend agreed that the organization needed to correct the problems noted by the audit team. In addition, we found that subsidiaries of the OICI were not submitting expenditure reports. Promptly after we left, the Director was terminated or transferred to other parts of the Reverend organization. When we completed our report, we referred the matter of the non-submission of expenditure reports to our counterpart AG Offices in Africa, and the final report to the Auditor General for further review and actions.

I still remember some of the -memos and correspondence I found in the files – rough language, no mincing of words, no diplomatic language, and the use of the "F" word was most frequent. I had never seen such language in official correspondence, and I never saw those terms used again in other organizations.

What is interesting is that once this job was over -- and although they had not wanted to be associated with any part of this assignment before -- every big wheel in the various offices (AAG, Investigations, Project Office, Investigations, others) wanted to either lead or march as a part of the triumphant parade. My reputation as a professional soared, and I had unwittingly marked myself to be assigned to do several more complex and unwanted jobs.

Part I. Audit Of Asia Foundation And Finding An AICPA Erroneous Ruling Which Affected A Number Of U.S. Government Agencies

As part of a four-man team, I participated in an AAG/ Washington study of the Asia Foundation in California – this was sometime around August

1976. The team consisted of Billy Ab. as the "Supervisor," me as a second, and Willy M. as specialist on contracts, and another junior auditor. The Asia Foundation was based in San Francisco, California, and Billy Ab only joined the team to see San Francisco.

<u>This organization was founded by the Central Intelligence Agency (CIA).</u> The CIA, USAID, and other U.S. government organizations had provided about $60.3 million over a 7-year period to finance programs covering numerous countries in the Pacific. Yet, no one had done studies to evaluate its technical programs or its financial integrity. Once again, people seemed hesitant to be assigned to such a complex – and supposedly sinister – organization. However, I my study of the Asia Foundation was a good one. The Asia Foundation was a well-run organization but also had complex problems. The Foundation employed exceptionally well-prepared personnel whose writing style and ease of the English language I still remember and wish that I could equal them; they were admirable and fabulous. The whole Foundation staff was fully cooperative with the team.

Nevertheless, the review resulted in my identifying a most unusual situation that was caused by an erroneous ruling issued by the American Institute of Certified Public Accountants (AICPA) and which affected many of the U.S. Government organizations.

- Simply put, then, there is a difference between an "Obligation" (which is only a "commitment of funds"); a "Reimbursement" (which normally takes place after the Contractor or Grantee begins to implement the project and has made an "Expenditure"); and an "Accrued Expenditure (which normally takes place at the end of a period and has not yet been claimed by the Contractor.
- In instances – like the Asia Foundation – USAID "Obligates" funds at the time the contract or grant is signed. This means that it only sets aside the funds. The Asia Foundation began to sign "sub-projects" (many of them) with people and organizations in the Far East. These subprojects are then implemented during period which lasted months, years, and/or not done at all. Thus, these signing of the sub-projects only means that it is a "commitment" on the part of the Foundation. It is neither an Expenditure nor an "Accrued Expenditure." However,

according to the (at that time) erroneous ruling by AICPA, organizations were instructed that they could claim the commitment as an "Accrued Expenditure."

- My study of the technical sub-projects found that the Asia Foundation followed the "Accrual" form of accounting prescribed by the AICPA. Although Asia Foundation's sub-projects lasted three and four years and were sometimes cancelled, the Foundation was reporting all funding for activities as having been "accrued expenditures" at the time that was sub-obligating the funds for a project. The Foundation was declaring funding for a project as completely accrued -- even in cases where the project was canceled. In such instances, it kept the funds and did not return the money to USAID.
- Since Willie M. was a contract specialist, I confirmed the practice with him; he had seen this as the usual practice in several other organizations. However, he had not questioned it because the AICPA had rendered a ruling on the appropriateness of this method of accounting for the funds.
- To me, the theory and practice were not coordinated. In other words, USAID (CIA and other donor U.S. Government Organizations) was disbursing funds prematurely. And the Asia Foundation (and other Private Voluntary Organizations) was receiving the funds and investing them until the fund were disbursed by them to the subproject and/or then retaining them when the sub-project was canceled.

The problem affected several U.S. government agencies dealing with Private Voluntary Organizations (PVO) or those organizations which had similar programs. Once we got back to Washington, I wrote the problem up. Although there was some discussion on the subject, we finally informed the General Accounting Office (GAO) of the problem. The GAO confirmed the problem, got involved, and described the situation to AICPA on November 8, 1976. Once the AICPA became aware of the problem, they changed the rules. The monetary savings to USAID and the other U.S. Government agencies were probably incredibly significant. This was a terrific achievement which was deserving of an important award.

Yet, I was not to hear again about the disposition of the issue until February 1979. By then, I had been in Pakistan for one year and transferred to Egypt. Based on a cable request from the Inspector General (IG) seeking worthwhile achievements in the last couple of years, my name was submitted in connection with AICPA change to its rules. The Office might have gotten an award; however, I have never gotten even a simple honorable mention. This troubled me for many years. But like they say "C'est la vie." My feelings at this stage of my life are that I helped the U.S. Government save a significant amount of funds.

PART J. PLAN TO REVIEW CONTRACTS' OFFICE.[76]

During one of my assignments in the Washington Office, the office asked me to design a comprehensive review plan to evaluate USAID's Office of Contracts and Grants. One other person helped me. This huge office was managing requests from the technical offices, advertising for the services, identifying the best supplier to do the work, negotiating with that company or organization, and preparing the required legal document (contract, grant, Indefinite Quantity Contract or IQC, or other).

One of the first things we did was to determine the number of active documents (1,908) at the time and their total value ($635,407,000). These were the total active contracts, grants, and documents that the AID/W Office of Contracts and Grants had generated for the AID/W technical offices alone. It did not include multiple and bilateral agreements with the different countries, administrative costs, salaries, P.L. 480 or Commodity Import Programs, Cash Grants, etc. But the statistics give a feel for magnitudes and other interesting information related to this office.

Anyway, the active documents and total value were then reassembled into 12 different profiles so we could analyze the statistics from different perspective. Each of the 12 perspectives were then divided into internal controls points which needed to be evaluated for possible problems. Once all our study was completed, I handed the program to one of the supervisors

[76] Based on Attachment B of an Audit Plan For The Office of Contracts and Grant Management, dated April 20, 1977

(Russell A.); he was most impressed. I don't know whether the complete study was ever taken. However, Russell Aulik was so impressed with my plan and talked to me at length and many times. He and I got along beautifully.

- I was very fortunate that Russell was the person who looked at the Contract Office Program. After Egypt and Israel renewed relations, USAID activated an assistance program for Egypt. Russell was appointed as the Regional Inspector General in Egypt. He requested my transfer from Pakistan (next chapter) to become his second in command.

PART K. DISCUSSION ON EDUCATION POLICIES WITH AUDITOR GENERAL

There were other similar jobs, but I will not get into them. Anyway, after nearly three years of doing complex jobs and being on the road a great deal of my time, I wrote a memo to the AG (Harry Cr.); I complained to the AG that I had only been able to attend two-night courses and had been rejected for several short-duration courses. The guy did not even answer. So, I finally got fed up with the situation, made the necessary appointment, and complained to AG Harry Cr directly. This was a guy who had worked as a Senator's Aide; enjoyed his drinks and had replaced the previous biddy-eye nincompoop. That day, I found him equally non-responsive. With his bloodshot eyes, he listened to my litany of complaints and reasons why I should be allowed to be in a sedentary job and allowed to get my master's degree from a university. He nodded a few times and did not say much. All he mumbled was that he would investigate it. So, we shook hands, and I left.

PART L. EXILED TO PAKISTAN

Not a month went by, and the Executive Officer (a guy named Gene C.) called me to his office. He was clear and to the point – "You are being reassigned to Pakistan." My objections were strong and strenuous: "For medical reasons, my wife and family cannot be cleared for that post, and I already have been separated from the family while being assigned to Vietnam." Gene flatly told me: "We hire the employee, not the family -- you are going … if you don't like it, you can resign your commission…." Not being in Foreign Service himself, Gene was espousing a wrong tenet. So, he and I had a most unfriendly conversation exchange. However, with close to 24 years of U.S. Government service, I was not to make a stupid decision that would forfeit retiring in 5 to 7 years. So, there was no option but to go to Pakistan. **This also accounts for why I was never able to get a higher degree than my BBA. However, the superlative-job and educational-training I got has been extremely valuable.**

PART M. CONCLUDING REMARKS

Let me explain that an assignment to Pakistan was the equivalent of living in Russia and being assigned to Siberia. No one wanted to ever volunteer to go there for several reasons. First, two "memorable" and "difficult" guys – Jack R. and John E – oversaw, and managed, the regional office. Second, the travel factor was between 80 to 90% -- to countries that were backward like Afghanistan, Bangladesh, Nepal, Yemen, etc. Third, the Regional Office was in Karachi and not in Islamabad, where the U.S. Embassy is located. Fourth, in 1977 Karachi did not have good schools or health facilities.

In sum, as I saw it (and still do), this was not a routine reassignment; it was an exile because I had raised a policy issue – on enhancing the education of our people – which was not of interest to A.G. My treatment reminded me of a personality (Aureliano Buendia). In a book, written by a Colombian Author Gabriel Garcia Marquez called *Cien Años de Soledad* ("One Hundred Years of Solitude.") The book covers four hundred years of history in a fictitious location called Macondo. Here is a condensed version of the scene that comes to my mind:

- Aureliano Buendia had formed an army…. and had fought over twenty different battles. He had won all the battles; but was caught after the last one. His adversaries sentenced him to be executed by a firing squad. Placed against a wall in front of the firing squad, Aureliano put his arms across his chest to scratch lacerations on his armpits. The firing squad held their fire because they were thinking: "…poor guy, don't shoot yet, he is saying his last prayer to his God…." In turn,

> Aureliano was looking at the firing squad and thinking, "…Asi es la vida, tanto Joderse uno, para que lo maten cinco maricas…" (…This is the way life is, you work your ass off, so hard, only to be killed by five damn fools…" (Note: At the propitious moment, the battle was over, and Aureliano lived but was exiled to continue other projects…)

In my case, I had worked so very hard during my rotation assignment in Washington. I had reviewed organizations that no one wanted to touch. I had been instrumental in changing rules rendered by the AICPA, which affected a number of Agencies of the U.S. Government; I had designed an audit plan to do a comprehensive review of an entire USAID Contracts' Office; I had helped my friends in a 1976 futuristic vision of the enforcement of drug program, and I had done other good jobs. And now, I was being punished for speaking out on the need for a better education policy. So, without further ado, I will borrow Aureliano's thinking "…. Asi es la vida, tanto Joderse uno para que lo exilian dos cabrones…" But, unlike Aureliano, I was not saved by the bell. My first "Rotation Assignment" to Washington ended, and I was never able to upgrade my formal education or get my Masters' Degree.

But, let me end this chapter with the great irony that ensued after my transfer. While I was serving in Pakistan, Gene C. (the Executive Officer) was caught in a scheme related to his practices in awarding contracts; he was booted out of the agency and prosecuted for his criminal acts. Also, AG Harry Cr. moved or was forced to move to another agency. I have no pity for these two; they got what they deserved. Moreover, aside from the loneliness and the intensive travel factor, my tour in Pakistan (and the different assignments) was not at all bad. In fact, it was very decent (see next chapter).

CHAPTER TWELVE
IN PAKISTAN, ON SINGLE STATUS, VERY DIFFICULT TEAM LEADERS, EXCELLENT INVESTIGATIVE STUDY, VISIT TO A THATCHED BORDELLO, HIGH TRAVEL FACTOR, DECENT TOUR

PART A. INTRODUCTORY COMMENTS

During the one year that I was assigned to Pakistan, I only worked on three audits -- one was an investigative review that took eight months, and two others. Many diverse types of situations took place during those reviews. For this reason, I have divided and will describe the events into 10 Parts and many sub-parts:

- Part A. Introductory Comments.
- Part B. My Arrival in Pakistan and Meeting with Two Managers.
- Part C. Family Planning Allegations in Bangladesh and Pakistan.
- Part D. My return to Pakistan.
- Part E. Life in Pakistan.
- Part F. A Complex Agriculture Job in Yemen.
- Part G. A USAID Operational Expense Job Assignment in Afghanistan.
- Part H. Creation of the Office of Inspector General.
- Part I. My transfer to Egypt.
- Part J. My Concluding Remarks.

PART B. MY ARRIVAL IN PAKISTAN

Pan Am Lost Bags. Within a month of my talk with Gene (Executive Officer), I packed only my air freight items, bought and shipped a used Chevrolet Vega, and was on my way, on Pan Am Airways, to Karachi, Pakistan – all alone.

Arriving in Karachi with a carry-on bag, I found that Pan Am had lost my two bags. I was greeted at the airport by Gino P, a very jovial Italian friend of mine. Gino and his wife were past-middle age, and he loved to smoke and chump on cigars. His garrulous manner and funny contagious laughter were well known. He was a great friend, died a few years later, and is sorely missed. Anyway, he was, aside from the two Chiefs, the only person in the office at the time; all the staff was on assignments in Pakistan and other countries. Gino's greeting to me was, "Joe, you came alone, huh! What do you want me to fix you with: a little boy or a female lamb…" and then burst out laughing at his own joke. It was a reference that I would lead a very lonely and monastic life. (And I did).

They put me up in a huge, beautiful house. After leaving my carry-on bag in the house, I went to the office.

Meeting With the Two Managers. The greetings by Jack R and John E were quick and to the point. "Glad you are here. We have a lot of work where you can help…we have received a bunch of allegations that family planning commodities (condoms, oral pills, and others) are being diverted, converted into other things, and sold in Bangladesh, Pakistan, and India....get ready because you are traveling to Bangladesh, on your first job**, three days** from today. You need to find out what is happening to the Family Planning Commodities and if the condoms and/or pills are being converted or sold; in other words, what is happening to them? Give us your passport so we can get you a Visa and the air tickets." The meeting lasted about 20 minutes.

About the Office Managers. These were my assessments of the two managers I made after my return from Bangladesh.

Jack R. had a very nice wife but a very serious alcohol problem. He would come into the office, grab a coke, lock his office door, and by ten o'clock, his face would be red as a beet, and he was zonked. And he was one of those mean ones when they get drunk. He was later transferred to Panama, experienced all kinds of trouble, retired, and within a couple of years, died of alcoholic damage to the body.

John E had a very wealthy wife who was an exceptional stock market analyst, invested in only six stocks, had timing on those six stocks down to a science, waited for the stocks to hit low, bought, and got out when stocks hit high. Whenever she went to New York, members of the New York Stock Exchange would fully host her stay. She developed cancer and died a few years later. But John E. was quite different. He had an excellent technical background but was an extremely negative person. He would be agreeing with you and at the same time shaking his head in a negative manner. He frequently functioned as Monday morning quarterback and arguing with him always became heated. He was a hard supervisor. Neither Jack R nor John E was a good personnel manager.

Together, those two people were rough. However, to be fair, they had many countries to cover, and whoever was assigned there would be traveling 85-90% of the time. So, that was to be another of my assignment to Siberia for complaining to the Auditor General against his assignments and education policies. Or could the assignment to Pakistan have been planned because the job was too complex, and that office did not have enough or qualified people to do the job? To this day, I just don't know.

PART C. FAMILY PLANNING ALLEGATIONS IN BANGLADESH AND PAKISTAN

Trip to Bangladesh. Since Pan Am could not find my bags, it gave me $100 (or thereabouts) to buy some clothing. Buying clothing in Karachi is not as easy as going to a shopping mall in the U.S. I bought some mismatched shirts and trousers as well as some underwear; Gino loaned me a bag, and I was on my way to Bangladesh on the third day as planned. (Note: Pan Am eventually found my bags, made efforts to return them to Virginia, and finally delivered them to Karachi. I was not to see my two bags until I returned from Bangladesh close to 3 months later.)

Bangladesh. In 1977, Bangladesh was quite a backward country. Dhaka, its capital, only had two half-decent hotels. So, I stayed in one (The Parbhani Hotel). It was not the best, but, for me, it was adequate, and it was in the center of Dhaka. In fact, I was to stay in worse hotels in other countries later. Anyway, I had brought a bottle of Johnny Walker with me (just in case a Cobra bit me).[77] All alone in the hotel the afternoon I got in, I got a little ice, unpurified water, which gave me a gift of amoebic dysentery -- and had a few drinks.

The Memorable Beggar. The night was coming fast. So, before it got too dark, I decided to walk around the center of Dhaka and then eat. As I walked outside the hotel, I looked at the little shops that were now closing and milled with the huge multitude of people. I got tapped on the shoulder a couple of times.

As I turned around, I faced the most horrible sight that I had ever seen. It was obviously a man. However, **he had no face, his nose was destroyed, his bare eyes stared at me, and the fingers of his hands and feet were nothing but stumps.** If you have seen Michael Jackson's "Thriller," you will remember the scene where people, in torn clothing and zombie-like appearances, are coming out of the graves. This will give you a good idea of what I saw in front of me. It was a beggar, in torn clothing who wanted me to give him money. And for the first time in my life, I was staring at the face of a human being in the **last stages of leprosy**. **Pieces of skin seemed stuck in places where his face and hands had been.** I had never expected to see anything like that. The sight terrified me. Talk about hallucinating; my mind began to work overtime. I began to search my memory on whether I had taken too many drinks. Boy, I sobered up fast. Scared stiff, I got some money, gingerly passed it to him without touching him, and hurried back to the hotel. I was to see this beggar and other similarly deformed people affected by leprosy many times after that. Knowing I was an easy target, they would wait and follow me until they got my donation. Every time, I was terrified but full of pity. Even today, over 40 years later, I sometimes have nightmares; I see myself walking among the more deprived, and I still see the faceless and deformed persons affected by that terrible illness.

[7777] I used to drink like a fish; however, I stopped drinking over 33 years ago.

Yet, now I know a few more things about leprosy that I did not know then. First, the disease, also known as Hansen's disease, is caused by a bacteria called Mycobacterium leprae. For some reason, this disease has a very high incidence of occurrence in countries like India, Brazil, Myanmar (Burma), Nepal, Tanzania, Mozambique, and others). The number of lepers in Bangladesh rose from 11,500 people in 1996 to 14,500 in 1999, declining to 10,000 in the Year 2003. According to scientific writings and the World Health Organization, the disease, in most cases, is easily curable – when diagnosed early. Fortunately, in more recent years, there has been a definite decline in the rate of infections throughout the world – from 753,262 in 2001 to 296,499 in 2005. Let's hope that leprosy can soon be completely eradicated from this earth.[78]

The Bengali President's Visit. Although I soon found friends – that I had met in Vietnam -- who would invite me to their home for a drink or a meal, the days that followed were intense with activity at the U.S. Embassy, the USAID Offices, and many other related Offices. The allegations were, and I eventually found, that Family Planning condoms were being converted into "hand gloves" and sold. In addition, birth control pills were being sold on the open market instead of being provided free as required by USAID. The hard part was trying to understand the background of the program and get a feel for such a huge health activity. It would also be hard to develop an approach for the review to prove or disprove the allegations.

Since I was doing the job by myself, most of the time, I would go back to the hotel at night, continue to review more material, write as I went along, have a couple of drinks, go to a restaurant to eat, and come back. I would then have a few drinks and go to sleep.

One late afternoon, when I came down the hotel elevator, the doors opened. I saw the lobby basically vacant, with only an extremely well-dressed high-ranking military man coming into the hotel. As I stepped out of the elevator, two men in uniform pointed a rifle, spoke to me in Bengali (which I did not speak or understand), grabbed me by the arm, turned me around,

---

[78] Statistical and other information come from Internet www.cdc.gov/nczved/dfbmd/disease_leprosy-ti.html.

placed me against a wall, and did a body search. Confused, bewildered, and not knowing what was happening, I readily cooperated. One of the hotel clerks came to my aid and told the security people that I was an "American." I finally had the sense to ask what this was all about. I was told that the President of Bangladesh (maybe Shahabuddin Ahmed) was in front of me. I was quickly placed back into the elevator, and I proceeded sheepishly back up to my room. I ate much later that night. Security was tight because the previous President had been murdered two years earlier.

Regression Analysis. During the next few weeks, I analyzed all international agreements, and documents, talked to many people, accumulated all kinds of statistical information – population by villages, commodities being sent there, etc. -- and developed a type of statistical analysis known as "Regression Analysis" which gave me a lead on disproportionate commodity assignment by areas. Regression Analysis is an exceptional tool that I frequently used throughout my career; here is a very simplified example:

Village	Commodities	No. of Population	Factor	Regression
A	1000	400	2.5	37.2%
B	1500	500	3.0	44.7%
C	2500	800	3.1	46.5%
D	3500	950	3.7	54.9%
E	6000	250	24.0	357.3%
F	8000	450	17.8	264.7%
Total	22500	3350	6.7	100.0%

As shown, the above example includes the names of the villages, the number of commodities (separated by condoms, Pills, Foam, etc.), and a number of people in the village. The Factor represents the number of units per person in the village. The Regression Factor identifies villages receiving disproportionate amounts of commodities. Here are the conclusions of the above example. The proportion of commodities being sent to Villages A, B, C, and D are below 100% within acceptable ranges and thus can be discarded. However, Villages E and F -- with 357% and 265% -- represent possible problematic proportions that deserve closer scrutiny.

This is how I identified 21 (of numerous) places (clinics, areas, or villages) that showed a disproportionate number of commodities and needed to be personally visited.

Sterilization of Women. USAID assigned a vehicle and a driver/translator to me. Over the next few days, I visited all kinds of health facilities in Dhaka and close-by villages. One facility was carrying out a Voluntary Sterilization Program and other related family planning programs. As in other facilities, the doctors were very open with me. At the time of my visit, there were about 10 - 12 women waiting to be sterilized. The doctors asked me if I were willing to see the procedure. Since I had seen how IUDs are placed inside a woman in Costa Rica, I said I was game. The sterilization of women is very different than the placement of an IUD. The doctors made me wash, put on a sterilized doctor's gown, and participate in the laparoscopic tubal ligation procedure, i.e., closure of the fallopian tubes. The sight of the two small belly cuts, a little blood, and the inside of the women's belly made me somewhat woozy. In fact, my knees became weak.

The great thing is that at least I was able to get a feel for the sterilization process. After seeing the clinic and talking to the doctors, I could now discard this area from the overall objectives of the audit. There was no possible way commodities or services could be diverted through a women's womb. Also, the doctors gave me a first-hand seminar on how many condoms were defective and broke easily. They also discussed how easy it would be to turn condoms into latex gloves and for birth control pills to be sold on the market.

Visit to Villages. It was time to go to the villages outside of Dhaka. The first series of trips I took was to several places near the border with India. We did some of these trips by car, but others were done by rickshaw and sampan. They were rough. For instance, to get to the village of Heschel Bazar, in the Comilla district, the driver and I had to start at 6 AM, travel by road, rickshaw, and sampan, and then return by the same methods to Comilla to sleep. When I visited some of the villages (one example was Heschel Bazar) close to the Indian border, I felt most uncomfortable. What I saw in those villages was that the number of condoms sent to the village was excessively relative to the size of the population and that there had been no effort to account for the condoms. Moreover, the village did not have a warehouse to store the condoms. People acted oddly; they looked rough, and they did not want either to cooperate or provide information. For the first time since Vietnam, the back of my hair stood up, and I became afraid for our lives. We saw the places and left fast. There was something about those villages that were not right. Even the driver was nervous. We did not stay in them long enough to find out what it was – and I certainly was not going to stay around to see the smelting or techniques used to convert condoms to latex gloves, balloons, or whatever.

Human Rights Abuses. The second series of trips were to places very close to the border with Myanmar (at the time, the country was known as Burma.). That sure is a beautiful part of the country – very green vegetation, a lot of water, huge palm trees, little islands, shacks, and people living in the midst of them. Because at the time, the people lived on the little islands and did not have modern communications such as radios, they could not be informed about coming typhoons. Therefore, so many people die in Bangladesh during these and other natural disasters. Sometimes, we would stop, and I would go by sampan to nearby villages – in little island-like areas – which seemed to have been forgotten by the modern age (no electricity, gas, etc.) As we traveled by sampan through the many rivers, women (with their children) would come out of their shacks and look at us. They would quickly go back inside, cover their faces, hide their children, and then peek at us.

We eventually got to a Guest House--a nice cabin-- in the middle of nowhere. After we had been there a short while, a helicopter began to circle close by. The driver/translator quickly ran inside the house; I did not understand why. So, I sat on the balcony of the cabin and witnessed the things that were taking place. The helicopter came down and hovered around four feet from the ground. **Suddenly, a few prisoners, with their hands tied behind their back, began to be thrown out of the helicopter.** Without thinking, I took some pictures. Suddenly, a Bengali Colonel came up to me, and asked who I was and what I was doing there. I told him and tried to explain that I was not interested in his military operations. He took the camera, destroyed all my valuable film, and told me to leave the area immediately. **What I had just witnessed was a gross human rights violation by Bangladeshi soldiers who had captured Burmese people and were now dropping them from the helicopter with their hands tied**. When

I got back to Dhaka, I briefed my two or three interested offices on this incident.

The Thatched Brothel. That day must have been one of the craziest I have ever had in my life. I left the area without a word and arrived in the port of Chittagong (the second-largest city in Bangladesh) late that afternoon. The hotel was much better than the ones I had stayed in Dhaka. Just to keep your interest, that night, I wound up going to a house of ill-repute. Let me say this; going to any red-light district or a brothel is not my style. But it did happen. So let me tell you about it.

When I got to Chittagong and got to the hotel, I met a guy from another U.S. agency stationed in Dhaka. We had a couple of drinks in the hotel, chatted, ate, and then decided to take a walk. Walking along a street close to the hotel that night, some guy on a rickshaw (a three-wheel pedal bicycle with a seat for two on the back) asked us, "…you want to see Chittagong?" Not having anything else to do, we hopped on the rickshaw, and he started pedaling. My friend said something in Bengali or Urdu, and the guy smiled. He took us to this place. Let me describe the basic setting, and then use your own imagination. **It** was a place where the floor was muddy and dirty; the stench was just like a pigpen; the roof was thatched; there might have been 40 to 60 small (cubby) rooms in an extremely limited space, and each individual room seemed to have only enough space for one bed. The rooms were separated by wallpaper or thatched mats. Young girls (12 to 15 years of age) went in and out of those rooms with unkempt and dirty clientele. Strange sounds and moaning could be heard all over. Walking half-naked, sweaty, and dirty were two or three bearded and disheveled men wearing nothing but a thong-like – Tarzan style—a piece of clothing covering only their private parts and obviously stoned, zonked, and/or in some sort of a trance.

I took one look and saw the horrors of young children stolen, sold, or forced – by family needs or circumstances -- into prostitution. So, I decided right there and then that I would merely ask for a Coca-Cola. The young girls would come over in bunches of 10 to 15. They would touch and feel me all over. My friend had disappeared into one of the rooms with one of those young girls. So, I was asking for a Coca Cola and the girls kept trying to convince me. Some were brazened enough to reach into private areas – without eliciting any reaction. The "Madam" – a nice – oriental looking --

woman in her 30's -- kept eying me in a funny way. I kept asking for a Coca-Cola in English, and they kept jabbering in Bengali or Urdu. So, communication was zero. The madam kept pointing to one or another young girl and talking to me (expounding their virtues); I kept asking for a Coca-Cola. Finally, the Madam pointed at me and to her temple (like saying, yeah, I got an idea), went out, and came back in a short while. She motioned for me to follow her. I thought to myself: ". at last, I am getting my Coca-Cola." She took me to another room where some seemingly romantic music was playing, and in the center of the room were two gay guys dancing up a storm....

What came to my mind at that time was that the Madam's power of deduction was truly fantastic. She had seen that I did not seem to like girls. So, the next obvious conclusion was that surely, I must be gay. For the next hour or so, I sat in a corner on a stool, just missing a dunce hat to look more stupid, feeling completely out of place, desperate to get back to the hotel, afraid to leave by myself (muggings and murders were common, especially in a port city), hearing all kinds of noises, watching strange going-on, smelling the crud, anxious to take a shower and rinse the scene away, and sipping at the Coca-Cola that I eventually got. As I sat there, the Madam passed me a few times; each time, she would look at me; she would shake her head, and I kept wondering what was going through her mind. There was a virile man who had rejected the girls, then he had rejected the boys, and now sat on a stool, drinking a Coca Cola in a "first-class" house of ill repute. Was she impressed, bewildered, or did she think I was some sort of a weird Freak getting his kicks from listening to the sounds and/or enjoying the smell of the place? I just know that I have you laughing now.

In all seriousness, however, the conditions that these poor underaged girls and children are forced to endure are horrendous and an affront to any society. Some of these children are sold or voluntary sex slaves; others are victims of human trafficking. As stated in Chapter 3, "...Annually, between 700,000 and 4 million people are bought and sold as prostitutes, domestic workers, sex slaves, child laborers, and child soldiers...of these, between 14,500 and

17,500 ..are women and children who are trafficked specifically into the United States.... ."[79]

Whatever the case, they are all exposed to the HIV/AIDs Pandemic, violence, and a host of diseases. So, they need help, and with the way that the TVPA of 2000 has been changed and all the findings which now make the TVP Act of 2017 Law, hopefully, these poor girls and boys are now being helped. Please see Chapter 3 and the discussion about the TVPAs for the modifications and coverage.

That was the first time I visited such a horrible house of ill repute in a developing country -- and as you have seen, my Machismo was probably questioned. But Machismo is such a relative term – when viewed in the Middle East and the West. In Chapters 13 and 20, I will tell you about the cultural customs of men holding hands, hugging, and kissing other men on the cheek, and dancing with them at weddings. I have done that out of diplomatic and cultural necessities.

PART D. RETURN TO PAKISTAN

I worked around the city of Chittagong for a few more days -- and, no, I never again even got close to the Thatched Bordello. Two to three weeks later, I was on my way back to Karachi. I had been in Bangladesh for nearly 3 months. Because of the type of information that I had gathered, my friend Gino P. (now deceased) was assigned to help me, and we continued doing this type of work within Pakistan and other countries for 4 more months. Later, a new auditor (Guy 3) was assigned to help us, but he had a strange personality and was not much help.

Assignment as Sponsor. On one of my trips back to Karachi, I was assigned as a "sponsor" to a newcomer and his family. I will call him Guy 3, and he was coming with his wife and nine (9) children (you read right – 9). Extremely devoted Catholics, both the husband and wife, did not believe in family planning. Finding a house for them was awfully difficult. We

---

[79] An Internet Article called "USAID Combating Trafficking in Persons," www.USAID.gov/our_work/cross-cutting_programs/trafficking and a "Summary of the Trafficking Victims Protection act (TVPA) and Reauthorization FY 2017. And the Internet Section on "U.S. Code Title 22, Foreign Relations and Intercourse FindLaw"

eventually located a house that had six bedrooms, and the USAID General Services Group modified it so the family could fit in it.

- Guy 3 was really something. At the airport, he was extremely upset that the Agency could only provide him with a modified six-bedroom house. He had expected a bigger place. At the office, Jack R, John E, Guy 3, and I had a nice talk with him to clarify things. We explained to him the problems we had experienced in fixing the house for him and his large family; there was nothing more anyone could do. For some reason, the Office quickly assigned Guy 3 to help Gino and me. He turned out to be more of a problem than a help. During the review, I had done a sufficient amount of initial survey work to identify areas of concern that we needed to fully develop into findings.[80] I would assign him an area of concern and expect him to determine the magnitude of the problem for use in a finding. He would analyze the issue for maybe an hour or two, return and then tell me, "There is nothing there…." Wow! After talking to him and showing him the results of my initial work, he would finally tell me, "If I continue to develop all facts of that area, it will take me close to a month or two; the easiest thing is not to find anything. I need to get home…my family needs me…." Although I felt some pity for him, I quickly dumped him and avoided him -- to the extent possible -- as an assistant from then on.

A Suggested Way to Get a Confession. One odd situation took place in Pakistan. During the work there, we identified some persons responsible for diverting condoms and pills. Of course, they were not about to admit the crime because it either meant they would face jail or have their hand chopped off. They could also be facing death. The Pakistani lawyer assigned as a consultant told us several times: "Oh, hell, do not fuss too much about it; we can make him or them talk and confess very quickly. All we do in Pakistan is strip the person nude, hang him by his feet, whack him a few times all over the body and at the soles of his feet, and he will confess in a matter of an hour…." We gently explained that this type of investigative coercion is simple

---

[80] The initial phase of an audit is known as the "survey" phase. During the survey phase, the auditor is attempting to determine whether a problem does or does not exist. The main part of the audit is spent fleshing out the concerns or problems identified during the survey phase.

torture. Of course, we did not accept the offer. But it gives the reader some ideas about how some countries extract confessions from people. Are all those that are executed guilty?

Overall Remarks on Family Planning Allegations. We had a good time for the five months that Gino and I were on that family planning job. In Islamabad and other major cities, we stayed in first-class hotels. We were also able to frequently visit the U.S. Embassy compound, where there was a club that served alcohol.

Moreover, our work was very fruitful. We found very complex problems in Bangladesh and Pakistan and eventually wrote a number of classified and unclassified reports. We also provided needed information to other "special" offices to pursue the criminals. I never saw the final disposition of the cases because I was transferred to Egypt within six months after we completed the work.

At the end of the family planning assignment, I was still somewhat annoyed that I had been sent to Bangladesh only 3 days after arriving in Pakistan. But I was nevertheless happy about my accomplishments. I had seen a great deal of Bangladesh and Pakistan. I had learned a lot about family planning tools, and how pills can be commercialized, and condoms converted into latex gloves and then sold, diverted, and smuggled to other countries. I saw some memorable sights. *And, oh, yes, how can I forget – I had been to the best-thatched house of ill-repute of Bangladesh.*

PART E. LIFE IN PAKISTAN, A MOST INTERESTING EXPERIENCE

Life In Karachi. Since I was traveling 90% of the time, the 10% of the time I stayed in Karachi was not particularly bad. I moved to a small two-bedroom apartment in a small Pakistani compound – near a Mosque -- where I could hear the "Call to Prayer" many times each day. Some beautiful girls lived in the family compound. They spoke English but hardly ever spoke to me (one of the taboos).

The little compound had a guard who was somewhat deformed. He had a (slightly hunched back, arthritic-like hands, and one leg shorter than the other). He stayed alone at his post and liked to sit outside my window and serenade me every day with his singsong reading of the Koran. I enjoyed that very much. Sometimes, I would walk out, give him a Coke, and sit close by. I would just listen, record him, and let him know I enjoyed it. At various parts during his readings, he would stop, hold my hand, in the Pakistani form of friendship between men, and, in Urdu or Farsi, say a few sweet nothings (that I could not understand), maybe to let me know that he appreciated my friendship and for listening to his chants. I keep wondering how many times he might have told me to convert to Islam and its advantages – a simpler religious concept, there is only one God, Muhammad was his prophet, marriages are mostly arranged, a man can have up to four wives at one time, divorce is easy – just throw three stones, etc. However, he probably never mentioned the discrimination and treatment against women or the self-flagellation sacrifices of some Islamic groups (such as the Shia).

- I saw such fervent penance in one of my trips to Peshawar. While Gino (a coworker) went to other parts of Pakistan, and then I went to Peshawar. One Friday, while on the second floor of my "First Class" hotel, I heard a great deal of chanting and commotion. From the balcony, I witnessed a long parade of maybe 8 people in each row; most of them were grown men, but there were some younger people, all chanting and marching in cadence, flogging/whipping their bare backs with whips that had spikes. Some with knives were slashing at their heads. There was blood spattered all over their bodies, heads, face, and street. That parade lasted close to an hour, giving the reader some idea of the fervent belief that the Shia have. Each year, they celebrate the "Ashura," or the date when the favorite grandson of Muhammad (Hussein Ibn Ali) and all his family were killed and dismembered. The Shia believe that only the heirs of the fourth Caliph, Ali, are the direct descendants of Mohammed.
- What is amazing about this flagellation are the similarities to the Catholic custom that takes place each year in Taxco, Guerrero, and other parts of Mexico during the season of Lent. Just like the Muslims, the Catholics, at least in Taxco, march through the streets, chant prayers, and flog themselves in an identical manner. Their backs are bare; the whips have spikes; there is praying or chanting; there is

profuse bleeding, and pain. *But there is a tremendous and radical religious difference.* Although the floggings and physical damages are identical, one is for the death of a Muslim -- the grandson of Muhammad. The other is for the death of Jesus Christ – the representation of Christianity.

Since I am not the most religious person, the significance and the difference are difficult to decipher or understand.

Overthrow of the Prime Minister. The political situation of Pakistan is always hard to understand. Pakistan has always had multiple political problems; perhaps, it is because of the way its constitution is written, or maybe it is the way the government is structured. The military also plays a huge role, and corruption is a huge problem.

Anyway, when I got to Pakistan, Zulfikar Ali Bhutto, who had been President of Pakistan for two years, was now the Prime Minister of Pakistan. On July 15, 1977, the General of the Armed Forces, Muhammad Zia al-Haq, engineered a coup. He became Chief Martial Law Administrator and overthrew the Bhutto Government. As usual, the U.S. broke relations with Pakistan but later renewed them. General Zia pursued his quarry Bhutto through accusations of murder. Bhutto underwent a series of trials, was released and subsequently recaptured, endured torture (no water for days), and was then jailed some more. After I left Pakistan, Zulfikar Ali Bhutto was finally hanged on April 4, 1979. General Zia met his maker, on August 17, 1988, in a fiery airplane explosion and crash that also claimed the life of the U.S. Ambassador. Bhutto's daughter Benazir Bhutto took over her father's party and was assassinated on December 27, 2007. Thus, Pakistan is not a politician's paradise.

Talking about Pakistani law, justice is meted out in a harsh way. Every Friday in Karachi, the central plaza was always full. Fridays were the days when sentences were conducted for several types of criminals. Very often, the confessions to the crime probably had been coerced. Depending on the crime, the person judged to be the criminal, either received a number of lashes on their bareback, had his right hand (thieves), or his neck chopped off. Women who had committed adultery were stoned to death. I was invited to go see these proceedings, but I did not have that built-in curiosity. Although I read about the events in the local newspaper, I never attended such executions.

Golf Courses in Karachi. One of my friends asked me if I had brought my golf clubs and invited me to play at the Karachi Golf Club. We got there, and we got ready to tee off. I asked how many holes. My friend said there were nine, but they were a little rough. He said it with a smirk on his face – and I wondered why. I soon found out. There was no grass anywhere – just sand all over. The "greens" were made out of sand matted down with oil. Not being the best of players, I would hit the ball; it would go up, come down, sink in the sand, and not advance much. My score was very bad that day. They were equally bad the next two times I played there. Those were the only times I played golf on that Golf Course.

Ancient Colonoscopy. Anyway, since I was all alone, my office friends and their families would drop by my small apartment, have a few drinks, and keep me company. I was also invited to my colleagues' homes and cocktails frequently.

Since I was not a good cooks, I usually got into my old Chevrolet Vega and drove to a good restaurant. I would eat Nan and a good spicy chicken tikka or a chicken tandoori. I also enjoyed eating a good lamb or chicken masala, or a good curry and foul (beans). Man alive, being of Mexican descent and a lover of hot spicy food, I loved that hot-spicy Pakistani food. Before long, I ate hot peppers with eggs in the morning, spicy chicken curry at noon, and then spicy lamb masala or curry at night. At night I would chase the food down with some scotch and unpurified water. And so, the hot spices or the water – most certainly not the Scotch (of course not) -- were bound to affect my system.

- I noticed some bleeding when I used the bathroom. Scared, I went to the recommended Pakistani doctor. He was good and thorough. He poked around my stomach and asked a bunch of questions. Do you smoke? No. Do you drink? Like a fish (then). Do you have worries? Constantly. Have you ever had amoebas? Several times. What medications did you use to get rid of them? Johnny Walker red or black label scotch. Have you ever had an ulcer? No. Have you ever been diagnosed with cancer? No. Is your family here? No. Are you having sex? Sex, a foreigner in Pakistan; ask me another question. Do you eat spicy food? Love Pakistani food. He shook his head a couple of times, paced the office floor up and down, checked some books, gave me a dire look, and finally prescribed a full **colonoscopy**.

- A colonoscopy in those ancient times (1978) and in Pakistan was not the gentle procedure observed in the U.S. these days. As verbally instructed, I ate soup or something light for two or three days before the day of the procedure. Then, I went to the local hospital on the indicated day, took my clothing off, put on one of those crazy gowns that open on the back and expose your rear end, and laid down on a table. Without any explanation or further ado, the male nurses gave me a huge enema full of soap and water. That jug must have been 17 gallons, or so it seemed. Was it comfortable? Think again. When I was ready to blow up, I asked where the toilet was. The nurses gave me a nice surprise. The toilet was at the end of a half-a-block long corridor, not close by as I expected. Faster than Superman, I put on my pants (modesty, you know), tightened every muscle I could (yes, especially those muscles), shuffled down the corridor barefooted, and tried to open the toilet door. There was a further surprise: Someone was in there. By then, the nurses and non-patients had a laughter attack. Anyway, somehow, I held on. Someone else came running, as desperate as I was. I growled a couple of choice things in Spanish, English, Vietnamese, and Urdu --- No One, but No One, was going in there – but me. After the door opened, I rushed in. The other poor soul must have had fits. After sitting there for what seemed like an eternity, I went meekly, subdued, without a semblance of pride back to the procedure room and, scared, laid down on the table all over again.

- While I remained wide-awake, the doctor came with a 10,000 (or maybe, as someone else has said a 20,000) foot long black tube. Later, my best friend Carlos would coin the black tube a name: “El Negrete" (or the Black Tube). The doctor told me to bend my legs and began inserting El Negrete in neutral zone. As that tube advanced, the air was pumped to expand the intestines, and my eyes – wide open – almost popped out of their sockets. On and on and on it went. It seemed like the procedure would never end. There were times when I thought I was going blind, but on second thought, it was only that the procedure had made me cross-eyed. My thoughts ran wild. I kept imagining things. Any moment, I thought, that tube would come out of my throat. And then, as quickly as it began, the 25,000 ft long (by then, it had grown to 25,000 feet long, or so it seemed) Negrete was being withdrawn. Since air pumped in must always come out, the explosions that followed were most embarrassing and were heard throughout the clinic. But I was all smiles when the doctor told me that my stomach was slightly irritated by the spices, but I was otherwise ok.

I know you are laughing. Yes, the ancient colonoscopy procedure used on me in Karachi, Pakistan, was certainly an event to remember, but this procedure seems to have come a long way in modern times

Not surprisingly, however, I still love Pakistani, Indian, and Mexican food, as well as hot-spicy food in general. I eat them whenever I get a chance. Anyhow, now you know how colonoscopies were done in 1978.

PART F. A COMPLEX AGRICULTURAL JOB ASSIGNMENT TO YEMEN

A Complex Job in Yemen. After the eight-month job in Bangladesh, Pakistan, and other countries, I was assigned, with Carl K. as my assistant, to a complex job in Sana'a, North Yemen.[81] Since Carl was coming along, the job was about 1 ½ months long.

Carl K. was a very nice person whom I had met in Vietnam. His personal life was interesting. He had met his wife (Van....) while in Saigon, courted her, and married her. He liked to brag about the wedding night. They had stayed in Van's house. The morning after their wedding, he had come out of his room and showed Van's mama and papa a bloody garment, celebrating the fact that the girl had been a virgin. Since then, some of her friends have laughed and told me to disregard the "virginity" aspect of the story. Both Carl and Van departed Vietnam in 1975, just before the North Vietnamese conquered all of South Vietnam. Van had a younger sister (Kim) who escaped

[81] North and South Yemen were at the time considered separate coutries.

Vietnam with them. Since the U.S. Government only permitted born dependents to receive benefits (these benefits included travel, health, and educational benefits), Carl K and Van had gotten around the rules by legally "adopting" Kim as their "daughter." This is how they could travel together to different posts at U.S. Government expense.

Kim, a lovely girl, was about 16 years old. She would often come over to my apartment and talk to me at length. It was obvious that Kim did not like living in Karachi – she was too mature for her age and life was too restrictive. Also, Van (Carl's wife) was apparently carrying on an extra-marital relationship with a "Vietnamese Friend "--- a Catholic Priest based in Hong Kong. He frequently came and stayed in Carl's home. With Carl K traveling so much, he might have heard the rumors floating in the community but seemed comfortable with the arrangement. In any event, Kim would tell me that Van was not a very good person because she was very greedy, lied, cheated, and that she (Van) would sooner or later get into serious trouble. (Note: Van did eventually get into very serious legal problems. A few years after I retired from USAID, I read in a newspaper that she was to be tried in a court of law for something she had stolen from an assisted lady living apartment where she worked. I also heard that she tried to sever a finger from a dead lady just to take a valuable ring that the lady owned. However, I never found out what or the disposition of the case).

So, Carl K and I went to Sana'a, Yemen, by way of Saudi Arabia. Going back and forth through Saudi Arabia was always a real hassle. Even with diplomatic passports, we would not dare carry liquor or "dirty magazines" – and God forbid if your passport was stamped as having been to Israel! Even though we were in transit, the airport security – with their spotlessly white Galabias and red-checkered (headdress) Kafai's -- would confiscate our passport, make us sit in a guarded area, watch us almost every minute, just about escort us to and from the toilets, and return us our passports at the door of the airplane. Although we never got out of the airport, I will always remember Saudi Arabia with very negative thoughts and feelings.

We got to Sana'a and started work. Let me describe Sana'a as I remember it from 1977 as well as several years later when I would travel there from the USAID Office of the Inspector General's regional office in Kenya. Sana'a, at the time, was the capital of the Republic of Yemen. Sana'a sat on top of a mountain. The homes were really old, and many of the homes had windows somewhat lopsided. Most of the roads were normally unpaved and traveling outside Sana'a was hazardous. The altitude drops between the capital and the rest of the country in a precipitous manner. When traveling, you would encounter beautiful sights of castles built on top of hills and places that you would never expect.

The people were not the typical arabesque type. A little on the darker side, the Yemenis usually wore a quilt-like wrap-around type of dress and a headdress called a Kafai., The males also always wore a dagger-like "Gambia (or Jambiya)" in the center part of their torso; this signified their machismo. I saw an advantage to their quilt-like dress. Toilet facilities were unusual. Even at the airport, you would find the toilets to be a series of round holes on the floor with water around. Since they required squatting, the Yemeni dress was a definite advantage over pants. Anyway, once a week, the Yemenis would go to the center of town and buy "Khat," I understand that chewing Khat causes a "high" with some hallucinations.

Judging from the number of Internet sites today, Yemen has changed in ways that are good and not so good. The country remains beautiful but has been in a state of strife since 2011. In 1978, however, there was a saying**: "If Jesus Christ was to return to earth today, he would only recognize one place – Sana'a, Yemen….** "

Anyway, we started working in the USAID Office. It had no cafeteria, there was a small shack about a block away, so we would eat there. The owner/cook had been a thief; the evidence was that his right hand was gone. He made nice egg and/or tough steak sandwiches the best he could. I did not starve, and I ate there for more than a month.

Not a week had gone by, and Carl K got an "Eyes Only" Cable, meaning that only he could see it. When he came back, he was crying and told me that Kim had left home and was missing. They searched for her all over Pakistan, but it seemed likely that she had left the country. Her destination was unknown. I liked Kim very much, and I always treated her like one of my daughters. So, remembering the house of ill-repute of Chittagong, I really feared for Kim's well-being. According to instructions, Carl K. returned to Karachi to help with the search.

Once again, I was left alone. I traveled throughout Yemen and ate in communal Bedouin restaurants. These restaurants make exceptional cheese, lamb, and Nan food, and the food was usually shared among people in a group. We would sit cross-legged, in a circle, on the floor (no difference in ranks or jobs), with the food in the center, and dipped the Nan into the food with our fingers. I don't remember if everyone washed their hands, but we did not get sick. Also, the camaraderie that develops is extraordinary.

As usual, the study resulted in exceptional findings. I returned to Karachi. When I got back, to Pakistan, I was told that someone (maybe Van's Catholic priest friend) had bought Kim a flight ticket. She had traveled to Hong Kong, stayed there a few days, and was now, safe somewhere in the U.S. Since Kim was underage and a legal dependent (adopted daughter) of Carl and Van, they made legal efforts to bring her back to Karachi. I don't think that ever happened. Kim's safety in the U.S. made me very happy.

PART G. A USAID OPERATIONAL EXPENSE JOB ASSIGNMENT IN AFGHANISTAN

Afghanistan. My final assignment during my tour of duty in Pakistan was to Afghanistan as part of five-person team headed by Rick H -- a real fine person and an exceptional professional. Some decided to go by plane to Kabul. Three of us decided to go to Islamabad, the capital of Pakistan, by air and from there via road to see the Khyber Pass. Going from Karachi to Islamabad by air had its challenges sometimes. At that time, airline security was almost non-existent. Smoking inside the airplane was permitted. And there was one time when one person lit his little kerosene stove to cook his meals and almost burned the entire plane.

This time our travel to Islamabad was a breeze. Traveling via road in a USAID Chevrolet van was rough but not too uncomfortable. I vaguely remember passing Peshawar, a small city at the time and then maneuvering through the Khyber Pass. Traveling through the pass was a challenge because of the height of the mountains and the number of buses, trucks, cars, and people on that narrow road. But, other than some inconveniences, the trip was decent.

In Kabul, we stayed at the U.S. Embassy/USAID Guest House. All five of us drank like fish at night, so the stay and camaraderie were nice. Everything went smoothly.

Since the Guest House was close to the Soviet embassy compound in Kabul, we often took long walks close to the compound. One day, I remember taking a walk by myself. There were two couples talking on the sidewalk. The ladies were covered with a veil. As I was about ready to pass them, the ladies decided to say goodbye to each other and uncovered their faces to kiss each other. My mind still sees those beautiful green eyes and those beautiful faces. I will never understand why such beautiful women are forced to cover up their pretty faces in that manner.

Anyway, we left Kabul one day and it was just in time because shortly after our departure the Soviet Union decided to invade Kabul.

PART H. CREATION OF OFFICE OF INSPECTOR GENERAL

Transfer to Inspector General's Office. Let me back up in time a little. By the time I returned to Karachi from Yemen, the whole concept of the Auditor General had changed. As a result of the Inspector General Act of 1978 (as amended), we were no longer the Office of the Auditor General. The functions of the Auditor General were transferred to the new Office of Inspector General. Harry Cromer – the guy that sent me to Pakistan -- had been terminated nine months after my transfer. He was replaced by a new man (**IG#1**), who was now officially appointed as the Inspector General. **IG#1**, had been a Marine Corps General and, unlike Harry Cromer, was well qualified for the job, bringing good credentials to the organization. He lasted in that position for about 17 years and was well-liked for a few years. He was a good leader at the beginning and made sound decisions for a time. In chapters 16 to19, I discuss some aspects of **IG#1**s performance.

PART I. TRANSFER ASSIGNMENT TO EGYPT

When we returned from our TDY to Afghanistan, Jack R and John E called me into the office and gave me a cable from the recently appointed Inspector General. The cable said that since Egypt and Israel had signed the Camp David Accord and established a diplomatic relationship, USAID's assistance programs to Egypt would grow exponentially. For this reason, the Inspector General had decided to establish a new USAID OIG office in Cairo. Without delay, I was transferred to Cairo, Egypt as an Audit Manager, second in command to Russell A (the RIG/A there). In other words, I would be the Acting Deputy Regional Inspector General for Audit in Egypt.

PART J. MY CONCLUDING REMARKS

My transfer to Cairo, Egypt, was a blessing and a vindication. It meant that my family would be joining me as soon as medical clearances could be obtained, and I would not be traveling too much. **It also meant that as an Audit Manager, I was to be the Acting Deputy Regional Inspector General for Audit (DRIG/A) or the second in command of the biggest RIG/A Office. In fact, I was the first Mexican American to be assigned as de-facto Deputy Regional Inspector General anywhere with USAID.** This was an excellent recognition of my potential. One of my colleagues (Ernie G.) quickly bought my car (the Vega). I had bought the car for about $400; he gave me $200, and I was happy; the car had served its purpose and had not given me any problems. I was on my way within 15 days of being notified of the transfer. I had been in Siberia –oops, Karachi – a total of one year. I left some exceptional colleagues and friends; however, I can't say that Jack R and John E were my friends, but we did not have any significant confrontations.

CHAPTER THIRTEEN
IN EGYPT, UNDER NEW I.G., ACTING DEPUTY REGIONAL INSPECTOR GENERAL AND ACTING RIG, SELECTED EXCELLENT TEAMS, EXCEPTIONAL AUDITS AND TOUR

PART A. AN INTRODUCTION TO MY EGYPT ASSIGNMENT

Introduction. I was in Egypt three times – either on long-term assignment or on temporary duty. My first tour occurred when I was transferred from Pakistan in 1978, and I served there by myself for about six to eight months. After this initial tour, in July 1979, I went back home to Northern Virginia; I picked up my family and returned to Post. We remained in Egypt as a family until June 1981--before Anwar El-Sadat's assassination in October 1981. Towards the end of my second tour, two things took place: (a) I was appointed to an elite board to participate in an annual Personnel Evaluation Team to evaluate Personnel Evaluations in 3 or 4 FS Codes; and (b) there were some personnel problems in the Regional Office of Inspector General for Latin America. This office had been reopened again and was then operating out of Panama once again. However, the problems were very serious; accordingly, the IG. had once again closed that office, and now the RIG/LA was to operate from Washington D.C. As a result, I was transferred as a Deputy Regional Inspector General for Latin America (DRIG/LA) -- to smooth and help resolve the personnel problems. My final tour in Egypt occurred after I had retired from USAID. As an independent financial consultant, I was contracted by a Washington D.C. based contractor to be a part of a five-person team helping to develop a project designed to help Egyptian women in different ways. My participation was quick and insignificant but enabled Jerry, my son, and myself to stay in Egypt for nearly a month. Without a doubt, let me say that my assignments to Peru, Egypt, Panama, and Guatemala were the best overseas assignments I have ever had. From a family point of view, our time in Panama and Egypt can never be equaled. As the reader can well imagine, many different types of situations took place during those three assignments.

For this reason, I will describe some of the important events in the following 7 Parts and many sub-parts or sections:

- Part A. Introductory Comments.
- Part B. First Eight-Month Egyptian Tour (by myself).
- Part C. Brief Audit Examples of First Tour Reviews.
- Part D. My Home Leave and Return to Post with Family.
- Part E. Examples of CIP Survey and Reviews.
- Part F. Final Egyptian Tour (Visit) and Taxi Driver Hassan.
- Part G. My Overall Concluding Remarks on Egypt.

PART B. FIRST EIGHT-MONTH EGYPTIAN TOUR (BY MYSELF)

Introduction to the Egypt of 1978. Egypt's history and culture through its ages have been documented abundantly in many books that can be found in numerous libraries around the world. For this reason, I will not try to recount its fabulous history in this book.

Although the United States began providing Egypt with economic assistance before 1978, my personal experience in Egypt started in that year. It was a fabulous moment in the history of three nations. Three great statesmen-- Jimmy Carter, Menachem Begin, and Anwar El-Sadat-- had met in Camp David for 13 days and signed the Camp David Accords on September 17, 1978. On March 26, 1979, the same three leaders signed a peace treaty between Egypt and Israel. Before 1978, there had been seven intermittent short wars between the two countries. Thus, this historic Camp David Peace Accord ushered in a peaceful relationship between two nations that had not existed since the birth of Israel in 1948. Thankfully, even today, and despite the current political situation in the Middle East and in Egypt, the Treaty is still being honored by the two nations.

For the United States, the Peace Treaty represented an enormous international diplomatic coup. Israel and the U.S. were already staunch allies. In this new relationship with Egypt -- which is one of the largest Arab nations in the Middle East -- the U.S. was faced with peaceful opportunities but also with huge challenges. For this reason, the U.S. immediately committed an additional large amount of diplomatic, military, and economic personnel and resources to the Government and People of Egypt.

In turn, for Egypt, the renewed diplomatic relationship -- and, in particular, the increase of economic assistance provided by USAID was greatly needed and essential for a lasting regional peace. It would also demonstrate to other Middle Eastern countries how two opposing countries can co-exist without the fear of constant wars.

In such historical times, actions by the U.S. are usually quick – and this one was no exception. In no time, the U.S. began to tremendously increase its diplomatic presence as well as the USAID presence in Egypt and formulate the needed development economic programs that the country sorely needed.

As stated in the previous chapter, when this was happening, I had been assigned without my family to the USAID Regional Office of Inspector General in Karachi, Pakistan. By then, I had already been in Pakistan for nearly one year. My transfer to Egypt came with a sense of great urgency. In October 1978, I was given 2 weeks to wind up all my affairs. After being, without the family, and on travel status 90% of the time during the period I was assigned to Karachi, I felt extremely happy to be leaving this regional office.

Egypt was to be a fabulous assignment for my family and me. It lasted only three and one-half beautiful years. To make the story short: I was the de-facto Deputy Regional Inspector General (DRI/A/G) in Egypt while I was there. I was also Acting RIG/A/E for about 4 to 5 months whenever Russell, the RIG, went somewhere (Washington, or home leave, Rest and Recuperation, etc.). During the time I was in Egypt, we did some extraordinary studies.

Arriving and Living by myself In Cairo. My flight from Karachi to Cairo in late October 1978 was short and quick. I arrived in Cairo completely re-energized. I was met at the airport by Russell and Jean (his wife) and driven to a real nice hotel in the center of Cairo. On the way to the hotel, Russell told me I was to be his deputy and gave me a briefing on our office situation. He had hired one local auditor and a secretary. Four or five other U.S. personnel were to join us soon. We had a great deal of work to do. According to Russell, we had received two urgent requests for "assist-audits" from the RIG/A/Washington – one review covered Borrower/Grantee Contracts, and the other covered Participant Training Programs. In the assist audits, we were to do very extensive in-depth reviews, and any questions we raised would be replicated by other USAID audit teams on a worldwide basis. In addition to the two reviews, we had to do a survey, determine our workload, and establish work priorities. We agreed that our priorities were to: (a) help him hire 3 or 4 other local staff and one other secretary; (b) do the assist audits of the Borrower/Grantee Contracts and the Participant Training Programs of Egypt; and (c) make a survey of active USAID projects as well as determine the Egyptian government's economic assistance priorities.

I stayed in that hotel for a few nights until they found me an apartment in a part of Cairo called "Mohaddessin" (the Engineering City), in the center of the city. The hotel was plush. I had a room on the second floor, and to go to the restaurant, I had to walk down a stairway. As in Pakistan, the workdays were from Sunday to Thursday. We were off on Fridays and Saturdays. The first Saturday night in Cairo, I began hearing a great deal of commotion coming from the hotel lobby and restaurant area. And then, I heard a bunch of real loud shrilling screams. My imagination went wild, taking me back to my time during the Tet Offensive in Vietnam. I thought the hotel was under attack. The noise and screams continued, so I made my way to the stairs and peeked down to see what was going on. What a happy surprise! It was a beautiful wedding. And the screams, well, this was to be the first of many introductions to several religious, social, and cultural practices:

- This type of Egyptian "yodeling" is how they celebrate "happy events." Yodeling is an art where the women roll their tongues and make a real scary or happy sound.

As time went on, my family and I learned about some other good and bad practices. Here are some:

- With Sadat as President, the country was extremely friendly and peaceful. The crime was minimal. Foreign Women, particularly my daughters, were respected and safe.
- It is perfectly normal for like-sexes to greet or say goodbye to each other with a hug and a kiss on the cheeks.
- Like in other Islamic countries, arranged marriages are promoted because the vetting and matching – mainly by the groom's parents -- of the bride and groom is most thorough. For these reasons, marriages seem to last.
- As in other Islamic countries, in a gathering like-sexes keep themselves separated, and if there is dancing, men dance with other men, and women with other women.
- Ramadan represents a very Holy Month when the Egyptians fast for a complete month. At the end of Ramadan, wealthy Egyptians sacrifice an animal (or animals) and give parts of the meat to the poor.
- As in some Middle Eastern and African Countries where I served or went on TDY (Pakistan, Afghanistan, Yemen, Kenya, and others), parts of Egypt -- particularly in the villages – still performed a "surgical procedure" called "infibulation" (radical circumcision) on their female population. This practice goes back Thousands of years. Oftentimes, this surgery is performed when the female is still a child. In the case of infibulations, the female's genitals are either disfigured or, perhaps, mutilated, and the vagina is sewed up so that only urine can flow; these female parts are reopened once the girls are to be married. This ancient practice denies a woman full sexual pleasure and makes them an object – to be used by men for their pleasure and only for children bearing purposes. In Kenya, I was told that some circumcisions are done with extremely primitive and unsanitary surgical tools, i.e., a piece of glass, kitchen knives, etc.
- We also found some other practices, especially in the outlying villages, which we considered objectionable. Here are some examples: (a) female children were still denied an education, and (b) there were

honor killings of girls who lost their virginity before they were married.

- As we continued to live in Egypt, we noted two other unusual things. One was that most of the Egyptian population, especially in Cairo and Alexandria, lived in narrow and small houses which, from our point of view, were never finished. The houses always had a few steels meshes or bars sticking out – as if a second or third-floor construction was going to take place. When I asked about this unusual observation, the explanation some people gave me was that the city would assess an exorbitant tax if the house was totally completed. Minimal taxes were assessed for houses still under construction – boy, wouldn't it be great if U.S. cities would pass such ordinances?
- The next odd thing reminds me of the idiom, "…One man's trash is some other man's treasure…." Why? Well, because, back then, we noticed that the trash was always picked up on a daily basis, and the streets were always clean. Here is why: the cities had contracted with the "Zabbaleen (trash people)," who went around with their donkeys or carts and picked up all the trash. The Zabbaleen were the poorest of the poor people – about 50,000 of them – who lived in the outlying areas of the city. These people did not mind the dirty work. They would pick up the trash, take it back to their district, and sort them in different ways – iron, cans, aluminum, plastic, etc. They would recycle (sell) about 80% of the trash and either feed their hogs with edible "garbage" or use the rest as fertilizer. But…I understand that this type of recycling was discontinued between 1997 and 2003 – because the Egyptian Government did not want to address "…the Poorest of the Poor situation…." In addition, the Government felt it could modernize trash collection. As a result, the cities were inundated with trash and garbage on the streets. The cities and the U.S. Congress should learn a tremendous lesson from this.

My Apartment for Eight Months. In any event, I moved within a few days into a real nice 2-bedroom duplex in Mohaddessin that USAID had furnished. Living by myself, I quickly developed a routine of working hard, working late, reading Egyptian history, learning a little Arabic, and eating Egyptian food (in Cairo, Mohaddessin, or Zamalek), which is also in the center of

Cairo. I also took long walks and had my usual nightly drink of scotch and water. I visited the pyramids and other tourist attractions and did some shopping at the Khan El-Khalili market or other markets, usually on Saturdays.

Shopping at the Central Food and the Khan-El-Khalili markets in Cairo was always a riot. Price negotiations were intensive. Here is a sample:

Me (pointing to the item): Becam? How much?

Vendor: Echerin Piasters (20 Piasters).

Me (making a disappointed face): La, La (No) – hamsa (5).

The vendor would smile and laugh: La (No) – Ashara (10), and we would negotiate some and finally agree on a good price.

Sometime in January 1979, I asked Pauline to shop for a new car that we could use in Egypt. She (and the family) fell in love with a 1978 Dodge Challenger. It was a beautiful small car. The only problem was that it was only a two-door car and it got extremely crowded when all of us (6 people) made use of it. She then had the car sent to me in Cairo.

Meeting a Coptic Family at the Balloon Theatre. According to the Internet, the population of Egypt is composed of about 94% Muslims and 6 to 8% who practice the Coptic Religion. Without knowing the difference, Russell and I hired four persons who were practicing Coptic. I found there was a Coptic religion sometime in December 1978, when I met a member of that Church outside a live performance theater.

As I mentioned earlier, I developed a routine of working hard all day, going home, eating at home or in different restaurants, and then taking a long one or two-mile walk. A few times, I walked about two miles and looked at posters of the coming live performances in the "Balloon Theatre," which was located close to Zamalek. I wanted to see some of the shows, but they were all in Arabic, and I did not know whether I could follow the plays.

One time, when I was looking at the posters, I became aware that a young lady kept staring at me. Although I felt a little uncomfortable, I looked at her and nodded a "hello." Suddenly, she came over and said: "Salaam Al-akum, Etna Massari?" (Hello, are you Egyptian?) I said: "Al-akum Salaam, la ana no Massari." (Hello to you, no, I am not Egyptian.) Then, she said: "Etna Fahim

Arabi?" (Do you know Arabic?) I said: "Ana Amerikay, inti Fahim Inglese?" (I am an American, do you know English – for males, you say "Etna" and for females, you say "Inti'). She looked at me, flashed a big smile, and her English was flawless.

Her name was Shaddai Rizk. She had seen me a couple of times looking at the posters of the Balloon Theatre. Boy, in the next 20 minutes, she quizzed me to no end. I bet she found out a great deal about me – why I did not have blond hair, why I was in Egypt, whether I was married if I had a family and if they were in Cairo, etc., etc. She told me that she worked for an office in the center of Cairo and that her father had passed on. She lived close to the Balloon Theater with her mother and brother. Towards the end of our conversation, she told me that both she and her brother were going to attend a live performance in that theatre three days later, and she asked me if I would like to join them. I agreed to go with them with certain conditions: We would meet in a restaurant near the theatre; have an early dinner, and I would pay for all three tickets and restaurant costs. After some persuasion, she agreed. I gave her the money (the cost was extremely reasonable); she promptly bought the tickets, and I asked her to keep the tickets until we met on the third day.

As agreed, we met at a nice restaurant in the Zamalek area on the third day. We had a nice dinner and chatted. They were obviously sizing me up, I was evaluating them in an equal manner. They told me their mother had recent surgery (a hysterectomy) and could not come. They belonged to the Coptic religion and invited me to their apartment and church. They also told me that they were planning to immigrate to Europe, maybe Austria, within two months. My impressions of them were most favorable. During the fabulous performance, both Shaddai and her brother (Mikael) gave me briefings as the show progressed. The story being told was about fishermen on a small boat in the ocean and their inter-related love pursuits of beautiful women. The men wore the attire of fishermen –tight pants with a hanging garment between the legs -- and the young women wore flimsy attire, and all were just so beautiful. In short, the choreographic singing, dancing, and verbal dialogue were just awesome – and I found that I could follow the play. The performances at this theatre were always fabulous. I went to the theatre several times whenever the shows were changed. I also took my family to see some shows after they arrived in Cairo.

In short, we became good friends from then on. I eventually visited Shaddai and her family at their real nice apartment very near the Balloon Theatre. They also took me to St Mark's Coptic Cathedral. I learned a great deal about the Coptic religion. This is a very ancient religion that was found, apparently, in the second century A.D. It has its own Pope. At the time of my tours, the head of the Coptic Church was Pope Shinoda III. He was head of the church for 46 years and died on March 17, 2012. After he passed on, a new Pope (Tawadros II) was elected.

About a month after our first meeting, Shaddai gave me some additional background on her family. She told me that her father had died of something like cancer when she was a very young child. Before he died, his father made an agreement with his brother (Shaddai's uncle) whereby the brother would take care of his wife and family. Shaddai's mother, aunt, and uncle had agreed to the arrangement. After her father had passed on – and a certain mourning period had been observed -- her uncle and mother began a "Casa Chica Type of Arrangement." Shaddai asked me if these types of arrangements bothered me and if they existed in the U.S. and/or other countries.

I had seen these types of arrangements in Latin America, and even in some parts of Texas. I have described the arrangement earlier in this book. The man maintains his principal marriage (Casa Grande) but maintains a separate relationship (Casa Chica) on the side. He provides financial support to both families and sexual needs to both wife and mistress. The two families know of each other and are in full agreement with the arrangement. So, when Shaddai asked for my opinion, I told her the arrangement did not bother me. I also told her about the Casa Chica arrangements in Latin America and that I knew that the Islamic, Mormon, and Buddhist religions permitted a man to have up to four wives at one time – and for all "wives" and husband to share a single home. I saw that the arrangement -- made between the two brothers -- had been very beneficial, particularly for the children. Otherwise, the family, living in a country where women do not normally work and no longer have a father that is working and supporting the children, might have experienced poverty and a lack of education. They might have also suffered tremendously. Perhaps she was looking for some reassurance, but she was happy with my support and explanation.

In any event, Shaddai, her mother, and her brother (and his family) were good friends for about two to three months. They immigrated to Europe, and I lost contact with them.

When my family got to Egypt, we met other Coptic friends. My son, Jerry, had many Coptic and Muslim friends. The name of one was Ashraf. Pauline and Melissa, my daughter, found other members of the Coptic Church. One good friend was Robert Hester, who worked for an oil company. Robert's wife and their daughter, Roberta, were Coptic's. After we left Egypt, they invited Jerry to come to Egypt, visit and stay with them. The Heisters eventually returned to the United States. Jerry and I visited them at their home in Amarillo, Texas. They truly were exceptional people.

During the time that we were in Egypt, the Muslim and Coptic populations had a real nice relationship. However, things have deteriorated since then and have become difficult for the Coptic's in more recent times. For example, a Coptic priest sometimes sends letters to Jerry, giving him updates on the religion and requesting donations. In the letters, the priest said that Copts were being treated as second-class citizens: They were considered dirty because they ate pork. Muslim families were boycotting their restaurants, and they had to use segregated restrooms. In fact, I read that in 2013, churches and the homes of Copts were attacked. Moreover, a bomb or bombs were placed in the St. Mark Cathedral on December 13, 2016; the resulting explosion killed about twenty-five people and destroyed many ancient icons.

In ending this section, let me say that I remember my Coptic friends – Shaddia, her family, the Hester family, and others -- with great affection. I hope that the two religions find a way to return to the peaceful co-existence which existed during my tours in Egypt.

Composition of Audit Personnel. Immediately upon my arrival, Russell and I began to hire Egyptian professionals. We also decided we needed one other secretary to help us. I would interview a great number of Egyptians, narrow the selection, and then Russell and I would take in only the very best. In the next few months after my arrival, we were joined by four other Americans, and we began to operate with the following staff:

- The U.S. staff consisted of Russell A., Coinage G., Joe V., Wayne M., and Ben F., and me.

- The Egyptian staff included two secretaries (Agnes and Mariam) and five members of the audit staff: Amin S., Ahmed A., Haney L., Amer, and one other person whose name escapes me as I write this. Although we selected the very best, their accounting and auditing training was much different than the training in the U.S. Therefore, part of our job was to teach and train them. Some parts were funny. I recall one instance when I was talking about "Indirect or Overhead costs," and two of them looked at the ceiling. I had to explain what those terms meant and how those types of factors affected costs. Nevertheless, they learned fast.

Thus, Russell and I made an exceptional team, and we were able to develop one of the best Regional Inspector's teams that you could possibly imagine. Oh, I almost forgot! Yes, we also hired Mahmoud. He was one unforgettable person:

- Ah Mahmoud was something else. I was off on a trip somewhere (it might have been on home leave) when someone hired Mahmoud. He had been working with us a week when I got back and first met him. I talked with the guy for a few minutes. Right after the meeting, I asked Russell: "…who hired him, and how was he selected?" Russell told me and asked me why I was asking. I told him that I had a very eerie feeling about him. Russell gave me a big grin (I think that he also had mixed feelings). Sure enough, not a month had gone by, and Mahmoud began coming in stoned to the brink on Hashish. He would fight with our other staff, insult USAID people in different offices, and ask for classified information that he was not authorized to see. In short, he was just generally being a complete nuisance and was certainly totally unfit for the office. Russell and I talked about the guy and the problems he was creating for the office. Russell gave me the word to fire the guy. I brought him into my office and, in friendly terms, told him things were not working and gave him the only option – to resign voluntarily. He quickly said, "I will not resign." With the greatest of patience, I could muster, I hugged him and told him that as a friend, I was counseling him that his best option was to resign. I gave him a few reasons. When we went to talk to Russell, Mahmoud hesitated but eventually resigned. But this was not to be the last time we were to see him. **Someone in the Security Office forgot to collect his identification card. Mahmoud would frequently go into the Embassy or USAID compound, stoned to no end, roam around, and create serious problems. He was a very real security risk.** After we learned about the infractions, we took the required action, and the Security Office confiscated his ID. We never saw him again.

Here is a final note about the Egyptian staff that we hired. After I retired from USAID, I went back to Egypt to work as a Financial Consultant and visited the RIG Office. Although our original U.S. staff was long gone and Agnes had retired, one original secretary and four Egyptian auditors were still working within the team. In sum, we had hired a terrific local staff.

Helping President Carter on His Visit to Egypt. For a brief period, on March 8th and 9th, 1979, I was in a place and time when history was being written. I contributed my extra little grain of sand to the writing of such an event.

As I later wrote to my family, it happened like this. President Jimmy Carter and his entourage came to Cairo on the above dates to address the People's Assembly in anticipation of the signing of the Peace Treaty between Egypt and Israel. The U.S. Embassy asked our office (and others) to "volunteer" people to help as "couriers." Since I was by myself at the time, I volunteered to help out. My job was to carry messages back and forth from the U.S. Embassy to the Hilton, where most of the White House people were staying, and then carry suggestions or work from the hotel to the "Koubbeh" or Kobe Palace, where President Carter and all the really high-level officials were staying.[82]

I was given a high-level security ID pass to enter the Palace. My work began right after the President had arrived at the Kobe Palace. I was sent to the Hilton Hotel to pick up some documents. The first high-level White House staffer I met was Jody Powell, Carter's press secretary. We rode the elevator together. Since he did not know who I was, he kept eye me up and down and was not that friendly to me. After the staff gave me some documents to take to the President, the Egyptian driver drove me to the Kobe Palace alone. When we got to the Palace gates, another car was waiting in front of us. We parked

---

[82] The Koubbeh Palace is Egypt's principal guesthouse for high level dignitaries.

behind the car and noted that there seemed to be a real big commotion between the guards and the driver of the other car. I went to see why. Well, the problem was that the guard would not let the driver into the Palace because he was Egyptian. I looked inside the other car and who was there? It was Jody Powell and his bodyguard. So, I showed the guard my ID, got behind the wheel of the car, and drove all of us and the documents into the compound.

From then on, Jody Powell was a great deal friendlier. I saw him many times in the "Operations Room," and we chatted very amicably. Since I had delivered the messages, I had to wait for a response from the high-level officials. During downtimes, I had some time to see parts of the Palace. Security was so tight; there must have been a Secret Service or other security agent every 10 feet. In my case, they would eye me up and down, not knowing if I was an Egyptian diplomat, a famous reporter, an Embassy type, or just what. Nevertheless, I saw where the President was staying and briefly saw him in person. I saw where Cyrus Vance, Zbigniew Brzezinski, Hamilton Jordan, and others worked. One person that was very friendly with me was Phil Wise.[83] He talked to me for a long time, asking about Cairo and Egypt. I talked to Jordan for a while, he seemed to be awfully sharp. So, I got to see quite a number of high-level officials and a lot of the palace.

The Kobe Palace was most impressive. What a place! I had done a tour of the part of the White House that was open to the public in the 1960s, and the White House seems relatively modest compared with the Koubbeh Palace. The Palace had three levels and numerous, but I mean, numerous rooms. I counted about four different dining rooms. The grounds were perhaps three times as big as those of the White House. The gardens were just beautiful. The inside was really plush, and all the rooms were decorated with Iranian carpeting. The chandeliers must have been worth a fortune. Expensive mirrors were all over. In short, the Egyptian Government gave President Carter a place to stay that he must still remember.[84]

---

[83] At the time, Cyrus Vance was Carter's Secretary of State; Brzezinski was Carter's national security advisor and Jordan was Carter's Chief of Staff. Wise was President Carter's appointments secretary.

[84] Subsequently President Barack Obama was also a guest in this Palace during his visit to Cairo in June 2009.

There were four of us in the Operations Room, and on a few occasions, each of us took turns to make the run to the Embassy, and from there to the Hilton, and back to the Palace. All of us got very hungry. So, we ordered dinner from the Palace. It was chicken and lamb, with carrots, potatoes, etc. It wasn't the greatest meal; in fact, it was poor, but I ate most of it anyway.

At the end of the night, the four of us were given a "golden pen," which had "President Jimmy Carter" written on it. I kept the pen for a few years. Of course, the pen was not real gold; the gold color eventually faded, and I lost it in one of our transfers.

Anyway, I finally got home late that night. The following day I saw the Carter entourage again on the streets of Cairo. The crowds of people were tremendous – pushing, shoving, and the women were "yodeling." I had never heard such a massive "yodeling" by big crowds. When I first heard that sound coming from thousands of women at the same time, it gave me goose pimples. But this one was for a very happy occasion; the crowds and I were witnessing a great moment in the history of their nation.

That day, President Carter talked to the Egyptian People's Assembly. After that, he did a little sightseeing and then left for Tel Aviv, Israel. His trip had been an enormous success. The publicity he got was just fabulous. In sum, I am happy to say that, on March 8 and 9, 1979, I was in a place and time when history was being written. On those dates, I was able to contribute that extra little grain of sand to the writing of such a historical event.

Part C. Brief Audit Examples Of First Tour Reviews

Part C.1 Audit Survey, An Audit Plan, And Some Work

Our Mission-wide survey disclosed an already existing, but small economic program that was beginning to become huge in leaps and bounds due to the arrival of a vastly increased amount of new U.S. assistance. Our survey also showed that USAID's assistance was already having a beneficial economic impact on the people and the country.

The work was, to put it mildly, tremendously complex, and challenging. Our portfolio of projects to audit included many very complex, multi-level types of programs and projects worth several billions of dollars. The programs and projects covered a wide spectrum of the types of assistance typically given to "special countries" of strategic importance to the United States.

By then, the USAID RIG/A in Egypt was already heavily involved in audits of many kinds of programs and projects being undertaken by USAID in Egypt, among them: the two assist audits that the OIG in Washington had requested by Washington dealing with Borrower and Grantee Contracts and Participant Training; the construction of Grain Silos in two locations: those of the Commodity Import Programs; the Electrical Distribution program; and the road construction programs. We were also involved, among other things, in audits of USAID programs and projects to improve Egypt's transportation and education systems; reconstruct a crossing unit across the Suez Canal; improve rice cultivation; strengthen family planning efforts and other programs and projects covering many other areas. In conducting our audits of these complex programs and projects, we found plenty of serious problems – flaws in the design, planning, programming, or implementation of the programs and projects or financial mismanagement and collusion or design miscalculations by suppliers. For my efforts, I got several awards. Let me discuss some of the audits of USAID's programs and projects in Egypt that I did.

(Note: As stated in Chapter 3, USAID loans and grants usually contain clauses requiring that technical services, contracts, commodities, training, etc. will be sourced to the maximum extent possible in or from organizations in the U.S. As such, both the U.S. and the Host Country benefit from the assistance. On the one hand, the Host Country benefits in some way from the assistance. On the other hand, many of the services, commodities, or products come from the U.S. This process enables U.S. suppliers and contractors to participate in the foreign assistance process. This is an excellent policy because most funds that originate in the U.S. return to help the U.S. economy. As I said in an earlier chapter, I wish these cyclical returns could be made to have a more dispersive economic impact on more needy U.S. sectors -- such as our aging infrastructure, bridges, road, costly education, health, and others.)

PART C.2 AUDIT OF USAID/EGYPT'S BORROWER/GRANTEE CONTRACT SUPPORT.[85]

As mentioned earlier, when I arrived, the OIG in Washington, D.C. had made their instructions very clear: our priority was to do an assist audit, led by the staff out of headquarters of contracts signed by borrowers and grantees of USAID in Egypt. As we discussed in Chapter 3 of this book, these contracts are always part of a larger program or or several projects, and the "assist audit" was to feed into a larger audit led by audit staff from Washington of similar USAID programs throughout the world. As such, the information we gathered about USAID in Egypt was to be part of a broader-range report.

USAID typically awards its assistance to host countries in the following manner: (a) the Host Country proposes a given area that needs development; (b) USAID sends a team to design the program and/or project; (the study is usually thorough and identifies the resources that are needed); c) USAID and the Host Country negotiate a Loan or a Grant Agreement that includes the necessary conditions or reforms that the Host Country needs to meet prior to USAID's making any disbursements. The program and/or project begins once the prime awardee: (a) has been identified; and (b) the requisite contract or grant agreement has been signed. The prime awardee can be a ministry or agency within the host government or, more likely in recent times, a private-sector contractor or not-for-profit grantee. A contractor or grantee can also be a non-governmental organization (NGO) as well as a regional or worldwide entity such as the United Nations' World Food Program. In all cases, USAID has different options to disburse the funds – direct payments, direct letter of commitments, bank letter of commitment, etc.

During our review, we found that, as of June 1978, USAID/Egypt had approved 36 borrower or grantee contracts amounting to over $242.0 million. Of the 36 contracts, 33 were for engineering and professional services, and 3 were for construction. We selected 6 of the largest contracts representing 78% of all costs and examined each in depth. As discussed later, we identified "The Grain Silos Project of Egypt" as having extremely serious contractor and construction problems-- it reminded me of the Colombian Cali Sewerage

---

[85] Audit Report 6-263-79-1 Audit of USAID/Egypt Borrower/Grantee Contracts and Practices.

project that I had audited in the early 1970s that had been afflicted by a bad case of “Murphy’s Law.” Thus, it became an urgent priority once we concluded the two assist audits. In addition, we found that a contractor implementing Poultry Improvement Project seemed to be submitting questionable financial claims; we put this on our list of projects for review. In addition to these, we found 8 areas related to the 36 borrower or grantee contracts that the RIG/A/Washington needed to include in a worldwide review that they were conducting. I am including only the most important ones:

1. We found over $44.0 million in “unusual” and questionable Agent’s Commissions in the case of one contract or grantee that deserved a closer look by our special OIG Investigations Office.

2. The USAID Handbooks did not provide guidance to USAID/Egypt and other USAID Missions about their responsibilities for overseeing borrower and grantee contracts. As we later found out during our audit of the Grain Silos project (See Section C4), this lack of guidance created a situation where all three responsible entities -- the USAID/Egypt, the Government of Egypt (GOE), and the Letter of Commitment Bank -- had adopted a very “passive attitude” in the implementation of the project with adverse effects on disbursement and the construction of the silos and the implementation the Silo Project. Yes, the handbooks were in urgent need of change.

3. Moreover, the USAID Handbooks prescribed the wrong kind of mechanism to disburse funds to programs, projects, and contractors or for the purchase of commodities. In effect, the existing regulations erroneously prescribed a preference for using the Bank Letters of Commitment rather than the Direct USAID Letters of Commitment. As a result, we found this erroneous instruction caused a series of complicated problems – Numbers 4, 5, 6, 7, and 8 -- which follows:

4. There was a lack of needed controls over a contractor’s performance and, particularly, over disbursements and project implementation.

5. There was a very passive attitude on the part of USAID/Egypt and the GOE, and neither was reviewing, certifying, or even looking at the performance and/or documents submitted by contractors.

6. The above two defects had further adverse consequent effects in that projects or programs (like the Grain Silos) were being constructed or implemented in a very defective manner.
7. There had been $440,000 disbursed to a banking institution just for disbursing funds without monitoring or reviewing certifications. This type of disbursement of funds reduced the availability of funds – by this amount – which could have been more beneficial to the Egyptian people.
8. Finally, there was evidence that contractors were submitting erroneous and duplicating billing costs information.
9. None of the contracts included standard language requiring USAID to undertake an audit before approval of the final indirect cost included in the payment voucher. As a result, contractors were inappropriately claiming Indirect Costs both as a separate cost item and within the Indefinite Quantity Contracts (which already contain a negotiated Indirect Cost factor). In other words, this represented a duplicate payment for Indirect Costs. (Note: This type of problem seemed to be a patterned situation. Our question, from our observation in Egypt, was: Either this was a legitimate Contractors' error – or illegitimate planned action on the part of some contractors. **I note, with great concern, that during my final tour in Washington, I reviewed a contractor that kept this practice going for years. Unfortunately, I was taken off the job – "...as a punishment to me or defective judgments or experience of my direct supervisor (See Chapters 16 and 18 for details)..." and for that reason, I was never able to determine the full extent of the contractors having inappropriately claimed an "indirect costs factor" under the IQC's and a duplicate but separate indirect cost factor on top of all the IQC costs....in other words, this would have been a deliberate fraudulent claim.**
    a. **To me, and this is my suggestion: like I say in this part, this seemed like a prevailing practice by some of the USAID Contractors. Accordingly, a broad I.G. audit should be made to determine the magnitude, if any, of this type of fraudulent submissions.**

10. Finally, we found that the U.S. Congress had recently passed a law requiring that USAID assistance be directed to the "Poorest of the Poor." This type of assistance being provided to Egypt did not lend itself to this legal expectations and requirement.

PART C.3 PARTICIPANT TRAINING PROGRAM OF USAID/EGYPT.[86]

Our second priority was an assist audit of the Participant Training of Egypt. In this connection, RIG/A/Washington informed us that, as of June 1978, there were 2,600 participant trainees in the U.S. who had come from 89 different countries.

For our study, we requested that RIG/A/Washington to send us eight different reports, apparently generated for the USAID Office of Training, on the number of Egyptian trainees.

Normally, Missions and Host Countries include training of people, in U.S. Universities or facilities, as part of each individual Project or Program Agreement. In Egypt, however, some of the Participant Training was done through individual projects, but most of the training – about $600,000 at that time -- was being channeled and financed under an agreement called "Transfer of Technology and Manpower Development Project."

After doing our study, we submitted a memo report to the RIG/A/Washington summarizing a few different areas where questions should be raised during the worldwide Audit. Following are areas which concerned us.

First, we found the eight (8) statistical reports provided by the USAID Office of Training – through RIG/A/Washington, on the number of Participants – to be inconsistent, their accuracy unreliable, and the financial data was not integrated with the number of Participants. Here are some examples:

---

[86] Memo Report to RIG/A/Washington entitled "Leads for Worldwide Audit of Participant Training Programs.

a. We were given eight different profiles on the number of people in the Participant Training of Egypt. Four reports showed (that there were) 616 trainees in U.S. training programs; one said 287, another said 388, another said 742, and another showed 671.

b. No report showed a correlation between the statistical numbers of participants and financial costs. Both statistical and financial information on Participant Training was inaccurate and in need of better integration between financial and statistical.

c. The Agency had very weak accounting procedures in relation to Egypt's -- and worldwide -- Training Programs.

To us, three hypothetical premises needed to be reviewed closely: (a) inaccuracy of statistical and financial information related to training; (b) inaccuracies in the training information provided to the U.S. Congress; and (c) an urgent need for a computerized system integrating statistical information with financial costs.

Second, using other U.S. Government Organizations to do training – through the Resources Support Services Agreements (RSSA) – showed price inconsistencies and seemed to create an obviously serious cost escalating problem. For instance:

a. Costs varied among U.S. Organizations. For example, the monthly charge by the Department of Agriculture was $205 per participant. In turn, the monthly charge by the Department of Labor was between $550 to $1,215 per participant.

b. It seemed to us that there was a very persistent effort on the part of the training organizations to increase the scope of the training program. This resulted in two problems: (a) an unforeseen escalation of program costs, and (b) a distinct incentive for the training organization to keep the escalation going. i.e., the more the training, the more the "profit" to the organization.

c. The identification and selection process of the training universities and institutions needed closer examination and improvement. We found evidence that some training in U.S. Universities and in RSSA's were not well planned, and returned Egyptian participants – and even other countries – were complaining that their training had been "…a waste of time…"

d. As in the case of B/G Contracts, the type of people receiving training did not fit the "Poorest of the Poor" vision desired by the Congressional Law.

Third, there was an unusual problem where the questions should be addressed to the Office of Training. As mentioned before, the cost of the Egyptian Training Program was about $600,000. This cost was broken down into five categories – instructional costs, living allowance, recurring costs, one-time costs, and others. According to Agency Procedural Instructions, missions were required to send to AID/W, all funds -- obligated through the Project – in four equal installments. The Mission(s) funding responsibilities ended at this point. We saw defects in this system because:

a. The funds sent to AID/W were merely Projected Estimated Obligations and not actual costs.

b. Several Participants had never gone for the training, and thus actual costs had not been incurred.

c. Current procedures required the use of "Standard Costs," and the definition of this concept was unclear.

d. The Office of Training never accounted for nor ever returned any of the unused funds.

e. Thus, there were questions on the accounting and disposition of those used funds.

We raised two questions on this procedure: (a) does the Office of Training have adequate procedures to control costs related to individual participants who do not go to training; and (b) what happens to those obligated but undisbursed funds – are they de-obligated, or reprogrammed, or just how are those cost identified and what is there disposition?

In sum, we were also able to contribute several significant questionable areas – in the Participant Training Programs that needed to be looked at by RIG/A/Washington in their worldwide review. It is

unfortunate that I never got to see the results of the worldwide audits of these two areas. These were completed after my transfers or retirement.

PART C.4 AUDIT PLAN FOR AND REVIEW OF THE GRAIN SILOS PROJECT.[87]

Some background on this Project. In 1975, Egypt was importing nearly 75 percent of its food grain needs. By 1980, these types of importations were expected to be over 4.5 million tons. Yet, Egypt only had two-grain silo facilities – a 48,000 metric ton (m/t) complex in Alexandria and a 58,000 m/t complex in Cairo. Neither the Alexandria nor the Cairo silo complexes had any modern "ship to silo" unloading equipment, structures, or mechanized system. Moreover, there were serious problems with both (a) the depth of the harbor in Alexandria being too shallow and (b) the Quay number 85 used to unload the grain - this Quay was both too shallow and short. In other words, the loaded grain came in small ships that would dock in a shallow harbor near a short quay; Egyptian laborers would board the ship, bag the grain, carry them one by one on their back, and load them onto the transportation and distribution trucks. On the one hand, this helped Egypt in keeping its excessive numbers of unemployed labor force. However, these inefficient unloading practices created excessive and unwarranted "demurrage" costs – which USAID/Egypt and other assisting countries were paying.

For this reason, the USAID Mission and the GOE negotiated an $84.5 million project to upgrade and build more modern silo systems in both Alexandria and Cairo. Financing for this project was being done through a USAID loan (Loan Agreement No. 263-K-028) amounting to $44.3 million (in US Dollars of this amount, about the U.S. $6.1 million would be payable in Egyptian Pounds (LE 15.5 million). The remaining amount (about $40.2 million) was the GOE local currency contribution. The Project had the following objectives:

---

[87] Audit Plan for the Grain Silo Project. Dated 1979, and Audit Report No. 6-263-80-6, issued May 29, 1980, entitled "A comprehensive Review of the Grain Silos Project – AID Loan 263-K-028 at Alexandria and Cairo, Egypt, Implemented Under Host Country Contracting Mode."

- In Alexandria, the objectives were to (a) dredge the channels; (b) widen and deepen the harbor; (c) deepen and extend Quay No. 85; (d) add a modern 20,000 m/t structure to the existing complex; and, (e) construct a new and modern 80,000 m/t unloading and storage silo complex system which would have pneumatic ship unloading towers, conveyors, and other modern equipment required to unload ships more efficiently.
- In Cairo, the objective was to construct a new and more modern 100,000 m/t silo complex in Shubra (near Cairo).

As stated previously, our review of the borrower and grantee contracts revealed the Grain Silos Project to be in urgent need of a more comprehensive audit due to the number of odd and potentially serious problems.

When my team and I expanded our survey – the expansion included a review of files and documents, samples of financial transactions, analyses, evaluations, test probes, discussions, limited visits, etc. -- we found that our concerns were warranted. What I saw reminded me of the Cali Sewerage Program in Colombia that I described earlier. Our tentative assessment showed a project that seemed to have been afflicted by Murphy's Law, i.e., whatever could go wrong, went….

In such complicated cases, a good Audit Plan is so necessary. For this reason, and with my team's help, I prepared an 80-page "Audit Plan" -- hereafter also called a "work plan" -- for a very comprehensive review and evaluation. The plan provided the necessary program and financial background. It also called for contracting the services of an independent special engineer as part of our evaluation team and for the RIG in Egypt to manage the entire evaluation. In addition, the work plan called for the team consisting of audit personnel from different disciplines and locations in both headquarters and Egypt since the work would be done in different locations. It laid out a cohesive and well-coordinated schedule for phasing-in and phasing-out of all evaluation teams. The plan contained numerous segments which described each individual problem, the work that was needed to be done by the team members, and the final report or contribution that each team was to make. Russell and our staff reviewed the plan, as did the Inspector General, Office of Inspector General Policy and Plans in Washington, the IG's Office of Special Investigations, and others. **In sum, this was going to be (and was) one of the most complex reviews that anyone can imagine.**

Once I completed the Audit Plan, and it was fully staffed, Russell decided to take over its broad supervision and control. We assigned an Auditor-In-Charge (AIC) and an audit team to help him monitor and achieve all phases of this extremely complex review.

This action was taken because I was scheduled to go on home leave in June 1979. Upon my return, I was also scheduled to start to work on our next urgent priority, which was to do a survey and develop a similar work plan for an audit of the $1.5 billion CIP program in Egypt. As I will discuss later, the CIP had overly complex problems of its own, and we eventually released a series of reports on them.

In short, having developed the work plan for the Grain Silo Program and upon transferring the supervisory responsibilities to Russell, my participation in this review became limited to an exchange of further ideas, consultations by team members, problem-solving, and reviews in the preparation of the Record of Audit Findings or the draft report.

The Grain Silo review took nearly 12 months. The implementation of the audit occurred exactly as I had planned it. The Inspector General and/or his Deputy contracted the services of Converse Ward Davis Dixon Inc. (CWDD), a U.S. engineering firm, to help us with the engineering and technical evaluation. The I.G. also arranged for an engineer from USAID's Office of Engineers, Bureau of Development and Support to review and evaluate the procurement of equipment under the Silo Program as well as the sub-contractor's performance. All other teams were quickly assembled.

The work started in June 1979, and the final report was issued on May 29, 1980. During this time, the teams issued numerous Records of Audit Findings, short Audit Reports, and referrals to the Office of Special Investigations. In addition, with our approval, CWDD released an interim technical report.

Our final report[88] is over fifty pages. It is most complex, containing a great deal of technical and financial analysis that integrates different technical disciplines. For this reason, I am presenting the results in seven segments, which are further divided into two distinct sub-parts. **The excellent quality of the audit reflects the result of my survey and work plan and the exceptional work of the audit teams.** The first segment shows the *Audit Plan Observations* that we made in the work plan; the second shows the actual audit finding. Each is marked by a different distinctive symbol:

- ❖ **1.0 Audit Plan Observation.** The most important reason for doing a comprehensive project review was that the Agency's Handbooks did not provide clear guidance to USAID headquarters or the Missions about their responsibilities for overseeing borrower and grantee projects or contracts. As a result, USAID/Egypt had adopted a very "passive and hands-off attitude" towards this project. Since the Mission had the erroneous impression that it was not responsible for any part of overseeing the borrower or grantee project or contract, it was not fulfilling the Agency's inherent responsibilities for monitoring, supervising, and overseeing the financial and programmatic aspects of this complex project. The result was a project that had many complex problems. We felt that the Central USAID Agency needed to give specific guidance and directions to the Missions on a worldwide basis covering their responsibilities for overseeing the different phases of these projects.
- ❖ **1.1 Audit Findings.** The actual review confirmed our work plan observations. The audit team found that the Mission had, in fact, adopted a very passive attitude towards oversight of the borrower and grantee contract project. The Mission's position was that since this was a borrower and grantee project, the Host Country and consulting engineering firm were responsible for overseeing all project phases. As such, the Mission relied on others for feedback on problems with the project. The Mission's oversight was limited to a review of the periodic reports submitted by the consulting engineer as well as

[88] Audit Report 6-263-80-6 called "A Comprehensive Review of the Grain Silos Project – AID Loan 263-K-028 – At Alexandria and Cairo, Egypt Implemented under Host Country Contracting Mode."

occasional meetings with high Egyptian government officials. When CWDD reviewed the periodic reports, they found them to be infrequent, untimely, incomplete, inaccurate, and misleading. Thus, the Mission did not have an accurate picture of the project's progress and problems. It was clear, then, that the Agency in Washington needed to clarify the Agency's Handbooks because, as we stated in our audit, (a) "…the theory of Policy Determination 68[89] which at that time covered responsibilities by the Host Country contracting mode needs to be better reconciled to the realities of overseas conditions and day-to-day difficulties in implementing multi-million-dollar projects such as the Grain Silos…."[90]

- **2.0 Audit Plan Observations.** We observed during our work on the audit plan that the implementation of the Grain Silos project showed several problems. Already it was significantly behind schedule, and the process used to select the consulting engineer had been controversial, anomalous, and discordant. The GOE had made the final selection of the consulting engineer overriding the Mission's strong reservations about the selection. (See following Number 4.0). In addition, the correspondence files contained a series of allegations suggesting defective practices on the part of the project's contractors and subcontractors, and there were indications that these were also utilizing substandard construction materials as well as other more technical problems. Finally, we had observed many problems during our review of the borrower and grantee contracts, and the contractors and sub-contractors were using the same kinds of defective contracting procedures to design, supervise, and construct the Silos, as well as to procure the needed equipment and commodities for this complex project.

---

[89] At the time of our report, USAID's guidance for the Missions was contained in a Handbook that contained a series of Policy Determinations. Policy Determination 68 dealt with the Mission's responsibilities for oversight of country program, projects, contracts, and grantees. USAID's current "nuts and bolts" guidance (policies, procedures, and directives) are contained in its Automated Directive System. See https://www.USAID.gov/sites/default/files/documents/1868/501.pdf.

[90] Page 7 of A/R 6-263-80-6 covering the Comprehensive Review of the Grain Silos

- **2.1 Audit Findings.** In its review of the project, CWDD confirmed all of the tentative conclusions contained in our audit plan. CWDD did an extremely thorough review, visiting all the right places, performing the required technical testing, and making all the needed assessments. They found that the construction of the projects in both Alexandria and Cairo had major problems. As we had noted, the project was significantly behind schedule due to delays in the selection of the consulting engineer as well as the consulting engineer's deficient performance. Scheduled to be completed by 1979, the completion of the project was now extended to about 1982. CWDD found numerous consulting engineer supervisory deficiencies and construction defects. For example, CWDD found that some of the construction, including the quality of the coarse and fine aggregates, as well as the cement used, did not meet the required specifications.[91] CWDD also found that the filters for sub-drains used to carry water away from the silos did not meet specifications and that the workmanship and waterproofing of the silos were unsatisfactory.

- **3.0 Audit Plan Observation.** We observed during the development of the work plan that the Mission in Egypt did not think it was a priority to deepen the harbor or improve Quay 85 in Alexandria. For all intents and purposes, this work would probably not be done. **To us, fixing these problems was crucial; unless the harbor was dredged, deepened, and widened and Quay 85 deepened and extended, the construction of the silos in Alexandria would not be able to fully serve the real needs of Egypt.** Egypt needed large and heavily weighted ships to be able to navigate the harbor and dock near Quay 85. Egypt also needed to be able to use modern pneumatic towers, unloading equipment, and conveyors belts to unload and mechanically transport the grain from the ship to the silos for storage and from there onto the distribution trucks.

- **3.1 Audit Findings.** The audit confirmed what we had observed in the audit plan. The teams found that the work required to dredge, deepen, widen, and/or extend the harbor and Quay 85 in Alexandria was most

---

[91] Aggregates are granular materials that are mixed into the cement to form the concrete or mortar.

complex. The Quay was being enlarged, but it was not being constructed on the bedrock, so there was a question of whether it would be able to safely take the heavy grain loads. Also, the channel alongside the quay would not be deepened because this would destabilize the existing quay wall. In responding to our Record of Audit Findings, USAID/Egypt told us once again that the GOE was funding this part of the project, and for that reason, USAID/Egypt had no responsibility for this work. Later, USAID/Egypt reversed its position and agreed to find ways of achieving this part of the project.

- **4.0 Audit Plan Observation.** The selection of the consulting Engineer -- who was to be responsible for all phases of the project -- had been most controversial. The Mission in Egypt had expressed concerns about his qualifications at the time of selection, rating his potential performance at a low level. In addition, the members of the Mission's selection committee had written a one-page critique objecting to the selection of this particular company. At the time we put together our audit plan, his actual project performance had been the subject of very persistent questions.
- **4.1 Audit Findings.** The audit teams confirmed the observations we made in the audit plan. Five engineering firms had submitted bids to implement the Grain Silo projects in Alexandria and Cairo. The selection committee had been formed by members of USAID/Egypt and the GOE. During the original vote, the GOE had voted 9 to 2 not to accept the engineer that was eventually selected; however, during the final vote, USAID/Egypt placed the rating at "3," and the GOE placed him at "1." Both USAID/Egypt and USAID in Washington raised strong reservations over the selection of this particular engineering firm for a series of reasons. First, it had no experience with a project of this magnitude. Second, its planned approach was faulty. Third, its reliance on several supervisory subcontractors seemed unwarranted. Lastly, its planned time to complete the project seemed unrealistic. [92]

[92] Page 5 of A/R 6-263-80-6 A Comprehensive Review of the Grain Silo.

- **5.0 Audit Plan Observation.** There were allegations of a $50,000 "kickback" to someone for "arranging" the awarding of the consulting engineer's contract. Our initial review showed that the scope of work for one subcontractor was ambiguous. Moreover, the contract was signed on March 11, 1977, for an amount of $50,000. However, less than a month later, on April 6, 1977, this contract, which had been a fixed cost contract, was increased to $100,000 – and yet, there was no change in the scope of the work. In other words, there were strange correlations between (a) the reported kickback," (b) the unusual increase in cost, and (c) the ambiguity of the scope of work. There was one other problem: the Mission's disbursements for the project were being made through a bank letter of commitment, and there had been no review of the costs billed. The entire process had its share of problems.

- **5.1 Audit Findings. The audit team** conducted the financial work at the home office of the consulting Engineer, reviewing both direct and indirect costs. They disallowed a total of $112,800 in commission for an agent. They also found that about $7,000 had been paid to someone in Egypt. However, we did not find an exact correlation between the disallowed amount and the $50,000 increase to the subcontractor. RIG/A/W also found that the accounting system and records were inadequate and inaccurate. In addition, documents submitted, by the contractor, to support payments were erroneous. Current L/Com procedures were not followed. And there were other types of problems.

- **6.0 Observation in Our Audit Plan.** We observed in our audit plan that the consulting engineer was implementing the Grain Silos project, in addition to 12 other prime contractors and 6 sub-contractors. There were already rumors and allegations that construction was deficient, and that performance of the contractors and subcontractors was also deficient.

- **6.1 Audit Findings.** As mentioned earlier, the audit team fully confirmed the observations made in our audit plan. CWDD found problems with the quality of the construction, as well as the quality of the work being done in the sub-drain.

- **7.0 Observation in Our Audit Plan.** Due to a radical devaluation of the Egyptian Pound to the U.S. Dollar and other technical fine tunings of program requirements, the $84.5 million Program might now be overfunded. In this connection, in 1975 – when the Project was planned – the Egyptian Pound was strong, and the Rate of Exchange was $2.56 to LE 1.00. By 1978, the Egyptian Pound had been devalued, and the Rate of Exchange was now LE 1.42, which equaled $1.00. Let me explain it differently: if you converted U.S. $100 to Egyptian Pounds in 1975, you would only be able to buy the equivalent of $39 dollars in goods or services; by 1978, U.S. $100 would be able to buy $142 of the same goods and services – a very significant difference. Thus, the initial cost estimate assumptions were no longer realistic.
- **7.1 Audit Findings.** Our audit corroborated our observations. Because of the currency devaluation, eventual sub-contract costs, and other fine-tuning of information, the audit teams calculated that, as of February 1980, the total project costs would probably be around U.S. $38.0 million-plus about LE 19.5 million. I hope that the excess amount was used to help with the Alexandria harbor and Quay 85 problem.

In sum, the review of the Grain Silo was extremely complex. One lesson that was learned was that our audit survey was well-done, and it was essential to an exceptional plan of action. The composition, scheduling, and participation of the different disciplines and teams were crucial to the satisfactory contribution that we made in this Project review. I certainly hope that the recommendations made by us were implemented in a timely manner. If all went well, Egypt's economy should still be deriving great benefits from Grain Silo Projects in Alexandria and Cairo.

PART C. 5 AUDIT OF THE POULTRY IMPROVEMENT PROJECT

The design of this project was to improve and develop the field of poultry production because it did not conflict with land, which was being used, by the GOE, to plant the highly exportable and profitable cotton. By 1987, the GOE expected poultry production to be over 1.5 billion eggs and 600 million broilers.

We concentrated our audit on one Contractor because he seemed to be submitting unusual contract costs. Our preliminary conclusions were found to be correct. The Contractor's performance under the Project was very satisfactory. However, his fiscal and administrative responsibilities were questionable and bordered on fraud. Only a few examples are mentioned:

a. The Contractor paid his employees a Fixed Monthly Salary. His billings, on the other hand, were on the basis of time (in hours).

b. The billed hours were too excessive.

c. These billings were at Indefinite Quantity Contract (IQC) unadjusted type of standard rates.

d. This Contractor was never accounting for fund advances.

e. Some Employees were receiving excessive Per-Diem.

Our report made a series of recommendations, including (a) temporary suspension of the Contractor and all the subsidiaries; (b) disallowances of close to $115,000 and LE 10,000; and (c) further negotiations on about $75,000 and LE 45,000.

In sum, this project was a much simpler review. Hopefully, the GOE was able to complete the project in an expeditious manner, and it is now exporting cotton, eggs, and broilers.

PART D. HOME LEAVE AND RETURN TO POST WITH FAMILY

A Busy Home Leave and the Airport Ride in Cairo. During my tour in Washington, D.C., we had bought a house in Alexandria, Virginia. It was a nice house on the edge of a forested area where deer and other wild animals could be seen from our back deck. That is where my family was living and where I was going to spend my home leave.

Before leaving Egypt, I conducted a survey of USAID's CIP. I had noted that the available computer information in Egypt was disorganized and faulty.

Because the available information was so disorganized, it would not be helpful in the development of the "Regression Analysis" that we planned to use as part of the audit. The data also did not lend itself to the development of accurate financial data for use in the audit. For this reason, Russell and I sent a request for eight different "computer profiles" showing summary information of the Egyptian CIP. We sent this request just as I was getting ready to go on home leave. (Note: We eventually got the 8 computer runs; however, we could only use the information in a limited manner because the design of the Agency computerized system had not included the capturing – and integrating – of all the necessary cost factors in one essential computerized run.)

In any event, because of the late submission of our eight (8) profile runs, my home leave in the Washington area was an extremely hectic one. After a real busy "Consultation Period" at the RIG's headquarters in Washington, my periods of relaxation and reunification with the family were frequently interrupted by calls from the Office, asking me to come into the office the following day or asking for information, consultations, clarifications, technical inputs, or other questions related to the Egypt Office, Grain Silo, and/or the CIP computer runs that we had requested.

Nevertheless, I enjoyed being with the family. I was happy to see Joe, who was then going to – and graduated with honors from – the College of William and Mary. He was doing simply great in school. After he graduated from William and Mary, Joe served in the Peace Corps in Costa Rica and Ecuador and then returned to the U.S. to get his master's degree from the University of Kentucky.

I was also happy to see that Jerry had a great deal of musical talent. Before his graduation, I saw Jerry play the guitar and sing in a high school concert. He and Francisco (Paco) Ojeda, his guitar teacher and friend, played the song "If You Could Read My Mind," composed by Canadian composer and singer Gordon Lightfoot. They were great. Linda and Melissa were getting so tall and ever so beautiful, but neither of them was so happy to be going to Egypt. Pauline had done an excellent job of raising all four children.

By the time of my arrival, everyone had gotten their physicals and vaccinations. Since my home leave and Return to Post orders included everyone, all we needed to do was to pick a shipping company, let them pack, send our air freight, and store most of our furniture. We were able to go back to Egypt within the 30-day period of Consultation and home leave.

And, oh, yes, I forgot "Sarge" (our Panamanian-born German Sheppard) and "Spunker," our cat. Back then, there were no special dog cages, so we had a wire cage built for Sarge. In record time, we got all shots and clearances for the two animals. The poor animals were so confused when we went to the airport and got on the plane. Since Trans World Airlines allowed customers to carry small pets inside the plane, Linda carried Spunker in her lap all the way. Sarge was too big, and as a result, he traveled the long distance from Washington, D.C. to Cairo in the cargo hold.

It was a long flight, but we finally got to the Cairo International Airport, about 15 miles northeast of Cairo in a suburb called Heliopolis. We were met at the airport by a USAID Car. Since they did not expect us to come with a dog and a cat, we had to hire a taxi (a Mercedes Benz car) to take Jerry, myself, and Sarge. Because the Egyptians do not have too many dogs as pets, Sarge sat in the cage on the top of the car.

I will never forget that ride. That crazy taxi driver was going about seventy miles per hour, with an open window, laughing, pointing up to Sarge, and yelling at the top of his voice: "Kalb!" (dog) "Kalb!" "Kalb!" The dumb guy would giggle, laugh, and continue with his type of "rebel yell." This made me extremely nervous and angry. So, I got into a yelling match with that crazy guy. I kept telling him: "shuaya!" (slowly), "Shuaya" "Shuaya." He would laugh, tell me, "Inchala, enta raija El beit" (God willing, we'll get to your house), and I would counter, "Enta Mish-quays" or "Enta Magnum." (You are bad. You are crazy). But…. he never slowed down or stopped giggling all the way.

We finally got to our apartment complex. When we got Sarge down from the top of the car, that poor animal was all wobbly and dizzy from the long and harrowing taxi trip. And how was the wire cage? It was a miracle that the cage survived the Taxi drive; it was all crooked and bent. It went into the trash bin after that. I bet you are by now laughing, huh? Me too…now I can laugh about it -- but at that time, I was terribly upset.

Living in Maadi on a Fourth Floor Apartment. Large single-family homes with a big yard were not easily available in Cairo at the time. Most people lived in small and narrow row-type of apartments or townhomes. For this reason, USAID had rented a number of apartment complexes in a suburb to the south of Cairo, an area known as Mahdi, close to the Cairo American School. Mahdi is where most foreigners live. We lived in one complex – located at House 4, Road 216, Degla, in Mahdi – for three wonderful years. The building complex had four floors. Each floor contained 2 adjoining apartments, and each apartment had 3 bedrooms and 2 baths. To accommodate families with children, the apartments on each floor had been joined. Thus, we were assigned a 6-bedroom apartment on the 4th floor. In all my posts, the USAID always provided all furniture – not plush, but nice and tasteful. This apartment was no exception. It was a nicely furnished apartment; the only problem was that there was no elevator in the building, and we all had to walk up and down the stairs each time we wanted to go anywhere. Believe me, that kept us in shape – but it also got rough.

The building was occupied by three USAID families and one military family, as follows: (a) Major J. Stickle, wife, and two children; (b) A. Bisset, wife, and two children (Julie and Peter); (c) C. Raley, wife, and 3 children (Matt, Pam, and Alex); and (d) my family, Pauline, Jerry, Linda, and Melissa. As I said before, our son, Joe, was then going to the university; so he stayed back home but came to Egypt two or three times during the Christmas holidays and the summer of 1980. The only description I can give of my neighbors in the building complex is that all were highly intellectual and beautiful people. We all got along exceptionally well and had frequent complex parties.

The Cairo American School was about three blocks from the building. Cairo American School was/is an exceptional school – very modern, with a track, and a swimming pool, along with playgrounds, etc. However, there were no lights on the streets, and at night, it was dark. Normally the school was very safe; however, there were three instances of terror threats against the school and the children. The Egyptian Government assigned a platoon of soldiers to protect the school and kids. Otherwise, there was little semblance of violence in the area, and our children, especially the girls, could walk to the school and other places at night without fear of being hurt, raped, or kidnapped. In sum, the Egyptian people were fabulously peaceful and nice.

One perennial problem was/is that hashish was readily available everywhere, and I imagine, some of the kids in school tried it.

Since the four of us (as family heads) worked in downtown Cairo, USAID provided a shuttle that took all four of us from Mahdi to central Cairo in the morning and returned us home at night. USAID at the time was co-located with the Embassy. This was an excellent arrangement. Since we were only allowed one car, and we had transportation to work, our wives and families had personal car to go anywhere.

Abdu the Boab (Guard). Let me now talk about our Boab (watchman or guard). His name was/is Abdel-Fattah-Sabah Ahmed. We called him Abdu, and he was one of those fantastic people who would do just about anything to make your stay, in a foreign country, an easy one. Abdu's origin might have been Sudanese; his skin color was on the darker side; he was perhaps in his 40s; he was married and had 3 children. He had been a soldier and fought against Israel but did not hate the Israeli people. He was a Muslim, and the friendliest person with the greatest of personalities that you can possibly imagine.

All four of the families in the building liked him very much. Whenever the girls would go to the school at night, Abdu would pass the word out, and the guards would keep an eye out for them. Jerry and Abdu became exceptional friends. Every afternoon and part of the night, Abdu and Jerry would sit together, and Abdu would teach Jerry Arabic. And Jerry learned fast. For example, when he got to Cairo, he knew no Arabic and would ask me: "Dad, what are they saying?" Within a month, the tables were turned, and I was the one asking: "Jerry, what are they saying?" Jerry's Arabic became exceptionally good. Even after close to 40 years of being outside of Egypt, he spoke and wrote Arabic well (Note: As I explained in the Prologue and Acknowledgement and other parts, Jerry died as a result of a nurse's mistake in giving him a medication that was 10 times the strength prescribed. We miss Jerry terribly).

Abdu seemed to be good at just about everything. There was an empty lot next to the building, and I used to practice hitting a few golf balls. Abdu and

Jerry would later gather the balls. I kept seeing that Abdu would watch me. And me, I would hit sliders to left and right and never straight or for a long distance. One day, Abdu said, "I try?" So, I gave him my clubs and a few balls. Every ball he hit was straight and farther than mine. He later told me that he had been a caddy on a golf course. I quit playing golf sometime later, could Abdu's way of hitting those balls have been a subliminal message to me to quit? Just kidding! But…all kidding aside, Abdu was good.

When he saw that Jerry or I had to walk Sarge up and down the 4 floors, he volunteered to help. I was somewhat apprehensive and feared Sarge might bite Abdu, but Abdu readily took command of Sarge, and they became fast friends. Unfortunately, Sarge died from some sort of a liver infection about six months after we got to Cairo. We loved Sarge so much. Not knowing where to bury our dead dog, Abdu helped us. Abdu took us to the human cemetery – and the plots – where his parents were buried; there is where Sarge found his resting peace. Doesn't the reader find this action – burying an animal in a human cemetery and close to his parents – a fantastic way that shows Abdu's love for the family and for his very close animal friend?

On May 2, 1980, the Embassy fired Abdu because he was only contracted as a day person and not on a permanent basis. All the families in the building revolted. I wrote a memo, and everyone signed it; we met with Embassy officials, and we got Abdu back and in a permanent job. It was the right thing to do.

Abdu worked as a Boab for the building for the three years we were there. When we were transferred, we were sad to leave a good friend behind. About 17 years later -- during a temporary assignment to Cairo -- Jerry, a Taxi Driver (named Hassan), and I tried to find Abdu. We went all over but never found him. Speaking in Arabic, a few people said this to Jerry and me: "…What kind of people are you? You must be awfully nice people. What kind of people would search so diligently for a simple and humble Boab?"

Well, we searched for Abdu because we considered him an exceptional friend and loved him as if he was part of our family. Wherever you are, Abdu, know that we will always remember you.

Family Life in Egypt for Pauline, Jerry, Linda, and Melissa. As I said before, with Sadat in power, the country was generally very peaceful. The

Egyptian people were extremely polite, gentle, and friendly. Schooling for Linda and Melissa was exceptional. The girls could walk to school even at night without fear of harm. And, Abdu, our Boab, was exceptional. This is all to say that we had a fantastic tour in Egypt. Let me now just give you a quick oversight of how the family spent their time:

Pauline's Tour. Pauline quickly found a maid that would come each day, clean the apartment, and do some cooking. So, Pauline met with other women from the American community in Cairo and would drive the 1978 Challenger to Cairo's Central Market and Khan-El-Khalil to buy nice Egyptian antiques. Pauline was an exceptional buyer and had a good eye for the good stuff. One of the most valuable things she bought was an antique mirror – which we still have, what a fabulous buy! She was also an exceptional cook and, on several occasions, would host women – or our regular -- parties or give us all a terrific meal most times.

So, Pauline enjoyed her stay in Egypt. Only a few things marred her stay there. With her strong temperament, she frequently had disagreements with Linda and/or me. One other thing was more troubling. She was involved in a terrible accident very close to the apartment complex. One day, she was driving the 1978 Challenger on the main road of Mahdi to Cairo, when out-of-nowhere, some fool driving his truck too fast, crashed against the driver's side of the car. I was at work but was immediately notified. With one of my auditors, we took a USAID motor pool car to the accident site. The truck had "caved-in" most of the driver's side of the car. Pauline was in a state of shock. We finally got her out of the car. The window glass had shattered, and Pauline had pieces of glass all over her hair and body. Luckily, the 1978 Challenger had "safety glass," and Pauline was not cut. So, we took Pauline to the hospital. She was banged up a little but, fortunately, was not badly hurt. The hospital people checked her out, brushed some of the glass from Pauline's hair, and released her. The police had arrested the truck driver. So, after we took Pauline home, I went to the police station to file the necessary complaint. At the necessary "face-to-face confrontation," I asked the truck driver a few questions through my auditor: "…do you own the truck?" "La (no)." "…do you have a driver's license?" "La." "…my car is very badly damaged by your fast driving; do you have insurance to fix my car?" "La." "How do you plan to fix my car?" "Ana Mishfajem!" (I don't know). "Do you have a family?"

"Ay-gua." (Yes) The only last thing I could say to him was "Etna magnon!" ("You're crazy!") His eyes got wide, and he just looked at me. The police asked me what charges to file against him. I just said, "reckless driving. Keep him here for 2 or 3 days and release him so he can maintain his family." So, they released him from jail in three days. It cost me around $2,500 to order parts for the driver's side of the car and have it repaired. More importantly, though, I was happy that Pauline was not hurt. After the car was fixed, she continued to drive and buy nice things.

Jerry's Tour. Jerry had a fabulous time in Egypt. Like me, he grew to love the country and its people. As I said earlier, Abdu and Jerry became fast friends. Abdu taught Jerry how to speak Arabic and did a fantastic job. Jerry fit right in with the Egyptian society and made many friends. So, with Abdu's help and with the help of friends at the American University of Cairo (AUC), Jerry learned to speak and write Arabic extremely well. Jerry was a fan of musical instruments and learned to play the Egyptian Oud. I always thought the Oud was a bit odd-looking, although it is related to the lute. During the time Jerry attended the AUC, he played the Oud in a concert along with people who had much more experience playing the instrument. I enjoyed that very much, especially since most of the participants were singing American songs, playing the piano…. but only one American, Jerry, played the very popular Oud. The song he played was an old Egyptian love song, so the audience went wild – clapping, "dancing," and yodeling. I remember the sight and sounds so well.

During the time Jerry attended AUC, he commuted each day between Mahdi to Cairo. Because we only had one car reserved for Pauline, Jerry had to commute each day on the local "subway." The "local subway" was an old, rickety, and poorly maintained commuter train that was always overcrowded, with Egyptian men, women, children, and related "items" (animals, food, furniture, appliances, etc.), hanging from the doors, and pushing each other for needed space. It was at times uncomfortable and difficult, but Jerry remembered and cherished the experience for the rest of his life and would often talk about it.

At the University, students liked Jerry very much. One time, two beautiful Egyptian girls who were attending AUC made a marriage proposal to Jerry. They told him, "If you convert to Islam, you can marry the two of us…." This was not the only marriage proposal that someone in Egypt made to Jerry; as I will tell you later, Hassan (a taxi driver) told Jerry that he could marry his two daughters. Later in our tour, Jerry and a friend from Venezuela called Fernando traveled, by bus from Cairo to Jerusalem via the Sinai. As a family, we eventually made that same trip at a later time.

It's strange. But even today, the daily sounds coming from the beautiful Islamic Minarets through the voices of the Imams, calling the faithful for prayer, are still on my mind, as it often resonated in Jerry's mind for the rest of his life. Yes, Jerry (and I) loved our stay in Egypt very much.

Linda's Tour. As mentioned in an earlier chapter, we miss Linda terribly. Linda was a redhead, truly beautiful, extremely intelligent, creative, intuitive, and had a great outgoing personality. Although Linda had some difficulty getting along with Pauline, she and I got along beautifully.

In any event, Linda was 16 when we got to Egypt. Typically for her, she quickly made friends with all the kids in the Mahdi apartment complex. Linda, Julie, Pam, Peter, and Matt would hang around together a great deal of time. Peter and Linda liked each other very much and might have had a crush on each other. Since each floor had six bedrooms -- three bedrooms on each side of the narrow building -- the families agreed that the parents would be on one side and the kids on the other side. Boy, kids can be so imaginative and inventive:

- Since cell phones did not exist at the time, Linda quickly found ways to communicate – from our fourth floor -- with kids that lived on the first and second floors. How? She got a roll of thin rope, put a can, and they would pass notes down (or up) through their windows.

- Taking Spunker's litter box down from the fourth floor could have been a great hassle. However, this was no major problem for Linda; she **trained** Spunker (yes, the cat) to use the regular commode. That cat was smart. I wish we could train our current dogs to do the same…. ok, go ahead and laugh. You don't believe me? Well, a picture like the one that follows is worth a really top of the line laugh:

Linda Trained Spunker to do 1 And 2 On the Throne

Yes! Nowadays, kids are terribly smart. There were several times when the kids would ask permission to go to the Pyramids; we would drop them off, and without telling us, they would rent horses and travel around.

Linda was a very popular cheerleader and acted in school plays at the Cairo American College (CAC), located near the apartment complex in Mahdi. Let me tell you about the time she was on Egyptian Television. One day, Linda dropped by my office with a bunch of other girls. I was somewhat surprised. She urgently wanted to talk to me about participating -- together with all the other girls – in an Egyptian television skit that would advertise bathroom appliances. All the girls chimed in for me to approve Linda's participation. I gave her the required approval after checking with my staff and the TV station. So, all the girls participated in the advertisement; they danced a little and appeared to be singing a song. However, the station "dubbed an Arabic song" for the final advertisement. The advertisement was hilarious! We got a bang watching Linda, and the other cheerleaders do the advertisement skit; it played on the TV for a few months.

During the time we were there, the school held a couple of competitive sports events, which the school called "the Great Marathon." There were a number of different types of events -- swimming, racing, football, tennis, basketball, etc. Both Linda and Melissa participated in the Marathon events. Linda was a good swimmer and competed in the diving competition. She might have won the event; we will never know. Why? Well, Linda had a mishap. Ms. Raley – who was originally from Korea – had taught Linda how to do terrific "Kimchi" (a fabulously spicy dish made of cabbage, hot chiles, and other spices, extremely popular in Korea). Delicious! So, the night before the competition, Linda was chopping the cabbage, hot pepper, and spices, and almost chopped one of her fingers. The cut was so bad that I had to take her to the hospital, where they sewed her up. At the swimming competition, Linda could not do the trampoline handstands she wanted to do. She tried, but almost had a bad accident and luckily fell into the water. So, she had to give up the event. We were sad to see her lose, but she continued to make great "Kimchi."

Linda also enjoyed Egypt very much, and most of the kids in the school liked her very much. She was scheduled to graduate from CAC the following year, but my transfer in 1981 back to Washington prevented that. After getting back to Alexandria, Virginia, she went on to become a Cheerleader there and graduated from the Thomas Edison High School. I do miss Linda very much.

Melissa's Tour. Melissa was about eleven when we got to Egypt. Since she had learning disabilities, the CAC placed her in special classes. She did great. Melissa has always been extremely friendly, so she was a natural at making friends quickly. Alex and Melissa were school chums. Roberta and Melissa stayed in each other's home overnight frequently. Roberta's parents – the Heisters --were Coptic, Melissa would often go to the St. Mark Cathedral with these friends.

As I said earlier, Melissa also participated in the "CAC Great Marathon." Her event required her – and many others – to race around the one-mile track, repeatedly, until one by one would drop out from exhaustion. Since Melissa had never expressed an interest in racing -- nor participated in a racing match and had not gotten into shape to run great distances -- I figured that she would be among the first to drop out. Boy was I wrong! Round and round the mile-long track went Melissa. Looking back, seeing her run, and run, she reminds me of "Forest Gump," – the principal personality of the 1994 movie with the same name --when he was running across the U.S. Melissa never seemed to tire. Mile after mile accumulated. By the 14th mile, runner after runner had dropped out and then only Melissa was still running. So, I am very proud to say that Melissa was declared the champion. Her perseverance and determination to win the race were absolutely amazing. However, let me be clear about one thing: this was not the only time that she demonstrated such strong willpower. When we were in Kenya, during a later assignment, Melissa – with the wrong type of shoes and an unsuitable backpack -- was one of the few in her school to climb nearly all the way to the top of Mount Kenya. She also skied and learned how to ride horses in New Mexico, Colorado, and Virginia. I am so proud of Melissa particularly because – despite her disabilities and illnesses – she seems to always achieve whatever she sets her mind to do.

As I was writing this Chapter, Melissa reminded me of a time, when she was only 13 years old, and some older guy wanted to marry her. It happened like this. While in Egypt and she was 13 years old by then, she went shopping to Khan El Khalili with Pauline. Some rich looking Egyptian or Arabic looking man approached them and told her mama that Melissa was beautiful and that he would like to marry her. Of course, Pauline got all flustered and told the guy off. Probably the guy thought that Melissa was Egyptian, and he was rich enough to make a young girl his wife. In the U.S., this type of request would be indecent and subject to prosecution of the guy. However, this took place in Egypt and those types of marital type of accords, especially in the villages, might be considered an honorable arrangement.

Here is a remarkably interesting footnote. Around 1980, all the CAC kids wrote a bunch of notes; they placed them in a "Time Capsule" and buried them at the school entrance. The classes promised to meet in Cairo at the end of 25 years, or in the year 2005, open it, and celebrate. Unfortunately, Linda passed on in 2004. Melissa and all of us moved to Texas. I just don't know if any of the other "kids" went to this reunion. Perhaps, the "Time Capsule" is still buried in CAC.

Family Visits to Many Tourist Sights. During the time that the family was in Egypt and later – when Jerry accompanied me, in 1997, on a short assignment – we visited so many tourist sites in Egypt that I can't possibly remember all the names. Of course, we visited the Cairo Museum, the Pyramids at Giza, the surrounding villages, the step pyramid of Djoser in Saqqara, and others. We saw the fabulous "Sound and Light Show" at the Pyramids. Melissa and I rode horses and camels near the Pyramids. Melissa remembers two events at the Pyramid. One was the time when I was afraid that she would fall off a camel, so I rode the camel with her. A la "Lawrence of Arabia," I wore a "Kafai" or "Keffiyeh" (the Arab Turban Hat). One time, Melissa and I rented two horses near the Pyramids; one was a huge horse, and the other was a smaller one. I took the big horse, but the horse did not like me and started giving me problems. Melissa asked to switch horses and that was the end of the problem. Melissa rode the big horse just like a champion, and I rode the smaller horse. Looking back, the picture that comes to my mind is that of Don Quixote and Sancho Panza's ready to chase the windmills.

As a family, we also visited Luxor and the Valley of the Kings and Queens. We traveled by train from Cairo to Luxor during the Christmas season of 1979. Since the hotels in Luxor are always full, I made the required hotel reservations – in the best hotel and for the six of us (since Joe would be coming to Egypt for the Christmas holidays) -- way ahead of time. What an experience! First, the ride in the old and rickety train was not all that great. The second surprise was more stressful. The hotel was overbooked; our reservations were no longer honored; and, all other hotels were full. The hotel finally found a family that would rent us two bedrooms. In respect to the Arab customs, the males (Jerry and I) slept in one room, which only had one bed, and the girls (Pauline, Linda, and Melissa) in another room, which also had one bed. Joe had a sofa all by himself – Boy, what nights we passed! Despite this bad lodging experience, the visit to Luxor was fabulous. Among the sites (tombs, temples, etc.), we saw the Valley of the Kings, Queens, and Ramses Tombs, The Karnack, Valley of the Artisans, Colossi of Marmon, Temple of Hatshepsut, and others. Our visit to the Tomb of Tutankhamen (King Tut) was an experience to remember:

- Having been to the Egyptian Museum in Cairo and seeing "The Treasures of Tutankhamen," we were able to envision what Howard Carter first saw when he opened King Tutt's grave on February 16, 1923. Unlike another explorer (Giovanni Battista Belzoni), who opened the entrance of one of the Giza Pyramids with dynamite, Howard Carter was very methodical and systematic when he opened King Tut's grave. The sight he saw inside must have been overwhelming! He encountered the three sarcophagi containing the gold coffin where the well-preserved body of the King had laid. He also found a tremendous amount of golden and other artifacts – a chariot, shrouds, golden chairs, jewelry, beds, and huge amounts of other things – that the ancient Egyptians placed in the tomb for the

King to use in the afterlife. Tutankhamen reined Egypt around 1400 BC and died as a teenager from gangrene; it appears that he might have fallen off a horse and broken a leg bone. Infection set in, and he died. To be inside the tomb for the first time in thousands of years must have been mined altering. It is unfortunate that Carter and others died shortly after opening the grave; the manner of their death created the story that their deaths resulted from "King Tut's revenge...." Because of possible damage to King Tut's array of pictures and inside surroundings, we were unable to take pictures inside the tomb. Nevertheless, we are most fortunate to have with us the memory of our visual sight. It is an awesome experience for all of us.

After our visit to Luxor, we made other visits. For instance, Jerry and I visited El Alamein one time. Everyone who has studied the history of World War II remembers that German General, Erwin Rommel, invaded Egypt in January 1942 to capture the Suez Canal. There were two battles. The British Forces were able to stop the German thrust. The second battle is well known as the "beginning of the end" for Hitler and his desire to conquer the world. Jerry and I visited the museum, as well as parts of the battle locations. We also learned some more history about both battles. We enjoyed that very much.

Later, during my visit to the port of Alexandria, I took Melissa with me. After doing my work, we visited the beaches. I remember that the waves were so strong that I had to drag Melissa away for fear that she could be pulled into the ocean. Something funny happened one night:

- We stayed at what was considered at that time a real nice hotel. They gave us a nice room on the second floor. Since the hotel had no air conditioning, this room had two windows – one faced the street, and the other faced the rooms on the first floor (probably the hotel worker's rooms). Anyway, one night, around 1 or 2 in the morning, while I was sleeping, the people on the first floor began to have a party, singing, dancing, and yodeling. Melissa got very upset because of the noise and woke me up: "Dad, that noise is terrible. Can't you do something?" Let me now describe my appearance when Melissa woke me up and expressed such urgency. Dressed up in the nice white Pakistani dress that I used as my pajamas, I jumped out of bed as if I had gotten a terrible electric shock. Somewhat somnambulant, wild-eyed, trying to wake up, and my hair raised up and a mess, I rushed to the opened inside window, and yelled in Arabic for them to stop the noise. The party was so loud that they could not hear me. So, I got a roll of toilet paper and threw it at the dancing crowd. They looked up at me and you can imagine my appearance in center of the wooden dark frame of an open window. There I was in my white silk Pakistani dress, hair sticking up, half-sleep, wild-eyed, and appearing, in the center of the dark wooden window frame. I must have appeared like a portrait of an unsolicited evil spirit or a deranged monarch. What a terrible sight I must have been! Probably thinking they were seeing the devil incarnate, the party disintegrated fast. Poor people! Ok, go ahead and laugh. Melissa and I had a nice sleep from then on.

Short Rest and Recuperation For Family. After visiting Luxor, we visited many other tourist attractions and places. After my family had been in Egypt for about six to eight months, they went to Europe and the U.S. on an authorized short "rest and recuperation" period. As part of this rest and recuperation period, Melissa and Jerry went to England. Jerry, a great fan of the Beatles, wanted to visit Liverpool, but they settled for London. After visits to different places, there was no doubt that they were happy to return to Egypt and continue to enjoy the country.

At this point, my book returns to the professional work that I was doing in the country.

PART E. BRIEF EXAMPLES OF SURVEY AND REVIEW OF THE COMMODITY IMPORT PROGRAM (CIP)

PART E.1. AUDIT PLAN FOR AND REVIEWS OF CIP.[93]

At the time we were in Egypt, USAID's Handbook 3 and 4 provided the Agency's rules, background, and guidance, as well as a "Paradigm" to

---

[93] My 1980 Audit Plan for the Commodity Import Program Covering the nine Loans and one grant.

differentiate between "project" and "non-project" assistance.[94] Project assistance is usually designed to have a long-term economic impact. For this reason, Agency's rules, regulations, and handbooks call for an extremely strict and precise process of design and implementation consisting of several steps, including pre-design, design, contracting, implementation, and monitoring. The Agency's rules, regulations, and handbooks also required the contractor or grantee to accurately calculate the costs of the project.

By contrast, non-project assistance is designed to have a quick and short-term economic and positive balance of payment impact. Here is a brief recap of the three types of assistance. One type of assistance consists of massive cash transfer grants made to certain countries like Israel. This type of assistance is purely political and not normally subject to audit and review. The next two types of assistance consist of the CIP and the P.L 480 Programs. Funding provided under the CIP can be used to import a wide range of commodities, such as tallow (used to make soap), chicken, tin plate, coal, and other items, while the P.L. 480 programs are basically limited to agricultural commodities. The items imported under the CIP are quickly consumed in the host country. The P.L. 480 assistance helps U.S. farmers produce, sell, and/or donate agricultural items to needy host countries. .[95] Both types of assistance have a dual beneficial effect on the U.S. For example, this assistance provides sales income for U.S. farmers, and the host country gets really needed commodities that are normally quickly used by the people.[96]

Here is a brief background on the CIP that the USAID Mission to Egypt provided to the country in the late 1970s and the early 1980s. The funding for the CIP totaled $1.5 Billion and was being implemented through nine different loans and one grant. At the time of our survey and review (March 1980), USAID had disbursed over $1.0 Billion. Of this amount, only $68.0 million had been targeted at the private sector; the great majority of the importations

[94] You can also find the Agency's rules, background and guidance at the time on page 31 of this book.
[95] Information obtained from audit reports issued while in Vietnam and Egypt
[96] Of course, importing goods into a host country can have the effect of displacing domestic producers; however, in certain circumstances, for example, during periods of famine, the effect can be extremely positive.

had been provided to nine Egyptian Governmental Ministries, i.e., the public sector.

As was always the case, my survey of the CIP was done to cover situations (issues, problems, aspects, procedures, and/or systems) of the entire program. Therefore, my survey used techniques learned from many years of experience and expounded by me in a memo to AG/Policies in 1974: reviews of documents, analysis of internal controls, degree of checks and balances, evaluations, test probes, test visits, visual observations, discussions, etc. On this basis, my team and mostly, I prepared a 140-page Audit Plan. Aside from background and related information, the Plan described 47 different situations that needed to be examined more thoroughly. For example, I estimated that there would be about 4 to 6 different audits (and Audit Reports) which would cover (a) the Financial Procedures and Controls, (b) Project-Like Activities, (c) Non-durable and Durable Commodities, (d) Arrival Accounting and End-use of Imported Commodities, (e) Agent's Commissions, (f) perhaps one or two classified reports, and (g) a "wrap-around" Top-Managerial Report Covering Broad Agency Policy Implications. I estimated that all work could be done by six RIG/A/ Egypt personnel -- and I named them and their individual time estimate -- three RIG/A/Washington auditors and one member of the Special Investigation group. The total time to achieve the work was estimated at 4,612 hours, and I estimated hours by auditors and review areas. In other words, my Work Plan was precise and thorough.

Different levels of the IG reviewed the work plan. When the Inspector General's Policy and Plans office reviewed my work plan, they raised some concerns about the time that we would be spending on these audits. One persistent question was "...what if we don't find any problems...." I justified the time by pointing out that the CIP was a $1.5 billion program, and that the CIP was larger than 30 other individual projects being implemented in Egypt, all of which amounted to $1.3 Billion. I also showed them statistics comparing the CIP with the 30 other projects. Finally, I noted that there was no doubt that the CIP had serious problems – the plan showed them the problems. In sum, the Inspector General approved 4,612 hours for audits of the CIP.

PART E.2. LISTING OF FIVE AUDIT REPORTS ISSUED UNDER CIP AUDIT PLAN

In any event, the full-scale audit work went exactly as planned, and we eventually issued seven reports. The high-level "Wrap Around" report was never issued, which I will explain why later. Because of the voluminous nature of each finding in the audit reports, I will only mention the highlights of the following five different reports (certain terms – like Counterpart Generation, sugar mills, calciner furnaces, microwave systems, and others are described in the reports shown on the "footnotes"):

The CIP Financial Procedures and Controls Report. This report was about 40 pages long.[97] It described issues related to (a) AID's Accounting and Information System for CIP; (b) methods of financing; (c) advances and progress payments to suppliers; (d) rates of disbursements; (e) commodity losses; and (f) GOE local currency counterpart generation. The report contained 10 different recommendations.

The CIP Project-Like Report. This report was about 50 pages long.[98] It described issues related to financing, managing, and monitoring of: (a) project-like-type activities through the CIP; (b) a railway traffic control system; (c) ice-making plants; (d) boilers and sugar mills; (e) rotary hearth calciner furnaces; (f) microwave system; (g) vessel traffic management system; and (h) automatic bakeries. The report contained 15 recommendations and a great number of lessons learned (see my Concluding Remarks).

The CIP Non-Durable and Durable Commodities Report. This report was about 35 pages long.[99] It described issues related to: (a) the GOE Ministry of Electricity; (b) tractors; (c) busses made by the Ward Bus Manufacturing Company; (d) the importation of tobacco and related products; and (e) the high-volume requirements that diminished competition. In addition, this report contained 11 recommendations. In addition, I also found evidence of a very

---

[97] Audit Report No. 6-263-81-1 entitled "Audit Report on the Financial Procedures and Controls (all reports contained the numbers of the CIP Loans and Grants)."
[98] Audit Report No. 6-263-81-2 entitled "Audit Report on Internal Operating Procedures Applicable to Project-Like Activities of the CIP (loans and grants) "
[99] Audit Report No. 6-263-81-3 entitled "Audit Report on Internal Operating Procedures Applicable to Non-Durable and Durable Commodities, (Loans and Grants)"

extensive fraud being perpetrated by four or five suppliers – using bidding collusion techniques to keep increasing price (and their profit) -- on the sale of a certain product. These types of findings, and another similar one, were the subject of classified reports, special investigations, and certain types of sanctions against the suppliers. For my work on this audit, I got a letter of recognition.

The CIP Arrival Accounting and End-Use Functions Report. This report was about 20 pages long.[100] It described three issues related to (a) defects of a manual arrival and accounting system maintained by the Mission to track the arrival and disbursement of certain CIP products; (b) the design of arrival and computerized accounting system being developed by the USAID Mission in Egypt; and (c) lapses in end-use coverage by one Mission office. The report contained 10 recommendations.

Questionable Agents' Commissions. This report was about 20 pages long and contained high-level recommendations. In the case of Egypt, the great majority of the CIP was being imported by the Public Sector (GOE Organizations). Of all the CIP of $1.5 Billion, about $44.0 million were being paid for "Agent's Commission." Since the work of these agents was done in Egypt by (and for) GOE Organizations, the commissions were highly questionable. Some agents had all the characteristics of being employees or contractors of the GOE Organization that paid them the commission. For instance, these people worked inside the company and were paid only when the work was totally complete. In addition, since Egypt was considered a "Local Currency Excess Country," any "legal" commission should have been paid in Local Currency – by Egypt. There were other issues. The report contained 9 recommendations.

The "Top-Managerial Report Covering Broad Agency Policy Implications" Was Cancelled. As noted from the above summaries, all the CIP reports were exceptional. They contained noticeably clear and descriptive explanations of the many defects in how the Mission had approached, implemented, and adopted a "passive monitoring attitude" toward providing this type of assistance to Egypt. In particular, the Mission should have

[100] Audit Report No. 6-263-81-5 entitled "Audit Report Covering the Internal Operating Procedures Used by Management in the Arrival Accounting and End-Use Functions (CIP Loans and Grants)."

designed, planned, supervised, executed, and monitored the "project-like activities" as distinct projects. The Mission also should not have allowed the "haphazard" upward cost adjustments that we found in a few cases. We made similar comments in other reports. A good example was the busses made by the Ward Company. These busses were built for roads in the United States and not for the roads in Egypt, many of which were rough. The busses were also not built with tremendous passenger loading capacities needed in Egypt (I will explain more in my Concluding Remarks).

In any event, after we began issuing our audit reports -- and especially the report covering the "project-like activities" -- plans to issue a fifth report covering topics with broad agency policy Implications, also referred to "wrap-up report," became highly controversial – especially in the USAID/Washington high management circles. As a result, the Mission requested the USAID Assistant Administrator for Near East, asking us to refrain from issuing such a "wrap-up report." After the Inspector General evaluated the request, he raised several questions related to (a) criteria we were using (it was AID Technical Order (TO) Circular 24, AID Handbook 3, chapter 3, Appendix 3c; and AID Handbook 4). He also asked about other minor or misunderstood type of issues, questions, or wordings we had used in the reports, which we could explain. In any event, at the Inspector General's request and with our concurrence, the high-level report was never issued. I agreed with his decision. My concurring memorandum said: "The broad questions and issues have been covered in the individual reports. The Mission has begun to act on all the recommendations. USAID/Washington has been made aware of the problem having broader implications. In sum, I don't see much to gain from this office or the IG Organization in issuing this additional report…."

As the reader can well imagine, attempting to summarize all the issues contained in all the issued reports would be a very difficult undertaking. For this reason, my concluding remarks will describe just some of the lessons learned from our reviews.

Other Audits and Activities. We made numerous other reports. In addition, we had a memorable Christmas in Jerusalem, and I was appointed to participate in the 1980 Personnel Evaluation Panel (these two subjects are covered in two later chapters).

Jerry Pena And Unknown Tourists at Egypt's Sphinx And Pyramid

Author Jose, Jerry My Son, Hasan with Blue Cap and Group of New Friends Hasan Is Driver Who Wanted Jerry to Marry His Two Daughters

In Pictures, Ladies Doing Their Laundry and A Lady and Boy on Local Transportation These Are Common Village Sights in Egypt. This raises a question: How Can U.S. Aid reach this Numerous "Poorest of The Poor Population?"

PART F. FINAL EGYPTIAN TOUR (VISIT)

At this point, I will now jump ahead to around 1997. Jerry accompanied me to Egypt when I went there with a team of four women who were to design a project addressing problems faced by women in Egyptian society. My role was quick, insignificant, and not worth elaboration. So, Jerry and I stayed in Egypt as tourists for one month. During my week-long assignment, we stayed at the Semiramis Inter-continental Hotel of Cairo, an extremely nice, but expensive hotel. We did two things right after my assignment was over. The first was to hire a taxi driver for a month. The second was to rent a furnished apartment for one month.

We first hired the taxi driver. His name was Hassan, and he had a real amusing personality. This is how we met him. As Jerry and I walked out of the Semiramis hotel, Hassan asked us if he could drive us somewhere. The first thing we noted was that Hassan's voice, speech, and mannerism were almost identical to that of Anthony Quinn in the 1964 movie "Zorba the Greek." There he was, trying to convince us to hire him and at the same time fighting off the competition who also wanted our business. He won. So, we liked him immediately. He quickly found us a real nice two-bedroom apartment in the nice part of the Zamalek area of Cairo. We rented the apartment for a month right away. It cost us about $1,500, but this arrangement gave us privacy and flexibility, and we saved on hotel costs.

From then on, Hassan drove us everywhere, ate with us, and protected us. Every day, I would give Hassan a little money for gas and home expenses. He and I had agreed that I would pay him at the end of the month. Wherever he drove, Hassan always had two spare tires on top of his car; I asked him why. He showed me the four tires on the car – all were completely bald. Anyway, Hassan liked us very much, and he and Jerry spoke Arabic most of the month. Since Jerry had taken his movie camera, he would take pictures of Cairo, the surrounding areas, and every place we went.

Once again, we revisited all the usual tourist attractions. In addition, we went to some pyramids that are seldom seen by tourists. The Step Pyramid of Djoser is a very interesting construction; getting into the central part of the chamber is extremely hard because you need to walk down into the middle of the Pyramid and then climb up a ladder into the chamber. While Jerry waited outside, I walked to the center inside the pyramid. The inside of the pyramid gave me a claustrophobic feeling, so I was not about to climb the ladder into a burial chamber. After going out and viewing the Step Pyramid from the outside, we got into the car. Just as we were about to leave, some guy with a pistol **told** us he wanted a ride to Cairo. I sat next to the guy in the back seat. I noted that Hassan was somewhat nervous and kept eyeing him through the mirror. After we dropped him off, Hassan said he was a secret police officer – and a very bad man. Fortunately, nothing happened.

Hassan also took us to various mosques – the Mohammed Ali Mosque or Citadel, the Suleiman Pasha mosques, the Tomb of Gamal Abdel Nassar,[101] and others. Jerry and I will always remember our visit to the Sacred Madam Mufasa Mosque. Why? Tourists seldom get inside this mosque. Since she was a very close relative to the Prophet Mohamed, the remains of Madam Mufasa are buried and greatly venerated in this Mosque. Therefore, deeply religious Muslim people (mostly men) come to touch the tomb that contains her remains.

When Hassan took us in, with the permission of the Imam, we were shown all kinds of courtesies. After viewing, and touching, the tomb, the Imam made Jerry and I kneel, and he prayed or "blessed" us, kissed us on the cheek, and sent us on our way. The experience was something to remember. Hassan said that we were baptized into the Muslim Religion; I just do not know. All I can say is that it was a wonderful experience.

About two days before our return to the U.S., Hassan invited us to his apartment. He lived there with his wife and two daughters. It was a beautiful family. Maybe in their 20's, his two daughters were real pretty. Anyway, the family gave us a real nice dinner. After the dinner, Hassan – with his Zorba the Greek voice -- got his wife, the two daughters, and us in front of him. He told us that he liked Jerry and me very much. He then asked Jerry if he liked his daughters. Jerry admitted that they were very pretty. Hassan then told Jerry that he would be extremely happy if he married ONE and even happier if he married the TWO daughters. Boy, that proposal caused my jaw to almost drop! But I had expected that something like that might happen. Throughout our different conversations, Hassan had asked Jerry many questions and had mentioned several times that he had two young daughters that were not married – yet. So, thinking ahead, I figured he might ask Jerry to marry ONE – not TWO. Jerry and I had made tentative plans for a response. In my case, I had crafted, in my mind, an inoffensive discourse that said many words without any commitment and, in essence, rejected the idea. When Hassan made the proposal for Jerry to marry BOTH girls, Jerry looked at me to answer, and my mind got all muddled up. My response was perhaps somewhat lame:

---

[101] Gamal Abdel Nasser served as Egypt's president from 1954 to 1970.

- I merely said that Hassan had a beautiful family, that the daughters were just fabulously beautiful, and that such a sincere marriage proposal was appreciated. However, this offer had come at a time when Jerry and I were about ready to leave. We were honored by their feelings toward us, and we would give the proposal profoundly thoughtful consideration once we got back to the U.S.

Hassan looked at Jerry, and Jerry gave him a more direct answer:

- He told him that the daughters were beautiful. But having two or more wives violated the U.S. laws, our society, and our religious affiliations. U.S. people frowned at such arrangements. And, since the girls were both so beautiful, he would have great difficulty choosing one or the other. He was incredibly grateful for the consideration and would give it profoundly serious thought once we got back to the U.S.

Anyway, Jerry and I felt greatly honored by Hassan's feelings toward us and his sincere desire to arrange a marriage between Jerry and his two daughters. We just hope that we did not hurt the family's feelings in any way. Two days after the dinner, Hassan took us to the airport. On the way there, one of the tires blew. Very quickly, Hassan put one of the spares, and we got to our flight on time. Aside from the daily expenses I had given him every day -- and just before we went to the airport -- I gave Hassan about the U.S. $2,500 (about LE 7,500); he was extremely happy. That was our last visit to Egypt. Hassan, wife, and daughters: we will always remember you and be grateful for your generous marriage proposal.

PART G. MY OVERALL CONCLUDING REMARKS ON EGYPT

It got time when the Egypt assignment came to an end. Russell was transferred to the Philippines as the Regional Inspector General. Although I had asked to stay in Egypt, the Inspector General appointed me as the Deputy Regional Inspector General for Audits in Latin America, which would now be operating from Washington D.C. – for the following reasons:

- As I mentioned in Chapter 12, the two managers of the RIG/A/Pakistan were very difficult to get along with. They were very poor managers of people. Soon after I left Pakistan, John E., the deputy, was assigned as the Regional Inspector General for Audits in East Africa. In turn, Jack R. was transferred as the Regional Inspector General for Audits in Latin America – based in Panama. As you might have already surmised, his drinking and mismanagement of personnel soon got him into a great deal of problems with his staff and the Missions. Personnel morale was at an all-time low. The Office operated in constant anger, animosity, accusations, retributions, and some near insurrections. There were even one or two incidents when "...someone overturned a heavy desk in front of either Jack R. or his deputy...." According to my friends, it was a mess. With so much trouble going on in the office, the IG made the decision to close the office and have the office operate from Washington. As a result, Jack R. retired and later died (may he RIP), Dean H., the Deputy RIG/A, was appointed as the Regional Inspector General, and I was officially appointed as his deputy. Since the Inspector General had never had personnel complaints from the office of the Regional Inspector General in Egypt, I guess his thinking was that I could help (and I did) mold the staff into an improved and better working team.

Departing Egypt was very hard on all of us. Our tour there was an extraordinary experience. From a personal and professional point of view, my tour was fabulous. The family had an exceptional learning education and experiences which have improved their outlook on life.

What helped the most was that during the 3 ½ years that Russell and I were in Egypt, we were able to get and have exceptional U.S. Staff and hire the best staff in Egypt; we taught and molded the staff into an exceptional team. The importance of good management and two-way communication between managers and staff cannot be over-emphasized. On this basis, aside from the above-summarized audits, the audit team conducted many more exceptional reviews and reports. On behalf of Russell and myself, I do want to express our appreciation to all the team members – Coinage, Joe, Wayne, Ben, Ahmed, Amin, Haney, Amer, Dale, Agnes, and Mariam, who made our assignment and responsibilities a tremendous success.

And in my pursuit of improving assistance to Host Countries, I feel that we had left many lessons which were (or could be) learned by USAID in

Washington, the Mission in Egypt, and the GOE. Due to time and space limitations, let me include only a few.

a) The USAID Agency Handbook needed to prescribe clear instructions telling the Missions and Host Countries how to help plan, design, contract, manage, and monitor borrower and grantee activities.

b) The USAID Agency Computerized Accounting System – which had eight (8) separate sub-systems (to account for Egypt accountin)-- needed to be modified to consolidate all project cost elements in a single computer system.

c) USAIDs Training Office computer system was in urgent need of a radical improvement.

d) USAID's policies on the use of very costly intermediary financial or sales instruments– such as Bank Letters of Credit and agents' commission needed urgent modifications.

The Mission(s) also had a few lessons that each could learn:

a) Projects like the Grain Silos are extremely complex to implement, and the Missions needed to be more proactive in designing, directing, managing, and monitoring such projects.

b) "Project-Like Activities" needed to be: (1) managed as distinct projects; ((2) well-planned; (3) adequately justified; (4) implemented in a timely manner.

c) The Missions also needed to do a better job of preparing contracts for borrowers and grantees. They needed to ensure that suppliers were never allowed to control the direction and scope of activities and costs.

d) Using Bank Letters of Credit and paying agents' commissions in U.S. Dollars represented a very high cost and unwarranted procedure which also had a consequent reduction of benefits to the host country and its people.

e) "Durable Commodities" like the Ward Busses needed technical specifications to be more precisely written and in line with the host country roads, population use, and other conditions. As shown in our report, the Ward Buses were poorly suited for road conditions in Egypt and other developing countries. As a result, the Ward Buses were destroyed within 3 to 6 months of use by the rough roads, lack of maintenance, and the tendency to cram too many people into the bus.

f) The Agency and the Mission(s) needed to monitor contractors' billings to avoid situations like the one we found in the Poultry Improvement Projects – and the activities I found in Washington later – where contractors inappropriately included indirect and other costs that for all intents and purposes were fraudulent.

In sum, Egypt was an exceptional assignment, and all of us were sad to leave the country. We left behind some fine people and many exceptional friends. Jerry went back to Virginia in January 1981. Pauline and Linda left on June 1, 1981. Melissa and I left on June 28, 1981.

CHAPTER FOURTEEN
A MEMORABLE CHRISTMAS TIME TRAVELING BY ROAD FROM EGYPT TO ISRAEL

PART A. INTRODUCTORY REMARKS

The trip that we took by car, from Egypt through the Sinai Desert to Israel and back, will always remain in our minds as one of the most memorable Christmases of our lives. The highlight of that trip occurred at midnight on December 24, 1980, in Bethlehem -- inside the small room and place where Baby Jesus is said to have been born. This chapter is presented in 10 Parts.

- Part A Introductory Remarks.
- Part B The Beginning of Our Story.
- Part C Background on Israel and Egyptian Treaty.
- Part D Some Recollections about my Transfer to Egypt.
- Part E Our Trip through the Sinai Desert and the Skeletal Remains of War.
- Part F Border Lines Distinction between Egypt and Israel.
- Part G Getting around Israel.
- Part H Impressions at Birthplace of Baby Jesus.
- Part I Time to Return to Cairo.
- Part J. Concluding Remarks

PART B. THE BEGINNING OF OUR STORY

This story really began in 1979. It was a fabulous moment in the history of three nations. Three great statesmen had met in the White House and Camp David and had signed the first peace treaty between Egypt and Israel. The date was March 26, 1979, and those great statesmen were Jimmy Carter, the 39th

President of the United States; Meacham Begin, the Israeli Prime Minister; and Anwar El-Sadat, President of Egypt. This historic peace treaty ushered in a peaceful relationship between the two nations that has continued for the last 41 years. It is now difficult to believe that, in effect, between 1948 and 1978, there had been countless wars, conflicts, and scrimmages. According to the Internet, there have been at least four important wars between the two nations: (a) the Suez Canal Incident of 1956; (b) the six-day war of 1967; (c) the war of attrition of 1967 to 197; and, (d) the war of 1973.

PART C. BACKGROUND ON THE ISRAELI AND EGYPTIAN TREATY

For the United States, the Camp David Accord represented an enormous international diplomatic coup. Since 1948, Israel and the U.S. had been staunch allies--to the point where the United States provided F-4 Phantoms from its own active stocks during the 1973 war in order to ensure that the Israelis would not lose that war. In its new relationship with Egypt -- which, in terms of its population, is the largest Arab nation in the Middle East -- the U.S. was faced with a huge challenge. For this reason, as part of the Camp David Accord, the U.S. immediately committed diplomatic, military, and economic resources and increased the size of its diplomatic presence in Egypt.

In turn, for Egypt, the economic assistance provided by the U.S. Agency for International Development (USAID) -- under which I was employed as a Foreign Service Officer at the time (now retired) -- was greatly needed and essential to lasting peace. It also provides an example to other Middle Eastern countries of how two opposing countries can co-exist without fear of constant wars.

Given such a historic opportunity, the United States moved quickly. It established a large USAID presence in Egypt to formulate and manage the economic development programs that the country sorely needed.

PART D. SOME RECOLLECTIONS OF MY EGYPT ASSIGNMENT

At the time this was happening, I had been assigned, without my family, to the USAID Regional Office of Inspector General in Karachi, Pakistan. I had already been there nearly one year and had extensively traveled to a series of other Middle Eastern countries (Bangladesh, Afghanistan, Yemen, etc.). My transfer to Egypt came with a note of urgency. I was given 2 weeks to wind up all my affairs, pack up, sell, or take an old Chevrolet Vega I had taken to Pakistan, and leave. One of my friends bought my old Vega for a token of $200. And, after being on travel status 90% of my time, I felt extremely happy to be leaving this regional office.

Once my family got to Egypt for my Second Tour, we began to think in terms of going to Israel and research the possibility of going by car – to see the Sinai Dessert and anything that was left of some wars. So, around November of 1980, we decided to go to Israel for Christmas – by road. After doing all the necessary consultations and reservations (We made reservations to stay in a monastery in Jerusalem), I requested permission from the Egyptian Government on December 2, 1980, to take the road trip. The trip was finally approved by everybody.

PART E. OUR TRIP THROUGH THE SINAI DESERT AND THE SKELETAL REMAINS OF WAR

Our trip began around December 19. By that date, Joe, who was in college, had arrived from the United States. The six of us piled into the small 1978 Dodge Challenger and drove to Port Said and stayed the night there. We saw two Russian ships and others crossing the Suez Canal that night. Because the Ahmed Hamid Tunnel was still under construction (it was completed in 1981), we crossed the Suez Canal via a small ferry boat. And thus, began on that day, our journey -- into the bareness, and bad roads, of the desert of the Sinai. Many of the roads that now exist in the Sinai were non-existent at the time. It seems like we traveled on bad roads forever that day – zigzagging through villages and places in the desert with strange names (not too sure of the spelling): Bir-Gigaba, Bir-Atha Hamadeh, Bir Hassan, and finally to El-Arish. To a certain extent, Jerry guided us. He and a friend (Fernando), a Venezuelan who made his home in Egypt, had traveled by bus from Cairo to Israel. So, Jerry remembered some of the routes.

Looking back, crossing the desert between Port Said and all those small towns or villages was a tremendous education – there were all kinds of destroyed war carcasses – vehicles, tanks, trucks, jeeps, cannons, etc. – discarded after the 1967 and 1973 wars. The kids, what can I say about the children. Joe, Jerry, and Linda were enjoying the value of seeing the war carcasses and imagining the wars. Nevertheless, the trip was long, tedious, and boring – there was the usual yelling, hollering, fighting, and the perennial question – "when are we getting there?"

Part F. Border Lines Distinction Between Egypt And Israel

Anyway, after getting to El-Arish, we crossed the border between Egypt and Israel. In crossing the border, we were amazed at the difference in the way two countries can be distinguished -- in the dress, presentation, and comportment. Back then (hopefully changed by now), the Egyptian Guards' uniforms seemed rumpled and shabby, whereas the Israeli guards' uniforms were tailored, pressed, and sharp. Despite the treaty between Israel and Egypt, security in Israel continued to be extremely high. Jerry made the mistake of trying to get close to one of the Israeli Guards. Without hesitation, the Guard pointed the gun at Jerry and told him to back off, or he would shoot him. Boy, did I jump to the rescue. I told the guards that we were American Diplomats and that we were stationed in Egypt and visiting Israel for the first time. I quickly told Jerry never to approach guards like that. He never did that again.

Our road trip took us to a few small towns in the Gaza Strip – Khan Yunis and others. As we passed the towns, the Palestinian people would see our Egyptian license plates and yell to us: "Nasser, Nasser." Thinking we were Egyptians, we chatted with them and ate their food along the way. After passing several towns in the Gaza Strip, we finally were on Israeli roads. What a difference. The roads were nicely paved and well maintained.

If I remember correctly, we passed Beersheba and Hebron. We eventually got to Jerusalem and the monastery (whose name escapes), where we would stay. Every one of us remembers a series of things about the monastery. There were numerous other tourists from different countries staying there. The rooms were extremely cold. Melissa had been smart and brought a heavy blanket, so the girls slept together for warmth and comfort. At mealtimes, a person would ring a bell, and we had to rush to get good seats. One time, either Jerry or Linda, rushed into the dining area, knocked on a coat rack full of clothing, and felt so embarrassed; he/she sat and ate quietly that night.

PART G. GETTING AROUND ISRAEL

Using a tour company to get around, the next couple of days were busy for us. We made the rounds of tourist and religious attractions. We walked the 14 stages of the Via Dolorosa, where Jesus struggled to carry the heavy cross. We saw the Golgotha Hill, where Jesus was crucified. And we also saw the Church of the Holy Sepulcher; this is where he is said to have been resurrected. Pauline, Linda, and Melissa were so impressed that they kept touching and feeling the different stages of the Via Dolorosa Road. We then went to the Wailing or Western Wall, the location of the second Jewish Temple, which is strongly venerated by the Jewish people. After observing the religious rituals and touching them, we walked through a passage to the Dome of the Rock; my son, Jerry, told me its Arabic Name is "Qubits Al-Sakha," and it is venerated by the Islamic religion. After these visits, we also saw other worthy religious locations.

PART H. IMPRESSIONS AT BIRTHPLACE OF BABY JESUS

By then, it was December 24th. We ate dinner at the monastery, rested, and waited for the bus to take us to Bethlehem. All of us remember that the night was extremely cold, and it was raining hard. Indeed, it was the most miserable night imaginable. A few buses arrived at the Monastery. We were supposed to go on the "Catholic Bus." However, one of us – and we keep pointing fingers and placing blame or credit – made a mistake and got us on the "Angelica Bus." This bus was full of people from the Church of England. Since we were on the going by bus to Bethlehem and did not know any better, we made the trip to Bethlehem with the wrong group.

The mistake turned out to be a lucky one. Once in Bethlehem, we unloaded right in front of the Church of the Nativity. At exactly 12:00 midnight, we were inside the room where the Baby Jesus is said to have been born. All of us remember the numerous inter-related things: time, sight, a bright star, the red garments, religious artifacts, candles, smells, different decorations, small cradle, kneeling of all present, and loud and the silent prayers that were being said. We also remember the feeling we all felt of the apparent "presence" of a supernatural being among us. All of us – especially young Melissa – experienced an unusually glorious and peaceful feeling that cannot be easily described. This magic moment is firmly imbedded in our minds forever and it was to later affect my daughter, Melissa, and she is now a deeply religious person. Here is her testimony:

- "At the time that we went to Bethlehem (the House of Bread), I was only 13 years old. However, I remember getting off the bus, walking down the stairs, and together with the group, coming face to face with the alter in the place where Jesus was born. Just like my father described the setting, I felt such an indescribable feeling of peace and adoration within myself. The beautiful alter and the setting it represented showed me, a definite proof, on how the Lord was born in a quite common manger. Moreover, this baby boy was born from the Virgin Mary, without original sin, and without the regular birth pains. Saint Joseph became the Foster Father of Jesus. On that faithful day of His birth, the Stars lit brightly and pointed the way that the Lord would take all of us to ensure our salvation. There is no doubt in my mind that a King was born that day. I firmly believe that this moment in time was the primary guiding factor that gave direction to my life. The Lord Jesus, in all his glory, allowed me to see the future path for my life, and I am, like my father says, gratefully walking closer to God than many other people. God Bless everyone."

Since That Memorable Night in The Bethlehem Church of Nativity, Melissa G. Pena Has Been A Very Religious Person

As we walked out of the church, there was a ragged beggar sitting in the cold and the rain. Was he an omen of some sort? We never knew. Anyway, the next couple of days, we traveled in our car to many other places: wailing Wall, the Golden Dome, Tel-Aviv, Jericho, the Dead Sea, close to the Jordan Border, Nablus, and others.

PART I. TIME TO RETURN TO CAIRO

It was time to go back to Cairo. We followed the reverse route that had brought us to Jerusalem. When we got to the border between Israel and Egypt, we were told that a bridge to El-Arish had been destroyed by the rain and the flood. So, we turned back, and the Israeli soldiers told us of a small "vacation village" nearby. The village was called "Yemen or Yamen, or Yamet" Yamen turned out to be a life saver. Before the Six-Day War, Yamen, which had a sunny beach, had been Palestinian territory. After the war, Israel took possession and built a real nice series of single-floor apartments. Since it was winter and cold, Yamen had no visitors. During the first night, Pauline got very sick and had a high fever; the Office Manager called an ambulance. She was checked out, given antibiotics, and sent "home." We stayed in Yamen for three days until the road to El Arish had been reestablished. A few years after we stayed in yamen, the Israelis destroyed all the nice apartments before turning over the territory to the Palestinians and Egyptians. Those apartments were gorgeous; if they had been turned over intact to the Palestinians or Egyptians, they could be serving as a fabulous tourist attraction.

We had a big problem at the Egyptian border. Our son, Joe, who was, at the time, a student at the College of William and Mary, had been given a "One Entry and One Departure Visa" to Egypt. Since he had entered Egypt and "left" through Israel, the Egyptians would not let him back into the country. We spent six hours at the border until the Egyptian Ministry of Foreign Affairs approved his re-entry. We finally made it back to Cairo on December 30, 1980.

PART J. CONCLUDING REMARKS

Let me conclude this chapter by saying that during the time I was employed as a Foreign Service Officer with USAID, the family and/or I took numerous memorable trips around the different parts of the world. However, whenever we discuss old times, and take trips down memory lanes, we always return to this trip. Because of the political instability, wars, and violence that now exists in Egypt and other Middle Eastern Countries, we consider ourselves ever so fortunate to have been stationed in Egypt during more stable times. In fact, we were in Egypt during a time when it was quite a peaceful country. Peaceful relations between Egypt and Israel were in the "honeymoon stage" and thus good. Although the roads through the Sinai were rough, there was no threat of violence or harm. The political situation in the Gaza Strip was relatively stable and calm. And although the security situation in Israel was tight, our travel by car was never challenged. Of course, we continue to thank the person who got us on the wrong bus because we will always remember that on midnight of December 24, 1980, we were inside a small "basement-type" room where Baby Jesus is said to have been born. Without a doubt, we will always remember this moment in time for the rest of our lives.

CHAPTER FIFTEEN
AN ASSIGNMENT TO AGENCY-WIDE PERSONNEL EVALUATION PANEL A TERRIFIC PROFESSIONAL RECOGNITION

PART A. INTRODUCTORY COMMENTS

This chapter covers my assignment as a member of the 1980 USAID Agency-wide Personnel Evaluation Panel. This type of assignment represents a fantastic personal and professional recognition for a USAID employee. During the time I was in the Evaluation Panel, the Inspector General sent me a batch of 8 folders of General Schedule Personnel from another U.S. Agency (General Accountability Office – GAO) that he apparently wanted to recruit; I evaluated them after I had completed my work with the 1980 Panel, and I wrote the IG a Memorandum Report on my findings and thoughts. For this reason, this chapter is divided into 8 Parts:

- Part A Introductory Comments.
- Part B Brief Description of USAID Evaluation Systems in My Time.
- Part C My Assignment To the 1980 Personnel Evaluation Panel.
- Part D Panel Found Agency Needed to Establish a Uniform PER Evaluation System and Other Types of Other Challenges.
- Part E Our Panel Developed a Format Potentially Useable to Achieve Uniformity among USAID Evaluation Panels.
- Part F Memorandum Report Sent to Personnel Director.
- Part G Memorandum Report Sent to IG Designed to Improve Personnel Policies and Practices.
- Part H My Concluding Remarks.

PART B. BRIEF DESCRIPTION OF USAID EVALUATION SYSTEMS IN MY TIME

Just like the Department of State does, USAID also employs FSO and regular civil service (General Schedule Personnel) and, it also has Personal Services Contracts (PSC). Neither General Schedule (GS) nor PSC Personnel are evaluated by the FSO Panels. FSOs are the people that are normally assigned to many countries around the world; they serve as part of a "Mission" of their particular countries of assignment. This chapter will only deal with USAID's FSO Personnel Evaluation System.

Because of the international implications of our work, the FSO Personnel Evaluation Reports (PER of my time) were very thorough and strict. Briefly, PERs were prepared on a yearly basis. The immediate supervisor prepared a comprehensively written evaluation (this is a long dissertation that evaluates employees from different perspectives); the employee reviews and comments on the PER; a Reviewer then evaluates the PER. Once the PER is approved at the Mission level, the many Missions around the world send the PERs – numbering in the thousands -- to USAID headquarters in Washington. The PERs were then separated into the type of specialties (administrative, financial, programming, project, planning, capital development, etc.) called "Back-Stop Codes" (BSC) separations and given to different panels. These panels were separated by specialties according to the BS Codes. The panels consisted of high-level or field people with demonstrated experience, abilities, and independence of mind. The panels make decisions on promoting only exceptional employees to a higher grade. The panels also make decisions on what employees to keep in the same grade or even terminate extremely weak employees. Thus, assignment to one of the several Personnel Evaluation Panels was a very prestigious recognition for us – one that also carries a great professional responsibility to do fair, equitable, and unbiased personnel evaluations.

PART C. MY ASSIGNMENT TO THE 1980 PERSONNEL EVALUATION PANEL

While in Egypt, I was sent, on TDY, to USAID in Washington and assigned to one of the 1980 Personnel Evaluation Panels. There were four of us in the "Program Support Evaluation Panel." There was Richard Harger (a Mission Controller, now deceased), Arthur B., Dallas O. – both Arthur and Dallas had Executive Officers' positions, and me. We quickly selected Richard as the "Chairman." I knew Richard well; our friendship dated back to the time we served as "Special Envoys" together in Nicaragua right after the 1973 earthquake. He was an exceptional professional; I will always have fond memories of him.

When we first met, our first task was to see how many employees we were going to evaluate. Our count was 259 from the following Back Stop Codes (BSC):

BSC's	Discipline	No of Employees
03	Administrator	63
04	Controller	75
06	General Services	31
08	Audit and Inspection	56
91	Participant Training	3
93	Procurement and Supply	31
Total 259		

PART D. PANEL FOUND AGENCY NEEDED A UNIFORM PER EVALUATION SYSTEM AND OTHER TYPES OF CHALLENGES

The next action we took was to determine whether the Agency had a uniform evaluation system or policy in place and what other challenges awaited our work. We quickly found that **the Agency did not have a uniform or standard PER Evaluation Policy or plan.** As a result, **all the different panels**, including the four of us, had to create our own evaluation module and methodology. We also found a series of other challenges in our work, among them: (a) how to do the evaluations in an unbiased manner; (b) how to acquaint the Personnel Director with the need to improve future USAID Personnel Evaluation Practices; and how to get our suggestions to the Personnel Director so they could improve the situation for the future.

Because of this absence of guidelines and procedures, we struggled, for over a day or more, trying to find an equitable formula to evaluate in an unbiased manner all the 259 FSO Employees assigned to us.

PART E. OUR PANEL DEVELOPED A FORMAT POTENTIALLY USEABLE TO ACHIEVE UNIFORMITY AMONG USAID EVALUATION PANELS

The inter-exchange of possible methods among the four of us was thorough, analytical, incisive, and intense. As a result, we finally agreed on the following evaluation format that we would use. This is how we did our panel evaluations:

a) We divided the FSO by grade levels.

b) We evaluated each level in groups of 8 files.

c) We studied each candidate's work history and current PER.

d) We used worksheets to annotate our assessments.

e) Each panelist reviewed the eight in the group individually and ranked them.

f) Once we had reviewed the eight Personal Evaluation Reports (PERs), we discussed each one and then rated each one.

g) If any of the individual ratings seemed way off, we re-reviewed the 8 PERs or areas of deviations.

h) Once we all agreed, we divided them into categories A, B, C, etc.

i) We then reviewed the next 8 and so on.

j) After reviewing all the PERs, we re-arranged PERs by BS Codes.

k) This rearrangement afforded us an ability to review the individual by categories within the BS Code.

l) Using a scale of 1(for bad) to 10 (exceptional), each Panelist assigned a value to people placed in Categories A, B, C, etc...

m) If Panelists deviated by more than 2 points, we once again reviewed the PERs.

n) Once we had completed our evaluation of all the PERs, we computed numbers for the A and B categories, and the very best were recommended for a promotion. Category C represented FSOs that could stay in Agency but were not considered for promotion.

As can be concluded from the above, our evaluation was devoid of personal biases. Our secret deliberations took one month, and we reviewed each FSO's file a minimum of 3 times. Therefore, without getting into details, the four of us unanimously concluded that of the 259 FSOs evaluated, 110 were top-notch and promotable; the remaining 149 were excellent FSOs but should remain in their present grade.

PART F. A MEMORANDUM REPORT SENT TO PERSONNEL DIRECTOR

At the end of our evaluations, the four of us prepared a combined memorandum report and gave it to the Director of USAID's Office of Personnel Management. In it, we listed 8 areas where the Agency could improve the FSO rating and evaluation process. Among the 8 areas, we detailed our evaluation format and our conclusions and told the Director that the Agency needed to set up an Agency-wide policy establishing a "uniform or standard evaluating format" for all future panels. We also told the Director that he needed to determine how to compensate personnel who fell in Category C and thus showed limitations in their scope of work. Finally, we reported that the Agency should not write PERs on FSOs who had been in the Agency for less than six months because the short time frame resulted in ratings that were unrealistic because they were written using very conservative language detrimental to the new employee.

To the best of my knowledge, none of us were ever told whether the Agency adopted our recommendations. I sincerely hope that the Agency – as it exists today – has a standard evaluation policy.

Part G. Memorandum Report Sent To I.G. Designed To Improve Personnel Policies And Practices

Background Information. As stated previously, as I was doing the work for the Evaluation Panel, I got a batch of about 8 people working in another agency who were being considered for employment with our Office of IG at very high grades. I was asked to evaluate them and give my opinion on their capabilities. I did the evaluations right after completing my work with the 1980 Evaluation Panel.

Thus, after concluding my official duties in the 1980 Performance Evaluation Panel, I wrote a memorandum to the USAID Inspector General – which was cleared by the Panel and did not infringe on personalities or our secret deliberations. In this memo, I conveyed to him certain areas of concern regarding the IG personnel policies. Once I told him the positive impressions that I had about the panel, my memorandum discussed the following areas where improvements should be made to the policies and practices of our Office of Inspector General:

1. The IG Audit and IG Office of Inspection needed to establish a career ladder. I showed him the comparison between an IG FSO and an FSO

in another office. Without a career ladder, the file of IG FSO gave the image of stagnation, whereas the other officer showed impressive progressions. Thus, the IG FSO was at a disadvantage when it came to promotions.

2. **Regarding the eight persons who worked for another Agency (the GAO), I pointed out the following facts. To me, it seemed that the IG Office might be adopting a policy of obtaining General Schedule Personnel from other U.S. Agencies and converting them to FSOs at extremely high-grade levels. They had good backgrounds, but their high grades were loading upper FSO grades. This type of hiring of new personnel would eventually create – and did create -- a great morale problem for long-term FSOs who had served in several countries, been exposed to dangerous situations, and violated FSO rules. The practice also created confusing proposals for new assignments, PER preparation, and promotion situations. The solution, in my opinion, was for the IG to hire or transfer bright young people at lower grades; these younger FSOs represented the "…new blood needed by the Agency…." They would grow in exposure to USAID operations, experience, and grade progression.**

3. Moreover, the GS personnel that were being transferred, or proposed for transfer, as FSOs were at an age (near or over 55) when FSOs can retire. This policy needed very close re-examination because these high-graded people would provide very limited benefits to the IG Office, the Agency and the FSO career. In other words, they would come – and about 8 to 10 were eventually transferred in high FSO positions – stay(ed) for a short duration and retire. In fact, some converted from GS to FSOs, put in 2 to 3 years, and retired. To my knowledge, one or two never served on a permanent overseas assignment. These types of employment did not serve the long-term needs of either the IG or the Agency. In addition, their transfers from GS categories and transfers to high-level FSO positions could be a violation of the FSO Act.

4. Unrelated to the 8 GS persons, there was another aspect that needed to be addressed. This was that, for some reason, the IG Rating Officers,

and Reviewing Officers – in the case of both the IG Audit and IG Investigations Office – were writing the narrative part of the PERs using very conservative and non-committal language. In the case of other offices, they used very flowery and positive language, which created a better image of the Evaluated Employee. We needed to receive some training on how to prepare better PERs and a policy to further modernize and improve our education.

PART H. MY CONCLUDING REMARKS

As shown in this chapter, the assignment to one of the Agency-Wide Evaluation Panels was, to me, a terrific learning experience. Certainly, the Agency needed to establish policies that would enable all panels to use uniform PER evaluative procedures. Without such uniformity in procedures, each panel evaluated FSO personnel "…every which way…" using several different ways and formats -- even if they resulted in unfair conclusions.

As stated earlier, none of the Panelists heard from the Personnel Director. Therefore, I hope the Agency now uses uniform evaluative procedures in its performance evaluation panels. In any event, I will make a recommendation, in Chapter 19, for the current IG to evaluate procedures of this area.

In relation to the memorandums that I sent to the USAID Inspector General, he chose not to accept my recommendation and hired the eight people and converted them from GS to high FSO Grades. I certainly wish he had adopted my recommendations for improving IG personnel practices. I was never formally told why he chose not to adopt them. However, as shown in Chapter 17, 18, and 19, the people he brought tried to establish policies, practices, and procedures which were not beneficial or the type needed by the IG, the Agency, and/or the Foreign Service System. Once again, I voiced dissent against their erroneous actions, and – since the IG did not have a "dissent channel," I was callously punished for four or five years for expressing my professional opinions.

In Chapter 16, I provide evidence of my fabulous performance. Yet….and yet, the Chapter also shows the callous way in which I was told that I had been fired from the DRIG/A/LA position. Without a doubt, my challenge of the erroneous policies, practices, and procedures was the reason for the dismissal. Chapters 16, 17, 18, and 19 explain why I needed to disagree with the proposals that the 8 new people wanted to institute.

CHAPTER SIXTEEN
AS DEPUTY REGIONAL INSPECTOR GENERAL AND ACTING RIG/A FOR LATIN AMERICA, MOLDED AN EXCELLENT STAFF, EXCEPTIONAL ACHIEVEMENTS, EXPRESSED DISSENTING OPINIONS, RETALIATIONS TERMINATED ME AS DRIG

PART A. INTRODUCTORY COMMENTS

This chapter covers a period of 20 months when I was Deputy Regional Inspector General for Audit for Latin America (DRIG/A/LA). As mentioned earlier, there had been serious problems, in the RIG/A/LA based in Panama, between the Audit Staff and the RIG/A/LA Audit Managers. The RIG/A/LA had retired or been fired, and all the audit staff transferred from Panama to Washington D.C. Dean H., who had been DRIG/A/LA, was appointed as the RIG/A/LA, and I had been appointed as his Deputy. Our orders were to establish a better environment among the audit team, have more harmony within the Office, and improve audit production.

As I stated in Part G, Chapter 15, the I.G. had identified eight GS Personnel from GAO that he was thinking of transferring to USAID and converting them to a high FSO Grade. Although I advised him against doing that, he nevertheless refused my recommendation and brought them anyway. They were placed in an high position, trying to implement erroneous policies and practices. I objected to them. Since the I.G. did not have a Dissent Channel, I was callously terminated as a DRIG and continuously persecuted for the next 5 years. Accordingly, the following 9 Parts sets my exceptional performance (and that of Dean H) during Dean's time as RIG/A/LA and my time as DRIG/A/LA:

- Part A. Introductory Comments.
- Part B. Brief Reminder of My Qualifications.

- Part C. My Assumption as DRIG/A/LA.
- Part D. Areas Needing Priorities, Improvements, and Bottle Necks.
- Part E. Finalizing Four or Five Pending Reports.
- Part F. Addressing Bottlenecks.
- Part G. Profiles of Audits, Review and Surveys Worked as DRIG/A/LA.
- Part H. Two Examples of My Reviews.
- Part I. My Concluding Remarks.

PART B. BRIEF REMINDER OF MY QUALIFICATIONS

As mentioned in Chapter 13, Russell A. was transferred to the Philippines, Dean H. was transferred as RIG/A/LA, and I was transferred as Dean's deputy – with the official title of Deputy Regional Inspector General for Latin America. Since the RIG Office in Panama had been closed, we were now to operate the RIG/A/LA Office from Washington D.C. Although I had asked to be returned to Egypt in the same capacity, I was nonetheless happy to be appointed as the deputy for all Latin America. This was a tremendous recognition for my experience and talent. In this capacity, I was the first Mexican American to occupy such a prominent position in the U.S. Agency for International Development.

The facts were that I was extremely well prepared for that high position. I had been with USAID many years, served in many countries, previously held positions as Chief Resident Auditor in Peru, Ecuador, and Colombia. I also held the position of a Deputy Unit Chief during my tour in Vietnam, had done many complex surveys, audits, and reviews, and had just completed close to 4 years serving as a Deputy Regional Inspector General and Acting Inspector General whenever Russell was gone. So, I knew how to manage an office and work peacefully with our office personnel, Mission people – and the international community.

I had also made or had been involved in some of the most complicated reviews and evaluations that the Regional Inspector General of USAID had done. My findings had a positive impact on the way USAID disbursed and monitored its funding to implementing partners. *As the reader might remember from Part I, Chapter 11, in one instance, I was instrumental in making major changes to financial policies or guidelines dictated by the American Institute of Certified Public Accountants (AICPA). These were erroneous policies that enabled contractors to claim reimbursement – from USAID and other U.S. government agencies -- for "obligated" – and only potential costs -- but not actual or accrued costs. In actual practice, some of these future costs were never incurred – but the funds were not returned to USAID. Based on our findings, the General Accounting Office (GAO) recommended that the AICPA change this policy, which it did. Although I had been informed that I would be recommended for a "noteworthy achievement award," but the request fell through the cracks, and I was never given that or any other type of an award or recognition.*

In addition, during my tours in Washington, Pakistan, and Egypt, I was able to do numerous other types of most complicated reviews. These included the investigative review in Bangladesh and Pakistan; the assist audits for the Borrower/Grantee and Participant training; the highly sophisticated Egyptian Grain Silo's Audit Plan and participation in the review; and, finally, the Audit Plan and actual review of the Egyptian Commodity Import Program.

In sum, since I had experience managing offices and personnel, I would be able to help (and did) create a more cohesive audit team that would work harmoniously in Latin America. I would also be able to easily improve on the working environment in the office (and I did), which at the time was bad. However, as I soon found out, this was the easy part which I was able to accomplish without major problems.

PART C. MY ASSUMPTION AS DEPUTY RIG/A/LA

I left Egypt on June 28, 1981, and after three weeks of settling back into our old home in Alexandria, Virginia, I reported for work in my new post.

Although Dean H. and I had never previously worked together, he and I had corresponded while I was still in Egypt. We exchanged ideas about personnel, problems, and plans. As a result of this fine interchange of information, I was able to work extremely well with all the staff of the Office of the Regional Inspector General for Latin America.

I knew most of them, and most knew me. Carlos C. has always been like a brother to me; he and I worked extremely well together. Raul C. and Luis P. were local staff; Raul lived in Bolivia, and Luis lived in Panama; Both Raul and Luis P. liked to collaborate with me; Luis was one of those exceptional people. I knew Roland H. and William S. from Vietnam. I had previously worked with Edward St., Rodney M., and Elmer H. either in Washington or other posts. Thus, the transition was easy.

Our first official meeting was in a group session where we reminisced about some of our old assignments. In a very subtle manner, Dean and I requested their full cooperation. I told them that my door would always be open and that I would have an individual meeting with each one. This way, I could get a good background on the work that each was doing and discuss any issues they wanted to discuss. The group meeting was nice and easy. In the following few days, I met with each one. Everyone gave me full cooperation.

PART D. AREAS NEEDING PRIORITIES, IMPROVEMENTS, AND BOTTLE NECKS

My meetings with Dean and the staff were most cordial and productive. I quickly identified the following six audit areas and activities which needed improvements and/or our most urgent attention:

a) Our most urgent priorities were to finalize 4 or 5 reports.

b) We needed to do missions-wide surveys to identify problem areas for audits during the coming fiscal year.

c) Indexing of Workpapers represented a big bottleneck. There was no uniformity in the way work papers were organized. Work papers were organized and numbered using assorted styles. To make things worse, teams usually organized their work papers after they had returned -- to Panama or Washington -- from fieldwork to author their reports.

d) Reports of Audit Findings (RAFs) were haphazardly organized and not referenced.

e) Final Audit Reports were not balanced and analytical, tending to focus entirely on the negative.

f) Recommendations contained in our reports needed to be balanced, clearer, and more tightly focused.

PART E. FINALIZING PENDING REPORTS

At the time that I became the DRIG/A/LA, the Wang Word Processing Computers were just coming into use. The audit staff would author the reports on a tablet of paper, and then the administrative staff would type the reports into the Wang Word Processor, at which point I would then review the reports making any changes by hand. After I had written down my changes, the administrative staff would then retype the changes into the draft contained in the Wang Word Processor.

My review of the first two reports submitted to me followed the above pattern without incident. However, our secretary got sick and was absent for one whole week during which time we could not get a replacement. Since reports had to be issued, I decided to see if I could work on the Wang Computer. I had taken a typing course in High School. I had taken a computer course at the University of Texas. And I also had experience working with computers from the days when I had worked for the U.S. Air Force at the General Dynamics plant in Fort Worth, Texas. So, I knew the basic logic on how computers operated. However, I quickly discovered that the Wang-word-processors were a little different.

After receiving an hour-long demonstration from a secretary that worked in another department, I managed to get the hang of Wang. Of course, I made a few mistakes at the start, but I learned to use the system well – and from then on, I have exclusively relied on computers to write all my reports and my two book, *Inherit the Dust from the Four Winds of Revilla and this one*.

As I began to finalize the pending reports, Dean and I assembled teams and sent them to several countries to make the surveys in preparation for the Fiscal Year 1983 audit work. These Mission-wide surveys enabled us to identify problems affecting the various USAID missions in Latin America. From then on, our audit work was focused mostly on areas that affected

USAID on a wide variety of basis or to projects or programs which had serious problems.

PART F. ADDRESSING BOTTLENECKS

The first bottleneck that I addressed was the indexing of the work papers. Once I had a little time, I talked to all the auditors to find a uniform, simple-to-use system that everyone could use to index their work papers. Adopting a standard system of indexing work papers would help expedite the referencing and writing of reports.[102]. Although I liked using the "Block Numbering System," which assigns blocks of numbers to areas to be examined, this system of indexing work papers was too complex to teach, implement, and use in cross-referencing.

It was only when I got to Carlos C. that I thought his way of indexing showed a good beginning of what I was looking for. Between Carlos and I, we developed a nice and simple Work Paper Indexing System. This is the one that we adopted. Very briefly, documents and worksheets would be filed in "Folders." At least 19 Folders would have predetermined first numbers; these first numbers would be followed by a second, third, and fourth number – each had a different purpose. Here are the major examples of Folders or Files:

Material Description	File Number
Referenced Copy of the Final Report	01
Copies of Draft Audit Reports	02
Reports of Audit Findings	03
Survey and Audit Programs	04
Loan and Project or Program Papers	05
Loan, Program, Project Agreements	06
Implementation Letters	07

[102] Auditors index their workpapers to supporting evidence, which typically can include documentary, testimonial and photographic evidence. To ensure the report is factually correct and that the findings are well supported, as part of a separate process, an independent auditor or auditors that are not on the audit team will fact check or "reference" the report.

Administrative Files	08
Record of Conversations	09
Financial Information	10
Statistical Information and Analysis	11
Evaluation Reports	12
Audit Reports	13
Technical Assistance Contracts	14
Training of People and Participants	15
Procurement of Commodities and Items	16
Host Country Organizations	17
Counterpart Funds and Contributions	18
Mission Monitoring Efforts	19
Other Files are opened to accommodate Unique Situations	

a) The first work paper of each file represented a summary listing of its contents.

b) Work papers – that were to be accumulated during the audit -- were to be indexed before the documents were even read or, in any event, daily. Only minor filing or indexing would take place at the end of the audit.

c) As each work paper was accumulated, it was to be initialed, dated, and assigned a series of three numbers (thus, an example was a working paper listed as number 12-2-54-3). The first number (12) was the file number, or in this example, it was an Evaluation Report; the second number showed that it was the second document in the file, and the third number showed that it was Page 54 of the Evaluation Report.

d) If there was something in the Evaluation Report which was to be included in the different Reports of Audit Findings (RAF) or Audit

Report(s), a fourth number (3) would be added to the series. This last number (3) would represent the exact location of supporting statement or information to be included as Cross Reference in Reports of Audit Findings, Draft Reports, and the Semi-Final Report. In my case, I added the fourth number as I typed the Reports of Audit Findings (RAFs), and these followed all the way until we issued the Final Audit Report.

The system was easily adopted by the staff and worked well to save numerous hours that represented a great bottleneck in figuring out how to index and cross-referencing of Reports of Audit Findings and the Final Report. In other words, this saved the USAID Inspector General a fantastic amount of time and reduced indexing and cross-referencing potential problems.

(Note: The above was the indexing system I left in place at the time I was the Deputy RIG/A for Latin America. Unfortunately, new people that were recruited questioned it by saying that they preferred letters and numbers (the old-fashioned way), and I do not know if our indexing system was kept in place or if it was shelved. *To me, the simple system that we designed was a tremendous advancement in saving time and audit costs; it should have been kept in place.*

PART G. PROFILES OF AUDITS, REVIEW AND SURVEYS WORKED DURING TIME I WAS DRIG/A/LA

During the time I served as DRIG/A/LA, we formed a fantastic team, and we were fortunate to do surveys and/or draft reports covering 36 different reviews in many countries and sectors. A series of conclusions can be obtained from the thirty-six audits, studies, and surveys shown by the following profiles.

This first profile shows the number of audits, reviews, and/or surveys that we did for each country:

Country	Sector Covered	Numbers By Countries

Bolivia	Mission Operating Systems	
Bolivia	University of North Carolina	2
Costa Rica	Economic Survey	1
Dominican Republic	P.L. 480 Title II	1
Ecuador	Integrated Rural Agriculture	
Ecuador	TELACU Grant	2
EI Salvador	Agrarian Reform	
EI Salvador	Private Sector Survey	
EI Salvador	Public Sector Emp.	
EI Salvador	Trans and Rest	4
Guatemala	Impress Fund	
Guatemala	Municipal Earthquake	
Guatemala	ROCAP Survey	
Guatemala	Small Farmer Development	4
Haiti	Integrated Rural Development	
Haiti	P.L. 480 Title II	
Haiti	Survey	3
Honduras	Agricultural Research	
Honduras	Agricultural Sector II	
Honduras	Aguan Valley	
Honduras	P.L. 480 Survey	
Honduras	Survey	5

Jamaica	Economic Recovery	
Jamaica	Integrated Rural Development	
Jamaica	Rural Education Sector	3
Panama	Rural Access Roads	
Panama	Rural Growth Ser Centers	
Panama	Survey	
Panama	Watershed	4
Paraguay	Follow-up Review	1
Peru	Mission Operating Systems	
Peru	Sub-Tropical Development	2
Reg. Development Office	Caribbean Facilities	1
ROCAP	Regional Rural Agriculture	2
Special Studies	Miscellaneous IG/II Etc	1 Total 36

As shown by the above statistical profile, the distribution of our audit activities made in each country was as follows: Bolivia (2), Costa Rica (1), Dominican Republic (1), Ecuador (1), El Salvador (4), Guatemala (4), Haiti (3), Honduras (5), Jamaica (3), Panama (4), Peru (2), ROCAP (in Guatemala) (2), and others.

The above listing by countries was then sorted by the sectors that were being covered. To save space in this book, I will not present the details of the profile. But my conclusions are that we were able to cover the following sectors: Agrarian Reform and Agricultural research (5 audits, reviews, or surveys); Caribbean Facilities (1); Economic studies and reviews (2); Follow up reviews and Revolving Funds (2); Integrated Rural Agriculture and Development (3); Special Investigative Studies (1); Mission Operating Systems (2); Municipal Earthquake (1); P.L. 480 Title II (3); Private and Public Employment and Sectors (2); ROCAP (in Guatemala) Study and Agriculture (2) Rural Roads, Education, Growth, and Small Farmers (5); Mission-wide Surveys (3); and, Others (4).

Most studies (23) were being made within a range of eighteen to less than five hundred direct hours. The remaining studies were more complicated and required between 752 and 1763 or more hours.

In sum, the above statistical profiles speak well for the (a) leadership that Dean and I provided; (b) the exceptional team that we molded and formed; and (c) the excellent coverage – in the number of countries and sectors -- that we covered.

PART G. TWO EXAMPLES OF REVIEWS

Let me discuss two reviews that I particularly made. The first was a review of how the deterioration of Costa Rica's economy, and the Currency Devaluations had affected USAID programs and projects in that country. The second was a review of an overly complex audit of the Integrated Rural Development program being implemented by the Government of Ecuador (GOE) that USAID was partially funding.

PART G.1. DEVALUATION OF COLON IN COSTA RICA

Review of how the Deterioration of the Economic Situation in Costa Rica affected USAID programs and projects. For numerous years, Costa Rica was the model of prosperity, economic growth, and currency conversion stability. Thus, USAID's planning for programs and projects in that country normally assumed a conversion rate of 8.54 Colone's[103] for each U.S. $1.00. However, in early 1980, Costa Rica, like other countries in Latin America, began to experience an economic decline. As a result, the country had to devalue its currency; for example, Costa Rica devalued its currency (the

[103] The Costa Rican local currency is known as the "colon."

Colon) by 400% in only one year. This currency devaluation had a tremendously adverse effect on USAID's project disbursements. While USAID's planning documents had assumed the currency conversion rate would be 8.54 Colone's to the dollar, with the devaluation, currency was being converted at 44.00 Colone's to the dollar. Thus, this resulted in 35.00 Colone's per dollar being "saved," resulting in a residual accumulation of local currency in all projects that the Mission had. The USAID Mission to Costa Rica thus requested help in determining the (a) number of projects affected by this problem, (b) the total residual amount that was being accumulated, and (c) the different options available to dispose or minimize the savings.

Since most of our people were either doing surveys and/or audits, and the audit had a priority to be done and I could see my "Ticos" friends once more, I gladly undertook the assignment myself. Once I got to Costa Rica, I discussed the issues with economists, as well as with Mission personnel, including the Mission Director, program and project people, Controller personnel, and a host of others. Also, I performed a test of USAID's vouchers and other information. I quickly determined that the problem was very real; a total of 16 projects were affected; and, that the residual accumulations appeared to result to be over to be $6.9 million dollars just between January 1981 and March 1982. Moreover, I also determined that the 16 projects were being affected by the currency devaluation and that most were affected by a very significant amount. In effect, as of March 31, 1982, the unexpended obligations amounted to $54.2 million. Of this amount, about $42.0 Million was planned for disbursement in Colone's. Thus, my calculations were that if the remaining amount of obligated funds were disbursed at the new rate (46.46 per U.S. dollar), there would be an excessive accumulation of over the U.S. $8.4 million.

Determining the effects of the accumulation was quite easy, but the solution – how to dispose of the excessive accumulations – was less clear. I suggested and discussed the following with the USAID Mission to Costa Rica:

a) To continue to extend the timeframes for the programs and projects indefinitely or for specified periods of time until the accumulation had been reduced or disappeared.

b) Since these residuals resembled unliquidated obligations, to de-obligate all residual accumulations as they grew or at certain periods of time.

c) To reprogram the residual accumulations at certain times into faster-moving activities.

d) To convert U.S. Dollar reimbursements at the new official rate of exchange and allow the Costa Rican government to keep the resulting windfall.

e) To change and broaden the scope of the programs and projects to provide the Costa Rican government with a source of budgetary support that it could use for purposes that were not contemplated in the original agreement.

The Mission received well the complete study. However, we got busy with other activities, and we did not do a follow-up review to determine how the problem was resolved.

PART G.2. THE INTEGRATED RURAL DEVELOPMENT AGRICULTURAL PROGRAM OF ECUADOR 104

This complicated project represented a GOE (Ecuadorean) priority with two broad objectives: to reduce the isolation of the rural areas; and to curtail the massive migration of Campesinos (Rural People) from the rural areas into the cities. Among the program's objectives were the creation at the cabinet-level of a secretariat to develop and implement activities in 17 different areas of Ecuador, involving activities in agriculture, health, forestry, energy, rural technology, community development, and training. To finance such a complex program, the GOE received financial assistance from a slew of international organizations, including USAID, the Inter-American Development Bank, the World Bank, the United Nations, the Organization of American States, and West Germany among others.

---

[104] Basic information came from a draft audit report the author wrote in December 7, 1983, entitled "Draft Audit Report for the Integrated Rural Development Program for Agriculture (Project 518-0012, Loan No. 518-T-038).

Aside from helping to establish a cabinet-level Office of Secretariat, USAID was to finance and implement two "multidimensional Interventions" in the Salcedo and Quimiag-Penipe areas of Ecuador. These two areas were extremely difficult to work in because they were near the top (called Paramo by the Ecuadorians) of the Cotopaxi and Chimborazo volcanoes.

USAID's funding included support for the following subprojects:

a) Two irrigations systems and several tertiary canals.

b) Short and long-term credit for farmers, commodities, and technical assistance.

c) Financial and technical assistance for Ecuador government agencies and officials.

d) Marketing inputs for tree nurseries, animal reproduction centers, and road improvements.

e) Legal and other types of assistance to support the efforts of Campesinos to gain titles to their land.

f) Support for forestry and conservation.

g) Support for the construction of community participation centers.

h) Support for constructing health clinics and potable water systems.

i) Other types of employment opportunities.

As the reader might observe, these programs were "masters of complexity." The planning needed to execute the projects was most complex, progress usually slow, and an evaluation of achievements extremely difficult to determine. Throughout my years as a USAID auditor, I saw and evaluated these types of assistance, or broad sector approaches in Botswana, Costa Rica, Ecuador, Haiti, Honduras, Jamaica, and Yemen. In each case, I was able to show some commendable progress, as well as program implementation problems. In the case of the Ecuadorean Study, I was also able to recommend improvements in the programs or projects. The draft report that I submitted to the Mission and my office was 60 pages long. It included pictures of the project, as well as an analysis of the achievements and problems affecting the project. The report included nine recommendations. The Ecuadorean Mission made some laudatory and positive comments about me and the draft report.

Unfortunately, I did this study at the time when Dean was getting ready to resign from USAID. It is noteworthy to mention that to this day, I do not know whether he resigned or was terminated by the Inspector General. All I know is that his departure was surreptitious – and, without informing me (the DRIG/A/LA), he was immediately replaced. **At the same time of Dean's firing, resignation, and/or departure, I was immediately "fired" and immediately replaced as DRIG/A/LA. These actions were taken (a) during a time when I was away from my post (Washington D.C.); (b) I was already in Peru (my fourth country of supervisory visits); (c) after I had already completed a very complex audit in Ecuador; (d) immediately upon Dean's departure; (e) in a secretive manner; (f) without informing me in any way or form; and, (g) in a most callous, abrupt, undignified, and unceremonious manner.**

In any event, it was ironic that I had finished my work in Ecuador, and in my DRIG/A/LA capacity, had given the draft report (as a RAF) to the Mission, and I was already working in Peru on a survey or another review when a USAID Controller gave me a message telling the Missions – to tell me – that I was no longer the Deputy Regional Inspector General. Anyway, the new Regional Inspector General (Guy 10) – who had worked under me in Egypt -- and his Deputy (Guy 11) alleged I had violated protocol by submitting the draft Record of Audit Findings as a working draft report to the Mission. Together with others, they accused me of "Insubordination" and gave me a poor rating in my Personal Evaluation Report. To me, the way the actions against me were taken raises very serious questions on the management capabilities, "a lack of Class," and style of the head of the Office of Inspector General (the IG himself) and the fools that wrote the cable. In effect, someone did not have the guts, nor the Class, to call me back to Washington, face me and tell me to my face that I was being fired as the Deputy Regional Inspector General for Audits. They just did not know how to manage or supervise staff. In addition, the accusation made was ridiculous, as a matter of courtesy, auditors routinely inform Missions about the results of their work before ending their work. Moreover, I was still the Deputy RIG/A/La when I provided the Mission with the Report of Audit Findings which was the full report, I cover this in greater length in Chapters 17, 18, and 19 of this book.)

PART H. MY CONCLUDING REMARKS

I am very hopeful that this chapter left no doubt that Dean and I (especially me), we straightened out the chaotic environment that had existed in the Office of the Regional Inspector General when it was based in Panama. As shown in this Chapter, I found the six or seven weak areas, corrected six of them, and then formed a fabulous team. The profiles of reviews and audits show that the team gave us their full cooperation. Also, our 17-member team, Dean, and I did a fabulous job – during the 20 months, I was DRIG/A/LA -- covering the gamut of studies needed by the different countries-- the easy jobs as well as the most complicated ones. Belatedly, but very deservedly, I want to congratulate our 17-member team for a job exceptionally well done.

Despite all our successes operating as a RIG/A/LA in Washington D.C., I believe the I.G. had other plans which would affect us in an immense manner. It was during my tour as the DRIG/A/LA that I began to see some radical and adverse changes in the way the Office of Inspector General was managed. For instance, the Inspector General chose not to accept my recommendations (discussed in a previous chapter) and brought into our organization eight people from the General Accountability Office (GAO). He awarded them high-ranking FSO grades and assigned them to high-level positions.

It is noteworthy to note that the I.G. never assembled all the staff's and informed us of his plans to reorganize all offices. Without us being informed, by the IG#1 of any changes, the new FSOs began drafting and trying to implement policies, practices, and procedures that were sharply at variance with what I knew were good management principles. These new policies were issued while Dean was away from the Office, and I was the Acting RIG/A/LA. In such a capacity, I staffed the proposals and voiced the feeling of the staff and mine (Chapter 18 provides more details on these points).

Eventually, this resulted in adverse consequences for Dean H. and me. In effect, Dean H. -- who had a real unpleasant experience as the DRIG/A/LA while he was in Panama – either resigned (or was fired) and went to work for another U.S. government agency. In my case, and as stated in this Chapter, without the common courtesy normally awarded to a long-time FSO

Employee, I was replaced, in a callous manner, as a DRIG/A/LA -- after only 20 months on the job and despite the fabulous work we were doing.

From this point until my retirement, on December 31, 1989, I was the victim of various unfair wrongly harassed, persecuted, and a victim of various retaliatory actions. Here is a brief preview of what the reader will see, in more detail, in Chapters 17, 18, and 19:

a) I was required to meet, by myself and without the presence of my lawyer, in front of a group of about 7 people and defend myself from their false accusations of "insubordination."

b) The Office prepared but, after my correction of facts, apparently never issued a Letter of Reprimand accusing me of "insubordination."

c) My transfer to the Philippines was canceled, and I was, instead, transferred to Kenya.

d) Despite an obvious violation of "Conflict of Interests" and without IG#1 doing the firing, Guy 11, not only replaced me as DRIG/A/LA, but also prepared and submitted an adverse and false Personnel or Employee Evaluation Report (PER or EER) even though he had not been my supervisor during my issuance of 36 reports.

e) My former subordinate, colleague, and friend in Egypt, who had taken Dean's RIG/A/LA position, performed as the "Reviewing Officer" and knowingly "certified" as to the accuracy of the false EER.

f) My requests to be placed in another supervisory position or transfer to other offices were consistently denied.

g) At later dates, some of my work and my reports were canceled even though in some cases, I had found evidence of fraud or a need for changes in the program or a need to notify the U.S. Congress. The cancellation of some of my reports meant that some of my recommendations never saw the light of day.

h) Towards the end of my career – while stationed in Kenya -- I was also falsely accused of making fraudulent Government claims related to two Educational Allowance Grant awarded to my Learning-Disabled Daughter under the Special Handicapped Child Education Allowance (SHCEA).

i) Although rulings eliminated me from wrongdoings, the Office of the IG Investigations conducted a very defective investigation of me. It showed "my case" to over 29 USAID Officials in the IG's attempt to both discredit my qualifications and find anything where I could be formally accused of fraud.

j) Although the Office of IG Inspections had found no reason for pursuing or persecuting me, the IG took steps to send the case to the Office of the IG of Department of State for a final determination. Once again, the I.G. was told there was no case for prosecuting me.

k) It took one and one-half years for the IG Office of Investigations to close my so-called case after the Department of State had rendered its final opinion.

Yes, all the above reprisal actions against me took place – all because I expressed disagreements with the erroneous policies, procedures, and practices that the I.G. and the 8 new people wanted to implement.

Also, as I explained in my Prologue and because of the complexity and interrelations of the different issues that affected other people and me in a negative manner, I will present the details of my positions in three separate Chapters 17, 18, and 19. Whenever I can, I will use the first names to attribute events and/or personalities that affected me in a *positive manner*. However, whenever the events and/or personalities affected me in a *negative manner,* I will attribute these to a Pseudonym person (Guy Number X). In the case of the first USAID Inspector General, my reference to him will be "IG#1" or (Inspector General). I do this because most events took place 30 years ago. To me, the adverse issues and/or events are the ones I deem important. Making use of Pseudonyms or attribution system enables me to "…air my adversarial disputes…" but attribute the event to a nebulous Guy. If I were to use proper names, it could affect his/her current family, which is not my desire.

The following chart shows a list of Pseudonyms that I will use beginning in Chapter 17 and ending in Chapter 19. For instance, Guys 4, 5, 6, and 7, in the chart, used to work for GAO. They were converted, without following rules or actual USAID experience, by the Inspector General, to a high FSO Grade and appointed as Regional Inspector Generals in different locations. To avoid repetition of these facts, I will only say "New FSO appointed to X position." Here is the chart:

Guy Number	New or Old FSO, Designated Positions Filled by Employee
IG#1	The first Inspector General who is no longer with USAID.
0	Do not recall; he was in Vietnam
1	Do not recall In Vietnam
2	Do Not recall In Vietnam
3	An Auditor in Pakistan not related to I.G. Problem
4	New FSO appointed as RIG/ A/Washington, later to IG/Policy, and Procedures Office (PPO)
5	New FSO appointed as RIG/A/Senegal, then to Washington
6	New FSO appointed IG/PPO and then as RIG/A/ Philippines
7	New FSO appointed as RIG/A/Nairobi
8	A USAID Employee who was Deputy Director in RFMC and who questioned the SHCEA and SMA after Controller was transferred.
9	Joe Fe, an excellent New FSO who fits well with all our staff.
10	Old IG FSO. He replaced Dean H. as RIG/A/LA
11	Old IG FSO. He is not a nice Employee; He replaced me as DRIG/A/L. A. and prepared a faulty PER on me.
12	Old Time IG Office of Inspector General Investigations
13	Inspector with OIG/N/ He did crazy things for Advancement
14	The USAID I.G. Executive Officer in Washington
15	She replaced the Previous Executive Officer in Kenya

Chapter Seventeen
In Kenya, My Last USAID Overseas Assignment, Rough Family Situations Caused Their Early Departure, Excellent Office Managers First Year, And Unqualified Person Assigned As RIG/A/Kenya My Last Two Years

Part A. Introductory Remarks

"My Concluding Remarks" stated in Chapter 16 Part H presents a fairly brief "Preview" of the reprisals against me. I believe that all these reprisals had either the tacit or explicit approval or direction of Inspector (IG#1). In other words, since the I.G. did not have a "Dissent Channel" at the time, I was unfairly punished for dissenting on defective policies and things that were taking place within the Office of the Inspector General.

As stated in the previous Chapter, one of the "punishments" against me was a demotion from the position of a DRIG/A/LA to a lower operating auditor position. Another was the preparation -- by Guy 11 who clearly had a conflict of interest – of a false and adverse PER, and yet another was the transfer from the Philippines to Kenya. This is the reason why I decided to discuss my Kenya assignment prior to my discussion about the real cause of the problems. This chapter states how this – my last overseas assignment to Kenya – eventually turned out.

Here is a short background on the family that accompanied me to Kenya. When the Travel Authorizations (T/A's) were prepared, Linda had already graduated from High School, but was not yet 21 years of age. Since she was studying and working part-time, but not yet 21, she was correctly included as my dependent in my T/A. In other words, out of a family of 5, only Pauline, Linda, Melissa, and I were included in the T/A. As noted, Joe and Jerry were not included in my T/A. Let me explain why.

In the case of Joe – our oldest son – he was over 21 years of age, had already graduated from William and Mary (with Honors), been in the Peace Corps, and the University of Kentucky had accepted him for his Masters. Therefore, he was not included, in my Travel Authorization (T/A), as my dependent or for official travel. In the case of Jerry, he was not included in my T/A. However, Jerry traveled with us, at my expense because he had special mental problems. Pauline, Jerry, Melissa, and I arrived in Nairobi on July 31, 1984.

Because my tour of duty in Kenya turned out to be so complicated for my family and me, I present this chapter in 6 Parts:

- Part A. Introductory Comments.
- Part B. A Short Summary of Chapter Contents.
- Part C. Life in Kenya.
- Part D. Excellent Friends and Managers in First Year in Kenya.
- Part E. Assignment of a Clearly Unqualified Person as RIG/A/Kenya.
- Part F. My Concluding Remarks

PART B. A SHORT SUMMARY OF CHAPTER CONTENTS

Here is what each of the Parts will say:

Life in Kenya will include a description of our life in Kenya, our trips throughout Kenya, Melissa's schooling problems, Melissa's departure (together with Pauline) from Kenya earlier than the end of my tour. This part of the chapter also covers Jerry's return to the U.S and his aggravated illness once he got in U.S.

Thanks to my two great Friends and excellent managers (Mervin Boyer and Eugene Treasrau (now both deceased), we had an exceptional first year. Because of their leadership, we had a fantastic working audit team, working relations, achievements, and audit coverage.

Once Messer Boyer and Treasau left Kenya, the IG appointed a person (Guy 7) to fill the RIG/A/Kenya Position. This was a bad choice! This appointment was an unfortunate assignment because this person was clearly unqualified for that position. He was out of his element; and should never have been assigned as the RIG/A. Guy 7 was among the people hired from the GAO into high-level positions. This guy was the most unqualified Office Manager and Regional Inspector General that I worked with in my entire career.

PART C. LIFE IN KENYA

Housing. Kenya was a good post. We were assigned a terrific two-story home at 94 Spring Valley Road on the outskirts of Nairobi in a very fine neighborhood. It was a real nice four-bedroom house that included two separate small apartments for the two "live-in" servants we hired.

Cars. Before leaving the United States, we ordered a 1984 Peugeot sedan that had the steering wheel on the right side because Kenya had been a part of the British Empire, driving is on the left-hand side of the road. Since we would not get this car for three months, I bought a used Plymouth Volare from a departing employee of the U.S. Embassy. Once we got the Peugeot, we had many problems because anytime we parked it anywhere, someone would try to steal it. So, Pauline used the car very judicially. On weekends, we would use it to go to the national parks. However, most of the time, this car was parked in our garage. Just before I left, I sold it for almost the same cost we originally paid.

The Plymouth Volare provided excellent service for the four years I was there. It was a big car, and every morning, I would load it up with Peter, the cook's son, and pick a bunch of Kenyan kids who lived nearby and attended a school near where I worked. I would also use this car to visit the Kenyan game parks during the weekends. Further, into my story, I will discuss what one person from the USAID Inspector General's Office of Investigations tried to do to sabotage the sale of this car near the time I left Kenya at the end of my 4-year tour.

Pauline. Pauline's life was very pleasant during her time in Kenya. She already knew people there and they gave her a "Welcome to Kenya Party" soon after we got there. She interviewed a bunch of prospective "Servants" and hired Mary (the cook and clean-up lady) and Fennis – (the gardener and all--around helper) -- they stayed with me (and us) for the time (four years for me) we were in Kenya. Pauline attended many "coffee parties" and supervised Mary and Fennis. She did an excellent job.

Melissa's Situation. Melissa's situation is very complex, so this section is somewhat lengthy. Because of her learning disabilities, she was awarded two Very Special Education Grants (SHCEA) or (this was different than a SEGs). These became very controversial because this was a very special type of Special Education Grant for people with disabilities, which later, someone accused me of "…submitting fraudulent claims against the U.S. Government for her two SHCEA or Special Education Grants…and the SMA for my wife." This triggered a very exhausting investigation by the IG Office of Investigations (OIG/I) in Kenya and the U.S., which lasted over 3 to 4years. Of course, there never was any such intent on my part.

In any event, here is some background. Melissa was diagnosed as having very serious Learning Disabilities during her kindergarten period. So, before we left for Kenya, I wrote a letter to "John Martin" -- the USAID Kenya Executive Officer (USAID EXO, a real nice person and excellent professional), and inquired whether the International School of Kenya (ISK) would be able to teach Melissa given her Learning Disabilities. The answer was very positive; in other words, ISK originally said they could. However, once we got there, ISK administered a series of tests and told us that they could only take her for the School Year beginning in September 1984, but that she needed to go to the U.S. to a Special Vocational School for her final two years. I notified the USAID EXO of the huge problem, and we started to look for alternatives.

On March 18, 1985, I wrote a letter to the Department of State Medical Division and requested assistance in looking for a Special Education School for Melissa. On August 7, 1985, the M/MED/MHS (Dr. T.H.V) wrote a memo to the Admin Officer of the Embassy in Nairobi saying that Melissa "…meets the criteria to receive the **Special Handicapped Child Education Allowance (SHCEA)** and will be attending a school which meets her needs…." **(Note: my understanding at the time and still is that this SHCEA has very different rules than the regular Special Education Allowance as authorized in the Standard Travel Regulations. Yet, one person (referred to as Guy 8) from the RFMC, who also always seemed to have a chip on his shoulder and others seemed intent on "considering my daughter's**

situation as a normal child." According to him, he seemed intent on erroneously applying the standard basis as prescribed by the Standard Travel Regulations; without a doubt, this was the wrong way of dealing with a child who required special needs.)

In any event, the Washington Medical Division or someone in Washington searched and located the Brush Ranch School in New Mexico. On May 17, 1985, I applied for the Special Education Grant, and everyone approved the application. In other words, this approval was given by the Department of State Medical Division, the USIAID Executive Officer, the Regional Finance Management Center (RFMC), hereafter also referred to as the Office of the Controller, and others.

I was told that there were no funds to finance the air tickets for Pauline and Melissa, so without knowing when Pauline and Melissa would be returning to Kenya, I bought the two one-way tickets with my own funds. **Both Pauline and Melissa departed Kenya on June 14, 1985. Pauline and Melissa visited the school in July 1985, and the school accepted Melissa.** For this purpose, there were two SHCEA types of Special Education Grants awarded to her, and we had to sign two extremely strict contracts with the Brush Ranch School.

- **These two contracts were signed after consultations and the explicit approval from the USAID/EXO, RFMC, State Department Medical Division, and others. In other words, my wife and I were required to (and did) sign contracts with the Brush Ranch School before Melissa started classes. In part, the contracts stated: "…I understand that I am reserving a place for him/her for the entire school year and that I will be responsible for the full year's tuition unless I notify the school in writing to the contrary prior to July 1st (1985 and/or 1986). I agree that my obligation for the full year's tuition will not be reduced by withdrawal, dismissal, or absence for any cause since I recognize and acknowledge that such withdrawal, dismissal, or absence would not materially reduce the school's cost nor permit the school to recoup lost income and that therefore payment of the full year's tuition is the fair and reasonable measure of the liquidated damage which the school would otherwise suffer in such an event…."**

(Note: There was irony in the approval of the SHCEA, the SMA (discussed later), and the two Contracts signed between the Brush Ranch School and us (wife and I). These documents were approved as early as June 1985 by the Embassy, Department of State, and the Medical Division. They were also approved by the RFMC Director and Executive Office Director (both of whom were subsequently transferred from Kenya).

Although everyone had approved the transactions, the people who had approved them were transferred to other posts and were now no longer in Kenya. Thus, On January 27, 1987 (1 ½ year after others had approved), Guy 8 questioned the legality of all the transactions, and this decision was concurred by Guy 15. (Note: Guy 8 had been Deputy to the RFMC Director who had approved them and was no longer in Kenya, and Guy 15 was a new Executive Officer who replaced John Martin, the EXO, who had previously approved them and was no longer in Kenya.) Based on Guy 8's opinion, the former RFMC Director "…did not know sh..t from Shinola about regulations (his derogatory assessment of his previous supervisor) …" According to the reversed USAID position, both SEG and SMA would be completely disallowed. Moreover, the USAID Inspector General's Office of Investigations thoroughly and secretively investigated me. I discuss this in more detail later in Part D of this Chapter and in Chapter 18.

In any event, Melissa enjoyed her stay in Kenya, visits to the wild animal parks, being in ISK and participating in all kinds of extracurricular activities.

- One memorable extra curriculum activity was climbing Mount Kenya. Without adequate preparation – wrong shoes, heavy pack, no climbing experience, etc., etc. – Melissa was one of only 3 students from ISK to climb Mount Kenya all the way very close to the top. Amazing! Amazing!
- She also enjoyed going to the Kenya Animal Park, with me, and seeing "Sebastian." Sebastian was a small monkey that was in a cage. He had a rope that he would throw out to people and measure strength with all of us. We would pull at the rope to see who was strongest. Sebastian would prop his two hind legs on the rail, place his feet on the bars,

stretch his body in the air, and win every time. Sebastian's intelligence was enormous, and Melissa would be laughing all the time.

- Another memorable but very scary moment was when she opened the door to our car garage and was confronted by a horrible Black Cobra that rose three feet from the floor in a "ready to strike" pose. Melissa ran away and got Fennis, who went looking for the Cobra with a Machete. By then, the Cobra had left the garage and could not be found. Melissa remembers that very scary time even now.
- Yet, another Memorable but equally scary situation is that our car was once chased by a huge Rhino. I will provide some more information on Linda's situation.

In addition, we made several parties for the students attending ISK, and Melissa liked those very much. Away in New Mexico, Melissa attended the Brush Ranch School, learned how to ride horses, and study hard until she graduated from High School.

Jerry's Situation. Jerry had an exceptional mind. He was an outstanding musician, able to manage the guitar, Egyptian Oud, piano, trumpet, and other instruments. He accumulated tons and tons of CDs and vinyl records. As might be recalled, he learned Arabic; spoke and wrote it well. Also, he studied various religions – Catholic, Islamic, Indian, and Buddhism.

Jerry liked the Islamic Religion very much. While we lived in Alexandria, he would go to the Muslim temples and talk to them; one time, he told Melissa that he was going to convert to the Muslim Religion. Melissa told her mom, and Pauline went to the Mosque, quarreled with the Imam about entering the Mosque without a veil and then took Jerry out before he made firm commitments. Religions! Religions! Religions! I keep wondering why… if there is only one God…why must there be so many religions?

Although Jerry had graduated from high school and had studied at the American University in Cairo for a brief period and at the Northern Virginia Community College after that, he could not support himself. For that reason, we could not leave him by himself in the United States.

For that reason, Jerry accompanied us to Kenya. As I had done with Melissa, I asked our Inspector General Office and the USAID executive officer whether Jerry would be able to find a job in Kenya. The executive officer assured me that he could. When we got to Nairobi, Jerry found a job at the embassy and reported for work; however, he was fired the following day. He tried to get other jobs but was never able to find one. Jerry studied at home and was seen by a psychologist who was certainly not the best professional. She never diagnosed Jerry correctly. She encouraged Jerry to smoke pot as she did herself. Until that time, Jerry had been addicted to cigarettes but had never smoked pot.

Less than six months after our arrival in Kenya, Jerry told us that he wanted to return to the U.S. to join the U.S. Air Force. He departed in November 1984. As they did for all older dependents, the USAID executive officer sent a letter to the manager of Pan Am, the official U.S. air carrier for U.S. government personnel assigned to Kenya, telling him that Jerry was my dependent and therefore eligible for the special fare. I purchased the $366 air ticket with my own funds. For doing this, I was accused, later, of violating "professional ethics because I was requesting a discounted airfare" and "…for trying to squeeze every possible advantage from my U.S. Government position…" – what an asinine Accusation!!! These discounted airfares were routinely given by Pan Am for all diplomats, and neither Pan Am Airlines nor I expected any favors from each other.

In any event, Jerry left for the U.S., applied to the U.S. Air Force, and was rejected. He had a nervous breakdown, was hospitalized, was diagnosed with mental illness, and Jerry began to live in our old home with Linda. The doctors prescribed medication for him but were not able to find the right ones, and for that reason, Jerry became suicidal. Jerry was in and out of the mental hospitals many times. The situation became intolerable for Linda, who was only 22 years old at the time. As a result, when Pauline and Melissa went back to the U.S., and Melissa began attending Brush Ranch, Pauline and I were in a terrible "…catch 22...situation." She and I wanted her to return to Kenya and for Jerry to return with her. However, the State Medical Division would not clear Jerry to return to Kenya, and Jerry could not be left alone in the U.S. And 22-year-old Linda could not be overloaded taking care of him. So, we were in a terrible predicament. For this reason, we both opted for her to stay in the U.S. for the time being. Until a much later date, our plans for her possible return to Kenya never wavered. Jerry's illness was out of control for close to 2 years. It was not until after I had returned to the U.S. on home leave and after being reassigned to Kenya in July 1986 that we took a trip to Austin, Texas. Towards the middle of August 1986, we went by car to Austin, Texas. Jerry was manic all the way. We eventually had to hospitalize him in Austin's Shoal Creek Psychiatric Hospital. It was there that one doctor (I wish that I could remember his name) prescribed an experimental drug called Clozaril. Jerry's mental situation improved sufficiently so that for a period of time he was able to work. He took Clozaril until he died on August 24, 2017. We miss him terribly.

From Austin, Pauline and Jerry went by plane back to Virginia at my own cost and I drove Melissa to the Brush Ranch School. While there, I met with the teachers and discussed Melissa's plan of study. I then drove back to Virginia. **In any event, <u>I returned to Nairobi alone on October 22, 1986</u>. I highlight the October date because later, there was a dispute on what date my wife had re-established residency in the U.S. In fact, during the investigation, there were questions raised, and claims made that Pauline had re-established her residency in the United States on dates which were totally erroneous; theories and financial assumptions were, in my opinion, wrong.**

To me, October 22, 1986, is the best date when we can all agree when she re-established residency in the U.S. I will discuss how the date that Pauline re-established residency in the United States became a point of contention between myself and the Office of the Inspector General, leading to spurious charges of fraud (See Chapter 18, Part K.)

<u>Linda's Situation.</u> Linda was authorized to live with me in Kenya because when my orders were issued, she was not yet 21 years of age. USAID in Washington issued the authorization on October 12, 1984, or just about a month after her 21st birthday (on September 3rd). She traveled to Kenya on November 10, 1984. She stayed in Nairobi for about 10 days and decided she had no job or future in Kenya. So, I bought Linda a one-way return ticket similar to the one I had bought Jerry. As I will discuss further in this book, the new USAID executive officer (Guy 15) and Guy 8 from RFMC later raised concerns about this.

In any event, during the time she was there, we took one trip to Masai Mara and a number of trips to the Nairobi National Park. She thoroughly enjoyed seeing the live animals. A curious and scary event took place in the Nairobi National Park one day:

- There were five of us in the old Plymouth Volare, including Jerry, Linda, Melissa, a Peace Corps Volunteer, and myself. The end of our visit was almost over when we spotted a huge Rhino walking across one of those unpaved roads we were about to go on. We waited until the big monster passed the road. We did not wait long enough. Big mistake! We got too close to his territory and distance. Since Rhinos can't see too well, he listened to our car's noise, he whipped around so fast and started chasing us. I pushed the gas hard, and we bounced on the road repeatedly, but he finally stopped chasing us. Boy! That was quite a scare. With that size and speed, he could have flipped the Volare very easily. From then on, Linda would refer to the Rhino – as Mr. Ma Goo (the comic character that could not see too well).

So, Linda's stay was very educational, which lasted her a lifetime.

As in the case of Jerry, the purchase of the tickets from Pan Am was the subject of allegations that I had violated "professional ethics for requesting a discounted airfare…" In Linda's case, the allegation centered on two facts: (a) that she had traveled using the ticket two months after she had become 21 years of age; and, (b) as in the case of Jerry, some officials alleged erroneously that I was "… trying to squeeze every possible advantage from my U.S. Government position…" because Pan Am had granted me a discounted fare – what a ridiculous Accusation!!! As stated before, for Jerry and Linda, Pan Am routinely provided discounted fares for all diplomats, and neither Pan Am nor I expected any special favor from each other. Moreover, Linda was on my travel orders and had been authorized to live with me. The fact that she traveled to Kenya after turning 21 seems, to me, an effort at a reprisal in order to damage the strong and favorable reputation I had developed during my 28 years with USAID. Let me be clear on one thing, I never had (and never would have) any intention of submitting false claims against the U.S. Government. In any event --as will be discussed further in the book -- the USAID General Counsel said this was a non-issue because "…the travel authorization was the determining factor and not her age at the time of travel."

Joe's Situation. After leaving the Peace Corps, Joe came to stay with us in Kenya for a period of time. I paid his fare to come to Kenya. He stayed with me in Nairobi for over six months. He obtained a contract with the USAID Mission in Kenya and was able to help the Mission in several ways. Moreover, we both had a really good time together -- going to the Parks, eating all kinds of wild animals (wildebeest, buffalo, crocodile meat, etc.) at a famous Kenyan restaurant that still exists called "the Carnivore." We also enjoyed eating at an Indian Restaurant near the Mission, which at the time was situated close to the U.S. Embassy. The same embassy was later destroyed by a truck bomb on August 7, 1998.

The Two Servants We Hired. During our first few weeks in Kenya, we interviewed several people to work as servants and hired two who remained for the four years of my tour.

Their names were Mary and Fennis. Mary was from a little town called Kituyi, northwest of Nairobi. She was a terrific cook and a fine cleaning lady. She had 2 sons – Peter and Joseph – who were exceptional kids. For some reason, Mary always referred to me as "Master."

- As I mentioned earlier about the kids I picked up and took to school each morning, Peter would be the first to ride with me. Every morning, he would look at me and observe all the things I did in the car. A few months after Pauline and Melissa had left Kenya, Mary came to me and said, "Master, Peter has been watching you drive each day, and he says that he could learn to drive like you very quickly." So, during that same weekend, I got up early and knocked on Mary's apartment and told Peter to come with me right after breakfast. We ate, and I took him to the Nairobi National Park. When we got inside the park, I said, "Peter, you take over the driving because I want to see the animals." He just smiled, and lo and behold, he had learned all my driving techniques; his performance was fantastic. From then on, we would go to the National Park frequently, and I would let him drive. In sum, he and Joseph were excellent kids.

Toward the end of my tour, Mary asked me if I could "loan" her about $200 to buy a little house and yard in Kituyi for her retirement. How could I refuse? For staying with us, and then with me after the family had left Kenya, I gladly gave her $300 to her. Before I left, I gave her more in severance pay for her services. I also got her a job with a couple who worked for the U.S. Embassy. She lasted some time in that position and then got a job with a friend of mine, Peter Greene. Anyway, after Peter returned to the U.S. and was stationed in Washington D.C., he (and his family) invited Marry to come to the U.S. As she was arriving -- at what she thought was her destination – she made a call to me. The first words she mentioned were "…Master, this is Mary from Kituyi…." Then she told me she was having problems because the airline would not let her leave the airport…." After I talked to the right people, I determined that the problem was that she was in Seattle, Washington and not in Washington, D.C." Thanks to the airlines, she was placed on another plane, and she finally arrived in Washington D.C. I sincerely hope that Mary and her family are well and have very productive jobs right now.

Fennis was our gardener. Fennis liked his women and his liquor. One Sunday afternoon while Pauline and Melissa were still in Kenya, Fennis walked into the yard trailed by a real pretty woman who entered his apartment. Pauline got up from where we were barbecuing some steaks, knocked on the door, and very strongly said: "…Get that woman out of there!" Fennis told her that the lady was "his cousin." Highly upset, Pauline got her out of the apartment. Once Pauline and Melissa had left, I was put on travel status a great deal. There were about 2 to 3 times when I returned, and my next-door neighbor (another USAID Family) would come, extremely agitated, and say: "Joe, you have to fire Fennis." Why? I would ask. She would tell me that he had gotten drunk and slept on the grass all night long. Needless to say, I never did fire Fennis for those infractions, but I did chew him out royally.

At the end of my tour, I got Fennis another job, but lo and behold, he was fired within a week – you guessed it: "For getting drunk…."

Hosting a Filipino Family Working for USAID/ Sudan. In addition to all the above things we did in Kenya, I hosted a Filipino (the Tabin Family) I met during my two trips to Sudan. Two of the ladies worked with USAID/Sudan's Accounting Office. Although I met all the family, only three of them – Emi,

Eddy, and Norma Tabin -- came to Kenya at a time when there were all kinds of food shortages in Sudan. They had been nice to me during my visits to Sudan, and they called me to see if they could come and make some pizzas and other food that they could cook and take with them. I was more than happy to host them. At the end of their tour in Sudan, all of them migrated to Canada and have lived there ever since. I last heard from them about 5 years ago. Very sincerely, I hope that all of you -- Emi (husband, daughter, son -- Eddy, Norma, and all family, are in the best of health these days and for the future.

PART D. EXCELLENT FIRST YEAR

When I first came to Kenya, the office managers were close friends of mine. Mervin Boyer was the Regional Inspector General for Audits, and Eugene Treasau was the Deputy Regional Inspector General. (Since then, both have passed on – May They Rest in Peace). Thus, for a period of the first year of my Kenya tour, they knew my capabilities and used them to the maximum. Both were exceptional office managers, and we had an exceptional relationship. We also issued excellent reports.

The office consisted of 12 professional auditors and 4 secretaries and clerical personnel. During this period, together with an assistant, we did reviews of different kinds of USAID missions in Botswana, Zimbabwe, Zaire, Tanzania, and Kenya. On my audits to Botswana and Kenya, Linda Brown (another auditor) helped me during the audits; she was a fabulous auditor. The last time I saw her, she was married and studying to become an Acupuncturist Doctor. Wish you well, Linda. All went well and the reports were issued on time and without any problems.

Aside from completing these audits, I did two things to improve the operations of the office in Kenya. I gave a lecture – and a paper copy of the lecture – to the staff on how to do audits using modern techniques related to computers. This lecture included information about the work paper indexing system and cross-referencing theory that I have already discussed in Chapter 16. The audit team liked the lecture very much.

- At some point right after my arrival, the I.G. Office decided to hire CPA Firms and later – based on my suggestions -- switched to retired USAID Auditors to do the financial reviews of contracts issued in Africa. Anyway, I was assigned to the Audit Manager's position of the "Non-Federal Audit Program" and sent to Senegal for two weeks to see how they did it. Although Guy 5 was the RIG/A/ for Senegal, he and I got along well on my assignment. Yet, I saw that they were using a very antiquated system and a wrong technical approach when using a CPA Firm. First problem was that they were doing it by hand and wasting time in doing a great deal of manual repetition. And second, they were allowing the CPA to survey, scope, audit, and all other work. So, when I got back to Kenya, I changed the approach; I did the survey, scope, and designed the audit. In addition, I designed a computerized system where the basic legal conditions to be included for each contract would incorporate into a Master Floppy Disk. Once the RIG/A Auditor (me as a manager) did a survey of the "Activity to be audited," the Master Floppy Disk" containing the basic legal language would be copied onto another Disk, and this second disk be used to add steps and work to be done by the CPA Firm. This system would save the repetitious work by hand that Senegal was doing and what Nairobi was about to do.

My assignment, as Audit Manager of the Non-Federal Audit Program, was for the rest of my duration in my Nairobi tour. I was given a superior rating in my PER's. However, my workload was heavy and although I frequently asked for a local auditor to be assigned to help me and for travel funds, the second RIG/A/Nairobi never gave them to me. Nevertheless, my performance was exemplary. For instance, here is a list of the work I had to do: (a) I surveyed the program to be reviewed, (b) developed the parameters of the study, (c) designed the duties of the Contracted Auditors in the PIO/T, (d) assisted in contracting the teams, (e) supervised the efforts of 14 members in about 5 teams, (f) monitored their progress, and (g) helped them to write the reports. Our efforts usually resulted in exemplary findings. In fact, during the time I was Audit Manager of the Non-Federal Audit Program," my teams returned a total $2,103,000 to the U.S. Government as a result of disallowances. Also, a

Collusion case involving "Tallow" that I found in Egypt, ten years before, was settled and the suppliers returned $575,797 to the U.S. Government.

In sum, we accomplished a great deal during the year when Mervin Boyer and Gene Treasrau were supervising the Office and during my remaining time when I was in Kenya.

PART E. THE UNFORTUNATE ASSIGNMENT OF AN UNQUALIFIED RIG/A

Unfortunately, both Mervin and Gene were transferred back to Washington within the year. Gene chose to retire rather than be treated the way I was. They were replaced by two of the GAO auditors which the Inspector General had brought into the agency. One auditor (Guy 7) who was brought in to manage the office in Kenya was probably the most unqualified person I have ever worked with. Here are four examples explaining how I reached this adverse conclusion about him.

First Example a Sudan CIP Report. Like the others from his group that the I.G. had recruited from GAO, he **had not** come through the ranks of the Foreign Service. For that reason, he did not have that certain "feel" for the type of situations and problems normally found by an experienced auditor with management experience who had come through the ranks. Second, his management style was questionable. For instance, I did an audit of the financial aspects of USAID's Commodity Import and Cash Grant Programs in Sudan. USAID had obligated over $700 million to the program – of which over $304 million had already been disbursed (by USAID). I had a number of negative findings, including five very significant ones: (a) Section 609 of the Foreign Assistance Act of 1961 did not specify that – and/or how -- the Government of Sudan (GOS) (and other countries) should accumulate and/or expend its counterpart funds; (b) the GOS had not collected or accounted for a minimum of $274 million in equivalent local currency; and, (c) without consulting the USAID, the Sudanese government had used the equivalent of about the U.S. $ 39.4 million in local currency as regular budgetary support. In addition to the findings related to the GOS, I had also found that the USAID Inspector General had not yet set up the required procedures – as prescribed by the Inspector General Act of 1978 – to review existing and proposed legislation and report to Congress concerning the impact of such legislation on USAID's administration of programs and defective parts of any legislative laws. Moreover, the Inspector General had not yet established a dissent channel as prescribed by the Foreign Assistance Act of 1961. These last two findings could have been sent to the I.G. in a separate memorandum report.

Over a period of six months after I had completed the audit and written the draft report, Guy 7, who was now the RIG/A/Nairobi, made me rewrite, repeatedly, the above facts six different times, adding over 450 more hours of useless work to the cost of the audit. He did not want to include the facts or recommendations related to the funding GOS or IG violations. Guy 7 threatened me several times by telling me that he would not issue the report if I did not agree to eliminate the recommendations. At the time, this would have been the third or fourth audit report (written by other auditors) that he had canceled since his arrival. I asked him to send the report to the Policy Division of the Office of the Inspector General for review and release. This guy had no USAID experience on this type of reviews and was so professionally insecure that he never took any action in this regard.

After the sixth time that I rewrote the same facts and recommendations, this guy and I had a "talk." Since the USAID Mission in Sudan had already reviewed and agreed with the findings in my draft report as well as with my recommendations, I told him that he should release the report without any further delay. If he wanted to make changes, it would be his prerogative. But, if the facts were not correct or if the facts could not be supported by my work papers, I would prepare "a Memorandum of Non-Concurrence" documenting my reasons for not agreeing to his demands. He did not respond right then to me. A few minutes later, he came to my desk and said in an angry voice: "Give me that fucking report and the work papers."

He and his crony, the apparently "Acting" deputy regional inspector general, rewrote that report, changing the facts and figures and eliminating all my recommendations. In other words, the audit report was "watered down" to the point where most facts were not supportable by any of my work papers. I was allowed to review, without any comment, the draft report that was to be re-sent to the Mission for comments. However, I was not allowed to see or comment on the final version of the report. I never knew whether a final audit report was ever issued.

On April 22, 1986, I wrote the promised Memorandum with the following subject line: "Statement of Non-Concurrence on Changes to Draft Report of Financial Procedures and Controls of the Commodity Import Program and Cash Transfer Grants of Sudan." The memorandum was addressed to the Regional Inspector General in Kenya (Guy 7). I sent copies of the Memorandum to Senator Richard Lugar, then the Chairman of the Senate Foreign Affairs Committee, and to Inspector General, as well as to Deputy Inspector General (James D.). The Memo and letter that accompanied it were lengthy documents and will not be included in this book. They provided the details of the information in the report on the CIP program in Sudan that was deleted, as well as the recommendations deleted from that report. Although I never got a response from anyone, it seems that the Deputy IG did review my original version and sided with me. In any event, my memorandum is part of the files for this book, and my plans are to donate all work papers and files to a university (maybe the University of Texas at Austin) or Library of Congress).

Second Example, a Survey of the USAID Agriculture Program in Yemen. Towards the end of my tour in Kenya, the office sent me to Yemen to do a survey of the USAID agricultural program in Yemen, which was being implemented by a consortium of 5 U. S. Universities. The auditing part of financial transactions was to be done by one or more CPA firms. However, the Mission rejected the idea of using a CPA Firm. So, plans were later changed to use Retired Auditors and the Programmatic Evaluation would be done by IG/Kenya. During this survey, I taught myself to use a computer worksheet and reconstructed the financial disbursements to each of the universities. I remember that they included universities in Texas, New Mexico, Arizona, and California. As required by the survey methodology, I went to the U.S., and accompanied by Mervin Boyer and the Inspector General's director of contract audits, we visited about 3 of those universities.

When I got back to Kenya, I continued writing the audit program for use by the private accounting firms or retired USAID Auditors that were to perform the financial audit. Because some of the audit objectives were to cover a financial review of the 5 universities, it was automatically a very complex and would require perhaps several CPA Firms. Thus, the audit program that I was writing would also be very lengthy and complex. Guy 7 asked for me to brief him on the program, and I did.

Here is a description of the status of the audit plan. As I saw things, the Yemen audit was going to be a fairly complex review because there were about 15 steps needed to be developed, people phased in and out, and everything needed to be coordinated: (1) there were 3 separate universities and a consortium (CID) involved in the project; (2) each university had its own separate financial accounting located in 4 different locations; (3) each university had its operating headquarter in separate U.S. locations; (4) each university would be working a separate – but not necessarily for an identical – part of the agricultural objective;(5) however, all the individual pieces would eventually a fitting part of the overall unified Project Objective; (6) each university had to work in the Yemen (same location) but not necessarily at the same time; (7) each university had to be able to communicate with each other in an integral and cohesive manner; (8) analysis on selection on whether how many (1 or 5) CPA Firms should do the financial reviews; (9) decisions on the selection of the CPA Firm(s) – whether one or 5 CPA firms, close to , or far away, from the location of the 5 universities -- had to be made; (10) completion of the field work that each CPA was to do had to be completed; (11) Contracts with the 1 or 5 CPA Firms had to signed; (12) someone, within Washington or RIG/A/Kenya, would have to be in charge, and coordinate, all 5 CPA or Retired USAID/IG Auditors financial reviews, and (13) that same person needed to be able to do a programmatic and evaluation of the project; (14) the financial reports from the 1 or 5 CPA Firms (or Retired Auditors) had to be analyzed, and some data might needed to be incorporated into the programmatic evaluation; and, (15) the final overall report had to be written, cleared and issued. Yes, the Yemen audit was to be a very complex review. To a capable supervisory level auditor, this would be a decent and doable challenge – provided the supervisory auditor (me) was given time to prepare a good and complete audit program, given the time, and given the manpower that was needed.

When he saw that it would be an overly complex job, he canceled the review as planned and did a modified version We did use two retired USAID Auditors (Jim B. and Ray C.) to do a limited part of the study. Jim and Ray, who I knew well, did an exceptional job and they got refunds of over $2.1 million previously mentioned. They also confirmed the conclusions that my survey had drawn, which was that the universities might not achieve all the program objectives. However, I do not think the overall Programmatic Audit was ever done in the thorough manner that was needed. It is interesting to note that I got a "Superior PER Rating" for my last year.

When I left Kenya, Guy 7, in his capacity of RIG/A/Nairobi, had canceled at least six different audits and/or reports. I have estimated the total cost of the six audits that were canceled at about $336,000, based on the number of hours wasted writing the programs and factoring into these costs' airfare, per diem, and other costs. Yes, a more qualified RIG/A would not have cancelled any of the six audits.

The Third and Fantastic Example -- The SHCEA Special Education Grant: Soon after writing my Memorandum of Non-Concurrence, Guy 7 either sent someone to talk to Guy 8 in the RFMC – or was asked by Guy 8 to send a person -- to talk to him about the SHCEA Special Education Grant for my daughter. I am not too sure how the conversation between Guy 7 and 8 initiated. But the talk did take place. I suspect that this was part of another reprisal against me. **The facts are that** Guy 8 had a serious proclivity for letting personal rancor prevail over professional objectivity. In my case, Guy 8 had a profoundly serious grudge against me because I had previously challenged – and made him correct -- some erroneous "assumptions and disallowances" that he and/or his staff had made on one of my travel vouchers; I will discuss this in Chapter 18 of this book.

In any event, right after Guys 7 and 8 had their discussion about SHCEA, Guy 7 went to the USAID Office of Inspector General for Investigations in Kenya (Guy 12) and told them that the RFMC Deputy Controller had made serious accusations against me alleging "…fraudulent submissions of claims against the U.S Government…" As a result of these meetings, the Office of Inspector General for Investigations launched a secret investigation of me. This investigation took place over a period of 3 to 4 years, and my name and the case were reviewed by over 29 USAID Officials. Some of them were repeatedly contacted with an obvious intent of proving a serious case against me -- yet, I was never told, by a USAID Official or anyone from USAID, that I was being investigated. As I will explain in Chapter 18, it was the Office of

Inspector General from the Department of State, very close to my retirement, that I first learned that I was being investigated.

While the investigation was taking place, Guy 8 from RFMC and the USAID Executive Officer to Kenya (Guy 15) reversed the prior (1 ½ year prior) approval, by the State Department Medical Office, and everyone who had previously approved both the SMA and the SHCEA Special Education Grant. On January 27, 1987, Guys 8 and 15 told me that the Special Education Grant and Separate Maintenance Allowance were wrong and that they would be issuing a Bill for Collection for the entire $45,000 within 90 days. They also said they planned to "garnish" every single monthly salary until I fully paid the entire amount.

Knowing that they were wrong, I told them they were wrong and that I intended to request a ruling from the State Department's Allowance Committee, which is charged for reviewing questionable rulings between offices and employees. I then wrote a long memorandum to the Committee, attaching 45 different cables and documents so that the Allowance Committee could examine and rule on the case.

The Fourth Example, Travel Authorization for Return to the U.S. Here is some background information. Whenever an FSO is assigned to an overseas post, he/she and his or her family are authorized, via the "Travel Authorization (T/A)" certain costs, including the cost of airfare, a certain amount of carry-on baggage, the cost of storing household effects in the United States, and the shipment of a certain amount of air freight. In other words, the authorized weight is radically different – much higher -- for FSOs with a family and the lower authorized weight for single FSOs.

Since my family was to live with me in Kenya, I had included airfare for my family, as well as the other items in my T/A since the plan was for all of us to stay in Kenya until my tour of duty was ended.

However, because my family had left early for medical reasons and their share of furniture and clothing was still in Kenya, the Travel Authorization that USAID were erroneously prepared and did not include air freight and/or shipping of any of my family's associated furniture. In other words, I was "declared" to be a "single person" and only authorized a Singles FSO's weight and cost. Obviously, this was wrong. I explained to Guy 7 that the travel authorization needed to be changed to include shipping of the furniture and other stuff for my family; however, to Guy 7, this information went in one ear and out the other without registering. He refused to make changes to the Travel Authorization. He did not care about the cost to me. I went around him and got the situation corrected. Nevertheless, this speaks volumes about his lack of management style.

PART F. MY CONCLUDING REMARKS

My tour in Kenya was mixed. On the one hand, we had a terrific time going to the game parks and seeing all the animals placed on this earth by God and nature. However, we had rough health situations that we could not have foreseen, or they could not be addressed in Kenya, and for that reason, Jerry, Pauline, and Melissa departed much earlier than expected.

From a work-related point of view, the first period – when Mervin Boyer and Eugene Treasau were heading the office in Nairobi – represented my usual excellent performance and happiness with the job. I missed their participation and their exceptional friendship that we all had during that period.

With respect to the auditors that replaced Mervin and Gene as the Regional Inspector General and the Acting Deputy Regional Inspector General, my opinion of them has neither changed nor mellowed since I left Kenya. Guy 7 was clearly the wrong person for the job. In any event, I was not the only one that questioned this guy's brain. A colleague who knew him from the time he was at GAO said, "I don't know how he got that position…he really should kneel down every day and give thanks to God for helping him so far…He just doesn't have it up there…."

CHAPTER EIGHTEEN
USAID INSPECTOR GENERAL RECONFIGURES AUDIT AND INVESTIGATIVE APPROACH, RECRUITS PERSONNEL FROM THE GENERAL ACCOUNTABILITY OFFICE, PLACES THEM IN HIGH FSO POSITIONS AND PURSUES TRAUMATIC REPRISALS, RETALIATIONS, INVESTIGATIONS, AND PERSECUTIONS, AFFECTING ME AND COUNTLESS OTHER EMPLOYEES

PART A. INTRODUCTORY COMMENTS

Background. This chapter is most complex because it integrates all the contents which briefly relate to the IG#1 persecutions and mentioned in Chapters 15, 16, 17, and new ones in this Chapter 18. So that the reader can fully understand the contents of the Chapter, these initial series of paragraphs represent a summary of all the things that I want to convey. So, let me begin at the top with the Inspector General.

At the time that the former Inspector General of USAID (hereafter referred to as the IG#1, Inspector General, or simply IG#1) joined USAID, he brought with him a great number of exceptional qualifications and compared to previous Auditor Generals, there was a very positive transformation to the office. Compared with the previous two Auditor Generals, this Inspector General was the first USAID IG. He was exceptional for about 7 years. As he continued in his tenure, however, he began to make changes that I did not think were good ones either for the Office of the I.G. or for the Agency. One example is that he brought an influx of eight civil service personnel from the General Accountability Office (GAO). To my knowledge, these people had never served in a USAID environment or in Less Developed Countries; he converted them from a GS to high-level FSO grade; he placed them in high-level positions. After that, with his tacit or implicit authorization, these new people began imparting or condoning negative actions on the part of these new FSOs. these actions were impractical and adversely affected the morale and operations of the IG Office and the rest of the USAID Personnel. When these people attempted to implement erroneous and deleterious policies, procedures, and practices, I was, at that time, the appointed DRIG/A/LA and was Acting RIG/A/LA (Dean was out of town) and, like my team, I believed (and still do) that those proposals were wrong. Therefore, as leader and representative of my team, I dissented. Unfortunately, my dissents were done at a time when the I.G. had NOT instituted a "Dissent Channel." My dissent was by means of memorandums addressed to the different new FSOs with copies to the Inspector General. My dissent obviously hit a bad nerve, and the I.G. and all-new FSO group did not like my objections. The Inspector General, through these new FSO's and two other long-terms FSO's-- began to conduct a systematic and sustained reprisal and punishment against me and possibly against Dean (the RIG/A/LA). In any event, Dean resigned or was terminated. In my case, my first punishment was my demotion as DRIG/A/LA. As the reader will see later, the way I was fired, from my position, was very shoddy. In effect, the IG#1 and his group waited until I was out of the U.S., on TDY, performing supervisory duties of my staff at my fourth Central and/or South American Country, and I had just completed a complex agricultural audit in Ecuador all by myself. Without decency, courtesy, a sound managerial Class, good managerial practices of informing me first, they sent a poorly worded cable to the Missions in Ecuador and Peru (no copy to me) telling them -- to inform me – first that Dean was no longer the RIG/A/LA and second that I, myself, was no longer the DRIG/A/LA. The Missions were to tell me that I was prohibited from sharing any information with them and to inform me to return to the U.S. immediately. By then, I had visited three countries, performed, and completed a complicated integral agricultural audit in Ecuador all by myself, and shared a Report of Audit Finding, which was the full audit report with the Mission in Ecuador.\. This was my third day of being in Pcru. So, I stopped working in Peru and returned to Washington. Once I got back to the U.S., I had to face a group of seven or eight people – all of whom had conflicts of interests against me -- and prove that the accusation of "Insubordination" was false. Then, for a period of four to five years, I was a victim of perennial persecution. Here are a series of examples. As I mentioned, I was demoted from my position. My planned assignment to the Philippines was switched and I was transferred from the

Philippines to Kenya. I was rated by the very person who took my place as DRIG/A/La and, despite the conflict of interest, he gave me a crummy and bad Personal Evaluation Report (PER). The way the PER was prepared violated all policies of Conflict of Interests. In addition, my transfer to Kenya was despite the possibility that the school there might not be able to educate my daughter, who has a learning disability. True to form, the International School of Kenya conducted a study of my daughter and the school found that she could go to that school for only one year. As a result, while in Kenya, my daughter received two Special Education Allowance Grants (known as SHCEA). I will explain what SHCEA is and how it differs from normal SEGs in Part H of this chapter. Despite approvals from several high Department of State, medical, and USAID Offices, Guys 8 and 15 erroneously reversed prior approvals and wanted to collect over $45,000 from me. With the help of an incompetent RIG/A/Kenya (see Chapter 17) and the rancorous Guy 8 (a Deputy Director RFMC), I was falsely accused of submitting false SHCEA claims against the U.S. Government. As a result, I was persecuted and secretly investigated by the Office of IG/Investigations for four years. My so-called "case" was shown, in some cases, "time and again" to over 29 USAID Officials with obviously explicit attempts to coerce their concurrence with the false accusations, erroneous interpretations of regulations, erroneously drawn or pursued conclusions, and misused legal statements that the investigators were pursuing. Yet, the OIG Investigations could only get a great variety of responses from the 29 high officials who saw "my case." The "case" was finally sent to the Office of Department of State I.G. and Ethics and Integrity Section for a final ruling. It was at this point that I learned of the USAID I.G. secret investigation. After looking at USAID Investigative Documentation, the Office of Inspector General of the Department of State sensed that the case was extremely defective and could not stand in a court hearing. As a result, a member of the IG Department of State called me and told me to get a lawyer; they did not want to nurture the false case against me any further. Once I hired a lawyer, she took over, and I never met anyone on my case. As planned, I retired from USAID on December 31, 1989. After my retirement, the ruling from the I.G. Department of State closed the case. Yet, it took the USAID I.G.'s Office of Investigations 1½ years to issue a "Notice of Action" and formally close the case.

As can be seen from the above summary, discussing the details of all these interrelated events is complex. It is for this reason that I needed to present the information together with two or three points that deserve further clarification in the following 12 Parts:

- Part A. Introductory Comments.
- Part B. The First USAID I.G., His Background, and His Transformation.
- Part C. Influx of GAO Personnel and Placement in High Positions.
- Part D. Examples of Erroneous Policies, Practices, and Procedures That New Personnel Tried to Implement.
- Part E. A Most Disrespectful Way that the Inspector General and his New Group Notified me that I was fired as DRIG/A/LA.
- Part F. In Kenya, RIG/A, (Guy 7) and I Strongly Disagree on Sudan CIP Audit; He Consults\ed Guy 8 and Instigates a Secret OIG Investigations on me.
- Part G. In Kenya, Guy 8 (or Staff) Made Mistakes on My Travel Vouchers; I Challenged Errors; His Rancorous Attitude Helps Guy 7 to Instigate OIG/Investigations Claiming that I Was Making Fraudulent Claims Against US Government.
- Part H. Background covering the Special Handicapped Child Education Allowance (SHCEA).
- Part I. Office of I.G. Conducts A Sloppy Secret Investigation of Me.
- Part J. Case Was Closed After I Had Retired.
- Part K Three Points Deserve Further Clarification.
- Part L. My Concluding Remarks.

PART B. THE FIRST USAID I.G., HIS BACKGROUND, AND TRANSFORMATION

A retired Marine Corps Lieutenant General, the IG#1 was appointed to the temporary position of Inspector General of USAID in 1977. Once the Inspector General Act of 1978 and the International Security and Development Cooperation Act 1980 were passed, the I.G. officially became the first USAID Inspector General.

At the time he was appointed, this I.G. had excellent military and political qualifications. He was born on October 3, 1920. He got his bachelor's degree from the Citadel in 1943. After receiving his bachelor's degree, he entered the Marine Corps as an artillery officer that same year. During the time he was in the Marine Corps, he got his Law degree from the Catholic University in 1953, and fought in World War II, the Korean War, and the Vietnam War. He also headed the Marine Corps' Personnel office and served as an assistant law clerk to a judge in the Marine Corps' Judge Advocate General Corps. He was promoted through the ranks in a fast manner, rising rather rapidly to the rank of Lieutenant General. After his promotion to Lt. General, IG#1 served as a military aide to Vice President Hubert Humphrey for 2 years, from 1965 to 1967. After leaving the Vice-President's service, this I.G. served in Vietnam and at Marine Corps Base Quantico, as well as at the Pentagon. He retired from the Marines Corps in 1975, having received many awards, including the Legion of Merit and the Distinguished Service Medal. As I stated previously, in 1977, he was appointed as a temporary Inspector General for USAID. Together with his USAID appointment, the names of the USAID audit field offices were upgraded and thereafter are/were known as Regional Offices of Inspector General.[105]

In sum, in 1977, IG#1 brought to USAID exceptional credentials for the position. He eventually served about 17 years or perhaps until 1994 in that capacity. In this book, I mention all this because of the transformation that occurred in his performance as Inspector General of USAID.

---

[105] Source: Https//www.washingtonpost.com/wp-dyn/cotent/article2007/11/12/AR2007111302232.html

IG#1 and I met several times. In Egypt, he praised us all for the fine work that he felt we were doing. I met him once again during my assignment to the Agency - Wide Evaluation Panel - I visited his office after writing him a memorandum on the outcome of the evaluation and promotion boards. He called on me several times to explain something. All our meetings were very cordial, and his questions were very incisive and to the point.

IG#1 was an excellent leader for the first 3 to 7 years during the time when he served as the USAID Inspector General. During those initial years, he saw how complicated, time-consuming, and challenging task USAID audit work really is, especially in the many countries (with their different governments, laws, social conditions, languages, restrictions, etc.) and that USAID operates in a very complex manner.. He also saw the limitations of his IG Office of investigations (OIG/I) in investigating, pursuing, and when requiring, prosecuting wayward foreign leaders who might have committed fraud. He saw how difficult it would be to hire a foreign country lawyer and a translator, learn about courts in different countries, and particularly the type of harsh type of punishments which could be expected, etc. How was he learning all these things? We were providing exceptional learning materials through our audits especially those that were dealing with the USAID programs in Pakistan and Egypt. Here are examples:

- Based on the work that I did in Pakistan and Bangladesh, he learned how easily birth control pills are sold on the illegal market. He also learned how easily condoms can be converted into latex gloves and sold by unscrupulous foreign business entrepreneurs for exorbitant profits. We uncovered other criminal activities, and this information was included in a series of classified memorandums for use by the USAID Inspector General's Office of Investigations. As discussed earlier, we also found evidence of outright fraud. This evidence involved collusion by and between U.S. suppliers to increase their profits; it also included the submission of duplicate bills hidden first as factors under Indefinite Quantity Contracts (IQC) and then billed as "Indirect Costs" for some projects.
- We also found evidence of improper planning and/or monitoring by USAID headquarters in Washington and/or by USAID Missions. For example, we found USAID lacked guidance in its Handbook for

effective project management; and that two-way communication between headquarters and the field was lacking. We also found that the Missions often adopted a passive attitude toward monitoring projects. In some cases, the Mission had deficient accounting systems.

- In addition, as discussed earlier, we found evidence of poor or perhaps very "astute" planning on the part of the host government. For example, (a) there was a questionable $44.0 million in Agent's Commissions paid to host country employees; (b) the shoddy work by implementing Engineers; (c) the passive monitoring of projects and/or programs that later became victims of "Murphy's Law;" (d) a lack of desires or perhaps a valid reason, on the part Egypt and perhaps other countries, to fulfill the "Poorest of the Poor" legal provision of the FAA. Our examples included cheap laborer costs paid at Alexandria Quays # 85 and the Zabbaleen (this is the name given to the Trash Collectors) and others.
- He learned that audits needed special skills. For instance, during our audits, we use a number of techniques, including surveys, audit plans, statistical sampling, and in-depth studies, to identify problems and confirm evidence of fraud; examples include evidence found by appropriate specialists, including engineers, investigators, and financial review specialists.

The lessons that we provided - Russell, me, and our Audit Team - during our tour in Egypt (and the other RIG/A's) were truly exceptional (just reread the Chapter covering our Egyptian tours).

Given his background and experience in the human capital field, it is my opinion that IG#1 might have been discouraged by the tremendous amount of audit work required to monitor USAID programs and projects throughout the world. He also must have seen the limitations that his Office of Investigation had in pursuing cases of citizens of foreign countries, i.e., the difference in courts, laws, punishments, and the necessity of employing translators.

As I understand it, according to his testimony before an Investigating Committee, IG#1 said that his office had substantially revised its audit approach away from audits of individually funded USAID programs and projects and toward a greater focus on agency systems to determine whether the appropriate controls were in place and functioning appropriately. [106]

- ❖ (Note: based on my experience, it seems that his approach left vacant in audit coverage of individually funded projects and programs. To me, the systems approach might cover some parts of the I.G. responsibilities. However, it disregarded the individuality of the projects which are usually designed in each country. These have their own transactions, internal controls, idiosyncrasies, goals, and evaluations, all of which will be the only measure of either success or failure of any project. I will have a further expansion on this at a later point in this chapter.

In sum, by 1980, he seems to have seen the avalanche of audit work required to monitor programs. It was at this point, he began to reconfigure the work of the Office of Inspector General; this included how his audit and investigative staff would carry out their work with the limited resources and the internationally complicated investigations of the OIG/I. This is the time he saw the need to bring into the organization the 8 to 10 older experienced GAO people, converting them to FSOs and placing them in management positions within the Inspector General. Why? He did this because the "old FSO timers" would be "too fixed in the old operational skills and ways," and the new people would be indebted to him. He could dictate his new policies, through this staff, without their attribution to him. And, he could also be assured of having control over them.

The Inspector General also got a bonus from the audits that we did of the borrower/grantee contracts, as well as the participant training and CIP audits, among others. With the results of these reviews, he also saw the easy control he could have by doing directed types of audits and reviews (like those done by the GAO). Moreover, this also gave him an opportunity to change the focus of the limited "investigative forces" from the very dispersive international scene to more on the personnel or "Ethical" matters on USAID personnel and less on questionable investigative cases related to foreign countries.

---

[106] Per the Senate Committee on Governmental Affairs, John Glenn 1992 Investigation Committee.

I discussed how I participated as part of an Agency-Wide Personnel Evaluation Panel, which without a doubt, this was a terrific professional recognition of my capabilities. Around the same time, IG#1 also asked me to review the applications of 8 civil service staff from GAO that he appeared to be planning to hire. Although he did not disclose to me that he would definitely hire these people, he thought that I would give the group a complete bill of health on his selection and my recommendation for him to hire younger and very bright younger auditors. However, as shown in Chapter 15, I gave him my honest evaluation of the 8 people submitted for my evaluation. In any event, he disregarded my recommendations. The rest is history – he hired them, converted them from civil service to FSOs, placed them in management positions above more experienced FSOs, and began systematically attempting to eliminate older FSOs who had been with the USAID for a long time. In addition, he began, in some cases, unfairly and without evidence to pursue any USAID employee who was violating employee integrity and/or ethics and to focus resources on anyone appearing to violate prescribed Agency Rules. And, although some were for valid reasons, too many were not, these were prolonged and vicious (as mentioned earlier, mine lasted between 3 and 5 years. Although I was innocent, my case was shown, without ever discussing it or consulting me, to over 29 people – probably to either punish me and/or to ruin my professional reputation.

Based on widely known public information, during IG#1's tenure, at least 8 USAID officials were investigated and prosecuted for ethical violations or fraud. Here are six examples:

a) A USAID accountant who worked in the Office of Controller who was found to have embezzled over $1.0 million and was sent to jail.

b) A former Inspector General Executive Officer who was getting kickbacks from contractors (he was fired and prosecuted).

c) A Mission Director in Costa Rica who was referring and approving participant training to his preferred religious association (he was removed as Director).

d) A Mission Director who used U.S. Government travel funds to visit a girlfriend in Hong Kong (no more details are known).

e) A USAID administrator who was Gay and had been fired by a university for having orgies with students. While in USAID, he appears to have been receiving "contributions" from an outside organization(s) (he quit or was fired).

f) There was also the case of a young OIG/I Employee in Kenya who was married. He was caught soliciting sexual services from prostitutes in different country. He was under investigation at the time of my retirement.

On the other hand, IG#! went too far in other ways. He or his managers let it be known that there were about seventy people in USAID that were being investigated. He also circulated a proposal to require most USAID project managers in the field or being considered for audit and staff in the Office of the Inspector General (more details are discussed later) to sign a sweeping "audit representation letter" stating that they had complied **with every provision of every agency policy and to take polygraph tests to prove they had. According to the Washington Post, USAID Employees "abhorred" this requirement.** [107]

- To say that USAID Employees "abhorred" is not an accurate statement. Most of us in the IG Office agreed with the idea of conducting audits of projects, including audit reviews, in the manner prescribed by USAID policy. However, requiring people: (a) to sign a letter saying that they had complied with every provision of all the Agency's policies; and (b) to agree to take a lie detector test to prove this was true – both the idea and proposal were, in my opinion and those of many others, simply preposterous, perverse, and an abuse of power. Aside from the six reasons that Patricia Del Bosque mentioned in her testimony, there are ample reasons for not requiring this. Here are some: Projects and Programs are developed under a team concept – contractors most times develop the concepts and parameters of the proposals, financial people prepare cost estimates and keep track of budgets and costs, negotiations with host countries take place, and rates of exchanges are affected by devaluations, changes in areas or

[107] https://www.washingtonpost.com/wp-dyn/content/article/2007/11/13/AR2007111302232.html

> locations of projects affect plans, or other types of changes, and many other reasons. To require the Director of a Mission, the Program or Project Officers, and Controllers to vouch for everyone's opinions and proposals is entirely wrong. Moreover, this requirement conceivably could violate the Fifth Amendment of the Constitution? As mentioned later, this requirement was first tried on us – the OIG Personnel – and my team refused to sign a "Proposed Contract." If that type of proposal was, without any hesitation, refused by OIG employees, I could see how nervous such a proposal was to the USAID employees.

The IG#1, I believe, was just really looking to find some type of an excuse – albeit an easy one -- to persecute, fire, and prosecute employees. **IG#1 justified** this conduct by saying that criminal conduct at USAID was phenomenal at the senior levels due in part to the large percentage of USAID staff at senior levels and the environment that USAID operates in. I wonder what basis the Inspector General had to make such a broad and general negative allegation. In my reviews over the period of 28 years, I found numerous problems. However, I do not agree that all the problems were due to malfeasance, fraud, etc., by the vast majority of USAID (and OIG) Employees. In any event, by the spring of 1992, the Office of the Inspector General's transformation was, apparently, complete, and IG#1 had become highly controversial simply because he certainly was no longer pursuing improvements over the way the USAID operated most of its programs. He was now focusing his office's efforts on USAID Employees.

Concerns about IG#1 conduct resulted in probes of his office by three government entities - the Senate Committee on Governmental Affairs, the President's Council on Integrity and Efficiency, and the GAO. It also resulted in a July 1992 *Foreign Service Journal* article entitled, "Inspecting the Inspector at USAID," as well as a *Washington Post* article entitled, "At AID, General and Troops Don't See Eye to Eye."

The *Foreign Service Journal* article said that some employees thought of IG#1 as being "... the Agency's J. Edgar Hoover ...suspicious, vindictive, eager to think the worst...." The same article said that the Inspector General saw himself "...as the righteous avenger...more like Elliot Ness rooting corruption in an Agency he believes is extraordinarily likely to yield to the temptation of malfeasance...." Based on the shoddy manner and relentless way that he and his OIG/I pursued me, I tend to believe the reference to J. Edgar Hoover was, in a great part, justified.

The May 1992 hearing, chaired by Senator John Glenn of Ohio, focused on serious allegations of misconduct on the part of the Inspector Generals of the Departments of the Army and Energy as well as USAID. At this hearing, Patricia del Bosque, the Vice President of the American Foreign Service Association, said that USAID employee confidence in the Inspector General system was non-existent and that there appeared to be widespread feelings of fear, mistrust, and intimidation on the part of USAID Employees. She also said that retired employees of the USAID Inspector General had reported that projects or programs were frequently chosen because they indicated that management could be exploited and reported on, not whether the subject matter was of important consequence to USAID's mission and operations.

- I wonder where Patricia got the information on how we selected projects or programs for audits. During the six-year period that I was DRIG/A for Egypt and for Latin America, we did Mission-wide surveys to determine which projects and programs had problems and which ones did not show problems. We then selected the projects or programs that showed the problems (review the Grain Silo Project in Egypt) – not because we could exploit or report on anyone – but because this is where we could help management the most. In other words, our audit selection was "…on the Exception…the activities that had the problems…" and we did it this way so we could use our limited audit personnel in the most efficient manner possible. In sum, our surveys were very objective ways focusing on problem situations and not a way to be critical of anyone.

In addition, Priscilla gave six reasons for objecting to the use of audit representation letters and polygraphs. For instance, she pointed out that many employees feared signing a document vouching for the truthfulness of information was dangerous because perhaps dozens of people often monitored parts of program implementation responsible for managing various aspects of a USAID program. She also noted that FSOs within the Inspector General were reporting that because the Inspector General had its own internal and independent personnel system, there was abuse in who got promoted and who were worthy of getting significant additional bonuses. She asked for a thorough review of the Office of the Inspector General to examine its policies, procedures, methods, and conduct. She suggested that the Office of the Inspector General introduce fairness and balance in its actions and become more open.

In his testimony before the Committee, IG#1 said that the Inspector General had instituted numerous measures designed to reduce or alleviate the adversarial relationship that the Office of the Inspector General had with USAID's employees, including more outreach and training. ***He did not respond to the allegations of abuse within the Inspector General's office, saying in his written statement that the Office's experience with whistleblower-related matters and issues was almost non-existent.***

- ***Based on my situation, IG#1's statements were true – only because I had, by then, retired and, seeing the way I had been treated, I.G. Employees were afraid of voicing exceptions. Nevertheless, I do know that (a) IG#1 subsequently dropped the requirement for the audit representation letter and polygraph test; and (b) the current Inspector General now has, in place, a "Dissent Channel" – the exact type of channel of dissent that I espoused, and that the IG#1 did not institute during all the times I objected.***
- To me, the persecution of innocent employees is very costly and not beneficial. Allegations are sometimes based on interpretations of regulations. Thus, they should be pursued with an open mind and up to the point of diminishing returns; they should be closed when solid information has been reached and/or when it begins to go against their human or employment rights. In my case, the Investigators talked to two or three people who told them that SHCEA grants were treated very differently than regular SE Grants. There were other points – when the I.G. was trying to find "unethical conduct" that OIG/I thought could be proven against me; they thought I had violated ethics when my daughter had gone to Kenya two months after her 21st birthday or when the airlines gave a discounted airfare. At several points, there were knowledgeable officials telling the I.G. Investigators that this was not a fact. The IG Investigators continued to pursue and attempt to coerce respondents with their faulty investigation.

Moreover, in his testimony (of the May 1992 Glenn Committee Hearing), IG#1 defended the use of the audit representation letters, saying they were not sweeping statements. He also said that the Inspector General had substantially revised its audit approach away from audits of individually funded USAID programs and projects and toward a greater focus on agency systems to determine whether the appropriate controls were in place and were functioning appropriately.

- ❖ Note: To me, it seems like the Inspector General would have liked to operate the IG audit responsibilities like GAO or more like an External CPA Firm. In other words, IG#1 would relinquish his Internal Auditor's part (identifying and doing individual audits of projects, programs, and activities having serious problems) of his Office's Responsibilities. However, I see great faults in this line of thinking. Based on my experience, USAID operates in a highly volatile and in many countries and areas, which have a great potentially corrupt international environment. In my way of thinking, if the Inspector General vacates (not do) his responsibilities for carrying out his Internal Audit functions (do audits on projects and programs which have problems), how – and by whom – will these functions be fulfilled? Who evaluates whether the project or program is on the right track and will achieve its desired objectives? Who and how will anyone, independently, know whether end costs and achievements equal the desired objectives? And, if the Inspector General will be relinquishing its audit responsibilities for doing internal audit functions of individually financed projects and programs, who in the Agency will take over these essential functions designed to ensure that projects, programs, and activities are individually designed and implemented in the most efficient, economical, and cost-effective manner? Unless the USAID creates an "Internal Audit Office" to implement the evaluative functions, yes, I see many problems with the approach that was tried by IG#1 and the staff that he brought in from GAO.

- ❖ To me, these vacancies of audit responsibilities expose the Agency to very wasteful policies, mismanagement, and fraud. Just review the "Grain Silo Project" or "the six reports covering the CIP" in Egypt and the canceled or water-downed audit of the CIP in Sudan. If it had not been for our surveys and audits, no one would have found and/or possibly) corrected all the financial and programmatic problems that we found in the survey and during the many months of our audit. Moreover, canceling audits and/or audit reports just because they are complex or because Guy 5 and Guy 7 had never seen situations like the ones, I found in my audit of CIP in Sudan are costly, unwarranted, and expose the United States and USAID as its representative to frauds and/or extremely bad publicity. THESE ARE THE TYPES OF AUDITS THAT WOULD BE VACATED BY THE IG SYSTEMS APPROACH, AS EXPLAINED BY IG#1 HIS MEETING WITH THE GLENN COMMITTEE. THE PROBLEMS WERE FOUND ONLY BECAUSE WE USED A COMBINATION OF A MISSION-WIDE SURVEY AND DID THE PROJECTS AND PROGRAMS REVIEW USING THE INDIVIDUALLY AUDIT APPROACH. IF WE HAD NOT FOUND THE PROBLEMS, THE ADVERSE CONSEQUENCE WOULD BE IMMEASURABLE TO THE U.S. AND THE EGYPTIAN PEOPLE.

- **Here is the way I see the way that the Office of Inspector General should conduct it audits. The IG Office must be assigned a combination of the External Auditor, as espoused by the IG in his congressional testimony, and the Internal Auditor Concept, which protects the USAID (and the U.S.) from frauds and mismanagement. And the best way to do audits in USAID is a six -- way approach: (a) do a mission-wide survey to identify and segregate projects which have problems and those that do not; (b) identify activities and projects which have systemic types of problems; (c) identify activities and projects which have individual types of problems; (d) Schedule and do audits of b (ones that have the systemic type of programs) -- these ones require broad Agency reviews; and of c; these ones must be done on an individual problematic project, program, activity basis) accordingly; and (e) since there are lessons to be learned from an activity that is going well, sample and do limited type of scope audits of activities and**

projects which seem to have no problems. If there are financial records, in other "Home Countries" to be examined, the Non-Federal Audits should be done in an integrated manner with the Programmatic Evaluations (I expand this explanation more fully in Chapter 19.).

In sum, I will always have fond memories of IG#1 when he first began work as the Inspector General and for the first 7 years. I searched the documents to see if this IG#1 had resigned or been fired after the committee sessions of 1992. However, I found nothing on that question. In fact, not even the General's Obituaries that I saw say whether IG#1 resigned or was fired as the USAID IG after 1992. However, there is an interesting correlation between the time the **Council of the Inspectors General on Integrity and Efficiency (CIGIE) was created around May 1992 and the time around the IG#1 departure from USAID.**

So, I continue to see some nice and positive actions as they relate to me only: Based on the recommendations of Russell A, the IG#!: (a) transferred me from Pakistan to Egypt; (b) appointed me as the Acting DRIG/A/For Egypt and Acting RIG/A/E when Russell was out of the country; (c) selected me for the 1980 Agency Wide Evaluation Panel; and, (d) selected me as the first Hispanic American Deputy Inspector General for Latin America.

However, his performance – and those of the GAO people he brought into USAID -- during my last five years with USAID left a great deal to be desired of a good leader. This included: (a) the shoddy way that he and/or the new group that took over the RIG/A/LA fired me from the DRIG/A/LA position; (b) the needless false accusations of "insubordination;" (c) the erroneous attempt at establishing policies, rules, and regulations which were tremendously prejudicial to the operations of the IG and Agency as a whole; (d) the perennial persecution and the secretive and shoddy way they conducted the investigation against me; (e) the unnecessary showing off "my case" to 29+ officials; (f) the delay in the closing of my investigation; and, (g) the needless persecution of many other innocent employees – including some of my friends. These actions left a great deal to be desired from a reputable leader. During this period, my family, some of my friends (and their families), and I greatly suffered. Therefore, I will remember that part of his leadership --

and part of my life – mostly with a certain degree of resentment. In sum, my overall feelings about IG#1 are mixed.

IG#1 died on October 14, 2007,[108]and has now been judged by the almighty Creator. May he now Rest in Peace.

I will now proceed to set the record straight as it relates to my treatment for the last five years of my career with USAID.

PART C. INFLUX OF GAO PERSONNEL AND THEIR PLACEMENT IN HIGH FSO POSITIONS

Civil Service Personnel Converted to FSOs. As mentioned at the conclusion of Chapter 16, I have assigned a Pseudonyms ("Guy X") to attribute events so as to avoid hurting the person's family. As I mention to the "Guys," here are some reminders:

- **IG#1 was the first Inspector General for USAID. He is no longer the I.G.**
- Guys 0, 1, 2, and 3 were not related to my problem with the I.G.
- Guys 4, 5, 6, and 7 used to have a GS grade, worked for GAO, were converted to FSO at high grades; and most were later named as RIG/A/Different Locations.
- Guy 8 was a rancorous and back-stabbing Deputy Director of the RFMC.
- Guy 9 Former GAO, nice person, and not related to my case.
- Guy 10 was a good person who served in Egypt under me; and, was appointed as RIG/A/LA.
- Guy 11 was NOT a nice person; His Narcissism played a huge role in his replacing me as DRIG/A/La and preparing a defective PER of me. He violated all conflicts of interest when he prepared my PER for this period; in my case, Dean should have prepared my PER and reviewer

[108] Read the Obituary for IG#1 as written by Washington Post and https://www.geni.com/people/Lt-General-Herbert-L-Beckington-USMC/6000003190132942l

should have been the Deputy IG#1. They were my legitimate Supervisors.

Challenges Which Plagued Me in Washington. During my last years I was the DRIG/A/LA, I faced 6 challenges resulting from the course IG#1had decided to take. Of particular concern to me were the practices and policies that the new GAO/FSO's employees tried to implement. Here is a summary of the different challenges:

a) I faced the challenge of having to curb IG#1's decision to place recently hired inexperienced civil service personnel from GAO in the Inspector General's Office at high positions, with authority over highly qualified, experienced FSOs. To me – and many other FSOs – this practice was unfair. As far as I know, before joining USAID, these GAO employees had never taken the rigid tests I took to join USAID or served in a USAID field environment or been exposed to Coup-de-tats or the dangers of wars. After joining USAID, many of these officials stayed for a short period of time with the USAID Inspector General's office and quickly retired; thus, they did not provide long-term benefits to the Inspector General, USAID, or the FSO Retirement System.

b) I faced the challenge of trying to discern why IG#1 and the Investigations Office focused so much time on prosecutions of long-term FSO employees even in instances where the regulations which often lack clarity and were confusing. According to statements made by someone, there were 70 "cases," and even the IG#1 said that corruption in USAID was remnant (just what were the basis for these assertions?

c) I had to deal with a group of the four (of 8) people who were brought in from GAO and given higher-level positions and greater authority than I had – especially because neither the I.G. nor his Deputy ever met with all the IG Offices and informed us that these new people would be in a superior position than us.

d) I faced the challenge of trying to halt the misguided change in audit philosophies that the Inspector General seemed to want to institute and that exposed the Agency to very wasteful policies, mismanagement, fraud, and the persecution of innocent employees.

e) I had to deal with a Guy 11 – a most ambitious, narcissistic, and sycophantic person who actively tried to undermine me. He eventually did replace me in my position as the DRIG/LA/A. And he then went on to even prepare a shoddy and bad PER on me.

f) I tried to ensure that the Inspector General instituted the Dissent Channel prescribed by the Foreign Services Act of 1980 and Section 105 of Public Law 96-465. These legal requirements protect the free expression of views and allow the resolution of differences and disputes – between employees and management or supervisors – in a harmonious manner – without fault, prejudice, or adverse consequence to the staff using the Dissent Channel.

PART D. EXAMPLES OF ERRONEOUS POLICIES AND PRACTICES THAT NEW PERSONNEL TRIED TO IMPLEMENT AND MY OBJECTIONS

As noted previously, I had been the DRIG/A/LA for about 18 months when the grapevine -- which seldom fails – began to be ripe with news that "…some civil service staff from GAO would be joining USAID at high-level Foreign Service positions. Based on this information and voicing the dissent coming from my staff, I wrote a memorandum to IG#1 and his deputy arguing against the transfer; however, I never received a response.

Some Issues with Guy 11. Once the rumors started, I noticed that Guy 11 – who was working in the Office of Policies and Procedures of the OIG – began an obvious effort of visiting my office under the guise of determining the extent to which the morale of the people of RIG/A/LA was improving. Since we no longer had a moral problem and neither Dean nor I had anything to hide, we gave him permission. Looking back and given his narcissistic background, we should have figured that; (a) he knew of the GAO people that would come in; (b) he knew the role each would play; (c) he was "casing" his new assignment to my position; and (d) he would probably be counted, from now on, to always take sides with the incoming GAO personnel.

Issues with Guy 4. After the new personnel had been brought into USAID, the first of these people to be introduced to me – as the new Regional Inspector General for Audits in Washington -- was Guy 4. Not even a month had gone by since his arrival when Guy 4 called a meeting of all the auditors in the Inspector General's Washington and Latin America offices to give us a lecture that he called "His Vision" of the way the Inspector General's Office was going to operate from then on. He seemed to "…be talking down to us…" as if he was the Deputy I.G. or, in any event, our supervisor and we all the experienced FSO as if worked under him. Let me clarify something that was never clear: Guy 4 was the RIG/A/Washington – this position had an equal organizational standing as those of the entire RIG/A's; that is, the RIG/A/LA, RIG/A/Senegal, RIG/A/Philippines, etc. He was never introduced as being in a superior position over the RIG/A/LA. And, to my knowledge, he never was.

After the meeting, Guy 4 and Guy 11 asked me to remain behind (Dean was not in town or in a course at the time, so I was the Acting RIG/A/LA. Right away, Guy 4 told me that he (and his staff) would be making a study of my office (the RIG/A/LA) to see why we were charging so much "indirect time" and why we were indexing our work papers using the system, I had prescribed (see Chapter 16). Guy 4 flatly told me that he preferred using an old-fashioned system he had used at GAO, which involved the use of numbers and letters in no systematic order.

Maybe he thought I would be very timid and submissive. He was wrong. He and I had a nice verbal discussion, and I told him not to waste his time on minor situations like he was mentioning. The Inspector General's Office had bigger problems which I cited. I promised to give him a memorandum detailing the audits and surveys that we currently had done or were underway as well as the actual hours spent on each. This analysis would eliminate some of the time that he would be wasting.

My Memorandum to Guy 4. With the help of Carlos and another person, I wrote a six-page memorandum to Guy 4 with a copy to IG#1. The memorandum provided (a) an itemized listing of all the audits that we had completed (see information in Chapter 16), studies we were in the process of doing, and the amount of time in hours spent directly on each; (b) provided an explanation of the indirect costs; (c) described the work paper indexing and filing system that I had instituted. In the memo, I also provided evidence showing how adopting our indexing system had saved the Agency a tremendous amount of direct and indirect time.

With respect to the **indirect charges, they were principally because one person – Don C. – had been mugged in Washington, D.C., and was partially paralyzed for the rest of his life. Don C. had been working in my RIG/LA when the mugging took place, and since he could never be assigned to overseas jobs, he now charged 100% of his time as indirect costs.** Most of the other Indirect charges were due to long-term FSOs who took Home Leave, annual, and sick leave and charged their time as indirect. All were legal and proper.

I ended the memo by emphasizing that while he and I had different work paper indexing systems, we should choose the system that represented the best for the Agency. I pointed out that my system was easier to teach and implement and saved enormous amounts of time. However, I never received a response to this memo, and no one ever explained their reasons for trying to return to an antiquated, confusing, and wasteful system.

Note: Curiously enough, after I was terminated as the Deputy Regional Inspector General, some auditors continued to use the work paper system that Carlos and I had designed.

<u>Issue Number 1 with Guy 6: Signing a Contract Requiring the Production of a Certain Number of Products</u>. Within a month of his arrival, Guy 6 tried to issue a policy requiring all auditors to sign a "contract" stating that he/she would produce a certain number of audits, findings, and recommendations. The proposed policy also authorized the Inspector General to use this information as a means of evaluating the employee's performance at the end of the year. When I saw the draft of the above policy, I told Dean that it was a bad policy and that I would not be signing it. He agreed with me in all respects.

Dean also told me that he would be resigning from USAID soon and that he would not sign what he called that "piece of crap." He also instructed me to take a supervisory trip to start or review the work that was taking place in El Salvador, Costa Rica, Peru, and especially

Ecuador. Ecuador had asked for a priority audit of a large Agricultural Project, but we did not have anyone to do the audit.

Based on our discussion, I assembled the staff, and we discussed the proposed policy at length. Every single member of my staff thought it was crazy and a horrendous policy. One member called it a "…knife with six cutting edges…" no matter how you held it, you would cut yourself. If one audit were highly complicated and the person failed to meet some or all the expectations, he/she could be pushed out from USAID. In sum, my memorandum mentioned how dangerous this policy was and that none of us were willing to sign such a contract.

Note: As a result, the policy was never issued. After I retired from USAID, IG#1 modified the policy so that it would apply only to Audit Managers, but again, it was controversial, and IG#1 withdrew it. As mentioned previously, IG#1 also tried to install a similar policy to Mission Personnel, requiring a "representation letter" and a Polygraph Test. Once again, this proposal was just too ridiculous. The IG#1 told the Glenn Congressional Committee that he had canceled the proposed policy.

Issue Number 2 with Guy 6: Proposed Change in Audit Approach. A very short time later, Guy 6 – probably at the instruction of the I.G. (who was trying to do only systemic type of reviews that I questioned earlier) -- tried to issue another policy. He proposed to change the entire audit philosophy. According to the proposal, audits would no longer emphasize evaluative types of reviews designed to evaluate the extent to which the program or project had accomplished its goals as well as the extent to which the program or project was being implemented in an economical, efficient, and cost-effective manner. The emphasis would now be on determining the latest financial condition of the program or project. Under his proposal, we would stop evaluating whether the program or project was meeting or had met its planned goals. **(As I wrote this portion of the book, it dawned on me that the IG#1 probably had in mind using Non-Federal Auditors to do the financial part of IG Audits; this revised concept was – at that time somewhat futuristic – and was not stated in the policy statement of Guy 6 or by anyone else. Therefore, we were all concerned on the change in Audit Philosophy expressed in the proposed new policy.)**

My Memorandum on Issue Number 2 to Guy 6. My memorandum to him and to IG#1 was very explicit. I pointedly told him in the memorandum that his proposal was unrealistic. In the memo, I explained that in my time with USAID, I had seen all kinds of projects and programs. I told him that a failure to evaluate what was being achieved compared to what was being expended and what was in the plans would not provide us with a realistic picture of what the program or project would be achieved in co-joined programmatically and financially. I provided the example of a hypothetical program or project plan developed under a given first Host Government only to be revised by a Dictator or Freely Elected Second Host Government. The original plan might have called for the construction of an airplane which could fly and be built at a cost of $ 2.0 million to USAID. When the succeeding Host Government came in, the new members thought the airplane was just too sophisticated, so they started eliminating bits and pieces -- first, the communications equipment was eliminated, then the flying instrumentation, then the landing gear and wheels; then the motors; finally, the wings. In the end, the succeeding Host Government had spent the $ 2.0 million; this is what the USAID Auditor would find under Guy 6's approach. However, he would not find that the airplane project had not met the project goal and that it could not fly. Under his approach, he would never be able to determine what had happened and why ***(I provided a good description of how "the effect to programs affects the financial and vice versa (Chapter 19)"***

Note: To my knowledge, this policy also died and was never issued. Nevertheless, IG#1 continued to espouse this theory and fill the RIG/A positions with GAO types who seemed united in this erroneous idea. Also, I don't think Guy 6 liked my logic or the analogy that I had used. Why? How can I be so sure? Well, he was instrumental in canceling my transfer to the Philippines, where he was to be the Regional Inspector General for Audits in the Philippines. I have you laughing, huh? Was it his way to get even with my disagreements? You bet you! In any event, Guy 6 served as the RIG/A/Philippines for 3 or so years and retired – you guessed it, as an FSO.

My Issue with Guy 5 took place after my return from my tour of duty in Kenya. Here is what happened. The problem he created seemed very whimsical and, in my view, represented an abuse of power. Auditors who found deleterious items (even large contractors' fraud) were withdrawn from the assignment (I was one of those). The justification for his action, as stated in the Monthly Activity Letter, which was sent to the IG, was that I was withdrawn from the assignment "…because he spent over 3,300 hours on this job and needs more training…"). Wow, how low and unrealistic, can a supervisor get! I had spent less than 150 hours on the job. This contractor was billing Overhead or Indirect Costs – both as a factor within the IQC and as a separate Indirect Cost Factor. In other words, Indirect Costs were billed twice. This was a true fraudulent claim against USAID. I had found the fraudulent condition, discussed it with Guy 5, and I was trying to determine how extensive the billings were. Guy 5 did not understand what I was doing.

- And, by withdrawing me from the assignment, the Contractor was allowed to continue submitting fraudulent billings to USAID. This is another excellent example of the type of IG vacancy of responsibility that I discussed earlier. If financial audits are to be done by CPA Firms, then the CPA firms must be sure of reporting events like the ones I found with various contractors.

My Issue with Guy 7 was discussed in Chapter 17, Part E, Audit of CIP in Sudan and Agricultural Project in Yemen. Another way that the former GAO people operated, as RIG/A's or in their positions of power, was to cancel or not issue good reports which might show a need for changes in policies or legislation, as in the case of the CIP Audit in Sudan or just too complicated as in the case of the Agricultural Project in Yemen. These are true examples of what took place back then; what a waste!

In sum and, in my opinion, neither the IG#1 nor none of the 4 GAO that the I.G. hired and placed in high RIG/A/ Offices brought with them, in the above policies, terrifically great ideas, which I could say that these would be "in pursuit for improvements" that would be greater than mine.

PART E. A MOST DISRESPECTFUL WAY IG#1 AND NEW GROUP NOTIFIED ME THAT I WAS FIRED AS DRIG/A/LA

After I turned in my critical memorandum to Guy 6, I began my trip to El Salvador, Costa Rica, Ecuador, and Peru, knowing of Dean's plans to resign from USAID. I found that everything was going according to plan in El Salvador and Costa Rica, and my teams were doing a great job. However, when I got to Ecuador, both the Mission Controller and the Mission Director asked me to see if I could do a short study on the "Integrated Rural Development Program for Agriculture of Ecuador (Project 518-0012)"[109] After talking to the USAID program managers, reviewing the documentation, and assessing the amount of time needed to do the work. I talked with Dean, and, with his permission, I undertook took the audit. I reviewed the agreements and all documents in the files. I reviewed the financial situation. I had discussions with USAID and GOE personnel. I visited the project locations. I saw the work that was being done, talked with people and technicians, took pictures, and evaluated the projects. Since I was on the road a great amount of time and there were no restaurants in sight, I ate my share of cuy (Guinea Pigs). I indexed the work papers and drafted the report as I went along. And I completed the audit work, including visits to the project sites, within 2 to 2 ½ week (my Spanish fluency was a terrific asset). Once I had completed the Draft Audit Report, I – in my DRIG/A/LA capacity - gave the Mission a copy (as a Report of Audit Finding) and proceeded to Peru.

As discussed in the Conclusion Remarks of Chapter 16, three days after getting to Lima, Peru, the USAID Controller (Mr. Arnold) called me into his office. He showed me a "cable" from the "new Regional Inspector General for Audits in Latin America (Guy 10) addressed to the USAID Missions in Ecuador and Peru – **no copy to me.** The wording of the cable was awkward and not well constructed. It "informed" the two Missions that neither Dean nor I were in charge of the office anymore **and to tell me that** I was no longer the DRIG/A. It instructed the Mission that I was not authorized to give the Mission in Ecuador the draft or the finished copy of the review that I had made of the "Integrated Rural Development Program for Agriculture of Ecuador (Project 518-0012)"[110] It also explained that Guy 10 (who had worked for me in Egypt and he and I were good friends) was the new Regional Inspector General for Audits and that his deputy (you guessed it) was now Guy 11. Moreover, the cable told the Missions to tell me that I was

---

[109] This information came from a draft audit report that I wrote in December 7, 1983, entitled "Draft Audit Report for the Integrated Rural Development Program for Agriculture (Project 518-0012, Loan No. 518-T-038).

"ordered" to return to Washington D. C. immediately. The Controller (a good friend of mine) and I had good laugh at how immature IG#1 and his new people really were. Mr. Arnold asked me: "…if the I.G. was going to "fire" you as Deputy Regional Inspector General, why didn't he just call you and tell you himself? …or asked that you return immediately because he had something urgent to discuss with you…." Moreover, I was not even marked for on the cable. I agreed that it was very unprofessional on someone's part. However, following the "orders," I returned to Washington the following day.

As a result of not going along with IG#1 and the New FSO's erroneous policies, **I was punished.** As soon as I got to the office, I found that Dean had apparently either submitted a resignation letter or had been surreptitiously fired. In any event, he was already gone to Colorado or another state. I also found that what had been our offices were now occupied by Guy 10 and Guy 11. I found my new desk near a corner.

Right away, some of my friends told me that there were rumors that there would be very serious retaliatory actions against me. They told me that Guy 10 and Guy 11 were considering charges of "insubordination." They also told me that my transfer to the Philippines was being canceled, and other actions would probably be taken. So, this timely information gave me a little time and valuable information for a meeting that was later called.

Sure enough, two or three days after my arrival, I was summoned to a meeting with about seven or eight persons, including Guy 14 (the IG Executive Officer who was presiding over the meeting) and Guys 4, 5, 6, 10, and 11. When I got to the meeting, all participants were there. Right away, Guy 14 told me, in firm words, that there were "indications" that I would be charged for "Insubordination" and that my transfer to the Philippines was now cancelled. He also said that I would be receiving a bad personnel evaluation for the year and others.

I immediately told the group that if I was to be charged for such a serious administrative crime as "insubordination," I did not want to say anything without my lawyer present. The room was incredibly quiet for a few minutes. In response to what I said, Guy 14 said that they were just discussing it but that nothing concrete had been firmly developed. He then said that the problem was that "…I had been told, by the new Regional Inspector General for Latin America not to share any information with the USAID Mission to Ecuador about the Integrated Rural Development Report, and that I had done so anyway.

I told them that their timeline and facts were wrong, and the charge of "insubordination" was entirely not supportable. I provided a sequence of events, noting that I was still the DRIG/LA when I had completed the job and was in Peru when I had been told of the cable. Moreover, the cable notified the Missions to inform me that I was no longer the Deputy Regional Inspector General. I told the group that this was not a good managerial practice and, having been with USAID so many years, I deserved a better way of informing people, like me, that they were being demoted from high positions. This was a fact. Up to that point, no one had sent me a cable or notified me in an official manner that I was no longer the Deputy Regional Inspector General or of any other orders. The room was once again deadly quiet.

Guy 11 broke the silence and said that he did not believe that I could finish a complex job, index papers, visit the project sites, take pictures, draft the report, and reference it – all in two weeks. As may be recalled, I had done all those things already and given the draft reports, in the form of a RAF, to the Mission during a time when I was still the DRIG/A/LA. Thus, I had the full authority to give the draft report to the Mission. I told the group that there should be no question over my authority to do so. Moreover, IG#1 and the new RIG/A/LA had the completed Audit Report. It was all my work. My being bi-lingual was always a tremendous asset. And I had spent many long hours doing all the work. It is at this point that they stopped talking about charging me for "insubordination" --- although I do not know if they ever put anything in my personal file on the subject without me seeing it.

During the rest of the meeting, I learned that none of the new FSOs wanted to work together with me. Accordingly, my proposed transfer to the Philippines would be canceled, and a new Post would be determined. The officials also said that my personnel evaluation for the year would not be too good and, if I wanted to, I could dispute it through the regular channels.

In sum, the attempted charge of "insubordination" was apparently dropped. However, certain actions did take place and affected the remaining part of my USAID career. These included: (a) demotion from my Deputy

Regional Inspector General position; (b) my assignment to a Junior Auditor position; (c) cancellation of my transfer to the Philippines; and (d) the preparation of a bad personnel evaluation prepared by you guessed it Guy 11 and "reviewed" by "my so-called friend" Guy 10. I challenged the PER, noting that I had been instrumental in straightening a morale problem that existed in Panama and issuing over 30 reports in 18 months. I also asked to be transferred back to Egypt, or to the USAID's Controller's Office, or at a minimum, to remain in the Washington Office. However, this request in the form of a memo was never answered, and instead, I was transferred to Kenya. I was eventually named, by Merve Boyer, as the the new and first Audit Manager for Non-Financial Audits for Kenya. And to this day, I still do not know if my files still contain that crappy PER or if it was deleted at the end of the second year as prescribed by regulations.

PART F. IN KENYA, RIG/A, (GUY 7) AND I STRONGLY DISAGREE ON SUDAN CIP AUDIT; HE CONSULTS WITH GUY 8 AND INSTIGATES SECRET OIG INVESTIGATION

Chapter 17, Part E, describes in detail and 4 examples, why I believe that Guy 7 was the wrong person to occupy the position of RIG/A/Kenya. Of the 4 examples included in the previous chapter, two of which relate to the investigations done by IG#1, through his I.G. Office of Inspections. Since Chapter 17 includes all details, the following two describe a brief account of what I said in the first and third examples.

An Example: The Sudan CIP Report. I had made an audit of the financial aspects of USAID's Commodity Import and Cash Grant Programs in Sudan. For this program, USAID had obligated over $700 million. Of this amount, over $304 million had already been disbursed. My draft report included several negative findings, including five findings that were very significant. For instance: (a) Section 609 of the Foreign Assistance Act of 1961 did not specify how Sudan's counterpart funds should be accumulated or expended; (b) the Sudanese government had not collected or accounted for a minimum of $274 million in equivalent local currency; and, (c) without consulting the

USAID, the Sudanese government had used the equivalent of about U.S. $ 39.4 million in local currency as regular budgetary support. In addition, I had also found that the USAID Inspector General had been negligent in certain ways. For instance, he had not set up the required procedures – as prescribed by the Inspector General Act of 1978 – to review existing and proposed legislation and report to Congress concerning the impact of such legislation on USAID's administration of the program and defective parts of any legislative laws. Moreover, he had not yet established a dissent channel as prescribed by the Foreign Assistance Act of 1961

Guy 7 had not liked and -- would not issue -- my draft report as I had prepared it. As a result, he had me repeatedly re-draft the report five different times. I would try to improve the way things were phrased, but not eliminate, the above key facts. By that time, we had added 450 hours more to the audit process, and he wanted me to re-draft the report a sixth time. So, Guy 7 and I had a "talk," and I told him that it was his prerogative to change the report in any way he wanted. However, if he eliminated facts and data and if my work papers could not support the changes to my report, that I would write a "Memorandum of Non-Concurrence." With some cuss words, he took my draft report and work papers. He and his crony re-drafted the report, changed facts, eliminated figures, and eliminated my recommendations. My work papers could not support the contents of the changed report that was eventually sent to the Mission. So, I wrote my Memorandum of Non-Concurrence.

The memorandum was addressed to Guy 7, the Regional Inspector General in Kenya. I sent copies of the Memorandum to Senator Richard Lugar, then the Chairman of the Senate Foreign Affairs Committee, and to Inspector General as well as to the Deputy Inspector General (James D.). I never heard from any of them. However, Guy 7 did not take my memorandum lying down. So, this is how the OIG/Investigation began.

The Third and Fantastic, Example -- The Special Education Grant: Soon after writing my Memorandum of Non-Concurrence, Guy 7 -- was either asked by RFMC to send – but in any event, did – send someone to the Regional Finance Management Center (RFMC) to talk about the SHCEA or Special Education Grant for my daughter. Right after that, Guy 7 and Guy 8 met and apparently talked together. I suspect that this was part of another reprisal against me. The RFMC officer (Guy 8) had a real serious grudge against me because I had previously challenged some erroneous "assumptions and disallowances" that he and/or his staff had made on one of my travel vouchers.

Right afterward, Guy 7 and Guy 8 talked, Guy 7 went to the USAID Office of Inspector General for Investigations in Kenya (Guy 12) and told them that the RFMC Deputy Controller had made very serious accUSAtions against me alleging "…fraudulent submissions of claims against the U.S Government…." As a result of these meetings, the Office of Inspector General for Investigations launched a secret investigation of me. This investigation took place over a period of 3 years, and my name and the case was reviewed by over 29 USAID Officials – some of them were repeatedly contacted with an obvious intent to coerce or to prove a serious case against me --- yet, I was never told that I was being investigated. We now continue with the role and rancorous participation of Guy 8.

Part G. In Kenya, Guy 8 (Or Staff) Made Mistakes On My Travel Vouchers, I Challenged Errors; His Rancorous Attitude Helps Guy 7 To Instigate OIG/Investigations Claiming I Was Making False USAID Claims

Guy 8 did not work for the I.G. He had been in Kenya four years and was the Deputy Director of the Regional Finance Management Center. He always had a chip on his shoulder and was nearly always "bad-mouthing" other people. He was also apparently angling for a Controller's position, which was a prestigious assignment.

The issues with him really began when my daughter, who was still assigned, according to the Travel Authorization, in Kenya, returned there during the summer months after the special school had ended the year. Melissa stayed there for a month or so. This coincided with the start of my Home Leave/and Return to Post Authorization.

Based on the Travel Authorization, Pauline, Melissa, and I were authorized and given airline tickets to travel from Kenya to Washington. After that, the tickets were amended to allow us to travel from Kenya to Washington and from there to Austin, Texas (my Home Leave of record). Since Pauline was already in the Washington area and later she, Jerry, and I travelled to Austin by car, Pauline did not use the tickets to travel from Kenya to Washington to Austin. Therefore, only Melissa and I traveled together from Kenya to Washington. We decided to go from Kenya to Austria. From there, we then traveled by railroad through various parts of Europe and left, on Home Leave, from France.

Once I had returned from my home and annual leave, I submitted my Travel Voucher along with an explanation of how I had substituted travel – as authorized by the travel regulations. I attached all the unused air tickets for Europe and while in Texas.

Guy 8 (or his staff) disallowed much of the cost of my travel, making many mistakes in their assumptions of how I should have traveled. They disallowed costs equaling to about $1,270, and based on their assumptions, I was not paid for my travels between different points. And they returned the tickets, related to Pauline, and requested me to get the refund – for about $4,000 of unused tickets – from the airlines.

I saw their mistakes and submitted to Guy 8 a memorandum itemizing the problems I had found. Among other things, Guy 8 was disallowing the cost of air tickets for Pauline on the basis that I needed to obtain a refund for the ($4,000) unused tickets since she had been in the United States to take care of Jerry. However, he failed to understand that the air tickets had been bought with funds that had been paid by the U.S. Government – not by me. Thus, it was up to RFMC -- not to me -- to cancel the tickets and collect the funds from the airlines. I had simply not used the tickets, and the funds belonged to the U.S. Government.

I do not know what Guy 8 was thinking because he was very annoyed with me for not accepting the disallowances. Later, Guy 8 and Guy 15 -- the Lady Executive Officer who took the place of John Martin, the former Executive Officer -- reversed all previous approvals for the SMA and the SHCEA. They questioned the legality – disallowed all costs -- of both the

SHCEA and the Separate Maintenance Allowance. As mentioned in Part F (above), Guy 8 apparently called Guy 7 (or vice versa) and, jointly, got the Inspector General's Office of Investigations to investigate me based on me having made "Fraudulent Claims against the U.S. Government" for the SHCEA Grants and SMA. The accusation was false from the start.

Guy 8 subsequently took the position that I had to refund the $45,000 corresponding for both SHCEA and SMA within 90 days. He also warned me that the RFMC would be garnishing all my monthly salaries until I fully paid the full amount.

I knew their position was wrong. As discussed in Part H of this chapter, the Special Education Grant for Handicapped Students (SHCEA) is guided by separate rules than the regular education grants, which were governed in a separate manner by the standardized regulations.

In sum, I wrote a very extensive memorandum detailing my position. I included over 44 documents detailing all conferences that I had with his predecessor and others within the Regional Financial Management Center, the Department of State's Medical Division, and others. I requested that the entire situation be reviewed and cleared up by the "Department of State Allowance Committee."

PART H. BACKGROUND ON THE SPECIAL HANDICAPPED CHILD EDUCATION ALLOWANCE (SHCEA)

Chapter 17, Part C, Life in Kenya, describes in detail the exceptional circumstances related to my daughter. For this reason, this (Part H) will just be a brief reminder on the background related to SHCEA type of Special Education Grants.

As stated in the previous chapter, my daughter was diagnosed with a Learning Disability in Kindergarten. My transfer to Nairobi, Kenya, was part of the OIG Punishment and was irrevocable. For this reason, and since I did not know whether the International School of Kenya (ISK) could accommodate her disability, I wrote a letter to a former USAID Executive

Officer (John M. – a fine person). I asked if ISK could accommodate her disabilities. The answer was positive. Shortly after our arrival in Kenya, ISK administered psychological tests and told us that they could teach my daughter only one year. However, she needed a Special Vocational School in the U.S. So, I notified the USAID Executive Officer of the huge problem, and all of us began to look for alternatives. This is where I begin my quotation related to my efforts and the granting of the SHCEA in place of a regular Special Education Grant (awarded for normal situations).

Begin Quote: On March 18, 1985, I wrote a letter to the Department of State Medical Division and requested assistance in looking for a Special Education School for Melissa. On August 7, 1985, the M/MED/MHS (Dr. T.H.V) wrote a memo to the Administrative Officer of the Embassy in Nairobi saying that Melissa "…meets the criteria to receive the **Special Handicapped Child Education Allowance (SHCEA)** and will be attending a school which meets her needs…." **(Note: my understanding – and everyone (in the Mission who approved the SHCEA) – was that this SHCEA has quite a different rules than the regular Special Education Allowance as authorized in the Standard Travel Regulations. Yet, one person (Guy 8) from the RFMC and others seemed intent on "considering my daughter's situation as a normal child" and erroneously applying the standard basis as prescribed by the Standard Travel Regulations; without a doubt, this was a wrong way of dealing with a child with special needs.)**

Continue Quote: In any event, the Washington Medical Division or someone in Washington searched and located the Brush Ranch School in New Mexico. On May 17, 1985, I applied for the SHCEA, or what everyone seemed to call the Special Education Grant, and it was approved by everyone. This approval was given by the Department of State Medical Division, the USAID Executive Officer, the Regional Finance Management Center (RFMC), hereafter also referred to as the Controller, and others.

Continue Quote: I was told that there were no funds to finance the air tickets for Pauline and Melissa, so without knowing when Pauline and Melissa would be returning to Kenya, I bought the two one-way tickets with my own funds. **Both Pauline and Melissa departed Kenya on June 14, 1985. Pauline and Melissa visited the school in July 1985, and Melissa was accepted.** For this purpose, there were two SHCEA or what everyone was calling Special Education Grants, awarded for her, and we had to sign two very strict contracts with the Brush Ranch School. (IF NEEDED, PLEASE SEE CHAPTER 17 FOR THE WORDING OF THE TWO STRICT CONTRACTS).

Continued Quote: (Note: The irony of the (SHCEA) was that the two Contracts between the Brush Ranch School and us (wife and I), and later a request for SMA is that although they were approved by everyone (as early as June 1985), both the SHCEA's and SMA's were later (on January 27, 1987) questioned by separate people from the same USAID Offices that had previously approved them. In other words, these were now questioned under a regular SEG. According to the reversed USAID position, both SEG and SMA would be completely disallowed. Moreover, without ever telling me, I was also thoroughly and secretively investigated by the USAID Inspector General's Office of Investigations. I discuss this in more detail in Part D of Chapter 17 and in this Chapter 18). End of Quote.

There are several conclusions to be drawn from Part H: (a) SHCEA was proposed and approved by the Medical Division of the Department of State; (b) the SHCEA type of education grant is treated differently than the common Special Education Grant (awarded to "Normal" children) which is guided by the Standard Regulations; (c) everyone was consulted and everyone approved -- regarding the special needs of my daughter and what became the SHCEA; (d) Guys 7, 8, and 15 were completely out of line – and plain wrong – in their reversal of everyone's approval. Thus, it follows that the launching of the Secretive Case, against me, by the Office of I.G. Inspections should never have been done.

PART I. OFFICE OF I.G. CONDUCTED A VERY SLOPPY SECRET INVESTIGATION

While my appeal for a review and a decision – by the State Allowance Committee -- was underway, the Office of the Inspector General, unbeknownst to me, was conducting a secret investigation of me. In a memo to Washington, Guy 12 or s**omeone in the IG told the IG in Washington that because of a conflict of interest -- the Inspector Generals should not**

investigate its own personnel. Despite this warning, the USAID IG conducted the investigation anyway. And it was not until close to my retirement that the IG finally sent a copy of all its investigation and a request for a final determination from the Office of the Inspector General of the Department of State; however, the State Inspector General seems to have reviewed the USAID IG documentation and was convinced that prosecution, in my case, was no where warranted.

It was from the State's Inspector General's Office that I learned that I was under investigations by the USAID's Office of Inspector General. In fact, the Department of State officer in charge of my case saw the injustice that was being committed against me and told me to hire a lawyer. He also told me that he did not want to talk to me without my lawyer present. I did just that, but never heard from him again (whoever you were: thanks for the excellent advice and help you gave me.). I subsequently hired a lawyer, incurring fees of around $3,000. Although I was innocent, I never got reimbursed for my legal expenses.

During my research for this book, I read most case documents given to me by my lawyer – and especially the "Reports of Interview" written during the three or four-year period of the USAID OIG/IG investigation. I was amazed at the number of variations in opinions expressed by over twenty-nine people that were shown – as I choose to describe it -- the "…Jose M. Pena Case…."

In fact, the Investigators either did not know or chose not to disclose some facts related to my case. For instance, most of the respondents did not seem to know that the investigators totally disregarded the recommendations of the State's "Allowance Committee." Based on the Allowance Committee decision and the opinion of the USAID Office of the General Counsel, the Director of Administrative Services had already decided to Grant a Waiver to me on all billings for the $45,000. In other words, I no longer should be billed for the amount stipulated by Guy 8. I do not know whether the Investigators either did not know of the waiver or chose not to disclose this fact to the respondents. Nonetheless, one thing that comes through is that the investigators were told about the difference between the SHCEA and SEG and should have disclosed this fact to the respondents.

Moreover, the Inspector General should have stopped the investigation once the collection waiver for the $45,000 had been granted. In his effort to punish me, as much as possible, the I.G. and his OIG/I continued to show the "Jose M. Pena case" to as many people (over 29) as possible -- thereby damaging my reputation of being a top professional person with extremely high, honesty, integrity, objectivity, and independence. This was the reputation that I had built throughout my career with USAID.

As stated above, I was really amazed that the twenty-nine theoretically well-informed officials who were shown the case were all over the place with their opinions, conclusions, and/or recommendations, for instance:

- Guy 8 was interviewed two times. Although he was a Financial Officer, he never mentioned the difference between SHCEA and the SEG or the "Administrator's Waiver." In both instances, he showed his animosity towards me and nearly called me a "crook," and was adamant in his allegations that I was submitting fraudulent claims to the U.S. Government.

- Guy 15 said she had been in Kenya for a brief period of time and had just "gleaned" at my case. However, her recommendation was that I should reimburse the U.S. Government the $45,000 anyway. How can a person just "glean" at an important case and quickly come to an adverse type of conclusion? Her conclusion is incomprehensible, unsupportable, and without any basis.

- Others were more guarded and took different positions: (a) one said that the original EXO (John M.) was completely wrong but that I should not be billed for the error; (b) others said John's position was correct and I should not have to pay; (c) One said that Guy 8 and Lady 15 were wrong; (e) some focused on insignificant issues – on my children's special airline rates; (f) some said I should refund the complete $45,000; (g) others said that I should be given a verbal or "Written Reprimand;" (h) others said that I should be given only a "Verbal Reprimand;" and, (i) others said they should close the case; (j) others had no opinion.

- Tom P. (an exceptional former Controller in Kenya and former supervisor of Guy 8) wrote a long cable, dated December 28, 1989, and explained that Jose M. Pena "…was honest and above board on his information… did not attempt to conceal material facts in requests of allowances or other benefits… (This cable by Tom P. was sent TWO DAYS BEFORE MY RETIREMENT). Here is my comment: "Tom: Thanks for the excellent cable."

- One official got close to a communications problem. He said that the problem had been created by some approvals being given in Kenya, and other approvals had been given in Washington. Here is my comment: This is a good possibility. The Medical Division of the Department of State recommended and approved the SHCEA and sent a memo to the Administrative Officer of the U.S. Embassy in Kenya; I do not know if this information was coordinated with Guy 7 RIG/A/Kenya and 8 in RFMC.
- Another Official also came close to another problem. He said that the Standardized Travel Regulations were changed frequently, and they frequently provided mixed interpretations. Here is my comment: The standardized regulations are changed frequently and written in legal terminology, which can create a great deal of confusion. I don't know if all the respondents had read the regulations before they were shown my case.
- Only one – Jan Miller, the GC/EPA lawyer got it correct. His explanation to two OIG Inspectors is stated later. Even after this exact explanation, the investigation continued. Here is my comment: Thanks Jan Miller for your exceptional research and explanations.

At this point, let me say this: with all the contradictions, confusion, and correct explanations, by Jan Miller, in place, I wonder how the USAID OIG/I Office thought they could build a solid case against me. Moreover, I wonder what basis would have been used by the I.G. to have ordered an investigation in the first place and a "Verbal Reprimand" against me in the end. We'll never know. The IG#1 never even discussed nor gave me the proposed Verbal Reprimand.

As I explain in my Concluding Remarks for this chapter, the whole investigation (and all reviewers of my case) took "…roads that no investigation should ever be directed to follow…." It sure was not an "independent and objective investigation..." The Investigators were told that the financial requirements for "Special Education Grants to Handicap Students" and the regular "Regular Education Grants" were different. Thus, using the provisions of the Regular SEG Standard Travel Regulations was erroneous.

In any event, the investigation was badly flawed from the start and, I believe, was a means of punishing me. It was supposed to be "independent and objective" but was far from that. The investigators were told from early in the investigation that they were using the wrong criteria, and they continued in their investigation anyway. Imagine all the wasted money spent trying to conduct such a flawed investigation!

Moreover, it is also my opinion that the conclusion drawn from this part is that based on the Legal Opinion of the GC/EPA, the OIG/I should never have been called to investigate such a clear case involving a difference between treating a "normal Education Grant' and "a Special Education Grant for Handicap Students." **In other words, GUY 7. 8 and Lady 15 were way off on their questioning prior approvals or to propose the disallowance of the $45,000 and my salaries be garnished. And, of course, they were also wrong in their position that I was submitting "...fraudulent claims against the U.S. Government...." It follows that the OIG/I investigation was flawed – and uncalled for -- from the very start. Their erroneous positions created a great deal of wasted time and funds for the U.S. Government**.

PART J. CASE WAS CLOSED AFTER I HAD RETIRED

The case was closed after I had retired and after the USAID Administrator, the Director of the Inspector General's Office of Investigations, and the Department of State Inspector General wrote memorandums to IG#1. The first two Officials told him that the maximum penalty he could give me was a "verbal reprimand."

- But....I wonder what would have been the basis for a "Verbal Reprimand." Just review the entire facts of the case – (a) my professional history and the work that I had done with the USAID for

28 years and the assignment to many countries; (b) the vicious and demeaning manner in which I was fired after molding an exceptional team, as DRIG/A in both Egypt and Latin America, and an exemplary way I was performing my job over a period of six years; (c) the vicious way I was mistreated for five years; (d) the false accusations of insubordination; ('e) the false and crummy PER filed against me; (f) the vicious persecution against me; (g) the false accusation of submitting false billing against the U.S. Government false claims; (g) the defective manner that the secret investigation was conducted; (h) the discussion of my case with 29 people; (i) and, my favorable prospects of pursuing a legal suit involving discrimination and defamation of character – yes, I wonder how my conversation with the I.G. and/or his group of followers might have gone – in front of my lawyer and an objective court Judge. In sum, there was never even a semblance to support a basis for any type of reprimand – much less a "Verbal Reprimand."

In any event, the USAID Administrator waived reimbursement of the $45,000 and said that I had erroneously been provided with $17,592,[111] but that the error was not the result of any inappropriate behavior on my part and that I had been above board in my request. The Administrator also recommended that the agency waive the recovery of these funds considering my record and the problems we were having with Jerry. From my standpoint, it was always our intent for Pauline to return to Kenya, and we applied for the separate education grant before that became clear. At the time that Pauline went to the United States, Jerry was going through an difficult time and had been in and out of several mental hospitals. There was no way Pauline could have come home at that time. In any event, I never received either a verbal or written reprimand. And, with only two exceptions, I never talked to the I.G., the GAO/New FSOs, or his investigative people after my retirement. One of the instances occurred after I had retired and was working under contract for the Organization of American States (OAS). I ran into Guy 5 at a training course sponsored by USAID. He told me that he had been placed in a corner

[111] This amount is also questionable. Everyone seemed to erroneously call either June 1985 or June 1986 as the "date when my wife re-established residency in the United States." The $17,592 is based on that premise and is wrong. The best date when she re-established residency is October 22, 1986. See my discussion later related to this point.

office and that his "talents" (whatever they were) were no longer being used. Imagine that! As the saying goes, what goes around comes around.

PART K. TWO POINTS DESERVE A NEED FOR CLARIFICATION

This part clarifies two issues that deserve final discussion: The first one relates to the date when my wife re-established residence in the U.S. The second one provides my final thoughts on the investigation initiated by Guys 7, 8, 15 and, the manner that the investigation was conducted by the Office of the I.G.

Without a Doubt, the Best Date When My Wife Re-established U.S. Residence Was October 22, 1986. The I.G. Investigators, the Legal Counsel, the Assistant Administrator, and others somehow reached the conclusion that Pauline had re-established her U.S. Residence on June 21, 1985, when she and Melissa departed Kenya, and/or June 27, 1986, when I applied for Separate Maintenance Allowance (SMA). These were all wrong calls. Here is a more complete explanation.

Of course, everyone knew that both my wife and daughter had departed – and their trip was financed by me -- on June 21, 1985; if I had given any other date, it would have been false. However, because of the unpredictability nature of my son's illness -- we never really knew how long our separation was going to be. Thus, these conclusions were wrong: (a) Pauline did not re-established residency in the U.S. neither on June 21, 1985 (departure date) nor June 27, 1986 (the retroactive request for SMA). My requests for SMA were purely based on a 20-20 hindsight. In other words, she had departed Kenya one year earlier and the T/A/'s still established her residence in Kenya. As a result, it was my belief that I was entitled to SMA for the past year..

Moreover, June 27, 1986, was not a predictor of Pauline's re-establishing residence or of how long she could be in the U.S. In fact, we were caught in a "Catch 22 situation." Pauline wanted to return to Kenya; I wanted her to come; she could not come because the Department of State would not clear Jerry because of his illness, and Jerry could not remain in the U.S. by himself because he could not survive his illness. Yes, that was a very intricate and difficult period of time to pinpoint the exact date when we can all agree on the famous "date when my wife re-establishes her residency in the U.S."

So, which is the best date to determine when we can all agree that Pauline re-established Residency in the U.S.? There is no doubt in my mind that the **"best date" to be when I returned to Kenya – by myself – or October 22, 1986. Why?** This date is the most accurate for the following reasons:

a) Any date before October 22, 1986, would represent a highly speculative idea, not one based on facts, because Pauline, Melissa, and I thought that they would be returning to Kenya once Jerry was stabilized.

b) The June 1985 and/or June 1986 represented a 20-20 hindsight request because we had been separated, by my job requirements and unusual circumstances, one year by then. It did not represent factual expression for re-establishing a U.S. Residency.

c) During these early periods of my son's illness, his illness had not been really diagnosed; the best medications had not been determined; and he was constantly in and out of the hospital with ideations of harming himself.

d) On the other hand, by October 22, 1986, the Texas Doctor had determined the correct diagnosis and prescribed the correct medication (Clozaril) to Jerry.

e) By October, Jerry was reasonably stable and his moods more predictable.

f) Pauline might have been had more flexibility and not necessarily as fully committed to stay in the U.S. to take Jerry to Mental Hospitals.

g) By the October date, Pauline and I had already signed two extremely strict contracts with the Brush Ranch School, and we could no longer withdraw Melissa from the school until she completed the whole year. Moreover, we could no longer request a refund for costs paid to the school.

h) Melissa had already started attending her final year in Brush Ranch and graduated from high school by the following year.

i) By the October date, Pauline and I had discussed the entire situation and made a reasonably informed decision that she would stay to monitor Jerry's and Melissa's situation very closely.

j) Finally --- I arrived in Kenya **alone** on October 22, 1986, and if someone had asked me at that time if Pauline and Melissa would be returning to Post, I would have given a "negative" response.

In sum, October 22, 1986, is the only date when all available facts met at the most realistic pivotal point. Therefore, I can categorically say that there was never any attempt and/or intent, on my part, to falsely claim any portion of either the SHCEA, also called the Special Education Grant, or of the SMA against the U.S. Government. Quite to the contrary – and as the General Counsel stated – all steps in requesting and/or claiming costs related to both SMA and SEG were relied on the advice of USAID top officials. It follows that the reversal of positions by the USAID Officials of January 27, 1987, was either designed as "C.Y.A." or a really mean action on the part of Guy 7, 8, and 15. But, as shown in this book, they were completely vicious and wrong.

The Final Point is whether Guys 7 and 8 were correct in calling for the Investigation and whether it was objectively conducted. As I said earlier, the whole investigation (and all reviewers of my case) took "…roads that no investigation should be put through…." It sure was not an "independent and/or an objective investigation.".

Jan Miller, the GC/EPA Counselor, explains it very clearly. At some point, the Investigators were told that the financial requirements for "Special Education Grants to Handicap Students" and the "Regular Special Education Grants" were quite different. Thus, using the provisions of the Regular SEG Standard Travel Regulations was erroneous; so, the investigation was flawed from the start.

Here is his rationale. According to a "Report of Interview" dated 10/24/1988, as written by J.A.C, an I.G. Inspector, this is what Jan Miller, GC/EPA, told two OIG Inspectors:

Begin Quote: "The requirements for Special Education Grants for the handicapped are different than those for a regular education allowance. He (Miller) provided a copy of an opinion (Note: This opinion was not made available to me -- Jose M. Pena) in which he discussed the

"parent, or step-parent" in the U.S. rule" the facts are somewhat different in that it is further complicated by a question of legal custody of the child. He wrote that in his opinion, Standardized Regulation 276.7 (the regulation that permitted Pena's Special Education grant) is the controlling regulation, as opposed to PM's (*initials not explained in document*) opinion that Standardized was the controlling regulation. In this case, the opinion was correct and the waiver to allow both the special education allowance and the separate maintenance allowance to be given was correct...." End of Quote

Mr. Miller continued by saying "...Pena's experience as an auditor should not be an issue. Just because certain classes of employees, such as executive officers, financial officers, and auditors, are able to read and understand travel regulations that should not make them suspect and they should not be treated differently...."

In sum, Mr. Miller believed that "....the recommendation for a Section 636(6) waiver was appropriate at the time it was made and did not believe there was any reason to change it...."

- ***Note two facts in the above information: first, this was the second meeting between the Investigators and Mr. Miller and there is an implication and effort by OIG/Investigator to get Mr. Miller to change his mind and render an unfavorable opinion in my case. Mr. Miller stood fast and did not change his opinion. Second, this information was given to the two OIG/Investigators on October 24, 1988, i.e., over one year before I retired. The I.G. Office should have stopped its investigation at that point; it did not -- what a waste of time.).***

In other words, GUYs 7, 8, and 15 were off on their position that the $45,000 be completely disallowed and my salaries garnished and also wrong in their position that I was submitting "...fraudulent claims against the U.S. Government...." It follows that the OIG/I investigation was flawed from the very start and that it should have been immediately stopped. Showing the case and trying to coerce an invalid conclusion – out of over 29 separate people – represented a very vicious and unwarranted effort on the part of the I.G. Office.

PART L. HERE ARE MY CONCLUDING REMARKS ON THIS CHAPTER

Let me make some very important points clear:

a) **First and foremost, allegations and reprisals – such as the way I heard that I was no longer the DRIG/A/LA, the demotion as the DRIG/A/LA, the accusations of insubordination, the preparation, of a bad PERs by a person who had a conflict of interest, switching of transfers, etc., -- represent a very immature, unprofessional, and a poor managerial manner of handling a clear differences in opinions and approaches to conflicting problems.**

b) **Second, there never was a basis for any dispute on either my request over my SHCEA (the Special Education Grants) or the SMA requests. The records show that I followed all the rules and that I was extremely careful in coordinating all my actions with everyone and getting their approval before taking the different actions. It follows that there was never any attempt and/or intent on my part to "...submit fraudulent claims against the U.S. Government...." This turned out to be a very costly allegation that was later pursued without any solid basis.**

c) **I believe that the exact proposal and approval of the SHCEA Type of Special Education Allowance Grant on the part of the Medical Division caught everyone off guard (because these types of grants were not normally granted at Mission levels) and gave rise to a great deal of confusion.**

d) **The rancorous way Guys 7 and 8 in calling my requests and billings as "fraudulent claims against the U.S. Government" were clearly erroneous and created an enormous waste of human efforts and costs. Moreover, the two actions taken by these two people were clearly reprisals that were based on rancorous personal feelings; these types of decisions and actions should not be even considered in making serious allegations similar to the ones in my case.**

e) **Launching of the secretive investigation of the case and showing my case to 29 different officials -- without considering talking to me or showing approvals granted by the Medical Division and all pertinent USAID Officials, Agency waivers, General Counsel's Opinions, and the misinformation related to the regulations – represent, to me, gross negligence, on the part of the Investigators, to actually determine the true facts over an assigned case, or a perverse intent to thwart the facts related to it.**

f) **Thus, it follows that the Office of the IG Investigation had no basis to open the case or should never have shown it to the twenty-nine officials in any event. Moreover, it should have closed it immediately upon reaching a number of points discussed throughout my discussion. In sum, the allegations were unworthy of either persecution and/or the investigation. The case should have been promptly closed.**

In any event, I learned that the case was closed, from my lawyer, about 4 months after my retirement.

Was the case really and promptly closed? Do not bet on it!

- **Even after my lawyer said that the case was closed, the I.G. Office of Investigations did not prepare a "Notice of Action" (NOA) until March 15, 1991, to officially close the case. This was 1 1/2 years after my retirement, and it came after the Department of State Inspector General, the Department of Justice, and the Public Integrity Section had reviewed the case, at the IG#1 request, to determine if there was a case for prosecution because of a criminal or an integrity violation on my part. The Department of State Inspector General finally informed the USAID I.G. that their findings were that the ".... allegations were unworthy of Prosecution."**

- **The Department of State Inspector General was correct. As I have stated all along, the case was flawed from the start. So, this was the end of the vicious reprisals, persecutions, and attacks on me....**

Even after so many years of its closure...once in a while...just once in a now fading while...I still look behind, first over my left shoulder, and

then over my right one…and very cautiously – and with a certain degree of anger -- say…….

"I hope so…The entire situation was such a terrible and uncalled for waste of human effort time and unnecessary costs!"

CHAPTER NINETEEN
MY FINAL CHAPTER WITH THE USAID SALIENT MEMORIES OF THE PAST AND VISIONS FOR THE FUTURE

PART A. INTRODUCTORY COMMENTS AND A BRIEF REMINDER OF MY TECHNICAL EXPERIENCE AND QUALIFICATIONS

Some Background. For those of You Who Did Not Have Time to Read All My Book, here is A Short Reminder of My Technical and Career Background. During my time with USAID, I served in the Office of Controller, in the Offices of two USAID Auditor Generals, and in the Office of the previous Inspector General (also referred to as IG#1, or IG) over a period of 28 years. Under the Office of Controller, I either worked as Chief Auditor (in three countries), Acting Controller, and/or Assistant Unit Chief (in Vietnam). I managed a great number of people; I worked on numerous types of audits; and, as a Foreign Service Officer, I received several promotions and various types of awards. Under the previous IG, I worked as Auditor in Charge, Audit Manager, and I was, for a period of six years, Deputy Regional Inspector General for Audit in Egypt, and Latin America. During my tour in Egypt, I prepared Audit Programs for the Grain Silo Project and the Commodity Import Program. Both audits were some of the most complex that USAID probably ever had. I received many accolades. When the Office of Panama developed serious personnel complications, its operations were transferred to Washington. I was transferred, as Deputy Regional Inspector General for Audit of all Latin America to straighten the personnel mess. Given my management style, I had no problem with the staff, and I was able to mold an exceptional team. We were able to complete 36 reviews, surveys, and audits during the 18 to 20 months I was the DRIG/A/LA.

As noted in Chapters 15, 16, 17, and 18, IG#1 chose – against my recommendations -- to bring in an influx of 8 General Schedule Auditors from GAO and appoint a minimum of 4 of them as RIG/As in various posts. To my knowledge, none of these people had ever served a full tour of duty in Less Developed Countries. One of them (see Chapter 17) was clearly not qualified to be RIG/A; two others were questionable. As such, they tried to introduce and implement policies and practices which were entirely faulty, erroneous, and inappropriate for USAID and to the Office of I.G. (I give examples in Chapter 18). Although the I.G. did not have a "Dissent Channel" which was required by law and as the current Office of I.G. now has), I spoke out against such faulty policies which the IG and his new group of staff were trying to implement. For expressing my dissenting opinion, I was demoted, in a most degrading manner, from the position of DRIG/A/LA, and for the next 5 years -- before the end of my USAID career -- I was viciously persecuted and falsely accused of different types of misdeeds. But I was not the only one receiving such bad treatment. According to the Glenn Committee findings, 70 other USAID employees were being investigated or prosecuted.

These were challenging years for me, other USAID Employees, the agency, and the Office of Inspector General. At the end of the secretive IG investigation, the I.G. of the Department of State told the USAID IG to close the case because "...the allegations were unworthy of prosecution...." So, the USAID IG closed my case. However, it took his office close to 1 ½ year after I had retired. I cannot say that I am glad to have played a role in the events that occurred during these periods. In fact, I am certainly glad this period of my life with the I.G. is all over.

It has now been well over 32 years since I left USAID. Yet, my love for USAID, as an organization, remains most vividly in my mind. This love exists despite the vicious and unfounded investigations, reprisals, and punishments which, the IG#1 and his supportive group of followers -- pursued against me in the last 5 years of my USAID career. How come? Because, my 28-year period of professional life –and the lives of my family – was, for most parts, tremendously educational, challenging, most productive, and beneficial to me, the USAID, and three other organizations I later worked for. I have a lot to be proud of. During my 28 years with the Agency, I advanced, in my profession and personal life, in maturity, expertise, grade, and responsibilities to the point that I not only supervised many audits but also directed several USAID audit offices in a few countries. I can proudly say that I became the first Mexican American to serve in such high positions as the USAID Deputy Regional

Inspector General for Audit (DRIG/A), Acting RIG/A, and as a Manager of the Non-Federal Audit Teams in Kenya. I served as a DRIG/A six years in this capacity in Egypt and in Latin America. I earned and got many awards and recognitions. I am also proud to say that I contributed (as the proverb says) "…my small grain of sand…" in support of President Carter and his staff during their 1979 historic visit to Egypt and Israel.

In USAID alone, I worked with and/or supervised over 200 professional staff, made many friends in several countries, and made numerous studies. These studies covered a great many different types of disciplines; I wrote countless reports amounting to numerous pages; I made over 1,000 recommendations to improve projects, programs, activities, and/or procedures; and I examined programs amounting to well over U.S. $5.0 Billion. During these examinations, I found programs that were being achieved in an exemplary manner, some which were very defective, some fraudulent incidents, and some which cumulatively resulted in significant refunds to the U.S. Government. As Manager of the Non-Federal Auditors, I managed 14 persons team and one team, made up by Retired USAID Auditors, found incidents which resulted over $2.9 million in refunds to USAID.

Even now, in my retirement, and, as I repeatedly say time and again in this book, I firmly believe that USAID is truly exceptional as an organization. Over the years, I met many extremely intelligent, diligent, and firmly committed U.S. and local employees. There is no doubt in my mind that USAID, as an organization, is fulfilling an exceptional function that was badly needed in my time and in today's world.

That the USAID and the Office of Inspector General can improve their operations, there is no doubt. Throughout this book, I have included different types of examples – related to financing types of techniques, projects, programs, activities, procedures, processes, and/or ideas – which were salient to me because they were exceptional, good but needed improvement, afflicted by Murphy's law, and/or ideas deserving of further review by USAID, for potential adaptation. This is the reason that the remainder of this chapter will present a brief recollection (including some repetitions) of the past and some of my analysis of salient examples discussed in the body of the book; this will be done in the following 8 Parts and many sub-parts.

- Part A. Introductory Comments and Brief Reminder on My Professional and Technical Background.
- Part B. Referrals to the Honorable USAID Administrator.
- Part C. Examples of Exceptional Techniques, Projects, and Programs (Hereafter also called "Activities").
- Part D. Examples of Activities Afflicted by Murphy's Laws.
- Part E. Theories and Ideas for Possible Adaptation in USAID Operations.
- Part F. Referrals to the Current USAID Inspector General for Possible Lessons Learned, Audits, Correction, and improvements.
- Part G. Referrals to the Honorable Chair of Council of the Inspectors General on Integrity and Efficiency (CIGIE).
- Part H. My Concluding Remarks.

PART B. REFERRALS TO THE HONORABLE USAID ADMINISTRATOR FOR POSSIBLE DISSEMINATION TO USAID STAFF

B.1 Exceptional Examples.

Background. In my years with USAID, I audited and reviewed many projects, financial techniques, and activities. In all these years, the Activities shown in (a) Part C were found to be exceptional; (b) Part D were obviously afflicted by "Murphy's Laws" and had a nightmare of problems; (c) Part E shows some theories, ideas, and concepts that I think USAID could potentially use. (Note: Way back in Chapter 3, I have included longer discussions on all these. To avoid the need to go back and review the extensive referrals, I will repeat certain background and quick reviews of the findings. However, to the extent possible, I will try to avoid repetition of all that I have already written. If the reader needs further information, the referenced chapter, and the following parts will give a very brief explanation of my opinion):

PART C. EXAMPLES OF EXCEPTIONAL TECHNIQUES, PROJECTS, AND PROGRAMS

C.1 Two Step Loans.

I was the Chief Auditor during my tour in Colombia. We had an exceptional U.S. and Local Audit Team, and my team and/or I audited ,many Projects financed with a technique called a "Two-Step Loan." Here is a nice example of how the two-step loan arrangement works: From 1968 to 1972, Colombia borrowed $55 million from USAID to implement nine different projects through the local organizations listed in the referenced chapter and part. The steps begin once the negotiations between the USAID and Host Country have been completed:

- Thus, under the first step, USAID signed the principal loan agreement with the Government of Colombia (GOC); at this level, the GOC was to repay the USAID loan in U.S. Dollars. The rate of interest ranged between .75 to 2.0%. The bilateral loan had a 10-year grace period. The Government was to repay the complete loan over a period of 30-40 Years.
- Under the second step, the GOC lent the funds to nine Semi-Autonomous Organizations under different local or U.S. currency, interest rates, grace periods, and term duration. For instance, the sub-borrowers were to repay the GOC in Local Currency. Their rate of interest was between 2.0 to 9.5%. They had a grace period of 5 to 10 years. And they were to repay the loan between 10 to 20 Years. The Local Currency repayments were deposited in certain Special Accounts.

In sum, as I see it, the beauty of the Two-Step Loans was/is that the Host Country benefits at five distinct levels and times during the different steps and procedures. Here is how:

1. **These are loans and the Host Country benefits in its repayments to USAID through the differentials in interest rates, grace, currency, and period of repayments.**

2. **The Host Country implements a series of programs. projects or subprojects that it sorely needs; in the case of Colombia, effects were evident in all departments and economic sectors.**
3. **Most risk resulting from currency devaluations is assumed – it seems to me – by the Host Country.**
4. **The sub-loans are repaid to the Host Country in local currency which is deposited into Special Counterpart Fund.**
5. **The Host Country own the Special Fund, in perpetuity, and/or co-owned and/or coordinated with/by USAID; this fund can be used for other projects and/or even as budgetary support.**

Here is my suggestion. In my opinion, the two-step approach seems like an excellent way to help Host Countries. However, I saw this technique used only in Colombia; perhaps some further research and fine-tuning might be needed in several areas – especially in relation to the fact that this is a Borrower/Grantee Type of Financial Technique where the trickledown theory is involved, and there is the possibility of commingling of different types of funds. More details are included in the referenced chapters and Parts. If the reader needs additional information on the Activity, this can be found in reference (Ref.) to **Chapter 3. Part G 3, and Chapter 8 Part J cover the Two-Step Loans.**[112]

C.2 The Private Investment Fund (PIF)

PIF is an exceptional example of financing activities using a Two-Step financing technique. PIF was created on February 28, 1963, and was administered by the Bank of the Republic of Colombia (BORC). [113] Our review of PIF showed the degree of sophistication that we encountered in some of our reviews during my assignment in Colombia. Here are some aspects: Although PIF was administered by the BORC, it was receiving funds (converted into Millions of U.S. Dollars) from (a) three USAID Loans -- some of the funding was through the "two-step" loan mentioned previously – ($11.6 million); (b) several local currency generated programs (like P.L. 480 and

---

[112] Information obtained from an Audit Report (No. 1-514-71-96) I did in March 15, 1971 entitled "Eleven Two-Step Loans of Colombia," P.2 and Exhibit A.
[113] A.R. 69-08, Results of Examination of the Private Investment Fund of the Bank of the Republic, Project 514-56-920-115.

counterpart funds ($60. Millions); (c) Interest differential (.5 million); (d) the Government of the Netherlands ($1.4 Million); (e) the Inter-American Development Bank ($3.0 Million); (f) the Government of Germany ($5.0 Million); (g) the World Bank ($37.5 Million), (h) the Colombian Social Security Ministry ($4.8 Million), and (g) others. In other words, PIF was receiving "investments" or contributions amounting to about $123 Million from various organizations. More information is found in Chapter 8, Part K covering PIF in Colombia.

From a Program type of view, the result of our examination showed exceptional achievements. Most of the funds were converted to local currency and used to make sub-loans towards achieving three different objectives: (a) diversification and export promotion; (b) elimination of shortages in the production of goods; and (c) Import substitution. Our 70--plus page report contained many statistical profiles of the sub-loans. We were happy to see that the sub-loans were having a positive impact on almost every department (equivalent to the U.S. States) of Colombia (Antioquia, Boyacá, Bolivar, Mata, Valle, etc.). Almost all the Colombian economic sectors were being affected in a favorable manner. Here are some examples: sub-loans were being made for: (a) agriculture (banana, sugar, cacao, etc.); (b) manufacturing and processing (textiles, clothing, etc.); (c) industrial groups (metal, machinery, electrical, etc.). Our sample included seventy sub-loans; these borrowers had increased exports, during a four--year period, from $4.0 to $20.0 million. There is no doubt that this program was benefitting the GOC and its economic sectors. Moreover, the rate of increase in exports was nice and the positive effects on employment of people, in the different sectors and departments, can only be imagined.

From a financial point of view, it looked, to us, as if all "investors" were contributing their grants and loaned funds toward a common purpose or for the same three objectives. As a result, we found a commingling of funds, and there was no separation between funding sources. Nevertheless, the degree of sophistication shown by this project is worth a review by USAID as a good lesson learned. In other words, PIF got financing from USAID through three loans, one was a two step loan, some came from local currency generated by P.L. 480, Title I, and still, others came from several different countries and international banks.

Here is My Suggestion. USAID might want to explore possibilities of creating projects which imitate the objectives and sophistication shown by PIF. Here is the start of an idea for further analysis.

1. The principal start of such a project would be to do it using the "Two-Step Loan" described previously in combination with local currency generated by P.L 480 or CIP programs.
2. The second step is to design objectives which would give a common purpose or the same objectives that will attract different "Investors" – to wit: convert different currencies to local currency and used to make sub-loans towards achieving desired same or similar country-related objectives: (a) diversification and export promotion; (b) elimination of shortages in production of goods; and (c) Import substitution.
3. The next step is to find the locations where commonality or similarity of purposes are present; **my bet for the good candidates for the possible project(s), like PIF, would be the six Central American Countries of Guatemala, Nicaragua, Costa Rica, El Salvador, Honduras, and Panama**. Why the five or six Central American Countries? The simple reason is that CABEI (see the next description) is most interested in the development of these countries and would probably be happy to be one of the "Investors" or as "the Administrator" for such a project and to attract more "Investors."
4. The next step is to attract several "investors;" aside from USAID, CABEI, IDB, and World Bank would potentially be exceptional "Investors" for the project.

If some sort of financial agreement can be negotiated among all the "participating countries," "Investors," on pooling and/or comingling funds, monitoring, procurement sources, auditing, and evaluations" the achievements and help to countries could be very significant.

C.3 Central American Bank for Economic Integration (CABEI).

CABEI is one of those lasting success stories. The concept for such a bank was first proposed by a group of Central American economists in 1948. The actual development of the idea began to take shape in the 1950s when the five Central American countries (Guatemala, Nicaragua, Costa Rica, El Salvador, and Honduras) began to negotiate the needed International Treaty. CABEI was finally established on May 8, 1961 and had two initial basic objectives: (a) to promote balanced economic development within each Central American country and (b) to promote Central American economic integration.

A comparison of the Financial Statements for the periods between December 2020 and December 2008 shows the following broad amounts of growth (in Billions of U.S. Dollars):

	Year 2020	**Year 2008**	**Growth in 12 Years**
Assets	13.2	5.5	7.7
Liabilities	9.6	3.7	5.9
Equity	3.6	1.8	1.8

A little more information can be found in Chapter 8, Part K, and I believe that its story must be told.[114]

Here is a suggestion. *In sum, the growth of CABEI is most impressive. I was one of the active participants in a comprehensive audit of CABEI. Our audit showed that some facts were evident. CABEI was conceived by the five Central American Countries and helped in its initial stages by visionary organizations like USAID, IDB, and others. It certainly seems like a healthy-going concern. Its success should rightfully be attributed to the forward visions of the Central American Countries, USAID, IDB, and others. I hope the success of CABEI can be replicated in many other countries. I also hope that CABEI accepts to be one of the Participants in a project that imitates the achievements of the Colombian PIF.*

---

[114] Information came from A/R 1-596-72-57, Our Review, where I was an active participant, of "The Central American Bank for Economic Integration through the AID Regional Office for Central America and Panama (ROCAP), various pages, filed in File on Chapter 3.

C.4.0 The "Malthusian Syndrome" Has a Hand in Hand Relationship with Demographic Growth and Food Production.

There is a definite inter-connecting relationship between (a) Unchecked Demographic Growth Situation; (b) extremely beneficial Agricultural Research; and (c) USAID emphasis on Agricultural and Livestock Projects. USAID is extremely aware of the degree of their interrelationship and makes strong efforts to help these sectors. The lynchpin that ties all groups is the threat that the Malthusian Syndrome may become a reality, and the population growth could greatly exceed the supply of food. The consequence will be Mass Starvation. Here are three examples:

C.4.1 Assistance to Organizations Working to Curb Unchecked Demographic Growth.

Reference is made to Chapter 3. Part I3; and Chapter 9. Part I. These chapters show assistance to the Costa Rican Demographic Association (CRDA). However, we should begin with a broad picture of the Demographic Situation. A quick review of the U.S. Census Bureau International Data Base[115] shows a very disturbing trend which is that in only 100 years – from the year 1950 to the Year 2050 – the World Population will grow from 2.7 billion to 9.7 billion, i.e., a phenomenal growth rate of 359%. Four countries will account for the most growth:

a) India – is the one to watch. It has a projected growth rate of 1.55% -- from a population of 1.2 billion in 2009 to a projected population of 1.8 billion by 2050.

b) The United States has a projected growth rate of 1.42% -- from 307 million to 432 million during the same period

c) Indonesia will be next at 1.30% -- from a population of 240 million to 313 million.

d) China, where the population was 1.3 billion in 2009, will grow, by only 1.06%, to 1.4 billion in the year 2050.

---

[115] U.S. Census Bureau, International Data Base Internet www.census.gov/ipc/www/idb/worldpopgraph.html

Yes, the demographic growth of the world population is very troublesome. Obviously, India has its share of problems trying to curb its population growth. On the other hand, China's population rate of growth, at 1.06%, is, at first glance, a desirable maximum or possibly less Worldwide goal to reach.

C.4.2 The Costa Rican Demographic Association

As mentioned in Chapter 3, USAID has been very keenly aware and has been fully supportive of organizations that have taken upon themselves the responsibility of trying to curb unchecked demographic growth in their specific country or on a worldwide basis**. One such organization is the Costa Rican Demographic Association (CRDA).** I audited CRDA a few years ago and was highly impressed by its operations. Thinking in terms of the way that the country's population was growing – fast and uncontrolled -- a number of doctors organized CRDA with a number of objectives in mind: (a) to make the public aware of the population problem, (b) to get women and people to join the organization, (c) encourage studies, and (d) provide needed commodities (condoms, pills, IUDs, etc.) to needy women.

As planned in the objectives, the right type of publicity directed to the right type of population and availability and provision of needed commodities and services went hand in hand and were imperative to the success of the program. Thus, the CRDA undertook the following uniquely and directed advertising radio (before the prevalence of TV) campaign to transmit messages to the population:

- Since TV was not in full swing at the time, the first step was radio broadcasts. These were first directed towards the general motivation of the middle and upper classes.
- The second step was to direct radio broadcasts at the middle and lower classes using messages that emphasized home and general comforts.
- During the third step, the radio broadcasts tried to reach men, women, teenagers, and professionals.
- At the same time, CRDA established an office, which also served as, a clinic to provide the needed information, services, and commodities; these items included birth control pills, injections, condoms, intra

uterine devices, and foams. At the time, CRDA was not providing women with sterilizations; these were referred to outside participating doctors.

At the time of my audit, CRDA had been operating for about 4 years by then; it was an acceptable country institution and growing. I saw and talked to many women who knew the location of CRDA, its objectives, and the services it provided. They saw the need for Family Planning, came willingly, and received the free commodities and services willingly and without shame or compunction. For instance, I witnessed the insertion of IUDs with the permission of and without any embarrassment to the lady.

Moreover, CRDA was beginning to have a certain degree of recognition from other demographic associations. For instance, CRDA was already receiving financial assistance from several organizations. They included USAID, the International Planned Parenthood Federation (IPPF), the Pan American Health Organization (PAHO), the World Education Inc., and the Swedish Government. I suspect that it now receives assistance from many others.

My evaluation was that CRDA was achieving its objectives. For instance, the Costa Rican population rate had decreased over a 10-year period, from 3.85 to 2.60. Thus, the massive, carefully focused, and multi-level publicity campaign was paying huge dividends. And USAID assistance seemed to be providing exceptional help in this area.[116]

Based on my 28 years of USAID work, I see immense importance in curbing unchecked demographic population growth. Thus, I strongly recommend that USAID continue to establish and support organizations, like the CRDA, to obtain financial resources from variously different organizations, continue promoting directed publicity, and make family planning commodities available in distinct parts of the world. **For example, USAID might want to coordinate a program with countries such as – India, Indonesia, and others -- that imitates the CRDA of Costa Rica.**

As stated above, the danger of not curbing an unchecked demographic worldwide explosion is the real possibility that, at some point in the future,

---

[116] A/R 1-512-72-113, USAID/Costa Rica, The Costa Rican Demographic Association, in Chapter 3 File.

there will be an insufficient supply of food to feed a burgeoning population growth. The unwanted consequence is that there will be massive starvation. This is the reason why USAID is an avid contributor to research and agricultural projects.

C.4,3 Agriculture, Livestock, and Agricultural Research

Reference to Chapter 3, Part I3, shows that USAID continues its exceptional efforts to help the Green Revolution by financing a great deal of research that is being done by Researchers of U.S. and International Universities and institutions.

A real example of when the "Malthusian Syndrome," which could have become true, took place in India in 1960. India began to experience extreme problems with its agricultural production and could not produce enough wheat to feed its exploding population. Massive starvation was just around the corner. Fortunately, the research of Norman Borlaug, a U.S. agronomist, paid off dramatically. At the time, Borlaug was employed by the Ford and Rockefeller foundations and at the International Maize and Wheat Improvement Center in Mexico (CIMMYT) to improve wheat production. USAID was providing research funds to CIMMYT at the time. Borlaug developed a type of wheat that could be harvested twice a year instead of once a year. However, to produce the wheat twice a year, there was a need for intensive fertilization and adequate irrigation. At the time, these research findings were a Godsend and helped India avoid massive starvation. This period is known as the "Green Revolution."

As noted in the statistical portion of this section, the population of India is projected to be around 1.8 billion by the year 2050. Thus, this means that India is having problems curbing its population explosion. Moreover, India is currently having complicated problems due to the overuse of pesticides and is apparently unable to use the fertilizer to the extent needed to produce wheat twice yearly. I sincerely hope that India finds a solution to its population explosion and agricultural production problems.

In any event, USAID does a lot to help agricultural research done by many universities and international organizations such as CIMMYT, International Center for Tropical Agriculture (CIAT), International Potato Center (CIP), International Food Policy Research Institute (IFPRI),

International Livestock Research Institute (ILR), and many others. As you re-read this book, observe the many examples or notations I give to assistance to the agricultural sectors and Livestock sectors.

C.5. Example of a Technique to Reach Poorest of the Poor

Chapter 3. Part G5 shows a unique way USAID Reaches the Poorest of the Poor. It is called the "micro-lending concept"" which will be explained in this part. When I first joined and was assigned to Peru, USAID assistance was granted using the "trickle-down economic theory," meaning that most funds were granted through governments and expected to gradually cascade to the different strata of the country's socio-economic structure and at some point, reach the poorest of the poor. I visited Peru several times during the time I was with USAID; to me, the rich were probably richer, and the poor seemed to have remained the same. These comments serve to say that the "Trickle-down Theory" had proved unrealistic.

C.5.1 Shift to Poorest of Poor

As I stated previously, this concept was changed in 1973 when the U.S. Congress passed a congressional mandate requiring USAID to redirect its efforts and emphasize the rural and the poorest of the poor. This new direction became a great implementation challenge because many countries did not have a good handle on the number of people in rural towns and villages. Planning and implementation for such types of activities were difficult.

The result was the development of very complex types of projects – like the Integrated Rural Development Projects in Ecuador and in different countries –designed primarily to attempt to help or affect some of those classified as the so-called "poorest of the poor."

Despite the complex concepts used in the early beginning of the 1973 Congressional Mandate, it came down to a simpler change in lending philosophy, as explained in the referenced Chapter and Part, that has made a huge difference for one segment of the poorest population. John Hatch and his FINCA International have done an excellent job in helping the villages in different countries. Please read that particular part and the procedures used to reach the poorest of the poor.

One article in a newspaper said that over 100 million of the "poorest of the poor" families have benefited from these types of programs. Another article, in the Nature Conservatory for August/September 2014 says that the micro-lending concept is being applied very effectively in the Samburu area of Kenya. According to the article, 2,225 women in 12 "conservancies" (areas being helped by the Nature's Conservancy Organization) were receiving micro-loans and training in accounting and marketing.[117] *The article does not say whether USAID is contributing funds or effort to this activity. Nevertheless, and not surprisingly, the women tend to repay their loans promptly, and the delinquency rate is only a minimal 1%. In sum, this is a fabulous program that provides exceptional benefits to the villages and poor people.*

Yet, I see some problems in reaching all of the desired "poorest of the poor" – without displacing either the informal sector or the poorest of the poor -- in all countries. Egypt and its Zabbaleen population with its Informal and Poorest of the Poor Population are good examples.

When my family and I got to Egypt, we noted that Cairo was always a clean city, i.e., the trash was always nice on a daily basis. To me, this seemed like a very odd thing. When I was told why Cairo was so clean, it reminded me of the idiom "…One man's trash is some other man's treasure…." Why? Well, because, back then, we noticed that the trash was always picked up on a daily basis, and the streets were always clean. Here is why: the cities and home residents had contracted with the "Zabbaleen (Garbage or Trash People)," -- who went around with their donkeys or carts and picked up all the trash. According to some articles, about 50,000 to 100,000, mostly Coptic Christians, live in the outlying areas of the city, called the Mountains of Muqaddam. [118] These people did not mind the dirty work. They would pick up the trash, take it back to their district, and sort them in separate ways – iron, cans, aluminum, plastic, etc. They would recycle (sell) about 80% of the 4,500 M/T of trash picked each day and either feed their hogs with edible "garbage" or use the rest as fertilizer.

---

[117] The Nature Conservancy, August/September 2014, p. 42.

[118] An Article Called "The Zabbaleen: The Unique Story of the "Garbage People of Cairo," by Dana Houshmand, April 12, 2019.

But…I understand that this type of recycling was discontinued between 1997 and 2003 – because the Egyptian Government wanted to modernize and did not want to address "…the Poorest of the Poor situation…." As a result, the GOE contracted with private trash collection companies from foreign countries to pick up trash via huge trucks and modern technology. **This displaced the Zabbaleen – for a time.**

However, the big trucks and modern technology could not get through the narrow streets of Cairo, the contract costs and fees were too hefty for the population, they missed the less expensive and daily collection of trash, and the people living in high-rises refused to take trash all the way down to collection bins, and many other efforts displaced or required by the foreign country contracts. As a result, the cities were inundated with trash and garbage piles, and piles were all over the cities and streets.

Zabbaleen are back in business. According to the articles, the contracts with the private companies of foreign countries ended in 2017. And guess who got back into the business of collecting the trash – yes, you got it right: the Zabbaleen. And, why not!

- The Zabbaleen community lives in the outlying parts of Cairo, in the foothills of the Muqaddam Mountains. They were well organized in the past and could easily be the same in the present and future.
- Here is one interesting point: the Zabbaleen meet both the Informal sector and the poorest of the poor classification of people. They collect funds from the trash collections – but, as I understand it, they do not pay taxes to the Government; thus, they meet the classification of the "Informal Sector.' They live in the poorest sections of the cities, among the collected trash and items to be recycled, where not too many people would dare live; thus, they fit the "Poorest of the Poor" classification. I could not find any information on whether these two classifications will change in the future and if the GOE will acquire their services.

Like I said, they are well organized. Men take turns in driving donkey carts or narrow motorized carts. For a contract with the city and an economical cost to the home resident, the men pick up the trash and/or even go through the high-rise buildings and pick up the trash. They take it to their home, divide paid amounts, and the women and children go through the trash, by hand and divide the plastic containers, tin, iron, etc. They have designed (and used) automatic tools and machines to compact the categories of items. They recycle the items, feed their hogs, etc. Although during the HN 1 epidemic, the GOE appears to have killed over 300,000 hogs belonging to the Zabbaleen, there is some evidence that hogs are still being grown by the Zabbaleen.[119] Now, however, with the COVID-19 epidemic, the Zabbaleen find that they need help coping with the numerous **amount of used syringes** found in the garbage and a possible epidemic of hepatitis infections as a result of being pricked by the used syringes. USAID could provide some sort of help in this respect.

Here is another example where people were displaced. It relates to the USAID Project for grain silos in Alexandria (Egypt) which I discuss in Chapter 13 covering Egypt. The project plans called for Quay 85 to be dug deeper and its size extended so that a ship could come in, dock, and be unloaded. There was an issue related to this portion of the activity. Why? It was because Egypt was using the labor efforts of a vast number of laborers to pack the wheat and/or products from the smaller boats, place the bags on the back of laborers, carry them out of the small boats, and place them on the trucks. In other words, this is the way that Egypt was able to employ the excess number of laborers. Mechanization of this type of unloading a ship would displace a sizable number of laborers.

The above examples represent exceptional lessons that should be brought to the attention of the U.S. Congress. I wonder how Egypt resolved the types of problems, and I wonder how many other countries have excessive population problems that – like the Zabbaleen and the labor situation in the Alexandria portion of the grain silos – don't mind collecting the trash and sorting it out and the laborers who otherwise might not be able to support their families.

It seems to me that there are also opportunities that USAID could help populations in Host Countries – like the Zabbaleen and the Alexandria Laborers without displacing their needs. I will provide some of my thoughts later; USAID could explore these possibilities.

---

[119] Ibid. Unverified facts came from the same articl.

C.6. Many Other Projects and Activities Deserving Mention

In my years with USAID, I saw and did many audits and reviews of projects, programs, and activities that at least deserve mention without much expansion. Here are some that come to mind.

C. 7 Nicaragua Earthquake of 1972

Together with Dick Harger (now deceased; May he RIP), I served as a special envoy to the assistance that USAID provided to Nicaragua during its 1972 earthquake. We witnessed the construction of over 11,135 home shelters for people who lost their homes because of the earthquake. These shelters were being modified and probably became homes to those people displaced by the earthquake.

C.8 P.L. 480 Title I, II, and III

Without fanfares, the USAID has used and uses the provisions of P.L. 480, Titles I, II, and III to provide, and has provided, food and agricultural products to a tremendous number of Direct to Recipients, Government Organizations, and Non-Government Organizations. This type of help has been provided over the many years, and I have seen how the food helps needy people.

C.9 Assistance Against COVID-19

As mentioned, USAID is a continually active organization that attempts to address Pandemics, like HIV/AID Pandemic, very quickly as they begin to take place. In this vein, as of September 22, 2021, for instance, USAID was (a) investing $345 Million to accelerate the Global Fight against COVID-19; (b) providing $2.8 million in assistance to Tajikistan; (c) providing $2.0 million to UNICEF and WHO to support against the Pandemic; (d) providing $1.0 million assistance to Timor-Leste to extend the reach of vaccination program; and, (e) providing both financial and informational support about the COVI-19 to about 120 different countries. In short, USAID is right up to par with detrimental epidemics.

PART D. SOME EXAMPLES OF ACTIVITIES AFFLICTED BY MURPHY'S LAWS

D.0 Murphy's Law. Here is a reminder of what the concept of Murphy's Law is all about. "…Murphy's law states that "Anything that can go wrong will go wrong…."[120]

D.1 The Mutual Savings And Loans Program in Ecuador

Chapter 6, Part G shows the USAID assistance to the Mutual Savings and Loans Associations (also referred to as MSL Associations) Program of Ecuador. This one was administered by the Central Housing Bank Program (EHB) of Ecuador.

The objective of the EHB program was to establish an MSL Associations System similar to the one that the U.S. has. The plans were designed by ICA and called for a US$10 million program. The development loan (No. 518-A-012) was awarded to the Government of Ecuador (GOE) on October 31, 1961. Under the terms of the agreement, (a) the DLF/USAID Loan was to be US$5.0 million; and (b) the GOE share was to be the equivalent of US$5.0 Million.

Here is a Short Preview of Our Findings. Our review showed a program that was experiencing the "classic "Murphy's Law" (everything that could go wrong -- went wrong). In effect, this program was filled with a nightmare of serious problems. Almost every program level and area we touched had problems.

The biggest problem with the program was that it was not properly designed and/or planned. The Implementation Letters were written in a very poor; they contained contradictory instructions and were defective in other manners. With only one U.S. Technician assigned to this complex Program, supervision, monitoring, guidance, and periodic assessments were generally not found by us. The desired sustainability factors (difference between earnings and operational costs) and limitations to prevent take-overs of the individual associations were not carefully researched, designed, and/or

---

[120] This definition was obtained from the Internet.

envisioned. Ambiguity in the way the Standard Regulations were written gave rise to a variety of interpretations which resulted in control and awarding of construction contracts, by the few families, of some associations in some areas.

In addition, the project was affected by other uncontrolled and conflicting contributions. For instance, the Government of Ecuador -- authorized by its Social Security Institute and the EHB – signed with the Inter-American Development Bank (IDB) a separate US $10.6 million agreement for the direct construction of housing units throughout the country. As a result – rather than supervise and implement the development of mutual savings and loan associations -- EHB became enamored with and more interested in constructing housing units all over the country. Consequently, EHB: (a) switched its emphasis from the USAID MSL Association loan project to the construction of the housing units funded by IDB; and (b) equally bad, it began comingling the different funds (AID, IDB, ISSC, and counterpart funds (i.e., generated repayments of principal and interest), and others into one account.

In short, our 102-page report showed the many problems and predicted the failure of several individual associations. Even when our recommendations were implemented, there were 7 failures of different associations. For example, I recently consulted the Internet and found that out of 12 Mutual Savings and Loan Associations that were operating at the time of our audit, only 5 now exist.

Lessons learned. Here are some of the Lessons Learned: (a) designs and plans need to be thorough and precise; (b) staffing levels need to be well thought out; (c) implementation letters need to be well written and precise language used; (d) sustainability differentials (interest and earnings to be collected from mortgages minus projected operating expenses) must be realistic and project safely sustain the operational capabilities of the association; (e) interest should be more or less compatible with those being charged by other banks; (f) limitations on awarding shelter construction contracts must be instated in both Loan Agreement and Letters of Implementation -- they should be explicit enough so as to prevent takeovers that took place in the MSL Association of Guayaquil; and, (g) the conflict of interest problem -- that the EHB had with the IDB housing program and with this project -- should not be in the horizon or allowed in the agreement.

D.2 The Cali Sewerage Project

Reference is herein made to Chapter 8, **Part L. shows o**ur review of the Cali Sewerage Program and shows a project that had also been afflicted by "Murphy's Law," i.e., whatever could go wrong, went… In effect, Chapter 8 and Part L provide a good background and our detailed findings.

Briefly, the project started in 1956. The original technical study was made by a U.S. Consulting Firm and updated by a local engineering firm. The U.S. firm recommended a type of Sewerage Plan, but the local firm contradicted it. It was financed through a two-step loan. Based on a preliminary design, the Cali Sewerage was to cost the equivalent of $5.5 million and be financed by (a) a $3.7 million loan from USAID and (b) $1.8 million from EMCALI. CVC estimated that the project could be completed in 20 months. As of October 31, 1969 (6 years later), the agreement had been amended once, and 11 Letters of Implementation had been issued.

Here was our overall conclusion on the Cali Sewerage. At our review cut-off, only one section (A the Cement Pipes) had been completed. Although plans called for completion of the Cali Sewerage in 20 months, the table, in Referenced Chapter 8, Part L shows that even after 6 years, the program was significantly behind planned construction schedule because of the numerous problems the details of which are mentioned in the referenced Part L and briefed here as follows: (a) the program was affected by a multitude of factors; (b) the recommended type of sewerage system prescribed by the U.S. Consulting firm was not followed and the modified system resulted in a costly construction; (c) between 1954 and our cut-off, the geographical population of Cali shifted and plans needed further modifications; (d) plans were made at a prevailing Rate of Exchange of 10 pesos to US $1.00 and there was a devaluation of the currency which increased the value of the dollar from 10 pesos to 17.71 pesos to U.S. 1.00; ('e) there were very serious issues with the selection , retroactive contracting, physical work, length of work, accomplishments, and amount of reimbursements of/to the Local Engineering Consulting Firm; and, (f) there was a difference between plans to obtain the USAID loan, migration of populations, and the actual implementation that was actually needed to construct the sewerage.

Our final conclusions were that the program plans did not seem to have followed the best "Critical Path" in the construction of this sewerage; in fact, the planned components seemed to be constructed in a haphazard manner. In our opinion, this program would, most likely, not be completed by the Terminal Date for Request for Disbursement (July 31, 1970). Moreover, the cost would probably exceed the new program estimate of $7.7 million.

Lessons Learned. There are tremendous amounts of lessons to be learned from this example. Here are some of them: (a) be extra careful about the degree of trust that USAID places on plans presented by the local organization for the loan approval and financing; (b) take very careful care of when the contract with the Local Engineering Consulting Firm is signed (this one was signed with a retroactive period of one year); (c) be careful with the periodic local Engineering Consulting Firm work (This one took an excessive period of time to complete the various phases); (d) the population shifted from the originally planned location to another; (e) there was a devaluation of the currency which favored USAID – yet, for some reason, U.S. Dollar costs increased, and the need for this currency were just too excessive; (d) the actual work seemed to be constructed in a haphazard manner; and, (f) the project was significantly behind schedule and would eventually cost much more than originally planned. In sum, be careful with these types of projects. If possible, be prepared to withdraw support.

D.3 **Trailer Homes (A/R 68-13) of Vietnam**

With the tremendous influx of USAID economic assistance and the proportionate increase in technicians coming into the country, there was a shortage of housing facilities in Saigon as well as in the different regions of the country. After France ordered all NATO forces out of the country, in mid-1967, the U.S. military in France declared 345 house trailers as "Excess Property." Since we could use the trailers in Vietnam, USAID accepted the Excess Property and arranged – through Procurement Actions -- to import all 345 of the trailers.

The importation of the trailers turned out to be a nightmare -- full of pilferages, complicated problems, and unplanned costs. Here are some of the problems:

a) When USAID inspected the 345 in France, they were being occupied by the U.S. military, and therefore, they were in an almost perfect state.

b) The 345 trailers were to be subsequently transported, by rail and/or trucks, via Frankfurt, West Germany, to the port of Antwerp, Belgium, for shipment to Vietnam.

c) By the time the trailers arrived in Frankfurt, almost all had been basically stripped. They did not have refrigerators, toilets, beds, sinks, floors, windows, etc.).

d) Of the 345 trailers shipped, forty-five were deemed to be a total loss in Europe. Some were cannibalized, and the remainder were scrapped.

e) The first shipment of 106 house trailers arrived in Vietnam. Once again, they were vandalized. Their windows had been broken, and the insides were once again stripped.

f) Of the 106 trailers that had arrived, 25 remained on the ship and were sent to one of the regions. Another 10 were placed on barges waiting to be unloaded.

g) The 10 house trailers that were placed on barges were lost for a few days. They were later found near a village about 3 miles down the Saigon River. You guessed it: The door locks had been broken, and the insides had been completely ransacked.

In sum, USAID wound up expending over $1.3 million in shipping and refurbishing costs. There had been pilferages in all phases of the shipments. Forty-five house trailers were declared a total loss in Germany. Many others arrived in Vietnam pilferage, extensively damaged, and/or damaged beyond repair. The furniture in the 10 house trailers in the barges probably wound up in homes or tunnels of the Viet Cong.

Lessons Learned. USAID needs to be very leery of accepting these types of excess properties – particularly if the items will be shipped through various countries. Also, now is a good time to begin planning the housing situation for the time when the situation **in Ukraine** normalizes. With Russia's emphasis on destroying residential buildings, the need for construction of houses and buildings is very much in the horizon. Plans for these future needs in that country should begin now.

PART E. THEORIES AND IDEAS FOR POSSIBLE ADAPTATION IN USAID OPERATIONS

E.1 Potential Expansion to a USAID Policy

USAID provides a great deal of assistance through Projects, Programs, and the Commodity Import Programs (CIP). I did and/or supervised many vast numbers of audits in my time. In my many years with USAID, I have always noted that there seems to be a great deal of confusion about the programs that it carries out; in fact, a great many people think that USAID "gives money away" to other countries. As you read my book, you will have learned that this line of thinking is a total misconception, and then I hope that you will agree with me that USAID has a fabulous policy in place for awarding assistance to countries. The policy prescribes a two-way beneficial effect. In fact, the assistance requires lending recipients to purchase, to the extent possible, commodities and technical assistance from the U.S. As a result, most financial assistance to countries returns – through contractual marketing procedures -- to help businesses in the United States.

Lessons Learned. The only exception I take to this policy is that I wish it would have more dispersive economic effects so that the U.S. aging infrastructure could receive – just like private companies and corporations do -- significant benefits or some participation in USAID Assistance Programs. My suggestion is for USAID to make a study on these possibilities; and coordinate its findings with the U.S. Congress.

E.2 Manner of Financing Technical Assistance May Have Potential Problem

Ref. Chapter 9, Part J. discusses our review of the 1972 Earthquake in Nicaragua. We noted that the Banco de la Vivienda de Nicaragua (BAVINIC) – who was to (and did) administer (provided the land, designed the shelters, contracted builders' services, provided engineering services, etc.) to build 11,135 home shelters urgently needed Technical Assistance (T/A) for its operations. Here were the problems: BAVINIC was delinquent in the collection of contracted rent and was not maintaining adequate records of the Trust Fund accumulations. In addition, BAVINIC's planning for the 11,135 constructed Temporary Shelters did not contemplate a sewerage system; this created major problems during the rainy season. And when the system was built, it was not well designed and needed modifications. Thus, the problem is clear: BAVINIC needed T/A in its operations. Yet, BAVINIC seemed reluctant to get the T/A from U.S. Sources. From what we gathered; the hesitancy was due to the following:

- The reason, as explained by BAVINIC, is that the salary and benefits of U.S. Consultants are extremely high – and they all come out of a loan that will eventually be repaid to the U.S. The GON and BAVINIC's position is, to me, clear. Much like the GON and BAVINIC, other Recipient Nations are equally reluctant to use **loan funds** to reimburse the high salary and benefits that a U.S. Consultants is usually paid -- especially if the financing is to be with a repayable loan.

<u>Lessons Learned</u>. If we were to hypothesize that if the T/A to be provided was to be financed in the form of a Grant or that the Recipient Nation could obtain the T/A at a lower cost from any other source (Colombia, Costa Rica, CABEI, etc.) --- then, we would probably conclude that the Technical Assistance would be more expeditiously accepted and used. To me, U.S. Consultants of 1977 were not competing on a level field, and USAID needs to look at this – If it has not been done so yet -- as an Agency-wide problem.

- **In my opinion -- if this problem has not yet been addressed – then either the appropriate USAID Office or the USAID Inspector General should undertake an Agency-wide study (a) to determine whether other Recipient Governments are also reluctant to pay the salary and benefits of U.S. Consultants when financing is with Loans; and (b) whether the U.S. Congress and/or the USAID need to change laws or policies so that T/A – which is available from U.S. Consultants – can be financed, or even obtained from other source places, under a more competitive mode.**

E.3 "El Otro Sendero"

Chapter 3, Part K, "The Other Path," is an excellent treatise on how to help the under-served informal sector. [121] As discussed in the referenced Chapter 3, USAID has been making in-roads with the poorest populations through its micro-lending programs. Yet, one segment of the population that remained elusive, and, in fact, had not been either reached or is in any event under-served -- during my time in USAID -- was the informal sector. In Less Developed Countries, the informal sector is usually "…composed of those people who, although pursuing legal ends, such as building a house …"[122] or operating a business (like the Zabbaleen of Egypt), have not met all of the legal requirements. *In other words, these are private persons who work for themselves, often without a social safety net, such as street vendors, bus/truck/taxi drivers, transportation carriers, carpenters, hairdressers, barbers, bricklayers, seamstress electricians, gardeners, garbage collectors, etc. Some countries, such as Peru, have large informal sectors. As may be noted in this section, the informal sector has numerous complex problems and challenges stemming from the lack of recognition of their work by the country's legal system.*

Near the end of my career at USAID, the Agency hosted a seminar to discuss critical issues facing "third world" development. The seminar's moderator was Dr. Hernando de Soto, an economist, and Director of the Institute for Liberty and Democracy (hereafter referred to as ILD) in Lima, Peru). ILD is a non-government, private organization that can be described as a "Think Tank." During this conference, Dr. de Soto presented a very provocative dissertation and then wrote a book[123], on the causes of Latin American underdevelopment and how the situation could be resolved. The title of the paper was "El Otro Sendero" (The Other Path). (Note: At the time of the presentation, there was a terrorist group called "Sendero Luminoso

[121] Two Books in Spanish "El Otro Sendero, and in English "The Other Path" written by Dr. Hernando de Soto were published 1986, are sold in Amazon.com and represent exceptional background.

[122] A Paper called Constraints on People: The Original of Underground Economies and Limits to Their Growth, written by Hernando De Soto.

[123] The Book is called (in Spanish) "El Otro Sendero," and (in English) "The Other Path" by Hernando de Soto.

(Shining Path)," which was Marxist-Leninist and advocated a radical change in Peru through violence and terrorism). *Thus "El Otro Sendero," espoused by ILD, offered an alternative to the violent one of the Shining Path. The ILD recommended solutions that seemed like a path that USAID could follow in its help to third countries.*

Lessons Learned. *This part is a "must-read several times," and the actual book bought and used. It provides exceptional information, ideas, and theories that the USAID, and other lending organizations, could probably adapt as part of their efforts to reach that most elusive Informal Sector. Here is what I said in the end part of Chapter 3, Part K.*

In sum, during my time with USAID, our efforts to help the poorest of the poor had not yet reached the vast majority of the population, which made up the informal sector. Looking at the conditions now, I still see tremendous lessons that USAID could learn from *El Otro Sendero* and other studies that have been made by organizations like the ILD.

However, as the reader can well imagine, helping the informal sector is a most difficult and complex area. But the Study by ILD shows some potential ways:

- ***One important lesson is that some governments, particularly in Latin America, may need a great deal of technical support themselves particularly in the areas of transparency, honesty, accountability, administrative reforms, decentralization of government, and simplification of laws, rules, and regulations.***
- ***Moreover, to influence and affect needed governmental reforms in Less Developed Countries, maybe USAID could help create, organize, support, and replicate (a) organizations, like ILD in the different countries, and (b) programs designed towards introducing sounding boards, like the "Everyone's Balcony." If the governments can be motivated to correct their defects, the benefits to both the informal sector and those countries will be immeasurable.***
- **One additional type of lesson was demonstrated in Egypt by the Zabbaleen (the Garbage Collection People). These people meet the classification of both Informal Sector and Poorest of the Poor.**

They were displaced by the Government of Egypt and wanted to modernize trash collection. The GOE contracted with trash private collection organizations from other countries. The consequence merited re-consideration in Egypt and other countries. Modern trucks could not maneuver the narrow streets of Cairo or the unpaved and rough roads of the country. Mountains of trash and gross accumulation of trash and dirt were all over Cairo and other cities. Effective in 2017, the modernization concept required by the GOE was apparently discarded --- and the Zabbaleen seems to be now the chosen few to go back to collecting trash.

- **USAID could help the Zabbaleen in a number of ways – (a) persuading the Governments to award special "Participant Training" and letting a few talented garbage sorters classes on modern techniques for separation of items; (b) by providing small and narrow trash motorized collection vehicles, (c) requiring the GOE to grant special tax subsidies or very long term periods before enforcing collection of a minimal tax, (d) designing systems to eliminate the health hazard caused by discarded injection syringes and protection of the exposure to hepatitis, (e) reviewing and improving on types of machinery and equipment used by the Zabbaleen to separate types of recyclable items; and, (f) others.**

E.4 Excessive Demurrage Cost

I noted that Demurrage Costs were being incurred in both Vietnam and in Egypt. There might be more places where this type of unwanted cost is incurred. Chapter 7 discusses Demurrage Costs during the war in South Vietnam. I saw Demurrage costs being incurred in the Alexandria Grain Silo. Because of the size of the USAID assistance program to Vietnam, and the competing requirements of the U.S. military, ship after ship would come into the port area of Saigon and remain unloaded for extended periods of time. In the case of the Egyptian Alexandria Grain Silo, Quay 85 was too narrow and not sufficiently deep. Thus, big ships could not unload directly to the port, and significant demurrage costs were being incurred. Ships are supposed to be unloaded within a specified period of time; any additional time needed to unload can result in additional costs during what is known as *the period – the*

"Demurrage Period." The party that charters the shipment typically incurs the Demurrage and must pay for it. Because the U.S. military had priority in unloading all arriving shipments in Vietnam and because the Alexandria (Egypt) ports were too narrow and not deep enough, USAID (and other countries) was the one that was charged with most of the Demurrage Costs. As one can just imagine, there were ships galore in the port of Saigon, and USAID was incurring exorbitant amounts of demurrage costs.

Finding a solution to this huge, costly, and really unneeded problem was essential as the costs were substantial. In Vietnam, all of us were encouraged to submit ideas about how to resolve this problem. Although I submitted three ideas, they proved impractical to implement. Without success, teams and committees were assigned the task of finding a resolution.

Lessons Learned. To my knowledge, we never found a solution to this type of unwanted additional costly problem. USAID needs to address this type of potential problem just in case it should develop in the future. In the case of Egypt, perhaps counterpart funds generated from the CIP Programs could be used to expand Quay 85 and make the port broader and deeper. Once again, like in the case of the trailer homes problems that I discussed before, USAID needs to study this problem before it takes place. Is Demurrage Costs being incurred in the Ukraine or some other place? See if this type of unnecessary costs can be reduced or eliminated (through a negotiated arrangements with the shipping companies or somehow0 for the future?

E.5 The Paradigm Might Need Updating

In Chapter 3, Part F, the Paradigm on type of project or non-project type of financing represents exceptional current guidance. However, it might be in need of expansion to accommodate the short and long-term types of projects. For instance, a poultry project has a shorter measurable objective. Some projects – like the Integrated Rural Development of Ecuador, where the objective is to reduce population isolation in the mountains and reduce greater migrations to the cities, have extremely long-term objectives. USAID should make a study of this area.

E.6 Using Rapid Assessment Statistics

To Determine Sizes of Villages

In **Part B.5.1 Shift to Poorest of Poor,** I stated previously that this concept was changed beginning in 1973 when the U.S. Congress passed a congressional mandate requiring USAID to redirect its efforts and emphasize the rural and the poorest of the poor. This new direction became a great implementation challenge because many countries did not have a good handle on the number of people in rural towns and villages. Planning and implementation for such types of activities were difficult.

During the time I was the Director of a Health Project in Guatemala, we had a similar problem. One of the objectives of the "PAI/TRO Health Project" was to vaccinate as many people as possible in the various departments and villages -- to the extent possible. The problem was that the country did not have a good handle on the size of the village or the type of people living in it. In fact, before my team and I restarted the project, Guatemala did not have a systematic manner of determining medical baseline information throughout the country. So, to resolve the situation, we contracted the services of an excellent medical doctor (Dr. Victor Lara) to teach and apply "Rapid Assessment" sampling techniques which provided previously unknown baseline information more quickly for the different parts of Guatemala. We provided "Cold Chain" equipment to the areas and trained many personnel from our team and Vaccination-related personnel from the Ministry of Health on the statistical technique and how to use it to determine the sizes and vaccination requirements of the different villages. I am happy to say that the "Rapid Assessment Statistical Sampling Technique" gave us a genuinely nice result, and we were able to raise the vaccination rate in the country (I discuss my tour in Guatemala in Chapter 21 of this book).

Lessons Learned: USAID could use the Rapid Assessments Statistical sampling techniques to determine the sizes and compositions of villages. While it may as a real good Population Census, statistical sampling techniques do provide an excellent "feel" for villages and places where real population figures are not available. I do not know whether Dr. Victor Lara would be available as a consultant to teach the technique. But, although I lost contact with the company, here is a possible information to contact: CLAPP AND MAYNE, INC. - SILVER SPRING, MD - Business Data, ww.dandb.com/businessdirectory/clappandmayneinc.. 8401 COLESVILLE RD SILVER SPRING, MD 20910 Get Directions (301) 495-9572....

Part F. Referrals To Current USAID Inspector General For Possible Lessons Learned, Audits, Correction, And Improvements

Objectives of This Part. I have two objectives in writing this part. First, I want to congratulate your appointment to your current position of Inspector General for USAID and several other organizations. Second, I would like to describe some of the problems of the past with hopes that you and your current staff can learn from them and improve, if needed, current operation and those for the future. I shall now start.

F.1 Vacancy Left If Audits of Individual Projects are Excluded And Principles and Use of Non-Federal Audits

Background. Chapter 18, about page 361, shows a discussion on why I thought that excluding "individual projects" from the regular audit – as espoused by the previous IG#1 approach – was faulty. The following provides more details on my opinion and describes the way that Non-Federal Audits should be done.:

In his testimony (in front of the May 1992 Glenn Committee Hearing), the previous IG#1 defended the use of the audit representation letters, saying they were not sweeping statements. He also said that the Inspector General had substantially revised its audit approach away from audits of individually funded USAID programs and projects and toward a greater focus on agency systems to determine whether the appropriate controls were in place and were functioning appropriately. My opinion on both points follow.

Letters of Representations. To me, IG#1 requirements for people to sign letters of representation and accept an obligatory lie detection sitting were completely haywire and wrong. As noted in Chapter 18, Part D, Issues with Guys 11, 4, 6, and 5, these people had tried similar gimmicks against us (RIG/A) before attempting them against regular USAID FSOs. We thought these requirements were out of line and possibly violated the fifth amendment of the Constitution. None of us – this included a former RIG/A/LA, our staff, and me (as the DRIG/A/LA) -- would even think or consider signing those types of requirements. As noted in Chapter 18, I am on record as a representative of the RIG/A/LA, in rejecting them in a total manner. There is no doubt that, in presenting these types of requirements, to the regular USAID Employees, IG#1 and his supportive staff was entirely out of line. I was happy that these requirements were withdrawn in front of the committee.

Concept of Doing Systemic Audits and Excluding Programmatic Audits of Single Projects. I have very a very serious disagreement with IG #1 on this point with IG#1.. It seems like the IG would have liked to operate the IG audit responsibilities like GAO or more like an External CPA Firm. As I understand it, he would substantially relinquish his Internal Auditor's part of his Inter-entity responsibility (Programmatic Type of Audits) in favor of doing broad types of systemic reviews to see if internal controls were in place. In fact, this approach – if done by itself -- gives me the "willies." **As I wrote this section, it dawned on me that the IG#1 was really talking in terms of using Non-Federal Auditors to do the USAID financial work. If that was his thinking; then, his thinking was futuristic, but it was only half complete. He was missing an especially important basic tenet for using NFA's, which, in my opinion, is this: In the case of USAID field missions – where projects and programs are used -- NF Audits should normally be done as an integral part of a project or programmatic evaluations. Why? Simply stated, USAID Programs and Financial Resources are intertwined. In other words, the two are co-joined with one-another because the achievement of program goals is contingent on availability and proper use of the other. Thus, they should be done together and not normally done in a separate manner. The point I want to make clear in theory and practice is the following inherited principle in auditing both financial and programmatic which is that:** ***Effects on Financial Provisions Affects Program Goals and Vice Versa (the effects can be favorable or unfavarable.*** **Let me show you three real examples of how the two parts (program goals and financial sources are intertwined and how they demonstrate the tenet I am talking about:**

- **In the case of devaluation of currencies in foreign countries, Costa Rica and Egypt are good examples. They devalued the currency which resulted in beneficial effects to projects where U.S. Dollars were converted to local currencies. In Costa Rica, these devaluations <u>affected sixteen different projects goals</u> <u>in a</u>**

<u>favorable</u> manner (see Chapter 16); in this case, the projects used ($8.4 million) less U.S. Dollars to implement the same original or modified project goals.

- **In the case of Projects or Programs affected by Murphy's Law, (discussed in my referrals to the USAID Administrator) the correlation between program and financial resources is also noticeably clear. In the case of the Cali Sewerage, alone, the <u>project goals were adversely affected</u> in several ways and there were significant delays in program implementation.** ***The effects on financial resources – even with certain country currency devaluation -- <u>were to increase costs</u> in a radical manner and there were other financial aspects which were questionable.***
- **In the case of the Grain Silo of Egypt, this one had all kinds of problems where the effects to goals affected the financial and program goals and vice versa. These problems included passive monitoring, currency devaluation, disallowance, defective construction, buildings with defective materials, wrong filters, weak cement, and many other administrative and technical defects.**

In sum, the above examples describe the inherited principle which states that the effects to the financial part of a project affects the financial and vice versa. They are intrinsically intertwined. This is the principal reason why I see great faults in this line of the IG#1 thinking. And, there are others.

<u>Other Reasons For Doing Both Systemic and Project Audits Together.</u>
Based on my experience, let me say that USAID operates in a highly volatile environment, and in many countries and areas, which have a great probability that local people will find ways to undertake corrupt and fraudulent practices. Here are just some examples: please review the situation in the Family Planning Review of Pakistan Bangladesh and my findings on the conversion of condoms into gloves or sales of FP Pills in the open market. The conversion of condoms was done in the villages of Pakistan and Bangladesh, close to India, and Burma (now Myanmar), and sales, at significantly high profits, were done in the cities. Another example is the evident fraudulent

billings in the Poultry Project of Egypt. I also found "Collusion among U.S. Suppliers." I could go on and on.

In my way of thinking, the USAID Inspector General has three equal responsibilities in the case of USAID Audits – one is the broad systemic situation (as espoused by IG #1). A second one is inter-entity or internal and evaluative audits of Activities, Projects, and Programs which show individual problems. And third is to carry out a financial review, now, apparently, done by Non-Federal Auditors (former IG Retirees or CPA Firms). Thus, the USAID Office of Inspector General cannot vacate either his responsibilities to carry out the systemic type or his Internal Audit functions (to do audits on projects and programs which have problems). Here are some questions I would have: (a) how else – and by whom – will these functions be fulfilled? (b) Who evaluates whether the project or program is on the right track and will achieve its desired objectives? (c) Who and how will anyone know whether final costs and achievements equal the desired goals and objectives? And (d) if the Inspector General will be relinquishing its audit responsibilities for doing internal audit functions of individually financed projects and programs, who, in the Agency, will take over these necessary and essential functions designed to ensure that projects, programs, and activities are individually designed and implemented in the most efficient, economical, and cost-effective manner? Yes, I see serious problems with the approach that was tried by IG#1 and the staff that he brought in from GAO.

To me, these gaps of audit responsibilities expose the Agency to very wasteful policies, mismanagement, and fraud. Just review: (a) the "Grain Silo Project," (b) "the six reports covering the CIP" in Egypt, (c) the canceled or water-downed audit of the CIP in Sudan, and (d) the Family Planning review of Bangladesh. If it had not been for surveys, audit plans, and our audits, no one would have found and (or possibly) corrected all the financial and programmatic problems that we found in the survey and during the many months of our audit. Moreover, canceling audits and/or audit reports just because they are complex or because someone – like Guy 5 and Guy 7 (who came from GAO) -- had probably never seen situations like the ones I found in my audit of CIP in Sudan are costly, unwarranted, and expose the United States and USAID as its representative to frauds and/or extremely bad publicity. In the case of the "Grain Silo," there were systemic and internal types of problems – for instance Project Supervision was "Passive," and the Project was full of problems. THESE ARE THE TYPES OF AUDITS WHICH, AS I UNDERSTAND IT, WOULD BE VACATED BY THE IG SYSTEMS AND, ONLY FINANCIAL, APPROACHES, AS EXPLAINED BY IG#1 IN HIS MEETING WITH THE GLENN COMMITTEE. THE PROBLEMS WERE FOUND ONLY BECAUSE WE USED A COMBINATION OF A MISSION-WIDE REVIEW AND DID THE PROJECTS AND PROGRAMS REVIEW USING THE INDIVIDUALLY AUDIT APPROACH. IF WE HAD NOT FOUND THE PROBLEMS, THE ADVERSE CONSEQUENCE WOULD BE IMMEASURABLE TO THE U.S. AND THE EGYPTIAN PEOPLE. JUST PICTURE THE BAD PUBLICITY OF A GRAIN SILO FALLING DOWN BECAUSE NO ONE CAUGHT THE BAD CONSTRUCTION OR FAULTY MATERIAL BEING USED OR THE QUESTIONED COSTS RELATED TO THE PROJECT.

IG Responsibilities for the Intertwined Features Found in USAID Programs In sum, as I see it, he Office of Inspector General must have a combination of the External Auditor, as espoused by IG#1 in his congressional testimony, and the Internal Auditor Concept, which protects the USAID (and the U.S. Government) from frauds and mismanagement (THIS INCLUDES BOTH FINANCIAL AND PROGRAMMATIC EVALUATIONS.)

Best Way to Meet USAID Requirements. As I see it, the best way to do audits in USAID is a six-way approach: (a) do yearly missions-wide survey to identify and segregate activities, projects, and programs (hereafter described as "all activities") that have problems and those that don't – this survey includes programmatic and financial; and, once these segregation take place, then: (b) identify all activities which have systemic types of problems; (c) identify all activities which have individual types of problems; (d) test the financial part of projects to test internal controls and/or find problems; ('e) do a select a limited sample of all activities which have no problems; and, (f) schedule, prepare and assign the teams and do audit taking different approaches. Here are the details to follow in each case:

- **For (b), i.e., all activities with systemic problems: these ones require broad Agency-wide reviews. The designs might need an**

audit program, with a listing of disciplines needed, coordination with all RIG/A's, etc.,

- **For (c)-- those Activities having individual type of problems: these types of problems must be done on an individual problematic project, program activity basis, and identification of location of financial records.**
- **For (d) --those activities not having problems: since there are lessons to be learned from an activity that is going well, sample and do the limited type of scope audits of activities and projects which seem to have no problems.**
- **For ('e) – the financial costs. As I see it, the RIG/A/Washington Office has its own idiosyncrasies and are not discussed herein. In the case of the field activities, financial reviews should be done as part of the project and programs. The use of Non-Federal Auditors (CPA Firms and Retired USAID Auditors) is an excellent addition to usually limitations of IG Personnel. FYI, I was the Audit Manager for Non-Financial Audits in Kenya. At times, I had teams numbering at 14 people, including the Mission's -- and my preference -- highly experienced retired USAID Auditors, and/or CPA Firms.**

Conduct of Audits. Most of the USAID reviews where problems are present should be comprehensive and evaluative in nature. Systemic types of audits should be carefully planned and coordinated with all RIG/A's. The reviews should cover all aspects of a project (managerial, program design, implementation, financial, usages, internal controls, etc.). After analyzing legal documents, applicable USAID Handbooks and Instructions, and background material and obtaining a working background, the team should make an assessment on whether: (a) the development activity (program, project, function, etc.) is/was/did achieve desired objectives; (b) Project or activity management was using resources in an effective manner; (c) the project was being implemented in an efficient and economical manner; (d) there was any evidence of misuse, waste, mismanagement, or fraud; (e) procedures and internal controls were adequate; (f) the organization was in compliance with laws and regulations; and (g) any aspect of the development activity, procedures, or functions were in need of improvement or change. In preparing for the audit, the team should review such documents as loans, grants, project agreements, contracts, project design papers, implementation letters, handbooks, evaluation reports, host country budgets, decrees, laws, procedures, etc. to analyze each program or project and then prepare and publish a comprehensive report. Some complicated activities may require preparing comprehensive audit programs, which include phasing in and out of different types of disciplines.

Principles on Doing the Non-Federal Audits. As stated earlier in this Chapter and same part, program goals and financial resources are intertwined. Effects on one affects the other – sometimes beneficial and others in an adverse manner. I previously showed three actual examples which demonstrate how USAID mission activities are so intertwined and how the effects on one affects the other. So, I will not repeat it any longer.

In sum, programmatic evaluations and related financial resources are inherently intertwined. However, the NF Audit Program must be more carefully studied and scheduled so that they are implemented while the Program Evaluation takes place. There follow examples of two ways that we did NF Audits in Africa in my time.

In the case of Non-Federal Audits, two approaches were tried in my time: (a) in West Africa (Senegal), they allowed the CPA Firms to scope their work, write PIO/T, do work, and write reports; this approach failed. In turn, in Kenya where I was the NFA Program Manager, I observed the basic tenet and did the NF Audits as a part of a Programmatic Evaluation. Accordingly, I did the survey, scoped the work to be done, wrote PIO/T, developed scope of work, helped in finding CPA or retired auditors, helped in wording scope of work of the contracts, indirectly supervised (kept in touch with the team) on the progress of work, and assisted in drafting the report. My last EER with USAID points out that my teams got over $2.9 million in refunds to the USAID. In addition, one of my teams, composed mainly of USAID Retired Auditors, found, as I had noted in my survey, that the

three universities, and CID, assigned to the Yemen Program, were not ready to implement such a complicated Program; that the program was not being implemented in efficient or economical manner; and, that some of the high costs were due to universities granting exorbitant salaries and bonuses. According to my EER, my teams questioned $741,000 of universities costs which needed to be refunded to the U.S. Government.

<u>Personnel Requirements For NFA Programs.</u> Yes, indeed, I am a proponent of the NF Audit Program. However, the Office of Inspector General needs to appoint, in each RIG/A Office, highly trained and skilled USAID Audit Manger to participate and manage, in every step of the process. Moreover, this NFA Audit Manager should have the title of second Deputy RIG/A, have at least two highly skilled auditors, and be adequately supported by administrative staff. It goes with saying that he/she should also be adequately supported with financial resources so that this small team can do their work related to do surveys, PIO/T, Scope of work, Contract, and supervise, and/or assist in the field work at same time as the other Programmatic evaluations are taking place, and the writing or feeding information for the reports or integrating it with the evaluations. In other words, the Manager of the NFA Programs has duties which are complex and must be coordinated with a number of other jobs going at the same time. (Unfortunately, I did not have all these logistical supports in my time – but I made it work in an exceptional manner and got a superior mention, in my EER's, from the Deputy Inspector General).

<u>Here is a word of caution on using NF Audits.</u> Unless the NF Audits will be conducted by Retired USAID Auditors, these types of reviews should not be made by CPA Firms when the surveys show some possibilities of fraud or when Missions – like in the case of Yemen – expressed concerns on using commercial CPA Firms.

After reading the above, please review Chapter 8, **Part N and O on the Conduct of Reviews and the Report Clearance Process in Colombia. This approach should be carefully studied and possibly adapted for use by RIG/As.**

F.2 The Grain Silos Project of Egypt represents one of the most complicated audits that USAID could have and shows different lessons to be learned.

Reference is made to Chapter 13, in Egypt, Part C.4 The Audit Plan for and Review of the Grain Silos Project.[124]

To avoid going back, here is some background on this Project: In 1975, Egypt was importing nearly 75 percent of its food grain needs. By 1980, these types of importations were expected to be over 4.5 million tons. Yet, Egypt only had two-grain silo facilities – a 48,000 metric ton (m/t) complex in Alexandria and a 58,000 m/t complex in Cairo. Neither the Alexandria nor the Cairo silo complexes had any modern "ship to silo" unloading equipment, structures, or mechanized system. Moreover, there were serious problems with both (a) the depth of the harbor in Alexandria was too shallow, and (b) the Quay number 85 used to unload the grain was both too shallow and short. In other words, the loaded grain came in small ships that would dock in a shallow harbor near a short quay; Egyptian laborers would board the ship, bag the grain, carry them – one by one, on their back -- and load them onto the transportation and distribution trucks. These inefficient unloading practices created excessive and unwarranted "demurrage" costs – which USAID/Egypt and other assisting countries were paying.

For this reason, the USAID Mission and the GOE negotiated an $84.5 million project to upgrade and build more modern silo systems in both Alexandria and Cairo. Financing for this project was being done through a USAID loan (Loan Agreement No. 263-K-028), amounting to $44.3 million (in US Dollars). Of this amount, about the U.S. $6.1 million would be payable in Egyptian Pounds (LE 15.5 million). The remaining amount (about $40.2 million) was the GOE local currency contribution. The Project had the following objectives:

- In Alexandria, the objectives were to (a) dredge the channels; (b) widen and deepen the harbor; (c) deepen and extend Quay No. 85; (d)

---

[124] Audit Plan for the Grain Silo Project. Dated 1979, and Audit Report No. 6-263-80-6, issued May 29, 1980, entitled "A comprehensive Review of the Grain Silos Project – AID Loan 263-K-028 at Alexandria and Cairo, Egypt, Implemented Under Host Country Contracting Mode."

add a modern 20,000 m/t structure to the existing complex; and, (e) construct a new and modern 80,000 m/t unloading and storage silo complex system which would have pneumatic ship unloading towers, conveyors, and other modern equipment required to unload ships in a more efficient manner.

- In Cairo, the objective was to construct a new and more modern 100,000 m/t silo complex in Shubra (near Cairo).

As stated previously, I was the DRIG/A of Egypt at the time and our review of the borrower and grantee contracts revealed the Grain Silos Project to be in urgent need of a more comprehensive audit due to the number of odd and serious problems. Briefly, there were two types of major problems: (a) a systemic problem was that both the USAID and GOE had adopted a very passive approach to the monitoring of the project; and (b) there was a nightmare of situations that clamored for a special in-depth analysis.

When my team and I expanded our survey – the expansion included a review of files and documents, samples of financial transactions, analyses, evaluations, test probes, discussions, limited visits, etc. -- we found that our concerns were warranted. What I saw reminded me of the Cali Sewerage Program in Colombia that I described earlier. Our tentative assessment showed a project that seemed to have been afflicted by Murphy's Law, i.e., whatever could go wrong, went….

In such complicated cases, a good Audit Plan is so necessary. For this reason, and with the team's help, I prepared an 80-page "Audit Plan" -- hereafter also called a "work plan" -- for a very comprehensive review and evaluation. The plan provided the necessary program and financial background. It also called for contracting the services of an independent special engineer as part of our evaluation team and for the Office of RIG/A in Egypt to manage the entire evaluation. In addition, the work plan called for the team consisting of audit personnel from different disciplines and locations in both headquarters and Egypt since the work would be done in different locations. It laid out a cohesive and well-coordinated schedule for phasing-in and phasing-out of all participating teams. The plan contained numerous segments which described each individual problem, the work that needed to be done by the team members, financial in U.S. Office, and the final report or contribution that each team was to make. Russell (the RIG/A at that time) and our staff reviewed the plan, as did the Inspector General, Office of Inspector General Policy and Plans in Washington, the IG's Office of Special Investigations, and others. **In sum, this was one of the most complex reviews that anyone can imagine.**

Once I completed the Audit Plan, and it was fully staffed, Russell (the RIG/A/Egypt) decided to take over its broad supervision and control. We assigned an Auditor-In-Charge (AIC) and an audit team to help him monitor and achieve all phases of this extremely complex review.

This action was taken because I was scheduled to go on home leave in June 1979. Upon my return, I was also scheduled to start to work on our next urgent priority, which was to do a survey and develop a similar work plan for an audit of the $1.5 billion CIP program in Egypt. As I will discuss later, the CIP had very complex problems of its own, and we eventually released a series of six reports (and some Classified) on them.

In short, having developed the work plan for the Grain Silo program and upon transferring the supervisory responsibilities to Russell, my participation in this review became limited to an exchange of further ideas, consultations by team members, problem-solving, and reviews in the preparation of the Record of Audit Findings or the draft report.

Lessons Learned. This audit took 12 months to make. With some minor exceptions, it followed my plan right to the letter of the word. The findings were almost exactly as I had predicted. The lessons learned from this audit were extremely valuable; we found design problems, financial ones, bad engineering decisions, bad quality of material, defective parts, poor construction, passive monitoring, etc.). In a complex review, such as the Grain Silo, a good survey is essential. An excellent Audit Program must be developed. The various types of needed teams (auditors, engineers, financial auditors, IG Inspectors, and others) must be planned, phased in, and phased out in a timely manner, and their contributions (RAF, reports, meetings, etc.) must be fairly exact and fit into each other at the proper time.

F.3 Indefinite Quantity Contracts (IQC's) Could be a tinderbox for Fraud and abuse

Just before I transferred from Egypt and then again just before I retired, I did two audits of Contractors having both IQCs and Reimbursement Types of Contracts. In the Poultry project of Egypt, we found the contractor abusing the IQC to no end. One of the problems was that he was paying his people in firm monthly salary and then billing USAID at the inflated number of hours and unapproved hourly costs. Another problem was that he was billing the inflated hours by all the IQC allowed factors (which include an Indirect Cost Factor) and then billing all costs by an additional independent Overhead Factor. In other words, he was billing erroneous hourly costs and then duplicating the Indirect or Overhead Costs. If I remember correctly, the Poultry owner was suspended for a time.

Just before I retired – when I returned to Washington from Kenya – I found a similar situation with another Washington Contractor. Although I found the situation, I was never able to find the full extent of the fraud because I was pulled out prematurely by Guy 5; this guy was brought in from GAO and placed in a supervisor's position in Senegal then in Washington. Although I explained the problem to him, he failed to understand the significance of it. His monthly report to IG#1 included a note saying that he had withdrawn me from the assignment because I had incurred 3,360 hours on the job and needed more training. **My comment: I had only spent less than 150 hours, and I had found a very serious fraud problem, and I did not need additional training to recognize a fraud when I saw it.**

My recommendation to you is to make an Agency-Wide fairly large sample Review of Contractors having IQC's Contractors. See what the sample shows and expand the sample if it shows a possible fraudulent trend. A second idea is to have a statement in all USAID contracts forewarning Contractors on preventing perceptions of frauds and possibilities of suspensions if such are found.

F.4 Indexing of Work Papers

As shown in Chapter 16, my staff and I designed a system of indexing work papers that was simple to use. Work papers were indexed in step with the progress of the audit. Moreover, specific areas to be mentioned in the RAF's and Final Report were cross-referenced in step with the progress of the work. This practice proved to be a tremendously accurate and valuable time saver. You might want to review our practice and see if it can save time if you put it into your operations.

F.5 Use of Regression Analysis Techniques.

Over many years, I made use of Regression Statistical Analysis Techniques to identify potential problem areas. I presented an extremely summarized version in my TDY to Bangladesh. When I was in Egypt, I requested a computerized system of CIP costs that could be used to simplify our audit of this type of program. I even wrote a paper on how to do it. My proposal was rejected on the basis that modifying the USAID computerized Financial System (of the time) was just too costly. You may want to explore this now.

F.6 Personnel Evaluation Panels Should Use Uniform Policy to Evaluate FSOs on a yearly basis

As noted in Chapter 15 and the following Part E, during my assignment to the 1980 Evaluation Panel, we found that the Office of Personnel did not have Uniform Policy to make EER evaluations, and each Panel had to develop its own system. You will find the details of the system we developed on: Chapter 15, Part E. Our Panel Developed a Format Potentially Useable to Achieve Uniformity among USAID Evaluation Panels. We wrote a memo to the Director of Personnel, but there was never a response from him.

According to Foreign Service Rules, EER to be evaluated in a fair and unbiased manner, there should be a Uniform Evaluation Policy; otherwise, positions and grades are not evaluated in a level field. You may want to look to see if there is now a uniform policy to do the evaluations.

F.7 Currency Devaluations Influences USAID Costs

As noted in Chapter 16, Part G1, the country of Costa Rica devalued its currency, and its effect was felt in 16 of its projects. Please read this example carefully. I have been in at least five countries have had currency devaluations. In such instances, Programs or Projects would require less U.S. Dollars to accomplish goals which had been set at a different Rate of Exchange. In the example of Costa Rica, the "Residual

Amount" that the 16 projects would have would be over $8.4 million. That is to say that the devaluation of the Colon resulted in less dollars being converted to achieve the original goals of the sixteen projects. I see this type of problem is remarkably like an excessive number of Unliquidated Obligations. But then again, this could a highly political decision between USAID and Host Country Governments.

Let me suggest that you study the example of Costa Rica and determine if this might be an USAID Agency wide problem to be scheduled for a straight Agency wide audit. However, I believe the U.S. Congress did not anticipate this in the FA Act. I believe you should take a look and if so, inform the U.S. Congress and recommend actions for disposals on "Currency Devaluations or Increased Valuations."

F.8 Awards and Recognition Should be Awarded Promptly

I have been troubled by two of my findings which warranted recognition and/or awards and were never given. Here is the first.

- **During the time I did an audit of the Asia Foundation, I was never recognized for finding a very serious financial problem. It was created by an erroneous ruling on the part of the American Institute for Certified Accountants (AICPA). This ruling prescribed the billing of "obligated" potential costs as if they were already expended. As a result, this organization (and several other U.S. Government contractors) was billing USAID (and other U.S. Agencies) for "accrued obligations" at a point when the cost of a sub-project was in the planning stage or the "sub-obligation phase." The Asia Foundation was/is an exceptional organization. However, it was merely following the AICPA ruling. This was an erroneous ruling that affected USAID as well as several U.S. Government Agencies. As a result of my findings, the AICPA changed its rulings. The change in the AICPA's ruling no doubt resulted in immeasurable savings not only for USAID but for many other U.S. government agencies.**
- **The second one relates to my finding of collusions between CIP contractors related to certain type of product that was being imported in Egypt. This was reported in a classified report,**

investigated by IG/OI, and it was settled by the companies refunding the amount of $575,797 to the U.S. Government. It took 10 years to settle the case and, I was eventually told that I was being recognized – but I was never even given credit or even a certificate of recognition.

You may want to make sure that all significant audit findings, such as mine, are promptly rewarded, to members of your team, either in currency, certificates, and/or honors.

PART G. REFERRALS TO THE HONORABLE EXECUTIVE CHAIRPERSON OF THE COUNCIL OF THE INSPECTORS GENERAL ON INTEGRITY AND EFFICIENCY (CIGIE)

G.O Objectives For Referral to the CIGIE

By means of these series of referrals, I hope that I can support some of the CIGIE Methodology Objectives 1 through 6 as stated in your charter.

First, I would like to congratulate you on your reappointment to the position of Executive Chairperson of the CIGIE. I certainly wish the CIGIE's creation, and your appointment, would have been established in the 1980s; this was a period when I was undergoing some rough times – for expressing dissenting opinions — at a time when dissenting channels, as required by law, were not established. I certainly could have used some help then. Nevertheless, I am happy that the CIGIE is now in existence.

Second, I hope that you and your staff review – and particularly your training department -- the contents of my book and Chapter 19 and get additional ideas – and pass them to USAID. Having worked in USAID for 28 years, I know what a difficult job USAID has and that it also could improve its management and operations of the U.S. Foreign Assistance Investments.

Third, please review Part F (Referral to the Current USAID Inspector General) to see if any of the ideas or issues I presented to him should be expanded, broadened somehow, or even perhaps, they might not be of any value anymore, and thus should be discarded. My explanation of those ideas and recommendations come from the way USAID used to operate 30 years back. As I said all along, my 28 years of working with USAID date that back that far. So, I might not now be dealing in much modern times and the focus that USAID now has for the future.

Fourth, I would appreciate it very much if your office reviews the proposal – once made – by the first Inspector General of USAID (IG#1), which relates to his audit approach. He espoused doing – and did -- only systemic types of audits and significantly relinquished his responsibility for doing individual projects which had problems. In one of his approaches – as prescribed, in a policy proposal, by a person who came from another agency – the IG#1 planned to do only financial audits without any evaluations on whether the Project was achieving or had achieved the desired objectives or whether the costs, program objectives and program achievements were in close parallel. His approaches were faulty. In the case of USAID and its operations in over 134 countries, the USAID Inspector General must have three interrelated responsibilities: (a) the external or systemic approach as was espoused by IG#1; (b) the Internal (inter-entity) Audit responsibility or audit of individual activities, Project, and Programs especially those having problems; and (c) the financial aspects. My explanation of my position is clear; actually, my proposal is that the approach should include 6 steps described to the current IG. As I see it, this 6-step approach will give USAID – and the U.S. Government – a good protection. Unless audits cover activities having a broad systemic approach, an audit of activities having problems, and a determination that financial expenditures, project objectives, and project achievements are in basic agreement, how else could the IG or anyone else ever certify that they are being implemented in an efficient, effective, and economical manner and that there is no semblance or evidence of fraud, waste, and abuse (This is a requirement under your Methodology Objectives 1 and 2 of your charter)? Please read my analysis of the principles involved in the use of Non-Federal Audits also

in Part F on the referral to the current IG. The reason I say this is that, in USAID, the Program or Project goals and the financial stipulations are completely entwined; thus Effects on One Affects the Other (see Page 457 for three demonstrative true examples). It follows that audit on the financial aspects should be a part of a Programmatic Evaluation of Projects.

Fifth, based on my own experience, I believe, that there should also be systematic period reviews of I.G. performance and evaluations; provisions for removal "for cause," and a fixed term – not to exceed 7 to 10 years for all appointed Inspectors General. Here is why I say this.

As may be seen from the Prolog of this book and Chapters 15, 16, 17, and 18, one of my objectives for writing this book is because despite my many years with USAID, my many assignments with and without family, my number of dangerous assignments and situations, my many professional achievements, my many awards, my progression in the Foreign Officer's ranks and positions, my demonstrated capabilities to work with people in many countries and all walks of life, and my proven abilities to implement duties of the high DRIG/A and Acting RIG/A positions which I occupied and/or filled for six-years – and only for expressing disagreements against erroneous policies and practices that the former IG and his newly hired supportive staff – wanted to implement. Only for disagreeing with him and his people, I was demoted in a most disrespectful and degrading manner. And, for a five-year period of my final career with USAID, I was targeted numerous times for harsh treatment, reprisals, false accusations, investigations, and persecution by a very secretive and faulty investigation. These vicious aspects, and very faulty conduct of a secretive investigation, lasted for such a prolonged period of time. Although the investigation was without basis and faulty from the start and, as conducted throughout, I incurred unnecessary expenses, and there was a very pronounced psychological impact on my family and myself. Such treatment was unwarranted and unnecessary. To me, this is a horrible aberration, in the way, a good office – and especially within the U.S. Government -- should not be carried out and, especially by such a prestigious and elite manner such as is that of an

Inspector General…But, it took place because IG #1 was allowed to occupy his position for 17 years (way too long a period of time).

Why was he in power so long? Based on my research, the Inspector General of the U.S. Agency for International Development is one of only 3 IG's (out of 73 IG's) who are appointed by the President, and only he can remove the IG for cause. At the time, the IG (and his supportive staff) was reprising against me, there was no mechanism to reach the President with my complaints. *His dictatorial type of persecution of people and actions fit the Proverb which states: "Absolute Power Corrupts, absolutely!" IG#1 became entrenched and thought he could do anything without being held accountable. But his occupation of the I.G. Position was too long.* And now IG IG#1 is no longer with USAID – and can no longer be removed from office. He was a good general and a good IG leader for a time. As you can see, despite my persecutions, my personal and professional feelings towards this person will always remain mixed. He has now been judged by a higher authority; may he rests in peace.

My current concern is that current IG's should not be in power for no more than 7 to 10 years. Moreover, there are certain procedures that the IG#1 should have established but never did. There are also actions that he took but should not have taken. This is the reason I would appreciate it very much if you would review the following negative features which affected the operations of the Office of USAID IG in an adverse manner. Here goes:

IG#1 was allowed to be in his position for 17 years -- way too long for anyone to remain in that position. In effect, during the time I served under him and I really wish he would have established the following -- but he NEVER did:

- ***Establish a "Dissent Channel" as prescribed by the Foreign Services Act, although I wrote to him about that situation a number of times. By not having a Dissent Channel, he had an absolute power to reprise, accuse, and persecute persons, like me, who spoke out against bad practices and extremely defective policies and/or people who his office perceived as violating ethical or integrity*** *requirements. (Note: I am happy that there is now such a dissenting channel in place under the current IG.)*

- *Establish a "Career Ladder" for the FSO personnel in the USAID Office of the Inspector General; I also told the IG#1 about this in my memorandum to him after I served in the 1980 Evaluation Panels. The adverse result was to give I.G. employees a picture of stagnation during the yearly EER evaluation and to place them at a disadvantage, for promotions or advancement, in comparison to other professions being evaluated. The solution is to hire young, top of professional graduates, even former Peace Corps Volunteers, and improve their analytical and managerial abilities through on-the-job training, experiences, formal training, and the ranks.*
- *Establish a policy where FSOs on rotation should be allowed to improve themselves by getting an advanced degree or to continue to provide the service of an elite employee, which is something that I asked for and was denied several times. This was the reason I was not even able to get my master's degree. I am happy to see that this requirement is now "Methodology" No. 3 of the CIGIE rules.*
- *Establish – as required by the Foreign Assistance Act of 1961 -- a policy or system which conveys to the U.S. Congress weaknesses of the Foreign Assistance Laws so that those problems can be addressed by the U.S. Congress. As shown in Chapter 17, I found a condition in Sudan which needed to be reviewed by the U.S. Congress; this condition created a situation where I wanted to present the situation one way, and the RIG/A in Kenya did not want to disclose it at all and apparently just keep it in the work papers (I was never allowed to read the final report so, I don't know how it was presented).*
- *Perform a review of the USAID's Standard Regulations. These documents are written in an overly complex legalistic manner, making them easy for misinterpretation. The career of a friend of mine was ruined by the conflicting or unclear clauses of regulations. As noted in my case, something went wrong in relation to the way that the standard regulation was either written or the way it was*

communicated; the distinction between a SEG (those granted to a normal child) and a SHCEA (those granted to a child with physical and/or mental disabilities) was always fuzzy. Everyone who, in one way or another, reviewed my case was thrown for a loop. Just look at Chapter 18, Part I, and OIG/I conduct of the investigation and the "consultations" – and responses – of the twenty-nine people who reviewed my case; I think you will agree that it is just amazing to see the great variety of erroneous interpretations, conclusions, recommendations, deviations, and others. Only one – a lawyer – got it right. In sum, based on the lack of clarity – and the way the inter-communications of these documents -- my career and reputation were also placed in a most precarious manner.

IG#1 also took certain actions which adversely affected the morale and operations of the I.G. and eventually affected the remainder of the USAID FSO Personnel and the USAID as an organization -- to the point that IG Auditors and Inspectors were, to put it lightly, feared and IG #1 was given bad names. In effect, IG#1 was probably not thinking much broader than the I.G. Office. My opinion was then, as it is now, that he:

- **Should never have adopted an operational philosophy that emphasized auditing the systems and relinquishing his responsibilities to audit projects and programs especially when they had problems and disregarding evaluative analysis to determine whether activities are being implemented in the most cost-effective, efficient, economical, and expressed or desired relation between cost and fulfillment of program objectives. This approach left the USAID, as an organization, in limbo; if the IG was not going to do these types of reviews, who then would do it, and how could the IG say whether USAID's programs were being implemented in efficiency and economical manner and/or that there was no waste, fraud, and abuse;**

- ***Should not have transferred the eight civil service employees from GAO into the agency and placed them in such high positions and with such high grades. Selections for FSO Positions have always been very strict. The staff the IG#1 brought in had probably never, to my knowledge, served in a USAID Field Office and a less*** *developed foreign country environment. He made a big mistake when he brought them in, converted them to FSOs, and then placed them in high-level RIG/A positions. At least three were out of their element. I had recommended to the IG#1 that we should institute a policy for employing professional auditors by hiring young and recently University graduates and bringing them along into progressive audit experience and grade progression (which also addresses the "Career Ladder.") To me, this is what the I.G. in USAID and other U.S. Government Agencies need.*

- *Should never have allowed one GAO/New FSO person to issue policy statements, in a futuristic use of Non-Federal Audit in such an unclear and nebulous and incomplete manner.*
- **Should never have instructed and/or allowed the GAO/New FSO people to issue proposed policies and procedures requiring audit staff and/or USAID Personnel to sign documents that could be used in a manner that could very well amount to a violation of the fifth amendment of the Constitution.**
- *Should never have permitted the new FSO people to cancel (see Chapter 17) very expensive audit work without consideration as to their importance or adverse effects on USAID and the U.S. Government. The RIG/A/for Kenya was very defective in that position and canceled a minimum of 6 good audit reports (this was about $336,000 in a waste of expensive audit effort).*
- *Should never have allowed at least one "New FSO" to order a professional person (me) away from a job where the Contractor was obviously committing Fraud – in an Indefinite Quantity Contracts (IQC) against a USAID Program. This new FSO later took liberties (lied) on the number of hours expended on the job.*
- *Knowing my professionalism and capabilities (from Pakistan, Egypt, and DRIG/A/LA, IG#1 should have questioned the notation in the Monthly Activity Letter, saying that I was being taken off a job because I had incurred a false 3,360 hours and I needed more training. This was ridiculous.*

These and other defects instilled concern and fear by the people in USAID to the point that three organizations were called to investigate the I.G. In the meantime, the operational weaknesses enabled him to pursue good people, USAID personnel and me, without fear of repercussion to him as a functional USAID official.

In sum, I hope that your office will see that all the above "pending" items have now been corrected. Moreover, my love and affection for USAID should be truly clear in this book and I hope that the animosity that was created by the IG#1 with the USAID, as an organization, has now been forgotten and the two organizations are now operating in a friendly and cooperative manner.

Since I am now nearing my 91th birthday, I would like you to know that – in suggesting all possible actions you can take on the above perceived problems – I really have no personal interest in returning back to work or an ax to grind; my quest for improvements are made because I believe they will be beneficial to you, the USAID IG, and USAID for now and the future.

PART G. MY CONCLUDING REMARKS

In closing, I have some extremely good news before I end this chapter:

a) **I am happy to note that the current USAID Inspector General now has a "Dissent Channel" in place and has positioned a person to be in charge of any information which requires an employee to be protected if he/she "Objects, dissents, raise concerns, takes issue, etc.…" with a policy, document, or practice. In effect, the Law/Policy was written as a result of the Whistleblower Protection Act of 2017, which states: "Employees of (different organization the IG is now responsible for) … (1) USAID; (2) the Millennium Challenge Corporation; (3) U.S. African Development Foundation; (4) Inter-American Foundation; (5) Overseas Private Investment Corporation; and, (6) their contractors, subcontractors, and grantees… can perform an important service by reporting what they reasonably believe to be evidence of**

wrongdoing, and they should never be subjected to or threatened with reprisals for doing so….."

Bravo! Bravo! Bravo! I am really happy that my failed efforts of so many years ago were finally accepted and corrected. I congratulate the current Office of Inspector General and wish it the best of luck in this really extended responsibility coverage.

In ending my narrative on my career with USAID, let me sincerely hope that the current USAID Administrator, the Office of Inspector General[125] and the CGIE continue to improve the operations of his/her office by correcting any additional defects I have pointed out in this part. Moreover, I sincerely hope that the CIGIE and the U.S. Congress change the law so that there are much lesser limits on the amount of time that an Inspector General stays on the job and that there are periodic checks and balances to the performance of the USAID Inspector General.

Let me end this portion of my book by saying that I am extremely grateful to the U.S. Agency For International Agency for giving me the extraordinary opportunity to work with such a fine organization – and be associated with so many exceptional people -- for my 28 years. I will cherish all these years – in my Pursuit for Improvement (to myself and the Agency) -- for the remainder of my life.

CHAPTER TWENTY
IN PESHAWAR, ON CIVILIAN CONSULTING ASSIGNMENT, A CAULDRON FOR WARRING MUJAHEDEEN FACTIONS, MY LIFE THREATENED PRECIPITATES EARLY DEPARTURE

After leaving USAID in 1989, I spent several years working as a consultant primarily in three places: Pakistan, Guatemala, and with the OAS. This chapter discusses my six-month assignment as a consultant on the Afghanistan Construction Logistical Unit (ACLU) in Peshawar, Pakistan. I worked in Peshawar in 1990 and part of 1991. At that time, we were trying to help the Russians out of Afghanistan, and the Taliban had not taken over it.

Peshawar is an interesting city; close to the Khyber Pass, it is about 500 kilometers from Kabul, Afghanistan. The road from Peshawar to Kabul provides a beautiful panoramic view of the mountains; I travelled it a few times and enjoyed visiting some of the roads and bridges then under construction. Here is an example of the type of bridges that we were constructing to make the transportation from Peshawar to Kabul or thereabouts, for the Mujahedeen much easier:

My assignment to the ACLU Project in Peshawar was hairy and felt more dangerous than when I had been in Vietnam. In effect, Peshawar was a boiling cauldron with all the warring factions in one place. The objectives of ACLU were to help the Afghan resistance (the Mujahedeen) recover from the years of Soviet occupation, which had ended in 1989.

During my time in Peshawar, I worked to develop and implement a computerized accounting and inventory system and worked to refine the mechanics of a type of health and life insurance which covered the Mujahedeen if they did not come back from their constant incursions to Afghanistan; this insurance was called Solatium Fund. In the performance of my job, I saw some of the projects being developed from Peshawar to Kabul; travelled to safe areas of the country; and made a few American, Pakistani, and Afghan friends. I also experienced the dangerous environment – and isolation – of being ever so very close to Afghanistan.

At the time of my assignment, Peshawar was a tinderbox. It was full of Afghan guerillas, all armed to the teeth, and crazily running around in trucks everywhere. The city was divided into factions corresponding to important warlords and the guerilla factions would many times fire their guns into the air (and sometimes at each other or anyone around). They would also cross into Afghanistan to do their thing. Many never came back; the Solatium Fund helped their families. Stray and aimed bullets abounded; a number hit my house a few times. Mujahedeen groups came and went to the ACLU Project to pick up financial and other help, so I might have met some of Mujahedeen main warlords. However, only the name of Gulbuddin Hekmatyar now sticks in my mind.

Anyway, we all lived a most restricted existence. The Chief of Party held only one party when I was there. It was attended only by Americans. The principal show was the Pakistani Cook marching and playing the bagpipes. He was good! Also, the following picture shows a going away party for the first Chief of Party. He was going to be director of a construction contract I believe in Greece:

He was the first Chief of Party when I got to Peshawar. He was a fairly good person, and the people liked him. So, they gave him a going away party and I appear a long way from him.

> Oh, yes, I almost forgot to tell you about the time I danced with another man. Well, a diplomat has to do unusual things. Let me tell you how it happened. Four of the U.S. Team – the Chief of Party, myself (as the second in command), and two other colleagues – were invited to a Pakistani wedding. The marriage of the couple had not been arranged because the two had grown together and knew and loved each other very much. In any event, the civil ceremony took place in a large building. The bride sat upstairs in a form that resembled a cocoon. We were permitted to see her, and she was beautiful. She had some water paintings (I don't recall what they are called) on her that were customary at Pakistani weddings. All the men were downstairs. The judge began the ceremony by explaining something about the couple. He opened the marriage book. The future husband, his father, and the bride's father signed the book – the bride never came

down nor signed that she accepted to marry. There was the usual yodeling, and the ceremonial marriage was over. Everyone was invited to the reception, which was held in the house of the groom. So, we went.

At the house, we ate good food and drank some excellent drinks. Then, the orchestra – well, ok, there were three people playing string instruments – and the music began. The invited ladies began dancing with each other. The men followed suit and started dancing together with each other. After a couple of turns, one of them came over and asked the Chief of the Party to dance. I said, "oh..Sh..t. will I be next…." Sure enough, the next guy came over and told me to dance with him. So, I did. Boy! Was I a good dancer! I made a few two steps and turns, a couple of mambo jam boo twists, wiggled my behind a couple of times, twirled around a couple of times, did a Paso Doble like Cantinflas, and begged the guy if I could sit down. Yes, it reminded me of my time when I auditioned for a Toreador. See, I have you laughing. But it did happen, and I did dance with another man. However, while in Egypt, I had learned that hugging, kissing, and dancing with others of the same sex is a very common practice, so, my dancing with another man in Pakistan was OK to me. My machismo remained intact.

The tremendous isolation in Peshawar caused frequent mental anxieties and stress. There was the nice American Club in the center of town for those that drank and chose to eat there. For those of us (like me) that no longer drank, life was more isolated. Also, no person dressed in Pakistani attire was allowed to enter the club. Not knowing this rule, I invited three people into the club. All were Americans who lived in Peshawar, but wore Pakistani dresses. I was reprimanded for it and suspended from the club for one month. Since I did not drink and normally ate in local restaurants, the suspension did not bother me -- although I felt the rule was most discriminatory to the other U.S. Citizens who chose to wear the local attire. I wrote memos fighting the rule, but lost. So, for the duration of my stay, I never returned to the club.

Peshawar and its isolation was hard on your mind. Several people "flew over the cuckoo's nest" and were immediately evacuated. One of my co-workers, for instance, kept jabbering about "...directing an army.." for a couple of weeks. Then, he had a nervous breakdown. As we helped him to the van that would take him to Islamabad (to be interned in a hospital), he once again told us to take care of "his army." Since our work was so interrelated with another agency (the Central Intelligence Agency) and no one was sure about the other's involvement, we agreed to "…take care of his army…." When we went to pack his remaining personal effects, we found "...his army…" in a clear attack mode. **It was an army of Termites eating the design of a tree into a beautiful wooden wall. In a highly creative manner, my co-worker designed a tree with different branches; each night, he would place toothpicks on that wall so the termites would follow his guidance.** They sure obeyed him and kept eating away at the tree design. This man obviously had an amazing creative ability; I hope he got well and used that mind in a more productive manner.

Yes! Indeed, I still feel that Peshawar was a more difficult assignment than Vietnam. Although I had a contract to stay there for one year, I stayed in this environment for only six months. My contract was terminated when a fellow worker was shot five times – but survived – and there began to be bomb threats, actual bombs, drive-by shootings, and wounding of other Americans, and my safety (and those of others) became an extreme challenge. I was "very politely" asked to leave Peshawar because "…your life cannot be guaranteed…." Needless to say, I was quick in my departure – the options were nowhere favorable.

And yet, I remember the assignment because it gave me a "feeling" of being ever so close to Afghanistan and to the violent situation which currently exists in the country. I can imagine the tremendous isolation of all U.S. Soldiers and American Citizens assigned there and feel even very happy now that the end of the situation in that country is over. In any event, here is wishing that all U.S. Citizens were able to get out alive from that country. We now need to be very alert to the crazy factions that want everyone to live as they did in ancient times.

CHAPTER TWENTY-ONE
IN GUATEMALA, AS DIRECTOR OF A HEALTH PROJECT, SELECTED AND HIRED OVER 50 EXCEPTIONAL STAFF MEMBERS, IMPLEMENTED EXCEPTIONAL PROJECT OBJECTIVES

PART A. INTRODUCTORY COMMENTS

This chapter discusses my assignment, under a contract with Clapp and Mayne Inc., as the Chief of Party (the Director) of the team to implement the Guatemala Ministry of Health Child Survival Project (also called PAI/TRO Health Project in Guatemala). This project was financed by the U.S. Agency for International Development (USAID), and my work began in June 1992 and lasted until October 31, 1993. The Chapter is made up of ten (11) Parts:

- Part A. Introductory Comments.
- Part B. Project Story and How I Got the Job.
- Part C. Project Objectives and Implementation.
- Part D Hiring of Project Personnel.
- Part E. Memorable Personalities and Events.
- Part F. Problems Experienced During Project Implementation.
- Part G. Some Examples and Pictures Taken From The Third (of 6) Progress Reports.
- Part H. Most Project Objectives were Achieved.
- Part I Activities Completed and Those Requiring Improvements.
- Part J. Public Health Administrator Needed in Second Phase.
- Part K. Concluding Remarks.

PART B. PROJECT STORY AND HOW I GOT THE JOB

The story of this Guatemalan health project is interesting. Financed by USAID, a different private company had started this 10-year project seven years earlier (in 1985). Fraud, misappropriation of funds, and general mismanagement were found in 1989. As a result, the project was suspended, and the first company was discharged. The project stayed dormant for over three years.

In any event, I was on my way to Peshawar (Pakistan), when Larry Posner -- the C.E O. Director of the company Clapp and Mayne Inc. -- asked me if I would be interested in being included, as a possible Chief of Party, in a proposal to restart and implement, the Guatemalan Health Project. Of course, I was interested. We communicated a few times during the time I was in Peshawar. The proposal was submitted, and Clapp and Mayne Inc. were awarded the contract. So, the termination of my ACLU contract in Peshawar was perfect.

As a result, I transitioned at the start of the Guatemalan Health Project in a most timely manner. In the Proposal, Larry Posner had identified eight possible Key People and several other potential candidates (a total of over 40 people). He had also been negotiating with Management of Science for Health (MSH) -- who became the subcontractor – and helped us implement the Project -- and three other personnel who came to Guatemala on TDY to help me start the project. With this essential staff, a temporary office in a hotel, and some ancient (and failing) computers inherited from the previous company, we were able to restart the project, find a permanent office, hire a team of over 45 people (doctors, nurses, administrative, etc.), molded them into a cohesive implementation force – plus the tremendous participation of Larry Posner – we prepared excellent work plans. We began the hard task of implementation.

PART C. PROJECT OBJECTIVES AND IMPLEMENTATION

Although the original proposal had contemplated four priority objectives, the USAID and MOH modified the Project and assigned seven priorities to us: (a) reactivate the project; (b) reactivate the cold chain, which included an

Expanded Program for Immunization (PAI); (c) repair and restore the transportation system of vehicles and motorcycles; (d) introduce a new element, which included The Oral Rehydration Program (TRO); (e) the procurement of computer equipment and establish computer rooms for/to Health Areas; (f) improve budget execution of the MOH; and, (g) support decentralization effort by employment and use of "Gestores" (Field Representatives) who were to be assigned to, and coordinate all requirements, in the 24 Health Areas.

PART D. HIRING OF PROJECT PERSONNEL

Luck and personnel experience seemed to be with me all the time, and using a Team Effort, we were able to fairly quickly hire the very best Guatemalan Staff. At this point, let me first say that I had a great deal of help from all the staff and in particular, from the personnel that Larry had selected in his submission for the project. The eight key people were truly great. So, with their help and my training, we interviewed hundreds of "Candidates" and eventually hired close to 50 of the very best people we could find. They included a number of disciplines, like, Doctors, Nurses, Community Organizers, Accountants, Supply Experts, Administrative, Clerical, and one Engineer.

At this point, let me recognize the following nine key team members: (a) Dr. Marco C, an MSH employee; (b) Dr. Lucrecia (Lucky) P., for Immunization and Oral Dehydration; (c) Licenciado (equaling to a BBA) Danilo M., the Design of MOH Accounting Program; (d) Lic Marco Antonio F, audit and valuable assistant; (e) Lic. Victoria G., Chief Accountant; (f) Lic. Jorge P., Procurement Officer; (g) Edwin C., economics and Computer Expert; (h) Miguel Angel P. Transportation Expert; and (i) my secretary (Carmen Morales). Together with all the personnel we hired, the contribution to the success of the project by the above nine people was most significant. Please accept my many thanks to all of you. Your contributions were fabulous, and I sincerely appreciate them.

PART E. MEMORABLE PERSONALITIES AND EVENTS

In relation to my experiences, as Project Director, here are some of the memorable events of the Project:

a. One of the Professional Doctors we hired was an extremely beautiful and intelligent lad doctor, but she had a temper and volatility that went with it. One thing that I remember was that when things did not go the way she desired, she would come into my office and give me her Letter(s) of Resignation. She and I would discuss the situation, and I would place the Letter(s) in my desk drawer. A few days later, she and I would talk again. I would emphasize that the project really needed her. I would then ask her whether she wanted to reconsider her termination from the Project. She would be really happy at the way I had asked, and she would readily accept to stay with the Project. Although she made some mistakes along the way, the letter would be destroyed; we would hug each other; and she would return to her desk and cheerfully continue to provide an extremely valuable contribution to the success of the Project. Yes! I remember Lucky with great fondness. Her tremendous intelligence, energy, and creativity were excellent contributors to the project. Together with Dr. Juan Urrutia (an expert on Diarrheal Diseases) and, with Leticia C, a Community Organizer, on the immunization campaign in El Peten, Lucky's performance was really superb.

b. When the time came to vaccinate people, we wanted to increase population participation, particularly in El Peten. Lucky volunteered to go there. We needed a Specialist in Community Participation. Luck was with me, and I was able to temporarily hire a lady to help Lucky; her name is Leticia C. Both gave tremendous speeches to communities, and the two were able to increase the vaccination in El Peten – this was something that made me proud and that the Ministry of Health lauded later.

c. In hiring people, I often allowed two or three people – normally, Jorge P., Marco F., and/or Danilo M. (May they now RIP) -- to be the first to interview the people. This method enabled the filtering of hundreds of people that did not qualify or were not what the project needed. One time, the two interviewed a substantial number of people and identified clearly outstanding one. His name is Edwin C. I hired him on the spot. He was an exceptionally bright person with education and experience in economics and computers. Although my Project Deputy was constantly against him, Edwin's contribution was tremendous. I consider him my friend. He, his wife (Myrna), and I still communicate with each other to this day.

d. I also hired a person who had an extraordinarily strong personality but was full of good ideas and usually found a solution to the many problems which came about in the project implementation. His name is/was Andres C. There would be many instances when we were trying to achieve a complicated part of a project, and he would come to the rescue. At our regular meetings, I would express my idea on how to achieve the activity in question. Andres would sit there, quietly listening to my ideas or alternatives. After the meeting, he would call me to one side, express his contribution, and/or give me 3 or 4 other alternatives. And, lo and behold – his ideas, and solutions, were better than mine; so, we would do it his way. He was an exceptional contribution to the Project, particularly when it came time to work on the "Cold Chain."

e. The Engineer was fabulous. We employed him under a contract for a short period of time. During that time, he visited the 24 Health Areas and designed the Computer Centers and where the computers and desks would go. We were able to complete this part of the Project. The health Areas liked these contributions so much that some wanted to name them "the Jose M. Pena Computer Center." How about them apples???

f. Needless to say, all our secretaries and clerks were essential people who made exceptional contributions to the success of the Project. In fact, I still have them as friends. Even after 28 years since I left the Project, I still call Carmencita M. and Rocio (her sister) occasionally; she was originally married to a person who eventually became the USAID Director in El Salvador and has 4 children. Carmencita, who recently got married and now lives in California. Vilma P. and I call each other frequently. I consider her a particularly good friend. I know her and her two grown boys (Eimer and Fernando) well; Eimer is now married (to Marjorie), and they have a beautiful little daughter (Abigale). Vilma and all her family contracted the COVID-19 but survived.

Let me also say that I had very few losses of Personnel. Personnel turnover was minimal. According to my Third Progress Report, there were six people who were either fired or resigned. Of the six, four did not meet project requirement and voluntarily quit. If my memory serves me right, the Engineer resigned for better employment. I had to fire two people. Here are my reasons; one was a female doctor whose paper Resume seemed impressive. However, we quickly found that she was not what we could handle in the project. As I later found out from her, she had experienced a marriage full of domestic violence. In fact, her ex-husband had twice tried to kill her – once throwing her from a second-floor balcony of their apartment and the other by shooting her. As a result, her mind was traumatized, her learning levels were less than optimum, and her actual work performance was defective. I agonized over my decision but concluded that the project could not carry such a load, and I opted to fire her. The man I fired had tried two times to alter invoiced prices, i.e., commit fraud. When the Chief Accountant told me, I warned him the first time and met him with his termination check the second time.

PART F. PROBLEMS EXPERIENCED DURING PROJECT IMPLEMENTATION

Implementing this huge project was not easy. As I pretty soon found out, my supervision and project efforts were affected by factors such as the following:

- With its previous sad experience, the USAID Project Officer all-too-often tried to micro-manage our efforts. As I mentioned later, the USAID Project Officer refused to transmit, to the MOH, my report on the Lessons Learned "During the Immunization Campaign." Not only did this type of micro-managed slow down the project process, but it prevented improvements that would benefit all future Immunization

Campaigns. Nevertheless, I included many of the "Lessons Learned" in my Third Progress Report.

- The Ministry of Health (MOH) Coordinator consistently wanted to be a part of all decisions. This was awkward, and sometimes, his positions went against project goals.
- On May 25, 1993, the Guatemalan President took dictatorial powers; there was a 20-day diplomatic rupture between the U.S. and Guatemala. All assistance to Guatemala ceased for that duration. I was immediately instructed to terminate all employees. However, having been through several diplomatic ruptures, I brought back everyone. I worked an arrangement whereby we would all cut our salaries in half for the duration of the diplomatic crisis. Everyone agreed to my proposal, and no one was terminated. Eventually, this was not needed. Afterward, the personnel changes of the new government cascaded many levels of the ministries. Even the "old" MOH Coordinator was out of a job.
- One of the most serious problems that the project faced was that Guatemala did not have a real good fix on the populations of the outlying areas and villages. We needed this information to allot refrigerators and to conduct the vaccination campaign. So, I talked to Larry Posner and explained the situation. His tremendous ability to produce solution became evident. Let me explain his solution. Like I said, one of the objectives of the "PAI/TRO Health Project" was to vaccinate as many people as possible in the various departments and villages -- to the extent possible. The problem was that the country did not have a good handle on the size of the village or the type of people living in it. In fact, before my team and I restarted the project, Guatemala did not have a systematic manner of determining medical baseline information throughout the country. So, to resolve the situation and with Larry Posner's contacts, we contracted the services of an excellent medical doctor (Dr. Victor Lara) to teach and apply "Rapid Assessment" sampling techniques which provided previously unknown baseline information more quickly for the different parts of Guatemala. We trained many personnel from our team and Vaccination-related personnel from the Ministry of Health on the statistical technique and how to use it to determine the sizes and

vaccination requirements of the different villages. I am happy to say that the "Rapid Assessment Statistical Sampling Technique" gave us a genuinely nice result, and we were able to raise the vaccination rate in the country.

- One profoundly serious problem was that my project deputy was an employee of a sub-contractor (Management of Science for Health Inc.). Narcissistic, by nature, his loyalties and harmony were at self-promotion and not with the project. Throughout the time I was Project Director, he was constantly attempting to circumvent my directions, issuing raw and unanalyzed statistical reports to the MOH, and working on activities unrelated to the Project. In addition, he went to USAID and tried to convince the USAID Project Officer that I was incompetent and to separate the PAI/TRO into two projects. Terminating his services -- which I wanted to do and would have done -- was not within my authority. Under such circumstances, working with him was a terrific ordeal. He was not a good deputy and certainly not a good or loyal employee. I said so in my End of Tour Report, and he was eventually dismissed after I left the project.
- One of the Consultants sent by the Central Office on TDY turned out to be a real pain in the behind. When I and/or anyone contradicted him – because his ideas were warped, , impractical, unworkable, and/or plain wrong – this guy would "fly of the coup." He would (a) leave the meeting; (b) berate me and the Guatemalan Professionals, telling all of us, "I have worked with the very best, and you people will never make it in this project;" (c) accuse us that "his efforts were not appreciated;" (d) threaten us by saying that he was getting on a plane and never coming back to Guatemala; and, (e) threaten to get on the phone and tell Larry Posner to fire me and others because we were all incompetent. The times he went through those unprofessional temper tantrums, I wanted to help him go to the airport and make him leave. He did call Larry Posner and accuse me of incompetence and probably convinced Larry to hire a Columbian Doctor who was his good friend.

As the reader can see, I had to walk that fine line of independence and the need to accommodate all divergent parties and situations. This took patience, diplomatic skills, ingenuity, and intrepidness. Thanks to my 28 years with

USAID, I had learned to use these many skills. It was in this manner that I was able to manage all these divergent personalities and ideas.

In any event, by the time I left, the project was achieving most objectives throughout Guatemala in an exemplary manner. Doing things as a Team Effort, we were able to do work plans, issue over six Quarterly Progress Reports, Financial Fund Accounting, and Area Visits were done routinely. Very significant advances were made in all priority activities.

Part G. Some Examples and Pictures Taken from The Third (of 6) Progress Reports

As I might have mentioned somewhere, during my time as Director of the Project, I prepared a total of five Progress and an End of Tour Reports. The Progress Reports usually contained over 50 pages, tables, and pictures. They are too long to be briefed for this book. Moreover, the End of Tour Report contains classified evaluations of all my personnel; the information in this report will not be mentioned in this book. What follows is a very brief synopsis of some of the progress made as March 31, 1993. The reports show the following:

G.1 Overall Administrative Matters

- A total of nine short-term consultants had come and participated in Project.
- We were still working with old type of computers, but new ones were on the way.
- Accounting software to account for grants, assets, and liabilities were in progress of improvements.

G.2 For the Expanded Program for Immunization (PAI)

- Our first participation in favor of the vaccination campaign included the distribution of the following refrigerators and cold chain equipment:
    - 335 refrigerators bought by the Ministry of Health were distributed.

  - 2500 Vaccine carriers bought by USAID were sent to desired locations.
  - 10080 of ice packs were distributed to needed locations.
  - 2500 A.I.D. Emblems were attached to the Vaccine Carriers.
  - Numerous amounts of syringes were distributed to all locations.
  - Six solar refrigerators were installed in isolated locations.

- The preparation for the campaign was most intensive. Numerous meetings were held and a total of 6 different actions that were needed for the vaccination campaign were taken.
- From our participations, we included, in the Progress Report, a total of 13 individual lessons that could be learned for future campaign. These lessons show many problem areas – funding, timely cross information, promotional and advertisement plans, lack in the distribution of syringes, etc.

G.3 For the Oral-Rehydration Therapy (ORT)

- This was just beginning, and I don't think we had hired the extremely capable (Dr. Urrutia). Dr. Lucky was doing an excellent job of organizing meetings, etc.
- Meetings were held to determine parameters of participation.
- Consultations were held with USAID, MOH, Maternal and Child Department, etc.
- Plans were started to carry-out training sessions in nine different locations.
- Studies were made to determine equipment needed and cost estimates.
- Meetings were held to learn and plan for promotional materials and approaches.

G.4 For Tasks Supporting Both PAI and ORT

- Diagnostic was completed of the vehicles that USAID had provided. The Progress Report showed that the MOH had a total of 169 units of vehicles bought by USAID.
- These vehicles were in sad shape and all needed to be repaired.
- By March 31, we had contracted with two mechanical organizations and they had repaired 24 vehicles. Some repairs were defective.

- We had also bought a huge number of spare parts needed to repair the vehicles.
- A total of seventeen motorcycles had been transported to repair shops.

G.4 For the Health Management Information Systems (HMIS)

- This part of the program was being implemented by our sub-contractor.
- The specifications for computers, printers, and peripheral equipment and software were developed and approved by USAID and MOH.
- All the equipment and software was now being advertised for procurement.
- Because of USAID Rules of waiting 45 days, required purchases were somewhat delayed.
- Obligatory notifications of Illnesses, stored in Carrion, were being retrieved.
- Plans to remodel the computer centers were now being implemented.
- Contracts to maintain and repair computer equipment were being evaluated.

G.5 For The Improved Administrative and Financial Management (AFM)

- The work required for this part of the program has been explained and was done under G.1 "Overall Administrative Matters and will not be repeated.
- System and procedures to manage grant MOH funds had been completed.
- Various systems and procedures that were needed late on had been identified.
- Reports prepared by this team showed that PAI/TRO funds disbursed to the MOH amounted to over $279,474.
- Four-two day workshops on financial management for health areas were attended, by 178 participants in four different Guatemalan locations.
- Procedures to manage counterpart funds were being systematized.

The distribution of refrigerators and equipment as well as the vaccination campaign were extremely well advertised and well received by the

Guatemalan elite and the people. See the photos in the next three pages from the Third Progress Report:

ANNEX I
PAGE 1 OF 3

Minister of Health and Deputy DGSS Director officiating at the distribution of 335 refrigerators, 2,500 thermoses and 10,038 ice packs to the Health Areas.

Dignitaries from AID and MOH preparing to distribute refrigerators and thermoses to the Health Areas. See Annex H for list of distribution. One transportation company -Transportes Diaz- transported all items to the 24 Health Areas.

ANNEX J
PAGE 1 OF 4

Mrs. Telma de Espina, wife of Vice President of Guatemala opens the Second Immunization Campaign in Boca Del Monte.

Part of the people waiting to have their children vaccinated in Boca Del Monte.

ANNEX I
PAGE 3 OF 3

Technicians in Sta. Rosa have repaired eight refrigerators and at same time trained five people.

Like these four unrepairable refrigerators in Sta. Rosa, others in similar condition should be discharged from MOH inventories.

PART H. MOST PROJECT OBJECTIVES WERE ACHIEVED

This is what I said in my End of Tour Report. Most objectives were achieved during my tour of duty. A Project in financial difficulties was restarted and is now being managed with dignity and in an honest manner. Staffing of the contract went from Zero to nearly 50 people who now serve in different capacities in the contract. All 24 "Field Representatives," or Gestores, are now in place. All components show major accomplishments. Two major studies covering the budget procedures and status of the MOH vehicle fleet have been completed. When USAID equipment is excluded, the Cold Chain System is now operating at 95% capacity. Statistics now show a significant increase in immunization coverage, particularly in El Peten. A National Plan for Control of Diarrheal Disease was approved with our blessing and is being followed. Our employment as an expert in Diarrheal Disease Control was a major coup. Repair of 29 vehicles and 78 motorcycles has taken place. A total of 24 Health Areas now have "Computer Centers," which were structurally modified and furnished with our assistance. The number of forms used in the SIIS, or Management Information System has now been reduced, and members of the MSH Group are teaching the areas on the use of changed forms. Significant advances have been made in the Improved Administrative and Financial Systems Component. In this regard, (a) the cycles and structures of the systems have now been identified and problems determined; (b) a major analysis has been completed of how the Annual Operating Plan Works; (c) Systems and subsystems to be used in various activities —budget execution, preparation of Orden De Compra y Pago (Purchase Orders), Revolving Funds, Private Fondos etc. – have been conceptualized and their design is being coordinated closely with the Health Areas.

My End of Tour Report also included (a) my evaluation of every employee contracted for the PAI/TRO Project; and (b) 12 different recommendations for the efficient use of essential people, problem areas that would confront its implementation, and some of the ways to solve them.

Part I. Activities Completed And Those Requiring Improvements

In an area called the *Expanded Program for Immunization (EPI or PAI)*, I cited a number of actions that were completed -- procurement, storage, arrangement for transportation, and distribution of 335 refrigerators, 2,500 vaccine carriers, 80 cold boxes, installation of three solar energy refrigerators, repair of cold rooms. This "cold chain system" is essential in every country to keep injectable and other medications refrigerated and safe. In other words, we had reestablished the "cold chain system" throughout Guatemala at over 95% efficiency. This degree of cold chain efficiency enabled the vaccination campaign coverage to be increased throughout Guatemala and, in particular, in such isolated areas as El Peten.

In the *Control of Diarrheal Diseases* component, we hired a Pan American Health Organization expert (Dr. Juan Urrutia), retired in Guatemala, who began training medical personnel in new techniques at all levels. In fact, we carried out a great deal of training in all parts of the project. The following shows one of the training sessions. We made many similar training sessions during my time in Guatemala.

The MOH transportation system had serious problems. Most of the MOH fleet of vehicles and motorcycles – which had been donated by USAID -- was in obvious need of repair, and they had been repaired by the time I left. These donated vehicles were supposed to be used, by the Area Chiefs, to support all the activities in their areas.

During the Immunization Campaign, we found that the Vehicles were not being used in its support and other situations which were in need of improvement in subsequent campaigns.

- **This prompted me to write a report – called "Lessons Learned in the Immunization Campaign." Instead of finding the report to be constructive, the USAID Project Officer called me on the carpet and chewed me out for writing it.** Let me explain what happened. At the time that the Campaign was to start, I prepared an informal questionnaire that my observers and I filled out wherever we went during the Campaign. Myself, I was able to observe the Immunization Campaign, which took place at three Guatemalan locations. As a result, my Team and I were able to detect good practices and areas in need of improvement. The bad defects could be improved for future campaigns. So, in my capacity as Project Director, I wrote the report describing the good parts of the Campaign and areas where improvements were needed.
- As we saw the procedures, there was a need to provide adequate transportation of Immunization Items to the campaign sites. For instance, in some areas, we helped take, in our Project Cars, such items to the campaign sites. Why did we have to use our vehicle to transport items needed at the campaign site? Simply put, some of the Area Chiefs were home, and the donated vehicles were parked in front of their homes (our verifications). As a result, my report included the fact that Area Chiefs were not using USAID donated and repaired vehicles to support the Campaign (which was true). Aside from the vehicle problems, there were areas that needed improvements. When I gave my draft to USAID Project Officer for review, she called me over to her office and royally chewed me out. Her position was that the Minister and the Area Chiefs would find the report offensive, and I – through my report – would cause a Diplomatic crisis to take place.

> Although I found the USAID Project Officer's position ridiculous, the report was never issued, and weak areas were never corrected. To this day, I am of the opinion that USAID should have sent my report to the new MOH Minister.

The *Management Information System* was particularly difficult to implement because it was not completely under my control. As mentioned above, this area had been subcontracted to another company (Management of Science for Health Inc.), and the person assigned as my deputy was out to promote himself; the project came out final best. Yet, with the help of the Engineer that I hired, we achieved the most needed actions -- modification of buildings and related structural, electrical systems, procurement, contracting, and distribution of close to 340 units of computer-related equipment (computers, printers, UPS, etc.), and distribution of over 552 units of furniture. In other words, we converted envisioned concepts – of both USAID and the Ministry of Health -- to established reality.

Before we came on board, Guatemala did not have a systematic manner to determine medical baseline information throughout the country. So, we hired an excellent medical doctor (Dr. Victor Lara) to teach and apply "Rapid Assessment" sampling techniques which provided previously unknown baseline information more quickly for the different parts of Guatemala.

In the most complicated area, relating to *Improved Administrative Systems*, all cycles, and many problems of the integrated system were identified and were to be worked on during the second phase of the project. We trained over 5,544 persons in administrative, management information, and medical processes.

PART J. PUBLIC HEALTH ADMINISTRATOR NEEDED IN SECOND PROJECT PHASE

Sadly, although we were achieving all objectives, USAID's plan called, and the Project Officer insisted on the second project phase to be implemented by a Public Health Administrator, i.e., a Medical Doctor. A person with such qualifications was hired in Colombia, and, since I did not have such a degree, my contract was not renewed.

PART KP. CONCLUDING REMARKS

As I said earlier, although most of our objectives were being achieved, and I felt we could have accomplished the Second Phase easily, the USAID plan for the Second Phase of the Project was for it to be directed by Public Health Doctor. I was terribly sad about that decision, so, as required, I left Guatemala in October 1993.

In recognition of my efforts, the going-away party, with Mariachis and dancing, and the dedication of the song "El Rey" (The King) to me will always be remembered. I was also given a number of Diplomas De Honor Al Merito from Guatemalan Departmental Governments and special portraits. Without a doubt, ours were great achievements, and I was extremely sad to leave the project and the Guatemalan people.

Here is one of the awards given to me by the Government of Guatemala. Please note the beautiful Quetzal (top left) which is the symbolic bird of Guatemala.

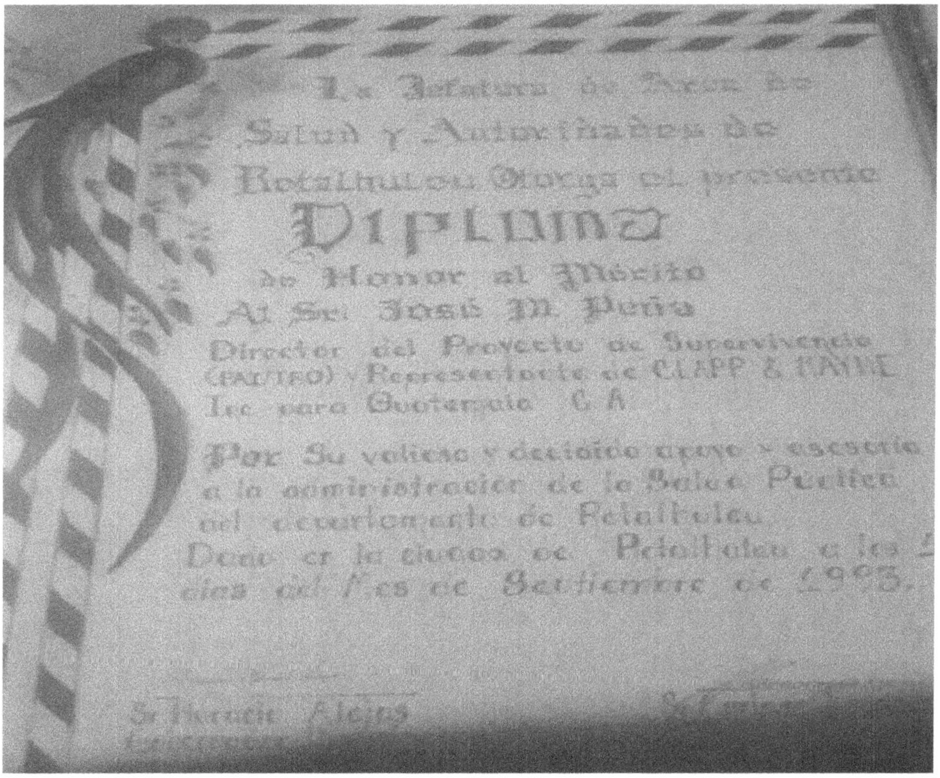

As I write this – nearly 30 years after leaving Guatemala – some of my Guatemalan employees and the Director of Clapp and Mayne Inc. are still my good friends. In other words, I still have good friends in Guatemala and communicate with them regularly. To end this chapter, let me say that this project completed most objectives in an extraordinary manner. We touched the lives of millions of people and improved, in a number of ways, the operations of the Ministry of Health. Let me, therefore, thank all my 50-member team who collaborated with me on this especially important project. I can categorically say that our achievements for our PAI/TAI Project and Oral Rehydration were truly phenomenal and that all of us should feel immensely proud to have done the job you did. I am certain that, through our efforts, we touched the lives of perhaps a million Guatemalans. And, Larry Posner, thanks for your great vision and help. Congratulations to all of you.

CHAPTER TWENTY-TWO
IN THE ORGANIZATION OF AMERICAN STATES, A VERY IMPORTANT INTERNATIONAL ORGANIZATION, AS FINANCIAL CONSULTANT, EXCELLENT PROFESSIONAL ACHIEVEMENTS, WROTE TRUTHFUL BUT HARD-HITTING REPORTS ON OAS, DECLARED PERSONA-NON-GRATA AS A REPRISAL

PART A. INTRODUCTORY COMMENTS

This chapter covers a four-year period (April 1994 to June 30, 1998) in which I worked under the supervision of the Office of the Inspector General of the Organization of American States (OIG/OAS) and I did my work through a series of "Contratos Por Resultado (a form Personal Services Contracts).

I want to make an important clarification on the administrative and operational conditions I found with the Organization of American States (OAS). This clarification is needed because the conditions presented in this part of my book dates back close to 25 years ago; in effect, this was the way this organization operated during the period 1994 to 1998. During this stated period, I made many audits and studies for the OIG/OAS. The individual results of the many reviews are a matter of record in OAS. These reports describe numerous problems found and they also detail recommendations that we (I did work through the IG) made to correct the defects. In drafting this part for my book, however, my review and analysis of most significant audits suggested that my presentation would be more beneficial to OAS – at this delayed stage and as an organization -- if I dissected my conclusions and presented them in the form of a broader perspective as viewed through a lens which emphasize meanings and implications, of all the combined audits, to the organization.

So, I reviewed all major studies that I did during the above period, and this is the big or broader picture that emerged from my analysis. It shows that the organization was in a serious need of improving its operations -- mostly as being conducted in the Administrative and Operational parts of the General Secretariat. In fact, the problems reflected that operations at this level were not being conducted in the most efficient, economical, effective, or even accurate manner. Here are brief examples that I will discuss in this book:

- Manpower (workforce) ceilings as set by the General Assembly needs re-examination and change.
- Some problems – like organizational locations of certain offices, especially the OIG/OAS, and Departments of Financial Services, Treasury, and Budgets -- represented conflict of interests and/or weaknesses of Internal and managerial controls to the organization
- Some employment modalities -- related to "Shadow Employees --" were illegal and the 19 modalities were too many and difficult to manage.
- A planned reorganization contemplated the eliminations of key positions, tasks, and functions, and others; these plans were a great danger to OAS and exposed the organization to potential errors, fraud and abuse. They also highlight serious Conflict of Interest Cases.
- Some controls over field projects – like financial unliquidated obligations and others – reflect a radical needed of improvement in managerial controls, procedures, and tasks at the central and field levels.
- Operational handbooks had not been modified for an excessive (17 years) time. To be useful, as operational instructions, these need to be current all the time.
- The parameters of authorities of at least one Assistant Secretaries needed to be curtailed and more clearly defined.

I hope that -- in the past 25 years since we made the individual Audit Reports -- OAS was able to implement the many detailed recommendations. Their implementation would go a long way in improving its operations In any event, the objectives in this book are to look at the composite broader picture that all our reports attempted to convey. In other words, since the individual audit reports, made at the time, contained the detailed picture of procedures in need of improvement, this book views the problems from a broader perspective – especially as to the way that some of the Offices of the General Secretariat were operating. Here is one other clarification: **my discussion related to the General Assembly is only limited to the way it was setting the Manpower Levels. Our studies did not go beyond this point or as to the highly important international political work of the General Assembly.**

IN SUM, *THIS BOOK EMPHASIZES THE BROAD PERSPECIVE OF THE EXISTING ORGANIZATIONAL PROBLEMS – MOSTLY AT THE GENERAL SECRETARIAT LEVEL -- IN THE YEARS 1994 TO 1998. SINCE THERE IS A NEED FOR A BROADER ATTENTION AND THERE MIGHT BE A POSSIBILTY THAT SOME PROBLEMS STILL REQUIRE CORRECTIONS, I WILL PROVIDE A COPY OF THIS BOOK TO THE CURRENT CHAIRMAN OF THE PERMANENT COUNCIL, THE GENERAL SECRETARY, AND THE U.S. AMBASSADOR TO OAS.*

Because of its complexity, this Chapter is divided into 16 Parts. Parts A through E discuss some necessary background information. Parts F through Part O discuss the broad problems affecting the organization. Part Q represent our concluding remarks which in effect are memories of the past – a broad perspective summary of the composite problems revealed by our review of all reports – and Our Visions for the Future and the broad recommendations which need to be implemented to get there. The listing of the 16 Parts follow: :

- Part A. Introductory Comments.
- Part B. Background and Organizational Charts of OAS.
- Part C. How I Came to Work for OAS.
- Part D. A New Inspector General Assumes Position.
- Part E. Composition of OAS/OIG Staff Members.
- Part F. Organizational Location of OIG/OAS.
- Part G. Audits, Studies, and Reports That I Did.

- Part H. Responsible Office for Implementing Project's Recommendations.
- Part I.. This Part Shows a Summary of the Most Important and/or Organizational-Wide Affecting Findings of Our Review. Details, Analysis, and Examples are Shown on Parts J to Part O.
- Part J. The Way the General Assembly was setting Manpower Ceilings Should be Re-examined. This Defect Filtered, Cascaded, and Created A Series of Problems to Most Parts of the General Secretariat (organizational) operations.
- Part K. OAS had 19 Different Contractual Modalities; They Were Too Many, and Some Were Illegal.
- Part L. OAS's Assets Were Erroneously Accounted For; Assets Valuations Were Under, Over, Inaccurate, and Some Were Omitted; Problems Greatly Distorted the Statement of Financial Condition of the Entire Organization and Their Certifications
- Part M. Plans by the Assistant Secretary for Management to Reorganize his Six Departments Were Most Defective; They Contemplated the Elimination of Key Positions, functions, and Were Extremely Risky to OAS.
- Part N. There is Conflict of Interests for the Departments of Financial Services, Budget, and Treasury to be under and report to the Assistant Secretary of Management.
- Part O. Parameters of Authorities of Assistant Secretaries Need To Be Constricted and Clearly Defined. For Expressing My Professional Opinions, in OIG/OAS. Audit Reports, I Was Declared a "Persona-Non-Grata" and Was Never Again Allowed to Work or Enter OAS Buildings.
- Part P.. My Concluding Remarks --- Memories of the Past with Visions and recommendations to OAS for the Future.

PART B. BACKGROUND AND ORGANIZATIONAL CHARTS OF OAS

As an Organization, OAS is made up by 34 Inter-American countries and dates to the First American International Conference conducted in Washington D. C. in 1890. Operating since 1948, the Charter of the Organization prescribes that OAS has the following seven objectives: (a) to strengthen peace and security of the continent; (b) to promote and consolidate representative democracy respecting principles of nonintervention; (c) to prevent possible causes of difficulties and ensure peaceful settlement of disputes; (d) to provide for common action in case of aggression; (e) to seek solution to political, judicial, and economic problems that could arise; (f) to promote, by cooperative actions, economic, social, and cultural development; and, (g) to achieve limitations of conventional weapons so as to devote larger amount of resources to economic and social development. In sum, OAS is an extremely important international organization.

We made our reviews at a time when the OAS Organizational Chart appeared like the one appearing on Telephone Book, dated October 1997. We are also including --for information purposes only -- the OAS Organizational Chart as it currently appears on the Internet. This chart does not include the organizational structure of the General Secretariat (administrative and operational side of OAS). As can be seen from the charts, (see next three pages), OAS is divided into two or three distinct but integrated parts: the General Assembly, its Permanent Council, and the General Secretariat. Because the General Assembly meets only once a year, the two distinct organization are intertwined by a Permanent Council. Briefly, the functions of the three cojoined parts of the organization were as follows:

- ***The OAS General Assembly*** – *The General Assembly is composed of high-level diplomats (Ambassadors, Ministers, Chief of Countries) from thirty-four different Latin America and Caribbean countries. It has many Commissions, Committees, Counsels, and Special Organizations – The General Assembly meets once a year and discusses, debates, and negotiates inter-country developments, future events, plans issues, and problems. One of the most important aspects* *of this part is to name the General Secretary, who serves as the Principal Head of the entire administrative and operational side of the institution. In addition, the General Assembly establishes budgets, important rules, regulations, operational policies, and staffing levels. The scope of our audit did not include the political side of the General Assembly. However, at the time of my audit, I found problems with the way staffing levels were determined and set. Career Manpower requirements to carry out the projects, operations, and administrative functions, in such a complex organization were not realistic and this broad problem cascaded down to most levels of the General Secretariat part of the organization. A comprehensive manpower study was urgently needed to guide the General Assembly in setting realistic and stable levels of personnel levels for the General Secretariat side of the operations*

- *The* ***Permanent Council is*** *a very important part of the organization. It is made up of Ambassadors of each country; it is always in place in case of emergencies or consultations.*
- *Once the OAS General Assembly elects, names, and appoints the General Secretary. He, in turn, names a cabinet and implements the Mandates of the General Assembly through his named Assistant Secretaries, Executive Offices, direct lines of reporting, Assistants Secretaries for Management, Human Resources, and many others.*
- *The Assistant Secretaries and many employees in many offices implement the instructions through a series of Directors (of Offices and Departments) who operate through the actual staff members and employees. At the time I was under an OAS Contract, the Operational Staff consisted of both career staff employees,* ***and personnel*** *contracted through – over nineteen contractual modalities.* ***As shown by the charts, the lines of reporting and the many structural organizational exigencies makes it a very complex administrative and operational entity.***

ORGANIZATION OF AMERICAN STATES

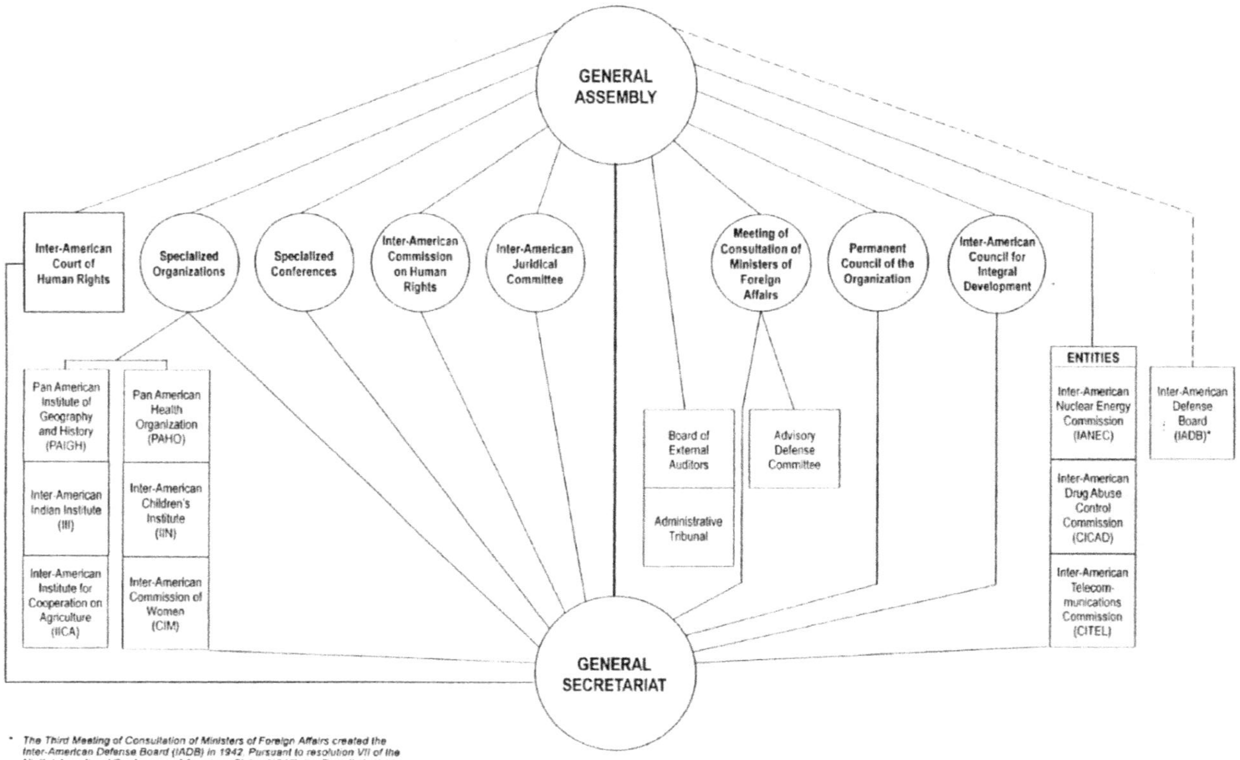

* *The Third Meeting of Consultation of Ministers of Foreign Affairs created the Inter-American Defense Board (IADB) in 1942. Pursuant to resolution VII of the Ninth International Conference of American States (1948), the Board's budget is included in the Organization's budget*

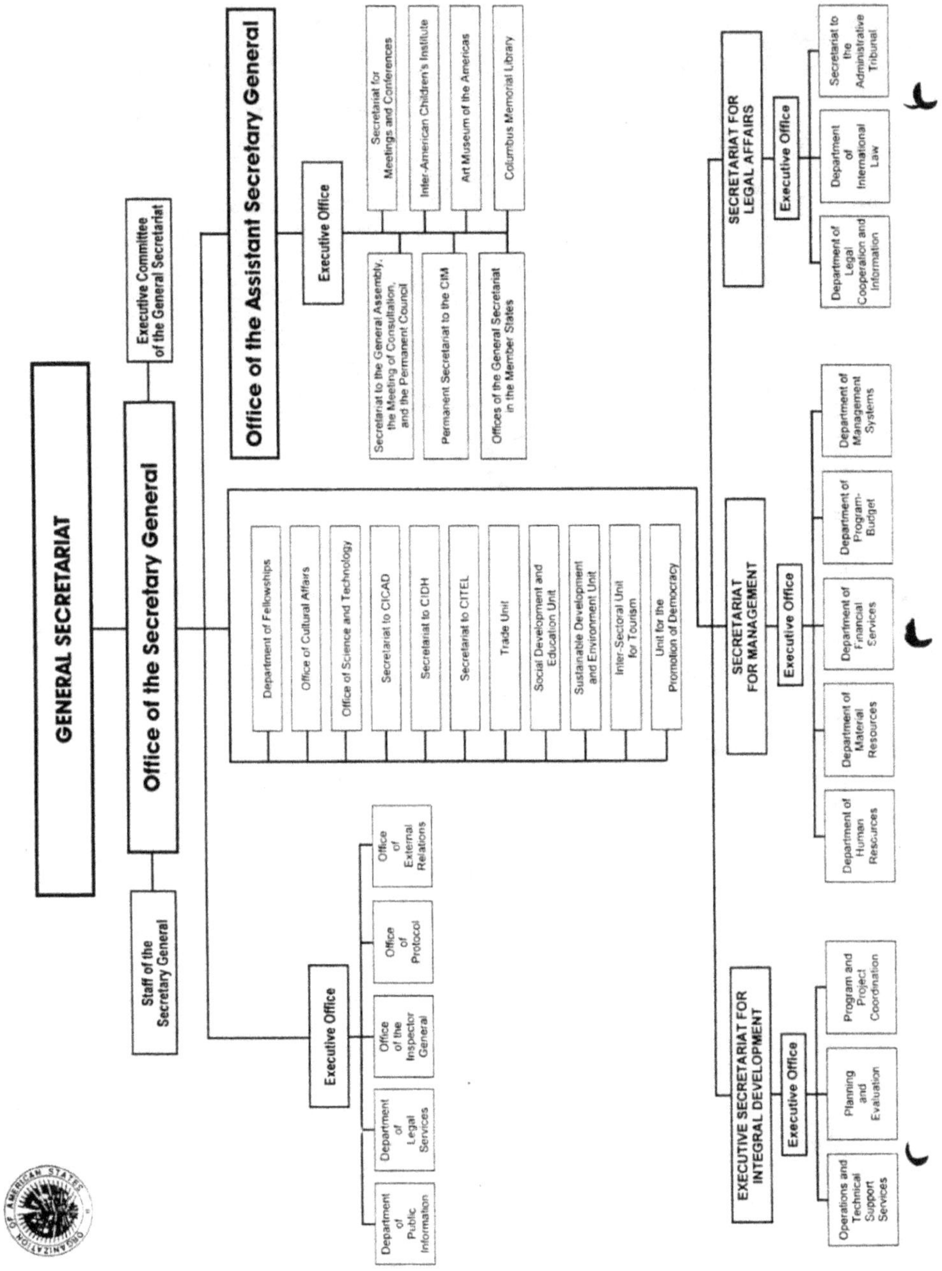
GENERAL SECRETARIAT
Staff of the Secretary General
Office of the Secretary General
Executive Committee of the General Secretariat
Office of the Assistant Secretary General
Executive Office
Secretariat to the General Assembly, the Meeting of Consultation, and the Permanent Council
Secretariat for Meetings and Conferences
Inter-American Children's Institute
Permanent Secretariat to the CIM
Art Museum of the Americas
Offices of the General Secretariat in the Member States
Columbus Memorial Library
Department of Fellowships
Office of Cultural Affairs
Office of Science and Technology
Secretariat to CICAD
Secretariat to CIDH
Secretariat to CITEL
Trade Unit
Social Development and Education Unit
Sustainable Development and Environment Unit
Inter-Sectoral Unit for Tourism
Unit for the Promotion of Democracy
Executive Office
Department of Public Information
Department of Legal Services
Office of the Inspector General
Office of Protocol
Office of External Relations
SECRETARIAT FOR LEGAL AFFAIRS
Executive Office
Department of Legal Cooperation and Information
Department of International Law
Secretariat to the Administrative Tribunal
SECRETARIAT FOR MANAGEMENT
Executive Office
Department of Human Resources
Department of Material Resources
Department of Financial Services
Department of Program-Budget
Department of Management Systems
EXECUTIVE SECRETARIAT FOR INTEGRAL DEVELOPMENT
Executive Office
Operations and Technical Support Services
Planning and Evaluation
Program and Project Coordination
ORGANIZATION OF AMERICAN STATES

ORGANIZATION OF AMERICAN STATES (OAS) NEW ORGANIZATIONAL CHART AS SHOWN IN INTERNET ON SEPTEMBER 1, 2022

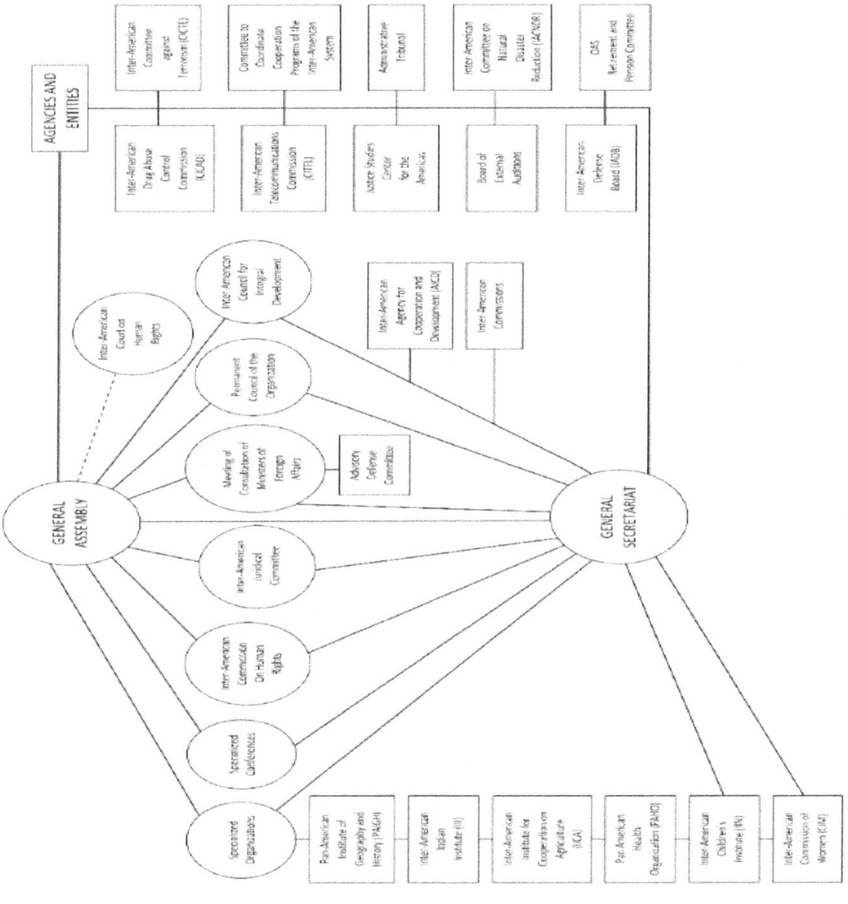

This Chart represents only the structure of the General Assembly. It does not include the structure and offices belonging to the Office of the General Secretariat – which does the supportive administrative and operational functions for the General Assembly.

PART C. HOW I CAME TO WORK FOR OAS

Professionally known as having been a trained auditor for 28 years with the U.S. Agency for International Development (USAID) and a Director for Health Project, and as mentioned in the Part A, I was contracted, during the period of 1994 and 1998, by the OAS Office of the Inspector General (hereafter also referred to as OAS/OIG) as an International Financial and Management Consultant. I did many audits and special studies during this time. This assignment came about because of my continued friendship with Mr. Alfonso Caycedo who recently passed on (May he RIP). He was my friend for many years and so, I will also referred to him as Alfonso or Mr. Caycedo" He was an exceptional person and friend. By way of information, Alfonso and fourteen other Audit Professionals had worked under my supervision during the time I was a USAID Chief Auditor in Colombia. In other words, we were friends for over 50 years, i.e., since the 1970's (see Chapter 8 of this book).

During the time we were in Colombia, I knew all my staff and their capabilities very well (and vice versa). So, I knew that Alfonso was an extremely adaptive learner, especially in of our type of work; he demonstrated extreme intelligence; and clearly showed all traits of a leader. His qualities could be described as: extremely intelligent, experienced, imaginative, analytical, decisive, and very personable. So, after my transfer to Panama, we stayed connected with each other. A bright young man, Alfonso immigrated to the U.S. and very quickly came to live in the Washington D.C. area and began working in OAS. When I was still working with USAID, Alfonso, his wife (Christel), and their now grown children (Pilar Nealis Caycedo and Juan Carlos Caycedo) and my family would meet and have parties and/or barbeques at his or my own home.

The years went by, and we continued our friendship. By the time I completed my work as Director of the PAI/TO Project in Guatemala in 1993, Alfonso had been the Acting Inspector General for OAS -- on and off – many times. By April 1994, he had been Acting Inspector General for a few months. When he found out I had returned from my tour in Guatemala, he called me and asked me to work in his office. I delayed at the time because I wanted to rest and wanted to do certain things around the houses in Virginia and our house in Austin, Texas. So, as soon as I completed my chores, I contacted him. Our business meeting took place in April 1994. I started work very soon after that. Alfonso worked as Acting Inspector General – and managed the people and office extremely well -- until his early retirement in early 1995. Let me say that I really enjoyed working with Alfonso during the time we were there. Since his retirement, we continued to be best friends and call each other frequently.

PART D. A NEW INSPECTOR GENERAL ASSUMES POSITION

When Mr. Caycedo decided to take "early retirement," Dr. Guillermo Belt (hereafter also referred to as either Dr. Belt or Guillermo) was assigned as Acting Inspector General – but reporting directly to the General Secretary. At the time of his appointment, Dr. Belt had worked with OAS in extremely high-level positions for over 35 years. He was a perfect fit to be the Inspector General (I.G.). Let me say that the 3-year period that I collaborated with him were fabulous. My assessment of him was/is that he is a most impressive and gifted person. A consummate diplomat, he is an exceptional bi-lingual speaker and writer. A most analytical person, his questioning was always incisive and perceptive. He is a very adaptive (quick) learner and quickly gets to the main points of the discussion. He has the Courage of His Conviction, and his decisions are always very precise and practical. He absolutely has fabulous intelligence and is an excellent manager of people and the I.G. office. His preparation for upcoming meetings is very thorough, and his conduct is very controlled, incisive, and comprehensive. His review and supervision during my field work and drafting of reports were very constructive and, they were sincerely appreciated. I thoroughly enjoyed working with him (and Alfonso). I certainly learned a lot from both. After completing 37 years with the Organization, Guillermo retired in June 1998.

PART E. COMPOSITION OF OAS/OIG STAFF MEMBERS

Despite its importance, the OAS Office of Inspector General (OAS/OIG) was small. It was made up of the following members: (a) Mr. Alfonso Caycedo, I.G. until the beginning of 1995; (b) Dr. Guillermo Belt I.G. until about June 1998; (c) Linda R., (d) Senior Auditor Ofilio P. B. (e) Auditor John S.; (f) Independent Consultant Jose M. Pena; (g) Junior Auditor Ivette A. (who came after I left); and, (h) the Secretary Gloria S. Except for me, all other staff members were Career OAS Employees.

Soon after I was contracted, it came to my attention that the OAS audit staff had not received any type of training since joining the OAS. As a result, I contacted the USAID Executive Officer at the time (Mr. John Popovich???) and asked him to invite us to the next USAID Training Program for the I.G. staff. It was a two-week course. All of us attended, and we all learned and enjoyed the short course very much. Note: **The GAO Office, several USAID Office of Inspector General, and the CIGIE have diverse types of training. Therefore, I would suggest that the OAS Inspector General should occasionally contact the USAID IG, CIGIE, and GAO, and get an invitation – for his/her audit personnel -- to attend planned training courses.**

PART F. ORGANIZATIONAL LOCATION OF OAS OFFICE OF INSPECTOR GENERAL

As previously stated, the Office of Inspector General and the two IG's reported directly to the General Secretary. In my mind, I always had three questions that relate to the politics that prevail in OAS (as an organization): (a) given the importance of this Office, why wasn't the OIG located at an organizational level where it reports directly to the Permanent Council; (b) given their expertise and qualifications, why were Dr. Belt (and Alfonso) appointed as only "Acting Inspector Generals;" and, (c) why weren't they appointed as a true "Inspector General???" The answers (b and c) are probably that both Alfonso and Guillermo were "career employees" and not

"Confidential Appointees." There follows some of my thoughts and opinions regarding to relocating the OIG to the most proper location.

In any event, here is my own rationale for asking the above questions on (b) and (c). After Guillermo retired, the General Secretary appointed a person who was nowhere close to being in the category of either Guillermo or Alfonso. I base my opinion on firsthand experience with the person because I once was asked to do (and did) a special "auditor to auditor review" of an audit made and the draft report written by this person. The audit techniques, coverage, and draft of the report left a great deal to be desired of an I.G.. Yet, this person was appointed to the coveted and prestigious position of a true "Inspector General."

To me, the process of this and other appointments, which I witnessed during my work, speaks volumes about the criteria used by OAS to make its appointment decisions. As I see it, nominations and decisions relating to Personnel appointments to high-level positions are based mostly on Political Consideration, involving the desire of the 34 OAS member countries and not necessarily on the exact qualifications and/or merits of the possible candidates.

In sum, here are my thoughts on the qualifications that OAS should require of an I.G. Candidate. In the case of the Office of Inspector General, its importance does not seem to be fully grasped at its present organizational location. This Office and the I.G. are in a position where at times, members of his office and himself will find facts and situations (like we found during my audits or, they could be in the future, potential frauds, embezzlements, etc.) that affect the organization in a broad or a need for specially handled manner. These types of observations, legal, or "delicate" matters – must, by their content or necessity, be reported and handled by the Permanent Council for disposition or next course of action. In such a case, the I.G. (and his staff) should be able to present those facts and not be subject to reprisals and persecutions of his people. As I will explain later in this chapter, I was the victim of such reprisal for expressing facts and Professional Opinions on legitimate defects which affected OAS as an organization.

- **Here is my opinion and recommendation. The selection and appointments, for an I.G. position, should be based mostly on**

professional qualifications, experience, the courage of conviction, and potential contribution to the Organization by the best and technically strong candidate. The I.G. should be able to serve a fixed term – say a maximum of seven to ten years – and not be subjected to being replaced every time a new General Secretary is appointed every 5 years. Moreover, the Organizational Position should be changed so that the OAS/OIG reports directly to the Permanent Council as representative of the OAS General Assembly. In other words, the selection, term, and higher position level of the OAS/OIG position will give him and his office the necessary stature, independence of mind, analysis, ability to express hard or difficult opinions, and the force of recommendations. He (and members of his office) should have immunity and relief from Political Pressures, reprisals and/or retributions that members or contracted personnel of a true Office of Inspector General must have. I will make a recommendation later.

PART G. AUDITS, STUDIES, AND REPORTS THAT I DID

Although I did many other reviews, the following table shows Major Audits and Reports – made by me, under contracts with the OAS Inspector General -- covering assessments, audits, reviews, and/or evaluations of systems, procedures, and Projects. The table includes the review, the number of pages in the report, the number of weak areas (issues or problems) found, and the number of Recommendations we made. These do not include other types of studies made by me and/or the many other audits and studies made by the Inspector General and/or his career employee.

System, Procedure, and/or Project	Pages	Problems	Recomendations
System on Flow of Funds and Payment Procedures	48	8	23
Management of Non-Expendable Properties and warehouse (includes Pictures, and Charts)	54	6	27
Assessment of the International Civilian Mission In Haiti Jointly by OAS and United Nation	71	8	26
Systems Used in Contractual and Employment			

Mechanisms by OAS	36	Too many	5
Second System Review of Flow of funds and Payment Procedures(incl. Graphs/Charts)	56	6	23
Assessment of Modernization Plans and Procedures On the Cycle of Funds	18	Suggestions	1
Covers Revised Policy and Costs of Official Headquarters Travel (a staff member helped me)	33	3 Broad Sec.	13
Covers the Trade Unit and Foreign Trade Information System (SICE) (incl. Pictures, Charts)	58	5	13
Covers the Assistance Program For "Demining" (Elimination of mines) in Central America Implemented by Promotion of Democracy Unit	48	8	9
Totals	422	44	140

As noted above, the above studies covered major systems, procedures, and projects which, for all intents and purposes, represented the "across-the-board" way the OAS General Secretariat normally operated. The above table shows that the reports: (a) gave Information and explained problems in 422 pages; (b) included discussion of 44 (and many more) problem areas; and (c) included 140 different recommendations and many suggestions.

PART H. RESPONSIBLE OFFICE FOR IMPLEMENTING PROJECT'S RECOMMENDATIONS

Because of the complicated way the Organization works, I made a separate analysis to determine who had responsibility for implementing the different recommendations. Here is a very brief synopsis of what we found in the above audits. Two projects were, in general terms, going very well. One project was on a borderline where serious problems were found, and its continuance was not guaranteed. At the other side, we found extremely serious problems – in the operations of the way the Office of the Assistant Secretary for Management (also called Management Officer or Management Office) operated; some problems (described below like the defective reports of the Statement of Financial Condition, recording of assets, and setting of ceilings) showed that they affected OAS as an organization in a serious manner. Here are our briefs of our four observations.

H.1 The Trade Programs Being Implemented By The Trade Unit And SICE Were Very Impressive

As stated in the above heading, this program was doing very well. Nevertheless, we did find certain areas where improvements were indicated. Therefore, we included 9 (of 13) recommendations that needed to be implemented by the Trade Unit and the Foreign Trade Information System (SICE). In the present case, there were a series of unique types of issues and problems that needed correction, and/or program improvements. For instance, the Secretary General needed to appoint a permanent SICE Unit Coordinator and take other actions which were needed by the Program. The Special Advisor for Trade and SICE needed to change some designs to the computer systems and others.

H.2 The Demining Program Was Achieving Its Objectives In An Excellent Manner

The Executive Coordinator for The Unit for the Promotion of Democracy was also assigned the implementation of 6 (of 9) recommendations for "**The Assistance Program for Demining (elimination of Land Mines) in Central America (PADCA).**" ***I visited the project, walked close to the mines, talked to officials and soldiers, and saw an actual demonstration where a mine was blown. On this basis, let me say that from a programmatic point of view, the achievements of the Demining Program had been excellent, considering the Life-Threatening Degree of difficulty which these tasks entail.*** The individua report contained many demonstrative pictures of the program. Nevertheless, my review showed several problems: (a) a need for refocusing the project to one of an "integrated and Multi-Disciplinarian Approach;" (b) one major problem was that one country (Costa Rica) was not making available the financial resources to the Project. For instance, it was not providing the required 3 emergency helicopters. Moreover, it was not providing the required accommodating housing and food for mine detecting dogs.. In addition, we found that the vehicles and furniture assigned to the Project were old and needed to be replaced. There were some other minor problems (Here is a photo of a field visit to Central American Projects:

AUTHOR AND HONDURAS PROGRAM DIRECTOR (NOT SHOWN) DOING A FIELD VISIT TO OAS'S LAND MINE ELIMINATION PROJECT IN THE MOUNTAINS OF HONDURAS. TO DEMONSTRATE THE PROJECT ACTIVITY, I WAS SHOWN AND CAN STILL HEAR THE CALL "FIRE IN THE HOLE" AND SEE ONE REAL LAND MINE EXPLODING. THIS IS AN EXCELLENT PROJECT. I INCLUDED IN THE OIG REPORT PICTURE OF PEOPLE MUTILATED BY LAND MINES. I HOPE LAND MINES ARE ELIMINATED WORLDWIDE.

H.3 The International Civilian Mission In Haiti (MICIVIH) Was Costly And Was In Danger Of Being Discontinued

The Executive Coordinator for The Unit for the Promotion of Democracy (UPD) had a responsibility to implement 25 different recommendations. At the time of our review, the UPD was under the direct responsibility of the General Secretary and was implementing **"the International Civilian Mission in Haiti (MICIVIH)"** that was being financed by both OAS and the United Nations. We found that the Project had very complicated problems which affected the financial and other resources of OAS. Here are some of the reasons. First, there was the possibility that the United Nations would no longer continue to provide financial contributions to the project. And second, OAS needed to re-design the Projects in different manners. For instance, OAS needed (i) to determine the effects of the earthquake that the country had experienced in that year; (ii) to reconfigure the Project in size and operational modalities; (iii) to reduce the excessive grading costs of the observers; and (iv) to develop work plans for the newly reconfigured Project. **Given all the problems this project had, I have no information on whether the Project still exists and/or if it has been changed or eliminated.**

H.4 Operations Of The Assistant Secretary For Management Had Serious Problems And Got Most Recommendations

Most – 79 (of the 140) recommendations -- were assigned to the Assistant Secretary for Management. This office is responsible for the operations of six important departments: (a) Human Resources; (b) Material Resources; (c) Financial Services; (d) Program Budgets; (e) Treasury; and (f) Management Information Systems. Our review showed extremely serious types of problems in all six departments. Our individual reports explained the reasons for the problems, and the degrees of responsibility to implement the recommendations. However, the findings in this office were highly representative of problems which were affecting the organization -– of the General Secretariat -- as a whole. For this reason, we outlined and will discuss them as shown in the following Part I.

Part I. This Part Shows a Summary of the Most Important and/or Organizational-Wide Affecting Findings of Our Reviews. Details, Analysis and Examples Follow in Parts I to Part O.

My book will analyze the reports -- where 79 (of 140) recommendations were assigned to the Secretary of the Assistant Secretary for Management -- in the following separate Parts because – the problems found in this office have major impacts or have their roots in reflecting the broader way that the administrative and operations was functioning. In other words, there was a lack of efficiency and economical way OAS and/or the General Secretariat, was operating at the time of our

audit. Briefly, the rest of our findings are shown in the 6 Parts (J, K, L, M, N, and O) stated in the beginning part of this chapter. We begin with Part J which follows.

PART J. THE WAY THE GENERAL ASSEMBLY WAS SETTING MANPOWER CEILINGS SHOULD BE RE-EXAMINED; THIS DEFECT FILTERED, CASCADED, AND CREATED A SERIES OF PROBLEMS TO MOST PARTS OF THE GENERAL SECRETARIAT'S OPERATIONS

The Way That OAS General Assembly Was Setting Personnel Ceilings was Faulty and Represented the Most Important OAS Problem. As noted in Part B of this Chapter, one of the functions of the OAS General Assembly is to establish the Personnel Ceilings Mandates for each year.

Our study showed that the most significant problem -- which affected the whole Organization -- was the way that the General Assembly was establishing or setting the required Personnel manpower requirement ceilings. In effect, the General Assembly was setting Personnel manpower (workforce) requirements based on an arbitrary mandated manner. It was setting the manpower ceiling in different ways. For instance, it sometimes sets them as a percentage of the budget and/or sometimes as a number of Personnel ceilings. For instance, between 1991 and 1994, the ceiling levels were set at a total of 725 Personnel. For some unknown reason, these ceilings were reduced to 595 in 1995 and "…in the most current year (maybe 1996), reduced ceilings to 470 positions and in another (maybe 1997) set the limit at 50% of the total budget for Regular and Voluntary Funds for personnel costs in both Object 1 (Personnel) and Object 2 (Fixed Term Personnel) …." These ceilings applied to categories, levels, and operational functions required by the Organization.

In other words, the Personnel ceilings (numbers, categories, and levels of employees) did not reflect the most realistic levels of Personnel that were really needed to efficiently operate the many aspects – such as Mandates, Projects, administration, operations, committees, exigencies and needs – required by the 34-member entity the General Assembly.

Therefore, we see that the General Secretariat is (and needs to be) a large and complicated Organization. In other words, as shown by the Organizational Charts, the General Secretariat must fulfill the mandates of thirty-four member countries and many committees. Our examination also showed that this problem affected the Organization, in several ways and manners. In effect, there were numerous coexisting adversely effects related between the ceiling levels set by the General Assembly and the numerous problems that affected the operational side of the Organization. I will only cite a few examples to show how:

1. **The Organization had an excessive number (19) of different employments and contracting modalities. Why? This was because once the General Assembly set the Personnel Ceilings Mandates – and if these ceilings were not realistic of the actual workforce needed by the operational offices (of the General Secretariat) – the operational offices tried to reach two "goals" or ways which (a) they complied with the General Assembly mandated ceilings; and (b) at the same time, they met the operational needs to do the two demands efficiently. This is how the cyclical yearly ceiling and growth of projects, activities, and situations created the progressive accumulations – and upward spiral of contractual modalities. At the time of our audits, the growth had reached the point where the nineteen contracting modalities existed. In sum, the accumulation of nineteen different employment and contracting modalities were caused by the unpredictable and unrealistic manners that General Assembly set the Personnel ceilings. Viewed in another way: workforce ceilings must equal the realistic needs of the operational offices to implement the complicated programs that the 34-member members of the General Assembly might prescribe. The problems created by this situation is better seen through various "Profiles."**

2. **Here is the first Profile on how the operational offices tried to comply with both "goals." To comply with mandated ceilings, the Management Officer was planning to reorganize his departments (Department of Financial Services or DFS is a good example) by arbitrarily eliminating essential functions, tasks, procedures, and**

positions. It was then planning to transfer General Services People to take over accounting positions and perform accounting functions; we were told that some people were not professional or trained accountants. In sum, his plans were haphazard, very defective, violated internal controls, and extremely dangerous for the organization.

3. Here is the next Profile. Certain key positions (like the Chief Accountant and 8 Accountants) -- which are needed in DFS to conduct important accounting duties and functions -- had been lost through retirements, resignations, or perhaps terminations. These plans were not going to replace them and were to be eliminated. In his effort to comply with the General Assembly mandated personnel ceilings, the Management Office was erroneously planning to abolish accounting positions which became vacant. Why? Once again, this was because the ceiling levels, and reorganization plans were wrong. The position of the Chief Accountant – who is equivalent to a Director of Finance (or Controller) in other organizations – was abolished; to us, this is a huge mistake; it is an example of a Conflict-of-Interest Situation – which we explain later. In fact, this elimination represented a very dangerous course of action which should not be taken. This elimination of positions and required jobs represent serious adverse effects on the work needed to manage the General Secretariat in a safe and efficient manner.

4. Here is yet another Profile where actions taken or to be taken have an adverse impact on OAS as an organization. The Department of Financial Services (DFS) was once again a good example of the effects caused by the cascading effects. The DFS was not fulfilling especially important functions – like reviewing travel vouchers, keeping track of project costs, of un-liquidated obligations, of travel advances, preparation of financial reports and statements of financial conditions, and others. Why? This was because it did not have the needed qualified personnel to do the jobs. In short, there were very serious gaps in the most essential functions of the DFS because of the way the Personnel ceiling levels were set by the

General Assembly and the way the Management Officer tried to resolve the perennial problems.

5. **The harsh realities for OAS were that Personnel needed in the Key Offices of the Accounting and Treasury was being reduced and in some cases decimated. Essential tasks, functions, processes, and procedures of the office were eliminated, thereby exposing OAS to potential financial embezzlements, frauds, and abuse. DFS represents an especially important department of OAS and merits consideration as a high-level department.**

6. **One question which keeps popping in my mind is why should the 8 key jobs be eliminated or not filled, when the Household Personnel of a High Official could be switched in contractual modalities? Here is a Good Example of How some needed positions could have been switched around and still comply with the OAS General Assembly Personnel Ceilings Mandate**. As explained above, the General Assembly practice -- of setting ceilings in an arbitrary manner -- adversely affects needed positions of career employees in many parts of the operational side of the Organization. In the case of this example, it affects the DFS Personnel within the Office of the Assistant Secretary for Management. For instance, as shown earlier, the Assistant Secretary for Management would not permit the DFS and Treasury Offices to fill 6 to 8 personnel and/or positions. These two offices had lost several positions due to the arbitrary setting of ceiling limitations or retirements. As a result, these two offices could not fulfill the very important functions needed by OAS.

- Yet, the case of an exceedingly high Organizational Official describes the solution to the adverse effect very clearly. As we understand it, several households needed for this high officer – like the Chauffer, house cleaners, etc. –were **established as career employees**. These employees contributed to the especially important comforts and well-being of the high official and his family. However, their "career employee status" reduced 5 to 8 operational career positions without really benefiting the actual operations of the organization. The rationale for this practice was to give them the same benefits that career types of employees normally receive.

- **To us, the solution in such cases as the above is clear. This type of category of Personnel could be better employed under a Borrowed Servant Contract (described later and, as we understand it, used in Argentina and Bolivia), where they get all salaries and benefits, they deserve. All these 8 career positions could then be transferred to the DFS and Treasury, where they are urgently needed. This way, DFS, and Treasury will render an actual benefit to OAS as an Organization. In implementing its reorganization plan, the Management Officer had not apparently considered this possible alternative.**

There was another conflict of interests in the way the Management Office was structured and violations of internal controls. For instance, placing the DFS as part of the Management Officer represents a very real conflict of interest.

In sum, procedures on the way that the General Assembly was setting the ceilings for the Operational Side (the General Secretariat Side) of the Organization was seriously flawed. As **a result of this major problem, the then Secretary for Management (of the General Secretariat) tried to find different contractual modalities to compensate for Personnel shortages and limits set by the General Assembly. This was one (of 3) the most significant problems and resulted in our finding defects in many areas we reviewed. Because of its importance, we made the requirement for a Manpower Study as Recommendation Number 1 in the issued report.** Here was the solution:

What the General Assembly – and the Operational side of the Organization under the Secretary General -- urgently needed was an Organizational-Wide Manpower and Organizational Structure Study. These studies would help everyone set Personnel workforce requirements in a more realistic manner. It would also re-structure the present organizations and improve operational efficiency.

PART K. OAS HAD 19 DIFFERENT CONTRACTUAL MODALITIES; THEY WERE TOO MANY AND SOME ARE ILLEGAL

OAS Had an Excessive Number of Contractual Mechanism Modalities. Because of the arbitrary way Personnel ceilings were set by the General Assembly, we were told during our audit that -- over an 18-year period -- the operations side of OAS had created a "yearly cyclical monster" that resulted in an ever-increasing number (19 at that time) of Employment and/or Contracting Mechanisms which were designed to employ or contract Personnel that was needed to fulfill the various functions prescribed or mandated by the General Assembly.

- Here is a partial list of the mechanisms: (1) Career Employees; (2) Career Trust Personnel; (3) Non-Career Trust Personnel; (4) Associate Staff Members; (5) Long Term Contract Personnel; (6) Short Term Contract Personnel; (7) Special Observers Contracts; (8) Contratos Por Resultado (Contracts Equaling Results or CPR's); (9) Miscellaneously Hired Contractors; (10) Borrowed Servant Concepts; (11) Other Informal Contracts; (12) Conference Contracts; (13) Borrower/Grantee Contracts; (14) a number of others.

In the case of the Contratos Por Resultado (CPRs), these border(ed) on unfair labor practices -- and based on Court Decision, most likely, were illegal practices -- because these were, in effect, "Shadow Staff Type of Employees." Their work is identical to those of career employees. However, unlike the career employees, the "Shadow Staff Contractors" did not receive any of the corresponding benefits (annual and sick leave, tax payments, Social Security Contributions, retirement pensions, etc.); these need to be paid by the contractors themselves. In sum, this is a most unfair Personnel Employment Practices.

In any event, the numbers of different contractual modalities were just too excessive, unwieldy, and difficult to manage. For this reason, we contacted several other International Organizations to see how they coped with this type of problem. As a result, we identified and included about 3 or 4 alternative solutions in the report. One was the way the U.S.

Agency for International Agency (USAID) uses the Personal Services Contracts (PSC). Another was the way the U.S. Treasury emulates USAID in the use of PSC's. Yet, another was the "Borrowed Servant Concept" used in Argentina, Bolivia, and CITAF (used by ECOSCO and Oil Companies). All three modalities award the same type of benefits people under PSCs as a career employee. Thus, all three-show promise as a solution.

One thing needs noted. When the contractual modalities are reduced and many may become legal and more permanent, then, there will, of necessity, require a greater increase to the costs of operations and financial benefits to the employees. Thus, finding a fair and economical solution to this problem is a great challenge but it is an utmost important one.

- **The report included three recommendations for action by the General Secretary. We asked him to appoint a Special Advisory Committee to (a) study this complex problem, (b) find a solution, (c) clear and coordinate findings with the Permanent Council, and the General Assembly; and (c) dictate the actions to be taken by the Operational Offices.**

PART L. OAS'S ASSETS WERE ERRONEOUSLY ACCOUNTED FOR; ASSETS VALUATIONS WERE UNDER, OVER,, INACCURATE, AND SOME WERE OMITTED; PROBLEMS GREATLY DISTORTED THE FINANCIAL STATEMENTS OF THE ENTIRE OAS ORGANIZATION AND THEIR CERTIFICATION

<u>This Was the Second Most Important OAS Problem.</u> Our audits showed the second most significant problem was that the OAS's Combined Statement of Assets, Liabilities, and Fund Balances (the Financial Statements) contained serious material distortions and showed an extremely distorted and very conservative OAS net worth. As a result, the

certification being made by the Board of External Auditors (Ernest and Young) was wrong.

Because of the complex nature of this finding, the individual audit report devoted twenty pages explaining the many problems, lack of applicability of certain Accounting Standards, and the erroneous certification by the External Auditors (Ernest and Young, Inc.), and the recommendations we made. For this book, I will only provide a very brief synopsis of the principal problems which the Organization had and what was needed to correct the situation. If more details are required, the reader should get access to this important report.

Briefly, we found that the Combined Statement of Assets, Liabilities, and Fund Balances reflected distorted and an ultra-conservative pictures of the true net worth of the organization – for several reasons. In our individual audit report, we questioned far too many things; here are major examples:

a. OAS used the Statement of Financial Accounting Standards No. 93 (FASB 93) to depreciate non-expendable property. Based on our conversation with other organizations, the FASB No. 93 was not being used by other International Organizations (like Pan American Health Organization, the World Health Organization, the World Bank, and United Nations, and others). In sum, the applicability and use of FASB 93 to OAS was questionable, and, wrong.

b. The depreciation of historical and/or buildings considered National Treasures -- at a time when buildings in the Washington D.C. area are appreciating at an accelerated rate -- were unrealistic. For instance, OAS records showed the following values for: (a) the Pan American Union Building at a ridiculous Zero; (b) the Administrative Building at $239,300; (c) the General Secretary's Residence at a mere $216,025; and (d) the Secretariat Building -- which was bought at a cost of $17.6 million -- at a mere $1.6 million. Moreover, OAS was taking erroneous depreciation on musical records and Works of Arts. **Yes, taking depreciation on such valuable property was totally unrealistic and wrong.**

c. The OAS's Columbus Memorial Library was not even included in the Financial Statements. Yet, it has an irreplaceable number of extremely valuable things and it had not been appraised. This OAS Library includes the building itself, books, Original organizational record, ribbons, antique bank notes documents dating back to the 16th Century, medals, and other unbelievably valuable items. Some of the smaller items were already valued at $20,000 and there were many other such similar items. **A more realistic appraisal on the value of this property will be extremely beneficial to OAS.**

d. There was an unaccounted difference of about $4.6 million between the inventory listings and financial statements. The problem was that the assets of the Executive Secretary for Economic and Social Affairs (ECOSOC) and the Executive Secretary for Education, Science, and Culture (EDUCICULT) had not been included. **Once again, the financial statements were understated by, at least, $4.6 million.**

e. In sum, there were many over, under, erroneous, and omitted distortions to the Combined Statement of Assets, Liabilities, and Fund Balances. Yes, the financial statements were totally understated and wrong. Thus, the certifications made by the Board of External Accountants (Ernest and Young) – attesting on the fair value of the net worth of OAS – was wrong.

The OAS/OIG (Dr. Guillermo Belt and I) met with Ernest and Young, the Department of Management Resources, Department of Financial Services on the above points. The presentation by Dr Belt, on this meeting, was most impressive and his incisive guidance left no doubt in anyone's mind on the severity of these problems. **There was a consensus agreement that the issues presented in our report were valid and accurate, that the Financial Statements were erroneous, and that the OAS General Assembly had become aware of our findings and was very concerned about the situation.** Also, the accounting firm of Ernest and Young stated and/or agreed on the following points: (a) that it had not been aware of the existence of either the valuable assets in the Columbus Memorial Library or the numerous musical books and record; (b) that it was aware that the Computer Information System had many problems; and (c) that the depreciation of valuable property – mentioned previously – was, in fact, unrealistic. Ernest and Young also stated that it used Section XIV.5 of the Budgetary and Financial Rule – and not FASB 93 – to require asset depreciation. However, they said that OAS had the option to change the rules; and that, if it did change the rules, the depreciation requirement would cease to exist. In my opinion, the best option to OAS is to delete the requirements to take the depreciation requirements on valuable assets.

- Our report included 8 different recommendations just on this finding. Three recommendations were for the Secretary for Legal Affairs, and five for the Secretary for Management. I will not discuss them in this book.

There were also five other findings discussed in the Review of Procedures Used to Manage Non-Expendable Property and Warehouses. They dealt with purging of excess property no longer needed by the Organization; finalizing and listing of all OAS items; listing of non-expendable items belonging to Projects; and, organizing items in warehouses in a more orderly manner. The report included 19 more recommendations that would correct all other problems.

Part M. Plans by the Assistant Secretary For Management to Reorganize His Six Departments were most Defective; They Contemplated elimination of key positions, functions, tasks, and were of great risk to the organization

A Planned Reorganization Was Flawed and Ill Planned. *As Stated Previously, We Found That the Office of the Assistant Secretary for Management Was Attempting to Re-Organize His Six Departments to Comply with Personnel Ceilings Set by the General Assembly. However, His Reorganization Plans Were Short-Sighted, Haphazard, Wrong, and Contained Absurd Eliminations of Key Personnel Positions, Tasks, Functions, and Required Procedures. We Evaluated the Reorganizations Plans -- Dated June 1996 and January 27, 1997 – Which Had Been Designed by the Assistant Secretary for Management. Audit Report No. SG/OIG/Audit-3/97 Pages 7 to 16, Details All the Defects We Saw and the Basis for the Following Opinion:*

- **The June 1996 reorganization plan being used by the Assistant Secretary for Management to reorganize the Department of Financial Services and his other departments were haphazard and did a disservice required for the efficient operations of the organization. The plans contained twenty-eight diverse ways to**

achieve the reorganization. For instance, he was just planning to eliminate positions, tasks, and functions in a very faulty manner. His approach to solve a deeply rooted problem was terribly ill-planned, wrong, and illogical. For instance: (a) the Chief Accountant's (a key) Position was abolished: (b) the flawed proposals caused the Chief Accountant and others to retire from OAS, and (c) Accounting Positions were to be filled with General Services (not accounting) Personnel; and (c) the Treasury Department was to be decimated. Details are explained more fully in the following parts.

Problems Related To the Department of Financial Services (DFS). The particularly important DFS had lost several positions over the years resulting from "early retirements" and "reduction in force" which were required by the limits on Personnel ceilings. **In the year of our examination, alone, it had lost eight different key accounting positions including the "early retirement" of DFS Chief Accountant. When this took place, the Management Officer resorted to abolishing the Chief Accountant Position. To us, this was a gross mistake and represents the "Conflict of Interest" that existed by DFS, Budget, and Treasury being under the jurisdiction of the Management Officer.**

The Former Chief Accountant told us that he had retired because the setting of the Personnel Ceilings was very arbitrary, and the reduction of Positions was too strict. He had submitted plans to the Management Officer – on how to reorganize his department – but the Management Officer had disregarded them. Also, he told us that when Positions became vacant, they were not replaced because of the General Assembly Mandated Personnel Ceiling Resolutions. Moreover, although DFS had the money to hire several accountants and had advertised for them – the Positions had been abolished. **As a result, DFS was not fulfilling extremely important accounting, auditing, and reporting functions. Also -- with the Chief Accountant now retired and the position abolished -- there were questions as to who would be preparing the "Combined Statement of Assets, Liabilities, and Fund Balances."** Who would monitor expenditures? Who would analyze unliquidated obligations so they could be reprogrammed? Who would keep track of travel expenses and many other functions? All these reductions were cascading adverse effects, throughout the OAS organization, due to the arbitrarily set ceilings.

Problems of the Department of Treasure. We noted that the positions of Department of Treasure would be significantly reduced and decimated. To us, this is also a gross mistake. The Treasury Department is also a particularly important Position and without adequate staffing -- important tasks in such areas as check signing, investments, banking, transfer of funds, control of Quota Receipts, etc. – may have to be delegated in an undesirable manner.

PART N. THERE IS CONFLICT OF INTERESTS FOR THE DEPARTMENTS OF FINANCIAL SERVICES, BUDGET, AND TREASURY TO BE UNDER AND REPORT TO THE ASSISTANT SECRETARY OF MANAGEMENT

As shown above, the plans contemplated by the Assistant Secretary for Management did not give due importance to either the Department of Financial Services (DFS) or the Department of Treasury. Essential personnel retired or withdrew from OAS; key positions and necessary tasks and functions were abolished; available funds to hire additional accounting personnel were denied or not approved; and the Department of Treasury was to be decimated. Let this be a lesson on a very descriptive presentation of a "Conflict of Interest" situation.

Aside from duties of preparing the Statement of Financial Condition, the DFS was delinquent – for lack of adequate personnel - - in reviewing travel vouchers, keeping track of obligations, and keeping management informed on delinquencies in the field and Washington-based offices on Unliquidated Obligations. Just see the following $8.8 million picture of the Unliquidated Obligations. Good management and closer monitoring of these funds could permit the OAS General Assembly or General Secretariat to reprogram them, to create, expand, or use the reprogrammed funds in many other activities, programs, and/or its own weak operational needs.

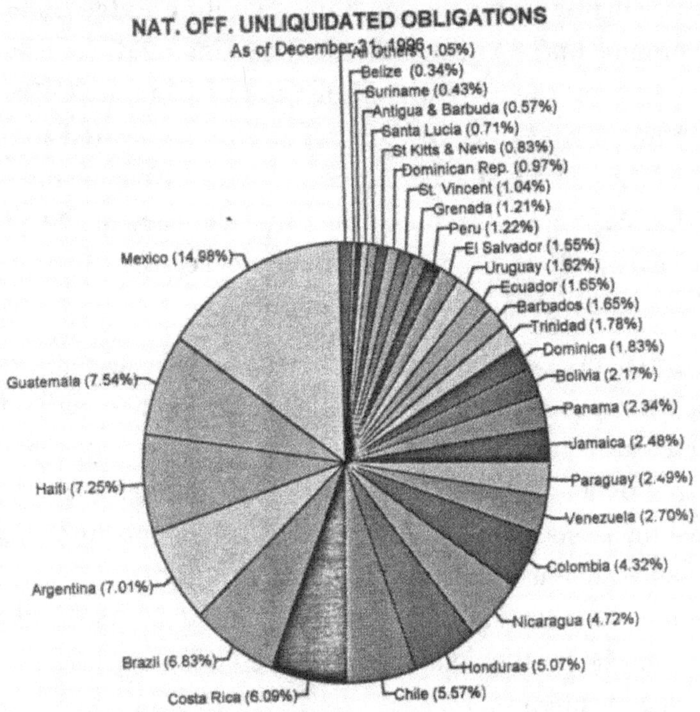

The indicators and supporting material seem to show a mixed bag of problems:

- As noted, OAS Mexico, Guatemala, Haiti, Argentina, Brazil, Costa Rica, Chile, Honduras, Nicaragua, and Colombia account for 69.4% of all Unliquidated Obligations.
- In terms of transactions, the majority are held by Nicaragua (386), Argentina (371), Guatemala (325), Costa Rica (312), Mexico (303), Chile (236), Honduras (227), Colombia (214).
- Many of the obligations were made in 1993, 1994, 1995, and early 1996.
- Many are small balances ($.01, $.95, $.10, $.60, etc) which suggest residual amounts which are no longer needed.

- **The DFS should not be under the Assistant Secretary for Management because there is a conflict of interest and violations of internal controls (just look at the elimination of positions, tasks, and functions, our observations on unliquidated obligations, or the problems noted in the Statement of Financial Conditions). I believe that the DFS should be renamed as the "Office of Financial Management Office or Controller" and relocated so that it reports directly to the General Secretary. This office performs extremely valuable functions which affect the accuracy of OAS accounting records and the Financial Statements certified by the Board of External Auditors.**

In addition, the Departments of Budget and Treasury are extremely important. They should not be placed in organizational position where it can be decimated and reduced in size. Also, this office needs people trained in accounting and non-accountants should not be transferred to this office. Yet, this is what the Assistant Secretary for Management planning to do. Because it manages investments, cash, and other financial situations which are important to OAS, this Office should not be under the Assistant Secretary for Management. The position and office should be separated from its current organizational position.

- **In sum, the way that the Assistant Secretary for Management was attempting to reorganize his departments and reduce processes, functions, and task was wrong, and, the General Secretary should view these types of plans with alarm because they represent a great danger that OAS does not deserve to have. Once again, the solution to the root cause was a Manpower Utilization Study that we have emphasized before.**

PART O. PARAMETERS OF AUTHORITIES OF ASSISTANT SECRETARIES NEED TO BE CONSTRICTED AND CLEARLY DEFINED. FOR EXPRESSING MY PROFESSIONAL OPINION AS INCLUDED IN THE OIG/OAS AUDIT REPORTS, I WAS DECLARED A "PERSONA-NON-GRATA" AND WAS NEVER AGAIN ALLOWED TO DO WORK OR TO ENTER OAS BUILDINGS

Background Information. Most studies I made normally required changes in how General Secretariat part of OAS conducted some of its administrative and/or project development affairs. But working in OAS can be difficult because it is an extremely political organization. And, as I said earlier, most high-level Cabinet positions are, apparently by OAS policy, made purely on political considerations. Once they are appointed to their high-level positions, some of these officials think they are so-called "kings." They certainly are not amenable to a strong criticism – especially when they "apply to him or her and might seem harsh but our professional criticisms are meant to be constructive. Some have no compunction to resort to unwarranted reprisals against the person(s) who dare criticize them.

Alfonso Caycedo and Dr Guillermo Belt were truly "Strong Inspector Generals" and having their support before they retired (and since I was under contract and not a career employee) helped a great deal (just look at the example when Dr Belt and I met the CPA Firm). With their support, I could usually call attention to OAS's weak areas; make the required number of recommendations; and the Assistant Secretary for Management (through his offices) and others would correct – or attempt to correct – the condition(s).

However, dealing with the Assistant Secretary for Management (also referred to as Management Officer), of that time, was always a very tough. As I understand it, this Management Officer had been a high officer in the U.S. Military for many years; had retired as a high-ranking General; and was a recent political appointee to his position. As shown in the Organizational Chart, he had six offices (one is not named), several departments, and many employees, reporting under him. So, indeed, he was an important Official. In sum, this may be the reason he always was hostile towards me and was hesitant to implement our audit recommendations. His office included certain departments – like the Department of Financial Services, Budget, and Treasury. In other organizations, these are especially important and are separate offices in themselves. As I stated before, there was a conflict of interest when OAS placed the DFS, Budget, and Treasury underneath the direction of the Management Officer.

In any event, before Dr Belt retired, I had found several major problems in the way the Management Officer (and his offices) operated his functions. Moreover, the way that he was trying to solve a perennial series of problems was wrong. These problems affected a great deal of the broad OAS administrative, financial operations, and operational departments. For instance, my reports affected OAS the most because they contained 70 (out of 79) recommendations that were assigned to the Management Officer. Consequently, we included the defects and recommendations in the five reports because:

- **The different audits and their respective reports -- when viewed together and from a broad perspective -- showed that OAS, and especially the offices of the General Secretariat, was not performing its Personnel allocations, managerial, administrative, financial, Activities, Internal Controls, and/or Operations in the most efficient, effective, and/or economical manner. Yet, the Operations could be radically improved if our recommendations were implemented. As noted earlier, the haphazard way in which staffing limitations and/or requirements were set by the General Assembly represented a huge problem for the operational side (Administrative, Financial, Treasury, Projects, Field Offices, and others) of OAS as an organization. Moreover, the problem permeated throughout the organization and included evidently illegal contracting of "shadow employees" who were doing "Career" type of work but got no benefits. Another major problem was that the Statement of Financial Condition did not represent a realistic financial picture of OAS as an Organization; there were financial items which were omitted from the statements; items which were understated and items which were**

overstated. The certifications by the External Audit Firm, as they related to the OAS Financial Statements, lacked accuracy.

When Dr Belt retired, however, the Assistant Secretary for Management (and the newly appointed Inspector General) no longer wanted the types of comprehensive reviews I made or to make those types of waves in the administrative areas. Reprisals were unmistakable. So, this brings us to a discussion of some of the other related problems we brought out in the reports; these problems affected the Management Office in unusual ways.

OAS Operational Manuals Needed Urgent Modifications. The Management Office was responsible for the upkeep of the OAS Operational Manuals. Our findings were that these important operational guidance for all the General Secretarial functions needed modifications and changes to reflect the most current operational practices and procedures. Although the need for changes to the Operational Manuals were discussed in our first report – issued October 28, 1994 – the manuals had not been changed in the ensuing two-year period i.e., as of December 1996. In fact, the modifications of important Operational Manuals had not been changes in 17 to 24 years and probably accounted for the gross understatement in the Statement of Financial Conditions and many other problems.

- **So, before the release of this book, the author had a chance to review some parts of the Automated Directive System (ADS) now being used by the U.S. Agency for International Development (USAID). Making use of computers and modern "paper-less" technology, the Bureau of Management is responsible for maintaining the ADS system on a current basis. When needed, the ADS is modified immediately; thus, it is always current. Based on this review, the author believes the ADS is an exceptional system and therefore, recommends that OAS review the procedures and adopts the major ADS theories in its operations.**

Problems Related to Unliquidated Obligation Balances. As shown in a previous chart (page 533), the Unliquidated Obligations Balances – at well over $8.8 million by Field Offices alone -- were extremely high at most levels of the central headquarters and all Field Office of OAS.

However, the high balances were due to a variety of reasons. At our request, the Field Offices sent us a listing of 15 reasons why the Unliquidated Obligations existed in the many Field Offices. Here is a synopsis of the reasons stated by them:

- **Reasons (1) Lack of Communication between Home and Field Offices; (2) Discontinued Funding Programs; (3) Late Funding Obligations; (4) Conflicting Policy Instruction; (5) Lack of Delegation of Authority to the Field Offices; (6) Centralized Control over Projects; (7) Poor Performance of Centralized Projects; (8) Field Offices Misunderstanding Expenditure Transactions Forms; (9) Plans not Carried Out; (10) Codes are Misinterpreted or Not Used by DFS; (11) Confusion on Authorities Over De-obligations; (12) No Action By DFS; (13) Normal Delays in Processing By DFS; (14) Shortages of Personnel by DFS; and, (15) Computer System Problems. Our report contains the detailed explanations for these Reasons.**

In sum, the principal reasons were lack of clear instructions by way of training, outdated handbooks, and manuals; a great lack of coordination between the Central Headquarters and the Field Offices; a definite need for cooperation and attitudinal changes from the staff; loss of Personnel by DFS; and a number of accounting errors made as a result of unclear instructions. As noted, some go back to outdated handbooks and instructions. Projects conducted from the central offices need to be monitored closely or the monitoring done by the Field Offices.

Weak Accounting for Advances. We found that Accounting for Advances was a very weak function and, as such, **was included in all three audit reports**; the reasons were also varied. However, they were primarily due to: (a) a lack of required personnel in the DFS; (b) a lack of clear instructions from outdated handbooks and manuals; (c) a need for training of the staff; (d) a need to require the staff to improve their attitude and coordination, and (d) compensating accounting errors which involved over and understatement of equal transactions posted erroneously to different employees and/or accounts. **Some practices by certain headquarter offices violated OAS rules and built-in internal controls. In fact, they were very dangerous to the Organization (the reports detail some of our observations).**

Problems Related to Travel Advances. Our first and second reports showed that accounting for Travel Advances (T/A) was not current. It was also erroneous. The reason was that the DFS had divested itself from doing a number of functional responsibilities: (a) voucher audits, (b) periodically needed reporting, and (c) other functional responsibilities. As a result, the Secretary for Administration had issued Administrative Memorandum Number 9 which attempted to decentralize responsibility for advancing, controlling, and reporting of Travel Advance. For instance, Travel Advances were authorized by the involved Office; a copy of the T/A was to be sent to DFS for accounting records; the actual cash advance was made by the OAS Credit Union, who, in theory, was to be paid $1.50 per transaction; after the travel was made, a Travel Expense Claim (TEC) was to be prepared by an Administrative Assistant; and, the TEC would be sent to DFS for the elimination of the Unliquidated Obligation. We were asked to evaluate the revised policy and costs.

We found many problems -- with the policy, procedures, and actual practice – stated in Administrative Memorandum No. 79. The DFS – which was under the Management Officer's responsibility -- needed to resume and fulfill its accounting, recording, auditing, and reporting responsibilities. Also, procedures were needed to be set so that the $1.50, per transaction, payable to the OAS Credit Union could be included as part of the T/A costs and could be paid in an orderly manner. The Department of Human Resources (DHR) needed to improve its Management of Chapter 9 "Common Services" Travel Transactions. The Assistant Secretary for Management needed to modify and reissue Administrative Memorandum No. 79 and conduct training courses for the staff on all phases of the Travel.

As mentioned earlier, we issued 70 (of 79) recommendations that needed to be implemented by the Assistant Secretary for Management. See Audit Report No. SG/OIG/Audit-3/97 pages 7 to 16, which details all the defects we saw and the basis for the following Recommendations Numbers 2, 3, 4, and 5. He refused to implement all four of them. These recommendations required the Assistant Secretary for Management to implement the following actions:

- **Recommendation No. 2; The Assistant Secretary for Management was to suspend efforts to (a) redefine tasks as described in a June**

1996 Plan; and (b) reorganize the Department of Financial Services along the lines of January 27, 1997, reorganization plan.

- **Recommendation No. 3: The Assistant Secretary for Management was to consider other ideas from the DFS -- which were already available to him -- to carry out a more balanced temporary reorganization of the Department of Financial Services,**
- **Recommendation No. 4: The Assistant Secretary for Management was to request the Department of Financial Services to redefine tasks and present a more realistic plan to automate, redistribute, outsource and/or cancel current divisional tasks.**
- **Recommendation No. 5: The Assistant Secretary for Management was to evaluate the possibilities of replacing the positions which were abolished or lost due to personnel retirement.**

(Note: After I was declared a "Persona-Non-Gretta (see next discussion and I had sent a letter to the General Secretariat, the same Assistant Secretary for Management that had listen my "in-person" critique at the Exit Conference and the new, and weak Inspector General wrote me a letter and said mine were mere "allegations." As noted in our Audit Reports and this book, I did see, evaluated, and can certify that the plans existed and that some actions such as elimination of key positions and functions were taking place).

The Way I was Declared a "Persona-Non-Gretta's, just before Dr. Guillermo Belt retired in June 1998, I completed my last report, as required by my contract, and I went on vacation. Because of the exceptionally nice feelings I had for Alfonso and Guillermo, I was not sure whether I wanted to work again for the OAS Inspector General because the person that took over the IG Office was, in my opinion, weak professionally, managerial, and personally. Moreover, the I.G. Office had lost prestige and personnel after Dr. Belt's departure. On the other hand, there were rumors that OAS and the Inter-American Agency for Cooperation and Development would begin their reorganization. And I did like the idea of working for some of the Technical Units. In any event, time passed, and I got a call on two separate days from an OAS Project Directors -- it might have been the Executive Coordinator for The Unit for the Promotion of Democracy (UPD); I just do not remember. The

Project Directors told me that they had read some of the reports I had produced, especially the Audits covering Deming and the other one on Trade and he thought I could help them in some areas. The first director asked whether I was available and if I was, could I meet him in his office. So, we talked, agreed on the price, and the contracts began to be drafted. A few days went by, and the first unit told me that "…they did not have money and could not award the contract to me…." It did not dawn on me that there could be another reason. The second Director called, and we agreed on the date for the meeting.

- **The day of the meeting came, and I arrived promptly at the agreed time. Everything seemed normal. In any event, the Project Director and I sat in his office, and he began telling me what he had in mind. The meeting had lasted no more than 10- 15 minutes when an OAS Guard came, interrupted the meeting, asked my name. And although my entrance to the building had followed routine procedures, it nearly caused an "international incident" as soon as people from the seventh floor found out I was inside the building. Security personnel came to check on me. As the Director began to draft the contract, the telephone rang, and conversations went back and forth, the second unit gave me another excuse for not giving me the contract. Security personnel promptly told me that I had to leave the building. I inquired why? The Guard just told me that someone very high-up did not want me around or for me to ever come back to OAS. The Project Director and I were surprised. Given no explanation, I thanked the Project Director and, as if I had committed a crime, the Guard escorted me out of the building. At the front door and in a polite way, he told me not to return because I would not be welcomed. Once again, he told me that some high official did not want me around. On February 1, I found out the obvious truth—that someone on the "seventh floor," maybe the Assistant Secretary for Management, his deputy, and/or someone else – opposed to granting me any additional contracts. The cover reasons were that I "had been saying some critical comments against the Oracle accounting system…and that I was walking around without a badge…." This**

was a ridiculous cover. I had made an assessment, given some ideas but I had left as this system was being designed – so I did not know much about the system. Moreover, I did have a temporary badge and was always accompanied by a member of a Unit. The facts were that the Units were told that if they awarded the contract to me, these Officials would instruct people in the Financial Services and everywhere not to cooperate with me.

Although I have never been told exactly who had declared me a "Persona-Non-Grata," to me, the retaliation by the Assistant Secretary for Management has always been clear. Mulling it over, I got angry at the unceremonious way I was ejected from the OAS Administrative Building. So, I wrote a couple of letters to the General Secretary (Dr. Cesar Gaviria). He never responded. **He passed my letter to the Assistant Secretary for Management, who passed the letter to the weak Inspector General. Both adopted the "cover" that (a) the two Officials from the Management Office "...denied the allegations (in the IG Reports??) ..." and (b) that the two-unit Directors (who almost wrote the contracts) had unilaterally made the decision not to grant me the contracts. Let me make one thing clear: the statements made in this book are supported by official OIG Audit Reports and were no "allegations;" they were systemic defects present in the operational system. Moreover, I hereby certify that I did see and evaluated the plans being contemplated by the Management Office. I had used professional audit analysis to find them and disclose them. Moreover, the two Unit Directors wanted my services, and there is no doubt in my mind that they did not make any decision to deny the contracts.**

On March 19, 2000, I wrote a letter to the then U.S. Ambassador to OAS and told him about the harassment I was getting in OAS. He promptly wrote me a nice letter, telling me that my information was serious and that his office had received similar information from other sources. His office would investigate it. In 2003, my family and I moved to Austin, Texas. So, I never again returned, worked, or wanted to work for OAS.

PART P. CONCLUDING REMARKS MEMORIES OF THE PAST, WITH VISIONS TO THE FUTURE

<u>Q.1 This Part Provides Memories of the Past.</u> This Chapter has shown that from April 1994 to about June 1998, I was contacted by the Office of the OAS Inspector General (as an International Financial and Management Consultant) to work under a series of Personal Services Contracts. During this time, I did many evaluations, audits, risk assessments, and studies covering: The Employment and Contracting Mechanisms, Management of Non-Expendable Property, Land Mine Problem, Trade Programs, Flow of Funds, Payment Procedures, Payroll, Inventories, the Internet, several Special Reviews, Procurement System, and Electoral Observations. Some studies resulted in changes in how OAS conducted some of its development affairs.

As an Organization, OAS can be divided into two or three integrated parts -- the General Assembly, the Permanent Council, and the Offices of the General Secretariat. Except for the way that the OAS General Assembly determines and mandates its career level of personnel, we did not cover any other functions of the General Assembly or the Permanent Council and have no other observation about them.

However, at the level of the Office of the General Secretariat, OAS needed to improve its overall efficiency, effectiveness, economy, and accuracy in many areas, and this is the reason some very tough-hitting conclusions were reached and disclosed in the Official Audit Reports issued by the then two Inspector Generals. Here is a sampling of what you have previously read in this book:

- OAS's employment and personnel practices were defective. Although OAS dates to the First American International Conference (1890) and is a solid organization that will be around for time into the future, its personnel ceiling – as set by the General Assembly – and the workforce required by the General Secretariat – are not in equilibrium; in other words, they are not based on realistic workforce utilization studies and have no flexibility to accommodate both program evolutions and legal compliance at the same time.

- OAS's Statements of Financial Condition were distorted – in fact, for more part, understated—because the Organization followed policies and practices not followed by other international organizations. For example, the Main OAS Building, a treasure in today's world, was valued in the Financial Statements, at Zero Dollars, and other buildings, in prime Washington locations, continued to be depreciated. The building and contents of the entire Columbus Memorial Library were excluded from inventories.
- Outsourcing of long-term functions is unfair to people, and some contracts are illegal because the practice violates U.S. Court Rulings. In fact, they are like the Microsoft labor practices, which the courts declared illegal; for example, OAS had people contracted through an employment agency working side by side and doing identical work as OAS full-time career employees. Yet, persons under contract do not get tax breaks, fringe benefits, and/or retirement benefits that the full-time person did. As in Microsoft, one faced the prospect of retiring a pauper, the other a millionaire.
- The Tax equalization program—where the U.S. Government reimburses the taxes to OAS employees so they can be tax-free – seemed to need reassessment and scrutiny. There were no audit reports issued on this issue. My brief 1995 survey showed possibilities that the U.S Government may be reimbursing more taxes than necessary. We found that the forms were done in an inappropriate manner. In fact, erroneous payments have been made and, overpayments have not been collected. A current, in-depth review was needed, and I highly recommend it. Because of the vested interests inside OAS, this study should be done by outside qualified sources and its scope should emphasize current practices, standard formularies, and calculation procedures.
- Other important observations included lengthy pipelines, poor program planning, huge "un-liquidated balances," poor reorganizational planning, and many others.

The above has been only a few of the many observations. They are not allegations. They are all facts, and systemic conditions, as found in our audits and included in official Inspector General Reports.

Nonetheless, OAS is composed by 34 different countries and political necessities requires the appointment of some high Officials who, once appointed, treat Organizational offices as if they were their very own "Fiefdom." I met and did collaborate with many solid professionals. However, at least one – the Management Officer, was not amenable to strong criticism and violations of sound internal controls, observation of proficiencies and separation of people and offices were clear.

We pointed out those serious problems in our Exit Conferences and in our reports. However, he refused to implement our recommendations. When these two fine Inspectors General retired, the Assistant Secretary for Management probably no longer wanted me to make the types of needed waves our reports were making. Political considerations and retaliation came fast and furious. Contracts ceased to come my way, and when one prospective PSC from a Technical Unit was a possibility, I was unceremoniously ejected from the OAS Administrative Building. Very obviously, I was essentially declared a "Persona-Non-Grata" and was never again allowed to enter and/or work in/for OAS.

Is this another example of "absolute power corruption?" Yes. However, it is unfortunate that I was treated in the above manner because there is no doubt that the audits, studies, and recommendations I made during my four years with the OAS Office of Inspector General – especially during the time when Mr. Alfonso Caycedo and Dr. Guillermo Belt ran the Office -- were extremely beneficial to the OAS as an Organization. Moreover, the reprisal actions against me by a narcissistic Official deprived OAS of the help I could have provided to the Technical Offices and the Field Office; these offices sorely needed – and had asked me to do this type of help

Q.2 Visions Towards the Future OAS Improvements. In my case, my pursuit of personal and professional improvements gave me an insight into the way this very important, but highly political, organization works. I was also able to reuse all the skills I learned in my 28 years with USAID. And in the case of OAS, the Organization benefited in diverse ways. Not having worked in OAS before, I brought with me a new and independent perspective that proved especially useful to the Organization. As a result, I have no doubt that the OAS needed – and still needs -- the types of in-depth studies we were able to make. As noted throughout this chapter, we found many major types of problems which affected most areas of OAS in a significant manner. Since this Chapter explains the problems, I will only cite major recommendations requiring OAS to review the following and, if situations still exist, address them because they are beneficial to the organization.

1. The way the General Assembly used to set Personnel Ceilings was faulty and was not compatible with setting realistic ceilings based on the ceilings needed by the operational units. Therefore, the General Secretary, in coordination with the Permanent Council and General Assembly, should obtain the services of a Professional Organization to make an organization-wide Manpower Study and (a) find a way to: desist from setting Personnel Ceilings in an Arbitrary manner; and (b) (b) find a more permanent, fair, and legal, solution to reconcile OAS's financial annual budgets and costs, as determined by the General Assembly, with the workforce needed by the General Secretariat, to implement its administrative and operational, and duties in an efficient, economical, effective, and accurate manner..

2. Find a legal, fair, efficient, and economical solution to avoid the cyclical process of creating and perpetuating the ever-increasing Employment and Contracting Modalities.

3. Curtail the nonsense of Officials reorganizing important departments – like the DFS, Budget, and Treasury – in an ill-conceived and haphazard manner.

4. Set parameters and inculcate high-level officials that reprisals and retributions are not within their purview of authority, especially reprisals against those professionals who are only trying to help the organization.

5. Relocate, empower, and staff with experienced professionals the Office of Inspector General so that this office has its professional personnel, authority, accountability, and reports directly to the

Permanent Council and to be independent, but cooperative with, the General Secretary.

6. Rename DFS as the "Office of Financial Management or Controller" or something similar and relocate the Office and empower it so that it reports directly to the General Secretary so it can fulfill all the very important accounting, reporting, auditing of vouchers, review and de-obligate unexpended funding no longer needed for projects, and preparation of Financial Statements.
7. Set and provide the needed number of Professional Auditors and Accountants to both the Office of Inspector General and the Department of Financial Services so they can fulfill their particularly essential functions.
8. Require the External Audit Board to do a more thorough job before certifying the Financial Statements and Net Worth of the Organization.
9. Stop taking depreciation on valuable buildings and valuable non-expendable property.
10. Improve the efficiency of the Department for Material Resources, so it can list and have an accurate accounting of Non-Expendable Property.
11. Update and modify outdated OAS Handbooks, Manuals, and Administrative Memorandums to reflect current operational instructions. As recommended earlier, OAS could radically improve its maintenance of Operational Manuals by adopting the modernization techniques used by USAID in its Automated Directive System.
12. Establish procedures to reduce and/or eliminate excessive Unliquidated Obligations on the books and reprogram or eliminate minor amounts in a timely manner.
13. Obtain the services of an independent auditing source, specializing in Tax Equalization Programs, to do an independent audit of current Tax Equalization Programs used by OAS to emphasize that current procedures, calculations, and practices are accurate.

The operations of the General Secretariat should have been radically improved if our recommendations had been implemented. However, our audit reports and recommendations were made many years ago. Since I have not had any further contact or access to OAS, I have no knowledge of the implementation status of the recommendations, and I can only hope that most of the recommendations were implemented.

If it has corrected or will correct situations, as indicated by us, then I certainly believe and hope that, at some time, between now and in the future, an audit team can honestly attest to the following positive opinion: " ....**We found that OAS was performing its managerial, administrative, financial, Activities, Internal Controls and/or Operations in the most efficient, effective, and economical manner...."**

At my age (90 years plus), I do not have any grudge or animosity to OAS as an organization. And, after having been to many countries in Latin America and the Caribbean, I will always continue to believe that OAS is a fine international organization and is needed by the 34 individual countries. For this reason, I want to express my appreciation for giving me an exceptional opportunity for working in it. My only two bad feelings is that (a) it appointed a high-level Official who could not accept duly made constructive criticisms; and (b) it allowed reprisals by this person or persons, to stain the good name of the Organization of American States.

Let me end this chapter by saying that the accomplishments of the Office of the Inspector General were the results of a team effort. So, I wish to recognize the help and contributions of Senior Auditor Ofilio Perez Balladares and John Sanchez. And let me just say that I thoroughly enjoyed the fabulous experience, leadership, help, contribution, considerations, and technical guidance that you – Mr. Alfonso Caycedo (may you rest in peace) and Dr. Guillermo Belt – gave me. I will always consider you both my real good friends.

THE EPILOGUE
SYNOPSIS OF MY BOOK, MY LIFE IN RETIREMENT, AND STATUS OF MY FAMILY

This will be the ending part of my book. It is divided into three parts: (a) synopsis of my book; (b) my Life in Retirement; and (b) the status of my family as of the writing of this book.

Synopsis of My Book. Since you have read my book, you have seen that I: (a) came from a humble family; (b) graduated from high school; (c) was in the U.S. Air Force for four years; (d) graduated from the University of Texas with a degree in Accounting; (e) worked four years for the U.S. Air Force as a civilian stationed in General Dynamics in Fort Worth; (f) joined the U.S. Agency for International Development where I worked for 28 years; (g) was stationed in 9 countries with my family; (h) was stationed in four countries and travelled on TDY to 26 other countries by myself; (i) made numerous review, evaluations, financial, special assessments, and others; (j) got many awards and rose through the ranks to serve as the First Mexican American to be a Deputy Regional Inspector General for Egypt and Latin America for six years; (k) had exceptional ratings for most of my career; (l) took various dissenting positions with proposed faulty policies; (m) became the victim of false accusation and a vicious reprisal actions which were unwarranted; (n) was a further victim of an I.G. Investigation which took 3 to 4 years to be resolved in my favor; (o) was cleared of all charges and retired from USAID; (p) worked as an International Financial Consultant for two companies; (q) was the Director of a Health Project in Guatemala and supervised the efforts of 50 Professional People that we hired for the Project; and, (r) achieved -- together with my team -- most Project Objectives and our performance was exceptional.

My last work as a consultant was with the Organization of American States (OAS). OAS is a fine international, but highly political organization, and I made a number of audits, evaluations, and assessments. I found numerous problems and wrote some hard-hitting but factual reports, which must have alienated at least one high official. In the form of reprisal – and for expressing my Professional Opinion -- I was essentially declared a "Persona-Non-Grata" and not permitted to either work for OAS or to even enter its building. Therefore I stopped looking for more consulting work, and also, I really wanted to enjoy my retirement.

Life in my retirement. Except for the death of three of my dependents (mentioned later), I have been and will continue to be happy in my retirement because most of my official and incredibly stressful Pursuit for Improvements has been fulfilled. In my retirement, I have found Peace of Mind; have done some genealogical and historical research; have written a combination of the genealogical and historical books **(Inherit the Dust from the Four Winds of Revilla**); given lectures using modern technology to discuss my book and conclusions of my research on the "The Battle of Medina;" written a number of articles; and I am extremely happy to have completed this book -- the title of which clearly expresses the fact that, in my life and my career, I was constantly "In Pursuit for Improvements" – for myself, for my family. For those Persons and Organizations, I touched. I feel certain that all my objectives in writing this book will help the younger generations to see how it is to work as a Foreign Services Officer and as an International Financial Consultant for over 38 years.

Status of the Lives of My Family. Pauline (my wife) and I were married 61 years and had four children – Joe, Jerry, Linda, and Melissa. We have two granddaughters – Estela Pena and Lauren Marie Bucher Delaney – and a great granddaughter (Natalie Marisol Delaney). Unfortunately, three members of my original family have died. So, let me first give you a quick update on Joe, Lucy, Estela, Lauren, Andrew, and Melissa, who are alive and well:

- Jose (Joe) M. Pena III is our first son. He is married to Lucy Sanchez Pena, and Estela is their daughter. Joe and Lucy are fantastic. Joe graduated, with a bachelor's degree, from William and Mary University and a Master's Degree from the University of Kentucky with very high honors in both universities. He was with the Peace Corps and served three years in Costa Rica and Ecuador. He is a top-notch professional and works for the U.S. Government Accountability Office (GAO) in Washington, D.C.

- Lucy Sanchez Pena is equally fantastic. Born in Peru, she graduated from the National University of San Marcos with a Degree in

Insurance Studies. She is a U.S. Citizen and has worked as a top-notch Administrative Staff Member for the Inter-American Development Bank for over 20 years. She is now enjoying her retirement very much.

- Estela Pena and her boyfriend (David Lantos) are studying at the same university and have set their joint eyes towards being top professionals in the future. From birth, Estela has always had a fantastic mind. I remember that she would watch a movie two times and would know the roles and words of most actors. Thus, she is beautiful, disciplined, highly studious, imaginative, and creative, and will be a top-notch professional someday. At this writing, Estela currently lives in California. She graduated in Linguistics from Santa Monica College, and she is now majoring in Psychology at the California University of Long Beach. David is studying to become a Chiropractor sometimes soon.
- Lauren Marie Bucher Delaney is the daughter of Linda (my daughter) and Kendall Bucher. When both Linda and Kendall died, she came to live with us. I saw her develop into a beautiful person. Lauren is married to Andrew Delaney. Lauren and Andrew can be described as fantastic persons – extremely disciplined, highly creative, imaginative, bright, fantastically intelligent, and have beautiful personalities. Lauren works as a manager in a private organization, and Andrew works for a Real Estate Company. At the time this book was being written, Lauren Marie and Andrew made me a Great-Grand Father to their daughter (Natalie Marisol Delaney). I love to watch her grow. She is just beautiful.
- Melissa Gisela Pena is my youngest daughter. She was born in Colombia while I was on assignment. She is widely mentioned in my book as having serious Learning Disabilities. Nevertheless, Melissa is extremely religious and is a person that is determined to succeed in life. For instance, she entered a running race in Egypt and won first place. She also climbed almost to the top of Mount Kenya – something that other kids could not do. She learned to ski and ride a horse. And she graduated from Brush Ranch High School. Recently, however, the death of her mother has greatly affected her, and her suffering is

intense. Knowing her, she will overcome that, and I expect she will forge ahead in life.

This brings us to my three original members who have died.

- *Pauline A. Pena, my wife for over 61 years, passed away on July 14, 2019. In life, Pauline and I had some marital problems due in part to my forced assignment separations. However, she was an excellent wife and mother to our children. She enjoyed living in Peru, Panama, Egypt, and Kenya.*
- *Linda Marisol Pena Bucher, my daughter, passed away on February 10, 2004. Linda was truly beautiful, creative, exceptional, and an inspiration to all of us. She and Kendall Bucher were married and had Lauren Marie Bucher as their only child. They were a beautiful couple, but the marriage had problems, and they divorced after being together for 15 years.*
- *Jerry (Gerardo) Javier Pena, my second son, died on August 24, 2017, as a result of a hospital nurse giving him an accidental overdose of one medication. Jerry had a fabulous mind, talents, skills, and attributes. You have read about him and his talents in the book. Despite his illness, he had an AA Degree in two professions; was an accomplished musician; played in school and University concerts; was fluent in three languages, and was asked by four Egyptian girls to marry them. Yes, Jerry was a great personality.*

We miss Pauline, Linda, and Jerry very much. The moral support and help they gave me during their lifetime were most needed and welcomed by all my living extended family and me. May they now Rest in Peace.

I hope you enjoyed my book. Y Muchas Gracias por leer mi libro. Thanks for reading my book, and Le deseo suerte para toda su vida. I wish you luck for all your life.

DETAILED TABLE OF CONTENTS

www.ingramcontent.com/pod-product-compliance
Lightning Source LLC
Chambersburg PA
CBHW060556120726
48002CB00010B/2705
9798218127084